THE LIFE AND TIMES

OF JOHN ROBBOY

THE LIFE AND TIMES

OF JOHN ROBBOY

AND HIS MISHPOCHA:

ORIGINS IN THE UKRAINIAN SHTETLS

KNYAZHE-KRINITSA AND SOKOLIVKA / JUSTINGRAD

Stanley J Robboy, MD
(with other family members contributing with their many stories)

ISBN: 978-1-7364009-1-3

DEDICATION

To our many ancestors from Kynazhe-Krinitsa and Sokolivka/Justingrad, who strove to assure freedom, economic opportunity, and education for their children. As economically poor were our forebearers, they celebrated life, community, justice, and Tikkun Olam in richness. May we, their descendants in the United States, Israel, Canada, Argentina, and elsewhere, live their philosophy and leave this world a better place for our children and their offspring.

Table of Contents

PREFACE

The stories in this book are mainly about [A026] John Robboy, my father, and:

His relatives, and inhabitants of [C01] Knyazhe-Krinitsa (hereafter called Knyazhe), the shtetl (small town or village) of his youth in Ukraine.

His family in [C02] Sokolivka/Justingrad, about which cousin [A457] Joe Gillman wrote in his study of the B'nai Khaim, and which is available online without cost.[1]

Father's family, friends, co-workers, and acquaintances in America.

Cousins and their experiences in Russia, when leaving, or in the new country.

As James Dupree, who helped me with the final edit of this book, said, "I loved learning about the history of your family. This compilation of stories from your father and others gives many unique perspectives of Jewish culture, belief, history, and experiences. With each person's voice and story, the book presents a more honest depiction of the Jewish community from the Ukraine to the U.S. It is amazing to see how many members of your family, whether close or extended or family friends, would proceed to have a major impact on the world, the U.S., or within the Jewish Community."

Dupree writes further, "I never knew about the Jewish communities within Russia. In school we were taught about Germany and the Nazis, but to discover that long before that, the Jews were being oppressed and killed in pogroms in Russia was eye-opening and brutal. I was amazed at the lengths many went to escape.

"The story of Vevel Kaprov's immigration, as well as the many other emigration/-immigration stories, and how much he and others went through to get to the U.S. (or Israel) were thought provoking.

"Joe Robboy's experience with communism was fascinating, and the relationship between communism and younger Jews, especially during the McCarthy era, was something unknown to me.

"This book gives me a better understanding of Jewish faith and philosophies and how those beliefs have led so many to practice medicine. John's experiences to enter the medical field were particularly enlightening. His observations of decades ago about the increase in Specialists over General Practitioners, and the failing quality of healthcare, were discomforting. His sentences, 'we are creating physicians' assistants instead of physicians; the art of nursing has been allowed to deteriorate; and just how we'll handle another pandemic flu remains to be seen,' have been answered by the events of 2020."

Remembering the past is good.
Understanding it is even better.

Stanley Robboy
Friday, February 12, 2021

OVERVIEW TO IDENTIFYING MEMBERS

Note: Each person has an ID number from [A001] thru [A835] sequential in a familial lineage. The editor, Stanley Robboy, is [A031], thus identifying himself as [A026] John Robboy's descendant. Only people mentioned in the text have received ID numbers. All further descendants appear in the appendices but without ID numbers. Chapter 3 provides more detail about the numbering system used.

To safeguard privacy, only descendants born prior to 1980 are listed. The editor would appreciate knowing of current names, births, and spouse names so as to keep the tree, which is separately maintained, up-to-date. Please send comments and updates to Stanley.Robboy@duke.edu

ABBREVIATED FAMILY TREE FOR

VOSKOBOINIK / ROBBOY / GERSON AND [C01] KNYAZHE FAMILIES, AND KAPROVE FAMILY LARGELY FROM [C02] SOKOLIVKA / JUSTINGRAD

ID	Family member	Spouse
[A001]	Laizer Eli Voskoboinik	Paya
[A002]	Yakov Hersh Voskoboinik	Aidi
[A003]	Haskel Voskoboinik	Faiga
[A004]	Donia Voskoboinik	
[A005]	Sarah Faiga Voskoboinik	Kalman
[A006]	Moshe Voskoboinik	
[A007]	Yossel Voskoboinik	
[A008]	Baila Voskoboinik	

BEN-ZION ROBBOY FAMILY

ID	Family member	Spouse
[A010]	Leah Voskoboinik	Ben Zion Robboy
[A011]	Shmiel Robboy	Malka Kaprov
[A012]	Khaim|Hyman Robboy	Rebecca Meshenstein
[A017]	Nessie Gerson Robboy	
[A023]	Tobie Robboy	
[A024]	Joseph|Yossel Robboy	Gertrude Gelman A2B2C2D1
[A026]	John Robboy	Sarah Shapiro
[A034]	Mordechai Robboy	Sarah Spector
[A035]	Nathan Robboy	Rhea Heiser
[A047]	Sylvia Robboy	Joe Isbitz
[A057]	Morton Robboy	Helen Heller
[A059]	George Robboy	Mary Frankel
[A064]	Rose Robboy	David Rein
[A071]	Dorothy Robboy	Nathan Strauss
[A075]	Eddie Robboy	Sylvia Davis
[A078]	Sosi Robboy	
[A079]	Mendel Robboy	Anna Desatnick
[A083]	Sidney Robboy	Eva Desatnick
[A088]	Benjamin Robboy	Irma Levin (→ Lee)
[A091]	Itzhak Voskoboinik	
[A092]	Shava	
[A093]	Dinah Voskoboinik	

GERSON FAMILY

ID	Name	Spouse
[A094]	Hanna Voskoboinik	Levi Gerson
[A095]	Avrom Shmiel (Samuel)	
[A098]	Paya Gerson	
[A099]	Fullie Gerson	married uncle
[A100]	Ruchel Gerson	
[A101]	Nathan Gerson → Kaffen	Anna Sobel
[A102]	Irvin Kaffen	Marg Grossman

MORE VOSKOBOINIK FAMILY

ID	Name	Spouse
[A105]	Golda Voskoboinik	1 Annulled
[A105b]		2 Meir Groysman
[A107]	Jennie | Shaindel VoskoboinikHarry Pritzker	
[A113]	Rayah	
[A120]	Pauline	Julius Friedman
[A128]	Haskel Voskoboinik →Weiss	Reva Leah
[A129]	Phillip	Elsie Schmuckler
[A139]	Dave	Mollie Broth
[A140]	Bessie (Betty Babe)	Jack Mesnick
[A148]	Hyman (Hy) Weiss	Sally Saltzberg

KAPROV TREE (B'NAI KHAIM)

ID	Generation		Spouse
[A290]	Khaim Kaprov	*1	Osna
[A291]	Yossel Kaprov	A1	Perl
[A292]	Rivka Kaprov	B1	Noah Dudnik
[A293]	Aaron Dudnik	C1	Cipa | Zipora Weinberg
[A323]	Isrul| Israel Dudnik	C2	Chana
[A326]	Chaim| Khaim Dudnik	C3	Brucha| Bertha [A413] Dolgonos
[A350]	Froim| Efraim Dudnik	C4	Sarah Dayan
[A355]	Leib Dudnik	C5	Tsiril Tichman
[A359]	Yankel Dudnik	C6	Leah _____
[A363]	Pearl| Mimi Dudnik	C7	Asher Gudisblatt
[A364]	Sarah| Sirka| Surcah Dudnik	C8	Zeina| Zoma| Zuma Sol Morrison
[A367]	Genendy Kaprov	B2	Shmuel Galak
[A368]	Israel Galak	C1	Rifke Shurak| Surak
[A398]	Khaim Galak	C2	Golda
	Yocheved Galak	C3	Abraham Skolnik
	Perl Galak	C4	Iskike
	Baruch Galak	C5	Yudis
[A399]	Leah Kaprov	B3	Dov| Beryl* Dolgonos
[A400]	Israel DolgonosàDouglas	C1	Tuba| Toby Mazur
[A413]	Bracha| Bertha Douglas	C2	Chaim Dudnik [A510] A1B1C3
[A414]	Itzhok Dolgonosà Douglas	C3	Esther _____
	Beila| Berta Kaprov	B4	
	Sarah Kaprov	B5	
	Rokhel Kaprov	B6	
[A419]	Beryl Dov Kaprove	A2	Dvossie Brodsky
[A420]	Khaye Golda Kaprove	B1	Velvel Gilman
[A421]	Khana Esther Gilman	C1	Isruel Tepilsky
[A422]	Pessie Kaprov	B2	Moshe Shestunov ⬚ Gillman
[A423]	Chaye| Haya Sarah Gillman	C1	Eliezer Pribludny
[A427]	Daniel Gelman	C2	Sarah| Sheva Kaprow ? Cousins

ID	Name	Code	Name
[A431]	Alta| (orig Baila Liba) Gelman	C3	David Hirsh Pearlman (h2 Alta)
[A457]	Yossel| Joseph Gillman	C4	Etta Judith Cohen Yustingrad
[A461]	Daniel (Rabbi) Kaprov	B3	Khaya
	Ettie Rachel Kaprov	C1	
	Khaim Kaprov	C2	
	Tobie Kaprov	C3	
	Gershon Kaprov	C4	
[A462]	Yenta Kaprov	B4	Yankel| Jacob Trachtman
[A463]	Motye| Max Trachtman	C1	Khana| Hannah Charnopolsky
[A470]	Zalman/Shlomo Trachtman	C2	
[A474]	Hyman Trachtman	C3	Edassy| Hadassah Kaprov (A7B4)
[A485]	Yossel| Yosef Trachtman	C4	Haika| Chaia Taratuta
[A492]	Shneur| Schnayer Trachtman	C5	Batya| Bessie Gelman
[A494]	Velvel| William| Feigel Trachtman	C6	Dvora| Dora Shapiro
[A500]	Ephraim| Frank| Froika Trachtman	C7	Fannie Pratter
[A501]	Girl Trachtman	C8	
[A502]	Leah Kaprove	B5	Itzhak Gelman (m Kishinev)
[A503]	Moishe Gelman	C1	Freda Grabois
[A505]	Rivka Gelman	C2	Yossef Galperin
[A506]	Motel| Mark Gelman (h2 Alta)	C3	Alta Perlman [A431]
[A507]	Genendal| Gwendel Gelman	C4	Shloma ____
[A508]	Yankel| Jacob Gelman	C5	Frima| Sarah Rabinowitz
[A510]	Itzik Gelman ?Rabbi	B6	Khana Sarah
	Velvel Gelman	C1	
[A511	Tobie Gelman	C2	?
	Daniel Gelman	C3	
	Hillel Gelman	C4	
[A011]	Malka Kraprov	B7	Shmiel Robboy
[A012]	Khaim| Hyman Robboy	C1	Rebecca Meshenstein
[A017]	Anna Nessie Gerson Robboy	C2	Avrom Shmiel Gerson
[A023]	Tobie Robboy	C3	
[A024]	Joseph| Yossel Robboy	C4	Gertrude Gelman A2B2C2D1
[A026]	John| Yankel Robboy	C5	Sarah Shapiro
[A515]	Avrom Ershel Rabbi Kaprow	B8	Sima Schwartz
[A516]	Fishel| Edward Philip Kaprov	C1	Malka| Mollie Molly Reich
[A522]	Dvossi| Dorothy Kaprov	C2	Yankel| Jake| Jacob Zitaner
[A526]	Moishe Kaprov	C3	
[A527]	Pessie| Pauline G Kaprov	C4	Frank S Lerman
[A528]	Gedaliah| Gordon,Rabbi Kaprow	C5	Gittel| Geraldine Shapiro
[A530]	Shmuel Abba Kaprov	A3	
[A531]	Gedaliah Kaprov	A4	Nessie __
	Abroham| Abraham Kaprow	B1	
[A532]	Gedalia | Gregorio Kaprow	C1	Sara Futeransky
[A552]	Shemariah Kaprov	A5	Perl
	Naftali Kaprov	B1	
	Yankel Kaprov	B2	
[A553]	Yakov Kaprov	B3	Hanna Litvak
[A554]	Samuel Kaprov →Kaplan	C1	Miriam Geisingsky
[A555]	Michael Kaprov	C2	Leah Grinberg
[A565]	Velvel Kaprov	C3	
[A566]	Ratsa Kaprov	C4	Samuel Berdichevsky
[A571]	Belchik Kaprov	C5	Chaya ____
[A573]	Khaya Kaprov	A6	
[A574]	Itzik-Yoel Kaprov	A7	Osna Kaprov
	Noah Dovid| Daniel Kaprov	B1	

	Yankov Moishe Kaprov	B2	
	Nehhama| Nachomi Kaprov	B3	Yossel Puchatilofsky
	Osna Puchatilofsky	C1	
	Gedalia Puchatilofsky	C2	
	Ethel Puchatilofsky	C3	Louis Dratch
	Nathan Puchatilofsky à Grossman	C4	Esther Kaplan
	Pinnie | Pinchos Puchatilovsky	C5	
	Leible Puchatilofsky	C6	
	Hadassah| Edassy Kaprow	B4	Hyman Trachtman-A2B4C3
	Khaim/Hyman Kaprove	B5	Mariam Yachnis (W2 Hyman)
	Leah Kaprove	C1	Louis| Pinye Brodsky
	Female, die	C2	
	Yitzchak| Isadore Kaprove	C3	Cecelia Friedland
	Menucha Kaprov	B6	
	Itzak Kaprove	B7	Leah
	Velvel Kaprov	B8	
[A577]	Isroel| Yisrael Dovid Kraprov	A8	
[A578]	Simkha Kaprov	*2	Fayge| Fegah
[A579]	Shlomi Kaprov	A1	Bassie| Buni
	Yoel Kaprove	B1	Dvorah Kaprov
	Samuel Kaprove	C1	Ida Trachtman
	Rose Kaprove	C2	
[A580]	David Kaprove| Caprov	B2	Ethel| Ette| Ete Rabinowitz
[A581]	Velvel Kaprov (Perepelitsky→Purpel	C1	Soybel Bergelson
[A588]	Khaim| Charles Caproff	C2	Pearl Shapiro
[A591]	Chavah Dvorah Kaprove	B3	Motel
[A592]	Moshe Kaprove	A2	Golda Rachel Schulnik
[A593]	Shalom Kaprove	B1	Fageh Haverback
	Rifki| Rose Ann Kaprove	C1	
	Yoel| Louis Kaprove	C2	
	Esther Kaprove	C3	
	Simcha/Samuel J Kaprove	C4	
	Sarah| Sally Kaprove	C5	Theodore Zisserson
	Abraham| Abie Kaprove	C6	
	Lillian Kaprove	C7	Ari Newman
	Mariam Kaprove	C8	Paul Shulman
[A594]	Schmuel Kaprove→ Cooper	B2	Sara Lasensky
	Frimi| Florence Cooper	C1	Harry Ari Fishman
	Simcha| Sidney Cooper	C2	Sadie Edna Ross
	Yoel| Joseph Robert Cooper	C3	Rita Dolores Aaron
[A599]	Simcha/Samuel Kaprove	B3	Sophie Fialky
	Fred Kaprove	C1	Mae Karp
	Ruth Kaprove	C2	Harold Alpert
[A600]	Chiki/Chava Kaprove	B4	Yisrael Weinekov
	Simon Weinekov	C1	
	Ruth Weinekov	C2	
[A601]	Esther Malka Kaprove	B5	Berel| Ben Varinsky
	Betty Varinsky	C2	Irving Shuman
	Philip Varinsky	C3	Dorothy Gomer
[A602]	Fegeh/Feika Kaprove	B6	Hershel Wolozin
[A603]	Eva| Chavah (Cooper) Kaprove	B7	Dave Herman
	Frederick R Herman	C1	Ilene
	Ruth Herman	C2	Morris Lift
[A604]	Rabbi Shimon Herman	C3	Charlotte Mae Golub
[A605]	Israel Kaprove	A3	Chiah |Chaia Dvorah
[A606]	- Avrom Kaprove → Caprov	B1	Sirke | Sara Sirota

16

	- - Bertha Caprov	C1	
	- - Elisa Caprov	C2	Samuel Gendelman
	- - Piñe Caprov	C3	
	- - Peisse Caprov	C4	
	- - Simón Caprov	C5	
[A607]	- Gitel Kaprove (?no such person)	B2	Zelik
[A608]	- Simcha | Simon Kaprove → Caprow	B3	Adela Grobocopatel
	- - Clara Caprow	C1	Luis Melamed
	- - Pedro Caprow	C3	Celia Kessler
	- - Adolfo Caprow	C2	
	- - Carlos Caprow	C4	
[A609]	- Yoel : Julio Kaprove → Caproff	B4	Maria Gelman
	- - Clara Caproff	C1	Marco ___
	- - Sara Caproff	C2	Abraham Nudel
	- - Fanny Caproff	C3	Yaakov Skiva
	- - Israel Caproff	C4	Betty ___
	- - Dorit Caproff	C5	
	- - Salomon Caproff	C6	Clarie
[A610]	Reichel| Ruchel Kaprove	A4	Pessie (Peyack) Sklar
[A611]	- Ezra Sklar	B1	?
	- - Michel Sklar	C1	
	- - Mendel Sklar	C2	
[A612]	- Chaim Sklar	B2	Perel Kaprov (see *3A5B5)
	- - Chiki Sklar	C1	
	- - Pini Sklar	C2	
	- - Nachomi Sklar	C3	
	- - Shayah Sklar	C4	
	- - Simcha Sklar	C5	
	- - ??	C6	
[A613]	- Baruch Sklar	B3	
	- - ??	C1	
	- - ??	C2	
	- - ??	C3	
	- - ??	C4	
[A614]	Hershel Sklar	B4	
	David Shapiro	C1	
	Ann Shapiro	C2	
	Bessie Shapiro	C3	
	Jeanette Shapiro	C4	
[A615]	Shayndel Sklar	B5	
[A616]	Fayge Sklar	B6	
[A617]	Chaya Sklar	B7	Schmiel _____
	Simon _____	C1	
	Shandel _____	C2	
	Ann	C3	
[A618]	- Yonkel David Kaprove	A5	
	Motel Kaprove	B1	
	Pini Kaprove	B2	
	Pesse Kaprove	B3	
[A619]	Chanah Dvorah Kaprove	A6	
[A620]	Yoel| Eli Kaprove	*3	
[A621]	Simchi Kaprove	A1	Fegah
[A622]	Leib Kaprove	A2	
[A623]	Chiki (Chayka?) Kaprove	A3	
[A624]	Raisel Kaprove	A4	
[A625]	Pinchas| Pini Kaprove	A5	Bat Shavah| Sheva

[A626]	Laiki Kaprove	B1	Mechel Shuman
	Pini Shuman	C1	
	? Son Shuman	C2	
[A627]	Bar Sheva Kaprov	C3	
[A628]	Nachomi Kaprove	B2	
[A629]	Chanah| Ania Kaprove	B3	
[A630]	Chrisi Kaprove	B4	
[A631]	Perel Kaprove (See Sklar)	B5	Chaim Sklar (*2A4B2
	Tubi Kaprove	B6	Pini| Pinchas Tishler
	Nusel| Nathan Tishler	C1	Fayge
[A637]	Dvorah/Dobi Kaprove	B7	Yoel Kaprove *2A1B1
	Bessie| Buni Kaprove	C1	Moshe| Morris Cooper
[A638]	Simcha| Samuel Kaprove	C2	Ida Trachtman *1A2B4C3D1
[A639]	Reiche| Rose Kaprove	C3	Benny Sadkin

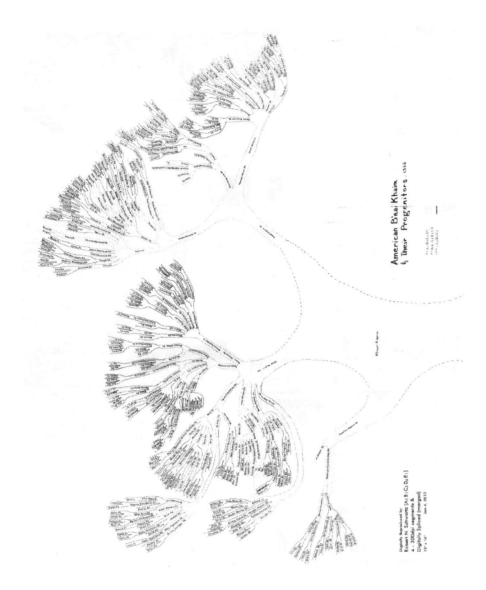

Fig -i-1: B'nai Khaim Family Tree (Joseph Gillman).

Note: See Appendix 3 for the expanded B'nai Khaim family tree, which contains two branches Cousin Joe Gillman did not include in his book. It also includes the entire Voskoboinik – Robboy clan

Background and Useful Information

#1 [C01] KNYAZHE-KRINITSA AND [C02] SOKOLIVKA/JUSTINGRAD: REMEMBRANCES OF A JEWISH FAMILY IN CZARIST RUSSIA AND INTRODUCTION TO MY FATHER, [A026] JOHN ROBBOY

[A026] John Robboy, my father, was 17 years old in 1910 when he and his brother [A012] Hyman (Hymie) left the atmosphere of pogroms[1] rampant throughout the Jewish Pale[2] of Settlement in Eastern Russia and migrated to the United States. He spoke fluent Yiddish and Ukrainian but knew neither Russian nor English. He began high school at age 21, a time when most students in the United States were already finishing college. He then attended college at Western Reserve University. His experience in medical school was not pleasant. The climate was hostile. Some faculty members were openly antisemitic and vindictively gave Jewish students failing grades to force their expulsion from school.

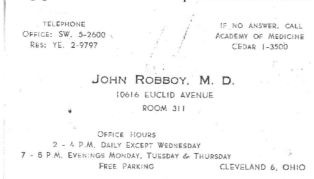

Fig. 1-1: [A026] John Robboy's business card, the 1950s

Father graduated from medical school at the University of Michigan in 1926 and, after completing his internship, began practice as a general practitioner amid the Great Depression. For the rest of his life, he continued as a family practitioner in Cleveland, Ohio.

---

[1] Pogrom, which means "to wreck havoc," describes violent riots aimed at the massacre or expulsion of an ethnic or religious group, particularly Jews. The term became generally popularized when describing the 19th- and 20th-century attacks on Jews who resided in the Pale of Settlement, which was part of the Russian Empire. Similar attacks against Jews elsewhere and at other times are now also called pogroms. Pogroms not infrequently culminated in massacres. Well-known pogroms in which our family died took place in Odessa and Kishinev. Lesser known ones destroyed [C02] Sokolivka/Justingrad and Uman. The Kristallnacht of 1938 in German was the most famous the Nazis organized. While over 90 Jews died, another 30,000 were arrested and interned in concentration camps. A thousand synagogues were burned and thousands of Jewish businesses were demolished.

[2] From the Latin *palus*, a stake, meaning an area enclosed by a boundary. The name, "Pale of Settlement" first came into being during [A278] Nicholas I's rule.

He and his extended family, his mishpocha, which grew over the years, lived initially in the city's Glenville and 105th Street area in Cleveland, OH, but later migrated to Cleveland Heights in the early to mid-1940s, University Heights, and Shaker Heights.[3]

The extended mishpocha affectionately called him "Uncle John." He was highly regarded in the family, as exemplified by an incident where a cousin was injured early one morning in an auto accident a suburb away. She lay semiconscious on the ground, bleeding and muttering, "Get Uncle John." The passerby knew this meant John Robboy.

Father wrote the stories that follow during the decade before he died at the age of 87 in 1980. He was correct when he wrote that he was then the only surviving member of the family who knew the full family tree. He was also one of the few members who remembered life in Russia at the turn of the century. Many family members who have already seen various portions of these materials have commented that they resemble the stories of [A830] Sholem Aleichem,[4] the Yiddish author, and humorist, and, indeed, they do. Since beginning the project, I, the editor of these memoirs, have found other stories that family members have written. [A457] Cousin Joe Gillman collected many of them. One substantial source was cousin [A487] Leah Trachtman-Palchan's remembrances.

The following passage from a letter John wrote to his cousin Joe Gillman, author of the book "B'nai Khaim,"[5] states well the philosophy found throughout the stories of Knyazhe, John's Russian experiences, and his new life in America.

> As I read your work on the B'nai Chaim, I reflect upon the simplicity and ease with which I write of my Knyazhe. Yours is a document for the world to read. It must be true and accurate factually. It must be in a beautiful style, excellent grammar, and above all, it must satisfy a need for the sociology student. My lot is entirely different. I am completely free and uninhibited. I have the freedom to exaggerate and to embellish my stories if I please. I may sentimentalize if I wish, roam to the moon and back again without anyone interfering. The colors of my characters are of my own choosing. They may be as black as the devil or as red as the Bolshevik. I may bestow my love or epithet on both. It is my privilege to call Knyazhe ugly and beautiful at the same time.

---

[3] Editor's note: Initially, America did not perceive the sudden massive and unexpected influx of the Eastern Europeans as a threat in America. Before 1880, the Cleveland Jewish population numbered 3,500 and were but an inconspicuous 2% of the city's residents. Forty years later, by 1920, another 85,000 Jews had arrived, mostly from Eastern Europe, and now numbered one of every 11 Clevelanders. To complicate matters, the German Jews, who had come earlier, disliked the newcomers as "different" and were refashioning the stereotype of the American Jew in a distasteful manner.

[4] Solomon Naumovich Rabinovich, whose pen name was [A830] Sholem Aleichem, was a leading Yiddish author and playwright. *Fiddler on the Roof*, the musical based on his stories about Tevye the Dairyman, was the first commercially successful English-language stage production about Jewish life in Eastern Europe. Sholem Aleichem also means "Peace be unto You." Of interest, [A405a] Moshe Fouks' great grandfather was Nissel Rabinovich, who came to Winnipeg around 1882. His older brother was Menachem Nukhm Rabinovich, the father of Sholem Aleichem.

[5] Joseph Moses Gillman, Etta C. Gillman, *The B'nai Khaim in America*: a study of cultural change in a Jewish group, Dorrance Publishing Co, Philadelphia, Jan 1, 1969, 168 pages, ISBN10 0805913157; ISBN13 9780805913156

Do you want to know how that is so? Frankly, I can't give you a satisfactory answer, but it is so. Did you ever see a character like [A326] Chaim? I admired him. He counted the eggs six at a time repeating one, one, one, two, two, two . . . then three and four, etc., for hours until all the eggs were counted. Never did he make an error in counting.

During the Czarist reign in Russia, educating the Jewish peasantry was officially and actively discouraged. The Decree of 1812 required all Jews to live in the geographic region called the Pale of Settlement, an area that today encompasses eastern Russia, Lithuania, Latvia, and much of Poland. For fear that educated Jews would think and that would lead to revolution, [A277] Czar Alexander I restricted organized schooling. Accessories of education, such as newspapers, were banned. Only a select few in high government were allowed road maps.

Father's stories appear much as he wrote them, except for consistency, spelling, and syntax. He wrote gracefully in a style that few native-born Americans ever achieve. In numerous instances, Father rewrote the initial drafts of his stories, adding new detail in subsequent drafts. Wherever possible, I have spliced the materials, sometimes extensively, to avoid repetition. Sometimes, this was not practically done, hence the duplication.

Many names have transliterated English spellings. For simplicity, but not always accurately, most all similar names are spelled identically. Thus, Khaim and Haim are spelled by the common Chaim. Many words in Yiddish, and names and places unknown to today's reader are referenced and footnoted. Wikipedia is the source for most; other sources are explicitly listed.

Father mentioned many persons only by a partial name or fragmentary identification; these remembrances were written primarily as anecdotes, not a genealogical study. As an aid, the appendices detail all known past and present members of the Voskoboinik, Kaprov (Kaprove), and Robboy families, and all other families mentioned. Each cited name appears in closed square brackets.

I hope that all members of the family will enjoy this book. Those who will ask, "Who am I?" will now know.

Stanley J. Robboy, MD
Chapel Hill, NC
January 2, 2021

#2 RUSSIA AND THE PALE OF SETTLEMENT
From Paul Johnson's *A History of The Jews*, © 1987 (pgs 357-365)
(Reprinted with permission of Harper Collins Publisher, New York)

It was in Tsarist Russia, however, that ill-treatment of the Jews was most systematic and embittering. Indeed the Tsarist regime epitomized for radicals everywhere the most evil and entrenched aspects of autocracy. For Jews, who viewed it with peculiar loathing, it was the most important of the factors driving them leftwards. Hence the Russian treatment of the Jews, horrifying in itself, constitutes one of the important facts of modern world history and must be examined in some detail. It must first be grasped that the Tsarist regime from the very start viewed the Jews with implacable hostility. Whereas other autocracies, in Austria, Prussia, even in Rome, had preserved an ambivalent attitude, protecting, using, exploiting and milking the Jews, as well as persecuting them from time to time, the Russians always treated Jews as unacceptable aliens. Until the partitions of Poland, 1772-1795, they had more or less succeeded in keeping Jews out of their territories. The moment their greed for Polish land brought them a large Jewish population, the regime began to refer to it as 'the Jewish problem', to be 'solved', either by assimilation or by expulsion.

What the Russians did was to engage in the first modern exercise in social engineering, treating human beings (in this case the Jews) as earth or concrete, to be shoveled around. Firstly, they confined Jews to what was called the Pale of Settlement, which took its final form in 1812, and which consisted of 25 western provinces stretching from the Baltic to the Black Sea. Jews could not travel, let alone live, outside the Pale except with special legal authority. Next, a series of statutes, beginning in 1804, determined where the Jews could live inside the Pale and what they could do there. The most damaging rule was that Jews could not live or work in villages, or sell alcohol to peasants. This destroyed the livelihood of a third of the Jewish population, who held village leases or ran village inns (another third were in trade, and most of the rest craftsmen). In theory, the object was to push the Jews into 'productive labor' on the land. But there was little or no land available, and the real aim was to drive Jews into accepting baptism, or getting out altogether. In practice it led to Jewish impoverishment and a steady stream of poor Jews into the Pale towns.[6]

The next turn of the screw came in 1827, when [A278] Nicholas I, one of the most savage of the autocrats, issued the 'Cantonist Decrees', which conscripted all male Jews from 12 to 25, placing the younger boys in canton-schools at the military depots, where they were liable to be forced into baptism, sometimes by whole units.[7] The government was also anxious to destroy the

---

[6] See Rowland RH, Geographical patterns of the Jewish population in the Pale of Settlement of late nineteenth century Russia, Jewish Social Studies 68: 207-234, 1968 for a broader discussion of Jews, trades and geographic areas of living.

[7] Editor's note: Czar Nicholas I's edict mandated that for families with two sons, one must serve in the military. Families with more than two sons, ages eight and older, must yield two. Hired kidnappers ('Chappers' or grabbers) snatched children and brought them to district assembly points. To assure that the parents could not find their children, they were sent to far distant places and given to peasants to raise until age 18 years. Commonly, the peasant hardly had food for his family, and so the strange child, and one Jewish at that received little care. Many died from starvation or beatings. The younger were commonly baptized. The older ones who refused "conversion"

Jewish schools. The authorities tried repeatedly to force Jewish children into state schools where the languages of instruction were Russian, Polish and German only, the object again being to promote baptism. In 1840 a Committee for the Jews was formed to promote the 'moral education' of what was treated publicly as an undesirable, semi-criminal community. Jewish religious books were censored or destroyed. Only two Jewish presses were permitted in Vilna and Kiev, and Jews were expelled from the latter town completely three years later. The government was quite cunning at dividing Jewish communities and setting 'maskils' (a person versed especially in Hebrew or Yiddish literature; an adherent of the Haskalah movement) against Orthodox. In 1841, for example, they put the maskil Max Lilienthal (1815-82) in charge of the new state Jewish schools, which were in effect anti-Talmud establishments designed, as the Orthodox claimed to offer their children to 'the Moloch of the Haskalah'. But he found the bitter battle which ensued too much for him and slipped out of the country four years later, to emigrate to America. The government also forbade Jews to wear traditional garments such as the skullcap and kapota. It divided them into 'useful' and 'useless Jews', subjecting the latter group to triple conscription quotas.

Gradually, over the century, an enormous mass of legislation discriminating against Jews, and regulating their activities, accumulated. Some of it was never properly enforced. Much of it was frustrated by bribery. Rich parents could buy Jewish children to take the place of their own in state schools or in the army. They could pay to buy legal certificates entitling them to travel, to live in cities, to engage in forbidden occupations. The attempt to 'solve' the Jewish problem created, or rather immensely aggravated, another one: corruption of the Tsarist bureaucracy, which became incorrigible and rotted the heart of the state. Moreover, government policy was never consistent for long. It oscillated between liberalism and repression. In 1856 the new Tsar, [A279] Alexander II, introduced a liberal phase, granting certain rights to Jews if they were long-service soldiers, university graduates or 'useful' merchants. That phase ended with the Polish revolt of 1863 and his attempted assassination. There was another liberal phase in the 1870s, again brought to an end by an attempt on his life, this time a successful one. Thereafter the position of Jews in Russia deteriorated sharply.

In the last half-century of imperial Russia, the official Jewish regulations formed an enormous monument to human cruelty, stupidity and futility. Gimpelson's Statutes Concerning the Jews (1914-15), the last annotated collection, ran to nearly 1,000 pages. A summary of the position, compiled by the English historian, Lucien Wolf, established the following facts. The Jews formed 1/24th of the Russian population. Some 95% of them were confined to the Pale, 1/23rd part of the empire, and of these the vast majority were trapped in the Pale towns and shtetls, forming 1/2000th part of the territory. A Jew's passport stated he was a Jew and where he might reside. Even in the Pale, most areas were banned to Jews, but 'legal' parts were constantly being eroded. Jews were banned from Sebastopol and Kiev. The Don territory was suddenly taken out of the Pale, then the Caucasian Kuban and Terek; then the Yalta health resort, a consumptive

---

were tormented, so few remained not "converted." These Jewish children could say goodbye to life. After training to age 18, they then served in the military for another 25 years. Few survived, but even if one found his way "home," after this term of service, he was old and broken down, lacking any trade to make a living. Parents of children so taken considered them gone forever. Parents would pray for a quick death for their child rather than having him endure the dragged out agony. Nicolas reported said he was satisfied if one soldier remained available for service from a hundred so conscripted.

Jewish student being expelled in the middle of his treatment when the decree took effect. Jews wishing to use the Caucasian mineral springs had to pass an exam conducted by an army officer. Some resorts were 'open' but had quotas; thus only twenty Jewish families were allowed into Darnitza in any one season. Other Pale resorts were banned to Jews under any circumstances.

There were privileged categories of Jews permitted to travel or even reside outside the Pale - discharged soldiers, graduates, 'useful merchants' and 'mechanics, distillers, brewers and artisans while pursuing their calling'. But they needed special papers, which were very difficult to obtain and had to be renewed constantly. All these categories tended to be whittled down, especially after 1881. Thus, ex-soldiers were suddenly limited to those serving before 1874. Merchants were abruptly forbidden to bring clerks or servants with them. Struck from the category of privileged artisans were tobacco workers, piano-tuners, butchers, galoshes menders, bricklayers, carpenters, plasterers and gardeners. There were particularly severe restrictions on women workers, except for prostitutes. (A prostitute who ceased to ply for hire was quickly spotted by the police and sent back to the ghetto.) A Jewish midwife privileged to practice outside the Pale could not have her children with her unless her husband was also a 'privileged person'.

Students who took their degrees abroad, because of anti-Jewish quota restrictions at Russian universities, were not entitled to privileged status. In the Caucasus, so-called 'Mountain Jews', who claimed their forefathers were deported there by Nebuchadnezzar in 597 BC, had rights of residence; on the other hand, they could not go anywhere else. Jews privileged to live outside the Pale were not allowed to have even a son or a daughter sleep in their houses, unless they too were privileged. In fact, privileged Jews faced an additional set of restrictions outside the Pale, and if they broke the rules were fined on the first offence, and banished on the second. The law on all these points was exceptionally complex and subject to endless changes by votes of the senate, ministry circulars, rulings by the local authorities or arbitrary decisions by officials high and low.

Enforcing these constantly changing codes was a nightmare for all concerned except the corrupt policeman or bureaucrat. Visitors from the West were shocked to see troops of frightened Jews being driven through the streets by police posses in the early hours of the morning, the result of 'oblavas' or night raids. The police were entitled to break into a house during the night using any force necessary and demand documentary proof of residence rights of everyone, irrespective of age or sex. Anyone unable to produce it instantly was taken to the police station. Jews were constantly humiliated in front of gentile neighbors, thus keeping alive the view that they were different, subhuman, and perpetuating the pogrom instinct. Even in first-class hotels, police stopped and questioned people on suspicion of 'Jewish physiognomy'. They were quite capable of banning distinguished foreigners, Oscar Straus, the American ambassador to Constantinople, being one victim. Jewish pianists were allowed to compete for the International Rubinstein Prize in St. Petersburg, but only on condition that they did not spend the night in the city.

Occasionally, the police organized massive 'Jew Hunts'. In Baku, police surrounded the stock exchange, arrested every Jew and took them to the police station where each was forced to prove his right of residence. In Smolensky district, at Pochinok, mounted police in 1909 surrounded the entire town but flushed out only ten 'illegals'; they had a big hunt through the woods and found 74 more. The Law of Settlement corrupted the entire police force, which milked the Jews. When business was slack, police chiefs would encourage Christians to draw up petitions calling for expulsions on the grounds that Jews were 'causing local discontent'. Then poor Jews would be thrown out and rich ones 'tapped'. The poor, returning to the Pale, became a growing social problem. In Odessa, for instance, over 30% were dependent on Jewish charities.

The residence laws, however, were only the beginning of the Jews' troubles. The government demanded fixed quotas of Jewish conscripts from the local communities. But these took no account of emigration. Jews should have provided no more than 4.13% of recruits. The government demanded 6.2%. Some 5.7% were actually produced, and this led to official complaints about the 'Jewish deficit' - provoking, in turn, antisemitic clamor that Jews evaded conscription. In fact, they furnished between 20 and 35% more than their fair share. From 1886 families were held legally responsible for non-service of conscripts and fined heavily; there was no possibility of successful evasion without massive bribes. But if the state forced Jews to soldier, it circumscribed narrowly how they did it. Jews were banned from the guards, the navy, the frontier or quarantine service, the gendarmerie, the commissariat and clerical grades. In 1887 they were banned from all military schools and army examinations, so effectively excluded from becoming officers. In 1888 they were banned from army dispensaries, in 1889 from military bands.

All Jews whatsoever were banned from any kind of state service in Moscow and St Petersburg. In theory, a Jew holding an MA or doctorate was eligible for certain posts elsewhere but, reported Wolf, 'without undergoing the rite of baptism it is well-nigh impossible for a Jew to fulfill all the conditions preliminary to employment by the state'. There was not a single Jewish teacher in the state system. There was no Jewish university professor and only a handful of lecturers. There were no Jews in the Justice Department, no examining magistrates, only one judge (appointed during the last 'liberal' period). Ministry circulars forbade the appointment of Jews as police inspectors: they were to be used only as spies or informers. Jews formed the majority of the urban population in six main regions and in many towns they were in a big majority, but they were not allowed to vote in municipal elections or stand for office; in the Pale government could 'appoint' them, up to 1/10th of the total. Jews were excluded from juries, from the boards of asylums or orphanages. From 1880 they were forbidden to practice as notaries and from 1890 as barristers and solicitors, without special permission - Wolf reported none had been given for fifteen years. They were forbidden to buy, rent or manage land beyond the immediate precincts of the Pale towns and shtetls. They could not even buy land for cemeteries. As with military service, Jews were accused of being unwilling to work the land, but in practice the regulations made this impossible, and wrecked the few Jewish agricultural colonies which had been established. Moreover, the fear that Jews would evade property laws by third-party transactions led to a mass of additional regulations covering partnerships and joint-stock companies. Hence many companies excluded Jews even as shareholders, and the fact was marked on share-certificates. Jews were excluded by law from mining industries, and a further set of regulations attempted to keep them from dealing in gold, oil, coal and other minerals.

Next to the residence qualifications, the antisemitic laws most hated by Jews governed education. Jews were excluded completely from such top training institutions as the St Petersburg Institute of Civil Engineers, the Army Medical College, the St Petersburg Electrical Institute, the Moscow Agricultural College, the St Petersburg Theatrical School, the Kharkov Veterinary Institute and the various colleges of mines. Their attendance at secondary and high schools was governed by the quota system or numerous clauses. They could occupy up to 10%

of such places in the Pale, only 5% outside and only 3% in Moscow and St Petersburg. The 25,000 'chedarim' schools, with 300,000 pupils, were forbidden to teach Russian, to stop children getting a secondary education. As a result of these measures, the number of Jews in the higher schools fell dramatically and parents fought desperately to get their children in, often bribing the gentile headmasters, who had a fixed scale of charges.

The anti-Jewish codes of Tsarist Russia thus succeeded, chiefly, in corrupting every element in the state service. They were an extraordinary amalgamation of past and future. They looked back to the medieval ghetto and forward to the Soviet slave-state. What they did not do was 'solve' the Jewish problem. Indeed, by radicalizing the Jews, they ended, it could be said, in solving the Tsarist problem. Despite all the restrictions, some Jews continued to prosper. Discrimination was purely religious and by getting themselves baptized, Jews could evade it completely, at any rate in theory. In Russian music, for instance, Anton Rubinstein (1829-94) and his brother Nikolay (1835-81), whose parents had converted, ran the Petersburg and Moscow Conservatories for many years and dominated the musical scene during the great age of the Russian symphony and opera. Even non-Christian Jews contrived to flourish in a rapidly expanding economy, being strongly represented in brewing, tobacco, leather, textiles, grain, banks, shipping, and railways and, despite the bans, oil and mining.

Hence the government code did nothing to reduce antisemitism. Quite the contrary. While baptized and smart Jews did well, the code impoverished or criminalized others, so ethnic Russians ended by both envying and despising the race, accusing Jews of being, at one and the same time, perfumed and filthy, profiteers and beggars, greedy and starving, unscrupulous and stupid, useless and too 'useful' by half. Russian antisemitism had all kinds of ingredients. The Tsarist regime persecuted other minorities besides the Jews but it was skillful at setting them off one against another, and in particular in inciting Poles, Letts, Ukrainians and Cossacks to go for the Jews. Indeed, Russia was the only country in Europe at this time where antisemitism was the official policy of the government. It took innumerable forms, from organizing pogroms to forging and publishing the Protocols of the Elders of Zion.

The object of the government was to reduce the Jewish population as quickly and as drastically as possible. A glimpse of the mentality of the Tsarist regime can be found in the diaries of Theodor Herzl, who interviewed several ministers in St Petersburg in 1903 to solicit help for his Zionist program. The Finance Minister, Count Serge Witte, by Tsarist standards a liberal, told him: "One has to admit that the Jews provide enough reasons for hostility. There is a characteristic arrogance about them. Most Jews however are poor, and because they are poor they are filthy and make a repulsive impression. They also engage in all sorts of ugly pursuits, like pimping and usury. So you see it is hard for friends of the Jews to come to their defense." When asked to what circumstances he would attribute this, he stated: "I believe it is the fault of our government. The Jews are too oppressed. I used to say to the late Tsar, [A280] Alexander III, "Majesty, if it were possible to drown the six or seven million Jews in the Black Sea, I would be absolutely in favor of that. But if it is not possible, one must let them live." Witte said further: 'the Jews are given encouragement - to emigrate. Kicks in the behind, for example."

The first modern Russian pogrom came in 1871 in Odessa.[8] It was instigated chiefly by Greek merchants. There was an ethnic element in most of the disturbances of the 1870s, Slav nationalists being particularly violent in their antisemitism. But after the murder of [A279] Alexander II in 1881, the state took over, and the 'kicks in the behind' followed in rapid succession. The major pogroms which began on 29 April 1881 were incited, condoned or organized by the Minister of the Interior, Ignatiev, an enthusiastic Slavophile. They spread over one hundred centres, lasted nearly a year, and in some cases involved huge mobs. Not only the government but the police and innumerable ethnic groups were involved. The far left joined in. The revolutionary Narodnaya Volya party incited the Ukrainians to kill the Jews in August 1881 under the slogan: 'Rise against the Tsar of the 'pans' (nobles) and the 'zhids' (Jews).' Great liberal writers like Turgenev and Tolstoi remained silent. The pogroms were followed by a mass of antisemitic legislation, known as the May Laws. Indeed, the pogroms were used to justify the legislation, the argument running: mob attacks on the Jews, while deplorable in themselves, indicate the extent of popular indignation against this anti-social minority; therefore its activities must be restricted. Of course the government inspired and permitted the mob action in the first place, and the whole aim of the regime was to bolster its crumbling popularity by attacking an easy target. The Nazis were to use exactly the same technique of violence-led legislation. Hence the 30 years 1881-1911 were a long calendar of anti-Jewish actions: 1882, May Laws; 1886-9, restrictions of Jewish entry to the professions and reduction of the Pale area; 1891, over 10,000 Jews expelled from Moscow; 1893-5, huge expulsions from non-Pale areas; 1894-6, introduction of the spirits monopoly, an economic catastrophe for the Jews; from 1903, a series of vicious pogroms, in which Jews were not merely robbed but killed. At [C14] Kishinev in 1905, fifty Jews were murdered and 500 injured. In [C29] Odessa, a four-day pogrom in 1905 killed more than 400 Jews. In Bialystok, the police and the army joined in the pogroms of 1906. From 1908 to 1911 there were more large-scale expulsions.

Hence from 1881, this vicious, mounting and cumulatively overwhelming pressure on Russian Jewry produced the inevitable consequence, a panic flight of Jews from Russia westwards. Thus 1881 was the most important year in Jewish history since 1648, indeed since the expulsion of the Jews from Spain in 1492. Its consequences were so wide, and fundamental, that it must be judged a key year in world history too. The first big rush to get out came in 1881-2. Thereafter Jews left at an average of 50,000-60,000 a year. With the Moscow expulsions, 110,000 Russian Jews left in 1891 and 137,000 in 1892. In the pogrom year 1905-6, over 200,000 Jews left. The exodus was by no means confined to Russia. Between 1881 and 1914 more than 350,000 Jews left Austrian Galicia. More Jews emigrated from Romania, where they were also under pressure. The net result was not to reduce the Jewish population of eastern Europe. In 1914 there were still five and a half million Jews in Russia and two and a half million in the Austrian empire. What the movement did was to take the natural population increase, some two and a half million, and

---

[8] Editor's note: Not only did the Greeks and Russians harbored religious antipathy towards the Jews, but another major background element was growing commercial rivalry in the grain trade. Czar Alexander II's assassination in March 1881 triggered mobs of peasants and new urban dwellers to attack Jews and their homes and stores. Beginning in Elisavetgrad, Kiev, and Odessa they quickly grew in scope. 219 occurred in villages, 4 in Jewish agricultural colonies, and 36 in small towns and cities. Some 35 Jews were killed by 1882 and many more were injured. In total 259 pogroms were recorded during 1881-1884. The material damage was considerable. Historians now believe the authorities did not instigate these pogroms, yet they occurred while those in government circles and the press blamed Jews for the ills the came as the result of industrialization and modernization.

transfer it elsewhere. Therein lay momentous effects, both for the Jews and for the world. We must now examine them in turn.

Of these emigrants, more than 2,000,000 went to the United States alone, and the most obvious and visible consequence, therefore, was the creation of a mass American urban Jewry. This was a completely new phenomenon, which in time changed the whole balance of Jewish power and influence in the world, and it came quite suddenly. The original Jewish settlement in America was small and slow to expand. As late as 1820 there were only about 4,000 Jews in the United States, and only seven of the original thirteen states recognized them politically. The slow growth of the community is hard to understand. As we have seen, there were few legal barriers to Jewish advancement.

#3 HELP TO IDENTIFY PEOPLE [Annn] AND PLACES [Cnn]

To aid in navigating the peoples mentioned, each person named explicitly in the text has a unique ID number [A001] through [A835]. All appear sequentially organized in the book's appendices. All geographic places in Russia are numbered [C01] through [C43].

Appendices:
A. Timeline of Father's life
B. Names, where a=spouse; b=second spouse
  [A001…105] Family in Knyazhe (Voskoboinik, Robboy, Gerson)
  [A160…275] Knyazhe residents (other than family)
  [A290…625] B'nai Khaim
  [A650…835] America, primarily Clevelanders
C. Shtetls, villages and cities mostly in Ukraine
D. Maps
E. Pogrom of Sokolivka annihilation
F. Headstones

Historical numbering

Cousin [A457] Joe Gillman, in writing his book about the American "B'nai Khaim," developed a numbering system with each letter representing a generation. Thus, "A" was generation "1", "B" generation "2", etc. Today we are at the 9th generation. The subscript 1 through "n" denoted the sequence of birth. The founder, Khaim, had no letter (pre-"A"). Subsequently, we found he had two brothers, requiring the awkward designation *0, *1, and *2. Further complicating this book's writing, new persons were included, who, while being John's relatives or acquaintances, were not of the B'nai Khaim. Hence, I've introduced a new numbering system. Thus, John is now [A026], but A1B7C5 in the Gillman book or *0A1B7C5 when accounting for the two new brothers discovered.

Numbering.

The spouse of each couple has the suffix "a." Second spouses, when known, receive the suffix "b", e.g., [A024b] is Bessie Kimmelman, who is the second wife of Father's brother, [A024] Joseph Robboy.

Our family records multiple marriages between cousins, e.g., Chaim Dudnik and Brukha Dolgonos. These unions present a logical problem in assigning identification codes. Using the system adopted based on birth order within a family, Chaim is [A326] as a Dudnik but [A413a] as a Dolgonos spouse. The male partner's code classifies most such unions.

Several relations were complicated and the numbering was handled in the manner thought clearest. This occurred when 1) cousins married other cousins for the second time or 2) cousins were adopted by other cousins. Examples are where: 1) cousin's [A431] Alta 2nd marriage was to her cousin [A431] Motel Gelman, and 2) adoption by others in the family ([A018] Nathan and [A021] Pauline Robboy) and [A360] Olga Dudnik.

Several others in this book's cast pose other numbering issues. Shmiel Robboy is a central descendant on one tree (Kynazhe/Robboy tree) but the spouse on the other (B'nai Khaim tree). Who should receive the primary designation, and who is the spouse ("a")? For simplicity, I report both Shmiel and his wife as [A011]. Both appear on both trees (Knyazhe families) and (B'nai Khaim) as primary.

Cautions: Many children and their many descendants are named for ancestors. I have tried with the numbering system to correctly identify each person as unique and appropriately within the numbering scheme.

Many individual persons have variations of the spellings of their names, depending upon who knew them. This William, Velvel and Wolf are the same and appear in the stories. Also the second name as listed herein is the same of the first but with a letter variation. I did not distinguish true middle names from the second variation.

Virtually every town mentioned has multiple spellings, and in many cases, unique cities exist with identical names. Sokolivka, used here, is currently on the English maps and in Leo and Diana Miller's book, "Sokolivka/Justingrad," but it is Sokolievka in Cousin Joe Gillman's book "B'nai Khaim." A second Sokolivka is located on the same highway, about 66 miles north (or 35 miles south of [C13] Kiev). According to JewishGen, there are 14 separate localities named Sokolovka or Sokolivka in the Ukraine. Such duplication should not be surprising. There are 28 Clevelands in the USA, 3 in the United Kingdom and 2 in Austrailia..

Knyazhe, the spelling adopted in this book, is how Father spelled the village. Its full name in Father's time as he and his family knew it was Knyazhe-Krinitsa. The JewishGen Gazetteer today lists it as Knyazhaya-Krinitsa (also as Knyazhe-Krynytse, Knyazhe-Krynytsya, and Knyash'ya Krinits) in the Cherkasy Oblast,[9] Ukraine 19113. Current Google maps spell the name as Knyazha-Krynytsa. A smaller village with a similar name, Knyazhyky, is nearby. A more major Knyazhe exists and is located about 350 km west, near Lyiv, an incorrectly is JewishGen lists members of the B'nai Khaim. A smaller town with the same name lies 40 miles north of that. Other names are Kniaze, Knyash'ye, and Knjaze.

---

[9] The administrative districts today in Ukraine from largest to smallest are:
  Oblast = province
  Raions or Region = district
  Misto = city/town
  Selo = village

The Family – The Shtetl

#4 [A026] JOHN AND SARAH ROBBOY'S FAMILIES

John's Introduction

My original intention was to describe my birthplace and the soil that endowed me with the qualities of its natural products. The products are not only the beets, cabbages, and onions but also the people, who, in all their humility, simplicity, and wholesomeness, grew more lovely and enchanted with time.

Like them, I never grew into prominence. Like them, my opportunities were lacking. So were my abilities and skills.

Like them, I tried my very best to carry out the mission assigned to me, honestly and ethically, and always strove to safeguard my integrity.

Maybe that is why some of my friends called me Honest John. [A710] Dr. Moses Garber, a physician at Mr. Sinai Hospital in Cleveland, always called me John the Baptist. When I entered the Shapiro clan, I was crowned Uncle John. To all others, including my colleagues, I was always known as plain John, and plain John suits me most.

Contrary to my original intention, these chapters have become a biographical sketch. It is not intended for publication since I lack the necessary skill. I only hope those who knew me and who are interested in knowing about their roots and the strength derived from that heritage will read it.

INTRODUCTION

My family came from two small towns halfway between [C13] Kiev and [C29] Odessa in Ukraine, Russia. They were [C01] Knyazhe-Krinitsa (meaning the Prince's Well) with about 30 Jewish families and [C02a] Justingrad, with about 800 Jewish families. Justingrad itself was adjunct to the larger town [C02b] Sokolivka. (See the footnote in Chapter #7 for a detailed origin of the villages and their relation to each other). Most town residents in all of these communities were farmers. A few of the family, the Dudniks and Galaks (later Galler), came from [C36] Uman.[10]

---

[10] Uman, located in central Ukraine, in what historically was the eastern region of Podolia, is one of the Cherkasy Oblast's (province) principal cities. It is the nearest major city near Sokolivka and Knyazhe. Dating back to 1616, Poland privately owned the city. From 1672 to 1699, it was part of the Ottoman Empire. Between 1726 and 1832, the Polish noble family, Pototski, owned it. In 1786, by which time Uman had grown in economic and cultural importance, Cossack rebels captured it during an uprising and purposefully massacred the Jews, Ukrainian Uniates,

CHAIM AND OSNA KAPROV

My maternal great-grandparents were [A290] Chaim Kaprov, [11] born in 1800 and [A290a] Osna, whose birthday is uncertain. According to modern texts, the name "Kaprov" was common in [C36] Uman and [C21] Lipovetz. It derives from the Ukrainian word "Kapravyj," meaning "pus-eyed." Alternatively, it comes from "Kapar," meaning "persons who became poor."

Fig. 4-1: [A574] Itzhak-Yoel Kaprov with unknown child.

[A290] Chaim was a candle maker. He lived at first in the village of [C02b] Sokolivka but later moved to [C02a] Justingrad (also Yustingrad), which adjoined, but was owned privately and open to Jews. Little else is known about him.

His children included [A291] Yossel, [A419] Beryl, [A530] Shmuel Abba, [A531] Gedalia, [A552] Shemaria, [A573] Khaye, and [A574] Itzhak-Yoel. [A290a] Osna died in 1842. Chaim

---

and Poles. Worse, the then military commander of the city betrayed the Jews present, permitting their murder in exchange for clemency towards the Poles. Some 20,000 Jews and Poles died. During the 20th century, Uman became linked by rail to Kiev and Odessa. The industrial sector quickly developed after that. The City grew to over 50,000 in 1914 from 10,100 in 1860 and 29,900 in 1900. Uman teemed with Jews during the 18th and 19th centuries. But during World War II, in 1941, the Battle of Uman took place. The Germans deported the entire Jewish community, murdered 17,000 Jews, and raised the town, annihilating the Jewish community and history.

Uman, to this day (9/2020), remains an important Jewish site, historically. With the current COVID pandemic still raging world-wide, the Ukraine, at Israel's request, refused the Breslov Hasidim and others from traveling to Uman for their annual gathering for Rosh Hashanah. It wa s felt irresponsible to allow gathering of thousands which would only further foster virus spread. Unfortunately, the Hasidim have refused to accept the verdict and instead joined the protest against the government. In Israel, this has proved problematic for the prime minister, Benjamin Netanyahu, because Uman is important to his voters. It seems struggles will always continue.

[11] In Wagner's memoirs, Khaim Kaprov is actually Chayyim Lichtzieher, Chayyim the Candle Dipper, whose little manufactory was where he made tallow candles, in those days the shtetl's only source of lighting., Kaprov is the literal translation of candle maker. https://www.jewishgen.org/yizkor/Sokolivka/soke001.html. It was in the early 1800s that [A277] Alexander I decreed all persons must have a surname.

took a second wife, [A290b] Edassey, who bore [A577] Isroel. Chaim died in 1869 at the age of 69.

[A419] BERYL KAPROV AND [A419a] DVOSSIE BRODSKY

Beryl Kaprov, John's maternal grandfather, was born in 1824. In later years, he developed a deep interest in the history and laws of the Jewish people. He spent much of his time reading the Bible. He was a small businessman.

Dvossie Brodsky was born in [C41] Voznesensk in 1824. Her father was the proprietor of a beet-sugar refinery. Her family's wealth provided her a large dowry; therefore, she was able to marry a "learned" man, Beryl Kaprov. (See footnote in Chapter 8.)

Beryl and Dvossie had eight children: [A420] Khaye Golda, [A422] Pessie, [A461] Daniel, [A462] Yenta, [A502] Leah, [A510] Itzhak, [A011] Malka, and [A515] Avrom.

Beryl died in 1908 at the age of 84, and Dvossie in 1894 at the age of 70.

[A010] BEN ZION ROBBOY AND [A010] LEAH VOSKOBOINIK

I know little about my paternal grandparents. Ben-Zion was a pious man who believed that everything happened because God wanted it. Leah, on the other hand, was less religious. Her last name, "Voskoboinik," which appears in the regions of Zhitomir, Starokonsk, Tarashcha, Berdichev, Bratslav, Proskurov, and Ol'gopol, comes from the occupational name, "wax- worker - or one who makes honey."

[A011] SAMUEL (SHMIEL) ROBBOY AND [A011] MALKA KAPROV

Samuel Robboy, my father, was born in 1862. He was an unskilled worker but well-educated in Jewish traditions and laws. Malka Kaprov was born in 1863. Her family, which was exceedingly religious, came from [C02a] Justingrad/Sokolivka. Five of her seven children survived: [A012] Hyman, [A017] Nessie, [A024] Joe, [A023] Tobie, and [A026] John. The two others died in early childhood.

Fig. 4-2: [A011] Shmiel Robboy and [A011] Malka Kaprov Robboy

Fig. 4-3: Robboy siblings, c1811. Top: L-R [A023] Tobie, [A026] John; Lower: [A024] Joe, [A012] Hymie.

Shmiel worked as a merchant. Later he and Malka opened a clothing store. She became a seamstress and taught her daughters, Nessie and Tobie, to sew also. The three worked in the store while the other children tended the animals or became apprentices.

The family came to America at different times when the children were in their teens.

Fig. 4-4: Circa 1912 or 1913;
Top: [A035] Nathan M Robboy, [A431a] Dov Pearlman, [A457] Joe Gillman.
Middle: [A527a] Frank Lehrman, [A026] John Robboy, [A023] Tobie Robboy, [A024] Joe Robboy, [A494] Willie Trachtman.
Lower: [A012] Hymie Robboy, [A011] Malka Robboy, [A011] Shmiel Robboy, [A018] Nat Robboy, [A017a] Nessie Gerson Robboy, [A021] Pauline Robboy.

JOHN ROBBOY

[A026] Yaakov ("John") Robboy was born in [C01] Knyazhe-Krinitsa in Ukraine in 1893. He began his education in a cheder (school for Jewish children teaching Hebrew and religious knowledge) and later went to other towns for further instruction. At age 16, he left for [C14] Kishinev to apprentice as a mechanic. He planned to remain there for three years, receiving room and board at the equivalent of five dollars per year, increasing by five dollars annually. He ended his apprenticeship after the first year and soon came to America (1910).

Within three weeks following his arrival to the United States (November 7, 1910), John began working for [A691] Dr. George Neil Stewart, Director, Department of Experimental Medicine, at Western Reserve University School of Medicine. The university doctors helped him learn English and his studies at school. He soon became an American citizen. After graduating from Central High School (~1914-1916), he began college at Western Reserve University (~1916-1921), but World War I interrupted this. John entered the Army as a contentious objector and served as a hospital orderly. In 1926 he obtained his Doctor of Medicine degree from the University of Michigan, after which he served an internship at the St. Vincent Hospital in Toledo, OH.

John married [A026a] Sarah Shapiro in 1936 and had two children, [A027] Myrna and [A031] Stanley.

Fig. 4-5: [A026] John Robboy, [A026a] Sarah Shapiro Robboy (born [A679] as a Shapiro).

John was a Judaic scholar. In later years he assiduously studied Biblical and Talmudic law and participated in activities at the Jewish Community Center in Cleveland Heights. He was a member of the American Medical Association and Phi Lambda Kappa, a medical fraternity.

Dad died in 1980 at age 87 at the Mount Sinai Hospital, where he had been on staff for more than 50 years.

THE BRUDNOS

"Brudno," the name of John Robboy's wife's family, is found in the region of [C37] Vilna and Oshmiany. It derives from "Brudnyj," a Belorusian word for "dirty," or "bad." The earliest ancestor was the renowned [A650] Rabbi Menashe (ben Porat) ben Joseph (1767-1831), who was the town rabbi of Smorgon from 1827-1828. Among the several children was [A651] Hannah, who married [A651a] Ezra Selig Brudno. Their daughter, [A652] Batya Brudno, who was [A026a] Sarah Robboy's maternal grandmother, married [A652a] Wolf Rogovin, who then adopted the name Brudno to avoid military service in Czarist Russia as an "only son." They came from [C40] Volozhin, Poland, where there was a famous yeshiva (school for rabbinical students and others interested in the Torah and Bible).

[A652a] WOLF BRUDNO (originally ROGOVIN) AND [A652] BATYA BRUDNO

[A026a] Sarah's maternal grandfather, [A652a] Wolf "Chulka" Brudno, was a most interesting ancestor. He was born in [C40] Volozhin in 1815 and married at about the age of twenty. He had at least five children, one of them being Sarah's mother, [A665.1] Esther-Rochel. According to family tradition, he had two wives with as many 18 children between them. The second wife was believed to be Batya's sister, [A653] Balebrine Rolnick. Wolf was 85 at the time.

Although lacking a formal education, Wolf was bright and served as a consultant to the town's nobility. His wit surpassed that of everyone there. The people of the region knew him as the "little bee" (Pezolka) – allegedly not for his sweetness, but his sting.

Wolf never had to work but was comfortably supported by his wealthy brother. He died in 1916 at the age of 101, outliving all but Esther-Rochel. [A674] Uriah Shapiro recounts the family legend that tells about how he lived so long. Wolf was old when the angel of death came to him and said it was time for him to die. He replied, "I'm not ready yet. Take one of my children. They are already old and have the same blood as me." The angel carried out Wolf's request and was given the same response every time he came for Wolf in subsequent years. Finally, when Wolf was 101 years old, the angel said, "I have already taken all but one of your children, and I cannot wait for you any longer." And so, Wolf died at an age unsurpassed by any of his descendants. His wit and his extreme longevity made him a family legend.

[A665.1] ESTHER ROCHEL BRUDNO AND [A665.1a] OSIAS SHAPIRO

Esther Rochel Brudno, [A026a] Sarah's mother, was born in 1865. She had no formal education but became a successful businesswoman. Esther was a talented singer and had a lovely "stage" voice. When in her twenties, the local Count wished her to attend a music conservatory for voice lessons. Still, her father wouldn't permit it because singing at the time was not considered an honorable occupation. Later, Esther acquired a boarding house that she operated for the students at the yeshiva. It was large, with 16 rooms and five gardens. It provided her with the substantial income she used to support her family.

In 1885, Esther married [A665.1a] Osias Shapiro (born in 1860), a student at the yeshiva. Osias continued to study throughout his life, working only for less than a decade. Esther became the matriarch who earned the family's support, headed the household, and raised the children. She and Osias had six surviving children: [A666] Jacob, [A669] Leo, [A674] Uriah, [A026a] Sarah,

[A682] Emanuel (Mannie), and [A686] Ezra Zelig. [A668] Chaim, [A673] Joseph and [A667] Chyeneh died in Russia. [A678] Rivka perished in a fire in the early 1900s.

[A026a] SARAH SHAPIRO ROBBOY

Sarah Robboy was born in 1900 in [C40] Volozhin, Poland (Lithuania), and came to Cleveland in 1906. After graduating from Central High School in 1918 and the old Cleveland Normal School in 1920, she taught in the Cleveland public schools, successively at the Dike Elementary School, Lafayette School in 1925, Warner School in 1933 and Stanard School in 1935. She and John married in 1936. She was a member of Pioneer Women and Hadassah. She died at age 78 of metastatic intestinal cancer.

Fig. 4-6: Sarah Shapiro Robboy, as a child and adult.

#5 ROOTS

I am now probably the only one left who can provide information about our progenitors -- The ROBBOY, VOSKOBOINIK, and GERSON families whom we left behind in [C01] Knyazhe-Krinitsa.

THE ROBBOY FAMILY

Rabei, the original Ukrainian name, means a mixture of colors such as checkered clothes or a freckled face. Later we Russianized it to Riaboy and Ryaboy and finally Americanized it to Robboy.

Grandfather [A010] Ben-Zion came from [C24] Monasteristshe, some 12 versts[12] from Knyazhe. He married grandmother [A010] Leah in Knyazhe, where he made his home. Here he was greatly respected and was treated as a cleric. Apparently, he had some learning.

Grandfather had a brother, [A091] Itzhak Voskoboinik, who lived with his family in Shukai Voda (Seek Water). One of Itzhak's daughters, [A092] Shava, later lived in Winnipeg, Canada, circa 1930. Cousin [A080] Phyllis Gomel knew more about her and her family.

Grandfather also had a sister, [A093] Dinah. She was widowed and had two daughters. All three lived in [C22] Lohahievka, some eight versts from Knyazhe.

After Grandfather married [A010] Leah Voskoboinik and settled in Knyazhe, they had three sons: [A011] Shmiel, [A034] Mordecai, and [A079] Mendel. They also had a daughter, [A078] Sosi, who died with her infant in childbirth. To my knowledge, these were the only fatalities that Grandmother suffered during her activities as a midwife.

Grandfather Ben-Zion must have had what was considered a good education due to the recognition and honor the local congregation bestowed upon him. He had a seat (pew) at the Eastern Wall and, on Saturday morning, had the honor of introducing the prayers by reciting the "Adon Olam."[13] He was a very pious, orthodox man, working hard to eke out a livelihood. All week long, he dressed simply and poorly as he walked from house to house. With basket suspended over his left elbow and staff of Moses in his right hand, he traveled all through the town collecting the freshly laid eggs. These he carried home, where he counted and placed them in large oblong wooden boxes to be picked up by the egg dealers.

All work stopped on Friday at noon, and by 2 p.m. he was on his way to the bathhouse for a shvitz (sweat) and scrubbing, following which he went home. By late afternoon, Grandfather was

---

[12] A Russian measure of length, now obsolete, used in Czarist Russia. It nearly equals a kilometer (1.069) and is roughly two-thirds of a mile (0.6629). Thus, like a square kilometer, a square verst roughly equals two-fifths of a square mile (0.4394).

s
[13] ADON OLAM (Heb "Lord of the World"), rhymed liturgical hymn in 12 verses extolling the eternity and unity of God and expressing man's absolute trust in His providence. Its main place now is at the conclusion of the Sabbath.

wholly transformed. He was now dressed in a clean suit, white shirt, and polished shoes as he hurried to the synagogue to meet his Sabbath bride.

Later in life, when his sight failed him, I had the honor to lead him home from the services and stay with him overnight. Grandmother would give me her special attention. Then I would accompany him back to the synagogue in the morning. The Friday evening meal was quite festive as it becomes the Sabbath. We sang the "Kol Mekadesh"[14] and the "Yom Zeh Mechubad."[15] In the morning, we chanted the Torah portion assigned for the week. Following

---

14

Who duly keeps Sabbath, who welcomes the Bride,
Who truly protects her, God's Law for his guide,
A guerdon as Abram's his faith shall provide:
So inch, in your tents, 'neath your banners abide.

Who yearn for Ariel rebuilded once more,
Take Sabbath in joy from the Torah's rich store,
Come, lovers of God, let us praise and adore
Our God Who gave rest to His people of yore.

O seek Him, ye children of Abram His friend,
Be glad Sabbath's frontiers and bounds to defend,
Too late is her coming, too soon is her end,
This day of God's making: let gladness ascend!

God's Law gave us Sabbath His Law be obeyed
A bride 'mid her maids in fair samite arrayed;
The pure are her heirs, they proclaim as 'tis said
"God rested and blessed all His works He had made."

All holy her night and all holy her day:
Then come, sons of Jacob, your King's word obey
Rejoice o'er your flagons, with feasting be gay,
All Israel united to rest and to pray.

Who know Thee, who guard Sabbath's twofold behest,
O grant them Thy mercy, O shorten their quest
For Salem rebuilt; in Thy light be they blest,
By Thy streams of delight bring them safely to rest.

Nor sowing nor reaping their Sabbath profanes;
They rest and they feast thrice with grateful refrains:
Their goodness a sevenfold radiance remains,
Their stronghold the Lord Who eternally reigns.

[This stanza contained in the translation but not in the Hebrew]:
Thy word make us pure as the sky, Thy pure veil!
O let Thy grace guide us as herds in the dale,
Reposing at ease, while the moonbeams grow pale,
On meads by still streams whose cool waters ne'er fail

Translation by Herbert Loewe, *Mediaeval Hebrew Minstrelsy, Songs for the Bride Queen's Feast*, published 1926.

Information:
Read or sung Friday night by many different tunes. Written by R' Moshe ben Kalonymus.

[15] Yom Zeh Mechubad-Sung during Shabbat, the words of which read:
This day is honored, above all blest
This day the God of the worlds did rest

You have six days to labor away
The seventh is God's, His special day

that, we left for the synagogue. Grandfather let me do all the leading and must have enjoyed my chanting, especially the trilling of the "Shalshelet."[16] I believed he depended on my leading him, but I realized it was probably part of his enjoyment as I grew older.

When I left for the States, Grandfather gave me his Tanakh (Bible) as a gift because, he said, "You respect books." Unfortunately, I had no time for these books, so I gave them to a Mr. Hirsch, an orthodox Jew, who I thought would enjoy them or at least give them to the synagogue library.

Grandfather died at 70 from a genitourinary problem, probably prostatic.

[A010] Grandmother Leah was a simple, humble, illiterate woman like most women in town, but she was a decent and loving woman. Possibly, she could read Hebrew, not necessarily knowing its meaning. Grandmother used her natural talents and became the outstanding midwife in town, a service she gave freely and gratis to whoever called for it, without discrimination. I knew many of the children she delivered. All were well. She delivered my two sisters and four brothers as well as me, and here I am at 84, testifying to her skill and ability. As she grew older, one never saw her, but rather only the numerous shawls, large and small, in which she wrapped herself. She was always in pain, complaining of backache. None of us there were familiar with hysteria, malingering, hypochondria, or just plain old age arthritis. We just laughed and teased the poor older woman. Grandmother lived to about 80 years of age. She became quite sick, weak, and lived her last days with her youngest son, [A079] Mendel. During the Russian revolution, when the family had to run for their lives, Mendel carried Leah on his back to [C36] Uman,[17] where she died.

No work on the Shabbat, O this obey
For in six He made all, by His behest

This day is honored, above all blest
This day the God of the worlds did rest

Eat tasty food, drink well and sing
For God provides, if to Him you cling
Clothing and food so nourishing
Good meat and fish to eat with zest

This day is honored, above all blest
This day the God of the worlds did rest

His glory is told by the heavens above
the earth is filled with His kindness and love
See: He made all, to the gentlest dove
His work is perfect, east or west

[16] Cantillation mark found in the Torah, but exceedingly rare. The Hebrew word שַׁלְשֶׁלֶת translates into English as *chain*, which shows the connection of the worlds by the links of a chain. The symbolism of the Shalshelet is that the subject of the story is wrestling with his inner demons and is undergoing some hesitation in his actions. It is rendered musically by a long and elaborate string of notes, giving a strong emphasis to the word on which it occurs.

[17] To the families of Knyazhe and Justingrad/Sokolivka, Uman was the "big city." Odessa and Kiev were mere names. Uman had no more than 30,000 inhabitants, but to our kinfolk, it was their metropolis. It was the city with the incredibly beautiful Sofievka Park, to our family, the eighth wonder of the world. During the pogrom, it had become the insecure refuge when enroute to Romania, America, and Israel from their burning villages.

Our father, [A011] Shmiel, was a timid, humble, and hard-working man. He received the education available in Knyazhe, but no skills. Father was pious and honest in all his dealings. He tried everything and anything possible but could not provide enough for his growing family. His good fortune was to marry a true woman of valor. She was not only good looking but also able, charming, and dynamic. Though Mother, like all Jewish girls at that time, was never sent to school, she somehow learned to read and immediately became the women's leader upon her arrival in Knyazhe. She also proved to be fruitful. Within some ten years, she gave birth to seven children, two of whom died early in life. The first two, [A012] Hyman and [A017] Nessie, were twins. Mother made numerous friends among the old and the young. She was vitally interested and helped all. She was devoted to all of the family members, maternal and paternal, and was loved by all. Mother also set the character of our home.

Father's inability to provide forced Mother to call on her inner talents to help maintain the home and family. By the way, this was true of many of the mothers at that time. When Hyman, the oldest child, grew up, he was sent to [C36] Uman, where he was enrolled in the Yeshiva. After that, he went to [C14] Kishinev, [C29] Odessa, and finally, in 1910, he and I left for America.

Sisters [A017] Nessie and [A023] Tobie, along with Mother, taught sewing. Together they carried on a sewing establishment to which they later added a small dry goods business. Father helped, which supplemented our income.

On reaching adulthood, Nessie married her first cousin, [A017a] Avrom Shmiel Gerson. Her marriage ended in divorce but was blessed with two children, [A018] Nathan and [A021] Pauline. Father adopted them and then brought them and their mother to the States as his children and as Robboys.

[A023] Tobie was a beautiful and gifted girl. Had she lived in a large city, she undoubtedly would have had the chance to develop her endowments. She never married and died a disappointed woman.

At 16 years of age, [A024] Joe left for America. Mother now felt the need to write. I wrote out the Yiddish alphabet for her, and she began to write slowly, sounding out the letters. Within a short time, Mother mastered the art and became our chief correspondent, keeping tabs on the family, scattered throughout the continents: Russia, North and South America, Romania, and Palestine.

Joe worked and maintained himself on various jobs: buttonhole maker, overall-maker, painter, and decorator. His mathematical mind helped him in paperhanging. With just a glance at a suite of rooms, he knew exactly how much paper he needed. His more experienced comrades were baffled by his ability.

Joe was a socialist and later joined the Communist party. He married [A024b] Bessie Kimmelman, an anarchist. Despite their political differences, they got along beautifully. Neither needed anything for themselves. They were devoted to all. During my several summer vacations from school, I worked for Joe until the trade union stopped it. Joe never paid me anything in wages, but for four years, he sent $40 or $50 every month to sustain me while I was in school.

As previously mentioned, brother [A012] Hyman and I came to the States in 1910. Hyman soon found employment with the H. Black Company as a cutter. Some years later, he married [A012a] Rivka Meshenstein, who also had come from a nearby shtetl in Ukraine. Like all of these villages, hers was rudimentary, with unpaved streets and without running water. Hyman then gave up his job and opened a candy store on Kinsman Road and East 77th Street, where he eked out a livelihood. They had a son, [A013] Bernard, who took up podiatry. Following Rivka's death, Hyman joined his son in Los Angeles, where he died in his 80s. Bernard now lives in La Jolla, California, with his wife [A013a] Rosalie and three sons. The oldest son, [A014] David, married [A014a] Deborah Herzberg. They live in Portland, Oregon, where they run a book store. The younger two sons, [A015] Ronald and [A016] William, are musicians. Ronald is a member of the San Diego Symphony Orchestra.

[A026] Three weeks following my arrival in the United States on November 10, 1910, and with brother Hyman, I found employment with [A691] Dr. George Neil Stewart, Director of the Department of Experimental Medicine and his associate, [A692] Dr. David Marine, at what was then Western Reserve University (Now Western Reserve – Case University.) I was known as Dr. Stewart's boy. My job was to care for the various animals used for experimentation. At first, I was most unhappy, but Tobie felt it would be the right place for my future development. She proved to be correct. These men were kind to me. Gradually, I assumed more responsibilities as they saw my progress and found me trustworthy. I became an essential member of a small group. My wages, which began at $20 per month, slowly rose to $80 a month by 1913, when I entered high school and worked half days at half salary.

Despite language and other difficulties, I did well in high school and later in college, medical school, and internship. Assuming solo practice in August 1927 was difficult. I did poorly until July 1936, when I moved to a better location. Four weeks later, I married [A026] Sarah Shapiro, and the entire world changed. My practice improved, Sarah made a beautiful home, and everything brightened. In due time, [A027] Myrna arrived, and then her brother [A031] Stanley J. Life assumed a rosier color. By that time, we had moved our home to Cleveland Heights, a suburb of Cleveland.

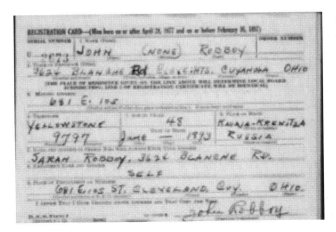

Fig. 5-1: Registration card (~1945)

Myrna grew up to be a beautiful young lady. She married [A027a] Herbert Groger, an attorney who owned and ran a travel agency. They gave us three splendid grandchildren: [A028] Laurel, who graduated high school in 1978; [A029] Richard, a sophomore at Exeter School in New Hampshire; and [A030] Debra, who entered junior high in 1977.

[A031] Stanley J. is (at this time of writing) an Associate Professor of Pathology at Harvard Medical School and Associate Pathologist at Massachusetts General Hospital. He married [A031a] Anita Wyzanski, who is now a practicing divorce attorney. They have two beautiful girls: [A032] Elizabeth and [A033] Caroline.

[A034] Mordecai, my father's brother, lived in [C43] Zashkov. He was an egg dealer, and I knew him slightly from his occasional visits to town. He is described elsewhere.

[A035] Nathan, who was also called N.M., was somewhat younger than I. He was small in stature, taking after his father, and even more vibrant than his father. I don't remember his going to school. He was an excellent horseback rider and popular in the town. The radical circle enlisted his help in spreading their leaflets in the neighborhood. My father brought Nathan to the States in 1912 as his son. Here he started shifting for himself, making a comfortable life for himself and his family, and eventually developed the Robboy Electric Manufacturing Company.[18]

---

[18] Additional history from [A035] Nathan's son, [A036] Mitchell, dated April 16, 2020. Father built his Remcraft Lighting business based on the training he received as a machinist after coming to the United States from Russia. [A010] Ben Zion Robboy brought him over as he was on the verge of getting into trouble with the Cossacks. His family had a farm, and he had become a superb horseback rider, a sport he continued to enjoy for the rest of his life. But in Russia, about the time of the Revolution, he was either caught or accused of riding his horses to distribute anti-tsarist brochures. He was set to be conscripted into the army (probably to get him killed). John sponsored him to come here and secure a job in Pennsylvania as a machinist trainee. I believe his farm machinery work helped him succeed, and he quickly became proficient with lathes, mills, etc. But he disliked the cold winters and so ended up in Cleveland. After a period, he started a business managing another electrician's wiring in new home construction. Part of that process required him to supply the lighting fixtures, which formed the nidus of his new company and manufacturing endeavor. The first store, then known as the Robboy Electric Manufacturing Company, was located near the lower end of Superior or Saint Claire Ave in Cleveland. And after a time, he moved to a building on Euclid Avenue just south of 55th Street. [A035] Stanley G, worked there as a teenager after school and weekends and received excellent machine training, learning also how to deal with the other employees. Nathan's 1st cousins, [A012] Hymie, worked there full time and for a while [A018] Nat Robboy. Even some of the younger Robboys worked there during the summer, including [A075] Eddie's son [A076] Marc, and [A026] John's son, [A031] Stanley J. worked there one summer. The Company was initially located in Cleveland, but later [A036] Mitchell moved the company to Miami and later Opa Locka, FL. Mitchell's son, [A044] Jeffery, is now the President. Today, it operates under the name, Remcraft Lighting Products, Inc.

Fig. 5-2: [A035] Nathan's family.

Fig. 5-3: Left: View from outside at 5900 Euclid Avenue, Cleveland. Right: [A035] Nathan with a customer.

Here I must say something about my parents. They were lacking in money but not in loyalty and spirit. They were ready to help each other at a moment's notice. I admire them for how they carried on under adversity.

THE VOSKOBOINIK FAMILY

		Spouse
[A001]	Laizer Eli	
[A002]	- Yakov Hersh	Aidi
[A003]	- Haskel	Faiga
[A004]	- - Donia	
	- - Daughter	
[A005]	- Sarah Faiga	Kalman
[A006]	- - Moshe	
[A007]	- - Yossel	
[A008]	- - Baila	
[A005b]		Boruch (h2 of Sarah)
[A010]	Leah	Ben-Zion Robboy
[A094]	Hannah	Levi Gerson
[A017]	- Avrom Shmiel	Nessie Robboy
[A018]	- - Nathan	
[A021]	- - Pauline	
[A098]	- Paya	Left for USA
[A099]	- Fullia	Uncle in Terlitza
[A100]	- Ruchel	
[A101]	- Nathan	
[A105]	Golda	Meir Grossman
[A107]	- Jennie	Pritzker
[A108]	- - Rose	
[A109]	- - Marvin	
[A113]	- Rayah	Shulman
[A120]	- Pauline	Julius Friedman
[A121]	- - Marvin	Susan Benjamin
[A122]	- - - Melanie	
[A123]	- - - Robert	
[A124]	- - Herschel	Shelly Skolnik
[A125]	- - - Stephanie	
[A126]	- - - Robin	
[A127]	- - - Ken	
[A128]	Haskel → Weiss	
[A129]	- Phillip	Elsie Schmuckler
[A130]	- - Harry	
[A133]	- - Herman	Jeannie
[A135]	- - Daniel	Karen Kilroy
[A139]	- Dave	Mollie Broth
[A140]	- Bessie	Jack Mesnick
[A141]	- - Rosilyn	Jack Sharwell
[A145]	- - Allan	Francine _____
[A148]	- Hyman	Sally Saltzberg
[A149]	- - Ronald	Doris Cohen
[A154]	- - Judy	Harvey Nudelman
[A157]	- - David	Eta S. Berner

Grandmother Leah Voskoboinik [A010] and her brother, [A001] Laizer Eli, are described below in this chapter. Her sister, [A094] Hanna, was married to [A094a] Levi Gerson, who, too, was an egg dealer. Levi was a sick man for many years, suffering from chronic lung disease. He was trying and mean, probably because of his illness. His oldest son, [A017a] Samuel Gerson, married sister [A017] Nessie twice and divorced her twice within three years. They lived together long enough to produce two children whom Father later adopted and brought to the States. Leah's other sister was [A105] Golda Voskoboinik.

Uncle [A001] Laizer Eli, my grandmother's brother, was patriarchal in appearance. He was a man who moved slowly and murmured, always pondering his thoughts. He was also the neatest man I ever saw. He had a business limited to two or three items: flour, oil, and grease for the wagon. When handling flour, he would don a clean jacket, covering his head and spine. One would see him carry a 100-pound sack of flour on his back, deposit it at the desired place, take off the jacket, and appear as clean as before he ever touched the bag. The flour was kept in an alcove at the side of the house. Next, he would measure off a quart or two of oil, never losing a drop or soiling his hands. The grease for the wagons was measured out from barrels in front of the house. He accomplished his deals so deftly that he never dirtied his hands nor clothing with any of these. He was always spotlessly clean. Apparently, the business was never rushing during the long warm summer day, for he still had time enough to rest on his veranda, warming himself in the sun.

He had no more education than any other man in town, but he had an excellent talent for embellishing rumors into exciting stories. He narrated them to us kids, especially when we found him on the veranda, hoping for a customer to come by. When I grew older and more appreciative of the man, I dubbed him the Hans Christian Andersen of Knyazhe.

His wife, Aunt [A001a] Paya Voskoboinik, was a simple, humble, illiterate, pious woman, a good wife, and a mother. She suffered from a chronic nasal obstruction, possibly greatly enlarged adenoids. She carried on silently with all her duties, and every Saturday morning, attended the synagogue. Though unable to pray, she listened attentively, as did most of the women.

Aunt Paya was embittered by the people who teased her by imitating her speech. She was sensitive. We knew it and further mocked her by imitating her. She, of course, was helpless. Occasionally our prayers would be interrupted by what appeared to be an earthquake, but it would only be a fight among the men. Soon all would go out into the street where they continued the strife by throwing epithets at each other. The women and children also joined in. This torture continued until Aunt Paya reached her veranda where she would turn about, lift her skirt, and thrust her behind to the people saying "Na," which translated means "Kiss my ass," thus always ending the fight. The "Na" intrigued me considerably. I wondered for some time what she was hiding behind that skirt. Hence, I spied on her whenever she climbed the stepladder to the attic or always managed to let her go up the ladder first. I tried to see what she hid underneath the skirt but never saw anything beyond her pantaloons.

Laizer Eli and Paya's oldest son, [A002] Yakov Hersh, married a beautiful young woman, [A002a] Aidi, who unfortunately was barren. Aidi was an educated, modern girl, able to write a letter. She could read the Hebrew prayer book and also knew a little arithmetic. To display her prowess, she would hand a complete account of her transactions from the Sunday bazaar to her husband. This action pleased him much, but Aidi did not realize the pitfall she created for herself. As time went on, her husband demanded the accounting, and it led to difficulties that, added to the fact that she was barren, ended in divorce.

The younger son, [A003] Haskel, married [A003a] Faiga from [C09] Christinovka. Faiga was not as good-looking as Aidi, but she was good-natured, attractive, cheerful, voluptuous and loving, and loved by all. She was full of vigor and charm. They had a cute little daughter, [A004] Donia, and were delightfully happy. Because I remembered her father's name, I was freed by an arresting policeman and saved from going to jail. Had he searched me, which he would have done if arresting me, he would have found me carrying a song in my pocket saying, "From the Ural to the [C10] Dunai, there is no one more stupid than [A281] Nikolai."[19]

Fig. 5-4: [A128] Haskel Voiskoboinik, later changed to Weiss. Circa 1915.

[A006] Moshe and [A007] Yossel were rejected by their parents. All and anybody in town raised Moshe. The peasants fed him, and he slept in their barns. Yossel fared somewhat better. [A001] Grandfather Laizer and [A001a] Grandmother Paya watched over him. When Moshe reached the age of military service, he drew the highest number. The quota was reached before his number was called, and he was now free. Moshe then left for Canada, where his mother and the other children joined him. He received them with all the love and kindness possible. They were a delightfully happy family.

THE GERSON FAMILY

[A094a] Levi Gerson was continually sick when I knew him and somehow faded out soon. He married Aunt [A094] Hanna, who was tall, thin, reasonably good-looking, and trying hard to eke

---

[19] See the Chapter, "The Cap".

out a livelihood. [A017a] Avrom Shmiel (Samuel), their son, married [A017] Nessie Robboy. Their marriage was a failure.

[A098] Paya's husband and their daughter left for America early in life and were never heard from since. She lived with the family.

[A099] Fullie, whose uncle lived in [C33] Terlitza, invited her to come to nurse his wife, who was dying from cancer. By the time the aunt died, Fullie had found herself pregnant. She returned home, intending to find someone to abort her. Grandfather Ben-Zion discovered this and objected to abortion as an act of murder. Instead, he convinced the uncle to marry her.

Our family helped [A101] Nathan to come to America. He soon found a job making caps. During World War I, he was drafted into the United States Army. Upon discharge, he opened a small factory of his own, married, and had a son. A short time later, he divorced his wife. Sometime later, [A816] Anna Minaker, a friend of ours, saw [A101] Nathan standing on East 105th Street smoking a cigarette when she was going to work. On returning at 6 p.m., she saw him standing in the same place. She reported this to sister [A023] Tobie, who verified the report. She then consulted me, who was already at school in Michigan studying medicine, and we both felt that Nathan needed psychiatric help. Tobie had him admitted to the Cleveland State Hospital. During my Spring vacation, I visited Nathan there. His attending physician advised me that Nathan should receive Veterans Administration (V.A.) compensation since the illness likely resulted from his army service. He advised me to look into the matter. Still, he warned me not to do anything without becoming the Executor of Nathan's estate, for, he said, "You are liable to get into trouble from which you will extricate yourself with difficulty." I turned this case over to [A295] Mr. Abe H. Dudnik, a young attorney and Mother's cousin, who, after two years of work, succeeded in getting a pension of $80 a month for Nathan and $20 a month for his son [A102] Irving.

Uncle [A128] Haskel Weiss and cousin [A035] Nathan (N.M.) Robboy refused to assume any responsibilities as Executors, and there was no one else for this job. I took on the responsibility, but Nathan promised to pay the expenses involved. Later he refused to keep his promise, though the amount was small – only $8. This refusal was an excellent experience for me. The hospital doctor's prediction was correct. With the first V.A. check arriving, all became concerned, for they thought I would abscond with it. The hospital sent in its full bill for some two years of care. The divorced wife and her sister, also cousin [A107] Jennie Pritzker, saw me, sister [A023] Tobie, and Attorney [A295] Dudnik growing fat on the enormous monies coming in from the government. They at least hoped for some crumbs for themselves. Since they were unwilling to help with the expenses, they had no idea what my obligations and duties were. The V.A., the courts, etc., had to and did approve every step of mine.

One rainy Friday evening, the divorced wife's sister called me to stop by on my way home. Naturally, I thought she wanted me to see someone sick in the family. When I arrived at her home on Lynn Drive, she simply told me that she did not wish me as Executor and asked me to give up the job. Neither she nor the divorced wife knew anything about what guardianship meant, what responsibilities it entailed, or that any debts had to be paid.

Soon after winning the claim for compensation, I wanted some advice about sending Nathan over to a V.A. institution. I went to talk to the Superintendent of the Cleveland State Hospital. To my disappointment, not one official knew anything about him. The doctor who once gave me advice was not there anymore. The Superintendent transferred me to one doctor, the latter to another. This repeated itself two or three more times. The only one familiar with the patient was the attendant, a massive, burly brute, who did not even care to treat Nathan gently during my presence.

I now had sufficient information and asked for his transfer to some V.A. hospital. Surprisingly and relatively quickly, he was relocated to Battle Creek, Michigan. Within days following his transfer, I learned that Nathan suffered from miliary tuberculosis, which killed him within three weeks.

The deceased was brought to Cleveland and buried. Now I had but one more duty to perform. I requested money to place a monument on his grave. This action the court had to approve. The divorced wife and her sister were there. The latter objected though I don't even know to what. On discovering who she was, the judge unceremoniously told her to leave the room at once and granted me the modest amount I had requested. I turned the few V.A. office dollars left over to the child [A102] Irvin. The V.A. office approved and closed the case.

Several years later, the child, now a grown boy, appeared in my office asking for an account of his father's case. My answer to him was to visit the V.A. office on East 14th Street, where all the facts in the case were available. He left my office. I never heard from him again. He assumed his mother's new married name of Kaffen. His full name is [A102] Irvin Gerson Kaffen, and he is in business in Cleveland. He has nothing to do with the family, feeling robbed and wronged.

THE ROBBOY FAMILY

		Spouse
[A010]	Leah Voskoboinik	**Ben Zion Robboy**
[A011]	- Shmiel	Malka Kaprov
[A012]	- - Hyman	Rivka Stein
[A013]	- - - Bernard	Rosalie Smotkin
[A014]	- - - - David	Rebecca
[A015]	- - - - Ronald	
[A016]	- - - - William	
[A017]	- - Nessie	Avrom Shmiel Gerson
[A018]	- - - Nathan	Rose Nedelman
[A019]	- - - - Nancy Ann	Mark W Cooper
[A020]	- - - - Marcia Lee	Jonathan Ames
[A021]	- - - Pauline G	Milton Siegel
[A022]	- - - - Donald R	Rosie Schwartz
[A023]	- - Tobie	
[A024]	- - Joe	Bessie Kimmelman
[A026]	- - John	Sarah Shapiro
[A027]	- - - Myrna L	Herbert Groger
[A028]	- - - - Laurel	
[A029]	- - - - Richard	
[A030]	- - - - Debra	
[A031]	- - - Stanley J	Anita Wyzanski

[A032]	- - - -	Elizabeth	
[A033]	- - - -	Caroline	
[A034]	-	Mordechai	Sarah Faiga Spector
[A035]	- -	Nathan	Rhea Heiser
[A036]	- - -	Mitchel	Leslie Shnader
[A037]	- - - -	Robin	
[A038]	- - - -	Jeffries	
[A041]	- - - -	Ryan	
[A039]	- - - -	Debra	
[A042]	- - -	Stanley G	Marion
[A043]	- - - -	Rebecca	
[A044]	- - - -	Rachel	
[A046]	- - - -	Michael	
[A045]	- - - -	Sarah	
[A047]	- -	Sylvia	Joe Isbitz
[A048]	- - -	Marilyn	Stanley Yellin
[A050]	- - - -	Stephanie	
[A051]	- - - -	Joseph	
[A049]	- - - -	Rhea	
[A052]	- - - -	Beverly	
[A053]	- - -	Rosie	A Waterman
[A054]	- - - -	Maurice	
[A055]	- - -	Shirley	Ira Manson
[A056]	- - -	Betty	Robert Koondel
[A056.1]	- - - -	Jennifer	Nathan Straus
[A071]	- -	Dorothy	Nathan Straus
[A072]	- - - -	Martin	
[A057]	- -	Morton	Helen Heller
[A058]	- - - -	Melvin	
[A059]	- -	George	Mary Frankel
[A060]	- - -	Rhoda	Richard Stamm
[A061]	- - - -	Blake	
[A062]	- - - -	Michael	
[A063]	- - -	Merle	
[A064]	- -	Rose	David Rein
[A065]	- - -	William	Joan Kest
[A066]	- - - -	David	
[A067]	- - - -	Marcia	
[A067.1]	- - - -	Robert	
[A068]	- - -	Susan	R Balyes
[A069]	- - - -	David	
[A070]	- - - -	Fred	
[A070.1]	- - - -	Gregory	
[A075]	- -	Edward	Sylvia
[A077]	- - -	Howard	
[A076]	- - -	Mark	Marilyn
[A078]	-	Sosi	
[A079]	-	Mendel	Anna Desatnick
[A080]	- -	Phyllis	Perry Gomel
[A081]	- - -	Francis	
[A082]	- - -	Bobby	
[A083]	- -	Sidney	Eva Desatnick
[A088]	- -	Ben	Irma Levin
[A089]	- - -	Stanton	
[A090]	- - -	Howard	

#6 [C01] KNYAZHE-KRINITSA AND THE FAMILY

Just how the name of my birthplace, Knyazhe-Krinitsa, came to be will forever remain undetermined. Suffice to say, Knyazhe still exists. It lies deep in Ukraine in the Province of [C13] Kiev, somewhere near [C36] Uman, [C38] Vinnitza and [C07] Berditchev. The region was the domain of the Polish feudal lord [A160] Krasitzki. His descendant, the current [A160] Graf Krasitzki, owned the entire township. I judge it was about a square mile in area. This was his estate. He also possessed much land and forests outside the town. One of the vast forests was near the [C24] Monasteristshe railroad station 12 miles away. A tall man with the biggest hawk-nose I ever saw, the Graf was responsible for converting Knyazhe into a township. He did this to retain his Jews, not because of special affection for them. He needed them, and they were not allowed by edict of the Czar to reside in villages. Though freed from serfdom in 1861, during the next 50 or so years until the Revolution, the Jews in [C01] Knyazhe-Krinitsa were still much under the Graf's rule and power. Like an island in mid-sea, his estate lay in the heart of the town and was surrounded by the peasantry.

Knyazhe was an unusually picturesque, slumbering, little town. It lay on a plateau at the foot of a very long high hill or low mountain with the Tykytch River[20] running through its entire length, bisecting it into two unequal parts. I am unsure if the Tykytch was a tributary to the Dneiper, Dniester, or Bug (editor, the latter). A bridge and dam at its mid-length served both to contain the river as well as to rejoin the divided parts. The town thus was given the shape of a huge letter "H." The long limbs formed the east and west sides of the town. The middle-connecting limb of the latter formed the bridge and dam to contain the river, which divided the town through its entire length. The four half limbs of the letter "H" were the streets named as follows:

Northeast limb --	Kashivka Street
Northwest limb --	Verbivka Street
Southwest limb --	Rinkivka Street
Southeast limb --	Utzelivka Street

The river was considerably widened between the northeast and northwest limbs by the bridge. Beyond the bridge, it ran through meadows, gardens, and orchards through and beyond the town. A road in the form of a widely opened letter "V" ran up the Northeast and Northwest limbs to carry traffic. This road was paved in 1907 or 1908.

Flanking the widened river to the west lay the Graf's huge estate. To the south lay the large marketplace.

---

[20] The Hnyly Tikych river, 157 km long, is a right tributary of the Southern Bug, the Tikych. The river's source is in the Stavyshche Raion (District), Kyiv Oblast, near village of Snizhky. A "right tributary," also known as a "right-bank tributary," is in orientation to the tributary's downstream current flow. According to the Michelin map of Ukraine (https://www.viamichelin.com/web/Maps/Map-Ukraine), the river flows through Knyazhe, and the other major homestead of the B'nai Khaim, [C02a] Justingrad / [C02b] Sokolivka, before turing north east, then east, and finally south. Just north of Novoarkhanhel's'k, it joins and becomes part of the Synyukha River. At Pervomajs'k, it becomes the Pivdennyl (Southern) Bug, meandering through [C41] Voznesens'k, and entering into the Black Sea near Mykolaiv.

The Graf had 11 homes scattered about the periphery of the place. Some of his workers and a few of his favorite Jews occupied these. These homes were extremely desirable because they consisted of three to four spacious rooms. There was also ample room for a cow and straw, wood with which to heat the house, a cellar, and a locker. These were luxurious homes in comparison with the one-room peasant huts, which were some 25-30 feet long by 12 to 15 feet wide. The oven was usually 25% of this room. In our home of 1900-1903, which I remember well, the beds occupied another quarter of the space, and the remaining space served as a dining room, bedrooms for [A017] Nessie and [A023] Tobie. [A024] Joe and I slept with our parents, and [A012] Hymie wasn't home.

The Graf's homes were much more desirable, and the rent, fortunately, was low. I doubt whether any Jew ever paid any rent after the first or second month. But once occupied, one was as confident of possession as if he bought the same with hard cash. The question was how to get in. First, one had to wait until there was a vacancy, i.e., someone had to die. Second, [A326] Chaim had to give permission, and Chaim did have two brothers, [A355] Leib and [A350] Froim, who needed a home. Elsewhere I will tell the detailed story of how we got the second half of the duplex where Chaim lived. There was a fight lasting two years between the Dudniks and ourselves over this move. It ended on Nessie's wedding night when all the Trachtmans were around, and the Dudniks would not venture to engage in a fight then.

The Poles working for the Graf occupied three of these homes: [A161] Pavlovsky, a manager of a sort, the mechanic, and the water carrier. The other homes were duplexes that were rented to Jews, usually Jews on good terms with the Graf.

Half of the duplex nearest the bridge served as a synagogue. It was an ordinary room with whitewashed walls that served us well for all occasions. Even the Jews of the neighboring villages came to us for the High Holidays. It was our Beit Hamidrosh (House of Study), the prayer House on weekdays, the Sabbath, and all Holidays, for Sabbath afternoon sermons by the Rabbi or itinerant magid (preacher). It served as our Beit Lamedroshand (town hall) for all major assemblies, for our Simhat Torah (Jewish holiday celebrating the conclusion of the annual cycle of public Torah readings, and beginning of a new cycle) pageant, also for weddings and any similar occasion.

A large room between the synagogue and the other half of the duplex was set aside for the ladies. This part also served as the public school. [A174] Aaron Korsunski, nicknamed "Gonta" because of his meanness and similarity to the infamous Ukrainian antisemite and murderer of the Jews in the 18th century occupied the other half of the duplex. Aaron always fought with us youngsters. Our best weapon was to hurl the eponym "Gonta" at him or to tease his daughter, [A175] Chaia, the cretin. The war between us sizzled all the time. Aaron was Jewish. He was an insignificant man and had nothing to do with the Graf.

The second duplex was also reserved for public use. One-half served as the public bathhouse, the other half as the residence for the caretaker. During the early days, my family lived with the caretaker's family. That is how I came to be born in the bathhouse, where I started on a career of public service almost immediately, as documented by sister [A023] Tobie.

The peasantry comprised a population of 2,000 to 4,000 and occupied the rest of the town. Following the abolition of serfdom in Russia by [A279] Czar Alexander II in 1861, each peasant family received some land in town and some in the surrounding field outside. How many acres of land this entailed I don't know, but the lots I knew were large. The peasants owned their land; the Jews, in contrast, were not permitted to own any. I am uncertain about their relationship with the Graf, but I know they neither rented the property nor shared the crops. Each consisted of a good-sized area for the family home, barns, stalls, and storage of grain. Next to the buildings was usually a large garden for the cultivation of cabbage, beets, radishes, onions and garlic, beans and peas, potatoes and other vegetables. Beyond the garden were substantial orchards with pear, apple,, and cherry trees.

Most peasants had at least two horses, a flock of sheep, many pigs, geese, deer, and chickens. The fields outside of town were used for the cultivation of grain: rye, wheat, buckwheat, oats, prosa millet (a tiny seed for kasha and as chicken feed), and some flax. The latter served for manufacturing linens.

With these resources, it is evident that the industrious peasant could do very well. However, having been robbed of initiative through the years of serfdom, many took to drinking and were poverty-stricken instead. Thus, the peasants were a very primitive but friendly animal. The peasant was kind, God-fearing, and amoral, but could be easily swayed and roused. By tradition, the Jew was not human to him. It was quite amusing to us to have peasants come up on summer days as we were sitting in front of the house and ask: "Are there Jews or people here?" He was not rude. It was asked in all innocence.

The Jewish population consisted of forty families, and about 165 men, women, and children. About twenty of the families occupied ten of the fairly comfortable homes that belonged to the Graf. Each consisted of a large living room, two bedrooms, and a kitchen. The others lived among the peasants in their one-room hovels. I really can't say that our Jews were either prosperous or poor. I know, however, that they did have a prosperity peculiar to Jews only, a prosperity rich in poverty and children. In reality, even our richest Jews were poorer than some of our poor peasants.

Pavements were not yet known in Knyazhe, nor were other modern conveniences such as plumbing, electricity, or even a privy. All roofs were straw-covered. The floors in the house and that of the large Dutch oven in the kitchen were of clay and had to be reconstituted or releveled once a week. We carried water by pail from the distant well in summer and in deep mud in autumn and in deep snows during the wintry cold frosty days. The kerosene lamp was still the mainstay of our lighting systems. But the springs and its warm sun rejuvenated us all, and, like the grass, we appeared happy and breathed the pure fresh air.

Jews were not allowed to own land or engage in certain activities or professions.[21] They were forced to depend upon their ingenuity to eke out a livelihood. Necessity forced their hidden

---

[21] John wrote that in Russia the Jew had but one profession open to him: rabbinism. Asked how he decided to enter medicine, he answered: In our free and wonderful American civilization all schools are allegedly open and free to all. Opportunities are present everywhere. In Russia we charged the civilization with failure to give these people the chance they sought. In our America where great educators and intellect abound, we thought and taught that all

innate qualities to rise to the surface when they were recognized and readily seized and utilized to advantage. That is how this small group of Jews came to provide all the varied services both Jewish and the much greater and vastly richer gentile communities needed for life. This group included the merchants, blacksmiths, furriers, carpenters, millers, egg dealers, seamstresses to sew their women's kaftans, the barrel makers, and shoe repairmen. It included cattlemen and dealers of the livestock, grain merchants, and winnowers of grain. The butchers supplied them with meats other than pork. It was the Jew who ran the flour mill and split the milled seed to provide grain for kasha. It was the Jew who skinned the dead animal when available, cured and tanned it making hides and sheepskin coats for the peasant, and who worked the thread of the sheep's wool into flannel as topping for these coats. The Jewish merchants and vendors provided grease for their wagons and oil for their lamps and other household necessities, combs, needles and thread, buttons, and even liquor, beer and soft drinks. It also included the saloonkeepers ([A326] Chaim and his brother owned the saloon, but the title, of course, was in the name of a gentile, as Jews were not allowed to sell liquor). The arendator[22] was also included. He was a leaseholder, i.e., the administrator of the mill, pond, and fish in the pond. The arendator did not necessarily have to be the Graf's manager. Thus, [A177] Shaia Korsunski was a leaseholder for a while, though he had no other privileges of the Graf. Lastly, this group provided services for the Graf, as well as general medical and obstetrical services.

The Jewish dealer bought the peasants' produce and collected the freshly laid eggs. The Jewish lessee owned the fish in the Graf's river and was the manager of the Graf's estate, the collector, and seller of his grains, his sugar beets, and his timber in the forests. These were a vibrant and ingenious group. As Jews, they were not allowed to live where there was no synagogue and bathhouse. Both requirements were met, and the excellent men in our community filled the needs.

The Jewish women always feared they might become tainted or unclean on their way home by encountering some pig or drunken peasant or some other unclean animal, thus annulling the purification of mikveh (ritual bath) and denying them the privilege of being with their husbands. All this could be obviated if the woman came in contact with something clean and innocent before venturing into the street. Since a child is most innocent, and Providence made me so readily available, I became the most sought after and admired servant in the cause. When I grew up and began to reflect upon my deeds and inclinations, I thought that this episode might serve as

---

schools and professions are open to all. How disappointing to find how these very forces (antisemetic policies and faculty) stand guard preventing this scum and vermin (Jewish students) from polluting the noble profession by various artificial means of percent norms and clandestine tools. Philosophically, he felt that the genius of man, whether in arts or science, is his great ability, drive and persistent stubbornness that should enable him to break through all difficulties and obstructions in his path. Every individual has some qualities which, under certain circumstances, could be made to rise to the surface and add much to our society.

[22] The arendator (literally "lease holder") (Ukrainian: "Орендар" (orendator), Russian: "Откупщик" (Otkupshchik)) was a person who leased fixed assets, such as land, mills, inns, breweries, distilleries, or of special rights, such as the right to collect customs duties, etc. Trusted individuals were often given such rights to collect rent or revenue and were allowed to keep a portion of the money in exchange for this service, sometimes as a reward for other services to the state. The practice is called "rent/revenue farming" (From Wikipedia). This practice was common in the Russian Empire, and Polish-Lithuanian Commonwealth, where Jews by law could not own property, and hence were forced to rent homes from a feudal landowner, who in turn had someone, often a Jew living there, manage the property for him.

a good explanation for my admiration of women and their beautiful breasts. Now, I feel, I may safely refute the theory advanced by the erudite Ph.D., Dr. Ashley Montague, a psychologist at Princeton, who in his article on "The Development of the Human Breast" (J Amer Med Assoc, Vol 180, June 9, 1962), ascribes man's desire to play with the breasts to the denial of the breast in infancy. To me, this is not at all convincing. My mother was quite generous in offering me her breasts, albeit empty. But she had nothing else to offer me except, perhaps, some curses. No, I am convinced that it was the beautiful women in Knyazhe who started me on the road of addiction, an addiction I still enjoy. I will always be thankful to them and will never forget and love them.

How early does memory develop? It is impossible to determine and is but one of many questions remaining unanswered in medicine. My memory goes back to about two years of age. Apparently, what happened was of sufficient significance to impress itself upon my mind. I remember exactly, and in full detail, how [A024] Joe and I followed [A017] Nessie, who was to drain the wine off the raisins in preparation for Friday's kiddush. In his desire to be first on the scene, Joe pushed me, and I fell, striking my forehead against the brick oven.[23] The next thing I knew, I was in bed with Mother applying cold towels to my head. There was not a doctor, feldsher (health care professional who provides various medical services limited to emergency treatment) or nurse in town. Mother was the chief consultant and best practitioner. In addition to the towels, she fed me candy, which served well for pacification. The candy consisted of small multicolored sugar balls contained in a small tin box with a central opening and thus served as a whistle. [A355] Leib Dudnik's supply of candy was soon exhausted, but the little he had served a noble purpose.

Forty years later, while in the doctors' lounge at Mt. Sinai Hospital, [A712] Dr. Sam Quitner noticed the scar above my left eyebrow. As he palpated it, he said: "You had a skull fracture." "Yes," I said and told him what happened. "There was no doctor in town?" "No," I said. "Well." he retorted, "That is why you are still with us." There is much truth in what he said. Actually, the fracture was limited to the outer table of the frontal sinus. It was, therefore, but a simple fracture and healed uneventfully.

There was no industry nor commerce, as we know it now, in our little towns. Also, there were no organized public school systems. The Christian children had a public school, but it was small and of poor quality. Actually, they were satisfied because all summer long the children helped their parents work in the fields and in the winter most of them hibernated as did their parents.

Education of the children was of primary importance to our folks, but how to attain it was a formidable task. They could only resort to the familiar cheder, and that is what it was, a schoolroom headed by a tutor (melamed), whom we addressed as rebbe (teacher). In actuality, there were two different tutors (melamdim), one for the beginners (dardaki melamed) and one for

---

[23] Decades later, Father describes the incident to a colleage at Mt. Sinai Hospital: How long our family lived in the bathhouse, I do not know, but I do know that at age 2 years of age, I sustained a fracture of the frontal sinus of the skull when my brother [A024] Joe threw me against the corner of the brick Dutch oven in our kitchen. Years later, when in the doctor's lounge at Mount Sinai Hospital, my colleague Dr. Kushner noticed the fracture, said I had a fractured skull, and asked when did this happen? I told him how and when it happened. He asked if there was any doctor there, and I said no. He replied, "That is why you are alive now".

the more advanced pupils. The melamed was usually imported and hired for the season. The parents paid a certain amount per child per season plus a stated number of days of room and board per child (usually being two weeks per child per semester). We had him both during summer and winter with but a short vacation during the holiday periods in spring and fall.

Space for the school was tough to acquire. We were fortunate that our public bathhouse keeper, [A202] Yankel Weinstein, was not only a devoted and loyal citizen but also a very kind and compassionate man. He felt compelled to share his abundant palace of two rooms adjacent to the bathhouse with the public. He made room for us. I remember that room as well as the teacher. He was a tall, slim man at the head of the table with his jacket off, the talis kotan (small talis) with fringe hung down. He held a bony pointer in one hand and rod in the other for any eventualities. The latter, however, was seldom used, for his sharp, rancorous voice or glance at us was sufficient to freeze all of us instantly in our seats.

The school for the advanced students was held in the ladies part of the synagogue. There, the rebbe (tutor) had a somewhat more difficult time in keeping order. Frequently, he resorted to a supply of fresh reeds he had taken from the lower part of the straw roof or simply to a strong ruler.

How long Jewish children went to school depended on the nature and economic status of the parents. Since there was nowhere to learn a trade or profession, some boys stayed on until late adolescence. Few girls attended school. There were two to three in my class. I was fond of them and enjoyed their company until I left for the States. Some boys acquired no skill. On reaching adulthood, they imitated their elders. They engaged in bartering during the bazaars that were found in the towns, buying and selling whatever came along, thus earning enough to eke out some existence. Some of them became vendors or small merchants.

Knyazhe was beautiful and fascinating. Other than for its unhygienic state, it was a most charming, picturesque little town. It would have been an excellent retreat or spa had it been in America. Nature here was in its full glory. Knyazhe was primitive, uncivilized, but wholesome. Its men and women were still as God first created them. The land abounded in grain, fruit, and vegetables. The river was full of fish, the sun warm, and the wind gentle. Yet Knyazhe was also filthy and destructive. Disease was rampant. Tuberculosis and typhoid fever[24] raged fiercely. Parasitic infection caused by the roundworm, which often resulted in bowel obstruction, was common. "Here live 2000 souls," read the signpost at the entrance gate to the town. To my knowledge, there was never any need to change this sign. Knyazhe lived up to the theory of "balance in nature." The dog, the bird, the cat, the rat, the pig in the mud, and the drunk in the rut all carried on, following the direction of their Creator.

In poverty, Knyazhe did not take a back seat either. In this, Knyazhe excelled. I can testify to that because my home constituted the charity organization of the town. My training in this field

---

[24] Typhoid is the infection caused by the bacterium, Salmonella typhimurium (S. typhi). The bacterium lives in the intestines and bloodstream of humans. It spreads between individuals by direct contact with the feces of an infected person. No animals carry this disease, so transmission is always human to human.

began during my very early formative years. I well remember gathering challah[25] during the wintry Friday mornings for Moshe Bear's family. [A180] Moshe Bear was the stepbrother of [A177] Shaia Korsunski, the wealthy citizen, who disowned her brother because of the latter's radical leanings. When the rich relatives refused to contribute their challah, I always promised not to forsake them in the time of need. This always proved to be a great remedy. It would frighten them to death, and they would come around immediately. In spite of all its ugliness and poverty, and although I have no one there now, I still long for Knyazhe. I would love to wade in the river, gather the leeches, eat the cabbage roots, and climb the cherry and plum trees. Silly fantasies and dreams.

The Tykytch River, which is about five miles long and some 1-2 versts (1500 feet) wide, swarmed with life. Carp, whitefish, mackerel, lobsters, turtles, and above all frogs, whose symphonies played at sundown, were as soothing to the nerves as the music of our finest orchestras.

True to our civilization, the poor only caught the fish but seldom ate them. The fish belonged to the arendator who shipped them to distant lands. Bathing in the river, however, was still freely enjoyed by all, but not due to the arendator's generosity. The latter was still too unaware. It had not yet dawned upon him to monopolize bathing. Have you ever bathed in the evening in the quiet waters, under starlight, with the breeze blowing softly and the waters flowing smoothly? There was but a ripple here and there from the splashing fish as they joined the chorus of the frogs and the swain which gathered to sing and dance on the meadows.

Knyazhe was made famous by its owner, His Highness, [A160] Graf Krasitzki. He was responsible for converting Knyazhe into a township and thus enabling him to retain his Jews whom he needed to run his estate. For who could run it better than [A326] Chaim Dudnik?

One of the important citizens was [A292a] Noah Dudnik, who married [A292] Rivka Kaprove, and had the following children: [A293] Aaron, [A323] Israel, [A326] Chaim, [A350] Froim, [A355] Leib, [A359] Yankel, [A363] Pearl (Mimi) and [A364] Sarah.[26] I remember Noah as a

---

[25] White bread leavened with yeast and containing eggs, often braided before baking, prepared especially for the Jewish Sabbath

[26] Editor's note: [A364] Sarah/Surcah Dudnik and her husband, [A364a] Sol /Zuma Morrison, resided in Knyazhe, as did her brother, [A359] Yankel Dudnik, and his wife [A359a] Leah at the time of the pogroms All knew of the lurking dangers, having been warned earlier of the perils of being Jewish. During one such pogrom, circa 1918, [A359] Yankel was murdered, for nothing more than being Jewish. What made the killing so much more pernicious was that it was done with Leah being forced to watch, and with [A362] Betty, the youngest child, sitting on her lap. Neither Leah nor Betty were injured.

Aunt Sarah and Uncle Sol were able to save Sarah's and Sol's two oldest children, [A360] Olga was then age 7, and [A361] Nathan, her brother, was around 11.

Together, they all escaped. Sol and Sarah and the children traveled by "foot," taking months to reach Italy, hiding as they went. Once there, a farmer, whom they met, permitted them stay in the barn on the property and work for them. Sol soon became adept in Italian having taken Latin earlier in school, possibly at the time he attended medical school, a rarity for Jews at that time.

tall, slim man wearing a yarmulke and pacing the floor as he supervised the workers baking matzos in his home for the Passover. His was the influential family in town. He lived in a large house the Graf owned. This house was the only inn in town, but guests were not too frequent.

Among some of the lovely stories worth knowing, one involved a visitor who stopped at the inn for an overnight stay. [A293] Aaron, a lad of 10 or 12 who was highly impressive, had returned from school, and the visitor engaged him in conversation. Aaron clearly made an indelible impression for the visitor returned some years later to claim Aaron as a husband for his daughter [A293a] Zipa Weinberg. That is how the two were married. It was a most pleasing marriage. No marriage ever blessed at Mount Sinai was finer or more successful than this one. It produced seven wonderful daughters and two fine sons: [A294] Gitie, [A298] Yossel, [A309] Pearl, [A310] Sarah, [A313] Golda, [A314] Dora, [A316] Dina, [A317] Harry, and [A320] Kay.

[A294] Gitie married a Dudnik (no relative) and later divorced him in Uman. [A295] Abe is her only son.

[A326] Chaim Dudnik was the third oldest son of [A292a] Noah, a central member of the community of previous days. He was one of the earlier settlers, but I do not know how he got to the Graf. Chaim was the outstanding intellectual power in town. He was a brilliant and self-educated young man who was much more worldly than his peers and soon became the right-hand man of the Graf. He was the natural product of time, place, and circumstances. He was shrewd, sly, cunning, mean, and sadistic. He was a 100 percenter as some might say. In about 1905, he became the Graf's manager and lessee of the mill and the fish in the River Tykytch, thus displacing the Korsunski family with whom he was constantly at war. Until then, [A168] Korsunski had been the Graf's right-hand man. No one else in the family had any contact with the Graf.

Chaim was always neatly and modernly dressed. In his association with the Graf, he made frequent trips to [C13] Kiev where he made various contacts that broadened his mind. He learned and spoke a fair Russian and was able to write a brief for the municipal court and even act as the advocate. Chaim owned a grocery store that his wife, [A413] Bracha, managed. The store was immediately next to the house. He also owned the saloon that his brother [A350] Froim managed. He was the congregation's most prominent member and owned a pew on the Eastern wall. He was also the arendator of the mill and pond in town. He gathered the grains from off the fields and the sugar beets from the plantation. He was in charge of the pasturelands, and the

---

The family grouping finally reached America and in 1922 settled in Niagara Falls, N.Y., which was nearby Buffalo where many of the Kaprov extended family lived. Sarah and Sol there formally adopted Olga, but [A361] Nathan did not wish that for himself. They all did, though, remain close. Nathan settled eventually in Chicago, while Sol and Sarah later moved to California. [A364a] Sol, likely, not being able to gain entrance to an American medical school, eventually became a pharmacist.

Olga later married [A360a] Sam Perman, another Russian émigré, who also became a pharmacist.

[A362] Betty, [A359] Yankel's and Leah's youngest child, remained and grew up in Russia. Sarah and Sol did everything possible to locate her, and after finding her, had her visit. When her own sons, [A362.1] Yanel Lupetsky and [A362.4] Feivil Lupensky, later came to the US (likely in the early 1960s) and became citizens, they brought Betty here to live (1973).

timber in the forests. He was the Graf's adviser at the stock exchange in [C13] Kiev. Because of these interests, he was always feuding with [A168] Dudy and [A177] Shaia Korsunski, each rivaling over their personal fortunes and interests. Each feared the other would encroach on their interests at the Graf's court. In this strife, the community was entirely forgotten.

Chaim married a cousin, [A413] Bracha Dolgonos, and had the following children: [A327] Fania, [A339] Yossel, [A340] Itzik, [A348] Betty. Bracha managed the grocery store they owned since Chaim was always preoccupied with the duties of supervising the Graf's estate, which he did for many years.

Chaim predicted to Mother that he would dispossess Graf Krasitzki and kept his prediction. The Graf's holdings did end on the auction block. Riches alone did not satisfy Chaim. He fleeced the peasants for which they did not like him. He also robbed the Graf and devised ways to torture his fellow Jews. A favorite trick of his was to deny the privilege of pasture for the cow of a fellow Jew with whom he wished to toy. With all the vegetation around luring the cow, no rope was ever strong enough to hold her down. Many a time, Father would return home, beaten up by [A164] Anton, whose garden the cow trampled and destroyed. To the sadistic Chaim, this was a great spectacle, very amusing and highly enjoyable.

Despite that, I loved Chaim and his children, especially as we lived under the same roof beginning when I was eight years old. I remained close to him for years after we immigrated to the States. Time healed wounds. We were always happy to see each other in Knyazhe and later in Buffalo. The same is true of the others in my family and the younger Dudniks, and now [A031] Stan has reestablished a close relationship with Chaim's grandson, [A457] Joe Gillman. Chaim was already old and harmless, but he still clung to the prejudices of the earlier days. When I asked him why he stooped so low as to mess around with the undignified character, [A183a] Russi, and actually had fistfights with her and her husband on Saturday mornings during the synagogue services, his answer was, "When a dog barks you must strike him."

How much Chaim contributed to the Jewish community, I don't know. He was, to my knowledge, the only rich one attending Saturday services. Somehow, for reasons I never knew, though, which I suspect were related to infringements with his privileges at the Graf, fistfights between him, the Gerson and Voskoboinik families would break out during Saturday morning services. No one knew the immediate cause of the fight, but the remote cause was always hazuhak (possession by birthright.) This was the principle of importance. To [A326] Chaim, who watched his interests vigilantly, this was of great importance, and anyone who dared to get to the Graf constituted a menace Chaim wouldn't tolerate.

Chaim usually was prominent during the verbal fights. All of our youngsters would be frightened to death and run outside of the synagogue once the clashes began. Once outside, the frightened children regained their composure and joined their elders in the chorus of epithets. Aunt [A001a] Paya, a tall, slender, devout woman suffering from a chronic nasal obstruction, once became involved in a fight with the [A292a] Bnai Noah, whose leading member was Chaim Dudnik. Thus, they threw the epithet "Blue Yakov Hershiva" (Blue wife of [A002] Yakov Hersh) at the Voskoboiniks while she retorted. "Dirty Gonif" and "Noah Gonif" (Noah, the thief). This continued until Aunt Paya reached her porch. There she felt as secure as a dog when he reached his home. She made a quick right turn, lifted her skirt, and thrusting her behind toward us, said "Na," and in she went.

Political parties were unknown to us in Knyazhe. I doubt whether anyone besides [A326] Chaim Dudnik knew anything about the structure of the Duma, Parliament, or anything about its members except perhaps that of Purishkevitch[27] of whom much was written and transmitted by word of mouth. Chaim was the only one in town subscribing to the "Friend," a Jewish newspaper. [A023] Tobie paid him 3 cents a copy to read it. The two of them and I were the only ones who read newspapers. Possibly, [A326a] Bracha Dudnik and their daughter, [A327] Fania, also read it. It was around 1907. The legendary deeds performed by the expropriation division of the socialist party, which by various tricks managed to elude the police or staged highly spectacular escapes from prison, were widespread among the populace. Even Zionism as a philosophy or party was unknown to our simple minds, though our people did long for Zion and kept on repeating, "May the next year be in Jerusalem." Yet Knyazhe had its parties. There were as many parties as there were families, and the feuding among them was as vicious as among the Kentuckians.

All week long, our people were preoccupied with eking out a livelihood. They went early in the morning to the synagogue, but prayer was swift since each had to run home to his task. But Saturday mornings were different. All were relaxed, at leisure, and a little diversion made the prayers spicy. I never knew just why or how things started. Suddenly we would become aware of some tumultuous vibration as if an earthquake had erupted. Soon chairs flew or actual fistfights broke out. Some of the women would rush in to help their husbands. [A183] Avrom Hersh was always the victim. His wife, [A183a] Russi, and daughter, [A184] Frima, would join the fight and [A225] Yankel Isaac, the clown, always managed to loosen Frima's skirt while she was busy fighting. The fistfight usually did not last long, but the verbal fight continued until all reached their homes.

Our police force consisted of but one officer. A fight among families was not his concern, and he was right. The argument would eventually come to a natural end. Even Frima would recover her skirt and her composure as well.

[A225] Yankel Isaac was a tall, handsome, slender, dark-complexioned, playful, and good-natured young man. He was the Walter Winchell of our town. He was completely illiterate but shrewd and clownish. Women were his hobby. Whenever he noticed smoke rising from the chimney of the public bathhouse, Yankel would take his position at the side of the store most centrally located so that no woman could escape his gaze. The struggle between him and the women went on for years. The young women tried to wear him out by delaying the trip until late, but Yankel was a patient man and always won.

[A292a] Noah's second-oldest son [A323] Israel died of tuberculosis, leaving a wife [A323a] Chana, a [A324] son, and a daughter, [A325] Charni-Gitel. The latter left to marry someone in

---

[27] Vladimir Mitrofanovich Purishkevich (1870-1920), a right-wing politician in Imperial Russia, who was monarchist, ultra-nationalist, antisemitic and noted for anticommunist views. In 1905 he founded the Union of the Russian People (URP), which advocated violent attacks against leftists and Jews

Argentina and was not heard from for years. All of us feared that she might have fallen victim to the white slavery then prevalent there, but her Uncle [A326] Chaim succeeded in tracing her whereabouts and found her well-married and well-to-do. She also had a fine family. One of her sons was a physician, I believe, in Buenos Aires.

[A221] Avrom Aaron was one of the oldest citizens in town and lived in one-half of the duplex where Chaim lived. On leaving Knyazhe because of advanced age, he sold his hazakah (monopolistic right given to a particular Jew to exploit a gentile's property) to my parents. This was accomplished in secrecy because Chaim would have disallowed it; indeed, he tried to do so later but failed after two years of fighting.

[A187] Gedalia Kapalushnik was the other influential citizen in Knyazhe. I saw him but a very few times. He was a tall, lanky man, neatly dressed. He had a neatly groomed beard and walked majestically with head lifted high, with the appearance of a cultured savant. I learned his relatives beat him, as they feared his superior ability and intelligence. He ailed from then on and died, leaving a wife, three sons, and three daughters in a highly precarious economic condition.

Gedalia's greatest enemies were his wealthy relatives [A168] Dudy Korsunski, an obese man, and [A177] Shaia Korsunski. Their riches gave them status as well as influence, even though they were not cultured. Dudy lived in one of the Graf's homes and owned a large grocery and hardware store. He considered the Graf as his personal property. Because of this, he always feuded with the Dudniks. This, therefore, brought about frequent disputes regarding the lesseeships between the two families. Dudy also owned the lumberyard fronting his home. It seemed to me that a fatty like Dudy could not run, hence I paid no attention to his admonition not to run up the piles of lumber he owned. To my surprise, he made me change convictions. He caught me and awarded me a spanking that I never forgot, and I vowed to leave his lumber alone.

[A187] Gedalia Kapalushnik and our [A197] Rabbi Yankel, our shochet (person who slaughters the animal in a manner proscribed by ritual), were more cultured than Chaim. Still, Chaim was worldly, cunning, and rich. How much Russian he knew, I don't know, but I can assure you that it was just minuscule. His wife, [A326a] Bracha, was barely able to read Yiddish, her prayer book, and write a letter. None of us spoke Russian. We spoke Ukrainian. [A023] Tobie and [A431] Alta spoke it well.

Just like [A168] Dudy Korsunski, he was corpulent to the point of dyspnea. His wife, [A168a] Tzirl, was thin and with a very long neck. She was a small woman and was as mean as she was lean. She had a large general store and warehouse of iron parts used by the blacksmiths. During the pogroms following the revolution, the peasants buried her alive. Unlike [A326] Chaim, who was smart enough to leave Knyazhe early, she was not so wise and paid dearly for that mistake.

Dudy's son, [A170] Bennie, was fat like his father and had a short neck. From this, I deduced that rich men have no necks. Of course, I learned that my deduction was entirely erroneous. Bennie was supposed to have had some illicit affairs with a peasant girl, [A233] Urpina. His cousin, [A182a] Boruch Mordechai, was aware of this secret and extracted an annual tribute for many years from Bennie. Father not only knew this but actually saw them consorting. Yet Father never mentioned this to anyone until years later in the States when he told me about it.

Bennie's youngest sister, [A171] Brocha, was as uninformed as all our girls. She was quite obese but beautiful and sweet. Naturally, she was her parents' darling. Brocha married a learned young man from the city of [C24] Monasteristshe and lived with the family in Knyazhe.

[A172] Mendel Korsunski, the Cantonist, entered the army of [A278] Nicholas I at the age of 17 in exchange for his younger brother, who was picked up by the catchers.[28] He never failed to tell us of his experiences during his army days. His wife, [A172a] Zipa, was born on the day he entered the army, and he married her 17 years later upon his discharge from service. Zipa was primitive, but a good wife, mother, and housekeeper. She, of course, could neither read nor write but always used many Hebrew expressions appropriately in her daily speech. I will never forget her excitement as she ran after the automobile that passed through town, screaming, "This is the devil, the horseless carriage, which killed my grandson in New York."

[A191] Isaac Shudler and his two sons, [A192] Samuel and [A193] Yakov, were grain dealers and winnowers of grain who worked on the estate of the grain owner. They were hard-working people and managed to live comfortably. They were not too upright in dealing with men, judging by the shady reputation they enjoyed. Isaac's daughter, [A194] Chaia, married a butcher, [A194a] Meir (unknown last name). The latter's reputation was also somewhat unsavory.

[A183] Avrom Hersh was a grain dealer. His wife, [A183a] Russi, was a noisy, quarrelsome woman. Somehow, they always managed to get into fistfights with the Noah clan. Exactly why was never clear to me. Probably they dared to attempt to invade the hazakah of the Graf. Avram Hersh belonged to the Ber Laib family.

[A252] Moshe was the town's outstanding melamed. He, too, suffered from chronic lung disease and was as mean and despotic as was [A094a] Levi Gerson. His wife, [A252a] Monicha, and the children had a most difficult time during his life and probably worse afterward. The entire family later left for New York City.

A colorful family was that of [A165] Hershel Korsunski. His was an incredibly pious family -- Hasidim -- probably followers of the Rabbi of [C23] Lubovich. They lived among the peasants, bartering groceries and other necessities for whatever the peasants offered. Their oldest son, [A166] Faivel, suffered from manic psychosis every spring. He was married to a girl from [C32] Tarashtscha, but during the psychotic attacks, he was always brought home to his parents, where two Jews armed with sticks would take turns watching him at night. On recovering, he returned to his family.

The younger son, [A167] David, was a zealot. His piety was far greater than was common here, and he was seen as not altogether well mentally either. His cousin, [A176] Esther, daughter of [A174] "Gonta" Korsunski, made fun of him and teased him a great deal. She would manage to

---

[28] Conscription into the Czar's meant lifelong deportation from one's home. All Jewish communities were communally responsible for supplying the required number of recruits. Boys aged twelve or older were required to serve, but not uncommonly, younger children were kidnapped to serve. In 1850 [A278] Nicholas I, decreed if the Jewish community failed to supply the required number, three men aged 20 or over could be taken into service, plus one additional person for every 2,000 rubles of taxes that were in arrears. Shortly after that, Nicholas decreed a relative could be seized in his place if the person failed to appear. The official community representatives might too be taken if the required number was not supplied.

sit in the doorway to the synagogue when he had to enter. She would jump up and plant a kiss on his cheek. He would then rush directly to the pond to wash his face. If he were inside, he would stay locked in for fear that she might kiss him.

[A217] Beryl Radlideciatnik, a cattle dealer, was another of our favored and colorful citizens. His wife, [A217a] Sossie, was disabled and bedridden for years, probably with tuberculosis. The oldest son, [A218] Shmiel, had a lame left arm, a result of a fractured elbow. The younger son, [A219] Yohel, a shoe repairman, suffered from tuberculosis. His only daughter, [A220] Tema, had a congenitally wry neck, possibly resulting from an injury at birth. Beryl himself was a strong, coarse, ignorant, poor, but honest man. I describe him more fully elsewhere.

Every Jewish community worthy of the name had to have a rabbi (spiritual leader), a synagogue, a public bathhouse, and a shochet to slaughter animals according to ritual in order to provide Kosher meat for its people.

[A197] Rabbi Yankel, referred to as the shochet, and the bathhouse keeper, [A202] Yankel Weinstein, were the two luminaries that I always suspected were specially created for us by God on his day of creation.

[A197] Rabbi Yankel was a tall, young, handsome man with an owl-like face, handsome nose, and deeply set eyes peering out from under bushy eyebrows. A well-groomed dense growth of beard and mustache covered the rest of his face. His beard converged into an inverted pyramid with its tip actually reaching his beltline. He had a wife and four children. [A198] Tevice, the oldest son, left town in pursuit of the cantorial art. The daughter, [A199] Ruchel, was good looking, but never won our affection. The two youngest boys were schoolmates of mine. Their father never failed to remind me that they were made of gentle material and admonished me to treat them kindly.

The Rabbi was a man of many qualities and accomplishments. He was our spiritual leader, teacher, and guide. He served as rabbi and shochet, slaughtering the animals as prescribed by ritual, thus helping two butchers to provide meat for both Jew and Gentile. He determined the kashrut of the animal when such problems arose. He was cantor, reader of the Torah (Baal Koreh), and leader of the prayers in services (Baal Tefilla). He performed marriage ceremonies. But he did not perform getts (document in Jewish religious law that effectuates a divorce between a Jewish couple) or funerals because our people were not sure of the name of the River Tykych flowing through town, without which none of the above could be handled. He also named the newborn children, circumcised the boys (mohel), and after that, performed their bar mitzvahs. He was also an excellent speaker. Of this, I became convinced during his campaign to improve the mikveh. Sitting next to Father, I listened to his sermons every Saturday afternoon for an entire summer. Although I slept through some parts, I can testify that his campaign in no way suffered. It was accomplished successfully. I immersed myself in it whenever the chance presented itself.

Despite all of his abilities, his salary was small. He was on a par with Yankel in poverty. The collection gathered on the eve of Yom Kippur contained little from the rich, and the poor had nothing to contribute. His primary income came, therefore, from the weekly slaughtering of cattle for the butchers and chickens for the Jewish families who required chicken for the Sabbath meal. During the winter months, he had frequent particular income. Many of our Jewish women would have him slaughter 20 to 30 geese on Saturday evening that had been fattening for weeks. This was quite an operation. The feathers and down had to be removed and separated, the geese singed and hung someplace where no animal could reach them until morning when the Jews from the neighboring town would buy them before [A269] Shalom, the tax collector, arrived. All of this brought some income. Occasionally there was added prosperity derived from the number of newborns, circumcisions, and weddings, which enabled the Rabbi to provide new shoes for his two younger boys for the Passover.

[A202] Yankel Weinstein was another able, colorful, and skilled citizen in town. He was the keeper of the public bathhouse and did a splendid job. In those days, providing water for the women's mikveh and the bathing of men on Fridays was not a matter of opening a faucet. He had to pull up the water by hand from a deep well. Yankel was also sexton (caretaker) and deacon of the synagogue. Here too, he excelled. To listen to him during the pageant on Simhat Torah eve, summoning the members of the congregation to honor the Torah, was listening to a great performer.

Another time for his performance was at weddings. Just before the ceremony, the bride sat surrounded by her girlfriends. A veil covered her hair and the badchen, Yankel,[29] recited rhymes, which had some bearing on her future life. The women all cried bitterly over her fate. His performance was always excellent.

Yankel was married to a little wife who was as good as he himself. She gave him seven sons and three daughters. Since supporting them on his salary was impossible, he was forced to use ingenuity. He skinned every dead animal found in town, cured the skins, and tanned them into pelts. He prepared them for use as sheepskins to be sewn into coats for the peasants. He bought yarn spun from sheep fleece and made a flannel lining material for these coats. To augment his income further, Yankel served as a night watchman to shoo away the fish poachers. He also helped his furrier sons in their business. He was the most compassionate man in town. When my parents couldn't find a home in which to live, Yankel was the only one in town willing to share his two-room palace adjoining the bathhouse with them. I was born in that palace and remember it. The population of the two families made a total of twenty. Despite all his activities, he could feed his children only buckwheat bread. In later years in school, we would exchange our wheat bread for their stale buckwheat, which was a treat to us.

Except for the few Jews who lived in the homes belonging to the Graf, which had three or four rooms, all lived in the single room peasant huts, where the oven took up about one-fifth of the area. The rest of the space had to accommodate all of the family's other needs of the family, such as the dining room and sleeping areas. It also had to accommodate the occasional visitors or guests, and during the coldest winter nights, even the calves. The Rebbe was entitled to a sleeping space of 2 weeks per child per semester. In the case of our family, we also needed space for a dressmaking establishment plus a whole dry goods business. This room was also [A017] Nessie and [A023] Tobie's bedroom.

---

[29] Jester, Yiddishized to mean a Jewish comedian, who with scholarly overtones entertains guests at weddings.

The carpenter, the furrier, the tanner, and the blacksmith, of which there were only a half dozen in town, were our only artisans and craftsmen. There were also two to three merchants. We had no barber, tailor, or shoemaker. Men cut each other's hair. For a finer cut, I walked some ten versts to the barber in neighboring [C22] Lohahievka. We now pity our children who have to walk a half-mile to school. There was no industry nor any substantial trade to learn.

The average Jew had nothing to do. Like Porgy, "He had plenty of nothing and nothing is plenty for him." He lived by ingenuity. Most men engaged in buying the grain the peasants brought to the bazaar. This was then sold to the richer dealer at a small profit. Some fellows became very slick, for their profits depended on mostly short weighing. Others, particularly the widows, were small vendors who displayed their wares during the bazaar days in easily constructed stalls or merely on the ground.

The hygiene in Knyazhe can best be described as nonexistent. Balance in nature had its full sway here. The town's population was stationary, while the two cemeteries grew to rather substantial sizes. We lived in symbiosis with all living things: horses, cows, pigs, sheep, dogs and cats, geese, ducks, chickens, and a myriad of lice, fleas, and bedbugs.

The dust was high, the mud deep. There was but one privy in town, a private one. Relief was obtained behind the houses in the open or along the riverbank. Tissue paper was unknown. In the summertime, the leaves came in handy. After dark, the women had to be escorted. That was a regular job of mine. I loved to escort [A229] Rachel Tzipes. At a later date, we had our own private privy. It was my job to empty the can in the river, for a consideration, of course.

The war against lice, fleas, bedbugs, and worms was continuous. No one will ever explain where our mothers gathered the energy to cope with all their hardships. Mother was a dressmaker and merchant yet found time and energy to keep the home and all of us clean. Once a week, she would dip our heads into a solution of kerosene. Not only were the lice killed, but the nits dissolved. I had to go to medical school to learn that.

Our mattresses were made of straw from rye stems because these stems were long, straight, and strong. The straw and the crevices in the wooden beds provided excellent breeding places for the bugs. Destroying the straw alone was useless. Mother always enlisted our help. It was a great sport to go over every crevice with a burning candle and watch these red round animalcules run for their life.

The roundworm was our everyday companion. A child sneezed and brought up a worm that was inches long or, upon vomiting, would bring up a coil of worms. This seldom made any impression on the child.

Drinking water came from the well. It was located at the lowest level of the town and received all the excrement the rains washed down. Typhoid, diphtheria, and other contagious diseases were widespread. We had no local doctor. Occasionally we had a self-styled feldsher. Mother was the foremost diagnostician and grandmother the finest obstetrician in town. For every newcomer, she merely had to tear another strip from the apron to tie the cord. To my knowledge, grandmother never lost a patient because of infection.

Hot water for baths was unavailable. During summertime, usually at dusk, we bathed in the river, nude. The men stayed at the outlet of the dam, where the river was deep enough to swim. Here many a child drowned. It was common to see the peasants throwing the child astride the horse and galloping away. It was quite an excellent resuscitating method. Women had their own secluded spot for bathing. It was in a beautiful, highly picturesque area. Many a time, some of us boys would descend upon them from the neighboring hills and keep them in the water or risk exposure.

The public bath was used more for ritual than for hygienic purposes. This was a unique institution because it also served as a meeting place. It was genuinely democratic. Here the latest political news, rumors of revolution, and the pogroms were reported and discussed, and the most recent war battles were fought in the most minute detail.

Food and clothing were the simplest. A garment was worn until it was utterly threadbare. This was true in Knyazhe as well as everywhere in Russia. I still remember the suit that [A213] Aaron, the furrier, wore every Saturday and on holidays. His daughter was married for years, but his pants that were made for her wedding day still had the original crease.

The food, except for the Sabbath, when the meals were festive, was as simple as the dress. It was, however, wholesome and not drab. Bread, cereals, borscht, kasha, onions, garlic, vegetables, potatoes and herring constituted the staple food. Eggs, dairy food, and meat were only for the more affluent citizens.

The Sabbath and holidays were welcome days. They provided not just rest but actual repose, relaxation, and tranquility. They were observed quietly and with serenity. For us, the growing youths, this was unsatisfactory. We were growing restless, imbued with new ideas that somehow permeated the air and penetrated even our little minds.

The evenings in Knyazhe were unforgettable. Millions of blinking stars studded the beautiful skies. The frequent displays of the northern lights, the Milky Way simulating broad highways across the sky, the mild rustling of the leaves, the murmur of the river, the symphony of the frogs, and the singing and dancing of the swain on the green hills showed Nature in all its glory.

Most towns and villages of the old Ukraine were isolated and lacked the organizational spirit characteristic of our present-day society. Natural talent and mutual aid were called upon and extensively exploited. The priest, the rabbi, and the melamed were the only professionals in our town. We had a limited number of artisans.

The furrier was outstanding among the artisans. We had six of them: [A213] Aaron Deutch and his son [A214] Mayer; the Weinstein boys, [A203] Shlomo, [A204] Chaim Hersh, [A207] Laizer, and [A208] Yossel. These men usually worked in the homes of the peasants, making sheepskin coats for them. It was quite common to watch these boys carrying many pelts draped over their backs as they traveled on foot from one peasant to another.

The priest and rabbi were the only trained professionals. All the others represented native talent that sprang from within like a natural spring. [A326] Chaim Dudnik represented legal talent and business acumen, grandmother the obstetrical, Mother the medical, and [A233] Urpina the poetic genius. Urpina always spoke in rhymes. Her rhymes floated from her mouth like water from the faucet. When asked what the faggots she was carrying were for, she answered:

Budiaki, prudiaki   Faggots and sticks
Shob ditiam chleba specti.   to bake bread for the kids.

A most outstanding talent was [A231] Musii, the bonesetter, who was an unlettered, heavily pock-marked drunk. Despite his large clumsy paws and massive fingers, he possessed great palpating ability with which to diagnose and practice minor orthopedics more deftly than the polished doctor in his area. His reputation was lesser than that of Reese, the bonesetter of Akron, Ohio, whom the U.S. Congress gave license to practice. But Musii looked for no honors, and the law never interfered with his practice. Musii was big with a broad chest. He slouched and moved slowly like a bear. His face was pock-marked and heavily bearded. His head was overgrown with hair that spread down over his shoulders like the mane of a lion. His hands were callused and spade-like. One rarely saw him all winter long. He might have been hibernating like some of the animals. In the summertime, one always found him fishing at the foot of the dam by the side of the mill. His requirements were simple. His home seldom needed repair or furniture replaced. His clothing was simple. His little plot of ground provided enough grain to sustain him for the year. His only needs were fish and vodka. When needed, the problem was not to find him, but to find him sober and how to keep him in that state. If paid in cash, he would immediately go to the saloon and then fail to return. When Mother dislocated her elbow, Father first bought a bottle of vodka, then brought Musii to the house. Before even seeing the patient, he was given his first drink as an incentive and then taken to the patient. After examining Mother's arm and making his diagnosis, he asked for a large vessel filled with hot water to immerse the arm to relax the muscles. After 15-20 minutes of soaking the arm in the hot water, he quietly and deftly reduced the dislocation. I remember that vividly, and I confess that most other physicians and I could not accomplish this as deftly as he. The more affluent people feared his hands and sought out physicians, but usually had less successful results.

Grandmother's obstetrics was, of course, primitive. The English leech already had forceps to help him.[30] True, Tristram did get his nose crushed, but grandmother had neither implements nor ether nor chloroform to accomplish even that. All she could do was to stand by the parturient, guiding and comforting as well as directing her in the proper utilization of her energies. Grandmother knew of no sterility. She tied and cut the cord by whatever means were at hand. Yet, frankly, I never heard of any of her patients suffering infection or injury. All her babies whom I knew were well and vigorous. Her compensation was the joy and happiness that comes with the first yell of the newborn. Judging by the demand for her services, she enjoyed a good reputation. No wonder she was thin and worn and always complained of backaches. We always laughed at her, but even the modern obstetrician finds a backache not an unusual accompaniment.

As the daughter-in-law of such an apt obstetrician, Mother proved herself equal in the field of medicine, with a particular interest in therapeutics. The present-day bombardment with newly

---

[30] A leech is a small animal which looks like a worm and lives in water. Leeches feed by attaching themselves to other animals and sucking their blood. Father also considered many in the medical profession to be leeches, bleeding the poor patient of money. In other words, a charlatan.

developed preparations was yet unknown. The remedies were few and simple, and she used them effectively.

Her cough mixture composed of eggs, whiskey and honey, was as good as any cough mixture today. I used her mustard plasters to advantage as late as the thirties and found them better and safer than the ready prepared ones. She used heat and cold extensively. Since no hot water bags nor electric pads were available, she made use of the hot moist towels, heated brick, and the heated cover of the earthen pot. Iodoform powder and carbolic acid sprinkle to control infection were standbys as well as ice chips for fever and salves consisting of flower, oil, and alcohol for boils. Her salves consisted of flour, honey, camphor, and alcohol, applied to the body. Kerosene was used against lice, fleas, and nits. She gave Eggnog for the weak and the undernourished. The above were simple remedies, of course, but these with good nursing, kindness, and devotion were her armamentaria.

When [A182a] Boruch Mordechai was stabbed one Sunday morning, Mother was quickly summoned. I still remember the swishing sound accompanying his every respiration. I don't know just what Mother prescribed, but I do know that the doctor, when summoned later that evening, was more helpless than Mother. The wound somehow healed and Boruch Mordechai soon resumed his duties in his butcher shop.

When [A298] Yossel Dudnik was run over by a wagon, Mother was quickly brought to the scene. She had his head packed in ice and kept him in bed. Yossel made an excellent recovery. Following the pogroms that came after the Russian Revolution, Yossel fled to Israel, which was then Palestine. I saw him during my visit to Israel in October 1965 and recalled this incident.

[A258] Rebbe Laib from [C03] Arotof was our first experience with a modern teacher. He was young, intelligent, and very kind. All of us were aware of this and learned to love him. He, in turn, loved us, though he found it difficult to discipline us. Each one of us was equal to him in physical strength, if not stronger. Whenever he attempted to discipline us, we would seize his hands and struggle with him until a smile would appear on his face. We knew then that he was conquered and would give up the struggle. In spite of that, we loved and respected him much more than any other rebbe we ever had. He taught us Hebrew and Hebrew grammar in addition to the Bible. Searching for some instrument with which to discipline us, the rebbe persuaded [A224] Shuke Gedaliah to surrender his strong oak ruler to him, and he began to make effective use of it. This, of course, the class couldn't tolerate. A meeting was held and I was selected to get hold of and destroy that dreadful instrument. By some good fortune, I found that one of our keys would open the school lock. The rest was simpler. I managed to get the ruler and, putting it into my pants, I attempted to walk out when [A202] Yankel Weinstein noticed my peculiar walk and insisted upon feeling my leg. He confiscated the ruler and also the key.

Among the few artisans in town, the blacksmiths [A205] Aaron Weinstein and [A195] Lemel Shudler were outstanding. Without them, the stetl's entire transport system was in danger of collapse. They did all the ironwork for the peasants, particularly that of shoeing the horses. It was my great pleasure to visit them at work. They were kind, friendly, and always welcomed me. I loved to stop at the smithy on my way to and from school, operate the bellows or do other things for them. In return, they taught me the latest songs. During one of these visits, we saw [A363] Pearl (Mima) Dudnik, a spinster, on her way to our home. The boys asked me to deliver their particular proposition to her, namely, they would marry her if she would give her nedon (dowry) to them. I ran home with the message as well as the songs, which I kept repeating since everybody laughed and seemed to enjoy them until Father slapped my face and silenced me. I don't know whether I ever returned to the smithy, but I do know I never sang their songs again. Besides, the smithy itself was soon abandoned. It developed that those two boys discovered a large load of desirable iron and steel in the warehouse of Dudy Korsunski. Since they thought they could make good use of it, they forged a key to the warehouse and helped themselves at night until they were discovered. To escape punishment, both fled to Argentina.

[A188] Moshe Kapalushnik, a boy of about ten years of age, was a born artist. He always led the boys much older and taller in parades across town while playing an imaginary trombone. I still see him dancing a kozachok (Ukrainian folk dance) more beautifully than I ever saw it since. He often entertained and charmed the peasants whom his widowed but proud mother, [A187a] Esther, was serving tea in a large living room that she had converted into a tea house for this purpose after her husband died. His kozachok was a masterpiece. He was a one-man show all through our childhood. The kopecks thrown at him during his dance helped sustain his rather large family during these difficult times. Unfortunately, his artistic ability was destined to atrophy because there was no chance here for its development. Some years later, all emigrated to America, where I expected Moshe to become another Fred Astaire only to find that he became an automobile salesman in Boston.

#7 [C02b] SOKOLIVKA JUSTINGRAD, HOW WE CAME TO BE....
[C02b] Sokolivka/Justingrad
Introduction by [A429a] Fern Mittleman from the memorial booklet about the B'nai Khaim Family Reunion held on August 17/18, 1991, Buffalo, NY

Editor's note: Sokolivka / Justingrad lies 120 miles south of Kiev, 20 miles north of Uman, and 160 miles north of Odessa.

In 1760, Francis Pototski, who owned the land on which the Sokolivka came to be built, issued a decree that permitted Christians and Jews to settle there and for three years remain exempt from taxes on specific goods.[31] Within five years, 585 Jews lived there. Sixty-five years later, in 1825, [A278] Czar Nicholas I, by edict, forbid Jews the right to choose their place to live (regular villages) as well as the occupations open to them. The area became a military settlement with all Jews expelled. The Sokolivkan Jews, fortunately were able to lease the nearby land situated across the lake and connected by a bridge/dam a quarter-mile long. The new lessees named the new shtetl, Justingrad, to honor Justina, the wife of the new feudal lord.

In 1852, Rabbi Reb Gedaliah Aharon, the famous Tzaddik (Hassidic spiritual leader) from Illintsi, and many followers also came to reside in Justingrad. The settlement grew substantially as both more Jewish and non-Jewish farmers came. Robust relationships developed in trade and in occasional employment between the Jews and non-Jews. By 1897 Justingrad had 3,194 inhabitants, of whom 2,521 were Jews. The shtetl eventually had four synagogues and 12 melamdim, each with its own cheder, libraries, schools, and banks.

Within years, life was to change once again. [A281] Czar Nicholas II had issued new edits making life for Jews in the area again difficult. While his government formally condemned the rioting, as exemplified by the Kishinev pogroms,[32] in private, Nicholas supported the mobs, viewing antisemitism as a tool that helped unify the people behind the government.

Emigration was increasing. The August 1919 pogrom wiped out 75% of the Jewish population, and the settlement ceased to be (Appendix E lists the names of murdered Kaprov cousins.) Destroyed were 400 houses, six synagogues, 140 shops, six tanneries, three carbonated water plants, a savings and loan association, a steam mill, and two bathhouses. By 1926, only 762 Jews remained in Sokolivka, constituting 25% of the total population.

---

[31] http://admin.lo-tishkach.org/Search/Search/ShowQryCemeteryTownPage.aspx?QryCemeteryAndTown=12004
Wikipedia (https://en.wikipedia.org/wiki/Justingrad)
Miller L, Miller DF: Sokolivka/Justingrad: A Century of Struggle and Suffering in a Ukrainian Shtetl, as recounted by Survivors to its Scattered Descendants. Loewenthal Press, New York, 1983 ISBN 0-914382-02-0
Gillman J, The B'nai Khaim in America: A Study of Cultural Change in a Jewish Group. Dorrance, Philadelphia, 1969. ISBN 0-8059-1315-7

[32] The infamous 1903 Kishinev pogrom may have had far greater repercussions than anyone ever guessed at the time. Col (Res.) Dr. Raphael G. Bouchnik-Chen of the Begin-Sadat Center for Strateguc Studies, who had served as a senior analyst in IDF Military Intelligence, presented an important explanation for the motives behind Japan's decision to launch a surprise attack on Russia that began the Russo-Japanese War of 1904-05.
https://besacenter.org/perspectives-papers/kishinev-pogrom-russia-japan/

On July 27, 1941, during World War II, the German soldiers came and occupied the area. Only 150 Jews were then living in Sokolivka. All Jews were quickly registered and ordered to wear the Star of David. On September 19, 35 Jews were killed during the first shootings. The remaining Jews were forced into the ghetto, which was then liquidated within the half-year. Although some Jewish artisans were initially allowed to live, by September 1942, many were shot, and by the summer of 1943, all the rest were murdered. During the Holocaust, in total, 146 Sokolivkan Jews were murdered. Cousins included in the Dudnik family [A355] Leo, [A356] Reva, [A357] Polya, and [A358] Chaya, a Dudnik [A360.9] son from Knyazhe, [A507] Grenedal, [A508] Yankel and Frima and daughter [A509] Leah Gelmans presumably still living in Sokolivka, [A398] Kaim Galak from nearby Uman, and [A503] Moishe Gelman from Kishinev.

Today, the former Justingrad is farmland and used for grazing the livestock from neighboring villages.

Sokolivka was a village in Russia. That is, the Jewish community referred to it as Sokolivka, but the Russians called it Sokolovka, and the Ukrainians called it Sokolivka.[33] Sokolivka lay on the right bank of the Konela river, a tributary of the Tykich Uhor river,[34] the county of [C36] Uman in the province or gubernia of [C13] Kiev.

Fig.7-1: Sokolivka countryside.

---

[33] Alternative names include: Justingrad (Formerly called), Justynhrad, Yustingrod (Polish), Sokolowka (Czech), Stara Vies (Alternative Name), Sukhovole (German), Zahojpole (Alternative Name), Zaluzie (Polish), Загайполь - Zagaipol (Russian), с. Соколовка - Sokolovka, Юстинград - Yustingrad (Russian), Соколівка - Sokolivka, Юстінград - Yustingrad (Ukrainian), יוסטינגרד, סוקוליװקה(Yiddish). http://admin.lo-tishkach.org/Search/Search/ShowQryCemeteryTownPage.aspx?QryCemeteryAndTown=12004

[34] Editor's note: According to Wagner, the 'Teich' actually was a pond, formed artificially by a dam or dike across a stream that came through the village of Popivka to the southwest, and 'De Brick' was really the dam of earth and brushwood, a quarter of a mile long. See footnote in Chapter 4. Also see the footnote in Chapter 4 that provides additional material about the River. The River's name found on Michelin maps is the Hornyi Tykich River, but on Google maps is the Hirskyi Tikych River.

It is not known how many Jewish families lived there in the early 1800s, when the first Jews settled there, or from where they came. They might have come from the West, Poland, Germany, Austria, or Hungary, or they might have come from the south, the Crimea from some Greek colonies on the northeast coast of the Black Sea. Persecution, antisemitism, expulsion from cities and lands kept the Jews always on the move.

And so it happened once again: forced exile. In 1835, [A278] Nicholas I, the tsar of all the Russias, issued one of his many anti-Jewish decrees (ukase) that Jews who lived in villages but neither owned nor cultivated land must be expelled to live in towns of their own. This new law affected about 35 Jewish families, according to Joseph Gillman, who authored *The B'nai Khaim in America.*

[A290] Khaim Kaprov, a candle-maker, lived on the other side of the bridge that connected Sokolivka on the east with open fields on the west. He lived in one of the two homes there, both owned by an absentee Polish landlord. The Jewish families moved across the bridge, established a community there, and renamed it [C02a] Justingrad (to honor the landlord's wife, [A160a] Justina (in Polish Justyna). In Russian, the town was Yustingrad, but the Jews pronounced it as Ustingrad and continued to refer to it as Sokolivka and to themselves as Sokolivkars. The Polish Gazetteer notes that Justyngrad was once known as Zahajpol and also as Sokolovka. [35]

The three dozen families of Yustingrad grew to over 500 families by the time of the first official Russian census in 1897. There were 2,521 Jews in a total population of 3,194.[36] The rest were peasants who lived in huts and farmed the fields on the outskirts of the Jewish shtetl.

---

35 According to an account of the town formation in the Mashabei Sadeh Memorial Book, the townspeople "never quite accepted the name of this settlement. They were people of Sokolivka, they and their forefathers, and so they also began to call the new settlement Sokolivka. The name Justingrad was used only on official documents and on letters sent by mail. It was inscribed in large letters on the sign of the drugstore and other community institutions.

36 Editor's note: A letter dated Dec 17, 1965 from the Chief Librarian, Slavic and Central European Division, US Library of Congress read: According to statistics based on the Pervaia vseobshchaia berepis naseleniia Rossiiskoi imperii 1897 g., Sokolovka (designated as a village by the abbreviation s.) had 2699 inhabitants, and Yustingrad (designated as a small town by the abbreviation mst.) had 3194 inhabitants. This information is from the following work: Russia. TSentral'nyi statisticheskii komitet. Goroda i poselaniia v uiezdakh imieiushchie 2000 i boliee zhitelei. S. Peterburg, 1905. 108 pp 32-33, Yudin H C0701.G4

In other sources, [C02a] Justingrad (transliterated Yustingrad or Ustingrad) was a Jewish shtetl in Ukraine that came into being after Jews were forced from their homes in the village of [C02b] Sokolivka (aka Sokolovka, Sokolivka, Sokolowka, Sokoliefka). While the two area are separately named, commonly the names were used interchangeably.

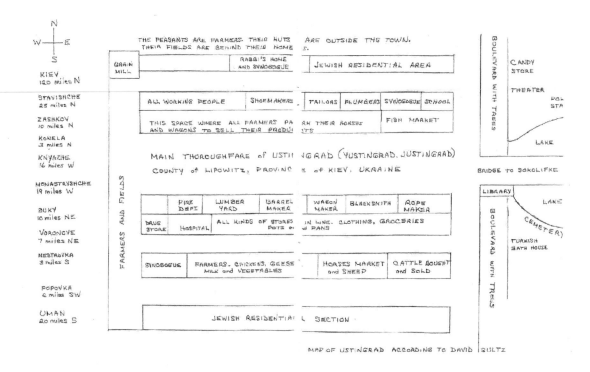

Fig. 7-2: Map of Justingrad (David Sultz), in Memories of [C02b] Sokoliefke/Ustingrad, B'nai Khaim reunion, Aug 17-18, 1991.

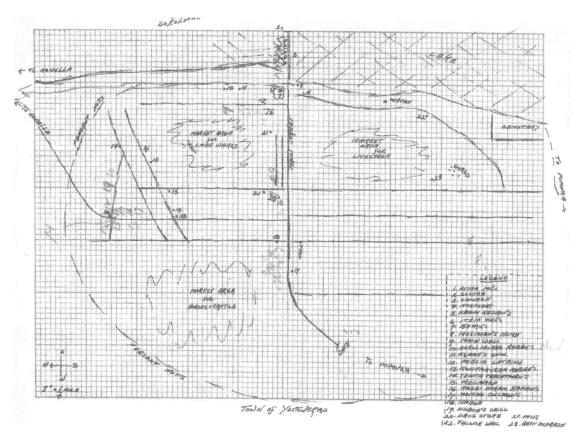

Fig. 7-3: Hand-drawn Map of Justingrad (Unknown author).

The closest large city to Justingrad was [C36] Uman, some 20 miles to the south. [C13] Kiev, 120 miles to the north, [C29] Odessa, 163 miles to the south and [C14] Kishinev, 164 miles southwest, were mere names of distant places to pass through on one's way to emigrate abroad.

The earliest immigrants to Buffalo from Justingrad, Abraham Criden and Shmuel Abba Cohen, arrived in 1903. Already here were Joseph Rachman and Moishe Tuchinsky from the neighboring town of [C17] Konela. The Erie County Naturalization Records indicated they came to the US and Erie in 1901. These men, in turn, encouraged many of their families and landsleit (Fellow Jews who came from the same district or town) to follow. More than 250 families eventually migrated to Buffalo from Justingrad and surrounding communities.

A landsleit society formed in 1913, the Ustingrader Unterstitzung Verein (Ustingrader Support Society), to aid the newcomers. When war struck Justingrad in 1914, the Russian Revolution in 1917, and the pogroms in 1919, the Ustingrader Verein found another purpose for their existence--supporting their brethren abroad.

Pogrom, a Russian word designating an attack, accompanied by destruction, the looting of property, murder, and rape, perpetrated by one section of the population against another, has come to mean attacks explicitly the Christian community carried out, accompanied by looting and bloodshed against the Jews in Russia between 1881 and 1921. The pogroms occurred during the periods of severe political crises in the country and were outbreaks linked to social upheavals and nationalist incitement in Eastern Europe.

It was the 6th of Av (August 4, 1919) when the first pogrom led by the rebel bandit [A284] Zeleny[37] terrorized the Justingrad Jews.[38] The first person killed was Rabbi Pinchas Rabinowitz. Looting and vandalism followed. Hostages were taken and then killed, and the women raped. The number of people who died during the two days varies, but the best approximation lies between 138 to 150.

After Zeleny's massacre, local gangs from nearby villages raided the town. For three months, from September to December 1919, the White Army [A285] General Anton Denikin[39] led passed through town several times on its way to fight the Bolsheviks. Many Jews fled during this time.

---

[37] Terpylo Danylo Ilkovych, also known as Ataman Zeleny (or Green) (1886 -1919) was the infamous commander of about 2,500 irregulars of Ukrainian peasant insurrection movement in Ukraine. He commanded at least 40 pogroms.
[38] See *Jewish Pogroms in Ukraine, 1918-1921*. Pogroms were recorded in 231 populated areas, some multiple times. Upwards of 1000 people were killed at a time for a total of near 100,000. Also see https://kehilalinks.jewishgen.org/pogrebishche/History/PogromsInTheUkraine.htm for terror Zelony's group spread.
[39] Followers of General Denikin, leader of White Russian Counter-Revolutionaries during the Civil War, 1919-20. Not only were they fighting the Bolsheviks, but the Denikintses, who were pro-Russian, also fought the Ukrainian nationalists and the Ukrainian anarchists, all of whom were killing the Jews. The Jews were seen as allied or even synonymous with the Bolsheviks. The Denikintses and two other groups, the Petlurtses, Makhnovtses murdered some 150,000 Jews as they rampaged the country. These groups were the forerunners of Hitler and showed they could kill wantonly as the civilized watched with indifference.

After Denikin's forces were defeated, they passed through Justingrad once again, on the 10th of Tevet, 5680 (January 1, 1919), burning homes and murdering some 200 people.

Justingrad thus ended as the people had known it for about 80 years. Most survivors moved to other communities, such as [C43] Zashkov, [C36] Uman, [C29] Odessa, and [C14] Kishinev, and finally to the United States, Canada, Israel, and Argentina.

This next wave of Sokolivkars arrived in Buffalo in the 1920s. By this time, the strong Yustingrad community had sprung up on the western side of Buffalo. A Sokolivkar shul, Anshe Sokolovka, had been founded in 1915, and a burial society, The Holy Order of the Living, had been established. Socially the Justingrad Society still flourished.

The children and grandchildren of these early immigrants looked back nostalgically to the close-knit Sokolivkar community that once was. A search for roots led some back to find relatives in the large cities of the Soviet Union. They were survivors of what was once Justingrad.

As for the communities of Sokolivka and Justingrad, Sokolivka today exists as a peasant village frozen in time, but the town of Justingrad no longer exists.[40]

---

[40] Sources:

Adler, Selig. From Ararat to Suburbia: The History of the Jewish Community of Buffalo. Philadelphia: The Jewish Publication Society of America, 1960.

Encyclopedia Judaica. New York: Keter, 1971, 16 vols.

Gillman, Joseph. The Binai Khaim in America: A Study of Cultural Changes in a Jewish Group. Philadelphia: Dorrance & Company, 1969.

Miller, Leo and Diana F. Sokolivka/Justingrad: A Century of Struggle and Suffering in a Ukrainian Shtetl. New York: Lowenthal Press, 1983.

Slownik Geograficzny Krolestwa Polskiego i Innych Krajow Slowianskich(Geographic Dictionary of the Polish Kingdom and Other Slavic Countries), 1880 -1904, republished in 1983 by Panstwowe Wydawnictwo Naukowe (State Publishing House for Scientific Literature), Warsaw, in 15 vols.

#8 [C01] REFLECTIONS ON OUR BEGINNINGS
(Letter during 1963 to Joe Gillman from John Robboy)

I find it difficult to criticize your "Soil" (the opening chapter in the book B'nai Khaim, which describes one branch of my family's beginnings). Though what you say is factually true, it is still inaccurate. It gives a distorted view of the people as if they were just emerging from the Stone Age.

Your story starts some 100 years before our time and brings us to our own generation. Judging by what I remember of [C02a] Justingrad and our folks, I would say that they were already far from savagery at the turn of the century.

The entire civilization was quite primitive, but new ideas were infiltrating everywhere, even reaching little Knyazhe. It was no accident that you rebelled. The whole world was awakening, and it reached us too. Religion was dominant in those days, but the faith of our ancestors was already more liberal than that of the Christians. Whether you agree with their beliefs or not, you will admit that their Sabbath and holidays were observed with sanctity. Their morals were of high quality. Then as now, criminality and venereal disease were foreign to the Jew. Already the family and its relationships were unique.

Weak as the schools were, our ancestors recognized their value and maintained them everywhere under great sacrifice, even in Knyazhe.[41] Indeed, they clung to prejudices and ancient practices, but they did value the doctor and sought him out in the cities. Our ancestors were clean. They understood cleanliness even then. "Cleanliness is next to Godliness" is what they said. No Jew was allowed to reside where there was no bath. The municipal bathhouse was a most essential requirement established by them then. The peasantry had none of these. Even the municipal bathhouse on St. Clair Street in Cleveland was not built until about 1915-8.

In manner, habits, customs, and dress, the Jews were also far superior to those of the surrounding population. Their poor were always remembered at Jewish celebrations, either by a feast or donations. Charity was practiced everywhere. Even in Knyazhe, [A011] Mother was the charity organization, and [A011] Father always roused the congregation to the need for Maot Chitim.[42]

I am convinced that we as well as our primitive ancestors were more advanced in thought than many in America today. In speaking of the environment, you unconsciously compare theirs with

---

[41] Letter from [A317] Harry Dudnik to [A457] Joe Gillman, dated 1963-04-07. Some members of [A293] Aaron and [A326] Chaim Dudnik families received some form of formal education in Russia: [A332] Polya, [A339] Yosif, and [A340] Isaac (Khaim's family), and [A316] Dina, [A317] myself (Harry), and [A320] Kenia in Aaron's family. Referencing the rest, home education covered many sins ranging in a wide spectrum from hilly-billy-type ignorance to serious teaching.

[42] The exact translation of Maot Chitim is "Wheat Money." This centuries old Pesach custom is an ancient religious obligation. Its traditional form was a response to the insufficiency of kosher, which was used for baking Matzah. During that time, poor families had to rationalize the amount of Matzah eaten, or survive without it altogether. Raising money for the less privileged families thus became an obligation, which has stood the test of time. In contemporary times, donating flour used in the preparation of Matzah became the norm rather than donating ready made Matzah to the poor families. Scholars argue that this was a way of ensuring that everyone took part in the preparation of the delicacy. In our current age, Maot Chitim has been greatly diversified. In most communities, food and other supplies are often distributed to the poor for free or at highly subsidized prices.

that of Fifth Ave. Poverty was rampant. To procure the basic necessities of life was their greatest preoccupation. They could think of no refinements. Yet despite all privations in the homes, even in our early days, we were already superior to those of the surrounding population.

The people I knew in [C02a] Justingrad exhibited the urgencies, restlessness, desires, ambition, activities, and accomplishments in no way inferior to those of our present day. You, yourself, are a good example of what I describe. Already at the birth of this century, Justingrad was a center of commerce. The city was teeming with wagon work, rope mills, horse-driven mills, and an extensive fishing industry. The town was thriving.

#9 [A010] GRANDFATHER BEN ZION ROBBOY (~1842-1917)

Nothing was known about [A010] Grandfather Ben Zion until he married [A010] Leah Voskoboinik and settled in [C01] Knyazhe. He was apparently educated in Hebrew lore for he was treated with esteem. Since he had no special skills and was free from false pride, he became an egg dealer.

Clad in his faded capote, frayed and bronzed with age, cord at his waist, baggy pants, and wrinkled shoes, Grandfather Ben Zion could have passed for Charlie Chaplin. His hair was clipped short, leaving two straight heavy earlocks flanking his leonine face. A large proboscis heavily studded with blackheads was topped with blue cylindrical glasses that covered up his intense eyes.

Grandfather was a lean man. This made him appear tall. Hard labor made him miserly and serious. I don't remember ever seeing him laugh. All this was reflected in his heavily wrinkled, deeply furrowed, weather-beaten face, a face splashed with cold water every morning, leaving all the grime on until Friday when prolonged steaming and soaping of the face prepared him for the Sabbath. Grandfather was the John Cotton of Knyazhe. He was honest, just, and deeply religious. His was a palpable religion with a God who was personal. He was in direct communication with his God three times a day. He had his pew at the Eastern wall and was honored by singing the Adon Olam when introducing the morning prayer in the synagogue. Nothing ever interfered with this relationship with God.

When his daughter [A078] Sosi died giving birth, it was God's will. When his son, [A079] Mendel, was drafted for military service, though the rabbi promised an absolute disqualification, it was God's decision and could not be questioned. When his niece, [A099] Fullie, returned impregnated by the uncle whose wife was dying from cancer, grandfather violently objected to abortion, as abortion meant murder to him. Instead, he took his niece back to [C33] Terlitza and married her off to the man in question as ordered by the laws of Moses and Israel.

All week-long life was simple and austere. Early, every weekday morning, one invariably saw Grandfather emerging from behind the Graf's estate dressed in an old faded capote, cap, and wrinkled shoes. The staff of Moses was in his right hand, and on his left elbow was a basket that held the freshly laid eggs he picked up among the villagers. These he brought home to be sorted, counted, candled, and packed in individual containers for the next dealer, the wholesaler, to pick up. Little time remained for anything else. Thus, time went on from Sunday to Friday noon, when the time came to make oneself ready for the Sabbath.

It was exciting to watch him on Friday afternoon. By 2:00 p.m., Grandfather was in the bathhouse. He was no politician. He came for a very definite purpose. He was to cleanse and purify himself so as to meet the Sabbath. He soaked himself long in the deep tub, soaped himself well, and then steamed himself on the very topmost bench. Always there was someone to rub his back well. Following this, he would immerse in the mikveh and then was ready for his bride. Then he would rush home.

Watching him at dusk on his way to the synagogue, one beheld a complete metamorphosis. Now he was clad in a clean black capote, a clean white shirt under it, a white collar about his neck, a black cap, a fresh talis katon (small talis), clean trousers, and clean newly polished shoes. Even the cord at his waistline was black and unfrayed. His face clean, all the blackheads were gone, and he was walking rapidly as if someone were running after him. Hastily he made his way to the Beit Hamikdash (synagogue) to meet his Sabbath bride.

When his vision grew dim because of cataracts, it was my privilege to lead him home. I would stay with him overnight. Actually, he needed no help. He merely enjoyed me by his side. I did not appreciate this until a much later date. We sang the "Sholem Aleichem, the Kol Mekadesh" (a song sung during the Sabbath) and the "Yom Zeh Mechubad" (Sabbath table hymn describing how God will provide those who observe this holy day with everything they need) as ordained by the sages. In the morning, we chanted the Bible, following which I took him back to the synagogue. He always let me lead him during the chanting. He must have had a lot of fun listening to my trilling the Shalshelet (cantillation mark found in the Torah). I know now that he knew all the songs as well as the Bible by heart. He did not need me to lead him. He was simply pretending that he needed my help by making me lead.

When the chanting was over, the two of us walked to the synagogue where it was his honor and privilege to sing the "Adon Olam." His rendition was as unique as he was himself. He sang it in a distinctive staccato arrangement that sounded like the pounding of a sledgehammer. It was his pleasure to sing the Adon Olam with such gusto that to this day, I wonder why the walls didn't tumble down. I am convinced that [A786] Cantor Saul Meisels could not do it as well.[43]

---

[43] Saul Meisels, for 37 years, served as cantor at B'nai Jeshurun Congregation, in Cleveland Heights, OH, and then Pepper Pike, OH. He was widely considered as one of the era's foremost interpreters of Jewish song. Ida, his wife, a composer of note, was well known for her arrangements of Jewish music.

#10 [A011] MOTHER (MALKA KAPROVE, 1863-1927) AND FAMILY

Nothing is known about Mother's childhood or adolescent years. Time and its upheavals obliterated all sources of information. Most of you are too young to have known Mother. Many of the older ones will agree with me that she was the queen of the family. Though not educated, like most women of her generation, she rose above her environment because of her intelligence, ability, and character.

Mother was the product of an ultra-religious rabbinical family of the town of [C02a] Justingrad. Her father, [A419] Beryl Kaprov, eked out a livelihood by selling dried salt fish to the peasants. He was a Hassid and great devotee of the Rabbi in town, [A242] Sokolievker Rabbi Pinchas Chochazoh, as were his three sons. [A461] Daniel, Beryl's oldest son and was noted for his scholarship, was chosen at the Yeshiva by some father as the husband for his daughter. [A510] Itzhak, the next oldest boy studied in town for some time and later, was a melamed in [C33] Terlitza. [A515] Abraham, the youngest, was ordained as Rabbi in the city of [C31] Stavishtsh but never practiced Rabbinism until, following the Russian revolution, he came to the States, where he was a Rabbi in Bangor, Maine.

Mother loved the family and was greatly devoted. She kept track of everyone and knew his or her birthdates. However, she seemed to have had no contact with her mother's people. Her mother, [A419a] Dvossie Brodsky, was the daughter of the famous Brodskys, proprietors of sugar beet refineries. Grandmother had two brothers, one an attorney and the other a physician. She came from a home of culture. The difference in the status of the two families as well as the distance from [C02b] Sokolivka or [C01] Knyazhe to [C41] Voznesensk, her birthplace (See Chapter #57), was substantial, thus estranging the families.[44]

---

[44] [A026] Father's maternal grandmother [A419a] Dvossie Brodsky, from [C41] Voznesensk, was part of the larger Brodsky mishpocha that controlled much of the sugar beet industry in Ukraine during the 1800s. No records exist that establish the exact genealogic relation of Dvossie and her siblings to the more extended and well-known parts of the family.

Our first glimpse of Mother is that of a rebel of her time. She had already reached adulthood. Her father announced her engagement, and Mother made the bold assertion that neither the engagement nor the marriage would take place unless and until she met and approved of the young man. Her rebellious stand, no doubt, was painful to her parents, but parents learn to yield. Mother had her way, and the wedding to Shmiel was duly celebrated in the year of 1882 or 1883.

Fig. 10-1: Brodsky synagogues in Kiev (Upper left) and Odessa (Upper right). Under the Soviet regime, the synagogue in Kyiv was remodeled to become a children's theater. In 1966, the time (lower row), half of it had been already restored as a synagogue. Courtesy of Antoinette Gray, a 6th generation descendant of Israel Marcovitch Brodsky, and William Gray, her husband.

Justingrad was a mostly Jewish city of some 800 families. It was a prosperous city teeming with industry, commerce, and culture. Sudden transfer to the small village of [C01] Knyazhe with but 30 Jewish families and no opportunities for earning a living or even a home to live in required much adjustment. The young couple made their home with the [A202] Weinsteins. Mother readily made friends, and though she had never gone to school, she became the reader for the women in the synagogue.

Opportunities for a livelihood were significantly limited. Employment was nonexistent, and what was available brought nothing but a starvation wage. In the meantime, Mother proved herself fruitful. Her first pregnancy brought twins. Five other children came in rapid succession.

Necessity is the mother of invention, and starvation stimulates resourcefulness. To augment their income, Mother tried manufacturing artificial flowers. This did not prove profitable, so she ventured into sewing. At this, she was quite successful. Not only was she making the caftans and skirts for the women but also pants for the men. We were quite amused by her tailoring. She never measured anyone and indeed, not even the men, who never needed fitting. All she did was to take one look at the man and knew exactly how much material to use. The cutting and sewing were then effortless. She made few errors, if any.

Now my people were one of the more prosperous persons in town. With time, the success of Mother's venture into sewing gave birth to a new idea, a dry goods store. She could then sell the material as well as make the garment. This latter idea was excellent, indeed, but the capital was lacking. At least 1000 rubles were necessary to start this venture, quite a sum for Knyazhe at that time. There were no banks to take out a loan. She devised a quasi-cooperative where some folks advanced her enough money to start the business. The friends and cousins included:

[A191] Shmiel Isaac Shudler- 200 R
[A002] Yacov Hersh Voskoboinik- 100 R
[A003] Cousin Haskel Voskoboinik- 100 R
[A168a] Tzire Korsunski- 100 R
[A172a] Zipa Korsunski- 50 R

These sums were repaid as the merchandise was sold, only to be reborrowed when necessary. Others in town used this practice, and flourishing businesses were thus established. The peasant women were also quite pleased. Now they were able to buy the material, which Mother and her daughters then converted into skirts and kaftan (long coat-like garment).

The situation improved so that they were even able to have a goat. All were happy. There was enough milk for the children and all. The wolf, too, was quite pleased. He soon helped himself. Father watched him carry the goat away but couldn't help any. It was a great tragedy, but a cow soon replaced the goat. The cow not only supplied the family with milk, from which we made butter and cheese, but some of the latter could be sold and added to the family's prosperity.

Years later, Mother organized a similar organization, a family loan association in Cleveland. Brother [A024] Joe was in charge. The stockholders, however, did not quite understand the idea, so the association was disbanded after several years.

Knyazhe never had a doctor or even a feldsher. About 1909, a feldsher did settle in our town, but he was an impostor. The doctor had to be imported from a neighboring city, and the price was prohibitive.[45] Innate abilities and mutual aid were sought out and utilized. Because of their kindness and particular inclinations, Grandmother [A010] Leah and [A011] Mother became the most respected doctors in town. Grandmother was the midwife and mother, the general practitioner. Neither of them had any medical or any other education. Their acquisition of the art came through inclination, supervision, and practice, a method common since antiquity. I don't know how many children grandmother delivered, but it was most of the town's Jewish children and all of the peasants' children who called for her help. Rheumatic fever[46] and contagious diseases were raging everywhere. Also, accidents were frequent occurrences. To Mother, healing was a work of love. Her acumen was sharpened by experience. She served gratis and freely to all.

The first beneficiary of Mother's healing ability was her friend, [A212] Sarah Weinstein. Sarah was a charming, attractive young woman, and, as frequently happens, these are the very ones caught in the web of life. Sarah was desperate, but Mother stood by her, helped to extricate her from the mire, and remained friends with her until Mother left Russia in 1912. I have a photograph of both of them.

Though preoccupied with her own problems, Mother never forgot those less fortunate than herself. It was but natural for her home to become the charity organization in town. When [A180] Moshe Bear and his family came to town, his wealthy relative and stepbrother, [A177] Shaia Korsunski, the arendator, refused to have anything to do with him. He was the outcast, the radical, and the socialist. But Mother knew hunger. I was drafted to gather challah every Friday morning for his family. The only ones reluctant to donate the challah were his wealthy relatives. Here, Mother's genes within me came to my rescue. I promised them help should they be in need. My promise frightened them into making contributions to bread.

Mother understood people, their vanity, and psychology. There was [A187a] Esther Kapalushnik and her husband, [A187] Gedalia. I remember seeing him walk to the synagogue. He had a majestic appearance, young, handsome, neatly dressed, and ambled with head held high. He was a polished, educated, and refined man, but ailing since an assault by his rich relatives, the Korsunskis, who saw him as a threat. When he died, Esther tried to maintain her family of six on the proceeds obtained from selling tea to the peasants, and from the pennies they threw at little [A188] Moshe, who entertained them by dancing the kozachok, while they drank the tea. The family was starving, but Esther's pride was unyielding. Mother's eye was discerning, but she couldn't break through Esther's pride. She thought of various schemes and finally had an idea.

---

[45] According to a letter from [A332] Polia Galler to [A457] Joe Gillman, dated 1988, Knyazhe had medical help of some limited sort for a short time (one year). [A327a] Yyova Morrison was not a feldsher, but served the town as one. After he married [A327] Fania Dudnik and moved to another city, his brother [A364a] Zeina (Sol) Morrison came to Knyazhe and opened an American-style drugstore. He had no right to issue prescriptions; he could only sell patent medicine and cosmetics. He married [A364] Sarah Dudnik Morrison, both of whom retired to Los Angeles.

[46] Rheumatic fever, an inflammatory disease, can develop when strep throat or scarlet fever, themselves caused by an infection with group-A streptococcus bacteria. It is rare in the US and other developed countries. The inflammatory condition, which incites the body to attack its own tissues, can lead to permanent heart damage, especially to the heart valves and heart failure.

She would advance money to Esther under the subterfuge that it came from her sister, [A189] Chaichik, in [C43] Zashkov.

Education of the children was of prime importance to all of our parents, and mine was no exception. Since my birth, the financial status of my parents had improved considerably, and they tried to give me all benefits possible. Opportunities in Knyazhe were limited. Hence other areas were considered. Here, Mother's charm, attraction, and powers of conversation served very well. Once on her way to [C36] Uman circa 1906-7, a young travel agent, [A237] Yankel Virin from [C02b] Sokolivka, engaged her in conversation. The mere mention of Sokolivka aroused her curiosity. She knew her genealogy well and found his proper niche in the tree. Within the next few weeks, I was dispatched to and enrolled in cheder at Sokolivka, where I lived with cousins Yankel and [A237a] Sarah Virin[47] for a full year.

In another chapter, I relate the humor and drama of which Mother was capable, together with the value of knowing one's genealogical tree. It also allowed her to demonstrate her powers of persuasion. This deals with how I ultimately was taught by my cousin and [A326] Chaim's nephew, [A401] Liova Dolgonos.

Mother had a strong character, high ability, and an abundance of energy. In addition to her usual activities of childcare, housekeeping, seamstress, and businesswoman, she was interested in animal husbandry. She also made use of this to augment her income. She was as proud of the appearance of our calf as if her child. The calf was never denied full-time suckling. Also, the calf was fed eggnog to assure an elegant shiny coat.

Milk was stored in tall earthen containers -- crocks -- until soured. The cream was then removed, the sour milk poured into large sacs and pressed into cheese while the cream was churned to butter. We always had a large brood of chickens about the house. None of them were ever slaughtered. We knew each one, as well as its hiding place, by name. When any one of the chickens was missed at breakfast time, I would always find it as well as the hidden eggs.

Fattening geese was a significant industry in wintertime. After some three to four weeks of proper feeding, the geese were slaughtered, always on Saturday night. They were then plucked, singed, and hung out to freeze. Come the next morning, the eggs, cheese, butter, the frozen geese with their feathers and down were sold to the folks who came to the bazaar. This provided an abundance of food and income for the family.

For holidays, and particularly for Passover, all the children, brother Joe and myself especially, dressed in new suits, shoes, caps, shirts with detached hard collars and shirt fronts. We did not yet know of ties. My great puzzle always was where did my parents find the funds to pay for all of this. I finally realized that their efforts provided funds for the clothes.

The communities were small and isolated, with none of the present-day communication facilities. Most relatives lived nearby. People were busy from sunrise to sunset. Lack of writing ability was of no particular handicap. Girls received no education at all, but Mother somehow learned to read the Bible, her prayer book, and Yiddish stories. In 1907 or 1908, when brother [A024]

---

[47] The relation on the tree is not certain.

Yossel left for America, Mother suddenly found writing to be a necessity. [A024] Joe was but 16 years of age, young and tender. Mother did not expect to see him again. She felt the need for personal communication sharply, so she faced this crisis and resolved it.

I remember distinctly writing out the Yiddish alphabet for Mother, sounding out the characters. Thus, she wrote the first letters in her life. From then on, she carried on an extensive correspondence with her children and all the relatives scattered throughout the United States, and even the different continents. Although Mother never went to school, she became the reader for the women in town. She was a gifted, dynamic woman, a good mother, and a good friend to all. Her home was always open to everybody in Russia as well as in America.

Mother believed in justice, and her sympathies were always with the oppressed. She was deeply religious and a devotee of her native Rabbi [A266] Rohbonchvamatz from [C24] Monasteristshe. She supported him as well as his son, [A267] Hoshuah, who emigrated to America following the Russian upheaval and lived in New York City. When the latter married off his daughter, Mother and some of her girlfriends went to the wedding to celebrate with him. Here the luxury and splendor were so overwhelming that Mother lost all faith in the Rabbi. She felt it was outrageous for them to live in such opulence on the sweat of other people.

Later in her life, when in Cleveland, Mother showed her feelings towards the usurpation of others. Strikes nowadays have no significant impact on us, but in our earlier days when our fathers, brothers, and sisters were working in the cloak, bakery, and other shops, strikes had a real meaning. The unions were small and weak and had no funds on which to depend. Strikes were dealt with viciously by the employers and the police. A strike was synonymous with war and starvation. There was then the cloakmakers strike against the Wooltex Company, the Belle Vernon Milk Company, and the Rosen Bakery. All were prolonged and violent. One baker was killed. The entire Jewish community was in convulsions. Mother then vowed never to allow the products of the latter two companies into our home.

Matchmaking was still in vogue among Jews in the latter part of the 19th century. Betrothal was based upon the qualities of the parents rather than that of the betrothed. Piety and learning were synonymous with culture and education. Hence families with rabbinical background or education were highly prized. That is why grandfather [A419] Beryl of [C02a] Justingrad and Grandfather [A010] Ben Zion Robboy of [C01] Knyazhe-Krinitsa met and agreed to the match in about 1883 and returned home elated as they announced the engagement of their children: Shmeil and Malka.

To Beryl's great surprise and astonishment came the determined and straightforward bombshell from the rebellious [A011] Malka, announcing no engagement unless she sees the young man and approves of him. How were we to appreciate the significance of her action, the shame, and the pain her parents experienced? Possibly the shame and pain experienced could be analogous to that of the mid-western farmer, the most American-of-all, who suddenly declared himself communist during the McCarthy period[48] of a few years ago in our own States.

But Beryl knew his Malka. A formal meeting was held, and Malka's approval obtained. I would have loved to have witnessed and listened to their talk. I visualize Mother as a pretty, vivacious, neatly dressed young lady whose piercing eyes mirrored her active mind and added great charm to her loving face.

Mother, in turn, became an excellent matchmaker. In fact, matchmaking became her particular forte. Her matches were of the very best. She couldn't leave the spinster or bachelor alone, and when she paired them, the match was always excellent. Only her son and daughter failed her and defied her services. Upon first coming to Knyazhe, Mother found Father's brother, [A034] Mordechai, eligible for marriage. She considered a young lady, [A034a] Sarah Spector in [C43] Zashkov, to be the right one. The two families were also suitable. The rest was simple. She dressed the young man appropriately, the meeting was arranged and a mazel tov followed. No match could be more exceptional.

Father's youngest brother, [A079] Mendel, was a tall, red-headed man with a long red beard and, though only 21 years old, had already finished serving four years in the Russian army. He was unworldly, clumsy, poorly dressed, and had no trade. Mother was quite worried about him. Again, Mother recalled [A079a] Anna Desatnick, in [C35] Tsibulov/Tzibular/Sibilev. She was a bit older but still a good possibility. Once the idea struck, the rest was simple. Mendel was fitted with a new pair of pants, a black surtout, new shoes and haircut, and off we went. This, too, was a happy match. The family later emigrated to the United States and now lives in Philadelphia.

But Mother's crowning success as matchmaker came much later here in Cleveland. [A819] Ben Bernstein, the "Pig," was a most unfortunate, extremely sensitive, shy, and depressed young man because of his deformed face. He presented an extreme prognathism, a condition in which his upper jaw protrudes forward, exposing a series of buck teeth and widespread nostrils sitting upon the protrusion, thus giving him the resemblance of a pig. By chance, Mother met the sister of a man who was a soldier in the army with me during World War I. She was an older girl, not good looking, but also very sensitive, shy, and lonesome. Immediately Mother recognized the lost rib and got busy looking for the rightful owner. Of course, she didn't have to search for too long. Mother managed to marry them off quickly. There never was greater joy anywhere, and we all rejoiced with them. They visited Mother on each of their anniversaries. Unfortunately, their happiness did not last too long. Mr. Bernstein died within a few years. I used to see the widow forlornly walking in the street.

---

[48] Joseph McCarthy, a U.S. Senator (1947-1957), began in 1950 fostering public tensions of widespread Communist subversion. He claimed that numerous Soviet spies, Communists, and sympathizers had infiltrated the government, universities, and film industry. The term "McCarthyism" came to mean demagogic, reckless, unfounded accusations, or public attacks about the patriotism of political opponents. The hysteria swept up several of our family. [A498a] Ken Goodman, a tenured teacher at the Torrance, Ca middle school, was called to the principal's office, where with FBI and State of California officers present, and was fired on the spot. His story is presented in detail in chapter #103.

She was intensely loyal and interested in her relatives. Her home in Knyazhe and later in Cleveland was open to all. Her home was the cynosure for all. She always had room and food for any who came. She mothered all and saw to it that each one in America brought his family. All loved and respected her. Not one defaulted.

Immediately after World War I was over, Mother made contact with Uncle [A502a] Itzhak in [C14] Kishinev. Our family was relatively prosperous during the war. I was in the army, but all others, including Father, were working. None had bank accounts. All monies were deposited with Mother. The Union Trust bank was then on East 105th Street and Pasadena Avenue, just two blocks away from our home. [A803] Mr. Zupnik, the teller, knew Yiddish and solved Mother's difficulties. All but two families had their husbands and fathers here.

Uncle [A079] Mendel and his family were delayed in crossing the border to Romania.[49] Mother sent money on three different times to [A091] Uncle Itzhak for transmission to Mendel. Since the latter did not arrive, he transmitted the sums to other relatives. Finally, the mission was accomplished. The family finally arrived. The folks are now gone, but the children are in Philadelphia. Recently one son, [A088] Ben, a chemical engineer, dropped in to see me. I was thrilled with him. I feel that the family is a great monument to Mother.

Uncle [A034] Mordechai died circa 1919 several months after having been beaten by the Cossacks in a pogrom. Aunt [A034a] Sarah Faiga, his widow, and her family were somewhere in Russia not long after trying to get to [C14] Kishinev and then to America.

The oldest son, [A035] Nathan, at that time, was at Lakeside Hospital, recovering from surgery on his knee due to an injury sustained in the U.S. army. (See Chp #61 for details of this story.) He was destitute, and no one knew when he would recover. But Mother had faith.

Greatness of soul supersedes all deeds. Is there anything greater than what my parents did every Sunday of the year? Ours was the only house in the town wide open from early morning till evening, welcoming all.

Imagine a little town where there is no pavement. Everything is muddy, dirty, wet from rain or snow, particularly in fall when the mud is deep or in winter when the snow is high. There is a bazaar in town. Small vendors are displaying their merchandise, and people from all the surrounding villages are swarming about. All are cold. All are eager to find a place to warm up or get a drink of water or to eat lunch.

At dawn each Sunday morning, Father would warm up the house, throw several large logs into the oven and allow them merely to glow so as to form hot coals. While he then fed the cow, Mother fed the geese, kept in cages for fattening, and then summoned her chicken for breakfast. Here I came in handy, rounding up any that were hiding somewhere in the attic. Then Mother milked the cow. While Mother prepared the meal for the family, Father, with his two sons

---

[49] [A083] Sidney, their son, later described the cruel antisemitic pogroms of the Czars. When a young boy, he and his family escaped from Russia by walking all night and hiding under barns during the day. Eventually he moved to the United States, married, had children, and started his own business, but he never forgot the faithfulness of his parents. (From https://www.shalomadventure.com/stories/prose/2086-sidney-robboy)

helping him, loaded the entire dry goods store onto a cart, and we pulled it to the stall in the marketplace.

All day long, the various vendors came and went uninterruptedly through our door. Some came but for a drink of water or to wash their hands. Others came to deliver their prayers. And some came just to warm up. At noon some munched on the sandwiches they brought with them and helped themselves to a glass of hot water or even tea from the samovar kept going for that purpose. Women vendors came to refill pots with hot glowing coals, which they carried back to the stalls to sit on for warmth. Throughout the day, Father would continuously fill two large barrels with fresh water for all to drink. This act required more than just opening a faucet. It involved many trips carrying two pails of water on his shoulders from a well about half a mile away. By the end of the day, after all the people had come and gone, it is not difficult to imagine how the house and clay floor appeared. Yet I never heard Mother complain or in any way object to what happened.

Our home was on the highway near the center of the town that led to the railroad station, and since my people stayed up late at night working, it was the only house lit up. Passersby, therefore, stopped here to rest or warm themselves. During the fall, the weather was tolerably cold, but the mud was frequently ankle deep. During the winter days, the cold was brisk, the frost sharp and snow up to the knee. The few minutes in our warm house, therefore, was as welcome as an oasis in the wilderness. Mother's hospitality was always warmly extended. Father also always cooperated, too. Within minutes the table would be set with samovar perking, black bread, butter, cheese, and eggs served. These happenings were the delight of my parents. True, many a traveler paid for all the courtesies, but payment never prompted these courtesies -- only the kindness and hospitality that comes from the depth of heart and soul. Here in the States, my people carried on the same way. All our cousins and landsleit (those from the same town or village in Europe as oneself) felt at home. They always felt welcome. Mother watched over them. She saw that they took care of their families and brought them here. Not one faulted. All relatives from either side were equally her people. It was through her efforts that two whole families, with brothers and fathers were brought to America to join us.

If I could paint even as poorly as I can write, I would put the following scenes of Mother onto a canvas. On Friday, after a full week of toil and hard labor, Mother, dressed in her finest with a silk shawl covering her head, sits with her two daughters at the top of the table. It is draped with a white tablecloth. At the head are two large challahs intended for Father. Smaller ones for the sons flank these. There are also wine and glasses for the Kiddush. On opening the door, Father finds his home warm, fresh, clean, brightly lit, with his queen sitting at the table, radiating happiness. He enters the house and chants, "Peace unto you! Unto you, Peace!" One feels, though can't see, an angel with wings outstretched gliding silently in the atmosphere above.

The departure of the Sabbath was proclaimed at dusk by Mother, always facing the window with hands clasped, imploring in an excellent soprano voice the God of Abraham, Isaac, and Joseph for her people everywhere. This song I found but a few weeks ago in the "Jewish Day and Morning Journal." I am translating it the best I can:

God of Abraham, Isaac and Jacob,   Usher in the coming week and luck,
Protect your people, Israel; in your glory   blending justice and prosperity.

and all the best in general.
Amen, Amen

Oh Dear Lord.
The suffering thou dust heal
The naked thou dust clothe
The hungry one thou feedest
Grant us lives in repose and dignity.

Oh, When the dove left Noah's ark
inquiry was made,
Dove, dove what will you bring,

the sweet leaf or the bitter one?
And the dove answered,
Better the bitter from God, Blessed be He,
than the sweet from man.

Oh Dear Lord
You are teaching Torah early and late
In you I trust
In you I feel secure
In you alone.
Amen

In the earlier years of my practice, before hospitalization and insurance came into vogue and when the hospital still had little to offer, people were more realistic in their attitude toward death than at present. They accepted the inevitable and preferred to die at home in their own bed among their loved ones. The doctor would not uncommonly sit at the bedside of the patient until he took his last gasp of breath. It was during these periods I came to realize that even in death, people could be great.

When Mother took to her bed, she asked me to keep her comfortable but not to dull her mind. This was a most challenging request in 1921 when there were no drugs to alleviate high blood pressure or dialysis for uremia. Mother was my very first patient. I had plenty of time also. [A023] Sister Tobie was unemployed and so became Mother's private nurse. We did our best to keep her comfortable, and her mind was never more lucid than during her two weeks in bed. We were amazed at the number and variety of friends she had. She named whom she wished to see, and we would bring them over. Mother had something to say to each one. Instead of gloom, she made this entire period seem like a party.

Ironically, she forgot confession. She realized this quite belatedly and asked for [A805] Mrs. Paley, whom we brought immediately. Mother could hardly repeat the prayers by this time. Mother was deeply superstitious, believing the various legends were current. We thought that she expected a revelation and was disappointed when it did not come, for her last words as she went into a coma were, "Heaven of heavens." The beauty and nobility of her character permeated all who knew her. None of us will ever forget her.

#11 FATHER (SHMIEL ROBBOY 1862-1933)

Little is known about [A011] Father's early childhood other than he received the best education possible in Knyazhe, which was slight. I don't know how long he went to school, but I believe it was until he was about 18.

As Father reached adulthood, it was time to marry. At that time, a young man or woman did not select his partner. It was the fathers of the two who decided upon the match. Invariably, it was based upon the status of the fathers (usually based upon their rabbinical or theological education). Already, then, things began to change, and Mother surprised all by her unusual rebellious stand. "There will be no engagement until I approve of the young man," she said promptly and vigorously. I can just imagine how that poor graced man felt, but he was forced to yield. Mother saw Father, and the engagement was held. Soon they married.

Father, as you already know, was not equipped for marriage. He was a gentle, non-aggressive man whose error was to marry a dynamic and attractive woman with whom he could not cope. He was not as vigorous nor active as Mother, and she overwhelmed him. Father was a good friend, an upright, honest man, and a devoted husband, but a poor provider. Despite this, there was never any friction about which we were aware. There was harmony in our home, but Mother was the master and set the tone in the household. He appreciated Mother's abilities and cooperated well with her. Mother, who relied on her own ingenuity, established a seamstress business with her two oldest daughters. It seemed a good move, and later she added a small dry goods store. Things now improved. Father was kind and respected by all of us to the very end.

Lacking any particular skills, Father at first could only follow the pursuits of all his contemporaries. He tried to earn a livelihood by buying and selling grain during the bazaar days. To eke out any livelihood, one had to learn the art of short weighing and measuring. This was beyond him. He did buy and sell whatever he came across at the bazaars. By the end of the day, luckily, there was often enough for herring and bread, and, occasionally, even for kasha (a dish originating in Eastern Europe, consisting of boiled or baked buckwheat.) Father tried hard at everything and anything that came along. He served as a miller and later, as a night watchman for the equivalent of $3.00 a week, shooing the poachers away along the shores of the river.

Father became a valued citizen and was concerned with the welfare of the impoverished. As a citizen and member of the congregation, he was respected by all. I remember how he would alert the group to the problem of matzos for the poor by withholding the keys to the ark until the promise of help came. Following this, he and cousin [A002] Yakov Hersh continued the campaign and spent days organizing and boxing matzos for all, including the poor. Incidentally, here I must say that the division of labor ascribed in making matzos did not originate in America with American genius. Anyone who witnessed its baking in Knyazhe would have found a most elaborate organization divided into its various departments with duties prescribed for each division and individual. Knyazhe, I am convinced, was the first in line, and her people must have brought the idea with them to America. At least 70 of our citizens, I determined once by count, emigrated to the U.S.

Father was a quiet, humble, good-natured man. It was interesting to find that he was far from timid in his younger years. He was the leader of the pupils' plan to avenge the rebbe's (teacher's) harsh discipline by pouring melted wax over the rebbe's head when he fell asleep. The plan worked.

The Jewish congregation in Knyazhe, as was characteristic of all Jewish settlements, conducted its affairs along democratic lines. That is how Father was elected gabbai (person who assists in the running of synagogue services), which occurred by the time that I was age seven or so. There were no membership dues. The salaries for the rabbi, the shamas (synagogue official who manages many of the day-to-day activities), and the expenses for the synagogue's upkeep, such as repairs, linens, and cleaning, were raised by selling pews, honors to the Torah on holidays and by voluntary contributions on the day preceding the Day of Atonement.

During the preceding year [A001] Uncle Laizer Eli was honored to the presidency. That year was long remembered in the annals of Knyazhe. It was a year of near calamity. All the officers remained underpaid. There was no linen, and the synagogue was run down because of a lack of funds. At the same time, under the list of expenses, there were overinflated bills as evidenced by 18 rubles for whitewashing the synagogue. Those of us who remember Knyazhe know that a load of lime sufficient to whitewash the synagogue for ten years was readily delivered to the premises for the munificent sum of 50 kopecks.

In contrast, during Father's presidency, there was great prosperity. Not only was the synagogue repaired and fully decorated, but also new linen was bought, and the rabbi and shamas were given substantial raises. Also, there was enough left to throw an elaborate party for all, serving herring and real vodka.

Gathering maot chitim was always Father's task, not that he wanted to nor for its honors. Rather, it was his task simply because no one else attempted to compete for his job. This was an annually repeated occurrence at about the same time of the year and under exactly the same circumstances. On Saturday morning several weeks before Passover, at a certain moment during the morning prayer, one suddenly became aware of a serious commotion and excitement. Soon one heard that the keys to the Ark were lost. Naturally, there could be no reading of the Torah. Also, the praying was delayed. The commotion kept on rising in pitch until Father, feeling the climax reached, would assert loudly that no keys would be forthcoming until the community provided the moat chitim. The congregation now would be thrown into even more violent commotion, excitement, and protestation when suddenly the Ark would open and the Torah delivered. What arrangements were arrived at I never knew. All I knew is that no one in Knyazhe ever failed to be amply provided with matzos for the Passover.

In 1902 Father was honored by being elected as mayor of the Jews. It is unclear what his duties or powers were, although there were probably not many. Once a year, he went to [C21] Lipovetz, the county seat where, for a ruble, the clerk recorded whatever vital statistics he reported. When I left for America, I took with me the book that Father used for vital statistics. Whether he made friends during his term, I don't know, but he certainly made no enemies. Later, when he served as our synagogue's gabbai, he finished not only with enough money to pay the rabbi and sexton but raised the salaries of both, and, as well, threw a gala party for the entire congregation. The man preceding him, his own uncle, was short of monies, but very high in expense.

On one Sunday during the summer, Father was put to the test. It was a beautiful day. I helped load the dry goods and pushed the wagon as he pulled it to the marketplace, where he erected our stall and put the goods onto the shelves as all other merchants and vendors did. Suddenly a general pandemonium broke out. The stalls were collapsing, and all were running as if from a great fire. Father did the same. Again I helped push the wagon; only this time, we went to the large barn of [A228a] Urpina Skrivenuk, our landlady. I did not quite understand what happened. Gradually the peasants learned where Father and his merchandise were. He unloaded the goods, spread it out on the floor, and carried on as if nothing happened, but it turned out to be a successful business day. In the evening, I learned that Father had heard the government tax inspector was on his way to town. The news swept the town like wildfire, and panic ensued. The inspector, who was met by deputy mayor [A326] Chaim Dudnik, proved to be a good man. He took a gift and left town. Years later, already a grown man, I learned during a conversation with Father here in America that the inspector was a man of thought and character.

Later in life, I discovered something about Father that is difficult to reconcile with his character. At 14 years of age, I spent a winter in [C43] Zashkov while attending school. A young, very beautiful and attractive woman by her endearing name of [A222] Pupa came to visit me. I discovered that Pupa was Father's first love. She was so impressive that I am confident I could still recognize her. The name Pupa certainly suited her face and appearance. Despite all taboos and even though boys and girls were strictly supervised so that they could not come close to each other, Father managed to get into her room at night by climbing through the back window. There is no doubt about his taste. Apparently, he was not as meek then as when I knew him.

When I was about eight years of age, a man charged with having stolen a cow was seized at the bazaar. To save himself, he confessed and stated that he sold the cow to the butcher. We had two such men in town. Both had their stalls near each other in the marketplace. The police, followed by the mob, led him there, and he pointed at [A194a] Meir, who happened to be first in line. Meir was a friend and neighbor of ours. Months later, Meir was summoned to trial with Father as a witness. Father gave him a strong alibi and rescued Meir from a long imprisonment. Years later, in America, Father told me that he felt justified in giving Meir the alibi, though Meir had an unsavory reputation. Father felt that the thief was led to him, and any butcher in his place would have been accused.

Later during my life in Russia, Father became an independent merchant. The family worked very hard to supplement their income by selling the surplus of milk, cheese, and butter. They also fed and fattened geese during the winter season. The geese would then be killed after four to six weeks, cleaned, and sold at the bazaar. Every little bit helped to improve their status. In 1912, they came to the United States to join their three sons and daughter who immigrated earlier.

In America, Father followed the traditional pursuits of newly arrived Jews. He peddled at first, then later tried the glazier business and finally found a job as a broom maker for a struggling entrepreneur. By then, Father already owned property. With five of us working, we decided to buy a home of our own and put it in Father's name. This arrangement proved to be a panacea for the struggling broom maker businessman whose loans were regularly underwritten and renewed by father. The two men became great friends. The business is now a considerable manufacturing concern in Cleveland.

#12 [A026] JOHN ROBBOY (1893-1980)

The struggle for life begins early. In fact, it starts immediately after conception. Actually, the state of health of the ovum and sperm even before conception may add much to the struggle. Nor is life within the womb a bed of roses. Throughout the pregnancy, the fetus may be subjected to numerous trials caused by mother's ailments or vagaries, but the greatest challenge of all is birth itself. The journey through the birth canal is beset by dangers such as disproportions, chemical changes, or injuries due to drugs or the obstetrician's poor skills. The leech only squashed Tristram's nose. The modern obstetrician dares more. The damage he inflicts may, therefore, be of a much more severe nature.

Our [A010] Grandmother Leah had none of the modern help nor instruments. She merely stood by guiding the patient without any interference. This fact explains my arrival during one early summer morning landing not only in [C01] Knyazhe, but, of all places, in the public bathhouse building.

The landing place itself presented a grave danger. Though beautiful and picturesque, Knyazhe was less than hygienic. On the one hand, this is where orchards, gardens, and meadows abounded, where the large river teeming with life flowed lazily through the town, where cows mooed, horses whinnied, dogs barked, and frogs filled the air with their symphony at evening. On the other hand, its people lived in symbiosis with all these animals, including the cat, the horse, pig, sheep, geese, ducks, and chickens, as well as with a great abundance of lice, fleas, and bedbugs.

The lovely birthplace was no accident. It was merely the result of time and circumstances. Knyazhe was in a perpetual housing crisis. The peasants built small huts for themselves only. The homes there, i.e., structures with more than one room, were few and belonged to the Graf. His favorite Jews occupied most of them. Some of the Jews learned to share what they had. [A202] Yankel Weinstein, the bathhouse keeper, whose family of 12 occupied the two rooms adjacent to the bathhouse, felt obliged, though for a consideration, to share part of his mansion with my folks and their little family that reached seven upon my arrival.

Though unwanted, my parents never rejected me. Only Mother saw no reason to make as much fuss over me as over the other four boys and, therefore, allowed the local mohel, whom she distrusted previously, to circumcise me. None of this disturbed me at all. If I am to believe sister [A023] Tobie, I stood pat on my rights objecting to mother's empty breasts and demanding food. Formulas for infants were yet non-existent, and wet nurses too costly and not always available. Mothers would masticate the bread and then feed it to the children as supplementary feeding.

While being an added burden to my folks, the beautiful women of our metropolis greeted my arrival with joy. They found the panacea in me in response to their prayers. Our women were in constant danger of having their purification despoiled by roaming drunken peasants, or dogs and pigs on their way home from the Mikveh. Now, immediate contact with the innocent, young child obliviated all fears. I was thus destined to public service since infancy, and I am delighted that I was instrumental in assuring these lovely women to nights of good sporting. I am only sorry that all their love and caressing were wasted on me then. I could have enjoyed them much more at a later date.

Just how long we lived with Yankel, I don't know but long enough to sustain a skull fracture when [A024] Joe pushed me against the brick oven. Mother's nursing, together with [A355] Leib Dudnik's candy, saved my life. Shortly after that, we moved into the home of [A228a] Urpina, widow of [A228] Uchrem Skrivenuk.

The very house I was born in served as my first cheder. Somehow there was room for everyone and everything in the one-room homes of our mothers. Can one imagine any of our modern mothers sparing even a part of her six rooms for the gathering of 25 to 30 children, all summer and winter long for most of the day?

My first rebbe was known as [A251] Katzap. I was then about four years of age. This distinguished appellation remains unexplained, for the rebbe in no way resembled the Katzap. The latter name was applied to the Muscovite, who was a heavy, strong, muscular, and pugnacious type who usually indulged in drinking, eating, and women. But our Katzap, as I remember him, was tall and thin, at the head of the table facing us, standing coatless with his small talis with fringe hanging down. He held a fishbone pointer in his hand and a rod in the other for disciplining if need be, but for which he seldom had any use. His strong, sharp, and raucous voice and menacing stare were sufficient to freeze all of us little monsters in our seats within an instant. That is all I remember of him.

One other bit of memory remains vividly in my mind. One of my schoolmates came to cheder, showing off a very attractive walking cane that was then in vogue. Actually, it was an iron rod run through a multitude of fiber rings. For some reason, he decided to crown me with it. But I escaped with but a scalp laceration. It was the thickness of my skull that enabled me to withstand this as well as later assaults.

In my days, the rebbe was seldom a learned man. Poverty, sickness, or ignorance, which rendered the man unfit for anything else, made him venture into teaching. Because of this, the instruction was poor and seldom went beyond the Bible. A primary function of the teacher was discipline, which mostly consisted of beatings. In this, most of our teachers performed excellently.

[A252] Moishe, melamed for the more advanced pupils, was our next rebbe. He was more scholarly than some others, but a good example as a disciplinarian. Though I was only about six years of age, I was already aware of his reputation. Therefore, when one fall morning Joe and I saw him coming to our home, we burst out crying. We knew he was coming to enroll us in his class.

Moishe was married. He had four children, two of whom were our playmates, and he lived in one of the typical one-room peasant huts on the Rinkivki River. This home also served as the cheder. Moishe was afflicted with chronic lung disease, always coughing and bringing up copious amounts of sputum. Apparently, he had advanced bronchiectasis and not tuberculosis for, to my knowledge, none of us ever became afflicted with this disease.

Moishe was as poor as he was sick. His wife, [A252a] Menicha, was forced to augment his meager income by selling soap during the bazaar days.

Added to poverty and his disease was the problem of handling the 20 or more of us "Angels." All of this was, without a doubt, highly taxing. No wonder he was highly irritable and would go into frequent rages. Yet he managed to control himself and attack his wife instead of his pupils. During the rage, he would throw anything at hand at her. Nevertheless, he did not neglect us either. Generally, he did not hesitate to discipline his pupils.

Once, when I reported that brother [A024] Joe was reluctant to return to school unless Mother gave him five kopecks for the afternoon snack, the rebbe disappeared instantly only to go back with a bunch of kropiva (poison ivy) in his hand. He then forced Joe to pull his pants down and lie down on his knee while he flogged Joe's behind for his misbehavior. He continued to spank him until Joe's hind part blistered into a giant balloon. What Joe looked like afterward, I leave to your imagination. However, the poison ivy plant there was less allergenic than the one we are familiar with here in Ohio. The skin would blister and itch but would clear in 24 hours. Joe made a speedy recovery and returned to school the next day.

The cheder was about a mile away from home. In the summertime, the trip was rather enjoyable despite the gauntlet we were forced to run to avoid attack by [A161] Pan Pavlovsky's dogs on the right and those of the priest on the left. In wintertime, being hampered by heavy clothing, boots, and deep snow, the problem was formidable. Mother always rose to the occasion and found a way to protect her offspring. Whether in Knyazhe or Cleveland, mothers are endowed with the same special feelings and sympathies for their young. Even our Mother Rachel, if one remembers the Bible, pleaded for special privileges for her little Benjamin.

To protect us from the blistering cold one Sunday morning, Mother decreed that Joe and I stay home. Joe and I were very pleased and prepared for an extended vacation, but to our great disappointment on Friday morning, Mother suddenly rescinded her decree. This was the week when we studied the chapter, Vayechee (last Torah portion of the Book of Genesis). It is the part of the Bible where Jacob gathers his children to bless them before departing to the world beyond. These blessings presented a formidable task. Not only was one to master this chapter by Friday, but we had to memorize all of the interpretations the rebbe gathered from Rashi and other commentators. Our consternation was extreme. To return to school that morning without knowing the required Bible part was tantamount to suicide.

Mother apparently was quite aware of this danger. She, therefore, fortified each of us with a silver ruble, and we went to school as if to the guillotine. When [A252] Rebbe Moshe saw us opening the door, he instantly turned crimson, and his lips began to quiver with anger, but Joe and I also knew our business.

The two of us, whether out of fear or just good luck, instead of removing our boots and coats, ran directly to the table and deposited the two rubles in front of the rebbe. Immediately a smile appeared on his lips. Moishe suddenly saw a week's bread and butter for his family. He softened, and we knew we were safe. No excuses were now necessary. He welcomed us now warmly, and we returned home happy and triumphant, as cheerful and gay as all other kids, free for the weekend.

Joe and I continued as his pupils until 1901 when he passed on to the world of eternal rest. Then the problems of our further education presented itself. To be sure I was entirely undisturbed when the town had failed to engage a rebbe for the coming season. But Mother made a speedy decision, namely, her greater family living in [C02a] Justingrad (Sokolivka). Any of her sisters would welcome her children. She decided to send Joe to [A462] Aunt Yenta and me to [A422] Sister Pessie, her favorite. She did not know that Aunt Pessie had died some months earlier. No one had informed her of that fact, in keeping with an old cherished tradition. Immediately after the holidays in early fall, the two of us were dispatched to Justingrad to assure our continued education.

Justingrad was a highly industrialized, nearly all Jewish city having beautiful homes and a multitude of goats. Though I missed [A205] Aaron, the blacksmith, whom I helped blow the bellows in exchange for teaching me the ways of life and the latest songs, I was well compensated in other ways. It was fun to play with the goats or to watch the artisans skillfully shape the spokes for the wheel or counsel [A485] Yossel as he manufactured long, thick ropes. Unfortunately, that was not my parents' intention. I was sent in quest of an education, and that is what I was going to get. Thus I found myself enrolled in the class of Rebbe [A257] Israel "Kiegele." I never learned why he received such an attractive nickname.

Rebbe Kiegele was a stern man. We were 20 to 30 boys of all ages and sizes sitting on long benches around a square table with the rebbe, rod in hand at the head of it, studying Judges. We were each to recite successively, the sentences in the text. Despite the rod, no one ever knew where the other left off. The rebbe thus was given his chance for exercise. School lasted until 8 or 9 p.m., and if it was not exactly efficient, it did have its purpose. Here I had my first lesson in social relations and blackmail. [A232] Tahatuta, who was at least four times my size, was sitting next to me and managed to rob me of what pennies Mother sent me by threatening to tell the rebbe. What he had to tell I still don't know.

Upon my arrival in Justingrad, cousin [A431] Alta Gillman, Pessie's daughter, welcomed me graciously and even provided me with a private room. Soon, however, Alta was confronted with a most perplexing physiological problem. I was accustomed to a warm home with plenty of warm bedding. How was she to know the effect of a cold room and scanty bed covers upon kidney functions? It must have been a nightmare for her as my revolt against cold was prompt and effective. To her credit, Alto never made me conscious of it. Those were the pre-psychiatric days when even psychologist or guidance clinics were not yet a futuristic dream. Quietly she managed to transfer me to [A515a] Aunt Sima Kaprov. My sojourn here was rather pleasant. There were cousins [A522] Dora and [A516] Fishel, both my age, and we were fond of each other. Fishel was even in my class with Kiegele. Friday nights were especially delightful as we were entertained by [A515] Uncle Avrom, who, with his beautiful and robust voice, rendered the Kol Mekadesh and the Yom Zeh Mechubad to our delight.

Unfortunately, the underlying environment, except for sharing the bed with Fishel, remained unchanged. Who was the culprit, and who was to accept responsibility for the wet bedclothes? That was the mystery, but Fishel, as the son, was always the recipient of the beatings. That Aunt Sima was desperate was quite obvious. To relieve her, I was now shifted to Aunt [A462] Yenta for weekends.

Aunt Yenta was an institution of her own. She was almost the ugliest woman I ever knew, but her kindness was unsurpassed. Though she had been a widow since the birth of her seventh son, she raised them all and taught each one of the children a trade or placed them in business. Hers was the only well-heated home, and there was plenty of black bread on the shelf and herring in the table drawer. What else did a healthy, growing boy need? Because I shared the bed with cousin [A485] Yossel, who was as warm as a stove, and covered with a down featherbed, the lake in the sheets suddenly vanished. In the morning, I was as proud as a peacock and happy as a lark.

The Sabbath was of particular significance for Aunt Yenta. It was not just a day of rest, but a day of repose, relaxation, and complete freedom from toil. She was dressed neatly. Her face was washed clean, and with a white shawl around her head, she almost looked beautiful. The synagogue was not crucial to her. She could neither read nor write anyway. It was her day to enjoy the children. Since I was the youngest one around, it was but natural for her to give me her attention. With me in her lap, while she combed my hair, I could hear her whispered prayer in between the crackling of the lice as she crushed them with her right thumbnail against the blood bespattered comb. But while the lowly pediculi presented no serious problems to her, for she knew how to cope with them, the annoying eruptions over my body and its accompanying pruritus baffled her. Salves were of no avail. The bath was therefore resorted to with [A494] Cousin Willie's help.

Willie was serious and had a job to perform. From now on for three times a week, he would meet brother [A024] Joe and me after school and lead us to the public bathhouse. He brought two herrings for admission, one for each watchman. I enjoyed the baths and steaming for some time until my schoolmate, to whom I had confided the secret, relayed the news to his father, owner of the bathhouse. The baths were discontinued.

How was I to know who the schoolmate was? What was worse, the eruption was spreading and growing more severe and annoying. Fortunately, the Passover season was near. Mother arrived, claiming both Joe and me. She took us home, lice and all, and immediately started a clean-up campaign of her own.

Busy as Mother was with business, dressmaking for her customers and general household duties, she always found time for the care of her children. Once a week, she would dip our heads in kerosene. She never failed to boil all linens, and for the bedbugs, she used the very latest of war-weapons, fire. It was a great pastime to help Mother with a lighted candle in hand, go through every crevice of the bed, and watch the red, flat-backed, multi-legged creatures run for life. No wonder that by Passover, the rash was gone, the head was clean, and I was able to sing the Had Gadya as vociferously as I did.

To supplant material for the dry goods business, Mother traveled to [C36] Uman or [C38] Vinnitzia about once a month. Being attractive as well as a good conversationalist, men sought her company during these trips. That is how she met a young travel agent, [A237] Yankel Vizin, by name, whose home was [C02b] Sokolivka. The name Sokolivka was quite familiar to Mother. She had relatives there and within minutes found the proper niche in her genealogical tree for him.

Now with the Passover duly celebrated, I was dispatched to Sokolivka for the continuation of my education. Since the Vizins had no children of their own, I was greatly welcomed by [A508]

Yankel and his wife, [A508a] Sarah, and I lived with them for a full year. That I enjoyed myself there is evident in that I have not the faintest idea of who the rebbe was or what the cheder was like.

The city of Sokolivka and its people were quite modern. Their homes compared well with those of Cleveland a few years later, though I do not remember what the plumbing was like. The people and the youth, in particular, differed very little from our own even at this late date.

I found here another family of cousins, a brother of [A237] Yankel Vizin, but by a different name. His first name, I believe, was [A238] Itzi, and he was a grain dealer. His oldest son, [A239] Abraham, was a medical student. We met during summer vacation. It was during this time that he worked for his grandfather, repairing the sacs for the grain. The middle son, [A240] Nyashke, a gymnast, was a busy, robust young man, handsome and majestic looking in uniform. He was always gay, cheerful, and most mischievous. His hobby was to tease [A237a] Sarah. He would raid her icebox whenever she had any worthy edibles stored away, despite all of her precautions. Sarah could never carry any grudge against Nyashke. The youngest son, [A241] Yossel, who was about my age and blind in his right eye, was not as handsome, but just as naughty as his brother.

All the children in town were lively, carefree, and spoiled, much like our own. To use the phrase of a Jewish alderman from pre-war Warsaw referring to American children, "They were children, not little old men."

After school, we all gathered at the candy store eating and drinking sweets. I had no money, but I learned the game and became fairly expert and a frequent winner. The Game - hard candy bars consisting of honey - were placed on the face alongside the nose. By manipulating the face and jaw properly, one was to catch the bar with his lips without the help of hands. My skill grew great. This game only proved the power of necessity.

The next [A258] rebbe, Laib, from the city of [C03] Arotof, brought a glimpse of light for us in Knyazhe. I believe he was with us for the two years, 1903 and 1904. He was a young, handsome, and gentle individual. He was orthodox, but yet more modern than some of the former rebbes and was the first one to teach us Hebrew and Hebrew grammar in addition to the Bible. He was also the first one who was unable to discipline us physically. Whenever he did attempt such regulation, we would seize his arms and struggle with him until he would begin to smile. That was our signal of conquest and safety.

Once he discovered that [A190] Shuke Kapaliushnik owned a strong oak ruler, he thought he could make good use of it and persuaded Shuke to give it to him. It was but natural that the kids should object to its use for punishment. After due deliberation, I was assigned the job of disposing of the dreaded tool. It just so happened that our house key fitted the lock of the cheder. Late one afternoon, I entered the cheder and, finding the ruler, put it into my pocket. Just as I was leaving the cheder, [A202] Yankel Weinstein came up and, noticing my peculiar walk, insisted on examining me. This resulted in confiscating not only the ruler but the keys as well. Eventually, the keys were returned, and I did dispose of the ruler.

School was five full days and Friday till noon. In wintertime, it lasted until late in the evening. The school was lit by kerosene lamps. The pupils, in rotation, provided the kerosene. The streets were dark. [A178] Ruchel Korsunski, [A177] Shaia's daughter, lived about a mile away from school and required an escort to protect her from stray dogs, pigs, or drunks. [A327] Fania Dudnik, the only other girl in school to my knowledge, lived closer. Secretly, there was considerable vying for the opportunity to escort [A178] Ruchel. Hence I kept myself alert and in readiness for the moment for the rebbe's call for volunteers.

This happened during the week of "Beshalach." The story of Jacob's return home with his four wives and his entire household was told in detail. Trying to appease his brother, Esau, whom he was to meet, Jacob sent him a handsome gift. Rashi, the commentator, elaborated extensively by giving the number and sex of the various animals sent. Amid this exciting and absorbing story, the quest for volunteers came up. Of course, I was ready and the lucky one.

Upon returning, I had enough time to recapitulate what I learned as well as to formulate an appropriate question. The rebbe and his class were outside waiting for me. On approaching closer, I called out loudly that I had a question to ask. Being of a more modern vintage, the rebbe would not refuse a pupil's question. Knowing that my question would call for punishment, I ran up the nearby hill and at the top of my voice said: "Rebbe, if 20 male sheep are required for 100 female sheep, how many boys are required for 100 girls?"

Once the question was delivered, I jumped double-quick and ran home with the rebbe after me. On reaching home, I went directly to bed, asking for no food, much to Mother's surprise. The rebbe, on the other hand, on reaching our home, saw the town policeman in the living room. With such a personage present in the house, the rebbe could not possibly disturb the peace. I was thus saved, though not for long.

To my misfortune [A172] Mendel Korsunski, the cantonist, happened to visit the school early the next morning. The rebbe seized the opportunity and told the entire story with a bit of embellishment in addition. The rebbe now put me on his knee and enjoyed a great picnic. My hind part still hurts. Nevertheless, I still love to think of the gentle soul [A258] Rebbe Laib was.

[A259] Rebbe Avrahom was our next teacher. He was much older and possibly better educated than Laib but apparently found us very difficult and irritating. He resorted to the stick and beat us mercilessly. He was a Litvak. Our pronunciation was very different from his, and although his chanting of the Bible was really beautiful, we just couldn't do as well. I am confident that this contributed to his dissatisfaction.

Our cheder was on the bank of the river. There were reeds all along the bank, and Rebbe Avrahom kept a supply hidden in the straw roof of the cheder. There were obtainable at any moment.

Once the old mother of [A174] Aaron "Gonta" Korsunski accused us of having stolen her ball of yarn. Without questioning, Rebbe Avrahom began to beat us like a madman. We had no idea why this was happening. Suddenly, amid the beating, he noticed the ball of yarn under Gonta's arm. The beating stopped instantly, which I am sure was out of embarrassment and not compassion.

I recall another one of the rebbe's beatings. He fell upon one of the boys and beat him until brother [A024] Joe protested. He then turned on Joe and continued until I spoke up in protest and received my share of the same. The family was just getting ready for the wedding of my cousin, I believe, [A511] Tobie by name, who was [A510] Uncle Itzi's daughter in [C33] Terlitza. For a moment I thought that trip lost, but I soon recovered and managed to go to the wedding. I never saw this family Kaprove again.

It seems that my folks were tired of looking for places for my further education and began thinking of launching me on a career in teaching. I remember standing beside [A194a] Meir, the butcher one Sunday afternoon at his stand at the bazaar. He was extolling my qualifications to the villager from [C19] Kuritna, who needed a tutor for his children. "He is not so erudite a boy as he is learned," he told the man. I passed, and that same afternoon the villager took me with him to Kuritna, which was some 3-4 versts from Knyazhe. It was a most glorious week for me. No one was concerned about my well being, nor was I ever fed so well. Yet the job did not appeal to me so that on Sunday morning, I just walked home. Thus ended my career.

The spring of 1906 brought shocking news to our little town. Our two richest Jews, for some unknown reason, abandoned all rivalry and made peace. As an expression of their peaceful coexistence, they imported [A326] Chaim's nephew, [A401] Liova Dolgonos,[50] an Odessa bookkeeper to teach their three children. The exclusive, ironclad contract assured them against the intrusion from any outsiders. Liova represented the modern teacher in contrast to the old-fashioned rebbe. Mother resented this exclusion and just refused to accept it. Upon learning the young teacher's name, she considered herself as close to a cousin as Chaim. She then managed to meet Liova and to talk to him about teaching me. Liova was sympathetic and promised to speak with his employers about me. He kept his promise that very evening, but his employers said this was an absolute impossibility because I was unruly, mischievous, and dangerous – a "shegetz" (Yiddish racial epithet for someone who is not Jewish). Liova, not understanding this charge, decided to investigate for himself, meet me and make his own decision.

I still remember the excitement and my trepidation until Liova arrived and asked me to go walking with him. The two of us walked over to the Graf's estate, where we talked. His approach was very sensible so as not to make me feel as undergoing examination. He was interested to know where my playmates and I gathered during our leisure time and about what we talked. I was quite at ease and told him of my dreams as well as those of my playmates. I told him that we felt forsaken, helpless, with no prospect of development and learning either trade or profession. Liova must have been unusually impressed, for after listening to me, he told Chaim that [A026] Yankel the "Shegetz" must be admitted to his class or he would leave the next morning. Apparently, Chaim and [A177] Shaia Korsunski realized they lost the cause. In fact, he actually packed and was ready to leave in the morning when his employers relented and acquiesced on

---

[50] According to [A402] Dave Douglas, his father, [A401] Liova (Louis), was then a young man of about 18 years, when he went to Knyazhe to teach the cousins. David believes his father said he had been sent to teach [A385] Morris and [A332] Polia Galler, who were cousins and later married. [A401] Louis was a bookkeeper for the Community Organization of Self Help, and based on this experience later became the bookkeeper for a bank, which at that time was an unusual position for a Jew. This allowed him to live in Odessa in a style normally and legally prohibited to Jews. They moved in 1921 to [C14] Kishinev, in 1924 to Romania, in 1924 to Vancouver, Canada, and in 1925 to Toronto. David moved in 1946 to Los Angeles, CA.

101

one condition. Mother must provide room for the cheder. One of our bedrooms, therefore, served the purpose.

That was the most successful year of all my schooling, and I excelled in all my studies. We studied Bible, the prophets, Jewish history, Hebrew and Hebrew grammar, Russian language, grammar and composition, Russian history, arithmetic, and geography. No wonder [A756] Miss Peiser in Cleveland thought I was entitled to enter highschool once I learned some English. I excelled in all the studies and behaved much better than [A327] Fania Dudnik, whom Liova was forced to punish frequently. Also, I enjoyed [A178] Ruchel Korsunski to the utmost! Incidentally, [A401] Liova and I remained great friends. I visited him some years later in Toronto. Unfortunately, he died very early from coronary heart disease.

A most unusual thing occurred during the second semester. The class was enlarged when [A364] Sarah Dudnik, sister of Chaim, was admitted. Sarah, who was older than the others, was coarse and illiterate but possessed natural intelligence and lots of cheer. Another young girl was the [A270] daughter of [A269] Shalom, the tax collector from [C22] Lohahievka. She had to live in our house, and Mother was forced to promise that I would help her with the work. As it happened, I did not like the girl, although she was good-looking, neat, and clean. I did not know of the contract with Mother. When Mother asked why I didn't help her, I said, "She stinks."

After [A401] Liova left Knyazhe, the question arose about continuing my education. The problem was, where? Here, [A034] Uncle Mordechai, Father's brother, came to the rescue. A new modern school had just opened in [C43] Zashkov. Mordechai was willing to have me as his guest. He only had seven little ones of his own. Certainly, Aunt [A005] Sarah Faiga would have no objection, and so he took me with him to Zashkov.

The school was of modern vintage and therefore opposed by the religious group. The faction had permission for a religious school only. The study of the Bible and other spiritual subjects was eliminated, and instead, replaced by the Russian language, history, and arithmetic. The two factions were at war continuously and caused police raids frequently.

I remember but three teachers. One appeared distinctly Russian and probably never had seen a Jew before or knew the Jewish alphabet. One taught singing and dramatics. He considered the Bible too advanced for children - a most revolutionary thought, particularly to the Orthodox at that time. The third teacher, [A261] Mr. Krasnyansky, a grand angelic man and fine teacher who was very much dedicated like our own [A682a] Aunt Helen. The moment he saw the police, he made us quickly hide the books, while he would turn to the blackboard and teach us the Jewish alphabet. Krasnyansky was an "externic," a term applied to students, Jewish students, who studied outside the school due to exclusion. [A261] Krasnyansky appeared for entrance exams to the University but failed each time until he finally gave up trying. Some years later, I found a Krasnyansky mentioned as [A282] Trotsky's bodyguard in Trotsky's "My Life." Could it have been the Krasnyansky I knew?

The school where I spent the year in Zashkov (~1908) was too elementary and hence unprofitable. I don't know what became of the school. My education was of extreme importance to my folks. Their economic status had improved considerably by this time. Since I was the youngest, they wished to give me whatever opportunity possible.

Mother, on one of her trips to Uman, by accident met a [A263] Mr. Schlemensohn, a grain dealer, at the railroad station of [C24] Monasteristshe. He was a rotund, pot-bellied, well dressed, neatly groomed, bearded man. He was friendly and responsive. It took but little time for Mother to discover that he had two sons, [A265] Misha, a medical student, and [A264] Aaron, a gymnast who would be willing to do some tutoring. The next I knew, I was in [C24] Monasteristshe to receive the benefits of education.

[A264] Aaron was an impressive looking young man. He was tall and broad-chested. His head was full of large curls, and he wore a polka dot blouse with a heavy cord around the waistline. The curls and his dress strongly resembled the familiar picture of Pushkin. Aaron and I met about once, sometimes twice a week in the besedka (garden house). The teaching, however, was not very profitable. Brother [A265] Misha visited his home infrequently for short periods. His arrival always caused excitement and commotion among the few Jewish girls there for they idolized him and managed to greet him upon arrival as well as on parting.

There were some youngsters there. They had a school of their own. [A178] Ruchel Korsunski and her brother [A179] Rachmiel were here also and lived in the tavern owned by their grandmother. I made my home in the same house. They brought me in contact with the other students. Some of the girls were quite attractive. I felt quite at home with them. When we ventured into the forest to pick cherries or nuts, my role usually was to lead the expedition. Possibly, this was one reason why the education was unprofitable. I did enjoy that summer and the girls in particular.

The Jewish population here was not high, but it was homogenous, consisting of fairly well-to-do, modern, and neither orthodox in either dress nor religion. Their affluence had its influence upon the children who behaved very much as our own do. All were interested in clothing, fineries, and luxuries. In Fall, a dance class was organized into which I was enrolled as a matter of course. A dance master was imported, but when classes opened, I found myself outside. What happened, I summarized some years later. [A023] Sister Tobie, at this time, was about 18 or 19 years of age and already a seamstress of note. When I was to leave home, she made a jacket for me. As a seamstress, she was able to cut the material for a blouse very well, but not for a boy's jacket. There was no pattern for her to get. Hence the jacket turned out like the top of a lady's dress - wide at the shoulders and narrowed at the waistline. Also, the sleeves were puffed somewhat at the top and narrowed down gradually as they reached the wrists. No doubt, I would have made an excellent dance partner. I don't know what effect this had on me, but I never cared to dance since.

I was now 16 years old. Even though education was highly valued by my parents and greatly stressed, it had been by necessity only elementary and limited to Jewish religious subjects. Further education was now abandoned, not because mine was considered complete, but because of the difficulties in pursuing it. The pre-revolutionary movement in Russia was at its high peak. Revolutionary ideas permeated the atmosphere. The repression from pogroms was giving stimulus to the Zionist movement. The Jews were most restless. The philosophies of Zionism and that of the Russian revolution filled the air. The Zionist slogans "Acquire a Trade" and "Return to the Soil" resounded loudly through the Jewish Pale, arousing response even from those who knew nothing about either philosophy or, for that matter, nothing much about Zionism.

The restlessness and criticism of the regime were sharp and universal as indicated by this random illustration: "What is new in the Duma (parliament). They just think and think, but never reach any conclusion." This is the thought of an illiterate peasant whom I met later. He was from the tiny village of [C27] Novosilka some 3 or 4 versts west of my home town and who looked upon me as a man of the world coming from the great metropolis of [C01] Knyazhe-Krinitsa.

Unable to provide me an education beyond the parochial level, my folks were forced to abandon their parental obligation and yield to the forces prevalent at the time. As there was no industry, no schools, nor any possibilities for learning a trade for a Jew or Christian in [C01] Knyazhe, I left home in September 1909 for [C14] Kishinev where I resolved to learn mechanics, the profession of respectability at the time. As a parting word, Mother said "do anything but don't become a tradesman." See Chapter #28 about the stay with my cousins [A502] Gelman.

The year in Kishinev was as enjoyable as all others. However, even good things end. It was time for me to return home in the spring of 1910, an event that nearly cost me my life.[51]

Life during these days was not pleasant in Knyazhe. One day, when returning home and on reaching the highest point of [C12] Kashivka, I was able to view the entire Knyazhe. Thus, I was able to see the tall, immense chimney, ghostlike, sitting on the spot where our home was. Just a few weeks earlier, a fire had consumed our home. Thanks to the peasants, they had rescued all our possessions. [A326] Chaim Dudnik, however, whom the peasants hated, did not fare so well. However, he was a favorite of the Graf who provided him with a different home immediately. Fortunately, [A235] Yudel, the pharmacist, out of gratitude to what our folks did for him when he came to marry [A235a] Frima, offered my family shelter during this tragic moment. Upon my arrival, naturally, I joined my family there. This home originally was the parochial school for the peasant children only. The Hromada (Public) allowed [A235] Yudel to make his home and pharmacy in the school, as there was no other home present. Father and I slept in part of the large room partitioned off from the other people. At dawn, Father would leave the house, driving the cow to pasture. [A234] Yudel's mother, who happened to live here too, knew the schedule, and hence managed to get by my bed and accidentally brush against my pillow and wake me. After repeating this three to four times, she exposed herself to me. I was still naive and pure. The fact that she was probably three times my age aroused my resentment. As a result, I grabbed her labia and almost tore them off. The poor woman couldn't scream and expose herself as the mother and daughter were sleeping behind the curtain. She was, therefore in great agony before I let her go. I am sure she was not functioning for weeks after that.

Soon, [A177] Shaia Korsunski moved his home, and we then became tenants of [A230] Lefko (~1910). His was a modern home consisting of a living room, bedroom, and kitchen. The tin roof gave some protection from fires. Shortly after we moved to this modern apartment, brother [A012] Hymie came home from [C29] Odessa, and it was decided that we should leave for America where opportunities for development were hopefully higher than in Knyazhe. Hymie had already served in the army. I was 17 years old. It was felt, therefore, that there would be no obstacles in permitting us to leave Russia. We were confident of obtaining a local passport since [A177] Shaia Korsunski was then the Meshtshamski Strosta (Mayor of the Jews), and I was a

---

[51] In Chapter #49, "The Cap", John tells of his parting experience, which nearly cost him his life. [A502a] Uncle Itzie bought him a cap, which to a policeman made Father appear to be a student revolutionary.

favorite of his. I liked his daughter [A178] Ruchel. He would have been happy to have me as his son-in-law, not only because of superior family stature but also because of my promising personal qualities.

Means of communication (telephone and telegraph) were not yet present here, while the best transportation available was on foot. Once the local passports were obtained, Hymie and I set out on foot for the city of [C35] Tzibulev some ten versts away to see the uradnik (a public person, usually involved in bureaucratic work). Thence we continued our journey to [C24] Monasteristshe, a distance of another twelve versts, for the office of the pristav (district officer). Usually, this office was the stumbling block. Fortunately, and purely accidentally, when I asked the clerk how long a wait we could expect before the passport will arrive, he unceremoniously answered that it all depends on the amount one pays. A ten-ruble note was now handed over. Nothing more was said. We signed papers, which included a note that I promised to return for military service at age 21. Within three weeks, the passport to leave Russia came, which truly was a record time. Mission accomplished, we left for home, a distance of another twelve to fifteen versts.

We reached Knyazhe late that afternoon. We stopped at the home of [A213] Aaron Deutch, the furrier, whose wife, realizing how tired and hungry we were, treated us to a sizeable black bread and a dish full of pickles. Never was a meal more appreciated.

Cousin [A237] Yankel Virin, steamship agent from [C02b] Sokolivka, made all arrangements for our travel through the H. Polk and Co. Time and comfort were of no importance to us. I had six weeks of fun greater than at any time in my life. I was all eyes and ears. The scenery changed daily, and there was so much to see.

On our way to [C20] Libow (Lviv), I was much impressed by the different types of passengers and dress and particularly by a group of Polish Jews who wore long capotes and small caps (kashkets). They were gesticulating a good deal, talked loudly and excitedly and used the "ai" in their speech. I could account for the latter as a matter of dialect, but the cap perched on the vertex of the calvarium I could never understand. The city was beautiful and had double-decker streetcars. Our inn, though, was far from a Statler Hotel (an important hotel in Cleveland), and the food was terrible. Such small things mattered little to us. We were supposedly quarantined for two weeks there, where we enjoyed the High Holidays.

From [C20] Libow (Lviv), we went by boat by way of the Visla River through the Kiel Canal. We stopped at Copenhagen, where the natives met us. They were very friendly and appeared as wholesome and clean as their landscapes. They introduced us to raisin bread.

We then crossed the English Channel, the passage proving rather rough. Many were sick, although I recovered readily. Soon I made friends with two young girls whose company I enjoyed throughout the journey. For meals, we formed queues that itself was fun. The food, even if not to my taste, worried me little. There was plenty of good herring on board. The journey lasted six days.

The train from Hull in England to Liverpool was beautiful, clean, and fast. The cars were divided into compartments for six passengers in each but lacked toilet facilities. Relief was thus unattainable until the train stopped at specified intervals.

In Liverpool, we were placed into quarantine for another two weeks. Our hotel was barely third class, and the food even worse. Even I discerned the difference, but there was plenty of plum jelly. In the daytime, we explored the city and always managed to find our way home. On Saturday, while returning from the synagogue, we lost our way as the street and court had the same name. We wandered around the city until late that afternoon, when a frocked gentleman in a high hat responded to the only English word we knew, "America." He took us to an arcade where everyone readily knew precisely where we belonged. We missed our dinner, but the trip was worth the loss.

At this inn, I was introduced to the diaper pin and its use. The innkeeper's daughter, a girl of 14 or 15, appeared far from clean. Her dress was all in tatters with possibly 100 or more pins holding the tatters together. Thus, I learned the use of the pin.

Liverpool stands out as unique. It is the only city I know where there were comfort stations at nearly every two blocks. Our big cities never provided such facilities to the great discomfort of many a person. Liverpool also provided the newcomer with a display of tremendous workhorses. I have never seen such horses since.

At least two incidents provided us some mirth during the quarantine in Liverpool. A scrawny little Jew appeared one afternoon and excitedly in a high-pitched voice tried to warn us of the difficulties we would face when attempting to enter the "golden land." Because of just such a minute, an absolutely munificent thing, he had been refused entrance. At the same time, he showed us the size of the "thing" by pointing to the tip of his little finger, repeating, again and again, the size and significance of it. I had no understanding at all about what he was talking. Tragic as this little man was, I couldn't help but to laugh. Finally, we realized he was denied entrance at Castle Garden (later known as Castle Clinton or Fort Clinton, which is a circular sandstone fort now located in Battery Park, in Manhattan) because of a tiny hernia discovered during the examination.

Another experience concerned the missionary. Immediately on stepping off the train in Liverpool, the "soul rescuers" showered us with New Testament booklets. Brother Hymie explained this to me. Now I knew who the chasers were.

Sunday afternoon, soon after the incident of the tragic little Jew, a well-dressed corpulent and big-bellied man in high hat appeared. Most of us were resting, some even dozing when he started shouting: "Young men, sleeping your days away! Come with me. I will entertain you." All of us were curious. I jumped off the bed, and before he could say, "Christopher Columbus," I was ready to march. He led us into a chapel where we sang hymns with the leader. Within a few minutes, one addressed us and started off tactlessly and foolishly sneering at Jewish customs and religious ceremonies. It was insulting. But what was interesting was that all of us, as if previously organized, left the hall, leaving him addressing the empty seats. He never came to us again.

The voyage to Quebec was difficult.[52] We were sent to Quebec because, allegedly, entrance to the States was simpler through here and worth suffering the few extra days on the boat. The Atlantic was raging fiercely. High waves threatened to break the ship, Megantic,[53] in two. All were sick and thrown about from side to side with each sway of the ship. Some of us recovered soon and turned the tossing from side to side into a game.

Fig.12-1 Steamship Megantic.

My appetite suffered little. The herring was plentiful and delicious. So was the rest of the food. To stimulate my appetite further, Hymie fed me wine, of which he carried eight bottles as gifts for the Americans. Because of the rumor that no liquor could be brought in, we disposed of the wine before landing in the New World.

After 14 days, we reached Quebec. At early dawn, we found our baggage lying on the dock and had it checked by the inspection officer. Our gear consisted mostly of perinas (feather bed covers, in Yiddish "perine"). Mother provided them to her sons to keep warm in America. Hidden in these perinas were some gifts for sister Tobie and her girlfriends. Then, as now, women used other people's hair to improve their hairdos. Thus, we carried several long braids, a pair of silver candelabras, and a few other little things. In addition, we brought a set of the Bible consisting of several leather-bound volumes. Grandfather entrusted these to me because he knew I respected books. The set was probably his wedding gift. Unfortunately, I had no time to read them, and finally, I gave them to our tenant, [A812] Mr. Hirsch, who I thought would have more

---

[52] Editor's note: Between 1880 and 1924, over 2 million Eastern European Jews emigrated to America. The modern technology using steam-driven engines had simplified the voyage of earlier centuries when ships had only sails, and the journey took weeks. Now passage across the ocean took only days. Steerage was cheap, sometimes for under $10. Of course, amenities like meals and attentive stewards were omitted, but for the Jews, this was not of concern, for they brought their own kosher foods. The immigrants lived in the holds and had to fend for themselves. Ironically, the immigrants were, in reality, only a convenient byproduct of the transatlantic traffic. Since the United States sent bulky raw materials to Europe, receiving in exchange only a smaller volume of finished goods, the Western bound vessels were considerably empty. Since immigrants could load and unload themselves, they were the most convenient, inexpensive, and handiest type of ballast capable of filling the half-empty halls. Indeed, they were walking weight That is why they were transported so cheaply.

[53] The SS Megantic, an ocean liner, carried on the passenger trade on the Liverpool-Canada route during the latter 19th and early 20th centuries. Originally to be named the SS Albany, the ship, while under construction, was sold to the White Star Line and renamed Megantic after Lac-Mégantic in Québec. The liner launched in 1908 with a 14,878 gross register tons weight and a net of 9,183 tons. The deadweight was 8,790 tons. Its load-displacement on a draft of 27 ft, 6 in was 20,470 tons. The overall length was 570 ft. It survived a German U-boat attack during World War I and retired from service in 1931 and scrapped in 1933. (Adapted from Wikipedia and NorwayHeritage.com)

opportunity to use them, or at least would turn them over to some library. We also carried two shawls, one large and one small. We wore these as mufflers about the neck.

Now at early dawn of Nov 7, 1910, Hymie with the large shawl about his neck and I with the little shawl wrapped about my neck searched for our baggage among hundreds of packages scattered over the long pier in Quebec. Here and there stood a clerk, who, when we approached, seemed to point at the shawl. Frightened, we left him and tried another one only to meet with the same results. Thus, we tried a third, fourth, and fifth man, thereby wishing them the very best until we stumbled on one who checked our baggage. Now we realized what truly was wrong and had a good laugh at ourselves.

We boarded the train and were on our way to Cleveland. Our worries, we thought, were over. Soon, however, we discovered that another inspection was due on entering the States at Niagara Falls. To avoid difficulties, we gave the large shawl to one of our girlfriends to carry, as it would be more natural for a girl to wear a shawl. We were now at ease and enjoying the trip.

In Buffalo, where the train stopped, we went down to see the station. Here we managed to get into a large room, the walls of which were lined entirely with mirrors. We had difficulty finding the exit. Finally, on extricating ourselves, we discovered the girl with the shawl had been transferred to another train going to Chicago. Without thinking, I ran across all the tracks in the railroad yard, jumped into the train, reclaimed the shawl, and swiftly returned to my train just in time. We wore our shawls all the way to Cleveland, not knowing that the customs point was passed at Niagara Falls.

We reached Cleveland in the early evening of November 10, 1910. There was no one to meet us since our telegram never reached our relatives. (It was a common practice for the sender to pocket the monies thus collected.) While searching for our folks, a 10-12-year-old boy spotted us. Being unable to converse with us, but realizing a possible good fare for his father, who was prohibited from collecting passengers at the station, promptly brought a police officer to us. As a result, not only were we brought to our destination, but we were not overcharged either. (Many immigrants were frequently mishandled and robbed as well.) Our arrival at the house of [A806] Dora Roodman on Scovill and E. 30th Street was a pleasant surprise for all.

The process of Americanization started immediately upon arrival with a hot bath and a large dose of Epsom salts to assure purification and elimination of all possible vestiges of the Old World.

The next morning my hair was cut. Then sister [A023] Tobie took me to the May Co for a completely new outfit. English was the spoken language, good or bad, with or without an accent, except for the older ones, few of whom could speak the new language. [A813] Young Ruskin taught me English phrases. Within a few days, I was a full-fledged citizen, "Going home to make some cigarettes."

Exactly three weeks later, on December 1, 1910, I faced my first boss in America, [A691] Dr. George Neil Stewart, physiologist and medical director of the experimental medicine department at Western Reserve University. Standing in the hallways on the stairway landing and facing me, he said, "What is your name?" "Jacob," I said. "Let's call him John," he retorted, and off he went. The name he had christened me was formally legalized during my naturalization process in 1915. I was John ever since to all. Only father would revert to Yankel during special excitements.

[A700] Charles Burn, a young frivolous good-natured, jolly Scot took me under his wing. The work required: general care of keeping the various animals clean, well-watered and fed following the specifications of [A692] Dr. David Marine, Dr. Stewart's associate, for each individual batch. Charlie taught me how to do things by actual demonstration, gesticulation, and naming of objects. He helped me buy dogs, cats, chickens, and rabbits. The white mice reproduced rapidly, obviating us from buying them. (See end of this chapter for additional details of John's job).

One morning as I attempted to do another part of my job, I saw a man dressed in a very long, worn, and faded coat going up the steps. I was sure he was one of the unwelcome drunks who used to try to enter the building and ran to pull him down the stairway. Fortunately, when he turned around, I beheld a very handsome attractive and commanding face that was radiating a glow resembling that of Moses when he descended Mt. Sinai with the tablets in his hands. It was a face I shall never forget. It was a beautiful, very expressive face, cleanly shaven, and with bushy eyebrows and two deeply set, sharp eyes. Sheepishly I retreated, as it was my boss, Dr. Stewart, whom I had not recognized and tried to pull down the stairs. This tall and proverbial frugal Scotchman had worn an old faded overcoat that probably was bought as a wedding gift. Of course, I retreated very sheepishly, but my co-workers [A700] Charles and [A701] Max Charkin had a good laugh at me.

Both Dr. Stewart and [A692] Dr. Marine were friendly and treated me gently and with kindness. Soon I became Dr. Marine's right-hand man, and he entrusted me with all his feeding experiments and other lab work. He and I would catch frogs in the East 79th Street Canal for use in the experiments.

The work and the men made a profound impression on me. Here I came in contact with the elite and the idealists of the profession. Besides Drs. Stewart and Marine, there were Drs. [A725] Salman, [A726] Foda, [A693] Frederick Clayton Waite, [A727] McLeod, our own [A728] Dr. Julius Rogoff, the chemist [A729] Zuker, and the great [A730] Dr. George Crile and his associates, [A731] Stone, [A732] Slom, and [A733] Mentin. There were also Drs. [A734] Richard Dexter, [A735] Clyde Cummer and many lesser lights.

During the three years on this job, I grew in stature. I became the valued and trusted worker of Dr. Marine. My wages had doubled, but I decided to go into medicine. I entered Central High School but continued to work for Marine in the afternoons. I ran the surgical suite and administered anesthesia during his surgical experiments. Both Stewart and Marine always displayed a paternal attitude towards me. Stewart arbitrated the difficulties between my co-workers and me and never failed to appease me when I asked for a rise in wages. Marine even corrected my classroom speech in which I described the operation for removing a goiter.

In 1917, I gave up my job and entered the Adelbert College of Western Reserve University as a pre-med student. On May 25, 1917, I was drafted for army service in World War I and sent to Camp Gordon, Georgia. Claiming conscientious objection in a court presided by Judge Mack of

Chicago, my plea was granted, and I was transferred to the base hospital where I became an orderly.

Fig. 12-2: John Robboy, when in the US Army, 1917.

It was a great experience to work at the hospital during the great flu epidemic of 1918. When the armistice was declared, I petitioned and was allowed to return to school. I did well in college and, except for my experience with [A736] Dr. Castile, who saw fit to keep me at school for an extra year for the sake of my maturation, the year was uneventful.

It is thus evident that the period of my sojourn in the States was one of hope, vigor, and development. It was a time of young people only. There were hardly any older people around or parents to inhibit us. We were all young, restless, and ambitious. Most spent the day in the factories, but in the evening, we all turned to schools, dance halls, concerts, theaters, and lectures. All theories, political, social, and economic, were enthusiastically examined, debated, and then carried home for further digestion and assimilation. All of us became familiar with outstanding world characters: writers, scientists, philosophers, teachers, actors, singers, and musicians. It was a period when pent-up energy was released, coupled with a freedom of activity, enthusiasm, and hope that made us float about like birds picking up the kernels of knowledge.

With this as background, I returned in February 1918 to Western Reserve University as a second-year undergraduate.

Appendix: A letter dated Nov 4, 1973, was recently found where John describes his work for Drs. Marine and Stewart.

From December 1910 to about September 1913, I worked for [A692] Dr. David Marine, then the associate of [A691]Dr. George Neil Stewart, director of the Experimental Medical Division at Western Reserve University. Dr. Marine was interested in goiter, a condition significantly prevalent in this region. His experiments were dietary in type. I couldn't speak English, at least for a few months. [A700] Charles Burns took me under his wing and taught me what to do. Neither of us knew the whats or whys, but we did as we were told.

As I see things now, Dr. Marine's methods were flawed, but he was fortunate in arriving at the proper conclusions.

We bought our dogs from the dogcatchers, paying $0.50 a piece. Most of these dogs had lived a clean and sheltered life but were now deposited here into small kennels with up to 15 dogs of all types and sizes.

The kennel was cold in winter and hot in summer. The floor was covered with sawdust. There was neither ventilation nor provision for natural relief. The dogs were fed a stew of bread and liver once daily.

We had to keep them for 14 days so that the owners could claim them. During these days, many took sick and died from fighting. After 14 days, we could use them experimentally, after which we moved them to kennels on the roof, where they received proper care. We had other animals as well: cats, chickens, white mice, and frogs.

Charles was given a certain amount for the chicken-feed every week. Marine found their crops (stomachs) empty and realized Charles had pocketed the money. From then on, I did all the feedings other than for the chickens. We divided the animals into several groups, the feedings varying by age. The liver naturally became more putrid each day. The poor animals were forced to eat as they were starved like prisoners in the Nazis' concentration camps. Marine did not find it necessary to explain to us what he was doing. Everything then was done as ordered. I never read his work then or since. However, he came to proper conclusions. Based on his work, salt is used today to prevent goiter. Nowadays, hardly ever is a person seen with a simple goiter.

In the early 20s, [A716] Dr. Persky and I would go to the nearby Gordon Park, and in five-minute intervals count the number of people and animals found with goiter. Goiter, then, was as prevalent among animals as among humans. [A730] Dr. George Creil Sr devised and perfected an operation for the disease. One hardly ever sees this today

Once, a reporter came snooping around and did write a report about what he saw. Foolishly, he was carried away by his own imagination and described what never occurred. Dr. Stewart laughed at him and allowed the press to print the article. Following its publication, the Protective Animal Organization wrote to me asking me to be more kind to the animals. We laughed at them and the information they received.

#13 [A023] SISTER TOBIE

This event did not take place in ancient nor medieval times but during the first decade of our present century when our primitive sanitation and the natural environmental forces helped determine our chances of survival. Medical science was still limited to prayer, exorcism of the evil eye, and a potion consisting of the Tatar's script boiled in water. Contagion and infectious diseases were widespread, particularly among the young, with consequent high mortality rate and even considerable morbidity. No wonder my two brothers died in early childhood. Sister [A017] Nessie was stricken with rheumatic fever, and later died from cardiac complications. [A023] Sister Tobie was attacked by smallpox but managed to survive with but two small pocks left on her face, thanks to Mother's excellent nursing acumen.

Children of our day and our environment had to assume responsibility for a livelihood early in life. When I was eight years old, sisters Tobie and Nessie were already sitting in their cramped positions on a bench, sewing garments for the peasants from early dawn until evening. Notwithstanding these hardships, Tobie grew to be a tall, straight, shapely and attractive young lady. She was gay and cheerful. She had long black hair and a charming face with vivacious black eyes that mirrored her sharp and active mind. Tobie grew beautifully as if to prove the superiority of natural endowments over the environmental rigors. She was outstanding among her girlfriends and like a long-stemmed rose in a garden of thorns. Additionally, Tobie was endowed with unusual artistic skill in sewing. Every stitch of hers was distinctive. She was recognized for her talent and became the seamstress in demand early in life among the more affluent citizens.

Tobie never went to school, which then was for boys only. Yet she learned to read and write. How, when, or where, she could give no account, nor could anyone else. She even taught the art of writing to [A218] Shmiel Radlideciatnik. His father, upon discovering his son's pursuit, was as frightened by this sacrilege as the average American was by the term, "Communism." Tobie was also the only one in town other than the family of [A326] Chaim Dudnik to read a daily newspaper, "The Friend," which she purchased from Chaim at three kopecks per copy after he had finished reading it. Besides Yiddish, Tobie also spoke some Russian and fluent Polish.

With the revolutionary ideas seeping in at this time, the youths, including Tobie, grew restive. She left for the big city, [C14] Kishinev. Unfortunately, this venture proved highly disappointing. Her cousins, the Gilmans, though having grown up in the large town, remained backward and more provincial than she, while cousin [A503] Moshe was annoying in his attempt to court her. She soon returned home. Here the atmosphere had become even more stifling than formerly. Tobie was now of age, and the young men in town, as well as those suggested by the matchmakers, failed to meet the qualifications she desired. There were, but two remarkable young men and both were from out-of-town.

[A412] Moshe Dolgonos, a sweet, handsome, charming, and gifted young gymnast from [C29] Odessa was spending his summer vacations in town. He was dramatic and entertained us all. He was responsible for introducing many of the new ideas to us and also brought some literary works with him. He gave us the opportunity to read an illegal history of Russia depicting the gruesome acts of [A275] Ivan the Terrible, the cruelties of [A278] Czar Nicholas I and the sexual aberrations of [A276] Catherine the Great. We also read the proscribed *Tragedy of Galileo* in manuscript form as well as some other books. Moshe loved people, and we loved him. His cousin [A327] Fania Dudnik and Tobie admired him. Unfortunately, he died early in life from pulmonary tuberculosis.

The other young man who impressed Tobie profoundly was cousin [A457] Joseph Gillman. Joe was younger than Tobie and resided in [C36] Uman, where he was struggling to obtain an education. Like Moshe, Joe also had no difficulties in conquering the weaker sex, but at the moment, Joe was interested in America and soon left Russia.

Within two years, in 1909, Tobie left for America and landed in Cleveland, where she roomed with Mrs. [A806] Dora Roodman, a friendly, matronly woman who remained a friend of the family until death. [A457] Joe was then at college. He was handsome, smart, dynamic, and progressive. He had numerous and varied friends. Tobie soon found work and entered night school, where she learned English. She mingled with many of Joe's friends, particularly [A807] Bessie Roodman, Joe's sweetheart, [A457a] Etta Cohen, whom Joe later married, [A728a] Rebecca Rogoff and [A809] Esther Zwick, all of whom were college or normal school students. One year later, brother [A012] Hymie and I joined Tobie and brother Joe, but we lived in separate homes until the summer of 1912 when, in preparation for the arrival of our parents and the rest of our family, we prepared a home for all of us. While waiting for our parents' arrival, Tobie suddenly became seriously ill. Joe Gillman enlisted the help of [A710] Dr. Moses Garber, a young practitioner in his first year of practice. Tobie was admitted to the old Glenville Hospital, where she underwent a hysterectomy by [A713] Dr. Krepehl and Dr. Garber. Hymie and I were given some enlightenment, but, strangely, brother Joe remained in complete ignorance. The family arrived when Tobie was still confined to the hospital. All of us rejoiced with the family, mainly because Tobie survived her ordeal.

Within a short time, however, possibly because of the shock, Tobie developed a toxic goiter. This time, fortunately, she fell into the hands of a more skillful surgeon, [A714] Dr. Skeel, at St. Luke's Hospital. The latter was kind and sympathetic to her and carried her successfully through this new ordeal. She now joined her newly arrived cousins, [A294] Gitie Dudnik, [A298] Pearl Dudnik, and [A310] Sarah Dudnik, in Philadelphia, where they helped her recuperate. She made a rapid physical recovery and returned home to Cleveland. However, she remained extraordinarily restless and never again found roots anywhere. She wandered from place to place. After living in New York, she was in Philadelphia, Chicago, Denver, San Francisco, and Los Angeles. She especially loved the West and visited all the scenic places many times.

Because of her skills, Tobie had no difficulty finding employment in any city she visited. She was able to make an entire dress as well as blouses, skirts, or suits, and even men's clothing. Her work was artistic and distinctive. Her girlfriends used to recognize garments that Tobie made and were displayed in Halles Department store's windows or on people seen in the streetcar. I remember a blouse Tobie made for [A021] Pauline, consisting of 100 or more pieces. It was as artistic a piece of work as any painting of some famous artist.

Tobie had a great obsession for remnants. When she came across one at a store, she immediately visualized Pauline or some other child or friend in the skirt or dress this piece would become. As a result, Tobie always had hundreds of dollars' worth of remnants in her possession. During slack periods, she would set up a shop at home for a few weeks. These periods usually were nightmares for all of us at home. Tobie had no business savvy. She tried to work at home in a manner befitting Hattie Carnegie or Adrian but at very pitiful prices. All were busy with her work. We would have to call the customers for fittings, pick up trimmings, or deliver garments. She, herself, would waste much time shopping for trimmings for the clients or serving tea during frequent fitting visits by customers. We were jubilant and felt emancipated when she closed up shop.

Tobie strove to enter the business world for a long time. The apparel business for infants and children was fascinating to her, and she approached the [A710] Garbers to help her in this venture. The latter would not support the idea, and Tobie never mentioned it again. Instead of business, the Garbers, as ardent Zionists, thought Tobie would be a suitable person to run a school for sewing in Palestine. This was a pioneering job and was appropriate for an idealistic Zionist. Tobie was tired. She felt unable to become a pioneer and dismissed the proposition. Instead, she went into business.

Early in the 1920s, Tobie acquired a Singer Sewing Machine Agency from a [A810] Mr. Sagolovitch on East 55th Street and Lexington, selling old and new sewing machines. Tobie tried to outdo the Singer Company. Machines were sold on payments of $3 a month. To get a discount, Tobie would pay the company the entire amount, thus assuming the risk of loss should the customer abscond. She also rented new machines out at similar prices. The neighborhood was already deteriorating. The people were becoming untrustworthy and transient. Since Tobie had little know-how and no power of repossession of the machines, many were lost. Joe and I were helpless in attempting to sharpen Tobie's philosophy or business principles. Fortunately, the business proved to be a gold mine despite all the losses.

Tobie's business ventures continued even in her later years in Los Angeles. Here she bought a home for herself and a lot for investment purposes. She disposed of both at favorable terms before entering a home for the aged. She wanted to buy a large building consisting of many suites, but [A024] Joe prevented the transaction because he would have had all the responsibility of looking after the property.

Tobie was much interested in social problems. Advocacy for the birth control movement was one in a particular area. On Easter Sunday, April 23, 1916, Mrs. Margaret Sanger,[54] the founder of the birth control movement in the US, visited from New York and delivered two addresses before packed audiences in Cleveland at the Chapel of the Unitarian Church and the Pythian Temple.[55] Later informal gatherings culminated on June 1 in a meeting held at the City's Union Club to initiate a birth control campaign involving doctors, social workers, and others. At a subsequent meeting held three weeks later at the Unitarian Chapel, the group formed an organizing committee and adopted an organization plan. It formally named itself the Birth Control League of Ohio. Tobie, a vital member of this initial group, was elected the "assistant

---

[54] Margaret Sanger (1879-1966) was an American birth control activist, sex educator, nurse, and writer. She popularized the term "birth control," having visited at The Hague in February 1915 where she had heard the physician, Dr. J Rutgers, giving the maternity nurses instructions on the "proper means and hygienic principles of the methods of Family Limitation." After returning to the US in November 1915 and bringing suit in the Federal Courts to permit her to open a clinic for birth control, which ended before it came to trial, she opened the first birth control clinic in this Country. The organization evolved into today's Planned Parenthood Federation of America.
[55] Sanger, M: Clinics, Courts and Jails, The Birth Control Review, 2 (3): p3 & 10, 1918.

secretary." Among the constitution's stated goals was: "First—The modification of existing laws in such a manner as to allow physicians, nurses, and other competent persons, to give information concerning methods of preventing conception."

The first 25-30 years of adult life were spent in various active radical social groups. She frequented the theater and concerts. She attended lectures and read the best of literature: Andreev, Chekhov, Gorky, Dostoevski, Tolstoy, Sholem Asch, Raboy,[56] Laivik, and many of the modern American writers. Though Tobie's penmanship was awful and her spelling atrocious, her letters had substance and a good deal of punch to them. She carried on an extensive correspondence with many of her relatives and friends almost to the very end.

Life embittered Tobie with the result that she developed a sarcastic, sharp, and lashing tongue. Despite this, she had an excellent faculty for making and holding friends. They were of all ages and levels of intellect. She was never alone. Wherever Tobie lived, even when rooming with others, her room was a home where she received friends. Even at the home for the aged, she made many friends.

Tobie bestowed her motherly instincts upon the Gillman children, [A458] Leonard and [A459] Robert when they were available; upon her nephew, [A013] Bernie Robboy; cousins [A496] Minnie and [A498] Yetta Trachtman and particularly upon [A017] Nessie's children, whom she considered as her own. All of them, in turn, gave her love and respect. Busy as Bernie and Minnie were with their own affairs, they watched over her to the very last.

---

[56] Isaac Raboy (1882-1944) was a American writer, whose most famous book, Der Yiddisher Cowboy, relates the adventures, loves, and mishaps of a young Jewish immigrant who actually became a cowboy on a horse ranch on the North Dakota prairie. The Raboy family originated in the same locale in Ukraine as the Robboys, and even had members of their family killed in the same pogroms as John's family, suggesting a probable relation somewhere in the past. However, the editor could not trace any blood link between the families, despite extensive correspondence with one of the older members. Cousin [A015] Ron Robboy, Hymie's grandson, many years later researched out the tragedies rumored in "Der Yiddisher Cowboy." Some of the missing cowboys who worked and disappeared from a neighboring farm suffered a cannibalistic owner.

#14 BROTHER [A024] JOE ROBBOY
Letter from [A496] Minnie Brandt (12/62)

Education: The men were the learned ones, studying in the synagogues. The women were the "breadwinners."

Joe went to cheder from age 4-15, studying Tanakh (Bible) and Gemara (rabbinical commentary on the Mishnah, forming the second part of the Talmud). Girls were not supposed to get an education, so they only learned from the men during their talks and discussions. Tobie did not go to school and only learned from her mother and father. She was taught words as she sewed alongside her mother. One of her mother's friends taught her at the age of 13. Tobie remembers that one family in the town received a newspaper once a month, and for several kopecks, she read it after everyone else in the family.

Fig. 14-1: [A024] Joe Robboy.

Work: Their mother, [A011] Malka, was a dressmaker. About 1905, they got a sewing machine. Most of their sewing articles were exchanged for food, such as flour, potatoes, grits, pears, apples, etc., from the peasants. Their father, [A011] Shmiel, was a glazier and later a manager of flour mills. He received a wage that was the equivalent of $6 a month.

Religion: Malka and Shmiel remained Orthodox Jews, even in America. Joe obeyed the rules and was religious for about three years in America. Tobie, however, rebelled. She remembers the children getting caught picking fruit on the Sabbath. At age 12, she remembers hiding to comb her hair or shine her shoes on the Sabbath. Even singing was forbidden, and she secretly did sing. Because you might entice the men, high collars had to be worn by the women. Bright colored materials and transparent materials were forbidden. These things bothered Tobie.

Epidemics: When Tobie was about five or six years old, she remembers a bad cholera epidemic in the town. My grandfather died of cholera. She recalled that some in her family had smallpox and diphtheria.

Revolutions: Revolutions did not hit their town. They only heard about them days later from travelers.

America: There was no work in Joe's town. Stories were spreading of revolutionists in [C29] Odessa, so his mother would not let him go there. Through cousin [A237] Yankel Virin, who was a steamship agent, a passport was obtained, and Joe went to Cleveland. America, to him, meant hard work, and if he had the opportunity, he would have returned home (1907). Tobie's father wouldn't sign for her passport, so she managed to obtain one for $25 and came to America under a different name, but with no difficulty came directly to Cleveland in 1909. Tobie left Russia for freedom from her family and the Czar, as she wanted education and travel (the Czar did not permit traveling). She wanted friends but found the ones in America very conservative. As Tobie began working, she made friends with those who had ideas similar to hers. She didn't get the education she wanted or desired due to family ties (having to help support them). In many families, though, everyone helped to support one member of the family through school, as in the case of [A026] John, whom they also helped get the person started in the profession.

See chapter 99 about Joe in America and Communism.

#15 UNCLE [A034] MORDECHAI ROBBOY
(Letter from [A026] John Robboy to [A048] Marilyn Isbitz Yellin, 18 Nov 1978)

I have good feelings for your mother, [A047] Sylvia Isbitz, and her father, [A034] Mordechai Robboy. They were humble but good people. Your mother's father, Mordechai, was employed as an egg dealer. His job was to pick up the freshly laid eggs from the smaller dealers in the surrounding villages. He had the chance to visit us in [C01] Knyazhe occasionally. Mordechai was small in stature, good-natured, cheerful, very active, quick-moving, and laughed and talked a lot. Once, he dropped in on us in early summer, probably in 1907. I was 13 years old and in search of a school for my further education. Since a new school had just opened in [C43] Zashkov, your grandfather offered to take me to his home where I could go to school.

He felt that it was not necessary to consult with his wife, your grandmother, [A034a] Sarah Faiga Spector, who was good and loyal and had only six kids to look after. A seventh would not make any great difference, and apparently, he knew his wife. She was just as tiny a woman as he was a man, and just as cheerful. She was uneducated, but that was true of all women since they never had schooling.

Fig 15-1: [A034] Mordechai and Sarah Spector Robboy.

She accepted me graciously as just another addition to her loving family. We enjoyed each other for a full year.

School didn't really amount to much, but I had a grand time. All the children loved me. [A035] Nathan and your mother [A047] Sylvia were my age and good playmates. Your Uncle Nathan was small, but strong and athletic, driving the horse-drawn wagon, as well as his father.

Though we were young, unsophisticated, and provincial, we were affected by the revolutionary spirit of the day. The radical groups rampant then throughout the province recruited kids like Nathan, who seemed innocent and would never be suspected. He was a handy courier for disseminating their pamphlets. Somehow the police became suspicious of his activities, and Uncle managed to extricate him from these circles before he became too involved. (See Chapter #5 with the footnote by [A036] Mitchell Robboy about his father, [A035] Nathan's activities.

In 1912 my parents brought Nathan as one of their sons to America. He was having trouble with his knee at that time as a result of an injury during army training. Years later, he was hospitalized to have his knee repaired.

After World War I ended and the pogroms began circa 1918-9, your grandfather was murdered, and your grandmother with her family had to be rescued. With Nathan in the hospital here in the US, there was little one could do. Fortunately, at that time, our family owned a $2,500 mortgage on the home we sold on East 39th Street, our sole nest egg. That was our only savings at that time. We offered it to Nathan to help him bring the family to America. But there was one provision: Mother was to buy the tickets for the family's passage. Nathan consented. It turned out to be a fortunate transaction. Within a few days following the purchase of the tickets, the president of the Merchants or People's bank absconded with all the money, ruining a good many Jewish widows, including his sweetheart, [A804] Mrs. Gabowitz. Fortunately, Mother's transaction ended successfully. The family arrived, Nathan recovered, and all turned out as planned. Eventually, Nathan paid off the entire loan during the ensuing years.

#16 SOME WORTHY CHARACTERS (B'nai Khaim)

My first contact with B'nai Khaim dates back to 1901 when I left to [C02b] Sokolivka in quest of an education. The progenitor, [A290] Khaim Kaprove of the B'nai Khaim, whom I did not know, was an innkeeper.

Grandfather [A419] Beryl Kaprove, then about 70 years old, was an old man and growing senile. Neither his children nor grandchildren understood his condition. They teased him a lot, telling him that he was pregnant. He was in great distress, wondering what he would do with the baby. Mother was very concerned with the situation but could offer no help since she had no room for him in her home. Grandfather was a learned man in Jewish lore and a Hassid, as were his five daughters and three sons.[57]

I saw [A420] Khaya Golda, the oldest daughter, in 1901. I remember her to be a dwarf who was also mentally unsound. When I entered the medical world in 1926, I diagnosed her as a cretin. Later, when I learned that she had married and had a daughter, I felt that the child probably was only cretinoid. Her daughter, [A421] Khana Esther, immigrated to America and raised a family in New York City. [A023] Tobie and [A457] Joe Gillman met her daughter and two sons.

[A422] Pessie was the best looking and wisest of all. She died a few months before I arrived in [C02a] Justingrad in 1901. Pessie married [A422a] Moses Gillman, a fine and cultured man. Moses or Moshe lived up to expectations. He was interested in public affairs but not his own. It was up to Pessie to eke out a livelihood by selling herring and dried salt fish to the peasants.

[A462] Yenta, the third daughter, was the plainest looking but the kindest of all. Her husband died early in life, leaving her with seven sons. Yenta could neither read nor write, but she had a fine mind and stamina. She managed her store, selling herring and dried salt fish, and trained her children for some business or trade. When I got to know them, three of her sons were already married. Her home was no different from those of her sons, except it was the only home that was warm and well-heated. There was always bread and herring in the table drawer within easy reach. Her life was simple. She toiled from early morning till night, until Friday when she changed entirely. By Friday evening, she had had her weekly bath, dressed in her finest and, with her white silk shawl covering her head, she appeared almost beautiful. While sitting at the head of the table, she listened to her sons delivering the kiddush (blessing of the Sabbath). Like the other women of those times, she was illiterate. This made no difference in her life. She didn't have to go to shul. Saturday was her day of peace and relaxation. She couldn't read, but she knew her prayers. With me on her lap, she was able to pray and delouse me at the same time.

Yenta married [A462a] Yankel Trachtman. Her sons all grew into fine respectable men, good husbands, and devoted fathers. [A470] Zalman, the oldest, was the only educated one. He was an ardent Zionist and immigrated to Israel, then Palestine, after World War I. [A463] Motie was a

---

[57] According to [A463] Motye Trachtman in a letter to his son, [A466] Morris), Beryl remarried twice after his wife, [A419a] Dvossie, died. The letter stated that after her death, he stopped on the way from the cemetery at a widow's house, knocked at the window, and asked for her hand in marriage. She was baking at the time, and grabbing a rolling pin, chased him all over the marketplace. "That is the truth. He must have been quite a guy in his youth. I remember him when he was very old and sick. Aunt [A515a] Sima took care of him. He was a pathetic sight at that time."

handsome, rotund young businessman, selling ready-made boots. He was kindness personified. Before leaving for the bazaar at 4:00 a.m., he always warmed up the house for his ailing wife and saw that there was water for the day. Returning home at night, he would clean the house for the next day. Following the advent of the Russian revolution, he emigrated with his family to the United States. Brother [A474] Chaim, [A494] Willie, and [A500] Frank had done so earlier.

I was particularly fond of [A485] Yossel. I always slept with him. Their home was warm, the covers sufficient, and Yossel himself as warm as a blanket. The result was a dry bed every morning, which made me happy. I always enjoyed watching him make ropes in front of the house. He also took his family to Palestine. I saw brother [A492] Schneir once in [C01] Knyazhe when he visited us while on furlough from the army. He was tall, heavyset, and very handsome. As a cavalryman, he wore his uniform with a sword hanging by his side. He certainly made an impressive appearance. I never saw him again as he remained in Russia. A letter from his son, [A493] Grisha, recently reached one of us in America.

[A474] Chaim, [A494] Willie, and [A500] Frank came to the States about 1911-13. Willie lived in Cleveland and Frank later moved to Olean, NY, not far from Buffalo. Willie's family arrived years later. His older daughter, [A496] Minnie Brandt, now lives in Los Angeles and is a teacher. The younger daughter, [A498] Yetta Goodman, received her Ph.D. and is involved with the education of children. All three boys received some schooling in the States and became small businessmen, eventually owning salvage yards. Willie, who could fix anything, was often seen driving his peddler's truck through town. Frank was also a vegetarian. He married [A500a] Fannie Pratter from Buffalo but had no children. Our family was always close to [A462] Yenta and her children. We loved them all. They were simple but honest, kind, and devoted sons, husbands, fathers, wives, and cousins. They managed to transfer all of these characteristics to their children, who are following in their parents' paths in love and loyalty to all.

Fig. 16-1: (L-R) Trachtman brothers, 1938: [A500] Frank, [A474] Chaim, [A494] Willie.

Fig. 16-2: [A500] Willie Trachtman fixing a tool, 1938.

I got to know [A502] Aunt Leah in 1909 when I lived in her house for a full year. She was married to [A502a] Itzhak Gelman. Leah was a pitiful-looking, simple, ignorant, and illiterate woman. She knew nothing, was stingy, but was a relatively decent housekeeper. She was also the most domineering overall. No one had any respect for her and called her all sorts of names. I was ashamed to witness these scenes. Aunt went to the market two to three times a week, always following a set route. Once, after some 30 years in the city, she changed her route and got lost.

Itzhak was a fine, respectable, honest, and kind gentleman who was a good provider for their family of three sons and two daughters.

He leased several suites on the corner of Kiev and Nikolev streets, some of which he also rented out. Uncle's apartment consisted of four spacious rooms. Facing the court was an enclosed porch or solarium that he used as the kitchen. The store was no bigger than ours is now. I don't remember how the home was heated, and it lacked plumbing. There was an outside, common privy court, and the water was in the center of the court. The shut-off faucet was of the winter type, i.e., it was 3-4 feet below the surface and was operated by a handle up above. When closed, the water in the pipe would empty itself through a small opening in the faucet. This would prevent the pipe from bursting in wintertime when ice formed in it. Aunt, therefore, watched everyone carefully because, during a period of 24 hours, there could be a loss of a pail of water that amounted to ½ cent.

Uncle Itzi was also a wine dealer whose word was as good as a written contract. He was too trusting. The sharpies in business took advantage of him and frequently cheated him. Once he returned from the bazaar extremely shaken by what he had observed. The peasants brought their barrels filled with wine for sale. All the barrels were standard size. The sharpies insisted that a certain 40-pail barrel was only a 20-pail barrel. The peasant almost collapsed from pain and indignation and was finally forced to yield to these sharpies. Uncle Itzi could do nothing to stop this injustice. He returned home, disturbed, and sick over what he had witnessed.

As a wine dealer and manufacturer of wine, he would buy the entire crop of the vineyard long before the grapes ripened. On another occasion, after making the deal, he came home to pick up his bankbook. Aunt [A502] Leah, however, refused to surrender it for fear that he would be cheated on the deal. He begged and pleaded but his son, [A503] Motel, and two daughters, [A505] Rivka and [A507] Genedal, all adults by then, sided with their mother and forced him to break the deal. I shall never forget that scene and the humiliation of the man. The poor man almost collapsed from anger and shame and turned to me saying: "I should have married your mother." The deal collapsed. Of course, he was cheated on occasion. He was a man of his word, but many businessmen, then as now, were sharpies lacking integrity. In spite of all this, he lived well and quite nicely.

Unfortunately, neither his wife nor children favored him. Uncle was a fashionably, neatly dressed man. He had a large, well-groomed beard and bushy eyebrows overhanging his deeply set eyes. He always appeared to be in profound thought. He spoke little and always finished his speech by a motion of his hand and grimace of the face. I liked Uncle and was fond of him, but I resented his way of describing the worldly qualities of young men. "He is the kind of boy who had already given up religion or prayer," thus intimating that he must be a thinking and progressive young man. This made a terrific impression upon me. As a result, I prayed every morning the way I have never prayed before or since merely to spite him.

[A503] Moishe Gelman was the oldest son and was married. Moishe lived in [C05] Bender and would visit his parents occasionally, bringing his wife, [A503a] Freda, and two children with him. He was supposed to be the crown of the family since he was in business. He suffered from and was always preoccupied with his bleeding hemorrhoids, which at that time presented a formidable problem.

122

The other children in their home, though living in the big city for many years, seemed more provincial than I. [A505] Rivka, who was the age of my sister, [A023] Tobie, or slightly older, was much like her mother, but more literate and more intelligent. She never worked as was the custom. I don't think she ever married. One of Rivka's great disappointments was the fact that I, a non-student, was able to help her brother, [A508] Yankel, a gymnast, and overshadow him scholastically.

Yankel was about one year younger than I. He was a young, cheerful, heavily freckled boy whom one couldn't help but love. He did well in school. He appreciated my help, and we were good friends. He always took me to the illusion (movie theater) with him. I saw my first movie in Kishinev. Like myself, Yankel attained his degree of MD and practiced in [C14] Kishinev or Bucharest, where the Nazis murdered him, his wife, [A508a] Sarah, and daughter, [A509] Leah during the 1942 invasion in World War II.

[A506] Motel had returned from Argentina, where he had worked as a carpenter apprentice before I came to Kishinev. Yet he remained more provincial than me. One Saturday afternoon, Motel, his friend, and I went to a beerhouse located on Pushkin near Alexander Street, as fashionable a place as Euclid and East 105th Street was about 25 years ago. Usually, we would have a beer and herring to eat. (They didn't know about corned beef.) While Motel's friend entered the store to buy olives and herring for the beer, Motel decided to relieve himself at that very corner. He found it perfectly natural to seek relief in such a way in the open, even at the most fashionable corner in the city. The policeman saw what Motel did and was ready to arrest him. The officer became confused, not able to recognize who the culprit was, and had to abandon the arrest. Motel was deathly afraid of the police. When the police officer would visit them under the pretense of examining the register, but in reality, reminding Uncle that a bribe was due, Motel would hide, petrified with fear.

[A507] Genendal was the younger of the two girls, but older than me. She was not bad-looking but was somewhat obese and lisped. She was not a good student. She attended a private gymnasium because she was unable to qualify for the public gymnasium. She did not do too well there either.

Though they lived in the big city for many years, all but Uncle were quite provincial. Uncle was in business and traveled about, so he was more worldly than the rest of them. He was also a most trusting and honest man. As a result of this, he was often taken advantage of and occasionally cheated.

After the pogroms and the revolution in Russia, the family reestablished contact with us. I was then in college or already at medical school. They appealed for help. We were comfortable, but not rich. The appeal from Europe was critical, and we helped all we could. Our feelings for the Gelman family were strong, and we sent them $500 or $600, a sum sufficient to cover the transportation for all three of them. I also wrote them, pointing out that Motel, as a carpenter, would have no trouble finding work, but that Genendal would have to work in a factory just as sister Tobie and Nessie were doing. I said if this is not to her liking, she should not come.

It so happened that [A431] Alta, Joe Gilman's sister, with others of the family were on their way to America. Uncle Itzhak's home served as a rest station. Here the girls confided to Alta that

[A011] Malka, they were quite sure, wouldn't let them go to work in a factory. [A507] Genendal also confided in Alta the fact that what I wrote to her is significant. Probably, Genendal thought that I wanted her for myself. This prompted me to write again that Motel, as a carpenter, would have no trouble finding work and must come, but the girls would find it difficult and should think it over. Possibly it would be better for them to keep the money we sent and not come. They took our advice and stayed home. Would she have escaped the Nazis? Who knows! Motel did come. Brother Joe found a job for him, and he is now in the carpenters' union. He did well and some years later married [A431] Alta and lived in Buffalo.

Because of the upheaval in Europe, we lost contact with the family in [C14] Kishinev, only to learn later that most of them had met violent deaths. I was never fully satisfied with this information and am eager to know exactly what happened to all of them as well as other facts. According to the family tree [A457] that Joe Gillman constructed, [A503] Moishe had quite a large family in addition to the two sons in America, one being [A504] Boris. [A505] Rivka apparently married. [A507] Genendal is not mentioned at all. [A508] Yankel was a practicing physician in [C08] Bucharest and had a daughter, [A509] Leah. Nothing is known about anyone else.

[A461] Daniel Kaprov, [A419] Beryl's oldest son, and [A515] Abraham, the youngest son, were ordained rabbis. Daniel acted as "dayan" (judge) for the Sokolivkar Jewish community for some years. I saw him but once. I am uncertain whether [A510] Itzhak, the second oldest son, was ordained. He was married, lived in [C33] Terlitza not far from us, and had three or four children. Our whole family traveled to the wedding of his daughter, whose name was also [A511] Tobie. The family was poor. Uncle subsisted on the salary of a melamed (teacher), which was usually meager. Fortunately, his wife, [A510a] Sarah, was frugal. She learned to manage on the income provided. I remember Mother commented on the thin slivers of cake that Aunt Sarah was cutting to make it do for the occasion. Tobie's young [A511a] husband was a shochet by profession. He visited us once and brought his violin, which he played beautifully. Since such art was unbecoming his status, he could only play for us at night with the assurance that all windows were closed.

[A515] Abraham was the youngest of the children. Although an ordained rabbi, he never practiced in Russia. I knew him to be a handsome, redheaded young man, cheerful, orthodox in his belief, yet sportily dressed in his surtout (a man's overcoat similar in style to a frock coat). He was a worldly man who maintained a business. On Saturdays and holidays, he was the cantor in the Kontokusaver shul. His voice was strong and beautiful. He was a good mixer and insofar as we knew, he was never afraid of women. When he came to Bangor, Maine, he served as a rabbi. Mother, and all of us, were shocked and disappointed when he visited us years later in Cleveland wearing his rabbinical hat and long capote. He refused to shake hands with the women. We all loved and enjoyed him, but I prefer to remember him as he was when he entertained us during my sister [A017] Nessie's wedding or on Friday evenings when he sang *Sholem Aleichem* or *Kol Mekadesh* during the meal.

#17 OPEN HOUSE

I was born and raised in an "Open House," i.e., a home the doors of which were always open to anybody who wished to enter. That, I thought, was true of all households, but which I found untrue as I grew older. Not only did I find our home different from others, but unique in character, whether in Knyazhe or Cleveland.

Elsewhere, I have described our town. About 15 of our 25 Jewish families occupied the ten homes scattered around the periphery of an open space as large as a double baseball field serving as the marketplace for the Sunday bazaars. Our home was somewhat off at the very edge of the field.

The bazaar constituted a most valuable institution for both the peasantry and the Jewish merchants and vendors of the surrounding territory. The peasants sought to sell their produce: grain, cattle, poultry, and other things. The merchants, in return, provided material for clothing, readymade boots, soap, needles, thread, and other articles needed for the homes. Even the butcher was there to supply the beef to a population that otherwise subsisted on pork only.

During the summertime, the trip to the bazaar was pleasant for all. In fall, however, the trip was an ordeal. There was cold, rain, and mud everywhere for pavement was yet unknown. The winters were bitterly cold, the frosts fierce and the snow deep requiring not just boots but valenki (a traditional Russian winter footwear, essentially, felt boots). Also, a place to run into, even for a moment, was extremely welcome. [A011] Father and [A011] Mother responded to this problem with unusual generosity and kindness. It was their open generosity, increasingly, that I came to appreciate as I grew older.

On every Sunday morning at dawn, Father would get the house warm, then fill the oven with logs of wood to burn slowly. That produced many coals. Next, he would fill 2-3 barrels with drinking water and prepare the samovar. Of course, he had to carry the pails suspended on a yoke over his shoulders from a well about one-fourth mile away. He repeated the trips until the barrels were full. That was no easy job either. This preparedness was all for the sake of the merchants and vendors who came from the surrounding towns for the Sunday bazaar. Men and women came all day long, particularly during the cold fall and wintry days. Some came to pray while others to drink a glass of water, to eat a sandwich and possibly a glass of tea, or just to warm up. Women vendors came to fill their pots with glowing coals and then returned to their tents with pots under their skirts to help keep them warm. On returning to the tents, they sat on these pots to keep themselves warm. I leave it to you to imagine what the house looked like after the day ended, but Mother and Father delighted in being of service to these people.

By the time Father had set up the samovar for tea, all of us children would have awakened, and Mother made breakfast for us all. She dispatched brother [A024] Joe and me to school. Next, she assigned work for her two daughters. Of course, the cow and chickens were not to be forgotten. They, too, had to be taken care of on time. Before leaving, we helped Father load his entire dry goods store onto a small wagon, which pulled to his tent in the market where he then displayed the goods. Later, Mother joined him for the remainder of the day.

While Mother and Father were away, the house remained open to all. Any observer could have seen many sights. They included sisters [A023] Tobie and [A017] Nessie sitting at the far end of the room sewing, an elderly bearded Jew with talis and tefillin muttering to himself as he was swinging side to side or back and forth, and some merely warming up or looking for a cold drink. One may be munching on a piece of bread he brought with him. Women seldom came to pray.

Sunday was not the only day during which our folks were busy. There was always plenty to do. Besides acting as the general practitioner in town, Mother was also the housekeeper. She never neglected her home or children. Mother possessed sharp, discerning eyes which told her who was in need. Dealing with a proud people who would rather starve silently than accept charity, she carefully and deftly handled each one of them.

In America, our parents soon recovered their balance and carried on with the open-door policy as in their Knyazhe. This open-door kept the entire family, now remote, close together. All the cousins and even landsleit were always welcome. Mother watched, counseled, and mothered all.

Father and all the children were employed, and though none made any fortunes, all deposited the little they earned with Mother. None had any bundles of their own. Mother, therefore, felt strong financially. All she lacked was the English language, but she did know her Yiddish. By good fortune, she discovered Mr. [A803] Zupnick at the Union Commerce Bank on the corner of East 105th and Pasadena Ave. Mr. Zupnick knew Yiddish well and was trustworthy. Mother was now happy. With Zupnick in Cleveland and Uncle [A502a] Itzhok Gelman in [C14] Kishinev, Romania, she had her grand time. She never rested until all the relatives possible to reach were brought safely to America. No wonder all our cousins, old or young, loved her. Our house was always open to them with the help and kindness in all of us. Here I must add that every penny advanced to any and all was repaid with thanks. Not one defaulted in any way, nor did anyone forget his obligations to his family. All this I feel certain may be to the credit of Mother's efforts.

Upon his arrival to the States, Father engaged in the profession usually reserved for the new immigrant, i.e., peddling. He pushed the cart for but a short time since it did not much appeal to him. Soon Father joined the Tetiiver congregation where he met his landsleit and people of his own type.[58] Here he met [A811] Mr. Leventhal, owner of the Sunshine Broom Co., who offered him a job in his factory. Though this job did not pay much, Father was happy. Also, the two men became good friends and were very happy with each other until the very end.

By this time, the family managed to acquire its own home in Father's name on E. 39th Street. Father was now a homeowner and, since Mr. Leventhal was as great a capitalist as Father, it was but natural for Father to underwrite the mortgage for Mr. Leventhal. Thus, one happily ran his business while the other enjoyed the job until the very last day of his life. Father died suddenly at about 7 p.m. after a full day's work.

---

[58] Editor's note: The [C34] Tetiiv community, located close to Knyashe and Justingrad, included members of our family. Several from [A105] Golda Voskoboinik's family died there during a pogrom. Three Tetiiv landsleit societies were located in Cleveland, New York and Buffalo. See, "What I remember: Clevelanders recall the shtetl," by the Jewish Community Federation of Cleveland in cooperation with the Western Reserve Historical Society, Cleveland 1985.

Father's highest wages reached $23 per week, but with all children working and depositing their earnings with Mother, there was enough to send to the relatives to escape the pogroms as well as enough to send me $50 per month while I studied medicine.

Is there any reason why I should not sing my praises to these people of mine?

#18 THE KAPROVS AND THE TRACHTMANS

Letters to [A481] Louis and [A481a] Bettie Trachtman, by [A471] Jacob and Ahuva Trachtman, Ramat Gan, Israel)

Letter 1 (undated)

I was happy to receive your letter and the lovely photograph of you and your son, who are the descendants of [A290] Chaim Kaprove. I heard from those who translated and read the letter to me that it was written in a style embodying great warmth. It is indeed a great pity that I am unable to read English and have to be aided by others. [A473] Eyal and [A473a] Janice, however, are only too willing to help me.

Dear Louis, you ask me to write more of what I know of the Village [C02b] Sokolivka, where your father [A479] Yankel Trachtman, was born, bred, and educated. When I saw the photo you sent, I saw your father as a young man, indeed, a Trachtman in all respects. I shall now attempt writing as much as I can recollect of Sokolivka as possible.

Sokolivka's real name was Justingrad. I shall relate this story of how it was named according to what I was told as a child. Between Sokolivka and Justingrad was a bridge, named on one side by a vast river, stretching tens of kilometers. On the other side of the bridge was a smaller river, spanning but a few kilometers. Between the great lake and the smaller river was a flour mill that utilized the water of the great river to activate the wheels that ground the flour for Sokolivka and the surrounding villages and areas.

Beyond this same bridge was a large area, already mentioned in my previous stories. This area was where Justingrad was founded. It was in about 1820 when a Czar ruled Russia. There were lesser stationed men called "Paritzim," who, like feudal lords, owned their own land, and could do very much as they pleased. In fact, many, many years ago, they even enslaved people. Now the land upon which Justingrad was built belonged to such a "Paritze," who was a friend to the Jewish people. Her name was Justina, and she wanted to establish a village of Jewish people here. Thus was the place named.

According to the information I heard, [A290] Uncle Chaim, after whom your grandfather is called, was one of the first Jews to settle in Justingrad. After him came others, and with time, it became a large, flourishing town, which in 1918 comprised about 500-600 families. All Jews who wanted to settle in [C02a] Justingrad would go to the Paritze's agents to lease land. For about 300-400 meters of land, the Jews paid annual dues of a few rubles.

As time passed, five synagogues and two bathhouses were founded. There being no private baths in the small town, the Jews utilized the communal facilities. Every Friday, the men would go to the larger bathhouse, while the women used the smaller bath that was opened twice a week for womenfolk. Now in Sokolivka lived a Rabbi who married a woman whose father built him a palace that stretched for thousands of meters. Within the grounds of his home was a synagogue that I've already recalled, his bathhouse, a wondrous green garden, and orchards filled with fruit. At this time, two-storied houses began appearing in the town, although not too many.

In about 1917 or 1918, when the war terminated, the Czar and his family were killed and the properties of the Paritzim were ransacked and the spoils divided among the people. After the revolution, uprisings began, and of course, the Jews bore the brunt of the eruptions. In the villages surrounding Sokolivka, attacks and killings already were rife, but Justingrad was as yet silent. The story goes that during the lifetime of the Rabbi, there were no killings in Sokolivka. This story penetrated the ears of the enemy, and the first group of rebels entering Sokolivka took it upon themselves to kill the Rabbi, then aged 75 years. They began robbing, ransacking, and raping, and as already mentioned in a previous letter, they took young people to the synagogue and held them for ransom. They then claimed after demanding the payment that they were going to recruit the young people as soldiers. We already know how the rebels took them to the outskirts of the town and murdered them. After this band of rebels, others came who ransacked what remained of the spoils. The straw that broke the camel's back, however, came in the form of the [A285] "Denikintses," that is, rightists who were thirsty for rule. They behaved just like the rebels, igniting houses and shops in the town and burning the place down. It was in about 1920 that the town of Sokolivka vanished. It existed all in all for a period of about 100 years. Well, this is the short story of Sokolivka, which was destined to the same fate as many other Russian cities like Justingrad.

Letter 2, dated 1979

I don't know, Louis, if you know much about the children of Chaim from whom were born the brothers Trachtman. The children of Chaim were named after Grandmother [A462] Yenta, who was one of Chaim's daughters, and of her, I shall tell a separate story.

She married a man named [A462a] Jacob Trachtman, who came from a town near to that of grandmother Yenta. Seven brothers and one daughter (who died) were born to them. He also died young. Each brother who had a son was named Jacob after [A462a] Grandfather Jacob Trachtman. I am probably the only one who remembers facts about the family Trachtman for as far back as my memory exists. I suppose that I was about five years old, and I will try to give you a taste of the story of the lives of the Trachtman family and children, especially your grandfather [A474] Chaim, who was named after the [A290] Chaim after whom everyone was named.

Your grandfather Chaim left Russia and went to America. Why he left Russia and what happened to the family when your grandfather was in America and how the family reunited and all went to America is the long history I will relate. But before this, I'll tell you about the Trachtman brothers as much as my poor memory and talent will allow. As I wrote in the beginning, Grandmother Yenta married a man from another town, and there were born to them seven sons and a daughter. The [A501] daughter died, and the grandmother became widowed at an early age, left with seven children, the eldest of whom, Uncle [A463] Moti, was then only 16 years old. Through her own powers, she brought the children up to be good people, and with the little she possessed, managed to feed them well so that all were strong and healthy as well as honest men. It is understandable under the circumstances they did not receive the education they would have liked for the reason that all had to leave home and earn their daily bread.

My father studied in the Beit Hamikdash (Holy Temple). This studying, of course, did not cost him money. The youngest brother, [A500] Ephraim, received a better education in comparison with the rest of the brothers. All knew how to read and write. This is briefly what I have to relate on a general basis about their lives.

And now about the house of your Grandfather Chaim. I hope that this story will be dear to you because it may be that I will tell you things that are new to you. Please make copies to send to your mother and brothers, Uncle [A482] Itzhak, sisters of your father and daughters of [A475] Haika of whom I shall mainly write. I met Haika's daughters in Israel, and also when I visited in America.

And now about the little town of Sokolivka. It was also called Justingrad. Founded 200 years ago, the children of Chaim were the first settlers there. Before this, they lived in a village near the area where the town was founded. One of the relatives from America, [A457] Joe Gillman, wrote a book in English about the children of Chaim. But according to my late son, [A472] Zvi, this man didn't know very much about the families.

The little town of [C02b] Sokolivka from when I remember it before World War I was where 400-500 families lived. Most of the Jews made their living from small professions and merchandise. Mostly, on Mondays, market day, farmers from villages in the area came to sell their products to the Jews, and in return, also buy the necessities from the Jews: groceries, clothing, and all kinds of things a farmer demanded. On the market day, many farmers gathered with horses and wagons, and the little town was built in such a way as to enclose the masses. There were large empty squares where the farmers used to put their wagons and buy the necessities. There was a particular square for grain products, one for the buying and selling of horses, for the selling of cows and pigs, and one for boots and wooden equipment the farmers used. Also, the Jews had a wide road where they sold groceries, materials, metalwork, and petrol and tar for rubbing on the wagon wheels. This road also had shops for salty fish, which was the Trachtman family's business. Grandfather Chaim was among them. The fish came from a distance of many kilometers from [C04] Astakhani, which is in Russia. There was also a road for the people who made the wooden wagons and also for blacksmiths, who together made wagons for the farmers.

Grandfather Chaim's house was semi-detached. It had a thatched roof, just like most of the homes built in the little town. Rich men and nice houses were few and far between. Most of the homes lacked fences. Grandfather Chaim's house included one large room, two bedrooms, a kitchen, and a storehouse for the wood needed in the winter. He, his wife and six children, two boys and four girls, lived there.

In 1911-12, Grandfather Chaim left Russia for America with the thought in mind of making some money there and then returning to his family in Russia. During this time, many Jews did the same as sustentation was hard for them. Antisemitism was rife. Grandfather Chaim needed 150 rubles for the journey, which was then equivalent to $95. Because he lacked sufficient funds, at least not enough to cover the whole trip, his brothers lent him here and there a bit, and so he collected enough for the journey. When he began earning money in America, he sent some home to Russia to support the family and also to repay debts. Your grandfather related the hard life that he passed in his first years in America when he stayed with us in Israel for a month. I said that it was the first month of his life that he rested. When he left Israel, he looked 20 years younger. He enjoyed the trip greatly. He spent the whole month with us and did not want to visit any other relatives. He said, "I like it here, so why should I go elsewhere?" This was because [A471a] Ahuva looked after him as a sister would. He only went to see your Uncle [A482] Itzhak Trachtman at his home and sometimes had lunch with him. That was because we lived in the same garden, as you know. He did not wish to travel to visit his brother [A485] Joseph, even for a few days.

Above I mentioned that Grandfather [A474] Chaim, when in America, used to send money to his family left in Russia. The family lived well, and he also paid back all his debts. But in 1914, the world war broke out, and the whole family experienced difficulty because no one could earn a substantial salary. To send money from America was impossible. Grandmother [A474a] Hadassah, Chaim's wife, had a shop, which was an inheritance from her family. On the market day, she had money for the family, but after a short period, she died. Her death was a great tragedy to all. My father was in the war, and life was not easy.

Uncle [A463] Moti, one of the richest brothers, and Uncle [A485] Joseph, who never had much, and Grandmother Yenta worked (she used to make brushes for painting, bought by Jew and gentile alike), all tried to help the orphaned children. Here I must tell you about [A475] Haika, who was admired by one and all in our town. Despite being only 14 or 15 years old, she bore the yoke and was both mother and father to the children. No words can tell of my praise of Haika. When I met her daughters, I saw Haika in them – quiet, pleasant, and loyal.

Fig. 18-2: [A463] Moti and [A463a] Hannah Trachtman, late 1920s.

Fig. 18-3: [A462] Yenta Trachtman. Fig. 18-4: [A462a] Jacob Trachtman.

Fig. 18-5: Trachmans, Top: [A467] Dora, [A468] Sam standing. Bottom: [A463a] Anna, [A463] Moti

Fig. 18-6: [A477] Jeannette Rosenbaum's maternal Kaprove family: Top: [A483] Bella Trachtman Foigelman, [A479] Jacob Trachtman, [A482] Isadore Trachtman, and [A484] Bertha Trachtman Levitsky. Bottom: [A478a] Harry Berman, husband of [A478] Golda Trachtman, [A474] Grandfather Hyman Trachtman, daughter [A475] Ida Trachtman, her husband [A475a] Samuel Kaprove, holding his daughter [A476] Edith Newler.

Fig. 18-7: [A475a] Father Sam Kaprove, daughter [A476] Edith Kaprove, later Newler, and mother [A475] Ida Trachtman Kaprove.

The most challenging situation was when the 1917 revolution broke out in Russia, and the rebels, called the "Jelyonim," came to our town, killing 140 people in one day. Among them was [A526] Moishe Kaprov, the son of Uncle [A515] Abraham, brother of Granny Yenta, who was then in America. They herded all the Jews of our town together and then demanded money for their release. After they received the money, they freed only the older people, but the young ones, those 18-40 years old, they said they were going to mobilize for war. They took them out of town, and near a canyon, shot and killed them all. Only one man survived, and that was by hiding among the corpses. This happened each time that the invaders came, robbing, raping, and killing.

The straw that broke the camel's back was the "Denikintses" who murdered nearly everyone in the whole town. The Jews had no means of livelihood, so we had to go to the gentile farmers and ask for a piece of bread. For each piece left at home, the second piece was given to Chaim's children. Also, we earned money from rejects made into oil. This we got from the father of Aunt [A485a] Haika, the wife of [A485] Yossel Trachtman, who had a little factory for oil making not far from Haika's town. Chaim's daughter never forgot this good deed. When [A485] Uncle Joseph was in Israel and times were hard at first, she collected dollars from all the family and sent them money from time to time.

All the Jews in the village suffered. Among them was Uncle Chaim's family, until it became known to us that one could cross the border to Romania, and from there, one could go anywhere. Also, we knew that Uncle [A502a] Itzhak Gelman, whose children and grandchildren are in America today, was the husband of [A502] Leah. Leah's sister was Granny [A462] Yenta. He had $10,000 with him to help the family of Grandpa [A474] Chaim. [A494] Velvel Trachtman's wife, [A494a] Dora, who by then was also in America, also helped. The aim was to cross the border and go anywhere they wished. Then Uncle [A463] Moti and the children went to America, and [A485] Joseph's family went to Israel.

Velvel was the father of [A496] Minnie Brandt and [A498] Yetta Goodman. They also had a brother [A495] Jacob, who died during World War 1. The $10,000 Chaim, Velvel, and Froika gave to Isaac. The Trachtman family was the only surviving family in the town, thanks to Granny Yenta. We sold all our property for next to nothing and went to the Romanian border. One can write a separate book about the illegal border crossing and hardships encountered. Today I am 77 years old. I was two years older than your father, but we grew up together, learned, and suffered all hardships together. I could write even more, for the Trachtmans have a long and fascinating history.

What I wrote and told about the happenings in our village happened to all the towns in Ukraine. Many Jews died, led to slaughter like sheep, unable to defend themselves. You must have heard about Chmielnicki (1595-1657),[59] the exile of Jews from England and France in medieval times, and the antisemites living in Russia about 100 years ago. You must have read about the Crusades, the Spanish Inquisition, and the greatest tragedy of all to the Jewish people, Hitler. You know of the establishment of the State of Israel, the nation that exists with courage and without fear. We managed to overcome all enemies who came to destroy us. An expression of this is the Jewish people returning to their land and spiritual birthplace. Today we see sophisticated weapons of immense power in a world that has diminished in size. Now we see the two choices the world has – that we develop into one nation of the world, or end up in a world destroyed by said weapons. We may believe the visions of the prophets prophesying the end of days, saying, "and the lion and the lamb shall live together in peace and harmony, and there will be no more wars."

Letter 3, dated November 1981.

---

[59] Bogdan Chmielnicki, leader of the Cossack and peasant uprising against Polish rule in Ukraine in 1648 which resulted in the destruction of hundreds of Jewish communities. https://www.jewishvirtuallibrary.org/chmielnicki-khmelnitski-bogdan-x00b0

We were delighted to receive your letter, Louis. In fact, our joy was double: Firstly, because it was from the son of [A479] Jacob, the 6th generation of the sons of [A290] Chaim, and secondly because it was written in Hebrew, in a beautiful script and style. All read the letter and wondered at the lovely Hebrew expression.

Your late father, may his memory be blessed, was younger than I by a few years, but we were educated together and learned together with the same melamed. Together, we went hungry during war-time and fled the invaders who came to our little town to rob, rape, and kill.

Every Sabbath, we would meet at Grandmother [A462] Yenta's house. Her small, narrow house had two rooms and a kitchen. The married son always lived in one of the rooms, and in the larger room (4x5m) stood Grandmother's bed, a table and two benches that could seat about ten people. We would gather there, parents and older children. Sometimes, there were not enough places to sit, and some would have to stand. Grandmother Yenta would give all something to eat, oven-dried black seeds that she prepared after she baked the Sabbath challah. She would also prepare tea, and because it was forbidden to light a fire on Shabbat, grandmother would make bottles of boiling water before the Sabbath and put them on the hot stove and cover them with cloths. Thus was the heat retained until the Sabbath eve when all her children and grandchildren would visit.

In the event of my reminiscing, some memories came to mind of the journey your grandfather [A474] Chaim and uncles [A494] Velvel and [A500] Froika traveled and what they took with them. There were, of course, no suitcases in the town; therefore, they made these themselves of wooden slats to form a crate inside of which they placed their tallit and tefillin. Other than the clothes they wore, they took a few extra items and a suit they owned. However, the main concern was for food, for the long journey ahead that would sometimes take one to two months. The ship had water, and the food available there was expensive, but not only that, it wasn't kosher. So, familial preparations were made for the trip. Everyone prepared a quantity of dried bread, and the travelers took with them a bag of this bread, dried fish, and dried sausage that they themselves made.

From your letter Louis, I understand that you plan to visit Israel. We will all be jubilant to have you with us. You write that your Father's sister [A484] Bracha, passed away. Let me wish all her family long lives, and please tell them that we all share in their sorrow. In your letter, you say Bracha was two when she came to the States. Grandfather Chaim left the town before the first World War broke out, and [A474a] Grandmother Hadassah was without a father for four years. Bracha, therefore, must have been a little older when she arrived in the States, perhaps three or four.

As I am now approaching the age of 80 years and am the only adult grandchild of the Grandmother who remembers her, I would like to make a family tree, from Chaim, after whom your grandfather is named until the present generation. My grandchild, Eyal, gave me an idea about the tree and will help me do it.

With the hope that my letter finds you all well, I shall now conclude.

Fondest regards from all the brothers and their families.

#19 [A494a] DORA TRACHTMAN, WIFE OF [A494] WILLIAM A2B4C6
by her daughter, [A496] Minnie Brandt

Education: Mother's oldest sister taught her to read. The women received no formal education.

Religion: The Orthodox religion forbade the reading of the Russian language, so Mother would hide under her bed or in the attic to read. It was forbidden to walk or dance with a boy, but in the larger city, such as [C36] Uman, this did occur. Mother's oldest sister never met her husband before her engagement, but Mother had already met her future husband, [A494] William. Our grandmother, [A462] Yenta, was engaged at nine and married at 13 while our grandfather, [A462a] Yankel, was only 15. All of Mother's family married before 17 years of age.

Work: Our grandfather studied while our grandmother supported the family with a grocery store. They were the first ones to have a threshing machine for wheat. One son lost an arm using it.

Epidemic: Our brother, [A495] Yankel, died in the 1918 outbreak of scarlet fever. Typhoid fever hit most of the family from 1917-1920.

Revolutions and Pogroms (1913-1920): Fourteen in our family died by 1919. Mother lived through three pogroms. She described hiding in a dark attic for three days with 30 adults and 17 children. With cherry jelly, they kept the children from crying, also giving each child a cherry whenever one started to cry. Looking out from the darkness, she could see the enemy sharpening long knives at the end of rifles while looking for Jews to kill. She described stores broken into, broken windows, puddles of blood and dead bodies scattered all over. She made a point of describing one wagon of corpses, boys 20 and 30 years of age. She remembered long lines of wagons leaving town packed with stolen merchandise from the stores and another row of carts coming in with corpses and wounded. She said it was indescribable. Mother, herself, was taken to the morgue once, and a young doctor noticed that she was still breathing. He took her out and saved her life.

Our father [A494] William left Russia to find work in America. Since his son [A495] Yankel was about to be born, our mother planned to follow a little later after the birth. But war broke out, and it took nine years until she was able to get to America. Since our mother couldn't leave, he took her sister, Ida Shapiro, to substitute as his wife since he had a passport for two. After their son died, Mother escaped over the border to Bessarabia and from there to Romania. She took two nieces, Ann and Frances, as her children, since their mother had been killed in the pogrom.

#20 [A462a] YANKEL TRACHTMAN
by [A463] Motye (Morris) and [A463a] Chana Trachtman

Rumors spread all over town. Whether it was true or not, I cannot vouch for, but I quote, "As long as I'll live, there be no bloodshed in [C02a] Justingrad." The rabbi was supposed to have said that. As the pogroms started throughout Ukraine, we had none till the rabbi was killed. The same band that killed the 165 boys killed him. He was the first victim. My father was the rabbi on Saturday evening. He jumped over the rail into the orchard and stayed until the bandits left. We, the rest of the family, hid out in a chicken coop next door. We don't know whether the peasants knew if we were there, but after that, any peasant we ran into gave us cover and some food. As we kept kosher, we usually wound up with pickle juice and stale bread, which was more than other Jews had. All this was in exchange for a shawl or some piece of linen, which the bandits overlooked.

The rabbi's grandson was murdered at the same time, but not until his family turned over his grandmother's tiara, set with diamonds and many precious jewels. I saw it many a time. As you probably know, she came from a very wealthy family. Her people were in the wholesale lumber business. They built for him the shul and all the estate. The fact that the bandits asked for the tiara shows you that the town peasants were involved, but not openly. Of the rabbi's four daughters, three were divorced and died of starvation after leaving town for the big city. His granddaughter followed the army, as she was not too moral before the pogroms, from the town gossips. The Chasidim said the same for the daughter. As a matter of fact, my brother, [A485] Yossel, after fighting with [A494] Feigel, demanded back his child, which she was supposed to have aborted. I overheard all of this from [A462] Mother talking with the town women.

As soon as the white army bandits, the "Denikintses," left the town, the Reds walked right in. There were few houses left, so of course, they paid us a "social" call. The officer in charge told the soldiers hands-off. All he wanted was men's underwear. As everybody was lazy, we showed all our empty drawers, and they left not touching a thing or anybody. After that, we had no more organized bands, but anybody that stayed in town was visited at night. They made sure no Jews remained. That was when my family moved to [C36] Uman. As I was the youngest and strongest, I used to commute back and forth for food. By that time, I was 16 years old. When bandits stopped the wagon searching for Jews, I was never recognized or exposed since I dressed in a potato sack outfit. [C36] Uman, the city, was in great chaos and destruction. There were lines for bread when it was available. Everybody went barefoot. My father wore a suit made from potato sacks. You can visualize how he looked, but fortunately, we were there only six months before we left.

When Hitler entered Ukraine, the Jews there still thought they would fare better than under the Communists. They refused evacuation. The peasants gave them over to the Nazis. We heard about it from Motel Kreideen, who wrote that the Jews were killed by the same people that killed Froim Grossman, and that he was killed by the peasants from [C02b] Sokolivka. By the way, this Motel spent most of his remaining life in and out of jail for speculating on anything he could find, including foreign currency. That was the only way he saved his children and grandchildren from starvation. He died after World War II at the age of 80 in [C25] Moscow.

My [A462a] father came to this country in 1923 with the entire family. He died of prostate trouble after three operations in 1925.

#21 [A468] SAM TRACHTMAN
by [A469] Marcia Trachtman Scheer

Letter To Stanley Robboy (Jan 3, 2020)

[A465a] Len Weinstock's wife [A465] Marilyn is my first cousin. Her mother, [A464] Rochel and my father, [A468] Sam Trachtman, were brother and sister.

I am the daughter of someone who grew up in Sokolivka. Sam Trachtman came to the US in 1923. His father was [A463] Moti and his [A462] grandmother Yenta. The only pictures I have from Russia are a picture of Yenta and a photo of Sam, his mother, his father, and sister, [A467] Dora, from 1922.

My dad spoke little about his life in Russia, as he was so delighted to be in the USA. He was a loyal American citizen who took me with him when I was a child, every time he voted. He went to whatever schools Jews could go to in Russia until he was 14. He knew little Russian but was fluent in Yiddish and could read Hebrew, though I do not believe he could speak or understand the language. When he came to America at age 16, he went to night school to learn to read and write English. He was not well educated but loved to read and was curious about everything. He worked incredibly hard as the owner of a small hand laundry store but was always content with life and never complained.

My daughter interviewed him when she was in elementary school. She asked him if he suffered any tragedies. "When I was a little boy, I was walking to my father's store. It was Monday, a market day, a hectic day. Every Monday was a market day. All the people came to sell their goods. It was now winter. For three months, people rode in sleighs. At that time, horses pulled sleights. All of a sudden, horses passed by me, and I was knocked down by the sleigh. The next thing I knew, I was under it. I was screaming like anything. I was between the horses. If they had run over me, I would have been dead. Somebody yelled, 'Somebody is under the horses. Save him!' Finally, they saved me. Nothing happened other than many bruises." It was a great story to tell a child. He didn't tell her about the pogroms and why they had to leave their home and come to America.

You might enjoy the answer to the question, "What would you do if you had a chance to live your life over?" "It was an okay life at the beginning, but once the war and revolution came, it was miserable. I don't want that part, but I wish the rest of my life."

#22 COUSIN [A457] JOSEPH GILLMAN
by John Robboy

The experiences of the day mold every generation. [A457] Joe Gillman was a product of his day. He grew up during a highly turbulent period in Russian history. The Russian revolutionary movement was near its peak when Joe was reaching maturity. New ideas and philosophies permeated the land, seeping into the provinces, including [C02a] Justingrad and even my [C01] Knyazhe-Krinitsa. As an alert, bright,, and dynamic youngster, Joe adapted many of the new ideas. He boldly and unceremoniously refused, when he was 12 or 13, to recite Kaddish (the prayer for the dead) for his recently deceased mother. This was a highly revered ritual and a painful blow to his family.

It is difficult for us to understand now the iconoclastic impact on his people. This action could possibly be equated to the son of the Oshkosh farmer declaring himself communist during Senator Joseph McCarthy's time. The air in Justingrad now was too stifling, and like Abraham, Joe left his home. He went to [C36] Uman in search of cleaner air and greater opportunities. As far as I know, [A313] Gita and [A309] Pearl Dudnik were the only B'nai Khaim engaged in business there; they ran a millinery store. But life here was tough.

Joe was the son of her most beloved sister, and Mother loved him dearly. She admired his appearance and bright mind but could help him very little besides patching his torn pants and giving him a few pennies during her frequent visits to [C36] Uman. Somehow, he managed to sustain himself while he studied bookkeeping and photography. America beckoned, as the atmosphere in [C02a] Justingrad became more stifling. He presented an ultimatum to his father, [A422a] Moshe: "Sell the house and take me to America." Before Moshe could digest this ultimatum, Joe had already crossed the border to Romania. Moshe had no alternative but to bow to Joe's demand. He joined his son, and they went directly to Cleveland, where there were relatives. Here Joe's physical and intellectual vigor rapidly unfolded. Like a plant exposed to fresh air and sunshine, Joe's chest expanded, and his eyes embraced an ever-widening horizon.

Though I had met Joe in 1901, I got to know him in 1910 when I came to America. Joe was young and vigorous, handsome, and dynamic. His ambition was great. He recognized no obstacles, and no job was unsuitable nor too difficult. He worked for his cousin Fox, sewing on buttons, sold books, was a lifeguard and taught night school. By 1910, he had already gone through Hiram College and was at Western Reserve University, where he excelled in his schoolwork and participated in extracurricular activities. He made lasting friends among the students and faculty.

The women were at his mercy. All fell for him, but he selected [A457a] Etta Cohen because of her profundity. He never regretted his choice. Etta bore him two sons, [A458] Leonard and [A459] Robert, who inherited the intellectual capacities of both parents, a great accomplishment indeed.

His struggle for existence never lessened. Demands of life intensified his battle. With a family to support, he still had to get his Ph.D. degree. As a social worker, he worked for the Railroad Retirement Board. He managed to get the desired degree from Columbia University and taught at the University of Pittsburgh. He was an economist for a New York business house, a superintendent of an Orthodox children's home in Denver, and also worked for the United States Government.

At near 70, he retired from his job but not from work. Since retirement, he has written two volumes setting forth his views and theories on economic phases, which my son, [A031] Stanley, predicted I would never understand but that he would. He had other publications, including one depicting the family, "The B'nai Khaim," in which he fulfilled my prediction that he would be the most outstanding character.

#23 [A457] YOSEL (JOSEPH) GILLMAN
by himself

[A457] Yosel, who started the permanent migration of the B'nai Khaim to America, was the same young man who, at age ten, tempted the Gods to slay him if he sinned and who three years later took a census of Justingrad. Now, at 18, he came to America, bringing his father with him.

Yosel-Moishe-Beryl-Chaim, the chain of patronymics by which he was known back home, came to the United States not because of pogroms or for business reasons. (Somehow, he had escaped the pogroms of his day. He always seemed to have left a town a day before a pogrom or came to a town the day after.) Nor had he engaged in any business ventures threatened by competition from the developing factory system. As a matter of record, at age 15, he had served as an apprentice in a dry goods store for one hour. He came to the store at sunrise as ordered and was greeted by the proprietor with a broom in his hands. "Here, Yosel," he held out a broom, "Sweep the floors!"

"I came here to learn the dry goods business, not sweep floors," I said, refusing to take the broom from him. Consultation between him and my relatives, who had arranged the deal, followed in no time at all. And in no time at all, I was gone from the store, back to my consuming love, books. Yosel-Moishe-Beryl-Chaim came to America for other, purely personal and selfish reasons.

As was the case of all Jewish boys at the time, I began cheder at age four. I remember that first cheder quite well. It was a large bare room, holding one long table, a long bench on either side, 12 to 15 children, ages four to eight, and a chair for the melamed, a tall, gaunt man with a motley beard, at one end of the table. A stick lay on the table in front of him. In one corner of the room stood a bucket of water from which the kids drank with a wooden ladle. In the winter, when it got freezing and was snowing hard, the melamed would let the family goat in to warm itself under the table. Our legs were not long enough to touch it. But we were reminded of its presence when it sneezed or passed gas.

Instruction consisted of teaching the beginners to identify the 24 letters of the Hebrew alphabet, its vowel notations, and how to form Hebrew words. Later would come learning – their meaning in Yiddish. Even though writing was not taught, I clearly knew how to write by age seven, since I was corresponding with my father, [A422a] Moshe, who had gone to work one summer as a day laborer in the vineyards around [C26] Nikolayev on the Black Sea. As a rule, it took most children the whole first school year to achieve this goal. The brighter boys (no girls were then sent to cheder) might get there in a few weeks. The very bright might go beyond and begin to read the Pentateuch (Five Books of Moses) by age 5. When that happened, as it did in my case, it was an occasion for celebration. My mother, [A422] Pessie, I remember, then brought an apron-full of goodies. The melamed supplied sweet cider, and the kids were given a half-day holiday to enjoy it all.

From then on, my progress in learning was rapid. By age six, I read Rashi, a Biblical commentator. By age seven, in another cheder, I began reading excerpts from the Talmud. At age nine, in a more advanced cheder, I read the Gemorah (Talmud). By that time, I began to fret with school boredom. I would know the week's lesson by Tuesday and saw no reason to listen to the others repeat it during the rest of the week. Often that meant playing hooky, sitting by the river, skipping pebbles over its smooth surface. Consultations between Mother and the rebbe brought a promise to keep me busy in cheder with special assignments.

By the time I was 12, the situation had become hopeless. The most advanced cheder in [C02a] Justingrad could not hold me, for two reasons. First, I had become interested in secular learning, i.e., the Russian language, arithmetic, geography, even German. Second, the poor old rebbe really had nothing more than the sacred lore to teach me. What's more, one day, I profaned by bringing a Russian grammar to cheder. I wanted to have something to do while the others droned away at the lesson for the week. That was more than the old fellow could tolerate. He tore the book out of my hands, threw it out of the window, and cuffed me. That was the end. No melamed had ever hit me before. I walked out and never entered another cheder.

The family then made two decisions for me. Until I was bar mitzvah, I was to continue sacred studies on my own in a shul under the general supervision of the elder scholars studying there. Then I would be sent to the Yeshiva in [C14] Kishinev to prepare for the rabbinate. My mother had a sister, [A502] Leah Gelman, living in Kishinev, and I would be entrusted to her care.

As it turned out, the shul idea was a total loss. I learned little there and increasingly cared less. My intellectual interests were now wholly absorbed in secular studies. My only vivid recollection of that shul year is the presence there among the elders of [A577] "Isruel Chaim," the stepson of [A290] Zeide Chaim's stepson. The story is that after [A290a] Grandma Osna bore [A290] Zeide Chaim's seven children and then died, Zeide then married a young, winsome widow, [A290b] Edassey, who had a son by her first marriage. When Zeide Chaim died, we learned he had left all his worldly possessions to this second wife and her son. This was [A577] Isruel Chaim, who apparently had nothing else to do all his life but sit in shul and study. A tall, redheaded man with a long red beard, he was imposing among the other, generally wizened older men. Besides, he had a sharp cleft at the fleshy tip of his nose. This is what I remember from my year at shul.

Three months after I was bar mitzvah, my mother died of pneumonia at age 56. Thereupon plans for the Yeshiva, Kishinev, and the rabbinate also died. Later that year, my father married a midwife from [C36] Uman. My elder siblings made life intolerable for her in Justingrad, so she took my father to Uman and I came along. Six years later, I left them and struck out for myself. My stepmother could see no reason why I should not go to work, the way her own sons did, instead of "messing around" with books and learning. For 3 ½ years, I did just that, "mess around" with books and learning. But then it became clear to me that the learning goal I had set for myself was beyond my reach in tsarist Russia. Being a Jew and being poor in tsarist Russia precluded that. I picked up my savings, five rubles, accumulated by teaching Yiddish, and set off for America. In America, I reckoned, a young man like myself could work for a living eight hours a day, sleep eight hours a day and study eight hours a day. The prospect was alluring.

Already when I was 16, I pleaded with my family to help me get to America. That plea was rejected on the insistence of [A462] Aunt Yenta. In America, she said, all that is sacred to a Jew dies. "Read," she said, "the letters [A470] Zalman (her son) has been writing." She clinched the argument with, "Yossel is already a half-goy. He shaves, to the disgrace of the family. In America, he would become full goy; no Sabbath, no kashrut – a goy!"

A year later, my brother, [A427] Daniel, turned down my proposition that he advance my share of the potential family inheritance, which I figured at 100 rubles, to pay my way to America. So on January 5, 1906, with five rubles in my pocket, a pair of tefillin, a pillow, and a change of underwear and socks in a gunnysack, I set off for America. How finally I got my father to join me in Austria six months later, with money to take us both as far as Ellis Island need not be detailed here.[60] On July 21, 1906, we got there with 65 kopecks between us. Other B'nai Khaim followed us.

---

[60] [A460] Daniel Gillman, [A457] Joe's grandson, relates the story is after both Joe and his father were in the US. Joe was offered a job with a gentile baker, and his father told him he'd go back to Russia if he took the job. Both being very stubborn, Joe took the job, and his father left. Joe's father returned eventually.

#24 [A457] JOSEPH GILLMAN
(From *B'nai Khaim*)

Joseph Gillman was born in June 1888 in Ukraine in the small town of [C02a] Justingrad. He came to America in 1906 at the age of 18 with no funds and began working at menial jobs in Cleveland, Ohio. With the bare equivalent of a high school education, he started promptly to learn English and to prepare for college. In 1908 he entered Hiram College, Ohio, and in 1913 graduated from Adelbert College of Western Reserve University with a B.A. degree.

While an undergraduate, he taught English to newly arrived immigrants in the evening. Upon graduation, he worked as a probation officer in the Cleveland Juvenile Court. His goal, however, was graduate study. In 1911, after marrying [A457a] Etta Cohen, both moved to New York City and Columbia University, where he received a M.A. in sociology.

During World War I, he served as a statistician in the Council of National Defense in Washington and as a senior examiner in the U.S. Shipping Board. Following the war and after his initial studies at Columbia, he changed his primary interest to economics and received a Ph.D. in that area, also at Columbia University. In 1926 he published the monograph, "Rent Levels in Pittsburgh and Their Causes."

Joe's varied experiences as an economist spanned a half-century. They included university teaching, commercial research for private agencies, extensive economic research in U.S. government agencies, and the writing of numerous articles in both American and foreign periodicals. He wrote several monographs, two award-winning essays, and two books.

Joe first taught at the University of Arkansas and then at the University of Pittsburgh (1921-27), where he organized and directed the Bureau of Business Research. In the government service, he was Senior Economist at the Railroad Retirement Board and Assistant Branch Chief in the Bureau of Planning and Statistics of the War Production Board. Before retiring in 1947, he was the Chief of Economic Analysis of the War Assets Administration. He was a member of the American Economic Association and the American Statistical Association.

Joe's writings reflect his wide range of interests. His earliest articles published in sociological journals concerned race and immigration problems. In the 1920s, he also published monographs on business barometers, the business cycle, and monograph housing and rents. In 1944, his essay "Demobilization and After" was one of 17 winning plans in a national contest on postwar employment. In 1947 he retired from government service to devote full time to writing, especially on economic theory and political economy. In 1958, after writing another award-winning essay, "Disposition of Excess Savings" for the Committee for Economic Development, his first book was published, "The Palling Rate of Profit." Not quite a decade later, in 1965, his second book, "Prosperity In Crisis," appeared. Both were translated into multiple languages.

Joe's study on the B'nai Khaim germinated some forty years before with his concern about immigration problems and cultural adaptation. The work was completed in 1967. In April 1968, Joe expectedly died. [A457a] His wife, Etta, who for many years served as a school psychologist in New York City, completed the work. Their two sons are [A458] Dr. Leonard Gillman, a mathematician, and [A459] Dr. Robert Gillman, a psychoanalyst.

#25 FAMILY GILLMAN
by [A457] Joseph Gillman

Mother, [A422] Pessie Gillman, was one of the few women in [C02a] Justingrad, who could read Yiddish. I remember how on Tisha b'Av evening, several women would gather around her in stocking feet (symbol of mourning) and listen to her read the story of the Temple's destruction, swaying and weeping until the tallow candles went out. She was a devout, but not a pious Jewess.

[A422a] Moishe Gillman[61], my father, was born in [C11] Gaicin, some 50 miles from Justingrad. He had been married at 17 and again at 19 before he married my mother. According to the story I learned as a child, his first wife died; the second he divorced. At age 20 or 21, he came to Justingrad to "look at" " a" prospective bride, my mother's eldest sister, [A423] Khaye, also a divorcee. When the young swain came into [A419] Zeide Beryl's store, where he was to meet the prospective bride, he saw [A422] Pessie, her younger sister, and fell in love with her, it seems, at first sight. She evidently reciprocated. They soon married and lived together for 33 years.

When my mother died, he waited only six months before he again married. This time, he married a midwife from [C36] Uman and moved there a few months later, taking me along. Four years later, he emigrated to America with me, leaving her behind. Two years later, he returned to her, divorced her, married another woman, divorced her after a few months, remarried the midwife, then left without her for America again, coming here in time to see me graduate from college. Soon after that, his midwife died in Uman. He remained here ten years, preparing boys for their bar mitzvah. When he was 75, he was hit by an automobile, later developed fibrosis of the lungs, and died in Cleveland in 1923 at age 77. Father was an observant Jew, but somewhat of a skeptic.

[A427] Daniel Gelman, my brother, was born in Justingrad in 1879 and died in Buffalo in 1958. Daniel's life was a hard one from his early childhood. He had to go to work when he was scarcely a bar mitzvah. The family had lost their miserable retail store during the depression of the 90s. After two or three years as an apprentice to a wainwright (a tradesperson skilled in the making and repairing of wagons and carts), perhaps for a ruble a week or even less, he struck out for himself as a rope maker, one of the first B'nai Chaim to work with his hands. When called for induction into military service, he simulated a hysterical hiccup and was rejected. A bribe of 50 rubles to the attending physician in the military hospital where he was sent for observation hastened the decision. Free of the military, he married [A427a] Sheiva. They had four children of whom two died in infancy. In 1911 he emigrated to America, leaving his wife and two behind. Factory competition and, in particular, the Depression of 1904-08, drove him out of his rope-making business. In Cleveland, he worked as a fruit and vegetable peddler. Then in Buffalo, he

---

[61] The "Gilmans" and the "Gillman" mentioned are not related names, though they may have been in an earlier generation. As my father told me the story, his own father's name was [A422a] Shestunov. As a boy of seven or eight, he became subject to conscription into the military regime of [A278] Nicholas I. That would have meant service for about 25 years. It happened that about that time a boy of his age named Gillman died in their town. A small bribe induced the town clerk to "bury" a Shestunov instead of a Gillman and the Shestunov boy became a Gillman. As my father was an only son, the Gilmans in this line cannot be immediately related to him. Nor were they related to each other. In the ship's manifest, my father spelled his name as "Gelman."

became a junk peddler, then a junk dealer, doing reasonably well and acquiring a couple of income properties.

Then came World War I, the revolutions and counter-revolution in Russia, and ten agonizing years before he was reunited with his family in Buffalo. When their eldest daughter, [A428] Gertrude, married, he was at last happy. But not for long, for she died in childbirth. From then on, life was black. [A427a] Sheiva (Sarah) Kaprove, his wife, died, and later his second wife died of Hodgkin's disease. His third marriage might have been more tranquil, but by that time, he was a broken man. Always one could hear him intoning a sad song, ending it with a deep sigh. His overriding concern was the well being of his grandson "Sonny," whom he and Sheiva raised when his mother, [A428] Gertrude, died.

Daniel always kept a kosher home, attended to his morning and evening prayers, and observed Sabbath and all the holidays, though he had trimmed his beard soon after he came here. He was active in establishing the [C02b] Sokolivkar Shul in Buffalo and was its president for several years.

Daniel was a wit. When in the hospital the morning after he had suffered a heart attack, the nurse would not give him salt for his oatmeal, he looked at her with his sad smile and said, "If Daniel cannot have salt in his oatmeal, then Good-bye Daniel Gelman." Half an hour later, he was dead.

In his will, he provided that no eulogies be delivered at his funeral. "Praise a man when he is alive," the will said, "When he is dead, who cares?" The will also stated that his casket should not be opened for a last look. "I want my friends to remember me as I looked when I was alive," it stated.

#26 [A431] ALTA GELMAN
by [A445] Ellen Rossen

Descendants of   **[A422] Pessie Kaprov and Moshe Shestunov → Gillman**

ID	Name	Spouse/Relation
[A423]	Chaye Sarah Gillman	Eliezer Pribludny
[A424]	- Rachel Strayer Pribludny	Morris Green
[A425]	- Bayla Liba Pribludny	
[A426]	- Khaim Strayer Pribludny	Masha Portnick
[A427]	Daniel Gelman	Sarah|Sheiva Kaprow
	- Gertrude Gelman Twin-1	[A024] Joe Robboy
		Sam Mittleman (h2 Gertrude)
[A429]	- - Gordon Mittleman	Ferne Elaine Phillips
[A430]	- Dvossi Gelman	Benjamin Kareff
[A431]	Alta (originally Baila Liba) Gelman	David Hirsh Pearlman [A506]
[A432]	- Abe Pearlman	Freda
[A433]	- - Annette Pearlman	Howard Stanley Lynn
[A434]	- - Shirley Pearlman	Joseph Amato, Jr
[A435]	- - - Cheryl Lynn Amato	__Ladawer
[A436]	- - Emanuel (Sonny) Pearlman	Simone Dechelle Wllingford
[A437]	- - - Vicky Pearlman	__Kuczynsk
[A432b]		Alta Baily (w2 Abe)
[A439]	- - Rita Sue Pearlman	Donald Mahle
		James Albin Bogart (h2 Rita Sue)
[A440]	- - - Lesa K Bogart	Greg Woyton
[A441]	- - - Barbara Mahle	Michael Marzec
[A442]	- - Joyce Pearlman	Michael Segulin
[A443]	- Beryl Perlman	Sylvia Plumka
[A444]	- - Arleen Perlman	Allen W Rossen
[A445]	- - - Ellen Marcia Rossen	David Maman
[A446]	- - - Sandra Rossen	Avner Lahrey
[A447]		Moriah Lahrey
[A448]	- Pessie Perlman	Jack Fox
[A449]	- - Robert Fox	Martha Kerner
[A450]	- - - Denise Fox	
[A451]	- - - Michelle Fox	Rick Moss
[A452]	- - - Julius Fox	
[A453]	- - Diane Fox	Irving Chaitoff
[A454]	- - - David Kaye Chaitoff	
[A455]	- - Marlene Beverly Fox	Richard Rock
[A456]		Motel Gelman (w2 is [A431] Alta Perlman)
[A457]	Yossel Gillman	Etta Judith Cohen

On Friday afternoons, as I slide the blue dinner napkin under the silver-plated forks, an apparition of my great grandmother, [A431] Alta Gelman, appears in the corner of the room. But she looks nothing like a ghost. Alta still has her long silky silver hair pulled up in a bun, and she is looking at me through her round silver framed granny glasses. "Azoy virgin shabbes tish, mina kind," she says. Tears well up in my eyes. I hear the words, but she has been gone for close to fifty years, and her voice is obscure.

Our annual family Passover Seder was always held in her home, a 1910 flat on Commonwealth Avenue in Buffalo, NY. I especially remember the perfect corners it had for stashing the Afikomen. After Alta's repeated appearances in my Jerusalem dining room, I decided to ask my mother about her own childhood Friday night dinners at Alta's home. "Who made Kiddush?" I asked her, my grandfather, [A443] Benny Perlman or Alta's second husband, cousin [A506] Motle Gelman.

Her response caught me off guard. "We never had Friday night dinner together with them! They went to sleep at 6:30 in the evening to get up before the crack of dawn to go to the market." It had always been clear to me that Alta worked Saturday mornings at the Broadway Market. Market day in Sokolivka was on Monday, but in America, it was Saturday. It never dawned on me that this had put a damper on Friday night dinner as well. I was taken back, but not enough to stop my barrage of questions. And Seder? It turns out that Alta held a Seder for the family every other year. So as to share Passover fairly with both sides of the family, my grandparents alternated between Buffalo and the Bronx. The next day I realized that I had missed the fine details. Who then with whom did Alta and her husband Motle have Seder on alternate years? When I ask my mother, [A444] Arlene, her response will most likely be her typical "I would rather say I don't know than give you inaccurate information." It is precisely this response that sets off my relentless chase on the net for even the most remote shred of evidence. With every census, picture, license, or certificate discovered, I get into their shoes, their heads, their veins, skin, homes, and beds but, more importantly, their hearts. What did they feel? When I weave enough of these threads together, maybe, just maybe, I will be able to tell their story. And I know that my conjecture will color some of it.

I have been investigating my family's genealogy for decades. Geni, Ancestry, My Heritage census records, newspaper archives, Ellis Island ship manifests, obituaries and more, fill my internet search history. There are so many unanswered questions, and I am waiting anxiously for the 1950 census to become public information. The hours spent searching wax, and when my husband, [A445a] David Maman, inevitably catches me on the net, he lets out an exasperated "I hope you are writing a book!"

Long before the internet, I plagued my grandparents with questions. "Koch lefel" (cooking spoon) was my well-earned nickname. I had spent much of my childhood years in both Alta's and my grandparents' home. Alta would sit me on her lap and read me "news" from the Forwards. I was notorious for turning my nose up at any morsel of food that wasn't candy, and more often than not, I was "read" an article about undernourished children who refused to eat. I can't recall my great grandmother emitting a single word about her life in Sokolivka. "It's not the first time, and it's not the last time," was her stoic response to mishaps and unfortunate events, however trivial or significant.

In contrast, her son, my grandfather Benny, the jack of all trades, mechanic and magician, entertained me with tales of his childhood in the small town of [C02b] Sokolivka. I must have asked a hundred times, "How did you get that long scar on your arm?" At ten, a Ukrainian nationalist had cut him with his bayonet. At my very own age of eight and nine, I heard the redacted versions. I always asked for more, but still listened to a lacuna filled account. They all ran for their lives, hiding in chimney' and closets. My grandfather remembered a little girl's mortifying screams, but not one kinsman dared to leave their hiding place to save her. When years later, I understood the implications, the visions turned hair raising.

Published historical accounts describe the village, the violent pogroms, and the Jewish families flee to safety. A child's mind can comprehend only parts of the horror and tragedy, but despite this, I believe that I had a reasonably clear notion of what had transpired. Later, in high school and college, when I had to submit family history papers, my grandfather Benny was the natural subject of my mismanaged interviews. "Mismanaged," as now I see that I left too many stones unturned, and too many questions remained unresolved. I was a smart-aleck ten-year-old when Alta died, but regarding my inevitable role as the family historian, I shared more with the Haggadah's fourth child, who didn't know how or what to ask. Now there is no one left with to elucidate, and when Alta appears in my dining room, I am too overcome with emotion to ask.

Out of the blue, my mother, [A444], Arleen Perlman, has started inquiring about her ancestors. I am afraid she is getting all the names straight, so when the time comes, she will be able to locate them in the white pages somewhere up in the clouds. I do not see this as a good omen, but don't acknowledge it when we speak on the phone. "What name should have been written on Bubbie's tombstone, Baila or Alta?" she asked. "Alta," I insist, as she went by Alta in all documents found online from ship manifest to her second marriage certificate. I do not recall anyone ever calling her Baila. Born about 1883, her original name Baila had been changed to Alta when she became deathly sick as a baby. Her father, [A422a] Moshe Gillman's (original last name Shestunov) 1923 death certificate in Cleveland lists Baile Liba as the deceased's mother's name. This means Bubbie had been named after her father Moshe's mother, and he had to surrender the namesake for his dear mother to a peculiar magical name that would fool the angel of death and protect his child's life. [A457] Joseph Gillman wrote that their mother [A422] Pessie Kaprov had buried five of her nine children (The names are not listed in our family tree). As Alta, Pessie's baby girl was her penultimate child, switching lovely Baila to old Alta was a no brainer. Alta definitely was an odd appellation for a child. Still, she actually did reach a ripe old age, and a half a century ago, I may have actually believed that it was precisely this legerdemain that had worked.

Fig. 26-1: [A443] Beryl (Ben), [A431] Alta, [A448] Pessie (Pauline), [A432] Avrum (Abe) Perlman, Sokolifka, 1911 (left), 1915 (right).

Fig. 26-2: [A448] Pauline Perlman in Cleveland, 1927.

Fig. 26-3: Wedding photo 1933 NYC, [A443a] Sylvia Plumka Perlman and [A443] Ben Perlman. Ben and father [A431a] David closely resemble each other.

The old photos were buried in the bottom dresser drawer in my mother's old bedroom on Hartford. After dinner at my grandparents' home, I would head upstairs to my mother, Arlene's old bedroom. After a few minutes of coloring quietly, I would inevitably turn to snoop in the dresser drawers. The old photos had always captured my curiosity, and till today, I cannot let them go. The earliest photo, taken about 1912, had been cut in two. If there was a Yiddish equivalent of "say cheese," it wasn't in the photographer's lexicon, and nobody is cracking even half a smile. Actually, two-year-old [A443] Beryl (Ben) has a small of a grin on his face. The photographer's head ducking in and out of the blanket may have amused him. Unlike his older brother [A432] Abe, he is unaware of their father's imminent departure. My grandfather is wearing a long dress, and his long blond curls indicate that he hasn't had his "upsherin"[62] yet. I will never know what my great grandfather [A431a] David Pearlman looked like in Sokolivka, as the figure next to the toddler has been cut out. Alta is holding her youngest child and mother's namesake, [A448] Pessie (Pauline Perlman), and on the right is my grandfather's five-year-old brother, [A432] Abe with a defiant look on his face. David was leaving his family in Sokolivka

---

[62] Haircutting ceremony practiced by Jews, but particularly popular in Haredi Jewish communities. It occurs most commonly when boys turn three years old.

and would be sending them tickets as soon as he had saved up enough money. No wonder they looked so grim. A mench tracht un Gott lacht. (A man's costume and God laughs.)

World War I broke out, and most transatlantic travels were suspended. It turned into nearly a decade, and the children grew up without their father. The thought struck me yesterday that as Alta's father, [A422a] Moshe and brother, [A457] Joseph Gillman had left Sokolivka in 1906, Pauline, Ben, and Abe probably never even met their grandfather [A422a] Moshe Gillman until they arrived in Cleveland. Zeide Leib, David's father, was the only grandfather they knew.

I had always known that my great grandfather [A431a] David Pearlman was the missing family member, and for the past fifty years, I have been searching for him. I looked high and low on immigration records and eventually found two possible David Pearlmans. According to one ship manifest, he had three brothers about whom I had never heard. According to the second, he had a wife [A431] "Baila" back in a place called "Sokolovka." The journey was long, and it is impossible to verify whether the site listed was a hometown or last residence before boarding the ocean liner. Clerks rarely knew how to spell the names of the towns correctly, so I temporarily settled on the latter.

At last, I thought, maybe I had found my great grandfather. And he didn't call his wife, my great grandmother, Alta. He referred to her as "Baila," which sounded so much more loving. Tentatively I settled for this great grandfather though inwardly admitting that the find was more than a bit "iffy." Years passed and then, while going through all the records on all the David Pearlmans available on FamilySearch.org, one late night in 2019, long after the date changed in the corner of my computer screen, just one more popped up and caught my eye. It was a ship manifest, and the port was Philadelphia, not Ellis Island. All along, I had been searching in vain on the wrong site. My fingers touched the computer screen. One David Pearlman, with the middle name of Hirsh (this was news to me), five foot six, (just like my grandfather Benny), with brown eyes and a wife named Alta, from the district of Kiev, landed in Philadelphia on April 16, 1913. And if I still harbored any doubts about his identity, he had $22.00 in his pocket, a ticket to Buffalo, and was heading to see his brother in law, [A427] Daniel Gillman. A smile spread across my face. I couldn't believe my eyes. I had finally found him and have since then traced his every move, from his arrival in Philadelphia on the Bresslau in April 1913 to his premature death in Cleveland, Ohio, in 1943.

I have examined that broken old photo countless times, but only recently, my eye caught one-minute detail – my grandfather's small hand is holding a man's knee. When Alta cut her ex-husband out of the photo, she intentionally left a jigsawed edge. She could not remove one more millimeter of David's presence without cutting off her son [A443] Ben's hand. Luckily for us, she had used good judgment, as he was our "Dr. Yignipitz," as he called himself when in fix-it mode. The man was a natural mechanic and had the hands of a surgeon. We believed that if he couldn't fix it, it just couldn't be fixed. The face that went with the knee was probably bearded, but I will never know for sure, as in the sepia photo sent to the family from Cleveland, [A431a] David Hirsh Pearlman had adopted the American clean-shaven look.

Supposedly Benny resembled his father David to a tee. They shared the same height, small muscular build, color, and, most importantly, a very prominent, somewhat bulbous nose. My mother recalls that they boasted the same circus tricks to entertain the children. The one I remember is the "airplane," with my grandfather lying on the floor, his legs at a 90-degree angle, and my stomach on the soles of his feet and my arms outstretched like an airplane. Years after Alta's ex-husband's death, a friend from the old country came to visit her. The father-son resemblance was so strong that when my grandfather walked through the door, Alta's friend fainted. I had heard this story countless times, and the possibility of a carbon copy or original of the love of my life has never stopped dazzling my imagination.

There is the family lore handed down, which are the stories we learned as children. Then there are the other versions we will never know. There are the documents that ancestors have kept, and then there are official records that are available as the years pass. In junior high school, I was warned by my favorite history teacher to look critically at all genealogical information about our class roots project and take much of it with a grain of salt. Our beloved grandparents might not remember the details accurately. And there was more than one reason that they never smiled in pictures. Not only was the family portrait a solemn occasion, but they also preferred to hide their rotted teeth. This did not sound outlandish to me as I clearly remembered my grandfather Benny and his mother Alta's false teeth placed in cups in the bathroom to soak overnight. And when Alta complained about a headache and said "mine cup teet mir avay," I was confident that she was talking about her teeth put away in the cup!

Sometimes, my teacher added, they might even quote fabricated names, dates, and places. Moreover, written records were not necessarily accurate either. They did not always understand the questions, and the clerks didn't comprehend their answers. And census reports? The details merely reflect the residents' claims. Oh, the wannabees. There were important reasons to become younger or older or even take a dead man's identity, like Mad Men's Don Draper.[63] I am not sure that our parents and grandparents were overjoyed with our new-found skepticism, but there was no road back to naivety. As per sifting through stories and files to find out the "truth," good luck!

The cantonists' 25- year service in the Czar's army was one the most dreaded nightmares of Russian Jewish families during the nineteenth century. My grandfather had told me stories of the "khappers" or "knoppers," as he called them. It wasn't until recently that I realized that many times the children were kidnapped by other Jews who were paid to keep other children out of the Czar's army. It turns out that about 200 years ago, great grandfather Moshe Gillman's grandfather, Shustenov, was about to be drafted when fortuitous tragedy struck and, the Gillman boy died. A clerk was paid for the dead boy to be buried as Shustenov, and the real Shustenov stayed out of the army by becoming Gillman. I can't help but laugh as I think of Ace Ventura's[64] outrageous Einhorn is Finkel and Finkel is Einhorn. [A422a] Zeide Moishe's children, [A423] Haya Sara, [A427] Daniel, [A431] Alta Baila Leiba and [A457] Joseph were born Gillman, and Zeide Moishe remained Gillman until he died in 1923 in Cleveland Ohio.

Inaccuracies were repeated in census after census, license after license until they appeared to be factual. I take this for granted. But I wish I had been forewarned that what one looks for can be right under one's nose. One may go out on the hunt to find details that were right in front of oneself, right from the beginning. Moreover, with time, one views each character, each photo,

---

[63] Fictional television character and protagonist of the series, *Mad Men*.

[64] Fictional film character, Ace Ventura, is a zany private investigator who specializes in finding missing animals.

every decision from a different perspective. And sometimes a small detail dismissed a hundred times before takes center stage. Even worse, decades can pass before suddenly, the vital connection is made before what was so scared at the time changed.

My initial searches on Ellis Island site immediately bore fruit. I knew the year and the name of the ship that brought Alta and her children to the United States. My grandfather had proudly remembered his ship, the Olympic White Star Liner – the Titanic's sister ship. I had forgotten that their ticket was tucked away in my old roots project. The tickets would have spared me precious time but denied me the delectable drama of the hunt. After hours of searching the Ellis Island site, I found their records. My throat constricted as the list opened on my computer screen. The children's misspelled names on the ship manifest were easily identifiable. Avrum was Avrun, Beryl was Beizel, Pessie – Pessia, - and Alta was Otta. In addition, someone had changed their last name from Pearlman to Perel. Alta, Abraham, Beryl, and Pessie arrived at Ellis Island on April 13, 1921. A day later, they were reunited with their husband and father. [A431a] David Pearlman had paid their way and was waiting for them in Cleveland. I was born on April 14, 39 years later. I wonder if anyone remembered that Passover morning, when my father called from the hospital with the news, that it was precisely the same date the family was both reunited and broken up in America.

Alta's Sokolivka was a small town not far from Rabbi Nachman's[65] [C36] Uman, in between [C13] Kiev and [C29] Odessa. Her ancestors from the Kaprov side had lived there for generations. [A422a] Moshe from [C11] Gaicin and [A422] Pessie from [C02b] Sokolivka were married around 1865. Alta's older sister Haya was at least fifteen years her senior. I had never noted their age difference until recently when I was looking for more about Motle or David, and my search suddenly produced [A423] Haya Pridludny (Pribludny). Unlike most of the relatives who gained entry to the new world through Ellis Island, Haya and two of her children, [A424] Rose and [A426] Haim, were processed in St. Alban, Vermont. They had been through Gehenna[66] in the pogroms of 1919. As [A457] Joseph Gillman and his father, [A422a] Moshe, immigrated to the U.S. in 1906, and [A427] Daniel and [A431a] David in 1912 and 1913, before World War I, the four men were spared the worst ordeals of the impending pogroms.

[A431] Alta, her sister [A423] Haya and sister in law Sheva and their children followed their men across the Atlantic close to a decade later.[67] They had escaped narrowly after burying their loved ones. Tragically, Haya arrived a widow with only two of her four children. Haya's daughter [A425] Baila Liba, who shared the same namesake as my [A431] great grandmother and her son [A432] Avraham (possibly, the same namesake as my great uncle Abe) along with their father Eliezer, were murdered in the pogrom. The two sisters, Alta and [A423] Haya Sara,

---

[65] Founder of the mystically inclined Breslov Hasidic dynasty, located halfway between Odessa and Kiiv.

[66] Gehenna is a small valley in Jerusalem. In the Hebrew Bible, Gehenna was initially where some kings of Judah sacrificed their children by fire. Thereafter, it was deemed to be cursed. In rabbinic literature, Gehenna is a destination of the wicked.

[67] Editor's note: Not uncommonly, only one family member, often the husband, initially came to America with plans to have the spouse and child follow shortly after that. But the years of World War I disrupted plans, and the remaining parents and children might stay separated for at least a decade with little communication. The new inhabitants worked exceedingly hard, and virtually every penny earned was remit for the rest of the family's passage.

were not on speaking terms. When had the animosity begun? Here the family lore and official documents do not jibe.

Where could they start to tell about their ordeal? How long did it take to put their nightmare into a narrative? The horror of their experience was indescribable. I suspect they choked on the words that could have revealed their ordeal to their men. As a matter of fact, upon arrival in Cleveland, Alta had separated from her husband [A431a] David so tout de suite (at once, right away) that I think he was spared the anguish and agony of their story. Did the children ever tell him? I doubt that [A443] Ben did. Perhaps their father [A431a] David heard it years later from [A448] Pauline or [A432] Abe. My hunch is they didn't have to say a word. All of the Sokolivkars, no matter where residing, knew precisely what had happened.

It wasn't the first time, and it wouldn't be the last time I heard Bubbie saying that rampaging marauders had a set scenario. Partial images sufficed to reveal the full horror. It is 1971. My parents and grandparents are dressed to the nines for the gala Hebrew day school fundraiser premiere of "Fiddler on the Roof." The film had received rave reviews, and the event was the talk of the community. But Anatevka's red thatched roofs on the enormous silver screen bore too much resemblance to those in my grandfather's squelched memories of Sokolivka. The bigger than life images of the shtetl together with the "mild" bowdlerized pogrom on the night of Zeitel's wedding were just too much to bear.

Benny headed for the nearest exit and took refuge in the lobby. Many other Sokolivkans had settled in Buffalo, and I knew them and their families well. I never thought to ask Benny if any other landsleit had joined him in the lobby of the movie theater that night. If so, I imagine they just stood in silence and rolled their eyes.

In August 1918, the pogrom led by Ukrainian nationalists began en route to [C17] Konela and ended with over 150 dead and hundreds raped and maimed. It resulted in a syndrome that had not yet been given a name but revealed ubiquitous manifestations: Insomnia, nightmares, repressed emotions, silence, vertigo, separation anxiety, panic attacks, claustrophobia, asthma, and more.

Then came the summer of 1919. There were the Nationalists and Bolsheviks, and the historians attribute different pogroms to each. It was all the "zelba zach" (for all the good they did me) for the Jews of Sokolivka. Alta and the children are locked in a crowded, stifling attic along with their neighbors and relatives. I believe I imbibed the plot and details before encountering the fairy tales, "The Three Bears" and "Little Red Riding Hood." The counter-revolutionaries were threatening to burn the men women and children alive. At the same time, the neighboring gentile homeowners pleaded with them to abort the plan as the fire would only spread to their homes. Thirteen-year-old [A432] Abe, refused to be burned alive and jumped out the window. Shots were heard, and [A431] Alta was sure her firstborn was dead. The homeowners finally prevailed, and the Jews were released. Downstairs, they couldn't believe their eyes. Abe, who was fluent in Yiddish and "Goyish," was waiting for the family in the yard below. Somehow, he had convinced the marauders that he had been caught up in the scuffle and had nothing to do with the Jews in the attic.

That was Benny's narrative. Alta never said a word. One Friday night, shortly after Alta passed away, we were gathered around the dinner table, reminiscing with [A448] Aunt Pauline from

Cleveland. "Remember," she turned to her brother Ben, "when they came through the town on horseback, and one grabbed Ma and galloped away?" My grandfather's face froze. I thought that he had shared his entire array of horror tales with me. But this was one that he did not want to remember, let alone share. I was on the verge of shaking my head and saying to [A448] Aunt Pauline, "And then what happened?!" I persisted. "The relatives chased them with money and jewels, and they let her go." That was the first time and the last time anyone ever mentioned the scariest moment of their lives. I never brought it up again.

[A443] Benny was notorious for making up Yiddish gibberish. He sang a children's nursery rhyme that made me roar with laughter. It sounded like a fifteen-syllable word with a flatulent center. Oxenabeeben fartzenatzegen loyfenatsupes. I never got a real translation from him and could never figure out the meaning. Over five decades later, I think I can break it up. I suggest, oxen and babes, horses and goats, running on two feet. My translation is not quite precise, and I doubt that Sokolivka was quite that bucolic.

Theirs was not the only town that had been burned down. [A431] Alta was one of the thousands who had to find an escape route. Jews from Ukraine were pouring into Romania, where the Jewish Joint Distribution Committee set up refugee camps. For the next two years, they hid in fields and barns, and in horse-drawn wagons covered themselves with straw, placing their fate and possessions in smugglers' hands until they reached Bucharest.

The journey began with the four Pearlman's heading toward the riverbank, where smugglers were paid to take them to the next safe place. It was a small rowboat and had room for only three more passengers. Alta's heart was between a rock and a hard place. Who should be left to wait on the river bank for the boat to come back? Leaving [A448] Pauline, a nine-year-old girl, was out of the question, and after the window incident, who could trust Abe to wait patiently? Did they exchange any words? Did either boy protest? She had no other choice. [A443] Benny waited days in the fields near the river until the men came back to get him. I would like to have been a fly on that riverbank just as he caught sight of their boat. All's well that ends well, but really [A431] Alta Baila Liba, how could you have abandoned our Benny like that? As a child, I had heard the story many times. Yet, I could never muster the nerve to ask her how she chose who to take and who to leave. The ripples of salvation grapple with the ripples of trauma. That fateful reunion with the smugglers would forever turn a boat on the water into paradise. Fishing and boating became my grandfather's haven.

The four Pearlmans continued to Rotterdam and then boarded the Olympic White Liner in South Hampton, England. Alta was seasick, and Ben ran free on the ocean liner. The Olympic White Liner was the Titanic's sister ship. One decade and one world war in its resume, it had probably lost much of its luster, but for Ben, the jaded but luckier sister was heaven. For the first time, he saw a man playing the piano. To add to Ben's fascination, the piano player was black, and he couldn't take his eyes off of the man's face. He watched well-dressed people strolling around the deck without a worry. And the motor room. The aha moment came when he decided to become a mechanic. Maybe not yet, but this was definitely the first time Benjamin saw a motor, and he must have fallen in love. On April 13, 1921, the four Pearlmans arrived at Ellis Island. From there, they continued to Cleveland, Ohio where [A431a] David Pearlman, [A422a] Moshe and [A457] Joseph Gillman were waiting for Alta and the children. The story goes that Alta's older sister [A423] Haya was waiting at the train station – and couldn't control the urge to tell Alta that

155

her husband David was betraying her. David met them at the station with a gold Waltham watch for the wife he hadn't seen in eight years. But Alta was indignant and threw it on the ground in a fit of anger. Ben picked it up and pocketed the treasure. I know the watch. Where did an eleven-year-old hide such a valuable piece? Did it need repair after being flung on the ground? Did hunger pangs ever tempt him to sell it? I will never know.

My grandfather [A443] Benny remembered that they were taken to David's home, and claimed they didn't sleep there even once. The house was clean and presentable, and it was apparent that the father they hadn't seen in close to a decade had prepared it for their arrival. The man had paid for four transatlantic tickets. Alta and the children were meant to join him in Cleveland years earlier, but Benny had a contagious eye condition that could have compromised their entry at Ellis Island. I often wonder if he was aware of the ramifications that delay had on their lives. Even if I had thought of it in time, the words would have never left my lips. In any case, David must have had much more than a token of intent to keep his family together. Fifty years ago, it hadn't occurred to me to ask where the four heartbroken souls went to sleep. I am still searching for the word that might accurately describe such excruciating disappointment.

I am a cynic and never hesitate to question family lore. I am well aware that it sometimes conflicts with official documentation. I also know that official documentation can be even more inaccurate than the colorful anecdotes. It's when you think you know that you don't know... you know? But, some stories have been passed down so faithfully and so often that I didn't give the accusation a second thought. Once again, I did not want to call it a night without a single catch. I had tried [A423] Haya Pribludna's name with the most impossible spelling variations imaginable, and ultimately, it was worth every flip and switch. There they were. She and her two surviving children were processed at St. Albans and entered the United States through Buffalo. She sailed alone, and her children, [A424] Ruchel and [A426] Haim, arrived on a different liner. Her brother [A457] Joseph had paid for their tickets. The price for the three ocean liner tickets must have been a hefty sum for her younger brother to finance. Maybe he asked his brother [A427] Daniel to share the burden, but Daniel had just paid for his wife and daughters' fares. [A422a] Moshe Gillman, her father, was indigent and couldn't have contributed much. Clearly, relatives pitched in to save their stranded families, but the ship's manifest only indicates that they have relatives who will support them in America. They do not mention the various Jewish refugee agencies that gave financial backing as well. These facts were all interesting, but the real curveball was the date of the Pribludnas' arrival – May 1922, one year after Alta had set foot in Cleveland. I had heard repeatedly that [A423] Haya was the catalyst in Alta and David's breakup, but now I realize that the bearer of bad tidings had to have been someone or at least somewhere else.

Nevertheless, in 1922, two years after [A431] Alta and the children arrived in Cleveland, she and [A431a] David divorced. The 1920 census showed that David was a boarder in Rosie Fernberg's home. She was the head of household with two small boys, and even if they were lovers, Rosie wasn't the one David chose to marry. Eight months after the divorce, David married Sadie Goldstein. I recently met David and Sadie's granddaughter, my first cousin, once removed, Doreen, who sent me photos of their graves. Naturally, we have different perspectives on Sadie and Alta. It is not sure, but Sadie likely was the other woman. I found David and Sadie's marriage license replete with addresses. Circumstantially speaking, in 1921, they probably were not strangers. With the gift of google satellite maps, I viewed their old homes while sitting on the other side of the world.

New alliances had formed in Cleveland. Young [A448] Pauline was taken in by David and Sadie. She and her children became close to David and Sadie's daughters and grandchildren. David was cut out of the family picture and rarely mentioned. Our Cleveland connection embraced Pauline and her family but didn't include David and Sadie. We also lost contact with Abe's family. I recently spoke to my second cousin, David, Pauline's grandson, whom I haven't seen in almost 50 years. It should have been obvious, but the thought had never crossed my mind [A454] David Kaye was named after David Pearlman.

They had reached the shores of the promised land, but Alta and the children were still starving. Alta eked out a living as a peddler, and the boys hawked newspapers on the corners of Cleveland's streets. The newbies tried to fit in. Alta noticed people making chewing motions with their mouths while walking down the road. Assuming this was American custom, she imitated them until realizing that she was the only one not chewing gum. Abe came home with another Clevelander's bicycle, and someone convinced Ben that the friendly American greeting was "go to hell." He fell for it. He also believed that gold lined the streets, and when he found a dollar on the sidewalk – he immediately dropped it into the palm of a panhandler. No worries – there would be more around the corner. In the long run, he wasn't mistaken. Once young Pauline applied so much rouge and lipstick that her big brother Ben panicked and slapped her across the face. It may have been out of concern for her reputation, or out of jealousy that she had the luxury of living in David and Sadie's home.

Once Alta intimated to my mother [A444] Arlene, "If I knew then what I know now, I would have done things differently." She just might have given David a second chance. Today I wonder if when she reached Cleveland, Alta didn't collapse. For a short period, the children attended the Dike Elementary School (Now Dike School of the Arts, 2501 E 61st St, Cleveland), where the boys sometimes got into trouble. Abe threatened his teacher Miss Rose, and Ben pencil-stabbed a boy who called him a "greenhorn." The principal, Martha Graham, hauled the greenhorn into her office, whispering, "too bad Ben, you are going to be put on a small boat by yourself and sent back to Russia." As a child, I cried every time he retold this story. She had to have known the circumstances. How could she be so cruel? In any case, Ben's "deportment" improved. He never got into trouble again until his dying day. By the time he left the Dike Elementary School, he had put his dexterity to better use and snagged a penmanship award. It was this steady hand that later removed splinters, planted flower and vegetable gardens, fixed cars, built planes for Curtiss, performed card tricks, spun tops, and upon request, repaired broken toys. No job was ever too big or too small. In the 1930 census, David Pearlman reported that he was married for the first time at age 16. And Alta? Her documents show she was 19!

Both [A431] Alta's and [A431a] David's tombstones support this information. I stared incredulously at the records. In 1901 [A422] Pessie Gillman died of pneumonia, and Alta and Joseph became orphans as teenagers. A few years later, Moshe Gillman married off his 19-year old daughter to a 16-year old boy. With no dowry, I suspect that there were few other options, and Alta didn't balk. While the Gillman's were destitute, David's father Leib, who owned grain mills, was a well to do man. The groom gifted Alta with a seal fur coat, which Alta, and to avert gossip and the evil eye, she wore inside out. I suppose that in Sokolivka, this made sense. In a place where a young child could be renamed Alta, the seal fur could be in, and the lining out. In addition to the mills, Leib owned or leased the land where kosher slaughtering was performed. They ate well, and my grandfather did not remember being hungry until the Russian revolution. Jealousy, perhaps this is how the rift between Haya and Alta began.

[A432] Avrum was born about 1906, and [A443] Beryl, about four years later. The story goes that while [A431] Alta was still nursing baby [A443] Ben, her stomach kept on growing larger, and she believed her days were numbered. Fortunately, the rabbi, who knew better, assuaged her fears. "Don't worry," he comforted her "in about four months, you'll have a baby." It seems that even over a hundred years ago, the village rabbi knew that breastfeeding was hardly a reliable form of birth control. His prediction came true, and [A448] Pessie was born a year after [A443] Beryl. David left the family for America sometime in 1912 or 1913, and Abe was probably the only child with real memories of him. Alta remarried in Cleveland, in December 1924, two and a half years after her divorce from David. She married her first cousin [A506] Motle (Max) Gelman, and the 1930 census shows Alta and her second husband on Pratt Street in Buffalo. Alta's older brother, [A427] Daniel, lived in Buffalo, and I imagine she preferred to distance herself from Cleveland. It seems that Alta was what my kids call a cougar. Marrying a husband three years her junior didn't faze her in the least. The census shows that like David, Motle was three years younger than his wife. He was a 36-year-old bachelor when he married my great grandmother. I was still trying to grasp the age difference when, suddenly, a thought crossed my mind. David and Motle were contemporaries, but Motle's family was poor and David was a rich man's son. It must have stung Motle when the rich boy took his cousin Alta Beila Liba. I've gone over the photos with a fine-tooth comb repeatedly. Motle was just as handsome, but even if he had harbored feelings for her way back then, Alta had no dowry, and he had no means to marry her.

I thought of my grandfather, [A443] Ben, who always showed affection for his attractive older cousins, [A427] Daniel's daughter [A430] Dvossie (Dorothy) and [A423] Haya's daughter [A424] Ruchel (Rose). I found a picture Ben had prepared to send to Rose, signed Love, Kid Beigel Dempsy. Maybe he got cold feet about giving her the photo, but he adored her nevertheless. The rift between the sisters is still unclear. Fortunately, their children harbor no animosity.

Did [A506] Motle have his eye on [A431] Alta all those years? He was a handsome young man and a professional carpenter to boot. Later, he was one of the few men in the family who had a vocation, and he was reasonably literate. Alta had been alone in Sokolivka for more than eight years. Did he happen by her house to see if she needed any repairs? Was he one of the relatives who took off after the horseman that galloped away with his dear cousin Alta? I can only wonder.

[A431] Alta and [A506] Motle were married for over 35 years but did not have children together. I want to ask, Alta, did you love him? And I presume that she did. My sister [A446] Sandra Maxine (Sara Malka) is named after Max and is the only namesake for his entire family. None of his siblings had left Ukraine. After the German invasion of 1941, three of the children were all murdered by the Einzatzgruppen. In 1922, they had stayed in the old country, but Motle left on his own for America. The news of Alta's divorce may have reached the refugee camp in

Romania. Perhaps, just perhaps, it was the love of his first cousin Alta that saved him from the fate that awaited his family.

Ben must have been visiting Alta and Motle on Pratt Street when he met his good friend Izzy Goldman. It's all in the census records of 1930. The Goldman's were Alta's neighbors. Is it the Izzy Goldman I knew? I called my mother, Arlene. "Did Izzy have sisters? What were their names?" Mom is a people person, so I was not surprised when she rattled their names off one by one. While looking back at the list to compare and a smile spread across my face. Without a doubt, it was the same young man – my grandfather's longtime pal and eventual partner in crime.

But then, I wouldn't call it a crime, and I am not even entirely confident he was truly a partner, even though part of me wished it to be true. When the federal census is taken, obviously, not all Americans can be accounted for. I have viewed census reports that include inmates of prisons and hospitals, but the homeless remain uncounted. [A443] Ben Perlman was a perfect example. In 1930 Ben was not listed as living in Buffalo with his mother, Alta, or in Cleveland with father [A431a] David or his married siblings [A432] Abe or [A448] Pauline Fox. The great depression had hit, and for all practical purposes, he was homeless. It is not clear where he lived between 1930 and 1933 when he met my grandmother [A443a] Sylvia Plumka in New York. They married in July 1933 at the Grand Concourse. Sylvia's parents made a wedding for them, but not one relative from Ben's side was able to attend. Alta and Motle remained in Buffalo. David, Abe, and Pauline remained in Cleveland. They couldn't spare the train fare for the trip or consider taking off from work.

[A443] Ben and [A443a] Sylvia made their home in Buffalo to be near [A431] Alta and [A456] Motle, who had a stand at the Broadway Market. The newlyweds rented a room on Spring Street from the Strauss family. Ben sold fruits and vegetables from a truck, eventually opening a wrecking yard. Actually, David, Abe, Ben, and Uncle Daniel were all in the scrap business. When my [A444] mother Arlene was born in 1937, the Perlmans were renting a flat on Sycamore Street, and the Gelmans resided on Adams. Ben and Sylvia sought better housing on Brunswick Avenue, and Alta followed suit. But it wasn't that simple. Upon finding the 1940 census records with addresses and all, I immediately called my mother Arlene to tell her the good news.

As usual, I had to fend a semisweet honey-coated barb, "Why do you care? You should have been someone else's daughter." And then she relented. "Of course, I remember Adams Street. That's where Alta and Benny had a nasty, screaming, name-calling fight." I knew that this was a rarity, and I had never witnessed one. It seems that while the Perlmans were visiting the Gelmans, little [A444] Arlene was playing in the yard, digging up the garden. When the owner noticed the damage and scolded her, Ben lost his cool and screamed back at his mother's landlord. In retrospect, perhaps the drama was a convenient setup. Alta would have to move immediately as Ben would never set foot in her home again on Adams Street. Not so nice words were exchanged and I can guess the coda. "I guarantee you. So help me, god." And that's how they ended up together on Brunswick.

Although [A444] Arlene was Alta's fifth grandchild, she was Alta's only Buffalonian "einekel,"[68] and they shared hours together daily, maintaining a unique relationship over the years. And Arlene was present during a second fight over a decade later. This time it was over Abe, who was planning a visit from Cleveland. [A432] Abe Pearlman had divorced his first wife [A432a] Freda and remarried. His second wife [A432b] Alva was not Jewish, and Alta was beside herself over his marrying out of the faith. Benny adored Abe and refused to accept any slight or insult directed at his older brother. The brother whose spirit and gall he admired, the one who nicknamed him "kilavotch" because of his hernia, he who once miraculously appeared at his side in the Cleveland market to cuff an assailant and saved his life. A verbal battle ensued, and this time Arlene was old enough to understand and remember the words that were being flung back and forth across the room. Ben prevailed, the visit took place, and Alta bit her lip. Sadly, in 1962 Abe died of lung cancer at a young age. Since childhood, he had survived a litany of perils and had always emerged valiant. I am afraid that Abe died before he and Alta could make peace. Alta, Ben, and Pauline were devastated. They had been through so many trials and tribulations together. If only he could have surprised them just one more time. Alignments, realignments. Ben collected his mother Alta from her flat on Commonwealth, and they rode in his 1960 white Buick to Abe's funeral in Cleveland. Speechless. I wasn't there, but I know how silent they could be.

Fig. 26-4: 1948 Engagement party of [A430] Dorothy Gelman Kareff's sister-in-law Natalie nee Kareff.

---

[68] A Yiddish word whose root contains a fundamentally Jewish idea. Einekel means "grandchild", and may derive from the story of Moses and the Burning Bush. Moses sees the bush burning it is not consumed. Grandchildren implies Jewish continuity, a legacy never consumed, but lasting forever.

Back L-R: Ukn, Ukn; Jerry Miller; [A430a] Ben Kareff (Dorothy's husband); [A429] Gordon Mittleman (Daniel's grandson); [A427] Daniel Gillman ; Ukn, Ukn, Ukn ; [A443] Ben Perlman
Front L-R: Ukn; Natalie Kareff Miller; [A430] Dorothy Gillman Kareff; Eilene Kareff Haber; Ukn; [A444] Arlene Perlman Rossen; [A431] Alta Gillman Gelman; [A443a] Sylvia Plumka Perlman.

Fig. 26-5: 1957 Wedding of [A444] Arlene Perlman and Allen Rossen:
L-R: [A455a] Richard Rock, [A445] Marlene Fox Rock, [A453a] Irving Chaitoff, [A453] Diane Fox Chaitoff, [A448a] Jack Fox, [A448] Pauline Pearlman Fox, [A444] Arlene Perlman Rossen, [A444a] Allen Rossen, [A443a] Sylvia Plumka Perlman, [A443] Ben Perlman, [A449] Robert Fox, Mrs. and Mr. Rock (Marlene's in-laws).

While living in the Brunswick neighborhood, Alta was a member of the Humboldt Orthodox Center synagogue in Buffalo, NY. Her first cousin, [A528] Gedaliah Kaprow, became the rabbi of the congregation and the family took pride in belonging to his synagogue. Like his cousins, he was a fellow Sokolivkan and survivor of the 1919 pogrom. In a bustling industrial city like Buffalo, with neighboring Niagara Falls, he was able to boast many influential congregants who were involved in Jewish causes around the world.

[A529] Shalom Moishe, their son, better known as Maurice, also became a rabbi. While a Commander and on active duty as the US Navy Chaplain, he gave the opening prayer to the US Senate on September 29, 2008.

Fig. 26-6: [A529] Rabbi Maurice Kaprow.

I am trying to piece the dateline together, and it looks like the spring of 1944 when the Germans were desperate for supplies, and they were willing to release Jews for a price. In 1944 my mother was in first grade, and her good friend and classmate was Deanne Abelson. The Abelsons lived next door to [A528] Rabbi Gedalya Kaprow, whose home was on Hamlin Road. [A444] Arlene and Deannie always walked home from school together, frequently stopping at the Kaprows' for freshly baked cookies. [A528a] Gerry Kaprow, an excellent baker, recalls my mom. The delicious baked goods may have been meant for the family as well, but I think first and foremost, they were intended for private meetings held by the rabbi at his home. These were desperate times. One day Arlene and Deannie had stopped by for cookies and happened on a quorum of men seated at the dining room table. Max Yellen, a prominent attorney, was talking about "buying" Jews. The girls ran home flabbergasted. How and why would someone buy Jews? The idea was hardly unfamiliar to their Sokolivkan relatives, but it is difficult to imagine how my grandparents explained such an outrageous notion to a pair of incredulous first graders.

In 1943 Alta's son, [A432] Abe Pearlman, and her son in law [A448a] Jack Fox of Cleveland were serving in the U.S. Armed Forces. In Buffalo, [A443] Ben Perlman was employed in the wartime industry, working the swing shift for Curtiss Aeroplane and Motor Company. He recounted how one of his co-workers would gently lean into his ear and whisper, "Hitler's gonna get you." Perhaps it was on one of those days that he welded a child-sized ring from airplane metal and engraved a heart on it for Arlene. In Cleveland, on April 14, 1943, [A431a] David Pearlman suddenly died at the young age of 55. He was driving his scrap wagon when he suddenly fell unconscious. [A452] Julius Fox was the family member present noted on the death certificate. I can't help but note the coincidence. This date was the same when he was reunited and separated from his family in 1921. Ben didn't want to be burdened with a suitcase, rolled up a change of clothes in what was yesterday's newspaper, and boarded the train to Cleveland for his father's funeral.

[A431] Alta and [A456] Motle manned their produce stand at the Broadway Market. They lived frugally but knew well that if you looked out for the pennies, the dollars would take care of themselves. As [A444] Arlene spent many an afternoon with her grandmother, Alta, helping her prepare for her citizenship test, which Alta passed with flying colors. She was also present when the accountant happily told Alta that she would not have to pay any income tax. This news was unacceptable to Alta, who insisted, "I want Uncle Sam to know that I worked!" And she did. I remember her stand on the Broadway Market, where she worked until her death in 1971 at the age of 85.

Last year during Friday night dinner, my mother's friend, Marsha, was reminiscing about her father, Izzy Goldman's Zionist endeavors. This included smuggling guns across Lake Ontario for the fledgling State of Israel on or about 1948. Marsha had even ridden in the passenger's seat, as an innocent-looking decoy while her father drove across the Canadian border with guns stashed in the back of the truck. "Didn't your grandfather have a cache of guns, she asked?" He was a jack of all trades, but I don't remember any guns, and neither did my mother. But Marsha insisted. "Your grandfather, [A443] Ben, was part of my dad's crew. There were five of them your grandfather, Harry B, and..." I have already mentioned Izzy and remember him, my grandfather's close friend, very well. The two young men who had met near Alta's house on Pratt Street became best buddies, married two Sylvias with almost identical hairdos and cooking repertoires, and went fishing together regularly on Lake Ontario. Strangely, I don't remember my grandfather ever bringing home fish, except as fertilizer to bury in the flower garden. Once, when I was on a boat in the middle of Lake Ontario with my grandparents and their friends, the motor suddenly died. The adults spoke nervously about waiting for nightfall to alert the coast guard with rescue flares, but I wasn't concerned. Grandfather Benny was on his knees with his head lowered into the hull where the engine was hidden, toiling patiently with a can opener. The roar of the motor, followed by applause, didn't surprise me. If I were Izzy, I absolutely would have wanted Ben Pearlman on my boat.

Was he, or was he not engaged in activity that violated the United States prewar neutrality laws? His status on Izzy's crew was circumstantial. [A528] Rabbi Kaprow was Alta's first cousin, and the entire extended family was his congregants. Like the Gelmans and Pearlmans, Izzy and Sylvia Goldman belonged to the Humboldt Orthodox Center and even lived directly across the street from the rabbi's home. Both Rabbi Kaprow and Max Yellen were notable leaders, engaging in refugee rescue, Zionist activities, and Jewish education. Over the years, Ben was a faithful supporter of all of their causes. I know Ben and Izzy were best buddies, and Marsha, Izzy's daughter, insists they were a team. In the worst-case scenario, they would have had the rabbi's support and Max's legal counsel. Arms smuggling was a felony, and even 25 years later, the smallest hint of admission could have incriminated several accomplices. I had interviewed my grandfather at length twice, in junior high school and college. I suspect he didn't want to get anyone in trouble. I habitually badgered him for more stories, but never once did he mention arms smuggling across the Canadian border, and now there is nobody left to ask.

In the late 1940s, a stroke left [A506] Motel paralyzed. Alta took him to a private facility in the New York area for rehabilitation, but the efforts were to no avail. For about a decade, he was mostly homebound, and Alta ran the stand at the market single-handedly. They moved from Brunswick to Commonwealth in the North Park neighborhood. Their home was near the corner of Commonwealth and Hertel, just a few doors away from the Sokolivkan Anshe Emes Synagogue. The house I remember so well was a turn of the century two-family structure, replete with fireplace, balcony and owners, Annie and Benny Kassirer – who treated Alta like family.

Bubbie's house was a second home for Sandra and me. We were always welcome there and were free to play as we pleased. Our favorite game was running in circles on top of the living room furniture, jumping from sofa to armchair, armchair to the sofa and back again. Alta never complained. Upon departure, we got a hug and a kiss, and our great grandmother's formulaic send-off was "Ich dank der fer kimen un ich dank der for avec gayin." ("I thank you for coming and I thank you for leaving.")

In 1970, [A431] Alta suffered a heart attack and never fully recovered. The evening before she died, we had Friday night dinner while Alta slept in the bedroom that shared a door with the dining room. She wanted to die in her own home, and her physician Dr. Fracasso was holding her hand when she passed away that Shabbat morning.

Old-timers in general and Sokolivkans, in particular, are known to be stoic, and this was the first time I had ever seen my grandfather cry. Pauline was overcome with emotion. She fainted three times, once when her mother's body was removed by the undertaker, again at the funeral home, and finally at the cemetery when Alta's remains were lowered into the ground. Years prior, she had come by bus from Cleveland to visit her sick mother, leaving an ailing husband behind. When asked how she could leave a sick hubby at home, she replied without batting an eyelash. "A person can have several husbands, but you can have only one mother!"

The week of Shiva was over, and attorney Max Yellin had work ahead of him as Alta had refused to leave a will. He astutely asked if there were any other siblings not present or deceased. [A443] Ben and [A448] Pauline nodded, and Max notified Abe's Family. I had my own child historian's agenda. As [A444] Arlene and cousin [A453] Diane were packing up Alta's belongings, I insisted on being bequeathed three things; the old Victrola, Zeide Moishe Gillman's oval glass 1920 portrait, and Bubbie's silver-rimmed granny glasses.

Alta's death ultimately changed our lives in many ways. First and foremost, my parents' home became the center of family activity and holidays. Arlene gladly accepted her fate as the designated torch-bearer, and she has held it high carrying it way beyond expectation for almost half a century. The first holiday without Bubbie was Passover, and our Cleveland cousins joined us for Passover Seder. The [A454] Kayes (Chaitoff) and [A448] Pauline and [A448a] Jack Fox celebrated with us for the first time. It was just the beginning. The growing guest list and the table leaves were regular partners in a perpetual juggling act. Holiday and Sabbath tables were filled with guests that were family, friends, and strangers. This included aunts, uncles, and cousins from far and near, newcomers to town, neighbors, relatives and relatives of relatives, new and itinerant rabbis, cantors, students, and any new face in the Friday challah line at Schroeders Bakery. Once, my father, Allen, rose from the table and headed for the kitchen where he asked my mother, "Cookie, just one more time, what is the man's name who is sitting on my left?"

Alta had nine grandchildren. [A432] Abe Pearlman had five children, three with [A432a] Frieda: [A433] Annette (Lynn), [A434] Shirley (Amato), and [A436] Emanuel, and two with his second wife, [A432b] Alva: [A439] Rita Sue (Mahle) and [A442] Joyce Segulin). [A443] Ben and [A443a] Sylvia Pearlman had an only daughter, my mother, [A444] Arlene (Rossen); and [A448] Pauline and [A448a] Jack Fox had three children: [A449] Robert, [A453] Diane Chaitkoff), and [A455] Marlene (Zweig).

For the past two years, I've searched for relatives from both the Gillman and Pearlman sides that I had yet to meet. I originally knew the names of my second cousins from [A457] Joseph Gillman's B'nai Khaim family tree. Several of the Cleveland cousins had taken Ancestry or My Heritage DNA tests.

Fig. 26-7: [A432] Abe, [A434] Shirley, [A433] Annette, [A436] Emanuel (Sonny) Pearlman, 1943.

They, too, were searching for relatives, and I lucked out, though where I live in Israel, the kit is "not available." [A440] Lesa Jusko responded to my email, and we compared notes. Shortly after, while in Buffalo, I touched the phone icon on Facebook and presto – Lesa answered. We spoke for the first time -for almost an hour. I had also called [A435] Cheryl Amatto Lidawer and told her we were cousins and that I lived in Israel. "Cool," she said. Her husband was Israeli, and they had relatives from his side in Ashdod.

Cheryl was hosting a party, and we were cut short but became Facebook friends. Then I called again while in Buffalo, and we reminisced about our respective grandfathers and families. [A440] Lesa and [A435] Cheryl, first cousins, had never met each other. We all were eager to meet, but it was still winter, and the days were short, and we were unable to set a date.

My next Buffalo visit was in the summer, and on the fourth of July, my mother asked to visit her grandmother Alta's grave at the Sokolivkan cemetery, The Holy Order of the Living. Upon our return home, I decided to make one last attempt to find Doreen Friedman Zupan, David Pearlman's granddaughter from his second marriage with Sadie Goldstein. I found Doreen on Facebook and placed the call, not knowing where to begin to introduce myself should my cousin answer. To my surprise, she took the call. We had never met or even spoken before. She had just come home from the cemetery herself after visiting her uncle Abe's grave. My proverbial socks were knocked off. And then she Whatsapped me photos of David and Sadie Pearlman's graves. I stood with my mouth agape. A picture of David was on the monument. I possessed only one other, taken 20 some years earlier. The inscriptions confirmed the details I had already found. [A431a] David Pearlman's middle name was indeed Hirsh, and his father, my great, great grandfather was Leib. Sadie's grave shows that she had remarried. This finding explained why I couldn't find a trace of her after David's death.

Doreen, too was interested in a meeting. The reunion was taking shape. The next call was to [A451] Michelle Fox Moss, whom I had met with her family in Israel over twenty years ago. She, too, was planning to attend and was going to notify her sister, [A450] Denise Fox Brewster. Unlike the Buffalo Perlmans, the Foxes of Cleveland had maintained a closer tie with David Pearlman's family and knew Doreen Friedman from childhood. Our reunion group was growing. Hours later, while I was shopping at the store, Bed Bath & Beyond, my phone rang. The unidentified caller was my cousin [A454] David Kaye telephoning from Florida. Michelle had given him my number. I hadn't seen him for almost 50 years. Though our families had shared many an event, I had never really ever had held a conversation with David. I walked up and down the aisles oblivious to all around me. We laughed and cried while we remembered our grandparents, their love and attention, the delicacies served in their homes, and of course, their quirks and idiosyncrasies. David was too far away to join us, but he was very interested in connecting with the rest of the cousins of the Pearlman clan. Our venue would be the restaurant at the Holiday Inn in Mayfield, Ohio.

My mom had been expressing a wish to visit her great grandfather, [A422a] Moshe Gillman's grave in Cleveland, and I found a photo of his tombstone on A Million Graves site. We planned to drive from Buffalo to Chesed Shel Emeth Cemetery on Ridge Road in Cleveland and then meet our cousins the following day. And so we did. We parked at a plaza down the road from the cemetery in Old Brooklyn. I called an Uber car as evening was approaching, and I was apprehensive about being alone with my mother in a wheelchair, in an old cemetery, in an unfamiliar neighborhood near the railway tracks, as twilight was falling. The initially reluctant young driver took us right up to Moshe Gilman's grave and waited while I recited the El Maleh Rachamim (prayer for the departed) and grappled for a stone to place on top of the monument. I placed it next to another small rock that had already been left from someone else's prior visit and could not help wonder who could have recently paid their respects at Moshe Gillman's grave before us. I have a hunch it may have been cousins [A429] Ferne and Gordon Mittleman.

The next day, 15 of [A431] Alta Gillman (Pearlman) and David Pearlman's grandchildren and great-grandchildren and their spouses met. My initial contacts were [A435] Cheryl Amato Lidawer and [A440] Lesa Jusko, Abe Pearlman's granddaughters, women my age whom I had never met until that day. Cheryl brought [A437] Vicky Pearlman Kuczynski, [A436] Emmanuel Pearlman's daughter, and his ex-wife [A436a] Simone. [A440] Lesa brought her husband [A440a] Greg, sister [A441] Barbara Mahle Marzec, and aunt [A442] Joyce Pearlman Segulin. [A431a] David and [A431] Sadie Pearlman's granddaughter, Doreen Friedman Zupan, brought her daughter, Tracie Strong Corbin. [A451] Michelle Fox Moss was there with her husband [A451a] Rick, and she Skyped with our cousin [A454] David Kaye (Chaitoff) in Florida who was too far to join us in person. Susan Kassirer Hyman (whose parents rented a flat in their two-family home on Commonwealth to Alta) and her son, Ari, also attended. Of the nine grandchildren, my mom [A444] Arlene and [A442] Joyce are the only two still alive. Excitement was in the air, and we were all overcome with emotion. Time flew as we shared photos and memories and created a meaningful bond with our new found relatives.

A few months later, my sister, [A446] Sandra Rossen Lahrey, who also lives in Jerusalem and I had an "overlap visit" in Buffalo, and we made plans with the cousins to meet for lunch midway between Buffalo and Cleveland.

This time, not all were able to attend, but Sandra, her daughter [A447] Moriah and I, met Cheryl and Vicky halfway between Buffalo and Cleveland, in Conneaut, OH. I cannot describe how thrilling it was to introduce the cousins to my sister and niece, family members with 6000 miles between us, whose lives are so diverse but yet the same.

Years of research produced a lot of detailed information about people I loved and about others whom I could never have ever met. I am hooked on genealogical and historical research. Every detail and document found gives me a buzz. Clearly, it was bringing relatives together face to face and creating new ties that were the real rewards for the endless hours spent surfing on the net.

#27 [A502a] UNCLE ITZ (ITZHAK GELMAN)
(Letter dated 1963 to Joe Gillman from John Robboy)

Uncle [A502a] Itz from Kishinev was a good-natured, just, honorable, and religious man. He was much more worldly than anyone of his family, though they were young, and [A506] Motel had already been as far as Argentina. Uncle Itzhak was in the wine business and even manufactured some of it. For one or two days, I took part in treading the grapes. The process was extremely unsanitary. Believe it or not, I was actually in the wine to my waistline. Uncle was also his own traveling salesman. He visited our province annually. That is how I came to know him before going to [C14] Kishinev. He would send us some 15 to 20 pails of wine for Passover, an amount sufficient to supply our Jewry for the holidays. This gift presented a problem to my parents because it required much vigilance.

Our post office was in the [A160] Graf's home. Our ordinary mail was retrieved there easily. For safety's sake, Uncle would send the bill of lading by registered mail. This required the Graf's signature. If the latter was out of town, we couldn't get the bill of lading until he returned. Uncle was warned and urged to mail the statement differently. Once Father actually rescued a load of wine from being sold at auction two weeks after Passover. This was the first and last time Jews in [C01] Knyazhe drank real wine all year round.

Whenever Uncle wanted to describe the progressiveness of a youth, he would picture him as one who discarded prayer and religious activities. That angered me so much that when I came to Kishinev, I prayed daily for an entire hour, though at home, I had long given up praying except when mother would so force me. Mother always reminded herself of this fact late at night, accuse Father of contributing to my delinquency, wake me and force me to pray.

Uncle himself prayed every morning. His prayers, however, were very short, or so it seemed to me. However, he was religious. He went to shul on Saturday. I remember one of his debtors offered to pay his debt while Uncle was on his way to shul Friday evening. Uncle refused to take the money because he would have to carry it on Saturday. Unfortunately, he never saw this debtor again.

He was a respectable and honest man. His word was as good as gold. He trusted people and relied on words and promises. He was, therefore, frequently cheated. The family knew about it and tried to control his transactions. However, they were too backward in that respect and simply didn't have any inkling of the business world.

Uncle couldn't stand the gross injustices he saw committed. Once, he came home from the market, sick at heart, and unable to quiet himself over what he had witnessed. Wine was transported in barrels. These were well standardized so that any child knew the size. The peasant brought in a 40-pail barrel filled with wine, but the dealers insisted it was only a 30-pail barrel. The peasant cried, crossed himself a million times, stating it always was a 40-pail barrel, and everybody in the world knew it contained 40 pails. He begged them to see it again and again but to no avail. He had to acquiesce and sell it as a 30-pail barrel.

I think he had much trouble and certainly carried an enormous burden when our families were fleeing from Russia and came to him. There were no complaints about him or any of his family.

We were angry with him for charging our folks when he cashed the checks we sent them. We did not realize that he had to pay the bank. He delivered every check to our relatives and helped them all. He also kept some of our folks in his home for weeks. It must have been a nightmare.

One more thing. When contact with him was re-established after World War I, Mother told him about all of us, finishing by saying that her [A026] Yankel goes to cheder. He knew that meant medical school. To this, Uncle wrote, "My [A508] Yankel is in the Medical School. He is the best student in Ukraine."

#28 [A026] JOHN ROBBOY'S APPRENTICESHIP IN [C14] KISHINEV
(Letter dated 1975 to Joe Gillman from John Robboy)

My education came to a halt by the summer of 1909. My parents had tried hard. They had sent me to Sokolivka, to Zashkov and then to the railroad station of [C24] Monasteristshe, where I had a private tutor, but all with poor results. They finally decided I should acquire a trade. It was then they dispatched me to [C14] Kishinev, where I was well-received, but my Gelman family there was unimpressive, indeed disappointing, to me even then. Within 2-3 days, [A502a] Uncle Itzie had me apprenticed with a [A246] Mr. Shankman for three years. Mr. Shankman owned a mechanics shop on Pushkin St near Kiev St. My pay was 5 rubles for the first year, 10 rubles for the second, and 15 rubles for the third year without room, board, or any other benefits.

The shop was small but apparently of some reputation. The work we did, in plain English, was blacksmithing, only instead of making axles and horseshoes, we made parts for roofs, wine presses, etc. Iron stairways and lanterns for buildings were manufactured here. The group also did much repair work in the homes such as plumbing and unplugging sinks, making keys, and repairing electric bells. I did a considerable amount of these repairs and quickly learned the tricks of the trade.

There were six workers in all. Three were apprentices like myself. One of the other apprentices, coincidentally, was also named [A249] Yankel, only he came from [C15] Knyazheki, a village in Podolia. The chief mechanic was also named [A247] Yankel. I worked with him and learned to use the hammer efficiently and rhythmically under his guidance as he struck the anvil while turning the hot iron from side to side for me to strike it. Of the other two, one was a great designer but unreliable because of drinking. He designed a monkey wrench, the like of which I have never seen since. He also developed a winepress for which I drilled the holes. I found that type of press in widespread use in the States.

Electric bulbs were found only in the homes of the wealthy. They operated on wet batteries. Salt deposits would form on the zinc plates, which then interfered with the current. The plates had to be scraped, cleaned, and water and salt added. As one couldn't charge enough to make it worthwhile to clean the battery at home, we always carried it to the shop, thus enabling us to charge an extra 8-10 rubles. Making keys was also quite profitable. I did a good deal of this work. No wonder [A246] Mr. Shankman magnanimously doubled my wages to 10 rubles that year even though he knew I was not to return in the coming year.

The family accepted and treated me well, although I was never sure just how welcome I was. Clearly, [A502] Aunt Leah had the worst of the bargain. I suffered from nosebleeds occasionally. But now working with the bellows, also stoking the hot irons with a massive sledgehammer, caused frequent bleeds at night during my sleep. In the morning, Aunt Leah had the job of cleaning the bloody pillow. Honestly, I was never made to feel inhospitable despite the trouble.

But if Aunt Leah might have been unhappy with me, some of the cousins were not. Cousin [A508] Yankel certainly was not. He was somewhat younger than me by one or two years and was a student sophomore in Realni Utshilistshe (junior high school). The two of us were on particularly good terms as I was able to help him solve some of his mathematical problems. Though cousin [A505] Rivka resented that I was able to help her brother whom she thought of superior knowledge, Yankel not only did not resent it but truly appreciated my help. Therefore, he treated me frequently with admission to the illusion (movie) on Saturday nights. Besides, it was here where I saw legitimate theater for the first time.

Fig.28-1: A2B5 Gillman Family, L-R: [A505] Rivka, [A506] Motel, [A502a] Leah Kaprov, [A507] Genedal, [A502a] Itzhak Gelman, [A508] Yankel.

[A505] Rivka was possibly the age of Tobie or somewhat older. She did not work. Jewish girls didn't do such things. [A507] Grendal was younger and attended a private gymnasium.

The oldest cousin, [A503] Moishe and his wife [A503a] Freda, lived in [C05] Bender. They came to Kishinev often, where Moishe visited the doctor for treatment of his bleeding piles (hemorrhoids). Since I was a budding mechanic, his wife brought the flat iron for me to repair. She was so pleased that she gave me 17 kopeks, which was the cost of a theater ticket. This was the first time for me to visit the theater. It was a Jewish theater named after the woman who owned it and was located on the corner of Kiev Street and Pushkin. I remember seeing a Ukrainian play there that I enjoyed immensely. I still remember the heading of the song: "Za Zto" (why or what for). Returning home late that evening and trying not to wake the family, I managed to get into the yard by crawling through the space below the gate. Thus ended a perfect day.

[A506] Motel had already been in Argentina, where he worked as an apprentice and had returned home. On Sunday, he would occasionally take me along when we would meet with one of his friends in a beer house. There, we would have a beer and herring. (They didn't yet know about corned beef.)

Though they lived in the big city for many years, all but Uncle were provincial. Uncle was in business and traveled about, so he was much more worldly than the rest of them.

Following the revolution in Russia and the pogrom, Motel, Rivka and Grendal worked to come to America and asked for help. Our family was by then comfortable but not rich. The appeal from Europe was great, and we helped all we could. I was then in college and possibly already at medical school. Our feelings for the Gellman family were warm, and we did send a sum sufficient to cover the transportation of the three mentioned. I personally described what awaited the girl, that she will have to work just as Nessie and Tobie did in factories.

#29 [A317] HARRY DUDWICK ON B'NAI KHAIM
(Dated Oct 27, 1963)

The following are comments about the opening chapters of your book, B'nai Khaim in America.

The sudden upsurge of correspondence with the army, following the outbreak of the first world war, spawned a new local "industry" operated exclusively by (but not for) the Jews. One or more "gramotniy zhidok," as they were called, sat on the steps of the local post office, day in and day out, writing letters for the illiterate peasant wives and parents to their husbands and sons at the fighting front. The running price was 10 to 15 kopeks per letter, including the address. Being semi-illiterate (or functional illiterates) themselves, those Jewish "writers" would not always follow the dictation verbatim but blandly proceed to use the words and phrases they knew how to spell. Fortunately, this did not make much difference to either the sender or the intended readers, as very few received those letters anyway.

Manual workers, skilled and unskilled alike, were always the bottom men on the ghetto totem pole. This is from my personal experience.

As a youngster, I had a nice and legible "pocherk" (handwriting). Therefore the local "prisyazhniy poverenniy" (lawyer-politician in charge of litigations, land disputes, passports and a million other things) invited me to fill out the passport blanks for would-be Jewish travelers. The latter invariably requested they be listed as "prostak" (literally a simpleton, but implying an "odd job man" which many frequently interpreted as something more "dignified" than a manual worker instead of shoemaker, carpenter, etc., which they actually were).

Knyazhe had a provizor-feldsher-doctor for some years, a pharmacist married to a female B'nai-Khaim descendant. He not only filled the prescriptions he had himself prescribed but also administered to the ailing peasants. His "practice" also extended to curing the peasant girls of their chastity.

Lastly, [A325] Chama-Gitie Dudnik married a farmer somewhere near Buenos Aires and was later joined by her younger brother [A324] Khaim. We heard that Uncle [A326] Khaim ([A340] Isaak Dudnik's father) found their address and even heard from them.

#30 [A399a] DOV "BERYL" DOLGONOS
by [A402] David Douglas

My great-grandfather was Dov or "Beryl" Dolgonos, after whom [A328] Donald Morrison and [A402] I were named. He lived in the shtetl (village) [C28] Ochhmativ. I don't know his wife's name ([A399] Leah Kaprov). He started the name Dolgonos when he was officially "adopted" by a childless couple in order to avoid military service. Families with only one-son were exempt. As the parents had two sons, both were subject to mandatory military service. I hope [A026] John Robboy's records will divulge his real surname and find for me my original roots (unfortunately, the original name remains unknown).

Fig. 30-1: 50th wedding anniversary of Dave and Leah Douglas. 1934.

Dov (Beryl) had three children:

1. My grandfather: [A400] Isrul (Israel), who married [A400a] Tuba Mazur (Major)

2. A daughter: [A413][69] Bracha, who married a cousin, [A326] Chaim Dudnik

3. Another son: [A414] Itzhok, who never left Russia.[70]

---

[69] Cousins who married have two designations. For example, Bracha Dolgonos Dudnik is [A413] born as a Dolgonos (Douglas), becoming [A326a] as a married Dudnik.

[70] [A402] Dave Douglas remarks on the Dolgonos family that remained in Russia, circa 1964
I have completely lost tract of this branch of the Dolgonos family that remained in Europe.
The information supplied herein is the result of sketchy bits gathered from non-tree members of my family.

It seems that cousin [A418] Josip Dolgonos, whom I never knew, was killed as a youngster by a horse carriage.

I remember well cousins [A415] Lisa, [A416] Sonia, and [A417] Abram Douglas, but have not corresponded with them since leaving Odessa in 1921 (my age 10). Abram was about a year older than I, Sonia was somewhat older than Abram, and Lisa was the oldest - hence I placed their birthdates as 1910, 1908, and 1906 respectively.

I don't remember hearing Grandpa or Dad speaking of Dov, but I might have told you the story that a poor Russian peasant told me that his father was an employee of Dov's. Hence, I presume it is true that he was involved in the Tsarist Concession in Ochmatov.

Isrul and Tuba Dolgonos (later known as Israel and Toby Douglas) had six children; three died very young, one died at age 21, and two survived.

1. My aunt: [A405] Polia (Pearl), who married [A405a] Mischa Fuks (Fouks) .

2. My father: [A401] Liova, who married [A401a] Golda Moldawsky (also Mauldaur) of [C16] Kodima, and who changed their names in Canada to Louis and Alice Douglas

3. My uncle: [A412] Mischa, who died from pneumonia at age 21 without heirs.

Fig. 30-2: [A405a] Moses (Misha) and Paula Douglas in Odessa May 19, 1909.

Fig. 30-3: Moses and [A405] Paula Fouks with Baby [A406] Jack, 1912.

A cousin of mine, related to me through my grandmother (Mazur), informed me that the Nazis killed both Lisa and Abram (D-3 during their occupation (1943-45).

Sonia [A416] seems to be the sole survivor. Except for the surname of her husband, I know nothing about her, except that she is an Engineer, of some kind.

Neither do I have any information as to whether Abram or Lisa were married and/or whether they had any children.

I recollect that grandfather [A400] Isrul used to correspond with his brother, [A414] Izchok, and I recollect that he was quite disturbed one day, many years before the war when he received a letter from his brother advising him that it was most embarrassing for him to receive letters from America. He wished him well, would be thinking of him, but said it best if they stopped corresponding with each other. And this was the last I have heard told about that branch of the family, except that there were reports that Izchok and his two children are now dead.

Except for [A416] Sonia, I would not care to try and locate them by correspondence, as I have nothing in common with them now, and furthermore it could prove embarrassing, if not fatal, for them to receive letter from this terrible capitalistic country. I have no interests there and why should I place them in jeopardy?

Fig. 30-4: [A405]
Polia Douglas Fouks
and Morris.

Fig. 30-5: [A401]
Liova (Louis)
Douglas.

[A400] Grandpa had a small factory of "Washing Sodas," whose products were delivered locally by horse and buggy. He and his brother, [A414] Itzik, were partners. I remember that part of the label on their package read: "Bratya Dolgonos" (translated: Brothers Dolgonos). An interesting sidelight was that Grandpa was reputed to have been a "clever" businessman, and he did become very wealthy by standards of that time. I often wondered how he could have accomplished that with that small, unimpressive hole-in-the-wall of a factory. Many years later, he recounted to me how he became wealthy.

It seems that in the vicinity of Odessa, there is a land-locked lake. At some past time, it had been part of the Black Sea. It became separated, and after years of evaporation, its water became saturated to the point one needed only a shovel to "mine" pure salt. Several salt distributors skimmed off the clean salt and sold it, leaving large mounds of "dirty" salt alone in their yards. It included some amounts of sand from the lake bottom. Land was cheap at the time, and it was cheaper to leave these vast mounds of dirty salt than to have them moved away. Since these mounds were useless and had no value, grandpa knew that he could profit if he could find a use for that junk! He experimented with it and eventually came up with something that was cleansed of the dirt and sand, but it had a very odd and bitter taste. He submitted samples to a lab and discovered that he had come up with Epsom salts. The salt companies were delighted to get rid of their nuisance mounds for nothing, and Grandpa shipped Epsom salts all over Europe. It did not take a genius to discover that the barrels of Epsom salts paved a road to riches, primarily when the cost of 5 kopecks to prepare could be sold at 50 rubles.

[A026] John Robboy had already confirmed that his relative, [A401] Liova Dolgonos, my father, was a bookkeeper. That was before my time, but I had known he was either the bookkeeper or manager of a "G'moones Hesed," a sort of embryonic combination of Jewish club, credit association, and a savings and loan. Later, dad accepted a job as a bookkeeper, senior bookkeeper, or bank manager of a privately-owned bank in the tiny town of Ezina on the west bank of the Dniester River, across from Ribnitza, on the east bank. My own recollection was at the age of about four, we lived in a rear apartment on the premises of the bank where Dad was the bank's manager. The owner was [A268] Mr. Ochanowich, a Russian.

Some of my memories include:

1. A machine, a large press, in the bank was used for duplicating written documents. The original was heavily written on a thin paper, under which was placed, facing the underside, an indelible carbon paper. This produced a reverse image on the paper's underside, which became the master copy. Then the master was placed against a clean sheet of slightly damp paper and set between the pages of a heavy book, several hundred pages thick. The book was then placed between the lower and upper sections of the press, after which a rotary wheel at the top squeezed the upper section. This method created a reverse image of the original master reverse image. This was copy #1. Repeating the process produced additional copies, each a bit fainter. The process was slow, producing only a few legible copies.

2. I remember my Dad taking me, all bundled up, on a sleigh, over the frozen surface of the River Dniester, and seeing crowds of young children and others skating all around us.

3. I remember my father losing control of the pedals as he sped downhill on a bicycle. He crashed into a barrel located at the downspout of a rain gutter and fell headfirst into the barrel. Inside the barrel was a broken rusty stave, and Dad lost a piece of his chin, the size a dime, in his encounter with it. His doctor "reattached" his severed chin piece, but, for the rest of his life, he shaved carefully around the protruding reminder of his reckless cycling.

4. We had a large kitchen because I remember entering where our very buxom maid was talking to someone while breastfeeding her baby. I so vividly recall my being fascinated by that sight, as though it happened only yesterday, and bug-eyed, I slowly approached her. When I got within a few feet of her, I remember her removing her nipple from the infant's mouth, pointing it in my direction, squeezing it and drenching my face with her milk.

I next recall living in [C29] Odessa, next door to my grandparents, starting in about 1917. Their address was Provianskaia 15, in an apartment building of some 26 units. The apartment was on the right side of the two second-floor apartments as you face the rear from the entrance. We lived next door to each other with my parents occupying the apartment on the left. In 1918, my mother, brother and I were smuggled out of Russia. We joined her father in Romania, who had fled a year earlier to go to Palestine, which he never reached. We lived in Romania for about three years and then moved to Canada, first to Vancouver, where we joined the Fouks family and then in 1925 to Toronto. In 1946, my wife, two children, and I left for Los Angeles.

Sometime after that, my grandparents decided to migrate to Palestine. I don't know whether they left legally or fled much like we did, being smuggled from the country. But I know that they somehow found themselves in Istanbul, Turkey (known as Constantinople) at the train station, where thieves snatched their suitcases from their hands. Two of their bags contained their life savings of foreign exchange. Suddenly my grandparents were penniless. They finally landed in Palestine and lived there for several years, when my aunt, [A405] Polia Fouks, who lived in Vancouver, received special permission from the Canadian Government to bring her parents to Canada. It is interesting that after a long life of affluence and through the most trying times in

Russia, they lost all in one split second. As long as I remember them, neither Grandpa nor Grandma ever mentioned the subject to us.

My grandparents came to Canada about 1928 or 1929 to join their daughter, Aunt [A405] Polia Fouks and her family.[71] [A405a] Mischa Fouks was a small business meat wholesaler (Alberta Meat Company, 8 Water St, Vancouver). Grandpa, then in his 50's or early 60's, got into the business, buying the raw skins from uncle Mischa and processing them into leather and selling them. In 1932 or 1933, they decided to move to Toronto, where I lived. I am confident that my father had died by then, and that my being the love-of-their-lives, was the only reason for their leaving Vancouver. It did not take Grandpa long to find a suitable partner and get into a business, establishing the Ontario Monument Co, manufacturing, and installing Jewish cemetery stones.

Fig. 30-6: 1923 Top: [A410] Gertrude Fouks, [A404] Harry Douglas, [A411] Arthur Fouks; Front: [A408] David Fouks, [A402] Dave Douglas, [A406] Jack Fouks.

---

[71] [A405] Paula Dolgonoss (Douglas) married [A405a] Moses Fouks in Edmonton, Alberta, Canada on June 11, 1911. Moses had emigrated to Texas from Odessa, Russia, initially in 1908 and then, after his second cousin wanted him to marry one of his daughters, he found his way to Alberta, where his best friend, Grisha Olyan, had moved. Paula traveled by herself to Edmonton to marry him. Sometime during 1912, Paula returned to Odessa to be with her mother, [A400] Tuba and father, [A400a] Israel, when she was about to give birth to [A406] Jack. After several months, she returned to Canada with the baby. Paula was exceptionally intelligent, strong-willed and a determined woman. She had two more sons, [A408] David and [A411] Arthur, one daughter, [A410] Gertrude Zack, and ten grandchildren. Jack was born in Odessa on Dec 28, 1912.

#31 [A401] LIOVA DOLGONOS → DOUGLAS
(Letter From [A402] Dave Douglas To Joe Gillman, Sep. 15, 1964)

Regarding my late father's writings ([A401] Liova (Louis) Douglas), I have a brief outline of his reactions to the pogrom of 1905. It is part of an analysis of events from 1905 to 1920 (or 1924). He wrote little about himself. Few are endowed with as many virtues as he had. He was a giant of a man, a model of honesty and integrity, a person of quick wit and deep intellect, a moralist and an idealist, yet tolerant of human shortcomings. He stood head and shoulders above the crowd, yet he loved all people and, more particularly, his own people. He was a dedicated Zionist. He was a leader among men since his youth. The Jewish community, but particularly the Zionists of Toronto, mourned him when he suddenly died at 45.

Born in 1886, in [C28] Ochhmativ, he had a substantial Hebrew education. He spoke fluent Hebrew to his dying day, although he finished only the 7th of 8 years of Gymnasium. He became a bookkeeper, and before reaching the age of 30, he became a bank manager (a Jew in Russia!). A year or two later, he became the general manager of Mesaksudy Tobacco Company of Odessa (a Jew in Russia!). He left this employ and, within a brief period, became a millionaire (buying tobacco in Crimea and on the open market). The revolution brought his personal business activity to a halt. He was the first to organize a co-op market (similar to the supermarkets in the U.S.) in [C29] Odessa under the auspices of the Revolutionary Government (Kerensky or Bolshevik). He later left this and organized a successful factory to manufacture shoes of which there was then, and there still is a tremendous shortage. Rejecting Bolshevik indoctrination and refusing to remove his Jewish and Zionist mantle, he was scheduled for execution by the "comrades" for his activities in white-collar executive positions and for having been a "capitalist" before the Revolution. He fled Russia in 1920, aided and abetted by "comrades" who respected him despite their ideological differences.

Fig. 31-1: [A401] Liova and Golda Douglas, at engagement ~1910.

Fig. 31.2: Douglas family ~1917 L-R: [A402] Dave Douglas, [A400] Israel Douglas, [A401a] Golda Douglas, [A404] Tzvi (Harry) Douglas, [A401] Liova Douglas, [A400a] Tuba Douglas.

Broke, but not beaten, and armed and financed only with his intellect, boundless energy, and ingenuity, he organized and successfully conducted the manufacture of trousers in Turkey. Subsequently, he left for Romania to join the rest of his family, who had already left for America. Between 1921 and 1924, he established a lumber yard in Chisinau, Romania (with two partners), and made this business grow to become the largest yard in that city. His partners paid him 2,000,000 Romanian lei for his one-third interest in that business; such was the genius of his business acumen. That was my father, the businessman. Within one year, he was almost broke again in an import business (from the Orient), and he took a job at $40.00 a week in a travel agency in Toronto. He worked for three years and then opened his own office. In 1928-9, he earned $10,000 during the first year in that business. The year 1929 saw the Great Depression set in and the closing immigration to Canada, but he still kept a successful money-making enterprise. He had a heart attack, which slowed his pace, and three years later, this chapter closed.

Fig. 31-3: Douglas family ~1925. L-R: [A401] Liova and Golda Douglas, [A402] Dave Douglas, [A404] Tzvi Harry Douglas.

Fig. 31-4: [A402] Dave Douglas and [A402a] Rose Starkman at the first date.

His Zionist activities, which started at an early age, saw him, a blond, blue-eyed, pug-nosed youth (his appearance belying his Semitic ancestry) traveling illegally from small town to small town. There, with youngsters, he held forbidden meetings and preached the gospel of Zionism – the return to Israel. This activity he pursued all his life. In Odessa, Father was a member of the Yavne Synagogue, the hub of Odessa Zionist activity. His friends, who frequently visited our home, included some of the top Zionist world leaders who emerged in that era. They included: [A824] Chaim Nachman Bialik (Poet Laureate of Israel),[72] [A825] Dr. David Rebelsky (prominent Canadian Zionist), and even [A823] Vladimir (Zvi) Zhabotinsky,[73] with whom Dad always argued, for even then, Zhabotinsky was a firebrand and a dynamic speaker. To his dying day, he was still central to our community's Jewish life. When Chaim or [A826] Nahum Goldberg learned of my father's death, his comment was, "Far Vus Ot Ir Gelost Douglas 'n' Shtarben . . ." ("Why did you allow Douglas to die?")

It is impossible to pay tribute or enumerate all of Father's activities in one or two pages. Although very young, Dad was held in such esteem that he was often asked to be the sole judge at a "Din Torah" (Rabbinical Court). During his management of the shoe factory in Russia (during the famine of 1920), he managed to find jobs for some Zionist buddies so as to get them food coupons. [A825] Dr. David Rebelsky, a prominent Canadian Zionist, was among them. Dad made him the secretary.

Dad's Zionism went beyond the desire to help others go to Israel. His life's ambition had been to go there himself, so my early and only education in Russia was in Hebrew, not Russian. During Dad's lifetime, he had made three futile attempts to go to Palestine (as it was then known). While in Odessa, before the Bolshevik regime, father purchased a factory of folding beds for shipment to Palestine. We were supposed to have sailed together with the cargo, only to be frustrated when the Bolsheviks untimely captured Odessa one day before our sailing date. We made a second attempt in 1920, after Dad fled Russia. He had arrived at Jaffa's port on the day the Arab riots broke out. The authorities refused to permit the passengers to debark. He was then shipped to Egypt, refused permission to land, and ended up in Turkey. The third attempt occurred when we resided in Romania. Dad sent a substantial amount of lumber to Palestine, hoping that by establishing a commercial relationship, he could eventually transfer his interests there. He was unable to travel with the lumber because of our illegal refugee status in Romania, so he sent a relative by marriage ([A333a] Aron Milstein, who was [A332] Polia Galler's brother-in-law and [A333] Sarah's husband). Once again, riots broke out, business was terrible, and Dad lost most of his investment in that venture.

At home, Dad was a traditionalist. We went to Synagogue for Rosh Hashanah, Yom Kippur, and Passover only. We always had a seder. However, Dad worked, rode, and smoked on the Sabbath.

---

[72] From [A403] Myrna Koffman nee Douglas (Dolgonos in Odessa) (2020-01-01). My father was [A402] Dave Douglas and his father, [A401] Louis Dolgonos. Apparently, he was a leading Zionist in Odessa and good friends with [A824] Chaim Bialik and [A823] Vladimir (Svi) Jabotinsky (also known as Se'ev Zhabotinsky). He sent many waves of Jews to settle in Israel but stayed in Russia due to his business. The family left Russia in the middle of the night; My dad was 10 years old; his brother was 5 when the Communists came for the family. (An employee tipped them off.) They got on a boat and left for Romania. They remained there for 2 years, after which grandfather left for Israel, but there was the first Arab uprising in Haifa so the boat couldn't dock. Instead he docked the boat in Damascus, returned to Romania and then left for Vancouver where my grandfather's sister, [A405] Polia, lived. It interested me that other members of our "mishpocha" also left for Romania. The Dolgonos family were close to the Dudnik family and "Mima Bruch" told me she was going to bake for my wedding. Sadly, she died just before I married, which was 60 years ago. I knew [A332] Polia and [A385] Morris Galler well and their children; My parents knew all of Polia's siblings and I remember being told of the shooting in the pharmacy in Buffalo.

[73] Ze'ev Jabotinsky was a Zionist activist, orator, and writer who founded the Betar Movement. He was also a soldier who founded the Jewish Legion during World War I.

I do not believe he observed the kashrut, although our home was kosher. I think it was more of a habit than anything else.

The product of a fantastically revolutionary, evolutionary, and changing era, my father shall always remain to me a powerful symbol of rugged individualism, deep intellect, high idealism, profound morality, and unquestionable integrity. That was my father. Today he is only a memory, and it may take many generations before our family produces another person to fill his empty shoes.

#32 [A326] CHAIM AND [A413] BRUKHA DUDNIK
by [A332] Polia Galler (A1B1C3D2) and Others

Editor's note: Chaim Dudnik and Brukha Dolgonos, as cousins who married, present the logical problem of assigning identification codes. Using the system adopted whereby the code rests on birth order within a family, Chaim is [A326] as a Dudnik but [A413a] as a Dolgonos spouse. The male partner's code classifies most such unions.

My parents had twelve children, only seven of whom survived through infancy. We lived in [C01] Knyazhe-Krinitsa. The River Tykytch divided the town. On the higher bank of the river ran a long street; on the right, it was called Kashivka, and to the left, it was called Virbivka. Only one Jewish family that of the "shochet" [A197] Rabbi Yankel lived on Kashivka.

Fig. 32-1: Dudnik family 1912 in Knyazhe Krinitsa
Top: [A327] Fanya, [A339] Yosef, [A333] Sarah, [A332] Polia.
Middle: [A326a] Brucha w baby [A349] Vera on lap, [A326] Zaide Chaim, Chaim's mother [A292] Rivke.
Foreground: [A348] Betty, [A340] Itzik, [A346] Liza.
Note: Vera did not survive infancy.

I vividly remember the anguish and fright we children experienced when anticipating the trip to the shochet every Thursday to have him kill a chicken for the Sabbath. The Christian children were waiting for us with their dogs, throwing stones at us and calling us vile names.

On the lower bank of the river was the central part of the town, where the Jewish population lived. On the shore were the synagogue and the bathhouse, which was heated for everyone only on Fridays. For extra money and our family, it was also open on Thursday.

There was a large square from which the streets connecting Knyazhe with nearby towns radiated. On one side of the square was the large house of my grandmother, [A292] Rifke Dudnik, which was a boarding house. There was a large shopping center, including a saloon, a drug store, and two general merchandise stores. On the other side of the square was a beer cellar that belonged to my father. Next to it was our house, consisting of two rooms with a kitchen. On the other side of this "duplex" was a similar home of two rooms with a kitchen, in which the family of [A011] Malka and [A011] Shmiel Robboy lived. Near the house was our general merchandise store.

On the third side of the square was the church, and on the fourth, the road to the [A160] Graf's estate where [A326] Father was the manager.

Every Sunday, there was a bazaar on the square to which people from the nearby communities brought their wares. This market was the primary source of revenue for Knyazhe. During the week, the town was peaceful, clean, and beautiful. Thick woods and colorful gardens surrounded the shtetl, and "quiet flowed the Tykytch." The river was the life of the town. It abounded with fish, the rights of which were Father's, and its waters operated the mill, the rights of which the Graf also gave to Father. In the winter we went ice-skating on the frozen river, and we swam in the river in summer. The happy voices of children filled the air.

On Rosh Hashanah, the Jews, dressed in their best, came to the shores of the river to "shake off their sins," making resolutions to be good and to live in peace with each other. But it was soon forgotten. After the High Holidays, when they came to the synagogue on Friday, the battles of who should be the "speaker of the house" began anew. They also argued about who deserved the honored seat in the synagogue. Since my father was the wealthiest and most cultured Jew in Knyazhe, he had his way, and he settled all the disputes. He was the counsel of the town, the attorney because he had "good connections" with the proper authorities. Being the manager of the Graf's estate (the Graf owned the shtetl and, for that matter, its people), Father could always defend and guard their interests. The Graf was seldom at home. He lived abroad, spending more money than he had, draining the people with taxes. He was always in debt to Father. Father was the letter-writer and reader. He was the only one to get a Jewish newspaper from Poland, so the people came to him for news and advice.

He was respected and well-liked. He also had his enemies among the Graf's servants, partly because of jealousy and partly because of antisemitism. They learned from infancy that the Jew was the cause of their misery.

Every night, I used to wake up in fright, looking out of the window and expecting that something terrible was about to happen. Perhaps it was because our maid used to tell us stories about witches, robbers, and bad people, which she herself also believed.

One cold winter night, I awoke to find our house on fire. There was no fire equipment. The Church bells began tolling, and the whole village awoke and came running with pails to fetch water from the river. Our neighbors and we carried out as many belongings as we could save. In a short time, our house, and others burned to the ground. One of the Graf's servants was caught and accused of being the arsonist.

The [A160a] Grafina, the Graf's wife, offered Father a house near the estate. It was a beautiful home, surrounded by an orchard and a large garden. We were delighted there, but not for long.

In the spring of 1914, Father, Mother, and my two brothers went on a trip to Palestine. Father wanted to give the boys an education there. Before leaving Palestine, Mother changed her mind, and they all returned, arriving on the day before World War I broke out. The life in Knyazhe changed. The men went to war, and food was requisitioned for the army. Of course, the Jews were blamed. It became unsafe to live in Knyazhe. We moved to [C36] Uman and lived there from 1915 to 1918 comfortably. We all went to school. Father was still wealthy, but this lasted only until a year after the Revolution when Father lost everything he had possessed – the mill and real estate in various cities. Then the pogroms began in Uman. The town changed hands almost every week.

Father sent the older children to larger cities, some to [C13] Kiev and some to [C29] Odessa. For a full year, we had no contact with each other. In 1918 Father bribed a railroad official who put mother and the younger children in a sealed car bound for Odessa. Having been a capitalist, Father could not get a job. Starvation and sickness spread over the land, and our family was no exception.

Father and Mother began to speculate, selling sugar, salt, and other hard-to-get commodities. When that became impossible to do, they began to sell whatever they could of their belongings in order to survive. [A385] Morris, myself, my sisters, [A327] Fanya and her family, [A333] Sarah, and our two brothers decided to leave the country, however dangerous and challenging it might be. Morris had two brothers in America, as did our brother-in-law, [A327a] Lyova (Leon Morrison,[74] Fanya's husband). (A footnote explains the relation of the Morrison and Astor clans.)[75] We hoped, once out of the country, we could get in touch with them and, with their help, get to America.[76]

---

[74] Steve Chernoff (schernoff@chernoff.com) has spent 40 some years researching the Morrison family tree. Please contact him for further information.

[75] 2010-01-04 [A329] Leonette Morrison clarifies the Morrisons -Astor relation. Sasha/Alex Morrison (not part of the B'nai Khaim) was [A328] Donald Morrison's uncle as a half-brother to [A327a] Leon Morrison. As Sasha and Donald were of the same generation and close as friends, and as Alex Morrison, the uncle, was 3 years younger than his nephew Donald, Leonette thought of him as Dad's cousin.

Donald was close with his 9-year younger first cousin, [A334] Alex/Sasha Milstein - son of [A333a] Aron and [A333] Sarah Dudnik Milstein. Both together attended the Chicago Medical School, and during that time Donald lived with the Milsteins, Sarah, Aron, Alex, and [A337] David/Duzzy. Donald's mom ,[A327] Fanya Dudnik Morrison, recently widowed, was still in Buffalo.

Now to clarify the half-brother bit, and the Morrisons/Astors. Eli Morrison and Anna Astor, both widowed and living in Ukraine, married and blended their families. Eli already had several children: Leon, Sol/Zoma, Rona/Ronia, Meyer, Sylvia/Tzipa, Melvin/Misha, Mary/Mania (later Wichman,) and Rose (later Freedman) Morrison. Anna had her son, Henry Astor. Later they had Alex Morrison together. Later still, to add to the confusion, Rona Morrison and Henry Astor, stepsiblings, fell in love and married; hence she became Rona Astor.

Anecdote: Leonette and brother [A330] Elliot (Morrison) spoke about eponyms for great-grandfather Eli Morrison ("Zaide Luvid") and great-grandmother Anna. As a toddler in Buffalo, she commonly visited them where they always greeted us warmly and brought out a box of chocolates. Alas, my parents prohibited me from eating them, believing (incorrectly) I was allergic. Instead, I received a tangerine. No wonder it took decades for me to appreciate the then-hated tangerines.

[76] Per Leonette Morrison, December 31, 2019, is the 80th anniversary of the death of my grandfather, [A327a] Leon Morrison, who married [A327] Fanya, daughter of [A326] Chaim and [A326a and A395] Brucha Dudnik. She was living in Knyazhe when they met, telling Leonette (her granddaughter) that he travelled extensively giving advice, and that their relationship began with a spirited discussion (or argument) about censorship in then-Tsarist Russia. (He favored; she opposed.) She married at 18, on or about April 15, 1913, and gave birth to [A328] good Donald on May 5, 1914 in Justingrad/Sokolivka. (Side note: Donald's naturalization papers said "Odessa, Russia" and in both the Kaprove and "Moroffsky" databases the birth city was Uman, but several of the matriarchs confirmed he definitely was not from Uman, but rather from the village, Justingrad/ Sokolivka.)

Leaving our parents and two younger sisters, [A346] Liza and [A348] Betty, in Odessa, after indescribable hardships, we succeeded in coming to America. Fanya and her family settled in Buffalo, and Morris and I went to Chicago. [A333] Sarah married [A333a] Sol Morrison in Romania and remained there for seven years until she and her family came to Niagara Falls, NY. They later moved to Los Angeles, CA. [A340] Isaac and [A339] Yosef, went to Palestine. Our family members who remained in Odessa survived in part from packages we managed to send them, but they starved most of the time.[77]

[A333] Sarah Dudnik, [A327] Fanya , her husband [A327a] Leon, and their young son [A328] Donald came to Buffalo via Bucharest and London, starting in 1918 and arriving about 1922. Leon's pharmacy degree from Russia was not honored here. He thus had to repeat the degree at the then University of Buffalo (now SUNY at Buffalo.) He most likely opened his store in the mid-1920s. On June 4th, 1930, he received patent #277,385 for a tonic under "Leon Morrison, dba The Russian Drug Manufacturing Company, Buffalo, NY."

Fig. 32-2: Chaim and Bertha Dudnik family, Buffalo, 1934.

Top
[A348a] Leon Hayman
[A346a] Edward Julius Schwartz
[A327a] Leon Morrison
[A328] Donald Morrison

Bottom
[A348] Betty Dudnik Hayman
[A346] Liza Dudnik Schwartz
[A326] Chaim Dudnik
[A348.2] Mimi Hayman Brown
[A326a] Brucha Dudnik (Dolgonos)
[A327] Fania Dudnik Morrison

---

[77] Others were forced to wait also. In a letter dated Apr 25,1996, [A384] Gary Zaika states: My grandfather, [A381] Yochanon Galak (Galler) could not leave Russia with the rest of the family. It needed 70 years for his daughter [A383] Rifke Galak, (my mother) and son [A382] Lazar, (my uncle) to reach the United States. Now the whole Galak and Zaika families reside in New York (Brooklyn) and suburbs (Merrick).

Fig. 32-3: [A413] Bubbe Bracha and [A326] Zaide Chaim Dudnik

Fig. 32-4: Buffalo Jun 26, 1947 [A346] Liza and Edward Schwartz 20th Wedding Anniversary.
L-R
[A328a] Shirley Morrison (née Mizes)
[A348.8] David Hayman
[A347] Robert Schwartz
[A348.2] Mimi Hayman Brown
[A346a] Edward Julius Schwartz
[A346] Liza Dudnik Schwartz
[A348] Betty Dudnik Hayman
[A348a] Leon Hayman
[A340] Itzchak Dudnik
[A328] Donald Morrison

Fig. 32-5: Left: [A327a] Leon Morrison and [A327] Fanya Dudnik Morrison, c 1936.

Fig. 32-6: [A346a] Julius Schwartz, [A346] Liza Dudnik Schwartz, [A328] Donald Morrison, unknown man, [A327a] Leon Morrison, [A327] Fanya Dudnik Morrison.

Fig. 32-7: Left: [A332] Polia Dudnik Galler and sister [A327] Fanya Dudnik Morrison in front of Morrison's Drug Store, [A327a] Leon Morrison background, [A328] Donald Morrison at bat in junior Yankees uniform, 1926.

Fig. 32-8: Right: [A328] Donald Morrison (Yankees baseball uniform, Age 12), with cousin [A386] Vivian Galler (Age 2) (later Korn) 1926-07-07.

One of the younger descendants, who never met [A326] Chaim but had many fond memories of [A326a] Brucha remarked that Brucha, when seeing the smiling infant face, said "she smells." She remembers Brucha, herself and her parents dressed for a wedding in 1952. They were in a hotel room, possibly for [A392] Buzz and [A392a] Enid Galler's wedding, in Chicago. Brucha was then living in Chicago, and they had traveled from Buffalo. Some years later in 1954, when living in Lompoc, California, she came to visit for several summer months. She loved to grow strawberries and cucumbers, among other things. She pickled the cucumbers and watermelon rinds and put them up in canning jars. She also made cherry "varenishkas" and cherry "perishkas." The varenishkas (aka varnishkes, vereniky)[78] were like sweet kreplach (i.e., dumplings,) either boiled and then served with sour cream on top or pan-fried like pot stickers.

---

[78] http://www.cookitsimply.com/recipe-0010-01370s8.html

The perishkas (a variation on pirozhki, pierogi) was a filled pastry, made with a yeast dough.[79] So yummy. A master needleworker, Brucha also crocheted collars (like what Ruth Bader Ginsburg wore over her robe, except they consisted of metallic thread with dangling fake pearls) for all the B'nai Khaim women and girls on the West Coast.

Fig. 32-9: Family of [A327] Fanya (Fanny) Dudnik and her husband, Leon Morrison
Top L-R: Meyer Morrison, Fanya Dudnik Morrison, Rona Morrison Astor, Henry Astor, Sylvia (Tzepa) Morrison Marks.
Middle: Leon Morrison, Anna Hoffman, Astor Morrison, Elia Morrison, Sol (Zoma) Morrison
Front: Mary (Manya) Morrison Wichman, Rose (Rosa) Morrison Freedman, Melvin (Misha) Morrison
Note: Missing are Sarah Dudnik Morrison (1890-1978), aunt of Fanny Dudnik Morrison and sister of Chaim and Efraim Dudnik, who married Sol Morrison (1890-1970), Leon Morrison's younger brother, who in the photo sits on the right.

In 1923 a friend from Chicago sent my parents papers and the fare to come to America, and they managed to get permission to leave the USSR. They arrived within three months, settling in Buffalo. Without knowing the language and without a trade, they opened a fruit store in a Polish neighborhood, which was all they could do to earn a living. Father spoke fluent Polish. They lived there comfortably until 1934, at which time they decided to visit their sons in Palestine. They spent five years there and returned to America in 1939 on the day that the Nazis declared war on Poland. In 1940 Chaim and Brucha moved to Chicago and opened a grocery store, working most diligently (especially Mother). Father still could not get used to this kind of work. In 1943, they retired and moved in with us.

---

[79] https://internationalmenu.com/pirozhki-with-cherries/

On April 1, 1945, Chaim passed away at the age of 75. Brucha continued to live with us, every few months visiting one or another of her daughters. She passed away on September 22, 1957, at the age of 84.

Fig.32-10: [A386] Viv Korn, [A389] Victoria Korn Lerner, Lia Korn, Four Seasons, Beverly Hill, Dec. 28, 2002 (Marriage Vicki and [A389a] Andres Lerner).

Fig. 32-11: [A333] Sarah Dudnik Milstein, Jan. 30, 1928, by Polska Apteka, Polish Apothecary.

#33 [A298] COUSIN YOSSEL (JOE) DUDNIK
Letter dated 1963 to Joe Gillman from John Robboy

The relationships are confusing to you. [A294] Gitie Dudnik was a sister of [A298] Yossel. They were the children of [A293] Aaron Dudnik, son of [A292a] Noah, and [A292] Rivka Dudnik and brother of [A326] Chaim Dudnik.

[A298] Yossel was the oldest son of Aaron, and until his brother [A317] Harry was born, he was the only boy among many girls. Altogether, there were two boys and seven girls in the family. They were born and raised in the forest of Sumivka, near [C36] Uman, where [A293] Aaron was the manager. All of them had innate abilities and charm. Joe was no exception. As the oldest and a son, Joe received the best Jewish education possible. At a later date, the family moved to Uman. There, possibly, he obtained a bit more education. As far as I know, he had no formal training.

He was both handsome, charming, and outstanding in their family. He left for America about 1907-8 and landed in Galveston, Texas. Thence he made his way to Philadelphia. Like all of our youths at the time, he was radically inclined. He joined the anarchistic group, the "Radical Library." In 1912, his sisters [A294] Gitie, [A309] Pearl, and [A310] Sarah arrived. They introduced him to one of their shipmates, [A298a] Minnie, whom he married. Soon they all moved to Cleveland. All of them, including Joe, worked in the garment factories. [A023] Tobie found them the jobs.

Following the revolution in Russia, Joe, his wife, and child returned to Russia at Russian expense as expatriates. He found his family poor and his father sick. With [A401] Liova Dolgonos, his cousin from [C29] Odessa, he engaged in smuggling tobacco. Shortly after this, he managed with the help of the U.S. Government to return home with his wife and child. He joined in a business where he was as slippery as were a good many of his relatives.

Joe's accomplishments were commonplace. He became interested in philosophy, and I believe he translated some works into Yiddish.

It is the younger Dudnik generation that is getting somewhere now. The older ones had no better opportunities than we did. Some made advances by mere shrewdness and being unscrupulous.

#34 [A581] VELVEL PURPEL
by [A585] Nancy Kaprov Gore

Reprinted from https://nancygore.wordpress.com/ (Family and Personal Stories)

Legacy By Days (Nancy Kaprov Gore)

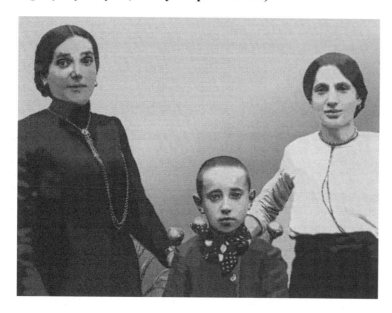

Fig. 34-1:   [A580a] Ethyl Rabinowitz Kaprov (mother), [A581] Velvel KAPROV, and[A579a] Bassie Kaprov (grandmother).

The characters in my grandfather's Ukrainian story are the stiffly dressed ones from an old photograph. My grandfather stands between his mother and grandmother, their hands at his back. On this day, my grandfather's mother wears a simple white blouse and black skirt. Her dark hair pulled back, her small lips almost smile. There is darkness above her eyes. My grandfather had baggy jacket buttons under his chin, where the scarf is tied around his neck. He leans slightly toward his mother. Large ears protrude from either side of his shaved head, eyes narrow. His lips slightly frown.

"I knew what was coming," he says decades later when asked why he looked so sad.

My grandmother's family owns a lumber business in this village, putting her in a class above my grandfather, but still, they know each other by sight. A day comes that my grandfather stands by a brook and sees my grandmother in the market. Her beauty strikes him, and at this moment of this day, he knows he will marry her. He knows he will.

How he could imagine such an unlikely possibility that 4,000 miles of travel will make even more staggering, I do not know.

Another day comes. The day he most wants to forget. The day he hears, "di koassax kume" (the Cossacks are coming). And he won't speak of what happened. And on this day, he runs.

He moves slowly through Romania, Belgium, and Cuba. He works in a Cuban cigar factory, buys passage to the US, and, one day in 1922, he lands in Florida precisely one day before my grandmother arrives in New York.

And the day comes, when my grandfather and grandmother are married. It is 1925.

Fifty years pass, and another day comes. I am 8 years old, give or take. The smell of boiled chicken from my grandparent's tiny kitchen mingles with my grandmother's perfume, which mingles with the strong scent from their blue toilet cleaner. That they are now living in this Cambridge high-rise, reserved for older and disabled adults, creates a sense of relief so palpable, I can't help but wonder how bad their last apartment must have been.

My grandmother clucks a bit as she talks. One of her thumbs is shorter than the other, round at the top with one small fingernail sticking straight up like a small upside-down carpenter's nail. I used to think all grandmothers smelled of chicken, clucked their teeth, and had one thumb different than the other. Later I learn that her clucking is a result of ill-fitting dentures and her thumb the result of a sewing factory accident.

And a day comes that my grandmother dies and another six weeks later, my grandfather. His letter awaits me when I come home from his funeral. I had sent him a quote about the importance of friends, and he'd written back. He explained that he took my letter to a senior's activity in his building and read it in front of "all those people." He was amazed at himself and the kindness of his neighbors. He declared he wasn't going to "let the parade of life pass him by."

And on this day, 40 years later, I imagine a conversation with my grandmother.

"Please tell me about [C43] Zhaskov," I say.

"Ach. Let's not talk about it. Why would you want to know such tsuris (troubles)?"

"Because you survived! You survived. And we carry that survival with us. And what you don't share becomes heavy and dark. And, most of all, because I want to know your strength."

"Now listen, you're talking nonsense. It's no good. Enough already. Here, I baked you some cookies. Tell me about Vermont!"

And on this day, I imagine she is finally provoked. "I know what you think! You think it was fear that strangled me. Meshugenah! Fear? Fear can be forgiven. But hate? Hate is unforgivable. And Zhaskov? Hatred ruined it. You don't think there are evil people, but you weren't there. I spit at the evilness!. Zhaskov? It's where I learned to hate. Hate was more powerful. It was hate that destroyed Zhaskov and hate that kept me alive. Hate is contagious like that, and I have had hate in me all my life. You have seen hate in the world, and you have your fear. You can have your fear. I had my hate."

#35 [A581] VELVEL KAPROV'S IMMIGRATION STORY
by [A584.2] Rachel Purpel

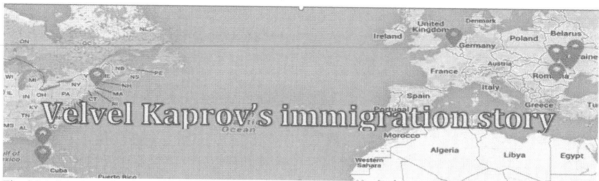

Fig. 35-1 (Map): Velvel Kaprov's immigration route.

This account summarizes what is known so far about [A581] Velvel Kaprov's journey from the "old" country to the new. Maps are included where possible. Further map exploration is available at https://www.google.com/maps/d/edit7midHZoxlzFyX53AY.kv1Jts48vVmo. (For street view, click on a place, and then click on the corresponding Google+ page. From there, go to the map and get to Street View.)

Origins

Names and aliases

- Velvel Kaprov = Birth name according to family. Velvel is Yiddish for "Wolf " and often used for William.
- Volco Caprov = Name listed on Antwerp police file. "Volco" is a Yiddish nickname of Velvel.
- Israel Perepilitzky = Name on passport used to enter the U.S., possibly "borrowed" in some fashion from the similarly named Izrael Perepelitchi.
- Israel Purpel = Naturalized name.
- William Purpel = Name he called himself in the U.S.

Birthplaces and dates

Date	Place	According To	Presumed modern place	More info
	[C43] Zhaskov	Family tradition	Zhashkiv, Ukraine	
1906	Kalarash Bessarabia	Antwerp police file	Cälärasi, Moldova	kehilalinks.jewishgen.org/calarasi/homepage.html
~1904	Boukovine, Romania	Passport	Historical region now divided between Romania & Ukraine	en.wikipedia.org/wiki/Bukovina kehilalinks.jewishgen.org/sadgura/reischtoronto.html
2/2/1904	Chernovitz, Romania	Naturalization papers	Chernivtsi, Ukraine	Chernivtsi, Ukraine was part of Bukovina, under Romanian rule from 1918-1940) www.bukowina.org.il/Cernovitz.html

Family members:

	Born	Presumed modern place
Father: [A580] David Caprov	Kalarash Bessarabia 1881	Calarasi, Moldova
Mother: [A580a] Ette ("Ethel") Rabinowitz	Kishinau Romania	Chisinau, Moldova en.wikiDedia.org/wiki/Chi%C8%99in%C4%83u
Uncle: Nuchum ("Nathan") Rabinowitz*	Konela, Russia 1885	Konela, Ukraine (21 km to Zhashkiv)
Uncle: Sander Rabinowitz*	Calarasi, Romania 1889	Calarasi, Moldova Residence: (Also from "Jaz, Romania" Iasi, Romania – 1921)

* Mother's relatives; not B'nai Khaim.

Câlârasi, Moldova as his most likely David Caprov's birthplace given

(1) some information from the passport and naturalization papers is false;

(2) some information from the police file is true;

(3) Sander Rabinowitz pointed to "Kalarash" as a birthplace

Relation of locations to each other.

Fig. 35-2: Key cities

Immigration

Velvel left home at a young age and slowly made his way to America, first to Bucharest to obtain a passport and visa, and then to Antwerp, where he doubtless intended to board a ship for America. Instead, he ended up in Cuba a year later with a new identity: "Israel Perepelitzky." Coincidentally – or not – a young man named "Izrael Perepelitchi" with a strikingly similar profile and journey was in Antwerp at the same time.

Antwerp authorities tracked immigrants passing through their city, and (conveniently for us) retained files on them. Those files include addresses in Antwerp for the two immigrants just steps from each other. Both were by the train station, where likely many other immigrants stayed.

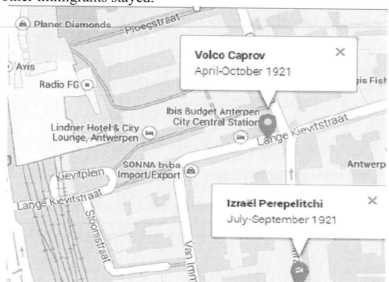

Fig. 35-3: Street map

Whether Velvel borrowed Izrael's name in some fashion is unknown. Note that only the name is the same (though spelled differently); other identifying details are different. Where did the other details – birth date, birthplace – come from?

"Volco Caprov"	"Israel Perepelitzky"	"Izraël Perepelitchi"
Birth: 1906	Birth: 2 Feb1904	Birth: 17 Feb 1902 Per naturalization papers: 15 Dec 1898
Birthplace: "Kalarash, Romania"	Birthplace: "Chernovitz, Romania"	Birthplace: "Winnitza, Ukraine"
Antwerp police inquiry regarding whereabouts: Requested: 12 Dec 1921 Respond: 23 Dec 1921		Antwerp police inquiry regarding whereabouts: Requested: 1 Dec 1921 Respond: 8 Dec 1921
Passport 90414	Passport 34304	Passport 4266
Romanian passport 90414 issued by Minister of Interior, Bucharest, Mar 9, 1921. Visa 2002 by Belgian Consul in Bucharest	Romanian Consul General issued on Oct. 9, 1922, in Havana; US Consulate stamped on Oct 25, 1922	Romanian passport 4266 issued by Prefect Chisinau Romania on Jul 5, 1921. Visa 4872 by Belgian Consul at Bucharest on Jul 11, 1921.

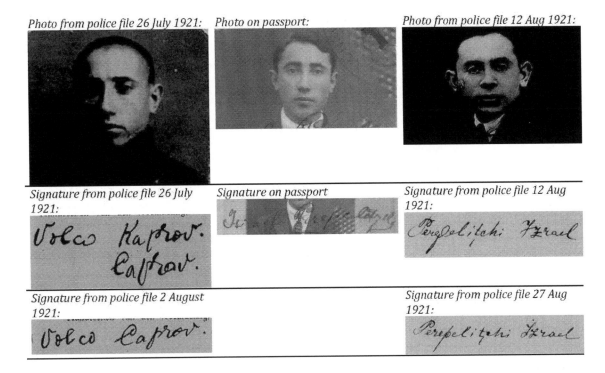

Photo from police file 26 July 1921:   *Photo on passport:*   *Photo from police file 12 Aug 1921:*

Signature from police file 26 July 1921:

Signature on passport

Signature from police file 12 Aug 1921:

Signature from police file 2 August 1921:

Signature from police file 27 Aug 1921:

Fig 35-4 Photo from police file

Journey

Why didn't Velvel board a ship to America from Antwerp? How and when did he lose his passport? How and when did he get a new (false) passport? (The signatures were identical to those shown, but why do the dates differ Aug 2, 1921, and Aug 27, 1921. Those questions are not yet answerable. We know little about his journey, but the following retraces his known steps.

Fig. 35-5: (Map) Antwerp address given in the police file.

Fig. 35-6: Today's view of Lange Kievitstraat 104, 2018 Antwerpen, Belgium.

How and when Velvel got from Antwerp to Cuba is unknown. There is a mostly illegible comment in his police file indicative that illness delayed the journey. Regardless, a one-year gap exists from the last record of him in Antwerp and the first in Cuba. His passport indicates he lived at 20 Christo, Havana. No Google street view is available in Cuba, but two guesthouses are listed on the block.

Twice weekly, the SS "Cuba" (P&O SS Company) traveled from Port Tampa to Havana via Key West and returned. "Steamboat Day" witnesses experienced joyous and exuberant reunions between friends and relatives who lived in the sister republics, separated by only 90 miles of water.

Fig. 35-7: Ship "Cuba" on which Velvel left Cuba on Nov 3, 1922, and arrived in Tampa on Nov 5, 1922.

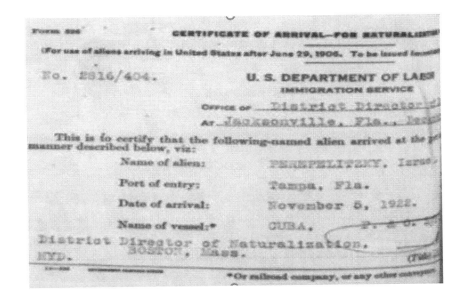

Fig. 35-8:
Immigratio
n
document.
2816/404..

Immigration timeline

Note: The names are those in official documents:

- "Israel Perepelitzky" = Passport of Velvel Kaprov
- "Israel Purpel" = Naturalization papers of Velvel Kaprov
- "Volco Caprov" = Police file on Velvel Kaprov
- "Israel Perel" = Naturalization papers of Izrael Perepelitchi
- "Izrael Perepelitchi" = Police file on Izrael Perepelitchi

Velvel Kaprov		Izrael Perepelitchi	
Date	Event	Date	Event
		Dec 15, 1898	Israel Perel born Winnitza, Ukraine
		Feb 17, 1902	Izrael Perepelitchi born Winnitza, Ukraine
~1904	Israel Perepelitzky born Boukovine, Romania		
Feb 2, 1904	Israel Purpel born Chernivtsi, Ukraine		
1906	Volco Caprov born Calarasi, Moldova		
Mar 9, 1921	Volco Caprov Romanian passport issued in Bucharest; Belgian visa issued in Bucharest		
April 1921	Volco Caprov arrives in Antwerp		
		Jul 5, 1921	Izrael Perepelitchi Romanian passport issued in Chisinau
		Jul 11, 1921	Izrael Perepelitchi Belgian visa issued in Bucharest
		Jul 20, 1921	Izrael Perepelitchi arrives in Antwerp
Jul 26, 1921	Volco Caprov police info file #1		
Aug 2, 1921	Volco Caprov police info file #2		
		Aug 12, 1921	Izrael Perepelitchi police file #1
		Aug 27, 1921	Izrael Perepelitchi police file #2
		Sep 21, 1921	Izrael Perepelitchi left Antwerp

197

		Oct 1, 1921	Israel Perel emigrated to U.S.
		Oct 9, 1921	Izrael Perepelitchi arrived NY
Oct 10, 1921	Volco Caprov left Antwerp		
		Dec 1, 1921	Police inquiry into Izrael Perepelitchi
		Dec 8, 1921	Police response to inquiry about Izrael Perepelitchi
Dec 12, 1921	Police inquiry into Volco Caprov		
Dec 23, 1921	Police response to inquiry about Volco Caprov		
Oct 9, 1922	Israel Purpel Romanian passport issued in Havana		
Oct 25, 1922	Israel Purpel US visa issued in Havana		
Nov 3, 1922	Israel Purpel left Havana		
Nov 5, 1922	Israel Purpel arrived Tampa		

Family connections timeline

Although Velvel seems to have traveled alone, his journey was made in the context of his family members' trips. For some insight into the "why" behind the "when" and "where" of his journey, the timeline below shows the whereabouts of various family members during these years. This information comes from immigration records only and may or may not be entirely accurate.

Father [A580] David Kaprov	Step-mother [A584b] Beile (Waxman) Kaprov step-brother [A588] Chaim Kaprov	[A581] Velvel Kaprov	Uncle: Nuchum Rabinovitz	Uncle: Sander Rabinovitz
~1880: Born Cälärasi, Moldova	~1877: Beila Born "Dubora"	~1906: Born Calarasi, Moldova	~1884: Born Konela, Ukraine	Mar 1889: Born Calarasi, Moldova
Oct 13, 1912: Resident of Sokolivka; sailed from Hamburg to Buenos Aires?*	Dec 24, 1911: Chaim born "Dubova"			
Jun 27 – Jul 13, 1913: Resident of "Dubowe"; sailed Hamburg to Quebec*				
1921: Living in Quebec at Rue des Fossé (#12 or #20).	May 8, 1921: Arrived Quebec	Mar 9, 1921: Bucharest Apr – Oct 1921: Antwerp		Mar 5 to Apr 1921 Resident Iasi, Romania; Sailed with wife & daughter from Antwerp to New York to join brother Nathan Robinson.
		Oct 1922: Havana, Nov 3-5, 1922:		
		Sailed Havana to Tampa		
			May 5, 1926 & Jan 4, 1928 Witness on Sander & Israel's naturalization petitions, respectively	

* Two immigration records are a good match for David Kaprov; whether these refer to the same person is unknown. Perhaps David went to Buenos Aires for a time before coming to Quebec.

Record 1: Hamburg to Buenos Aires Oct 1912		Record 2: Hamburg to Quebec Jun/Jul 1913	
Name:	David Kaprow	Name	Dawid Kaprow
Departure Date:	Oct 13, 1912	Departure Date	Jun 27, 1913
Destination:	Buenos Aires	Date of Arrival:	Jul 13, 1913
Birth Date:	~1882	Birth Date	~1878
Age:	30	Age	35
Marital Status:	Married	Marital Status	Married
Residence:	"Justingrad" (Sokolivka, Ukraine) from which many Kaprovs came Close to Zhashkov.	Residence	"Dubowe" - appears as the same place Beile and Chaim cite in their arrival records; its modern equivalent could be any of several areas.
Occupation:	Tailor	Occupation	Tailor
Port of Departure:	Hamburg	Port of Departure	Hamburg, Germany
Port of Arrival:	Boulogne; Southampton; Coruna; Lissabon; Rio de Janeiro; La Plata	Port of Arrival	Quebec, Canada

Assuming that at least one record is a match, it appears David left the country when Velvel was only about six and his other son, Chaim, was just a baby. Velvel most likely lived with his mother, Ete, and grandmother, Rachel Sirota, at the time.

Family stories say that Velvel's mother, Ete Rabinowitz, died in a pogrom and was the catalyst for his immigration. Beile, Chaim, Velvel, and Sander all journeyed in the spring of 1921, though it is unclear who lived where at the time. A massive resurgence of pogroms occurred throughout the region in 1919, mainly subsiding by the 1920s.

Though an estrangement existed between Velvel and his father's second family, Velvel provided his father's address in Quebec to Antwerp's authorities as 12 Rue des Fossés (though Beile's passenger arrival record states it as 20 Rue des Fossés). Was Velvel initially intending to join his father?

If not, was he planning to join his Uncle Nuchum, and why didn't he travel with his uncle Sander and his family? Did they get separated, or were they just not living nearby at the time? Sander was living in Iasi, Romania, which is quite close to Calarasi.

The "new country."
Velvel, Nuchum, Sander, Beile, and Chaim all made it to the new country. Velvel joined his uncles in the Cambridge area, and [A584b] Beile and [A588] Chaim joined Velvel's father [A580] David, in Quebec. Velvel lived with his new identity for the rest of his life, though he called himself William, as a sort of middle name, and named the store he later owned "Willy's Creamery."

#36 [A079] MENDEL ROBBOY'S GREAT ESCAPE
by [A088] Benjamin Robboy's son, [A090] Howard Robboy

Editor's note: The Russian Revolution, which followed World War I (1914-1918) was a time of enormous political and social revolution across the Russian Empire. It began in 1917 with the elimination of the monarchy. The Civil War ended in 1923 after the Bolsheviks had established the Soviet Union. Five other Soviet republics were born then also: Armenia, Azerbaijan, Belarus, Georgia, and Ukraine.

Father's grandparents, [A010] Ben Zion Robboy and Leah Voskoboinik, had six children; three boys, one girl, and two infant twins who had crib deaths. The youngest boy was [A079] Mendel. His son, [A088] Benjamin, was born in 1913 and was about 8-10 years old (1921-1923) when what followed occurred.

About 1920, an agent came to Mendel's home in [C01] Knyazhe and said he was to be drafted into the Russian army. Mendel would have been about age 35 at the time. The service for Jews so inducted was typically 25 years long. At that time, Mendel had a long red beard, for which the town citizen had named him, "the rabbi."

After a one year absence, Mendel suddenly reappeared at home and knocked on the door. [A088] Benjamin, Mendel's son, not knowing who the stranger was and fearing he was a burglar, grabbed something handy and hit Mendel over the head.

The family quickly decided it was time to flee, understanding that if Mendel didn't return and was found at the house, he would be considered AWOL and would receive severe punishment.

During their escape and to escape notice, they spent the days in the basements of sugar beet warehouses that Jewish families owned (not so different from the loose-knit "Underground Railroad" so famous in the US during the Civil War). Under the cover of night, the family traveled from one shtetl to the next, ultimately reaching freedom. This movement went on for over a year, until one day, the family was caught.

Mendel was put up in front of a firing squad, and death was to be immediate. Luckily, someone, possibly a friend, perhaps a protector Jew, effected an idea. While bringing the soldiers some whiskey, unbeknownst, Mendel escaped. [A079a] Anna (Mendel's wife), [A080] Phyllis, [A083] Sid, and [A088] Benjamin (their three children) watched as this occurred. The group continued until they found a contact whom they could bribe and who could transport them over the Prut River, which separates what is now Moldova from Romania. Benjamin, at the time, was so scared that a pillow had to be put over his mouth to muffle the sound, lest they be given away.

At this point, the family deemed it best to split up. Anna, Benjamin, and Phyllis went to Bucharest. Mendel and Sid traveled to Cluj-Napoca, which was the second-largest city in Romania. They all had to remain there for another 18 months until the papers they needed from home could be brought over. During this time, they peddled fruit and bagels and sold orange drinks at the open market to earn a living. But this also was not easy for making a profit, they had to resort to unscrupulous practices. Sugar was more expensive than artificial sweeteners. And as the artificial sweetener was much cheaper, that is what Mendel used to sweeten the drinks. The problem that it was illegal to do so. Guards would come around periodically and check the juices to ensure that real sugar was being used. If caught, the stand was closed down, and the proprietor received a hefty fine. Since the market was both big and open, the trick was simply not to get caught.

Finally, they were able to board a ship, but before it sailed, they were forced to disembark. There was the concern that someone who had boarded had an eye disease, which was highly infectious. As had happened in the past, when ships came to the United States, the passengers mandatorily went through customs and health inspections. If an infectious eye disease was discovered, the passengers would be denied entry, and the ship then forced to return to Europe with its passenger load. And, to make the situation worse, the passengers had to pay an extra fare. The family thus had to wait for a second ship, the SS Canada.

Fig. 36-1: Steamship Canada.

The travel time involved was slightly more than one month. The ship first stopped in Alexandria and then to Constantinople, where everybody mandatorily disembarked. While there, all were disinfected for lice. A warning, some learned, was that the disinfectant would discolor/destroy the leather used in their shoes.

The travel to the United States was in steerage class, which was so typical for all immigrants. Having no money, uncle Sid would sneak up to the floor with a higher class cabin and abscond with enough food to feed the family.

Upon arrival in Rhode Island, it was found that Ben had contracted the mumps, and so he was forced to remain in Providence for another week. Meanwhile, all of the other family members left for Philadelphia, which must have proved an interesting dilemma as none spoke English.

Ben has many memories of witnessing the pogroms that occurred in Knyazhe when he and his family lived there. In particular, he remembers one specific episode where the Cossacks stormed in, found women with relatively long hair, tied the hair of the four women together, hitched the women to horses, and dragged the women face up until they died of their bruises and treatment.

Like so many other of the senior members of our extended family, Ben would not relate his experiences to any of his children until Howard was already age 32, which meant that Ben then was about age 64. Also, Ben, Howard related, refused to eat cornbread as long as he knew him. As it turned out, for during the two years Ben and his family hid and were trying to reach America, cornbread was the principal food available.

#37 [A350] FROIM (EFRAIM) DUDNIK

[A350] Froim Dudnik, who is described elsewhere in this book, was a gentle and good-natured fellow. His brother was [A326] Chaim Dudnik, who was the foremost Jew in Kynazhe. Chaim lived in a duplex, which [A160] Graf (Krasitzki) owned. Rarely did a home become available. The one that did was the half that cousin Chaim occupied. Froim desired it, but little did he know that [A011] Malka and Shmiel Robboy, [A026] John Robboy's father, wished it also. The fight is described elsewhere.

Some years later, the family of Froim's and his wife's family, the Dayans, emigrated to Israel. But life is never simple. [A350a] Sarah Dayan Dudnik had died during her fourth birth in [C36] Uman, Ukraine just before the planned immigration.

Concerned that Abraham and Chaya Dayan (Sarah's parents) would be denied immigration certificates due to their old age, Froim and Sarah's children were registered as Abraham and Chaya Dayan's children. The Dayans and Dudnik children emigrated to Israel in 1922 and settled in Nahalal (15 miles SE of Haifa) with Shmuel Dayan leaving Efraim Dudnik behind in Ukraine. Only after settling in Nahalal did the Dudnik children officially change their surname back to Dudnik.

[A351] Noah Dudnik, Efraim's son, drowned accidentally shortly after when in the Jordan River. [A350] Efraim Dudnik emigrated several years later and settled in Tel Aviv. But [A352] Tzipora and [A353] Miriam, his daughters, remained in Nahalal until graduating high school, and then stayed with Efraim in Tel Aviv until they married (around 1930).

Unlike the Dayan family who immigrated to Israel, most of Efraim's siblings and cousins (Dudniks and Kaprows) went to the USA.

Efraim Dudnik's brother-in-law, Shmuel Dayan, was the father of General Moshe Dayan (1915-1981), who became the Israeli Defense Forces Chief of General Staff, and for the government, Minister of Defense and Minister of Foreign Affairs.

Fig. 37-1: [A350] Froim (Efraim) Dudnik (1874-1954) with wife's ([A350a] Sarah Dayan Dudnik) family, c1812. Top (L-R): Eliahu Dayan (Sarah's brother), Bela Dayan Hurwitz (Sarah's sister), [A350] Efraim Dudnik.

Middle: Batya Dayan (Eliahu Dayan's wife), Chaya Dayan (Sarah's mother), Abraham Dayan (Sarah's father), Sarah Dayan Dudnik (Efraim's wife, pregnant with Miriam).

Front: Tzipora Dayan (Eliahu's daughter), [A829] Moshe Dayan (Eliyahu's son), [A352] Tzipora Dudnik (Efraim's daughter), Bat-Sehva Dayan Markowski (Sarah's sister), Yehoshua Dayan (Eliahu's son), [A351] Noah Dudnik (Efraim's son).

Note: Sarah's brother, Shmuel Dayan, not in the picture, had already emigrated to Israel to prepare for the rest of the family's coming.

Fig. 37-2: [A829] Moshe Dayan.

#38 [A120] PAULINE VOSKOBOINIK
By [A124] Harry Friedman

[A001] Laizer Eli Voskoboinik, described elsewhere, was the oldest of seven siblings. Two others were [A010] Leah, from whom the Robboys descended and [A105] Golda, whose family is the focus of this chapter

Lazier Eli determined, likely about 1880-1890, that it was time for Golda to marry. She objected to the concept that someone could force her into marriage, and so was one of the earliest known feminists in the family (but by no means the last). At one point, Lazier slapped her, telling her he had chosen her husband. She replied that if forced, she would get the marriage annulled, which she did. Golda refused to remain in such a union. At some later time, she visited in [C34] Tetiiv, a village some 15 miles north of Knyazhe and there met [A105b] Meir Groysman, whom she did marry. He was older, learned, and prosperous, based upon his dress in the accompanying figure.

Every year Meir contracted with neighboring farmers to purchase their entire crops of fruit, be it apples, pears, etc., to be delivered in the fall after the harvest ended. Also, Meir owned an inn in Tetiiv plus a bathhouse and stables.

Fig. 38-1: Voskoboinik siblings and family in [C34] Tetiiv: [A113] Rayah, [A105b] Meir Groysman, [A105] Golda, [A120] Pauline.

Golda and Meir's oldest daughter, [A107] Jenny, was born in 1888. At some time, when Jenny was a young adult, she argued with her father. Her younger sister, [A113] Rayah, born in 1893, had been permitted to enter the pharmacy school in Kiev. In itself, this was most unusual, for admission to such a school was exceedingly rare. Such an event happened only to families of wealth or who were well-connected and permitted to travel and live in these cities. Unless she were given the chance to attend such a school, Jenny declared that she would leave for America, and she did. As Jenny had left before Pauline's birth in 1903, the two never met until after 1922, by which time Jenny was at least 34 years old.

A pogrom came to Tetiiv during Pesach, 1920. Meir was home ill when the bandits burst in and ransacked the home. They hit him so severely in the head that he died from the blow several days later. Pauline, then age 17, was hiding beneath the bed. Though not discovered, the event certainly traumatized her for life. Fortunately, at that moment, the Bolshevik soldiers had come and put down the pogrom. Pauline and Golda left with the soldiers and went to a neighboring town. For a reason uncertain, Golda returned days later to her home, not realizing the marauders had not left. They immediately shot her. Pauline remained with the other refugees. Her sole possession was a feather pillow that she had grabbed from her bed when fleeing.

It was apparent to the group leader that they must leave the region. The leader of the group, a Jew, planned they would board a train to freedom, but not in the way we think of boarding. They would have to jump onto a slowly moving train that would be coming through the area. The leader demanded Pauline discard the pillow for there would be no other way for her to jump and hold onto the train's railing. She refused, saying that was all she had. In turn, she was told, if she wished to live, she must discard the pillow, and use all her strength to run and then jump onto the train. She grabbed onto a handle, and soon after that arrived at a safe house.

The next hurdle was to cross the Prut River from Ukraine into Romania. The idea of swimming across was unrealistic, and even taking a small boat across was dangerous as too many people drowned in that manner. Thus, the small group remained at the safe house until the winter when the river had frozen over. That permitted the group to cross the river safely to a hay wagon, the leader first having paid off the sentries on both sides of the river.

In Romania, Pauline sold cigarettes, matches, and whatever else street vendors might sell. During this time, many people offered to transport her to South America, where she could work as a nanny. Of course, Pauline was old and sufficiently wizened to suspect these offers were from pimps wishing to indenture her to a life as a sex slave. She knew that none of these offers were legitimate.

Safety came from HIAS, the Hebrew Immigrant Aid Society, founded in 1881 to assist Jews who were fleeing the pogroms in Russia and Eastern Europe. Money also came from an appeal to the Tetiiver societies, which had helped raise monies for this purpose. Cousins in the US, hearing she was coming, offered to adopt her. They gave her the nickname, Zlota, from zloty, which in Polish meant 'golden.'

The Soroky cousins from Tetiiv, now living in Akron, OH, agreed to sponsor [A120] Pauline. They then asked Jenny if she would wish to have Pauline stay with her because, after all, they were sisters. The only request was that sister Jenny reimburse the cousins for transportation. After Jenny moved, she learned she was to become the nanny for the children, [A108] Rose and [A109] Marvin.

Jenny's second child, [A109] Marvin Pritzker, grew up in Cleveland and later became a rabbi holding pulpits in Aliquippa and Homestead, PA. For 17 years, he served as the rabbi of the Beth Israel Synagogue of the Baron de Hirsch Congregation in Halifax, Nova Scotia.

Jenny's youngest child died at an early age from scarlet fever during an epidemic. Jenny was convinced that Rose had brought the disease home. Rose never married due to Jenny's never approving of any suitable match.

[A113] Rayah, after graduating from pharmacy school in Kiev, came to the United States, which was long before the pogroms kicked off in high gear. Even though she had been admitted to the pharmacy school, it was nothing like anything we all would recognize today. Jews, even if granted admission, were not permitted to attend classes in person. But they could sit for exams.

[A120] Pauline, after living with Jenny, moved with paternal cousins of her own age, Sylvia and Eva, to New York just before the depression was to begin. She worked making pajamas on the lower East Side in the garment factories. After returning to Akron, she found employment in the Akron Bag Company, a maker of industrial bags and sacks.

Pauline married [A120a] Julius Friedman, whom she met at a Jewish singles club (Kadima). His family had come from Tetiiv via Romania after surviving the pogrom and revolution. His father, Srul (Israel), had emigrated to the US in 1914, and now lived in Cleveland.

Like so many other émigrés from Russia, the first to arrive worked and saved to bring the remaining family over. One of Julius' brothers had been conscripted into the Tsar's army, where after nearly 25 years, he was to die at the hands of the Nazis at Babi Yar during the Holocaust.

All families experience likes and dislikes, which often remain hidden. Pauline met Julius Friedman and married several years after she had returned from New York. Little did anybody suspect that Jenny disapproved of the marriage because [A120a] Julius was a "shaygetz." He wasn't educated in Torah like her own husband. Although a scrap dealer, he knew his Torah. In the same vein, Jenny liked that Pauline's son was named [A124] Herschel, which incidentally happened to be the name of her husband. But she was not pleased that Harry's middle name was Volka aka Wolf, which was the name Julius's uncle whom she found unscrupulous.

There was also one last incident that eventually was solved and amusing. [A124] Harry (Anglicized) was born on August 3, 1940, but the obstetrician mistakenly entered the date of July 3, 1940, on the birth certificate. Harry was always curious as to why his mother was unwilling to change it once discovered. And Harry was all the more betwixt since his mother in her later years taught immigrants how to get their immigration papers filed and completed. Why would she not have this obvious error fixed? She was, after all, an American citizen. Pauline finally admitted that she had used false papers to enter the United States, and was concerned if that should be discovered, her citizenship might be revoked and she would face deportation.

Knyazhe, Sokolivka, and the Russian Homeland

#39 BIRTH

Often, a person ugly in appearance will be found compensated by a superior intellect. I remember reading a description of Karl Radek[80] as a man with a most repulsive face but of dynamic character and mind. [A282] Trotsky,[81] the great giant among the Russian revolutionists, was small in stature and poor in appearance but high in intellect and magnetism.

The Almighty dealt the same way with little Knyazhe. It was endowed with beauty and grandeur as if to compensate for the poverty and disease rampant throughout its boundaries. Lined with spacious meadows, gardens, and orchards, a river ran for miles long on both sides, bisecting the town into east and west, thus its full length. The response to the awakening in spring was an outpouring of life in all varieties and colors in the skies, on the ground and in the water. I was too young there to appreciate the biological resources that unfolded before my eyes, except that I was but a part of it all and enjoyed it immensely.

No sooner had the snow and ice melted, and the sunrays dried the mud than everything turned green. Already the birds flew in the air in formation, while down below there were the newly born colts, little calves, piglets, puppies and kittens, newly born sheep, goslings, ducklings, chicks and, of course, babies. Homo sapiens were to be distinguished and superior from lower animal life. In nature, however, man is but another animal and follows its laws to some extent, at least.

Thus, most mating is at a period that results in parturition in springtime. Parturition almost always throughout the animal world took place in privacy and during the dark hours of the night. Seldom, therefore, was one to observe the process of birth. To us youngsters, it seemed like a game of surprises as we walked out of the house to find a newborn animal that was not there the day before. There was a new colt or calf already up and running about, showing off to its mother. It was grand fun to watch them or feel their smooth, shiny furs. Frequently, it was the son or the bitch lying in some corner with the piglets or puppies pulling at the teats. The puppies were always of great attraction. One never failed to disregard the danger of being bitten by the mother, who was highly protective of her young at this time. The little lambs were especially cute. Covered with new black fur, karakul-like, they preferred to stay close to mother and seek security. The geese, the ducks, and their young instructively learned their way to the river. It was

---

[80] Karl Berngardovich Radek was a Marxist active in the Polish and German social democratic movements before World War I and an international Communist leader in the Soviet Union after the Russian Revolution.

[81] Leon Trotsky, b Lev Davidovich Bronstein (1879 – 1940), was a Soviet revolutionary who helped lead the October 1917 revolution and immediately became a leader of the newly formed Communist Party. He was the founder and commander of the Red Army. Once Stalin came to power, Trotsky was relieved of his positions and eventually expelled, living his remaining life in exile. He was assassinated a decade later in Mexico City by a Soviet agent. Trotsky's ideas, reflecting Marxist thought, opposed the theories of Stalinism.

incredible to watch them waddle across town to the river. We never understood how they learned to find their way, but they always managed to return home following a straight route as if laid out by the engineer. As Jews, we possessed none of these features.

My folks did have chickens and cows. Hence, I did have the chance to observe the process of birth. It was immensely satisfying to hear the first strike of the chick's beak against the shell of the egg. Soon they came rhythmically repeating themselves until the beak became more and more visible and until the shell broke and allowed the imprisoned weak, moist, grizzly little chick out. The mother now would transfer these little chicks into a box where within minutes, though still shaky on their legs, they would start pecking the grains of food mother prepared for them.

Only once I had a chance to observe the birth of a calf. Our parents were away to the bazaar when one of us children realized the great event was coming. Quickly we spread straw over the floor in the hallway and sisters [A017] Nessie and [A023] Tobie and brother [A024] Joe, and I assumed the obstetrician's role. Our excitement was extreme, even greater than that of the cow, who seemed to be very uncomfortable, moving and wriggling about and moaning with pain. It was a long and slow process. Bit by bit, the head advanced until it was finally delivered. Next came the body with its front legs folded against the body caudad and hind legs folded and pointed in a forward direction, i.e., cephalad. It was lean and wet. The delivery was a glorious moment. Even we in our ignorance and innocence were awed by it.

The mother next began to chew the cord, but we would not allow her to consume it or the placenta and quickly rescued the organs. The cow now turned to bath her body. Within minutes, the calf started to get onto its feet, first on its forelegs, then on its hind legs, but was unable to accomplish the task for some minutes. Apparently, the hoofs were too slippery. It would fall and then repeat the trial until after some 30 minutes when it succeeded actually to stand on its own four feet and instinctively pull at the udder of its mother's teats while the mother kept washing it with her tongue. Soon it was ready to walk and explore the New World. Twenty-four hours later, this little calf was running playfully about, entertaining not only its mother but all the children as well.

Calves were always our favorite pets. We loved to play and pet them. Our mother allowed plenty of milk for her calves and still supplemented their diet with eggnog, for she loved the elegant shine this gave their fur.

Among the new mothers at this time was also the cow of our neighbor [A326] Chaim Dudnik. Though usually contented, this one, following parturition, was generally extremely dangerous and pugnacious for two or three weeks. She was apt to attack and gore one with her sharp horns in her attempt to protect her calf. I had to run pretty fast when she charged. This cow and [A327] Fania, Chaim's oldest daughter, were born on the same day. Chaim would, therefore, never part with the cow regardless of the circumstances.

During my childhood, I never witnessed the birth of a human baby, but once did have the chance of hearing it being born. It was early dawn when nephew [A018] Nathan decided to enter the cruel world of ours. Brother Joe and I were outside the house, shedding tears and shuddering from fear every time sister Nessie screamed with pain. This seemed to have lasted a lifetime, but it ended suddenly, and all including us youngsters became jubilant. I was fortunate to see this happy moment repeatedly during my earlier days in practice when deliveries at home were a common practice. The physician who failed to experience such moments will have missed the greatest thrill, satisfaction, and inspiration medicine ever offered.

Spring never failed my birthplace with its crop of babies. A newborn was always an event for celebration. Since most people in the small town are more or less interrelated, the party was actually common to all. At the same time, the school children had a unique function to play regardless of the relationship. For us little ones, the event was of double interest.

During the lying-in period, the mother was always in danger and required protection against evil spirits. This was the duty and obligation of the abler schoolboys. Brother Joe, myself, and [A196] Chaim Shudler, therefore, had the honor of writing many prayers (Shir Hamaalots) on numerous sheets of paper. We posted these onto every door, window, chimney, or other opening leading into the house. Also, we pinned as many as could be provided onto the sheets suspended about the mother's bed so as to isolate her from the others in the house.

The sex of the newborn child did not minimize the joy of our people, yet for girls, the ceremonies were considerably reduced and simpler in form. The father merely had the child named on Saturday at the synagogue. For boys, the celebrations were more numerous and more colorful. During the Saturday morning services, the rabbi would name the child. Following the services, the father would invite the entire congregation to kiddush, serving wine and cake at the synagogue, or he would ask his relatives and friends to kiddush at his home where the service was somewhat more elaborate.

On Thursday or Friday, the entire clan of boys would visit the mother en mass. We sang the Shema and wished her health and happiness, for which we were treated with cake and wine. What was of even greater importance was that we were dismissed from school for the rest of the day. Wasn't that something!

On the first Friday evening before the bris, there was a "shalom zachar" (welcoming the male) greeting services. The adults were served cake, wine, and chickpeas (nahit). On the eighth day was the bris (circumcision, or brit milah "covenant of circumcision.")

Circumcision presented a serious problem in our metropolis. There was but one mohel, [A197] Yankel. He was Rabbi, Cantor, Reader (Baal Koreh), Slaughterer, Shamus, and Mohel. He was reputed not to be too proficient in his technique. Hence his results were reportedly poor. Mother, therefore, would not allow him to circumcise her darling boys, of whom she had four in all. For the first three, she managed to import a very special mohel, but by the time I arrived, she was so tired that she cared no more about whatever would happen. This time Yankel had his opportunity, and there I am to testify to the event.

The circumcision, which is the symbol of the Jew, fulfilled the covenant between Abraham and God and was a glorious celebration then in our little Knyazhe as it is now in our own land.

#40 A DREAM COME TRUE – A HOME

Dreaming is man's prerogative. It is the dream that stimulates him and spurs on his ambition to seek new conquests, new empires, and new worlds. Because of man's ideas, America was discovered, and now outer space is being explored.

Not all dreams need to be of lofty height. Our folks in Knyazhe also dreamed, but their dreams were simple and as humble as they were themselves. My parents, like the rest of the people in town, dreamed of a home. There were precisely eight homes in town used by the Jews, each having three to four rooms, as well as other conveniences man cherished. All of the houses belonged to the [A160] Graf. Before them, their fathers had lived in their homes. Thus, they came to look at the homes as their own because of what they termed "hazakah" (birthright). One had to wait for a vacancy to get one of these homes. This happened only when one died or left town because of age, but even then, there was usually a son, a daughter, or some other relative who received preference. A large sum of money was also needed to consummate the transaction. And yet they dreamed.

Our home was the half-duplex of the typical peasant hut owned by [A228a] Urpina Skrivenuk and consisted of one large room 25 by 15 feet. I remember this home very well. The oven took up about a fourth of the valuable space. The second quarter of the house had twin beds; Father and brother [A024] Joe slept in one and Mother and I the other. A table that mother and her two daughters used to carry on the dressmaking establishment occupied the third quarter. The last quarter housed a tall wooden case with shelves filled with dry goods and constituted a dry goods store. The remaining space, if one can imagine any left, was for customers, visitors, and friends. At night bed space was provided here for both sisters, [A017] Nessie and [A023] Tobie, to sleep in and for [A258] Rebbe Laib, who was entitled to two weeks room and board for each pupil per semester. Besides all this, there was the large tub, used for feeding the cow as well as the calf. And, during the cold winter season, the calf was kept in the house overnight. In spring, young chicks requiring special protection came in as well.

Brother [A012] Hymie was the only one who presented no particular worries. He was always away in [C36] Uman, [C14] Kishinev, or [C29] Odessa. When he did drop-in, there was a large trunk in the hallway that served as his bed. Under these circumstances, is there any wonder that families dreamed?

The excitement and emotional state mother was in on awakening early one morning in the late summer of 1902 was indescribable. Mother dreamt that [A221] Avrom Aaron was leaving town and offered her his home. She knew it was but a dream but couldn't dismiss it from her mind. She narrated her dream to Father and sat down to work beside her two daughters. Work, however, was impossible. Both father and mother kept peering into the window as if expecting someone. Somehow, their excitement was transmitted to us. All of us joined in the restlessness though Mother denied anything unusual occurring.

Thus, things continued for some time when suddenly Mother and Father saw two figures in the distance that appeared to come in our direction. "Could that be the old man and his wife?" They looked again. It definitely was a man and a woman. Father and Mother exchanged glances, "Is it really?" And real it was! Slowly the old couple made their way toward our hut, unaware of the strain and anxiety their expected arrival was causing. The two were welcomed and made comfortable, and, after the usual amenities, the old man made his proposition. He desired to transfer or sell his hazakah to Father. Because of infirmities of age, he contemplated moving to [C43] Zashkov, where he might live with his daughter, [A222] Pupa. The hydrogen bomb could have had no greater effect than the proposition made to my parents. But how to consummate the transaction was another problem. They knew that [A326] Chaim Dudnik would never allow them to move in. Chaim lived in the other half of this duplex. No doubt Chaim would prefer his brother or some other closer relative.

But this was a home for which it was worth fighting. It was the chance to change from our one-room home of our peasant hovel to a larger, four-room, more modern home, even if it was otherwise simple, as were all the houses surrounding it. It had a huge living room, probably 50 x 18 feet. There were two bedrooms and a large kitchen in addition to a substantial cellar, a fruit room and ample space for the cow, the calf, wood, and straw. Was God himself and not only his angels playing with them? Immediately, but very secretly, [A221] Avrom Aaron and my parents managed to obtain an audience with the Graf's aunt, who was in charge of these matters. Her approval was obtained so as to legalize the transaction.

It was now 1903, and the most challenging problem yet remained. Moving in had to be done secretly without Chaim's knowledge. And now, though you may not believe in miracles, one did happen. [A294] Gitie Dudnik, Chaim's niece, was to be married within a few days, and the entire Dudnik family would then be out of the city for a few days. Could there be any better opportunity?

Plans were all set, and everything was arranged. The moment the Dudniks left town, our loading started. I remember pushing the loaded wagon. Chaim was shocked when he found us as his neighbors across the hall. The mere audacity to perpetrate such an act was unforgivable. Chaim was shrewd and determined. He accepted the challenge and swiftly made his plans for combat.

At midnight his brother, [A350] Froim, in company with about half a dozen peasants, banged at the door demanding entrance to the house. He entered and moved some furniture into the bedroom, which he claimed as his. Chaim stood in the hallway, gleefully overseeing these maneuvers and enjoying himself. These scenes repeated themselves almost every night. Knowing that the neighbors and the peasants would come to his aid, Father wanted to fight this out once and for all, but all of us little ones, terrified by the scenes, would prevent Father from fighting. Mother would then appeal to Froim, who in reality was a gentle and good-natured fellow, but carried on with these excesses only because of his sadistic brother's instigation. Eventually, Froim would soften and leave only to repeat the same the next night.

The terror continued for two years until the time when our various relatives, the Trachtman boys, in particular, gathered to celebrate [A017] Nessie's wedding. All had been fed and were in the highest of spirits by the time the newlyweds were escorted to their room. They then went to [A350] Froim's place, removed all his belongings, and circled about the adversaries' home until dawn. In the morning, Chaim and his brother found the furniture and all their belongings in front of the home. Chaim's defeat was now complete, and he capitulated. No invasion was ever tried again.

#41 [A202] YANKEL WEINSTEIN

Yankel Weinstein, "the Bader" (the bather), was so-called because he was in charge of the public bathhouse. Ever since I knew Yankel, he seemed to be an old man. From what I know now, he must have been about 40 years of age. Only the dress and his general poor grooming made him look older.

Yankel was married to a dwarfed woman who was also far from bright, but she made up for her shortcomings by giving him seven sons and three daughters. No wonder he was poor. To feed such a family required a considerable income even at that time. Yankel, therefore, resorted to a multitude of occupations. As indicated above, he was the keeper of the bathhouse, which was his principal obligation and which he never shirked. His duty was to keep the bathhouse running on Thursday nights for the women who wished purification, on Friday afternoon for the men when they were preparing themselves to meet the Sabbath Bride, and any time when it was also needed for purification.

It was no simple matter in those days to prepare enough water, hot and cold, considering that the water had to be drawn by pail from a deep well and carried to the tank, which had to be heated by wood. Yet, he never neglected or minimized these duties. Two kettles were always kept full. One was kept heated and ready all afternoon. Also, a brick wall was kept hot so it could produce steam by splashing water at the bricks. Friday afternoon was great fun for us youngsters. All afternoon we were free to jump from tub to tub, helping the elders bathing or to add hot water for them on request or to splash water to generate more steam or to run up the benches and scrub our fathers' and grandfathers' backs. Now following this sport, we returned home, donned our clean suits, polished shoes, and repaired for the synagogue where we sang the "Lecha Dodi" to meet the Sabbath bride.[82]

This job paid Yankel no salary, but the community gave him the two large rooms adjacent to the bathhouse, rent-free, in exchange for his services.

Such payment may not be much, but to find a home in our Knyazhe was a real accomplishment. To digress from the story of Yankel, my parents learned this by experience, for Knyazhe was always in a perpetual housing crisis. They had four living children, had already buried two, and Mother was pregnant with me and no home in sight. They were frantic. No one in town could spare any space for them, but Yankel Weinstein, the compassionate Yankel. He came to their rescue. He came offering them the privilege of sharing his castle with him. That is how I happened to be born in the bathhouse and introduced into public service immediately after. This act was really goodwill from God.

To supplement his earnings, Yankel was also a tanner. He would skin the animal as well as cure or tan the pelt. He also bought the thread woven from the sheep's wool to manufacture a course and dense type of flannel that was beaten into a compact material to blankets or serve as the

---

[82] Lecha Dodi ('Come my friend'), the hymn composed by Solomon Alkabetz, is sung during the synagogue service on Friday night to welcome the Sabbath.

fringe for the peasantry's coats. At times, he would even help the furrier in the actual construction of coats as well.

Yankel and my father also served as night watchmen for the arendator. Their duty was to paddle a boat all night long along the river's shores to scare the peasants away, thereby preventing them from fishing. Yankel, however, was too honest or too loyal and once ran after the peasants to recover the captured fish. He paid heavily for that and never tried it again.

Yankel was illiterate. Indeed, he was a genuine product of his people, pious but coarse and uneducated. I never saw him praying from an open book, and I am not sure that he could even read the Hebrew prayers. I'm confident he didn't know the meaning of any of the prayers. This was probably true of 95% of our Jews. Despite the illiteracy, Yankel was the deacon and the shamas (sexton), keeping the synagogue in proper order for the Sabbath, holidays, and all other occasions. His salary depended on the contributions the synagogue collected on the eve of Yom Kippur (Kol Nidre). Again, the collections depended upon the gabbai's goodwill as our uncle [A001] Laizer Eli exemplified during his regime when the treasury suffered a deficit. The congregation was astonished when Uncle brought a charge of 18 rubles for whitewashing the synagogue when fifty kopecks would have been plenty. In contrast, when Father was gabbai, there was sufficient money to raise the salaries of the shochet and the deacon and throw a gala party for the entire congregation.

One of Yankel's essential duties as a deacon was his performance during the pageant on Simchat Torah eve.[83] When standing in front of the ark, as deacon, he summoned the men with his loud, raucous voice, to rise and give honor to the Torah. He would gather the fathers and their sons one after another, calling with his voice that carried well above the commotion, "Rise Reb Yakov ben Reb Shmiel– give honor to the Torah." With only three or four scrolls present, the pageant lasted all evening. This allowed Yankel to carry on much like the leader at a square dance.

Yankel also served as badchen (jester, a Jewish comedian, skilled in tossing off rhymed patter extemporaneously) just before the wedding ceremony. Here he was quite an imposing figure. The bride was seated in the center of the hall, with all the women and curious children in the town surrounding her. At the ceremony, I believe that the bride's hair was clipped, and the veil put on while Yankel chanted his recitation in rhyme, and all the women sobbed.

Despite all his activities and various jobs, Yankel was a penniless man whose status did not improve until his children grew into merchants. Until then, Yankel could not even afford rye bread for his children. They ate buckwheat bread instead. Buckwheat bread is tasty when fresh and still hot, but later, it becomes unpalatable. To those of us who always ate rye bread, the buckwheat was a treat. Hence, we forever exchanged bread with Yankel's children during school hours. Milk, of course, was also on the prohibited list for Yankel's family because of the expense. It was only the fluid left after churning butter that our mother used to send over to Yankel. It is a thin tasteless liquid that we threw out or was useful in cooking.

---

[83] Simchat Torah or Simhat Torah is the Jewish holiday that celebrates and marks the conclusion of the annual cycle of public Torah readings, and the beginning of a new cycle.

When I got to know the family, Yankel's oldest son, [A203] Shlomo, was already married to a girl in [C33] Terlitza. I remember when [A204] Chaim Hersh, his second son, returned from military service. He married [A216] Rivka Deutch, the furrier's daughter. [A205] Aaron, another son, was blacksmithing together with [A195] Lemel Shudler. I used to visit them daily on my way from school and learned the latest songs from them. These, I much enjoyed for their unusual flavor. However, Father thought differently, and after a good thrashing, I stopped singing. [A206] Bessie, a daughter, married a soldier [A206a] Kleinman, a native of [C42] Yedenitz from Bessarabia.

[A207] Laizer and [A208] Yossel, two more sons, were furriers. Yankel frequently worked with them. [A209] Dvosia was a dwarf. She presented a particular problem when the family left for America. In about 1906 or 1907, the older children left for the New World. Two landed in Argentina; the rest went to Canada. About 1908 or 1909 Yankel, his wife [A202a] Faiga, the dwarfed daughter Dvosia with her husband and the younger children [A210] Nechoma and [A211] Ishika, left for America. Dvosia, however, was disqualified, and the father decided to return home with her. I will never forget this man when he returned. I don't believe I ever saw a more dejected individual in my life. Everybody sympathized with him and helped all they could. I was his private secretary. He did not need to dictate letters to me. All he needed to do was to give me a few statements. I did the rest. The letters were perfect and to his liking. I knew exactly what to tell his children. Maybe that is why his survivors are so friendly to me to this day.

#42 [A217] BERYL RADLIDECIATNIK

[A217] Beryl Radlideciatnik was the cattle dealer in town. When I first knew him, he was about 30 or 40 years of age but appeared at least 60 years old. He had been a cattle dealer long before I was born. He was a great dealer, and I am sure no dealer in America could improve upon him. He knew definitely that after parturition, a cow would give a good supply of milk provided, of course, the cow has sufficient food. His main difficulty was not so much with the theoretical knowledge as with the practical side of the question. Beryl well knew that to buy a cow, one needed money. He learned this long ago, for what silly peasant would sell him a cow without payment. Even then, it cost some 40 to 70 rubles. These were the days of high finance, indeed. In Cleveland, one could borrow from the bank or possibly a loan company, but [C01] Knyazhe had no banks. Yet business transactions and exchanges were always going on.

Our few Jews were quite enterprising. Most of them were in business with their capital in continuous circulation, and in rotation among them. It never came to a halt, not unlike our mother earth. Unfortunately, Beryl did not qualify in this rotational apparatus. Not that anyone questioned his honesty or character, not at all! Actually, Beryl never knew what dishonesty meant. He was an honest and pious man, who was, at most, the second generation past the caveman both in dress and behavior. Of course, he was religious, prayed three times daily, but whether he could read the prayer book, I have my doubts. I do know that he was otherwise illiterate. When his oldest son [A218] Samuel, at the age of 20 or more, persuaded sister [A023] Tobie to teach him the three Rs, Beryl was greatly perturbed. Beryl was much shocked and ashamed of public opinion, after which returning home from the bazaar at midnight, he found his son Samuel practicing writing.

Beryl's wife, [A217a] Sossie, was never well. I never saw her on foot or out of doors. She was bedridden for years, probably with tuberculosis. There was no doctor in town. A herring was the best medicine available. Beryl, on the other hand, was a vigorous and healthy man. He worked hard walking to and from bazaars in neighboring towns. For this, of course, he needed food for energy. But the food was costly, and therefore, he seldom tasted meats or other delicacies. Black bread and borscht were his mainstays, except in summertime when cherries were free for a pirog.[84] Pirogi are really what he loved and what wife wouldn't please her husband with a pirog or two? For Sossie, this was not difficult at all. She saw no necessity to prepare the particular dough, roll it, cut it into small sheets, fill them with cherries, and bake them into pirog. She devised her own short cut. After all, what shorter route is there than a straight line? Two to three pounds of dough shaped into a round Jewish pumpernickel cut open, filled with cherries and baked into a pirog cannot be beaten. Besides, one such pirog would be sufficient to maintain Beryl for the entire day. Now, you see, what a wonderfully efficient woman she was!

[A168a] Tzirel Korsunski, the wealthiest woman in town, couldn't accomplish such a feat. Her kreplach (small dumplings filled with ground meat) were tiny and so dainty, hardly requiring any

---

[84] Pirog is a baked case of dough with a sweet or savoury filling. Pirogi, which are common in Eastern European cuisines, are considered as "the most popular and important dish" and "truly national goods" of Russian cuisine and "ubiquitous in Russian life."

mastication. By some chance, Beryl visited her home at dinnertime when kreplach was served. "How many of these could you eat?" Beryl would jokingly reply, "A thousand or maybe more." When a plateful was served to him, he quietly flung them one by one into his mouth, gulping them down. Watching him was so amusing that she brought in the entire pan of kreplach, and Beryl, standing, gulped them one by one until all were gone.

Beryl had to eke out a living somehow, and he did it through dealing with cattle. But who would advance him the money when it was far from abundant? That is why he came to Mother. She always listened to his woes. She was the one who even made the pants he was wearing. The chance she took was lending him the money, even though she shared in the profit. This great tradesman had to dispose of his merchandise on the day he bought it. A 3 ruble gain was an excellent transaction, and when, by the help of the Almighty, a net gain of 10 rubles was realized, a blessing was delivered of a kind I never heard since I left Knyazhe. If by chance, the animal was not disposed of, it had to be brought home and then later taken to other bazaars. Since Beryl would have to feed it, the loss was proportionately more considerable than the highest profit. Now one realized why the blessing was so heartily uttered.

On one occasion, Beryl had two cows at one time. It must have been an event the Lord Himself ordained for who could have blinded Beryl for the moment so that he bought a cow with no horns. Actually, she was a beautiful cow, very well fed, and yielding plenty of milk. However, she failed to grow horns. And who would buy a hornless cow? Beryl now had to walk the cow home from [C35] Tzibular, quite a distance. The prospect of feeding the cow and walking her to the next bazaar or two presented a dilemma. Mother agreed to keep the cow as our own. The news of this transaction reverberated throughout the town. It was proof positive of our great prosperity. It also proved profitable, for she gave plenty of milk, cream, butter, and cheese and added to our income.

#43 [A184] FRIMA GERSON

Of all God's blessings, our people in [C01] Knyazhe enjoyed but two in great abundance: children and poverty.

These were pious people. They lived up to the precepts of "flourish and multiply", as commanded in the Bible. Therefore the Yankelach, the Ruchelach, and Taibelach (defined as diminutive) were quite numerous and the higher the number of these, the greater was the poverty. In fact, this was the only prosperity our folks knew. The children sustained by the fresh air, good food, and polluted water somehow managed to survive despite the great prosperity. As they grew, their hopes, ambitions, and aspirations grew with them. Like all others, they too grew up to recite the prayers to welcome the Sabbath and call out for the Queen of the Sabbath.

One of these young women was the heroine of our unfolding story. [A184] Frima, daughter of [A183] Avrom Hersh and [A183a] Russi Gerson, was an illiterate and uninformed girl as were most of her girlfriends in town. She was tall and dark, with good looks. She was already 20 or possibly 22 years old and in great danger of remaining an old maid. The worried parents scoured the entire vicinity. They were business people of a sort and willing to give a fine dowry, say 100 rubles or possibly even 200 rubles if need be, and even room and board for six months if necessary. Of course, they were not idle. They sought out the most prominent and most versatile shadchan (a Jewish professional matchmaker or marriage broker.) The search went on for months, and as the saying goes, "If thou seekest, thou shalt find." One beautiful wintry Sunday morning, the shadchan appeared in company with a young man, [A184a] Yudel, a feldsher from the city of [C28] Ochhmativ.

Dressed in a fox fur overcoat, tall karakul (pelt from a specific breed of sheep) cap, and well polished, high winter boots, he appeared as a prince no girl would ever dare to turn down. He was handsome. He had a fine, smoothly shaven face with a neatly trimmed mustache. He, too, recognized his long-lost rib at the very first glance. No time was wasted. A preliminary engagement was drawn up. A week later, his parents arrived, a formal betrothal was concluded, and the wedding date set.

If the problem above was difficult, the difficulties resulting following the engagement were sure to be formidable.

#44 PLUNDER OR LIFE IN KNAYZHE

Whether heredity or environment shapes the man, I leave the opposing factions to decide. The people among whom I was raised during my formative years were a people that were simple, illiterate, and bound to hard, consistent toil in a world still close to days of creation. They differed not in behavior, social and moral, from those of our people in the big cities of today, almost a century later. All the gossip, jealousies, animosities, injustices, and crimes observed here were prevalent there. Every person in town at one time had a derogatory epithet such as thief, cow, swindler, whore, and every dog carried the nuance of some individual such as mean, dull, lean, or sluggish to characterize him. The larcenous character of the rich was no different from those of today. They resembled the predatory bird that holds its victim in its powerfully clenched talons nibbling at its entrails until only the dry skeleton is left. They, too, hold on to the victim until its last gasp of breath.

Outstanding examples of these larcenous character types were [A326] Chaim Dudnik and [A168a] Tzire Korsunski, who owned everything of value in town. Chaim and his brothers owned two grocery stores, the saloon, the mill, and the fish in the river. Chaim was also the overseer of the [A160] Graf's estate, which included the fields of grain, sugar beets, and forests. Tzire owned the largest grocery store, a warehouse of raw iron, and parts for the smithy. Both robbed, plundered and fleeced all who fell into their hands. For these good deeds, they were favored with pews on the Eastern Wall and special honors when summoned to the Torah on Saturdays. This is often the only time he came to shul. The same sort of plundering goes on here in our sophisticated cities only on a larger scale. Nowadays, we honor the plunderers with plaques, lauding speeches, and elaborate dinners. The universal disease is we honor the rich for their amassing great wealth and not precisely for what they do for humanity with their substantial wealth. The difference from what was done in [C01] Knyazhe is in the magnificence of scale. The everyday folks, i.e., the peasants, were satisfied with simple pilfering. They were satisfied to pilfer a few fish for dinner or to sell the excess to the Jews for the Sabbath. To this end, they set up nets all along the river shore.

[A011] Father and [A202] Yankel Weinstein were night watchmen whose job it was to scare these pilferers away. Once Yankel dared to pursue these runaways, but after the beating received, he vowed never to repeat the pursuits again. Stealing, embezzling, and police involvement in crime were also common.

When a woman was arrested for stealing a bowl of dry goods, the goods were kept as material evidence. When she was released, there was hardly any material left to be returned. The pickpocket found the bazaar a most useful place and played his game cleverly. He would always employ the police officer as his bodyguard who would then come to his rescue and free him from the mob when caught.

The starshina (mayor) was also in charge of the government liquor store. He was a fine, reputable man but yet succumbed to the temptation of money. By the time he realized what was facing him, there was no way out. One morning he was found with his head stuck in a hole in the ice that covered the river.

The plight of the Jew was always grave. There was neither industry nor commerce. There was no way of learning a trade or profession. One was therefore doomed to eke out a living of some kind by tricks or cheating in the market during the bazaar days. The peasant had no idea of the market value of any of his products or produce. He always asked a fantastic price, and bargaining ensued until some agreement was reached, leaving but a very meager profit for the buyer. To overcome this, the buyer learned to cheat on weight or measure and thus eke out some sort of profit for the day. Occasionally the buyer would be caught and pay dearly for his actions. This happened to [A192] Shmiel and [A193] Yankel Shudler when a peasant caught them in the trap set for them in his home. They paid plenty and were very happy to get out from his clutches.

Love with all its complications was well known here. That [A233] Urpina, a peasant girl, had a son by [A170] Bennie Korsunky was a well-kept secret, which for his cousin, [A182a] Bouch Mordechai, extracted excellent compensation under threat of blackmail.

Crime of a more serious nature was also not uncommon. Brothers [A196] Hershel and [A195] Lemel Shudler operated the smithy in town. Both were healthy, cheerful, and friendly boys. It was my privilege to stop there almost daily on my way home from school and operate the bellows for them. In return, they would teach me the latest songs. They were well-liked by all. They worked hard and kept the transportation of the town going. The demand for their service was high and therefore required much in iron parts, i.e., supplies, all of which [A168a] Tzire monopolized and kept in her warehouse. They felt entitled to at least part of the quantity and proceeded to help themselves during the darkness of the night. To help them in their work, they even developed a code of their own. The younger sat in town, picked up the code, and used it though not knowing what it meant. This continued for some time until the police picked them up. The satsky (a minor police officer), carried only a stick, but in applying the latest method of torture, the babitz (rack), had no difficulties in extracting the facts. Thus, one afternoon the entire town was much frightened by the shouting made when these two men with anvils suspended from their necks were led through the streets.

The truth quickly dawned upon us, and though no one doubted their guilt, our sympathies were with the boys. No one felt that they were thieves, but only victims of their environment. We were happy to learn that they successfully escaped to Argentina.

Sometimes, accusations were false. One Sunday, during the bazaar, a rustler was captured and accused of stealing a cow. Realizing his expected fate, the rustler readily confessed, claiming to have sold it to the butcher. The mob now led the thief to the stalls of our two butchers whose stalls were next to each other. He happened to point to [A194a] Meir (Unknown last name), who was first on his path. Within a few days, father disclosed that Meir could not have been the guilty one because he saw Meir during the night when he was supposed to have met the thief. This alibi was strong enough to save Meir from years of imprisonment. Years later, here in the States, Father told me that though it was not beneath Meir to buy stolen goods, he felt that the mob had led the thief to Meir's stall. He was, therefore, not convinced of the truth and felt morally obligated to extricate Meir from a long imprisonment.

When or how elections were conducted, I am not aware, but Father was elected mestshanski storosta (mayor of the town) at least on two occasions. This is in contradiction to the chrestyanscy storosta (mayor of the peasants). Neither Father nor any other Jew knew his duties or his powers as mayor. They, therefore, limited themselves to the issuing of passports and vital statistics. The former presented no problems. During Father's regime, there was no discrimination, and no one experienced any difficulties in obtaining his passport. Also, fees remained at a minimum.

The storosta was entitled to a secretary. This office somehow fell into the hands of [A161] Pan Pavlovsky. This man was diminutive in stature, but with a beer belly larger than himself. He had not been sober since his early teens. He never kept books nor registered births or deaths because he was never sober. He presented a quandary. One had to tip him to induce him to register the birth. But once given a gift, he was sure to get drunk first and forged all registration. That explains why none of us had birth certificates. This latter fact was not limited to Knyazhe and led to peculiar and complex problems. Father found an easy way out. A bribe to the official in [C21] Lipovetz and all statistics were taken care of.

When reaching military age, the boys without birth certificates had to appear before a commission of physicians to adjudge their age. That is how brother [A012] Hymie was adjudged 18 when he was 21 years old and [A079] Uncle Mendel 21 when he was 17 years of age.

The problems presented were numerous. Each district had to fill a quota of recruits for the army. The boys drew numbers. Those with the highest had a chance to escape service. An only son or a firstborn son had special privileges and was drafted only when the others did not fill the quota. If they had no birth certificate, they lost these privileges. Rich men were able to buy these privileges. All sorts of manipulation and various complications resulted.

#45 [A555] MICHAEL KAPROV'S FAMILY:
CAPITALIST, WAR HERO, AND POGROM
by [A558] Gene Katzman

Editor's note: [A552] Shemariah Kaprov was the fifth of [A290] Khaim Kaprove's eight children. Virtually nothing was known about the branch until we heard from cousin [A558] Gene Katzman. In the early 1900s, this branch had become prominent "capitalists" trading in horses. Some were war heroes, but all but few died in the pogroms, and of the survivors, only a few survived the Nazis. Their stories are below. One member, [A556] Anna Kaprove, survived by sheer good fortune (See Chapter #105). Chapter 106 tells of her descendants leaving Russia in the late 1980s when the Soviet government officially again allowed Jews to emigrate. Cousin [A558] Gene Katzman recounts the stories told to him by cousins [A568] Anna (nee Kaprove) and [A567] Yakov Berdichevsky.

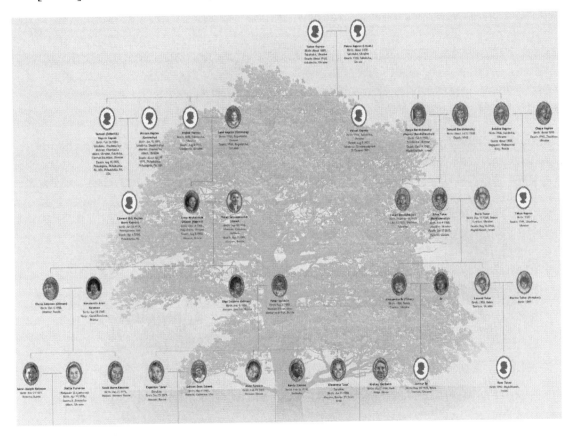

Fig. 45-1: [A553] Yakov Kaprov family tree

[A553] Yakov Kaprov (1860-1921) was one of the most important (if not the biggest) horse traders in Podolia, near [C13] Kiev, and one of the wealthiest families in [C02] the Sokolivka/ Justingrad village of the 1,000 Jewish families living there.

From about 1890 to shortly after 1910 and the beginning of WWI, Yakov would travel annually to Russia proper, which was unusual, for Jews were rarely allowed to move beyond the borders of the Pale. He first went to Tsaritzyn,[85] which was the railroad terminus and biggest port on the banks of Volga River. From there, he would travel about 800 miles to the east, and what is today's Kazakhstan. There in the prairie country, Yakov would purchase horses in the hundreds. He would hire the necessary people to help him herd the horses back to Tsaritsyn (Volgograd), where he would then have them loaded, having hired the entirety of the whole railroad train. The train went to [C36] Uman, the principal city some 30 miles south of Sokolivka. The Russian military itself was, in all likelihood, the primary purchaser of the horses. However, once World War I began, the military's need for horses jumped, and undoubtedly, the Russian Army appropriated most if not all of Yakov's horses and his horse business ended. It is unknown in what other companies Yakov had interests.

By 1914, Yakov's oldest son, [A554] Samuel, had left for the United States. Once settled in Philadelphia, he changed his last name to Kaplan.

Yakov's second son, [A555] Michael, was drafted into military service when he was 17 years of age. He was stationed in the region of Brody, an area about 40 miles northeast of Lvov and for some time near the Russia/Austro-Hungarian border. During a significant event in World War I, the nature of which remains unknown, he was awarded a high-level medal available to non-commissioned officers. Typically, it would have been the Georgian Cross, but only Christians were allowed to receive it.

A more chilling event occurred during this time. Michael was at the Brody front when something took his attention. He heard a whispering Hebrew prayer or a cry for help in Yiddish. None of his companions knew Yiddish, and so had no idea that the enemy troops had Jews in their ranks. In the dark without any of his compatriots knowing, Michael returned to the area only to find the wounded Austrian-Hungarian soldier who was a Hungarian Jew and who had been left alone. As befits a good Jew, Michael helped the fellow Jew by giving him the medical care available to him and provided him bread and other food. He also led him back close to Austro-Hungarian trenches. He knew that had he told any of his Russian compatriots of his actions, he, himself, would have been killed.

Toward the end of the war, [A555] Michael married [A555a] Leah Grinberg, who came from Pliskov, a small town in the Podolia / Kiev Gubernia. Leah's family was in the milling business and far better off than most other Jews.

But their life was soon to be torn asunder. After living in Pliskov for more than a year, and Leah giving birth to [A556] Anna, they came to Sokolivka in 1919 in time to die in a pogrom.

World War I had ended, but the civil war was beginning in Russia, which ultimately led to the formation of the Soviet Union. During this interregnum, would-be military leaders (a.k.a. Bandits) came and went, often monthly. The worst were [A284] Zeleny and [A286] Petliura (See

---

[85]Tsaritsen (1589-1925) was an early industrial city of Russia. After World War I its name changed to Stalingrad (1925 – 1961). The Soviets' Battle of Stalingrad and the invading German Army was one of the most bloody and largest battles in the history of warfare. Since 1961, the city's name has been Volgograd. The city lies on the Volga River's Western bank and is a major administrative center. It is strategically located close to the Don River.

chapter #54). The one theme all non-Jews shared, and that included many of the non-Jewish neighbors, was: "Everybody hates the Jews."

Michael Kaprov quickly became a leader of the Jewish Self-Defense Group in Sokolivka/ Justingrad.

And then came the infamous pogrom of August 1919, where Zeleny demanded 1,000,000 rubles, the sum of which was impossible to raise. Zeleny rounded up about 240 men and locked them in a house. Finally, 200,000 rubles were raised, but still, it was not enough. In retribution, ten men were murdered. Michael was one. When more money could not be raised, Zeleny killed another ten. Finally, he and his men went to various homes, killing and burglarizing at will.

Fig. 45-2: Grinberg-Kaprove family, C1836 taken in Justingrad.
L-R Top: [A556] Anna Michalovna Gilman (nee Kaprov), [A573] Chaya Kaprov, [A571] Belchik Kaprov; Lower: Raizel Berdichevsky, [A568] Anna Tokar (nee Berdichevsky), [A566] Ratsa Berdichevsky (nee Kaprov), [A566a] Samuel Berdichevsky, [A567] Yakov Berdichevsky.

Fig. 45-3: Grinberg-Kaprove family, 1926 taken in Pliskov.
L-R Top: [A555a] Leah Kaprov (nee Grinberg), Israel Grinberg, Basya Grinberg Ruvinsky; Middle: [A556] Anna Michalovna Gilman (born Kaprov), Surah Chaya Greenberg, Laib Greenberg; Lower: Manya Greenberg.

Fig. 45-4: [A566] Ratsa Kaprov and son [A567] Yakov Berdichevsky.

Fig. 45-5: Tokar family: [A568a] Boris, [A570] Leonid, [A570a] Marina, [A568] Anna, and [A569] Aleksandra (1985 in Belaya Tserkov).

[A553] Yakov, [A553a] Hannah, and several tried to hide in a crawl space beneath the home but were discovered. The problem when hiding was how to quiet the small children. To silence those who began to cry, the parents would stuff pillows into their mouths.

[A567] Velvel, who was then about 17 years of age, along with about 100 other youngsters, were taken to a nearby ravine. All were murdered when no money was forthcoming.

By the end of the pogroms, [A555] Michael and others in the family had died (See Appendix D). [A554] Yakov, [A554a] Hannah, [A555a] Leah, [A556] Anna, and [A566] Ratsa survived. Leah, with Anna, had returned to her parents and siblings in Pliskov. Yakov and Hannah could not bear the death of their two sons and soon also passed away. Ratsa and Belchik (who was then in Odessa) were the only two people who survived from what was once the prosperous and happy mishpocha that was called the Kaprov family.

Soon Ratsa and Samuel Berdichevsky married and moved to [C43] Zashkov to his family. Zashkov, a small town in Cherkasy Oblast, is the center of Zashkov district, located 10 miles north of Sokolivka. The first of their two children, born in 1928, was named to honor her grandfather [A553] Yakov. [A568] Anna, born two years later, was named to honor her grandmother [A553a] Hannah Kaprov. Samuel's father had built the home several decades earlier.

[A571] Belchik graduated from one of the Odessa universities with an engineering degree in making brad equipment. He married [A571a] Chaya, who was Jewish and grown up in the local community. In 1937, another [A572] Yakov entered the family. He was a full namesake to his grandfather [A553] Yakov Kaprov.

Despite the promising beginning, ugliness followed. Someone in Belchik's company falsely accused him, and after a trial, he was imprisoned for seven years in Siberia. Chaya and little Yasha (Yakov Kaprov) returned to Zashkov to reside with the Berdichevsky family. In June 1941, the Nazis invaded the western frontiers of the USSR, eventually pushing East. [A566a] Samuel was drafted into the Red Army, dying in 1943 during the war. At the end of June, Ratsa met a Sokolivkan Jewish neighbor, who, as a Red Army soldier retreating through Zashkov, told her that as the Nazis come, the locals were clearing the area for the Germans by rioting, burglarizing, and exterminating their Jewish neighbors. Ratsa quickly ran home and let [A571] Chaya and Raizel Berdichevsky (mother of Samuel Berdichevsky) know that they must leave immediately, and walk East to leave Ukraine, and get to the Russian proper. Chaya and Raizel refused.

With this new and alarming information, [A566] Ratsa, in contrast to Chaya and Raizel, immediately took both of her children, [A567] Yakov and [A568] Anna, and quickly left Zashkov, walking easterly. They covered 125 miles during the first month coming near Cherkasy. By chance, Ratsa saw a horse, and being a horse trader's daughter, knew well how to care for the animals. Thus, during the second part of their journey, they rode rather than walk. Soon they "rode" the next 200 miles to Kharkov where there was a train station. By train, they soon were in Central Asia, and by October 1941, in Samarkand, Uzbekistan, where they lived until early 1944 when Ukraine was Nazi free.

Chaya and Raizal's story ended tragically. The moment Nazis entered Zashkov, the locals drove the Jewish families from their homes and informing the German soldiers where to find the Jews. Some Ukrainians went further. They, themselves, killed their Jewish neighbors. The local neighbor who envied the house Samuel's father built, came over, and killed both women together, including the five-year-old, Yasha.

In 1944, when Ratsa with her children returned to Zashkov, they found the neighbor with his big family occupying the house. He claimed the house was his now, and "you Jews have the nerve to ask for it. You should be happy you got your life. You do not know when to stop. And now you want the house. What are you going to ask for next?" Ratsa left and found temporary lodging before finding a permanent home several years later.

Yakov later graduated from school and moved to Kiev, where he lived for some time before moving in 1973 to Israel. Ratsa joined him in Israel a year letter. In the mid-fifties, Anna Berdichevsky married Boris Tokar and moved to his town, Bila Tserkva, some 30 miles southwest of Kiev. In 1990, with their two children, Aleksandra and Leonid, the family joined Yakov in Israel. Ratsa died a half year before they arrived. Yakov, now 92 years old, lives in Migdal-Haimek, located 3 km north of Afula, Israel.

Some good fortune ensued. Laib Grinberg (1875-1941), who had become Greenberg, was [A555a] Leah's father and Anna's grandfather (not on the Kaprov side); his other children later prospered. Israel Greenberg became a well-known scientist specializing in physics. After having been admitted to a prominent physics institute in Moscow and himself already now recognized as outstanding, he led the other Greenbergs in the family to live in Moscow. [A556] Anna along with [A555a] Leah, Basya, and Manya Greenberg, thus came to reside in Moscow.

Russia, from after the pogrom era, the revolution and through the 1930s, became more "friendly" to Jews, especially to those who were not openly religious. During the 1930s, the population of Jews in Moscow numbered more than 500,000, which was exceeded only by New York City and Warsaw. Moscow had become a major Jewish center with two important Jewish theaters, Hodima (Hebrew) and Goset (Yiddish), as well as several Yiddish Schools and even several Synagogues. The Grand Choral Synagogue of Moscow was the home of the main Rabbi of

Russia and later of the Soviet Union, which might be unique for the Atheist State. By 1939 Jews had become the city's principal ethnic group. The city's population of Jews (400,000) was second only to Russians.[86]

See Chapter #105, which recounts the most unfortunate episode where grandfather Laib Greenberg (Grinberg), his wife Surah Chaya Greenberg, and other relatives went to attend a funeral in Pliskov in Podolie, just when on June 22, 1941 the Nazis invaded Russia during World War II. All were killed. Only Anna survived as she had remained home preparing for exams at the Moscow Medical University.

---

[86] In 1993, [A031b] Marion Robboy's cousin by marriage, Rabbi Pinchas Goldschmidt from in Zurich became the Chief Rabbi of Moscow. In addition to being the spiritual leader of Moscow's central synagogue, he headed the Moscow Rabbinical Court for all of the Commonwealth of Independent States (CIS).

#46 THE SABBATH

The Sabbath to our folks in Knyazhe was far more than just a day of rest. It was a day of relaxation and tranquility, a day of spiritual communion with the One above. The Sabbath was not an unwelcome guest. Plans to meet the guest were continuously in the making. Already on Sunday, the preparation for the coming Sabbath began. It was on an early Sunday morning that Mother, before going to her stall in the marketplace, managed to buy a chicken for the Sabbath.

Father always prepared his wine for the Sabbath kiddush on Monday. This was the best wine obtainable in Knyazhe. Actually, it was but an inferior aqueous extract of raisins. Whether the blessing of "hagafen" (Blessing over the wine)[87] was appropriate was never questioned.

By Thursday, the echoing footsteps of the guest reached into every Jewish home in town. By noon Thursday, it was usually my task to carry the chicken to the shochet over on the east bank of the river for slaughtering. In wintertime, this was not a task; rather, it was an enjoyable exercise. All one had to do was to cross the river on the ice. Not only was this a simple matter, but it also gave one the chance to count the holes in the ice the fishermen made in order to follow the direction of their nets. There were also the bubbles to count in the ice made by the breathing of the fish (my first lesson in ichthyology). Sometimes, some of my colleagues and I even had the opportunity to observe the fishermen as they brought the big net filled with splashing fish, frogs, turtles and lobsters, up through the ice. The latter were given free to all who wanted them. The Jew wasn't allowed to eat them, and some of the fishermen were unsure what to do with them. Occasionally, some youngster would burst in sudden outcry, but this never disturbed anyone for all knew that the strong jaws of a pickerel (a type of fish) had caught some youngster's finger.

In the summertime, the trip to the shochet presented a somewhat thorny problem. One had to cross the bridge and walk along the foot of the hill to get there. The peasant boys, as if keeping watch, were waiting for the Jewish boys to come by. They would then throw rocks or descend upon us and actually have us run through a gauntlet of whips. During the dry season, we walked along the river bank and thus escaped from their view. The game for outwitting them was, therefore, a continuous one. Occasionally, merely singing the following song contented the boys:

Szid, szid, cholomei- (Derogatory term, meaning Jew)
Suspended himself on the rubel- (Pole used for holding straw)
The rubel broke
And the szid croaked

By Thursday afternoon, the preparations had advanced considerably, and there was feverish activity everywhere. The chicken had already been plucked, cleaned, singed, opened, and contents examined for any abnormalities. When perchance any defect was discovered, the bird was quickly dispatched to the rabbi to determine its cash worth. With these preliminaries done, the more definite steps in koshering were to follow. The crop (stomach) and the intestines were removed and discarded, the bird split wide open, the large neck vessels removed, and the legs cut off. The fowl was now immersed and soaked in water for a prescribed time. Next, it was

---

[87] Blessed art Thou, LORD our God, King of the universe, Creator of the fruit of the vine.

thoroughly salted and spread out on a board for one to two hours when it was washed and ready for cooking on the Sabbath eve feast. The legs had their terminal toes and nails cut off. They were then scalded in hot water, following which the entire skin was removed. They were ready for the ptcha (jellied calves feet) to be served for the Sabbath morning meal.

By Thursday evening, if one happened to enter our kitchen, he found a whole factory at work. There was the large round deep tub on the table filled with darkish dough. It was rising high because of the unusually good yeast mother always used. This was the dough for rye bread used for baking during the weekdays. Next to this tub was a shallow oblong container filled with white dough that rose rapidly. This consisted mainly of white flour imported directly from the mill at [C02b] Sokolivka, for mother's challah had to be absolutely white in honor of the great guest.

At the other end of the kitchen, one was apt to find Mother rolling an especially prepared egg dough into a thin round sheet which, when finished, was folded over and over again upon itself until it formed a multi-layered roll. This was cut swiftly and very deftly into thin strings no more than one-eighth of an inch wide. These were the noodles for the soup and the kugel for the Sabbath meal. When mother retired on Thursday nights, I never knew, but when I got up on Friday mornings, the fire was already going in the oven, and it was hugely amusing to watch the sheet of red flame spreading across the dome of the large oven. The large round loaves of bread already sat at the far end and along the sides of the oven. Meanwhile, the challahs in the form of twists resembling braids were fed into the center of the oven. From time to time, the challahs were brought forward and painted with the yellow of the egg, then returned to the oven where they assumed the golden-red color, not unlike the cheeks of our beautiful Jewish maidens.

Despite the relative poverty of our shtetl and our folks, Mother ensured we always ate well, especially on the Sabbath. This day, for us children, was a treat. What she prepared was so very tasty.[88]

No beehive was ever more active than our folks in Knyazhe on Fridays. Old and young were busily engaged in the duties of the day, and no one shirked. Each one worked furiously to reach the common goal. Sisters [A017] Nessie and [A023] Tobie were hurrying since early morning to finish the garments promised for Friday. Mother, busy as she was in the kitchen, would join her daughters to give them a bit of assistance whenever possible. At the same time, she also managed to handle whatever customers came to buy dry goods when Father was not available. He supervised the housekeeper as well.

Every cleaning-woman put in a full day's work removing whatever had accumulated during the whole week. A final deed was to reconstruct the pripetshik (hearth of a clay or stone oven) that

---

[88] Editor's note: Father always spoke most fondly of his Mother, extolling her virtues, often in comparison to others. As one example, Father tells of his surprise 85th birthday when [A682a] Helen Shapiro, [A674b] Sally Shapiro, their men, and [A662a] Esther Fallenberg honored him. "They brought a large cake topped with cream and decorated with strawberries. [A026a] Sarah made tea and we ate and drank to a very lively l'chaim though there was no liquor around. [A675] Dottie and [A675a] Jack Dannhauser sent greetings by mail. It really was a most beautiful party and to my memory the first birthday party since my bar mitzvah which was just as beautiful and also without any liquor. [A011] Mother had made 500 or more cheese kreplach, sufficient to feed the entire congregation."

was made so famous by the song, "A small fire burns on the pripetshik and the house is hot." Yes, it as well as the floor in the living room had to be reconstructed, releveled, and repainted every Friday due to the week's wear.

[A011] Father, too, had no idle moments. He had the most difficult tasks. He had to chop the wood so as to prepare the fuel for the oven. In wintertime, he was to warm up the house before the others arose. During the winter, he also had to provide feed to last at least for two days for the cows, chickens, and geese. His most strenuous task was to provide enough water for all of us and the animals for over the Sabbath. In itself, this was a formidable job. The water had to be brought by pail from the well that was about a mile away. Besides, he had to look after customers and attend to various other minor matters.

The only two children free from labor were brother [A024] Joe and myself. Yet we were not completely free. Our Friday mornings started with a special breakfast consisting of a large buckwheat biscuit served with sour cream, a truly delicious meal. Following this, we left for school, where we chanted the Bible and recited the kiddush. This had to be at least near perfect to assure the rebbe could present us for examination before our parents on the Sabbath afternoon.

By Friday afternoon, a complete change in the preparation took place. Until then, all preparations were environmental. From now on, we attended to the self. Certainly, no one would leave his home unprepared for an expectant guest or fail to prepare his own self. By 2 p.m., the entire Jewish male population, with the exception possibly of [A191] Isaac Sudler and his two sons who were usually late from work, were ready to retire to the public bathhouse for a thorough cleaning and scrubbing before meeting the honored guest. Before leaving the house, the Sabbath clothes were brushed and laid out and ready for use. The shoes and boots were cleaned and polished and set aside for use upon return from the bathhouse. Now, all the fathers and their sons, each carrying towel, soap, and underwear, hurried from various places to the bathhouse.

There was [A326] Chaim Dudnik with his two sons, Father with his two sons, Uncle [A001] Laizer Eli, [A003] Haskel and [A002] Yakov Hersh, [A227] Shimon Pessis, and [A172] Mendel (the cantonist). Only at this time of the week did Grandfather emerge from behind the Graf's estate without the staff of Moses in his right hand or the basket on his left elbow. He had only a shirt, soap, and towel. What glorious afternoons those were. There was no school since noon. We junior citizens were free to mix with all. We could add hot water to the tubs of those who wanted it, jump in and out of anyone's tub, run-up to the top-most shelf of the steam room or simply throw water at the hot stones so as to produce more steam.

The bathhouse provided a marvelous opportunity to learn about both the latest politics and the latest events of the day. [A326] Chaim Dudnik, the only subscriber of the newspaper "The Friend," would tell us all the news of the day. Since sister [A023] Tobie bought the paper from him after he finished reading it, I also had the opportunity to read it. Now we gleefully recounted the feuilleton (newspaper or magazine portion devoted to fiction, criticism, or light literature), which under the caption of Rossi and Pini by [A830] Sholem Aleichem depicted the Russo-Japanese war battles in Manchuria. [A172] Mendel, the cantonist, added a bit of reality by describing to us the geography of Siberia he frequented and recited the various privations and tortures he experienced during his 17 years of military service as a conscript during the reign of [A278] Nicholas I. In addition, Uncle [A001] Laizer Eli, our Hans Christian Anderson, never failed to elaborate and embellish some of the rumors about the pogroms in [C14] Kishinev, [C29] Odessa, and elsewhere.

With the cleansing and purification over, all rushed home, donned the Sabbath clothes, and hurried to the synagogue ready to meet the long-looked-for guest. Our shul was a simple one. It had no decorations. It consisted of one large room with hard benches for pews. There was a simple ark, a cantor's stand, and a table at the center of the room for reading the Torah, but the place was clean, well lit, and inviting. We sang a specific song: "Come, my friend, let's meet the bride the Sabbath."

Thus inspired, we all returned home. I remember our home on Sabbath eve well. On opening the door, Father found the large living room brightly lit up. It smelled clean and fresh. Mother, dressed in her best and with head covered with a white silk scarf, sat at the table waiting for him, looking more beautiful than ever. She was indeed a beautiful queen. Though we couldn't see them, we were able to feel the angels hovering over the atmosphere.

A white cloth covered the table. There were two large challahs, each flanked by a small one for brother and me at the head of the table. The two sisters sat next to Mother. The candlesticks with seven candles, one for each in the family, added to the solemnity of the evening. No wonder Father sang his Sholem Aleichem so lustily. Each of the males now recited the kiddush. We washed our hands and made the HaMotzi[89] (Blessing over the bread). The family was now ready for the Sabbath meal.

The Sabbath meal was always extraordinary. It was a feast as becomes a great guest. There was gefilte fish (a poached mixture of ground deboned fish, such as carp, whitefish, or pike) with horseradish, noodle soup and chicken, noodle kugel, and finally tzimmes.[90] We felt like singing, and we did Kol Mekadesh and the Yom Zeh Mechubad, although occasionally brother [A024] Joe and I staged a little fight over the silver spoons and forks of which there were but two of each and which we monopolized as our own. By now, the older folks were tired, but we, the younger ones, were not ready to retire. We gathered to play in the moonlight, particularly in the summertime.

We arose early in the morning to chant the Bible before leaving the house. Father would not eat before praying, but we youngsters were served breakfast. During the fall season, there was a special treat for us, baked sugar beets, which we picked from the sugar beet caravans as they passed through the town and for which the drivers whipped us plenty as we attempted to pull the beets.

Grandfather always introduced the Sabbath morning prayer, an honor granted him for scholarship and piety by an Adon Olam that was as unique as he was himself. That the walls of the synagogue did not collapse as a result of the staccato hammering of this song merely testifies to the builders' great structural techniques. The prayers then continued until noon. We never

---

[89] Blessed are You, Lord, our God, King of the Universe, who brings forth bread from the earth. (Amen)
[90] Traditional Ashkenazi Jewish sweet stew typically made from carrots and dried fruits such as prunes or raisins, often combined with other root vegetables

hurried in Knyazhe. Actually, we enjoyed our sessions there. For us youngsters, including [A223] Yudel Dectar, [A196] Chaim Shudler, brother Joe and myself, there were special honors.

Often, for some unknown reason, mostly in the summertime, whether inspired by the prayers or only in search of excitement, an upheaval with fistfights and throwing of chairs would suddenly break out as if an explosion of some kind took place. And always [A183a] Russi and her daughter, [A184] Frima, were the heroines of the fight. Also [A225] Yankel Isaac, the clown, never failed to unbutton Frima's skirt during the conflict. This event added flavor to the observances of the day. The most exciting moments came after leaving the synagogue. Now the youngsters also had the chance to join the fight and throwing epithets at each other as they were going home.

After this, the p'tcha,[91] the grated radish, and the cholent (traditional Jewish stew) were most appreciated. The older folks now retired while the younger ones went out in search of entertainment. We went to the Loo (the orchard) where the fruit was available or to some peasant for watermelon. Mostly, however, we were content with munching sunflower seeds which we illegally carried in our pockets on the Sabbath. Many a time, we were forced to read "the ethics of our fathers," and occasionally, the rabbi had us exhibit the knowledge acquired under his tutelage to Father.

Mother's plaintive prayer to the God of Abraham, Isaac, and Jacob always signaled the end of the day. She always peered through the window and clasped her hands while singing plaintively in a high soprano voice imploring the Almighty to look kindly upon her and her household. Soon father arrived. All gathered about him. When in the presence of a candle made from several strands of cotton impregnated in multi-colored wax and woven into a single candle, he chanted the Havdalah (service marking the end of Shabbat). The Sabbath was now over. Immediately all returned to their usual labors and chores of the week.

The parting of the Sabbath was ushered in by an activity characteristic of the beehive. [A017] Nessie and [A023] Tobie resumed their work at sewing. Father immediately brought fodder for the cow and watered whatever livestock was around. Following that, he brought fresh water for tea and put up the samovar. Then he began filling the barrels with water in preparation for the visitors at the Sunday bazaar. Joe and I were dispatched to bring the tall wide-mouthed jugs filled with sour milk up from the cellar. Mother now skimmed the cream off into a particular bucket in which the cream was churned until butter formed. After removing the butter, the remaining fluid was then either thrown out or given to [A202] Yankel Weinstein for further use. The sour milk remaining after removal of the cream was fed to us as a repast for the evening meal. What was left was dumped into long sacks and pressed into cheese. With this done, we all relaxed. We now drank tea, with lemon and pieces of sugar on the side, and sometimes bread and butter with sweet tea. This time was considered a luxury and indicative of prosperity. No wonder [A168a] Tzirl Korsunski, the rich lady in town, could not condone us such privileges. Now my addiction to hot tea in a thin glass with lemon and sugar on the side is well explained.

---

[91] P'tcha or galareta is a traditional Ashkenazi Jewish dish prepared from calves' feet, a type of an aspic. The name derives from the Turkish words paça çorbası, or "leg soup."

In wintertime, the process was considerably altered. The fattening of geese was a significant industry in Knyazhe. I don't know how much profit there was in it, but it was plenty of work. A batch of geese would be fed for three or four weeks. Then on the parting of the Sabbath, the shochet would come and slaughter twenty to thirty of them at a time. The feathers would then be plucked and down separately, cleaned, dressed, and readied for sale on Sunday morning. This was some job. All the females, including [A178] Ruchel Korsunski, would pitch in to pluck the geese. After cleansing, some of the geese were sold whole. Others had the skin and fat removed and sold for a drobniak (a Polish low-value coin). The fat was then rendered and sold separately at a later time. The gribenes (crisp chicken or goose skin cracklings with fried onions, a kosher food akin to pork rinds), we enjoyed ourselves. When all was done, the geese were strung up by the neck in a cold place to freeze, and where no dogs, cats or other animals could reach them. Somehow, there seldom was any difficulty in disposing of them all early in the morning even before [A269] Shalom, the tax collector, had any chance to determine the number slaughtered. Unlike Uncle Sam, our collectors had neither policy power nor Uncle's efficiency. He thus lost out a good many times.

God, the Almighty and Merciful One had but two thoughts in mind when in His wisdom, he decreed that the Passover be celebrated in the spring. 1) The spring is the period of the great awakening and therefore was the most appropriate time for a nation just emerging from its early infancy to celebrate its birth. 2) He foresaw the plight of my people in [C01] Knyazhe and wanted them to have the opportunity to join the grand celebration.

The preparation for the forthcoming event started immediately after Purim and was a month full of excitement and high activity. Matzos, of course, were the first on the agenda because matzos presented a formidable problem in those days. We had no Manischewitz (leading brand of kosher products based in the United States, best known for its matzo and kosher wine) at that time. Even ready ground flour was still unavailable. It was somewhere about 1907 or 1908 when the first matzos were imported from the neighboring town of [C22] Lohahievka. Furthermore, no families required five pounds. Our own family only consumed three pounds of matzos, although we always ran the risk of falling short.

Our people were humble, unsophisticated, and knew nothing about organizational society. We had no constitutions, presidents, committees, nor secretaries to record the minutes of our meetings. The problem of matzos, therefore, started annually anew, from scratch.

[A011] Father and his cousin [A002] Yakov Hersh were usually the first ones to arouse the people from their inertia. They were the first ones to visit the flour mill. Here they would have the first grinding stone in the front part of the mill thoroughly cleaned from its accumulated hametz.[92] Then it was roughened with hammer and chisel as required for such a job. Now the specially gathered wheat was dumped into the funnel, whence it was fed for grounding into flour, then assembled into clean sacks and carried to a safe place.

The baking of matzos required a spacious area. The most favorite was the home of [A187a] Esther Gedalia Kapalushnik, which lent itself well for the purpose at hand because of its size and layout of rooms. Though the people knew nothing of organized society, they were not devoid of the sense of organization, imagination, coordination, and even efficiency. Baking the matzos resembled an efficiently organized factory. There were departments with foremen, supervisors, division of labor, and labor-saving devices that were crude, but in essence, no different from the chain belt system devised by Mr. Henry Ford (automobile manufacturer) of a later day. The reason the Soviet authorities failed to include the chain belt in their list of firsts was not from being unaware of the fact, but rather that they feared that the Jews, particularly those of our Knyazhe, might yet stage a revolution in a moment of pride and stimulation.

There was the overseer or general manager. His duties were to see that all the various utensils, appliances, and tools were prepared and assured there was plenty of water and firewood as well as sufficient tables and workers for the tables. There was the mashgiach (Jew who supervises the kashrut status of a kosher establishment), whose duties were limited to ritual specifications.

---

[92] Baked foods, such as cakes of breads, requiring the use of leavening agents were forbidden for Jews to consume during the Passover festival. Hametz are the forbidden foods.

There were the siever, the mixers who mixed the flour and water, the kneaders who kneaded the mixture into a dough, and the cutters who cut the dough into equal-sized pieces. These were then dispatched to the rollers, who were our young maidens. They were lined up beside the temporary long tables, and each was equipped with a roller pin. The daughters rolled these pieces of dough into matzos and transferred them to the last tables where the baker's assistant equipped with hand-operated spurs took over puncturing the matzos to prevent blistering.

The matzos were now ready for the shibers (bakers assistants who put bread into the oven.) Father and [A002] Yakov Hersh were equipped with two long-handled, oar-like spades. The distal end of one was the size and shape of a matzo and sieved to transfer the latter from the table to the spacious hot oven. The second terminated in a long narrow point and served to turn the matzos over from side to side, thus preventing charring.

Father and Yakov Hersh were young, healthy, and enduring men who managed to face the blistering heat for many hours and days until all the matzos were done. During this entire process, the finished product was gathered into large, clean sheets and carried to the respective homes where the matzos were stored carefully upon a dense layer of hay.

Shmurah matzah ("watched," meaning the ingredients – the flour and water – are watched from the moment of harvesting), presented an even more formidable problem than the ordinary ones to box. The ritual requirements were exhaustive. The wheat had to be of a specially select type. The girls handling the matzos had to be virgins and could not menstruate while handling the matzos. Since only an insignificant number were required, our people had them imported from [C22] Lohahievka, regardless of price.

During the weeks before the Passover, our entire Jewish township experienced a complete transformation, purification, and rejuvenation. My parents concentrated and limited their activities to the last few days before the Holiday.

The entire home, every room, ceiling, and walls had to be whitewashed, the clay floors reconstructed, releveled and repainted. The linens, curtains, beddings, and such other things had to be washed. The washing was done at the river where while watching [A017] Nessie, I caught hundreds of leeches and stored them in my talis koton. If one managed to attach itself, I did not panic nor search for salt to force its release but merely removed it by hand. The beds were taken apart, washed, and cleaned. All the crevices were washed with boiling water and later gone over with a lit candle to assure the absolute destruction of any animalcule that managed to hide someplace. New straw replaced the older straw serving as the mattress. We had no Sealy, i.e., the company manufacturing an orthopedic posture type mattress then. Every piece of furniture was washed, cleaned, and polished while the furniture in the kitchen was scrubbed with a sharp knife so as to remove the surface layer. Then boiling water was poured over it, and a hot iron was allowed to glide over it presumably to keep the water boiling longer. Finally, the oven and the pipe chuck were reconstructed and repaired, and all pots, plates, and other utensils washed and stored away for the week.

During the last 24 hours, there was hardly any cooking done, and all dining was limited to but one little corner of the house.

On the night before Passover Eve, we followed father through the ceremony of Bedikat Chametz (searching for hametz). As he gathered the pieces of bread previously scattered, he put them all into a large wooden spoon, which the Rabbi then received for proper disposal.

The activities of the last day started at early dawn. All Passover utensils were brought out from hiding, washed and cleaned. Specific articles, cutlery, for instance, were koshered for the Passover use. These were thoroughly cleaned, polished and then placed in a deep hole in the ground into which boiling water was poured and again. A hot iron was inserted to prolong the boiling.

The tables were covered with clean boards over which the table clothes were spread. [A010] Grandfather's table was covered with hay first, then boards, and finally the fabric.

Everyone in the household was busy as well as cooperative. Father had all the arduous duties. He had to prepare water for tea. The well was about one to two versts away. He also had to provide sufficient water for the poultry and the cow to last for two days. The well for drinking water was but a half verst away. He also had to prepare enough feed for these creatures. The poor cow was forced to live on hay only during the holiday, while all of us were feasting. There was also farfel[93] and matzos flour to be prepared for the various dishes we loved. This last job was usually mine. I spent hours pounding the matzos in the large wooden mortar with the heavy pestle until there were sufficient farfel and flour to meet the needs of the day. I repeated this job daily. I loved the kugel and cakes, which were fluffy and tasty.

By mid-afternoon, we were ready for the bathhouse, getting ourselves prepared for the occasion. When done, we rushed home to don the new garments every child had, which were a new suit, dress, shoes, and cap. We boys even had disposable paper collars and chest fronts. I don't remember having ties. Now happy and excited, we all ran to the synagogue to display our new garments and to compare prices. To this day, I don't know how our parents were able to pay for all this, but we were delighted, and with this joyful spirit, we returned home for the seder.

---

[93] Small, flake shaped pasta used in Ashkenazi Jewish cuisine, made from an egg noodle dough and frequently toasted before being cooked

#48 FROZEN JEW FOUND NEAR TOWN

Our folks in Knyazhe were not learned. They knew little of erudition but did absorb the excellent teachings and morals of the sages and lived up to them.

Life and death were equally sacred to our people and to which there should not be interference. That likely explains my people's attitude and the Jew's attitude generally to the physician. To them, the doctor was the messenger of the Almighty Himself, accompanied by the Archangel Raphael, who brought the ill both aid and succor.

Murder violated all the moral and ethical principles they were taught for generations and was therefore profoundly abhorrent to them. Imagine, thus, the impact when we learned that the body of a Jew found just outside the city limits was likely murdered.

It was early one winter morning when the messenger sent by [A168] Dudy Korsunski arrived calling father to his house. This, in itself, was unusual. In deference to the man, Father responded only to return in a most perplexed manner. Many questions presented themselves: 1) Why Dudy, a man never interested in any of the public issues, suddenly the prime mover of the subject? 2) Why did his son-in-law, a resident of [C22] Lohahievka, the administrative center, find it necessary to come and notify Dudy about this man even before the body was found? 3) How did the corpse get to where it was found? 4) Why was Dudy insistent the body be buried in [C24] Monasteristshe rather than Lohahievka, the usual place where our dead were normally buried?

There were questions that Father and some of his pals pondered in secrecy, a secrecy that spread as if by a sound wave through the entire Jewry so that even I became acutely aware of all the implications. No consent could be obtained to transport the body to any place other than Lohahievka. There were no mere doubts or objections. Murder was suspected. By noon of the same day relief finally came when, by order of the Pristor, a high district official, who arrived in town, drove directly to Dudy's house and decided that the body should go to Monasteristshe. That indeed was a great relief. Now that problem of internment was settled, [A011] Father and [A001] Uncle Laizer Eli were to transport the body the next morning.

While the arguments were on-going, the body lay on the floor in the ladies' section of the synagogue. Brother [A012] Hymie and one of his friends kept watch. Ordinarily, during the long vigil, the attendant recites the psalms as required by ritual, but these boys did not know of rituals. Each was provided with a heavy bat as if to ward off some animal that might bite. Thus, they stayed on monotonously looking at the dead Jew. Once, during the night, they were nearly given the opportunity to exercise their powers had not their sixth sense interfered. This was when, as the body thawed, the arms and legs moved. Frightened by these movements, thinking that the Jew may be reviving, or possibly by some magic in action, up they jumped ready to strike him with their bats when they realized that he was dead after all. Nevertheless, they remained quite vigilant until morning.

By morning they were relieved of their fears and duties when the body was lifted from off the floor to the wagon. Father and Uncle [A001] Laizer Eli served as escorts. Upon arrival to [C24] Monasteristshe, they naturally picked the most strategic place not to arouse the town. No particular difficulties were now encountered since the order for internment emanated from the pristor himself. It was Uncle's chance now to capitalize on the occasion. In this, he was an expert. Leaving Father in charge, Uncle went out searching for opportunities. This was not difficult. There was mercy, charity, and long life to sell, and what Jew was to refuse such bargains. Uncle was thus busy all day selling pie in the sky and, as usual, pocketed the receipts.

The puzzle resolved at a later date. Two Jewish beggars came to Lohahievka. One evening during prayer at the synagogue, one beggar accused the other of having stolen his $300. The assembled Jews put the accused through a third-degree, beating him to insensitivity. Realizing that they had killed him, they became panicky. The body was transported and left outside the bounds of Knyazhe. Then they frantically implored Dudy to help them out of the dilemma. Whether Dudy's son-in-law himself was actually involved in the murder, I don't know.

#49 THE CAP (THE SHTREIMEL)

To my knowledge, the cap originally was a protective device for the head and was used in inclement weather. More recently, it has become decorative, used particularly by our female partners. In the past, the cap had a symbolic character. E.L. Peretz beautifully depicts the shtreimel's power.[94] At the turn of the century, the Russian police invested the cap with their own imaginative powers, the revolutionary power. Anyone wearing what resembled a student's hat was suspected as a dangerous revolutionary and carefully watched. I became aware of this menacing power of the cap in the early spring of 1910.

I had completed my first year of apprenticeship in [C14] Kishinev and was returning home for the Passover. Due to my highly satisfactory performance, [A246] Mr. Shankman, my employer, had actually doubled my wages for the year. Instead of five rubles, I now carried a full ten rubles home as wages for the year's work. Room, board, clothing, and other incidentals did not concern my employer, not even the fare for home. I still wore the black velvet jacket that was designed and made by Sister [A023] Tobie. It was the jacket with the tight sleeves, puffy at the shoulders, and fitting snugly at the waistline, the very same jacket that disqualified me from the dancing class the year before at the railroad station. But I needed no other clothing. The only thing lacking was a cap. [A502a] Uncle Itzhak, therefore, decided to provide the deficiency as a parting gift.

Thus, the two of us started out on the crucial mission of procuring a cap. We thought that going to the store would be a simple matter. I would have never imagined so many differently shaped or colored hats on earth. There were the ordinary caps Jews wore as well as beautiful silk types. There were police caps, army caps, and students caps of all varieties. It was the most bewildering. After a long period of hesitancy and indecision, we decided on the black, wide-brimmed cap with uplifted front and the shining visor. It blended with my jacket. It added to my stature. Suddenly I grew tall. I felt great. I wondered whether Napoleon felt the same way? I was thrilled. It felt great the next morning with my newly acquired cap on, valise in the right hand and sock containing a cask of wine thrown over my shoulder. I boarded the train home.

The ride was pleasant. The train was fast and smooth. I was cheerful, enjoying the scenery along the road until late in the evening when the train reached [C09] Christinovka, where I was to change trains after a wait of several hours. Like all stations, this one was spacious and because of the late hour, practically empty. There were plenty of benches from which to choose.

Using the cask as a pillow and the cap over my face to shut out the light, I lay down, reflecting upon the various experiences of mine about which I was to tell my boyfriends. And there were many interesting ones to tell. The very first one was the privilege accorded me together with many other Jews to escort [A283] Krushevan,[95] the vicious antisemite, whose newspaper, the

---

[94] A fur hat worn by many married Haredi Jewish men, particularly, although not exclusively, members of Hasidic Judaism, on Shabbat and Jewish holidays and other festive occasions. The shtreimel, although generally worn only after marriage, in some communities, boys wear it from the age of bar mitzvah.

[95] Pavel Aleksandrovich Krushevan (1860 –1909) was a journalist, editor, publisher and an official in Imperial Russia. He was an active Black Hundredist and was known for his far-right, ultra-nationalist and openly antisemitic views and was the first publisher of *The Protocols of the Elders of Zion*.

"Drug," spread venom through the land to his grave. I was acutely aware of what he represented, and I readily fell in the step of the funeral march. I saw the city of Kishinev with its many beautiful streets and buildings, the spacious and beautiful Alexander and Pushkin streets, the great city garden or park with the band playing, and thousands of people parading in its alleys, or the homes in which I was working. I even worked in the mayor's mansion, which he won in a game of cards, the splendor of which and its parquet floors I still remember. I saw the Katorga (prison). I was to the theatre both Jewish and Ukrainian and even watched the actors doing their makeup. I also frequented the illusion (movie house). I also had the opportunity to hear [A250] Zeidel Rovner (1856-1943), the famous cantor, on account of whom I split the entire seat of my pants when I jumped the fence trying to enter the synagogue without a ticket.

My experience as an apprentice consisted of the iron stairs that I helped to build and the enormous lanterns for the roofs of the tall buildings. I helped at plumbing, made keys, and repaired electric bells.

While I was thus carried away by my puerile notions, the alert gendarme spotted my black cap with the shiny black visor. "A dangerous revolutionary, no doubt." Completely surprised, I received his brusque order, "Get up!" Frightened? Indeed, I was. But he gave me no chance to stay afraid. He showered me with questions until finally, he asked for my passport. Finding my passport had expired, he went into a rage. My argument that I saw no necessity to renew the passport, which was but 24 hours overdue when I was on my way home made no impression on him, and he ordered me to the police station.

All my dreams were now shattered. The problem now was how to dispose of the revolutionary song in my bosom pocket with the gendarme behind me. This was a very familiar song, mincing no words. It read, "From the Ural to the [C10] Dunai, there is no one more stupid than [A281] Nikolai." Imprisonment in Siberia was facing me, but there was nothing that I could do. And so with the cap on, valise in the right hand and sack with the cask of wine over my left shoulder, I started out trudging across [C09] Christinovka toward the station. New visions came to my mind now. I saw Mother in the courtroom, crying, pleading for her baby boy. I saw myself traveling on foot from town to town all the way to Siberia.

Various visions came one after another when suddenly, and entirely unexpectedly, came the question, "Do you know anyone here in Christinovka?" "Indeed I do," I snapped. "I know [A245] Zanvel, the commissioner. His daughter [A003a] Faiga is married to [A003] Haskel, my cousin." "Then why didn't you say so before?" the gendarme answered. "A friend of Zanvel's is my friend as well. Go back to the station." My reaction to this was almost paralytic in character, but I managed to return in time to board the train for home. I saved the song and still have it in my possession as my souvenir.

#50 FORMER DOCTORS

Reporters in Jewish newspapers love to tell us of how physicians were altruistic in bygone days and compare them with the mercenary ones of our times. This was a particularly favored theme during the great Jewish immigration episode in the early days of our century. It repeats itself frequently to this day and particularly now when the image of the physician is at its lowest. Throughout the land, the physician is under attack. Two to three years ago, the "Reporter," a liberal labor organ, painted the doctor in the ugliest of colors: Incompetent, mercenary, robber, and cheat.

As a general practitioner for 37 years now and rubbing shoulders with colleagues of various specialties, I see the physician in an altogether different light. I see him as a kind, sympathetic, very earnest man trying his very best to help the patient and family, though I am by no means denying the presence of the charlatan in our midst.

The laypeople, including the reporters, are woefully uninformed, and I wish to refute these allegations by describing three physicians of the older days.

The city of [C43] Zashkov in the province of [C13] Kiev was fortunate and happy with [A271] Dr. Kuzminsky. He was a man of about 40 and married. I don't know whether he had a family, but a house was given to him. There was no rent to pay. The upkeep of the home was minuscule, the furniture and decorations meager and dress simple. He needed no full-dress suits, no ties, nor various colored shoes. There were neither theaters nor movie houses. He had no charity drives to support nor income or property tax to pay. He had no nurse, stenographers, bookkeeper, or any other aides. Medical supplies were at a very minimum, and, I believe, he had a horse and buggy. Under these circumstances, he kept his fees small. They were deposited in a receptacle in a corner on the table.

Actually, Dr. Kuzminsky did not need the money. He was bestowed with gifts: Rye, wheat, corn, eggs, chickens, ducks, cabbages, radishes, onions, gourds, beets, potatoes, apples, pears, and cherries. Any wonder that he sent a couple of chickens to the poor patient who failed to compensate time for his last visit?

In contrast, there was [A272] Dr. Braverman, an ophthalmologist practicing in [C36] Uman. Mother took me to see him in 1910 to have my eyes examined before I left for America. Dr. Braverman was a handsome, corpulent young man, who was sportily dressed in a tan summer jacket and sat in an attractive office that smelled of phenol. His hands were soft and clean, his nails polished and manicured. I am confident he seldom touched a patient for fear of soiling himself. This man did have to pay rent for his office, as well as for other services. And he liked to attend the theater and concerts. Also, he had no peasants to bring him gifts of produce. His visit then was 5 rubles. How charitable he was, I don't know.

Incidentally, in Uman, we stayed at an inn run by a friend of mothers. I lay on the floor and never slept for a moment. There were no bedbugs, but large black beetles in the thousands came toward me. All night long, I kept warding them off. Sometimes I wonder whether it was a dream, but the picture remained so vivid in my memory that I can't accept it as a dream.

The city of [C22] Lohahievka had a doctor of yet another type. Lohahievka was about 8-10 versts from Knyazhe and provided us with various services:

1. Lohahievka provided Knyazhe with a burial ground for the dead since we had no Jewish cemetery.

2. Divorce court. No divorce could be granted in Knyazhe because the river in town was nameless. This must have been erroneous, for I learned later that the name of the river was the "Lazy Tykytch."

3. Medical services. We had no physician in town. Actually our folks could not afford the doctor's services and usually resorted to that of the feldsher. Of the latter, Lohahievka had two. One was [A273] Tzentlor, who was a medical aide and a kind man. The other, [A274] Faiga, was considerably less able than Tzentlor, yet loved by all because of her kindness.

The doctor from Lohahievka, on the other hand, was far from the type we idealized. He was a man entirely imbued with the spirit of importance and hence would not condescend to travel in an ordinary wagon. One had to send a modern carriage for him and pay 10 rubles for his visit as well. Though 10 rubles was an immense sum for any of our folks to pay, it was easier to raise the 10 rubles than to find a suitable carriage. The only carriages available were those of the Graf, and I believe [A177] Shaia Korsunski. When cousin [A004] Donia took sick, her father, [A003] Haskel, knowing that Shaia's son was also ill, waited patiently for Shaia to send for the doctor. To his great disappointment, the doctor refused to see Donia. Haskel begged and implored the doctor and even assured him the full fee but met with an absolute rebuff. Haskel now protested, asking to explain why he visited the peasant's child on a previous visit when Shaia brought him to town. His answer was a very plain and understandable one, namely, "The peasant won't send for me, but you will," and off he went home. Haskel did send for him.

My thesis is that doctors are human beings and behave like humans. The last doctor practiced under conditions not unlike those of [A271] Dr. Kuzminsky, but he lacked the kindness of feelings and the heart of Kuzminsky.

#51 THE DRAFT

Knyazhe was the recruiting center for the district. I'm not aware of the name or extent of the region, but I know it extended as far as [C02a] Justingrad, [C28] Ochhmativ, and possibly even further.

The recruiting took place in the fall of the year. Two to three thousand boys accompanied by one or both parents would gather here for the occasion. Since no hotels were available, the Jewish boys got whatever accommodations were possible, mostly space on the bare floor. They were given good food, of course, during this entire period, which usually lasted about a full week. The selection was determined after the physical examination that a committee of physicians carried out. This took place at the Prisudstva, a beautiful building that was part of the [A160] Graf's Estate.

The draftees were divided into three categories: only son, first-born sons, and all others. The difference was that the last group had no privileges. All boys drew numbers. Those with higher numbers had a greater chance to escape the draft, for as soon as the quota was filled, the selection was discontinued, leaving the remaining ones free or discharged. The draft seldom reached the top categories.

The scheme, though superficially democratic, enabled the well-to-do to place their sons in the privileged categories and to escape the draft through the old and tried methods of influence and bribery. It also led to the development of informers and blackmailers, a profession the Jews vehemently hated.

Brother [A012] Hymie, as the oldest son, was entitled to the privileges of the second category, but his rights were lost because his birth was not registered. My parents, therefore, tried to influence and bribe. The [A160a] Grafinia promised to talk to one of the doctors. Fearing this insufficient, they bribed another doctor. They based their hope upon the injured left scapula Hymie suffered in childhood, which he was able to thrust out at will but was otherwise of no consequence. At the examination, the two doctors were antagonistic to each other, with Hymie suffering the consequences.

But [A006] Moshe Kalman was more fortunate than his cousin Hymie. Moshe was also a first-born son. For some reason, his parents rejected him. His grandparents raised him, and he grew into a tall, husky boy who fared considerably worse than any stray dog. Everybody knew him and, out of pity, gave him food, cast-off clothing, and allowed him to sleep in their barns. Thus, Moshe grew up and was summoned for the draft. Moshe claimed no privileges while his parents were very eager for him to enter the army. The upshot of the story was that Moshe drew a very high number. The quota was filled long before reaching his number, and Moshe was now a free man. The Weinstein boys, now in Winnipeg, heard the news and remembering Moshe's plight, enabled him to join them. Interestingly, this same Moshe later brought the mother who rejected him previously to Winnipeg, where he treated her gently and royally despite all previous inequities.

To serve in the army was a tragic event for the Jew. This was not due to Jewish disloyalty to the government but to the exact opposite, the government's disloyalty to the Jew. The government mistreated the Jews in the army as well as in the community.

Many boys resorted to various bodily mutilations to escape the draft. A favorite one was to rupture oneself, but the most common mutilation was ear puncture. Once the ear was punctured, it was necessary to prevent the hole from closing. Dropping alcohol into the ear accomplished this. It would whistle as it emerged through the drum opening. It also served to keep the opening intact. It was amusing and yet tragic to watch the boys in line already up the steps and almost ready to meet the examiner unable to produce the whistling just at the critical moment.

Some boys tied off a nerve or muscle in the leg, causing a limp. Others cut off their right index finger or the large toe of the foot. Many boys went on starvation diets and no sleep during the summer months preceding the draft. This was an extreme process requiring strong character because starvation entails voluntary control while sleep does not yield to volition. The boys would fall asleep wherever they happened to sit, stand, or lie, and the poor mothers frantically tried to arouse them. I saw this quite familiar experience performed on rabbits in 1912 in the laboratory of [A730] Dr. George Crile. It took much effort to arouse these animals once they fell asleep. At first, some of these boys were successful in their efforts. Soon the doctors realized what the boys were perpetrating, and they referred them to the clinic in [C30] Szitomir where, in attempting to undo the mutilations, they were crippled for good.

Only one boy to my knowledge actually succeeded in outwitting the commission of physicians by a unique and skillful trick. Our cousin [A427] Daniel, brother of [A457] Joe Gillman, playfully imitated the hiccoughing of a girlfriend of his when it suddenly dawned on him that he could possibly make use of it in his attempt to escape the draft. He began practicing the act until he developed a crow, strongly resembling that of the cock. The examiners were much baffled by this unusual and strange malady. In all their erudition, they never came across this type of symptom, and they could ascribe no serious implication to it. Still, they felt he couldn't possibly stay in the ranks of soldiers and therefore discharged him. Cousin Daniel used to entertain us with his crowing. None of us could ever reproduce it.

#52 [A333a] GRANDFATHER ARON'S HORSE, COSSACKS, AND WORLD WAR I
by grandson [A335] Norman Milstein

Editor's note: The Cossacks were, to many, the signature of death. They were to be avoided at any cost. Their presence, especially when on a rampage, for many meant imminent if not an instant demise. We had one other cousin, [A035] Nathan (N.M.) Robboy, who was a superb rider when in Russia. Despite some rumors, there is no evidence he ever was a Cossack, although undoubtedly, his riding skills made him capable of being one. There is another family name, "Raboy", some of whose members came from the same locales as our family. One child, Isaac, came to America and wrote a well-known book called "The Yiddisher Cowboy," which told of his exploits when he hired himself out in one of our US midwestern states. The Steven Spielberg digital Yiddish Library I424I, Sokolivka Memorial book, lists two Raboys, Blume and Fishel of [C43] Zashkov as perishing in the [C02] Justingrad/ Sokolivka pogrom.

Strange are the ways of fate. I owe my life to an epileptic horse who died long before I was born. How can this be? Well, you see, my grandfather, [A333a] Aron Milstein, was one of the last of the Romanian Jewish cowboys. As you might expect, there weren't many with which to begin!

Somehow, someway, somebody from my family had finagled a deal whereby we could administer the vast landholdings of a dissolute nobleman. This nobleman wanted nothing to do with running his estate. He just wanted to spend his time squandering his riches elsewhere. The estate he ignored encompassed more than 100 square miles, including tracts of forest, vast vineyards, and grazing lands. The only way to oversee this vast territory was on horseback.

My grandfather grew up riding and observing highly skilled equestrians. His horsemanship was locally legendary. He could hide his body against the side of a galloping horse as Native American warriors used to do. He could whirl back and forth from one side of the horse to the other while it was running. He could leap into the saddle or dismount by vaulting over his steed's head. He could stand on a racing horse's back. He could turn and ride backward on his mount. These sorts of skills were characteristic of Cossacks, not Jews. My grandfather was unique.

When World War I began, the tsar's men combed the country to conscript the finest horsemen for the Russian cavalry units.

My grandfather's conspicuous qualifications attracted their attention, and so he became the only Jewish cavalryman in a Russian mounted brigade headed for frontline duty. It's difficult to imagine how lonely and frightened he must have been. He was only 19 years old, forced to fight alongside strangers who despised him because he was a Jew. Immediately, he faced disaster. Antisemitism was rampant in the cavalry, and my grandfather found himself assigned to an epileptic horse, an animal given to furious and unpredictable fits. Only one man, a retired soldier, had ever been able to ride this horse safely. To make matters even worse, my grandfather's fellow soldiers jeered him. "The Jew would get his alright!" My grandfather leaped to safety the first few times the horse collapsed with convulsions, but sooner or later he was going to have a nasty fall.

Then a strange thing happened. The retired soldier approached my grandfather. "Hey, Milstein! You have the best horse in the regiment. Maybe in the whole Russian army. This horse could save your life over and over. But you got to know the secret. Maybe I should not do this, but I like the way you ride. You are a real horseman! Get me drunk, and I'll tell you the secret."

My grandfather took this fellow to a saloon, where he purchased some powerful alcoholic truth serum. The retired soldier quickly became nearly incoherent. "What is the secret?" my grandfather demanded.

The retired soldier produced a little flat rock from his pocket and slipped it into my grandfather's hand. "This is secret!" he muttered.

"What kind of secret is this? It's just a little flat rock!" My grandfather was flabbergasted.

"That horse's head will sway a little before he has his fits," the soldier explained. "Take this rock and give him a good knock between the ears, and he'll be fine! Hide the rock in your palm when you knock the horse, so nobody knows what you are doing. That way, nobody else will learn the secret. Nobody else will be able to ride this horse. You got the best horse. You want to keep him!"

My grandfather took the rock. He wondered if the retired soldier was a lunatic or if the fellow was just playing a cruel joke on him. He doubted the little rock would be of any use, but why not give it a try? During drills a few days later, he noticed the horse's head swaying just a little bit. He palmed the stone and gave his mount a sharp rap right between the ears. Sure enough, the swaying stopped, and the horse settled down.

Call it a quirk of fate or cosmic justice, but my grandfather ended up with the most exceptional horse in the regiment. The epileptic horse could thread his way through the trenches with astonishing agility and jump dangerous obstacles with ease. He was courageous, steady, and wonderfully evasive under fire. My grandfather lost track of the number of times the horse saved his life.

Finally, after more than two years of action, this heroic animal was shot out from under my grandfather, who vaulted safely to the ground. The tide of battle moved on, and my grandfather was left behind with his dead friend. He collapsed on his horse weeping and remained there for two days. His faithful companion was gone.

Afterward, my grandfather rejoined his regiment, and after many more brushes with death, including a terrifying year in a German prisoner of war camp from which he escaped, he returned home safely. Ultimately, he came to the United States after Romania became too dangerous for Jews.

So, it's true. I do indeed owe my very existence to an epileptic horse!

#53 WORLD WAR I, THE REVOLUTION, AND POGROMS IN RUSSIA
by [A471] Yacov Trachtman

I am starting my memories at the beginning of the First World War. Up to that time, we lived in [C02a] Justingrad. My brothers were in America because they wished to avoid the Russian army. When the war broke out, I was visiting my mother's brother and his family, which consisted of five daughters and one son. Only one daughter survived, and she is in Israel with her family. I was visiting a village near [C36] Uman when the war was declared. My uncle brought me back to the city for my father, [A470] Zalman, to take me home. Men mobbed the town wishing to enlist for service. It was impossible to walk. All talk was about how Germany, with her new weapons, would destroy Europe.

I was eleven and scared to death. I thought we would never return home to the family. We finally did return, and the town looked quiet and peaceful. We were far from the front and thought it safe. We lacked newspapers. The Hebrew paper to which father subscribed had ceased. All the news was by mouth. Everybody thought that Germany would soon conquer all of Russia. The Jews, hopefully, expected utopia as the Jews in Germany had it so good in those days. The townspeople continued about their business and, strange as it may seem, business was quite good. Everybody waited for the war to end, so there would be a market in which to spend money. But then the Revolution broke out. As far as we in town were concerned, it was a huge surprise and shock. The tsar was eliminated. The peasants became petrified as they had no one for which to pray. You'd think the tsar worried about them.

All I knew about the Revolution was that we made flags with the slogan, "Long Live Liberty." Frankly, few of us knew what the slogan meant. I was then 16 years old, and we did not realize we were the tsar's slaves. We took all for granted. We thought we had worse things to worry about than politics. While all of us marched to the market with our flags screaming "Hurrah," an old drunken peasant stopped by to watch and said it was not yet time to celebrate. It is before the chuppah (wedding canopy).

All the Jews in town were to recall his words many times during the coming bitter years. From then on, we started to run like squirrels in a wheel. We ran without purpose. The first band of bandits picked up 165 Jewish boys. First, they asked for ransom, and when every penny in town was gathered, they shot them all, the finest and smartest the shtetl possessed. My brother was fortunate. They stripped his clothing. It took him five days to get some old pants and get home. All this time we were sure we would never see him again. He never was the same, and I guess none of us were. [A466] Morris and I still scream in our sleep. I always run and can never find a door through which to escape. That is an experience!

After the big pogrom, we found that every few days, another band came for money and lives. That persisted for two years. We ate what we could scrounge. In the fields, we would eat a few potatoes, but of course, we had no chance to cook. As soon as we lit a fire, a new band appeared, and we would have to run again. Our final experience was when the White Army retreated, followed by the Reds. The whole town was, by that time, practically destroyed and burned. The houses on our block were spared because the peasants were afraid the fire would spread to their haystacks.

The few remaining families gathered on our block. There were twelve in our four rooms when the bandits entered. They put a rope around my father's neck, demanding to know why he was a Jew. One of the soldiers took off my shoes, and, being a gentleman, offered his gun to my mother and asked me to go with him. In the other room at that moment, one of their band came shouting that the Reds were here! They left us where we stood and ran. Of the twelve people that were in our house, five remained alive. One of the soldiers took the Rabbi's granddaughter across the street to a Christian's house to have some privacy. In the meantime, babies were being born, but dying just as quickly. In the big cities, there was a little better order, but people still died of hunger.

After this pogrom, we left and went to [C36] Uman. The beautiful city was in shambles. There were no living facilities, no food, and no order. I traveled to the neighboring villages, selling my remaining possessions for food. Our clothing consisted of used potato bags. My suit was the one my father wore too. One person sold something to someone, the other sold it to somebody else until it came to the original owner, and it started once again. Girls I grew up with became prostitutes and followed the troops. That was the only way one had a decent meal and some clothing. On my last trip from our town to Uman, I sold my father's house for a bushel of grain. I took the grain to the mill five miles away to have it turned into flour. When I got to the city, my parents met me at the gate, as that night five more Jews were killed. They were neighbors of my father-in-law. The big news was that David Chertow sent his brother-in-law, Futternick, to Romania to try to contact us. We now began our trip to the Romanian border.

When the Reds entered the town, among its officers was a boy from town, the [A243] Karolnick's son, [A244] Duddey Dubovis. His parents peddled corrals from town to town. He hated every Jew in town, and every Jew shivered when he passed by in his uniform with a sword. He had no father, and it was difficult for his mother to support three children. Duddy wanted to go to Uman to school like some of the boys but lacked means. Thus, when he got authority, he got even. My father had to go to beg from him for a permit to ship eggs to the depot. Without it, they would have been confiscated. He respected our family as we never had money, and none of us children were sent to the city. At the time, it was ironic. He acted like a lord, lived like one, and died like one with syphilis. Poetic justice was done. He was 22 years old.

#54 ANNIHILATION OF [C02b] SOKOLIVKA:
THE POGROM OF AUGUST 3, 1919
Reprinted with permission of: https://www.jewishgen.org/Yizkor/Sokolivka/soke019.html

World War 1 ravaged Russia from 1914 to 1917. Then came the years of 1919-1920, which were agony to the Jews of Ukraine. Various armed factions made war against the central Moscow government and each other for control of the region. Anarchy prevailed, local authority collapsed, every place was open to robbery and murder. In between their battles among each other, these various bands broke into quiet towns and reeked atrocities upon the Jews.

At first, the Justingrad community kept its spirit up. Chayyim Greenspan, who later settled in Buffalo, recalls: With twelve rifles, they set up a night watch, and stopped night robberies.

When the goyim of nearby villages came to seize their arms, they resisted. These goyim then grabbed some Jews, dragged them to the "Bridge" to throw them into the river. Fortunately, some goyim from Sokolivka proper at the other end of the "Bridge" intervened to protect their neighbors, and the other goyim left.

On another occasion, a bandit troop of 150 invaded the shtetl and demanded the people give up their clothing and boots to the bandits and pay a ransom of half a million rubles. This time the shtetl was saved by the courage of two men who slipped away and ran to [C24] Monasteristshe, where they made contact with the government forces (Bolshevik) camped there. When the bandits were making ready to let loose their terror of the shtetl, they were surprised by the arrival of a force of regular soldiers headed by a Jewish commander.

The people of the shtetl saw these deliverances as miraculous. From mouth to ear, the word was passed that Reb Pinchas'l the Rabbi had said: "As long as I live, no blood will be shed in town."

The Murder of Reb Pinchas'l the Rabbi

It was Shabbat Chazon, the Sabbath before Tisha B'Av 5679 (August 2, 1919). It was a pleasant summer day. People were relaxing after a week of fear and anxiety, walking in the streets, talking about the latest news. Suddenly about five o'clock, gunfire was heard at the western approach to the shtetl. A horde of the reb bandit Zeleny numbering in the thousands "announced" their entrance. At once, there was panic in the streets. People ran home in utter confusion, parents hunting for their children, children for their parents. Screams of fright rose everywhere. People locked themselves in their houses, women and children hid themselves in the cellars.

Towards evening, residents on the Rabbi's street heard the sound of horses' hooves and saw several mounted horsemen approaching the Rabbi's house. One of them went into the courtyard, up the steps, and opened the door. The Rabbi had just finished the 'Se'udah shlishit,' the third meal of the Sabbath, and was about to begin the Ma'ariv evening prayers. In the twilight dusk, the murderer came to where the Rabbi was sitting and shot him dead.

The intruders saw him fall, and they left without further violence or looting. We believe that the goyim of the vicinity told the bandit leader the town was under the protection of the Tzaddik (very righteous person, especially a Hassidic spiritual leader) who dwelled there. This murderer was sent to "remove" the Rabbi before they attacked the town.

The Massacre

During the night, looting and vandalism began. Sunday morning saw streets deserted, some houses already devastated. At daylight, a hunt and round-up began, the bandits seizing all young men, especially any from 18 to 30. They were dragged to the synagogue of the Tolner Chassidim and locked up there.

The bandit chief announced that a "war tax" was imposed of not less than a million rubles, to be collected and turned over in two hours. A communal worker, surrounded by armed bandits, went from home to home collecting the money. Meanwhile, the armed bandits were beating down the hostages in the synagogue using the prayer stands and then stomped on their heads.

Two hours passed, and when the sum demanded had not been reached, ten men were taken out and killed. Another hour passed, and another ten were killed. At noon the collectors returned to the synagogue, having amassed only about half the amount demanded. The bandit officer took the money, refused to release the prisoners, and gave the word to start plundering the houses.

The bandits spread out through the shtetl, broke into stores, looted the merchandise, beating people with their whips. There was shooting of men and raping of women. They spoke of killing all the men in the synagogue.

About five o'clock, the bandit horde began to move out of the town. They separated about a hundred and fifty young men from the rest in the synagogue and took them along as captives. At first, some thought that nothing serious would happen to them, because in another town Zeleny's gang had also seized a large number of young men, but only warned them not to help the Bolsheviks and turned them loose. Alas, on the captives of Justingrad, the wrath of the Lord descended.

When the captives were led out onto the "Bridge," some parents overtook them, and pleaded for their children, offering still more money. They were shot and thrown into the river; among these parents were Menachem Tchernus and Yitzchak Snitzer.

Some of the young men, seeing what was up, pleaded with Zeleny [96] to take them as recruits to his band. The murderer mocked their words and ordered them to be mowed down. A withering

---

[96] The book, Ukraine Terror and the Jewish Peril, 1921 (Cornell Univ Library #3 1924 078 399 890), compiled by the Federation of Ukrainian Jews in Aid of the Pogrom Sufferers in Ukraine, and including Memorandum on the Massacres of Jews in Ukraine, Paris, 10, Place Edouard VII. GENEVA, 16 December 1920, notes Jewish massacers occurred in more than 400 locales. Since December 1918 more than 30,000 Ukrainian Jews were murdered. In many cities the sieges were sometimes 4 days long, one lasted 10 continuous days. The reports describe the savagery:

"Up to the present more than a million Jews have been robbed and many of them have had literally their last shirt taken from them. The most refined tortures have been devised. Old men and children have been cut to pieces. Thousands of women and young girls have been outraged, and among these even little girls and old women. The victims have been terribly mutilated; the right arm and left leg have been cut off, or vice versa, the

fire was opened on them from a hidden ambush, from a machine gun concealed by bushes. The best of Justingrad's youth fell dead, many young fathers, the strength and glory of Sokolivka.

The shooting having done its bloody work, the bandits waded in with their swords to silence the voices of the dying, among whom there were some who with their last strength cried out the Sh'ma Yisroel, the martyr's creed, "Hear, O Israel."

One of the young men, Yitzchak Pushkalinsky, though severely wounded in the head, managed to drag himself out of the heap of the dead, and to reach the town. He died two months later in the hospital at [C36] Uman, but from him were learned the details of what had happened. The bodies were first found in a ravine by gentiles, who notified the town.

Chavye Shuman, four of whose brothers were among those killed, recalls: "The gentiles refused to bring the bodies to the shtetl. The Jewish population rented horses and wagons from them, and they brought back the dead. My father was among those digging graves for my brothers. Nachum, the apothecary, tried to help him with the digging. My father said to him, "Take it easy, Nachum, let me take care of my children. My brother Baruch, who was killed, was married and father of a little boy."

During World War I, during the German occupation, and during the first two years of the Revolution, there were practically no Jewish pogroms as such. (There were many in the earlier decades.) Of course, demoralized detachments of troops did commit excesses, especially during the period of demobilization. There were sporadic hits and always small scale, and almost always directed against Jews. The focus was on robbery and damage to property.

Russia then entered is its own civil war, the Revolution. Alexander Kerensky's short-lived transitional government of the Russian Revolution fell to the Communists who rose against them. Unfortunately, as the defeats became more decisive and the beaten troops began evacuating from the territories they had occupied, the more cruelly [A286] Symon Petliura's (1879–1926) defeated and irritated troops began to revenge their setbacks and hardships on the peaceful Jewish population. The Jews were now treated as Communists. The battle-cries, "Murder Jews and Communists!" and the "Jews are Communists!" soon sounded throughout Ukraine, instigating pogroms.

---

left arm and right leg; one eye has been torn out and the nose cut off. The houses in which the Jews took refuge were burnt, and all perished in the flames. The number of cases in which these unhappy victims were doomed to die a slow death of indescribable torture cannot be counted. Burning was the usual practice.

Besides physical torture, they were subjected to mental torture of a kind for which there is no parallel in history. Jews were compelled to dance and to sing in the presence of their torturers, to mock their own people and to praise their executioners; they had to dig their own graves and to commit shameful acts for the amusement of their murderers. These wretched people were forced to look on at the dishonoring of their daughters and of their wives, and children were compelled to hang their fathers. …

"The imagination of the greatest poet could not describe these scenes of horror. Dante's Inferno pales beside the realities of everyday life in Ukraine."

The pogroms of the Kiev region began on December 31, 1918, Petliura was a Ukrainian politician who had become the Ukrainian Army's Supreme Commander and the Ukrainian People's Republic President during Ukraine's short-lived sovereignty in 1918–1921. As his troops began breaking up, many of the leaders (called by their titles, "ataman" and "hetman" meaning "Cossack leader") began their own independent campaigns, mostly directed against Jews. Tens of thousands were killed, purposefully, to rob, rape, and damage both person and property. One leader was Zeleny, who led the initial massacre on Justingrad/Sokolivka. Two months later, [A285] Anton Denikin assaulted, which led to the community's ultimate annihilation.

[C18] Korsun, [C32] Stavishtshe, [C34] Tetiiv and [C36] Uman were several of our family's communities the pogroms also demolished.

The [A285] Denikin Atrocities

After Zeleny's massacre, the shtetl was raided often by local gangs from nearby villages. No day passed without some tragic event. So the year 5679 came to an end (September 1919).

On Rosh Hashanah 5680 (September 25, 1919), not quite two months later, the army of Tsarist Denikin passed through the shtetl on their way to fight against the Bolsheviks. Three Jews whom they chanced upon on the way they killed. Again, there was robbing, looting, setting homes afire.

In Denikin's days, there was total anarchy. From the old town of Sokolivka, hoodlum ruffians came night after night, rioted, attacked Jews, burned houses, to force the Jews to leave. Many families did flee at that time. This went on for about three months.

The Denikin forces were later defeated. On their retreat from Byelo-Tserkov, they again passed through Justingrad. Once more, they began with burning homes, and this time they ended killing some two hundred. In the severe frost, the Denikin forces seized Jews, dragged them to the ice of the frozen river, and stripped them naked where they froze to death.

The shtetl was in ruins. The community of stunned mourners, crushed by these disasters, wandered around in a delirium of despair. The ground burned under their feet. They fled, some to nearby Uman, others to [C29] Odessa, crowding miserably into emergency shelters in the synagogues. Many decided to leave the country, making their way on foot overland to the Dniester river, the Romanian border. Risking their lives in the river crossing, they filtered stealthily across the frontier and reached Romania, penniless and starving.

Families broke up. Some, who had relatives in America, were able with their help to cross the ocean to the United States. A few families, after great hardships, managed to reach Palestine (as it was then known) and settled there.

The End of the Shtetl

It is now impossible to obtain details about how many families remained after the mass exodus, or how they lived from 1920 to 1941. What is known is that the Nazis, when they invaded, found some remaining Jews in Justingrad/Sokolivka. And they were all murdered.

A young woman physician of Yehoshua Abramov's family hastened to Sokolivka after the later Nazi defeat. She found not one living former Jewish resident. The houses were empty ruins. The gentile residents of the town told her that the Nazis led the surviving Jews to the forest and forced them to dig their own graves. They then shot the adults and buried children alive. No one knows what share the local gentiles had in this final massacre.

#55 [A515] AVROM KAPROV
By [A523] Shirley Charm

[A515] Avrom Kaprov, born in 1867, was the youngest of [A419] Beryl and [A419a] Dvossie Brodsky Kaprov's eight children. In 1912, their oldest son, [A516] Fishel Kaprov, then about 17 years old, emigrated by himself, sponsored by an aunt on his mother's side who already resided in Boston. Within two years, by 1914, his savings were sufficient to aid Avrom to immigrate. The only vacant rabbinical position that the Orthodox rabbis in Boston knew was in Bangor, ME. No one else desired it. And so, Avrom became the first rabbi ever to serve the Bangor community, and possibly the first rabbi to ever serve in Maine.

Fig. 55-1 Kaprov family in Sokolivka, 1913. (L to R) [A527] Pessie (Pauline), [A526] Moishe, [A515a] Sima (Mother), [A516] Fishel (Edward), [A515] Rabbi Avrom Kaprov, [A522] Dvossie (Dorothy), [A528] Gedalia (Gordon)

As with his son, Avrom lived frugally, saving his monies and sending some home to help his family. The plan was to save sufficient funds to bring the rest of the family over. But life goes as planned. World War I began, and despite its ending several years later, the pogroms and the Bolshevik revolution's stirrings had commenced.

One day in early August 1919, two of the children, [A526] Moishe and his sister, [A522] Dvossie, were returning home when suddenly Cossacks (a term loosely applied to the peoples involved in the pogroms) appeared and began to chase them. Understanding how serious was the predicament, Moishe bravely told his sister the bandits would likely come after only one of them, and almost certainly him because he is a male. He ensured she escape, and indeed, he was killed momentarily. This killing was the beginning of the infamous pogrom that demolished the town of [C02b] Sokolivka. Dvossie was one of the few survivors, and later, she had to go to the town's morgue to identify and confirm that the body was that of her brother from the many there. The trauma left her permanently scarred psychologically. Appendix D lists all of the townspeople who perished.

[A515a] Sima, her mother, understood the implications immediately. She and her entire surviving family needed to leave immediately, which they did. The family traveled by foot the 150-mile distance to Romania. Unlike some of the other family members who experienced horrifying times crossing into Romania and many difficulties before arriving in America, Sima

253

found help there from members of the Joint Distribution Committee. The "Joint,"[97] as it was better known, supported the family through this short period and enabled them both to locate Avrom and resettle in America. The money Avrom had saved afforded tickets to bring the remaining family to Boston. In 1921, finally, after a seven-year separation, Avrom and Sima were reunited.

Fig. 55-2. [A515] Avrum Kaprov's Family at [A527] Pauline Lerman's wedding, c1835.
Top row: [A522a] Jacob Zitaner, [A528a] Geraldine Kaprov, [A528] Gedalie Kaprov
Second row: [A527a] Frank Lerman, [A527] Pauline Lerman, [A517] Irene Kaprov, [A516a] Mollie Kaprov.
Front row [A522] Dorothy Kaprov Zitaner (later Charm), [A523] Shirley Zitaner, [A515a] Sima Schwartz
   Kaprov,[A515] Rabbi Avrom Kaprov, [A518] Gerald Kaprov, [A521] Rhoda Kaprov, [A516] Edward Kaprov.

With the family now in Bangor, Fishel had also established himself as a rabbi and mohel. Avrom and Sima's home was the extended family's center. Due to Avrom's position, it was the center of the Jewish community also. [A523] Shirley, their granddaughter (who was [A522] Dvossie's

---

[97] The Joint Distribution Committee (JDC), or Joint as it was commonly known, was founded in 1914 initially to assist Jews who lived in Palestine under Turkish rule. With the outbreak of World War I it expanded to assist the Jews in Russia and the Central and Eastern Europe, providing them food, medicine, and various other critical aids. The organization, and a spinoff, the American Jewish Relief Committee, began with moneys donated by Jacob Schiff and Felix Warburg, American philanthropists later related by marriage to the editor. By 1920, the JDC had disbursed over $22,000,000 to help provide relief across Europe.

daughter) spent much time there and heard the stories, debates, and the types of questions Avrom put to the family continuously.

As the only rabbi in town, Avrom conducted many marriages. He presided as well over the divorces, issuing the "get," the Jewish divorce decree. Without disclosing actual names, Avrom presented at his dinner table many of the problematic issues the cases raised, asking questions and opinions of the assembled. In one particularly amusing remembrance, the husband wished to obtain a get, but when pressed, professed he shouldn't be saying anything bad against his wife. Shortly after granting the get, Avrom asked the man if he would now answer the reason behind wishing to obtain the get. The reply, said succinctly, was now that he was divorced, he had no business to be speaking negatively about his former wife.

With World War II taking place, Avrom was especially busy involved in so many marriage ceremonies. The young soldiers going off to war desired to be married before embarkation. The family kept Shirley busy helping the family make all the wedding preparations since so many of the affairs took place in their home.

Fig. 55-3. 1950 25th wedding anniversary of Pessie Kaprov Lerman
[A516] Fishel Kaprov, [A457] Joe Gillman, [A528] Gedalia Kaprow, [A527] Pessie, [A515a] Sima Kaprow.

Fig. 55-4: 1957 88th birthday, [A522] Dvossie Kaprow Zitaner, L-R
Top: [A527] Pessie Kaprow, [A523] Shirley Zitaner Charm, [A525] Elizabeth Charm, [A524] Susan Charm.
Front: Sarah Zeldis Charm, [A522] Dvossie Kaprow Zitaner.

Avrom remained healthy until late in life when he suffered a major heart attack. A cousin who had just left the Army stayed with him until he was well. Sima was skinny and in good health, despite having known gallstones and being afraid to have them removed. She died of pneumonia at age 77.

Fig. 55-5: [A527] Pauline (Pessie) Kaprov, C1825, Portland ME.

Fig. 55-6: [A515] Rabbi Avrom and Sima Kaprov, 1946.

Shirley related one amusing story about her grandfather, [A419] Beryl Kaprove, who one of the eight children of the original [A290] Khaim giving rise to the B'nai Khaim. In Knyazhe, Khaim used to sleep by the stove in their home, for that was always the warmest place. One morning, as he did daily, he went to shul, but on this particular day, he did not return home. When the family began their search for him, they found him in jail. The police were asked why this happened. They answered he was stopped and asked where he was going, but he did not know, so they put them in jail. When Avrom, the son, asked later why he didn't tell the police he was coming home from shul, he answered, "But I didn't come home. I went to jail. How did I know where I was going."

#56 [A326] ON CHAIM DUDNIK:
LETTER TO JOE GILLMAN, 1962

The family scattered once the pogrom began. Some members went to [C13] Kiev and others to [C29] Odessa, but virtually all lost contact with one another for a year or more.

In 1918, Chaim's daughter wrote, "Father bribed a railroad official, who put Father, Mother, and the young children in a sealed car bound for Odessa. Having been a capitalist, Father could not get a job. Sickness spread on her land, and our family was no exception.

"Father and Mother began by selling sugar and other hard to get commodities. When that became impossible to do, they began to sell whatever they could, hoping only to survive. The only way out now was to get away to America.

"Leaving our parents and their two younger children, and after indescribable hardships, we secured our coming to America. Some of our family came to Buffalo. Others went to Chicago."

By 1923 most of the family reached America.

To earn a living, Chaim and his wife settled in a Polish neighborhood in Buffalo. They did reasonably well, and in 1934 they went to Palestine with their sons and remained there for five years. They then returned to the United States, moving to Chicago, where they opened a grocery store. Mother especially worked hard. Father could never get used to that kind of work.

In 1945, at age 75, Chaim died. Twelve years later, in 1957, Bracha died. She was 84.

#57 [C41] VOZNESENSK

[A419a] Dvossie Brodsky was born in [C41] Voznesensk in 1824. Her father was the proprietor of a beet-sugar refinery. Two brothers of whom we know were an attorney and a physician. As her family's wealth provided her a "substantial" dowery, she was able to marry a "learned" man, [A419] Beryl Kaprov.

On February 3 and 4, 1993, a friend traveled to the village to determine if anyone had remembrances of the Brodskys, then or now. She met the mayor. The city now has about 50,000 inhabitants, few if any Jews, and no synagogue.

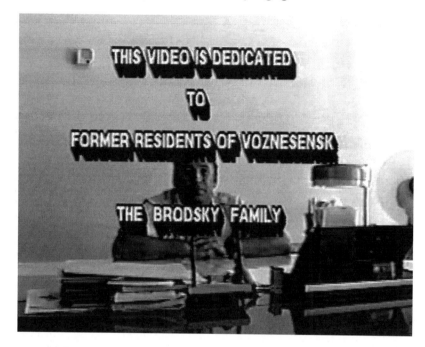

Fig. 57-1: Voznesenck Mayor honors the Brodsky family.

The cemetery from pre-World War I, the burial home of all Jewish residents, had long been destroyed. A shoe and woodworking factory now stands in its place. When World War II took place, the invading German Army devastated most of the town. The town's cemetery has a section for the Jewish residents. The cemetery is all that remains of the Jewish community. An older woman, Tamara, who lived next door to the cemetery, remembered that there were some Brodsky's interred there. Still, she did not know their first names and whether they were related in any way to the family ancestor Brodskys. In reality, the name Brodsky, during the late 1800s and until the Holocaust, was exceedingly common, much like Smith is in the United States today.

Fig. 57-2: Jewish section of Voznesensk cemetery.

Fig. 57-3: Tamara, a woman whose home neighbors the cemetery.

Voznesensk is a bucolic region teeming with wildlife, especially flocks of geese.

Fig. 57-4: Pastoral setting. Flocks of geese are common.

The citizens of the town with whom our friend met were extraordinarily friendly. They were most generous and openhearted. If one were asked to see a telephone book, more likely than not, one would receive the telephone book, even if it were the only one available in the house. The economy at the time was also in the doldrums. Inflation was a major issue, and anything needed was exceedingly costly.

The homes in the town ranged from poor and needing repair to being substantial. The children were clean and well-fed.

Fig. 57-5: Poor portion of the town.

Fig. 57-6: School children. The background shows a horse-drawn wagon.

Animals grazed freely wherever they wished.

Fig. 57-7: Cows wandering.

To a large extent, the village still resembled scenes as if taken from the play and movie *Fiddler on the Roof*. The standard mode of transportation for many was still the horse-led hay wagon.

Fig. 57-8: Horse-drawn wagon, a common form of transporation.

America

#58 WHY THE B'NAI KHAIM EMIGRATED AND ACCULTURATION IN AMERICA
(Adapted from *The B'nai Khaim in America* by Joe Gillman)

Editor's note: Throughout this book, the stories of why our family members left Russia to come to American carried a strong overtone of pogroms and the political hardships many experienced. But cousin Joe also describes more emphatically the economic opportunities that our ancestors believed America offered. Rokhl Kafrissen, in her column, *Rokhl's Golden City: An American Tale*, asks whether the stories about Jewish immigration to America a century ago, though popular and well known, were right ("persecution hypothesis")? She writes that the overwhelming driver of mass migration from the Russian Empire was the search for economic opportunity. In the early 1900s, the United States had virtually no limits on immigration (until it did, in 1924), and Jews arrived as white Europeans, which meant that their entrepreneurial opportunities were virtually unlimited. The Jews who came to America in that period were "pretty damn lucky."

But with a few decades, "they really were trying to kill us. And the United States very firmly closed its door." According to The United States Holocaust Memorial Museum, "In late 1938, 125,000 (German Jewish) applicants lined up outside U.S. consulates hoping to obtain 27,000 visas under the existing immigration quota. By June 1939, the number of applicants had increased to over 300,000. Most visa applicants were unsuccessful. At the Evian Conference in July 1938, only the Dominican Republic stated that it was prepared to admit significant numbers of refugees, although Bolivia would admit around 30,000 Jewish immigrants between 1938 and 1941." See https://www.tabletmag.com/jewish-life-and-religion/299642/an-american-tale

Hard times and pogroms swept over Russia from about the 1880s onwards. By the early 1900s, the upheavals in Russia were great. This agricultural country saw the beginning of and was becoming industrialized. Factories had begun to replace home-made labor, and this affected the livelihood of artisans and shopkeepers with whom the peasants traded. The livelihood of the Jews was affected, and the depression between 1899-1909 was continuous. The Jews became the scapegoats for the peasants' discontent, and the cry arose, "To America."

Justingrad, during those times, was a ghetto town, virtually a feudal, agricultural setting. Life was medieval. Most everybody was poor. Some peasants were slightly better off as they had farms and food. Most Jews were artisans, carpenters, shoemakers, tailors, small shopkeepers, and traders. The B'nai Khaim were generally poorer than the other Jews, as they disdained hard labor.

All the B'nai Khaim were scrupulously orthodox. All ancient rites were observed. Most believed in the supernatural and shared superstitions. Disease was rampant as sanitation was nonexistent. The infant mortality was high. A medical student came periodically for short times.

Most community members were illiterate or semi-illiterate, especially the peasants. Jewish boys, ages 6-13 years, attended cheder (Jewish school) and were required to learn the Prayer-book in Hebrew, at least to read it. Some went for further Hebrew study. A few had a secular education. Most learned to figure mentally. Many could not write numbers. After 1900, girls were admitted to cheder, and even some secular education was introduced. Few learned to write, even in the mother tongue. Most spoke Yiddish and the peasant Ukrainian dialect. A few of the family married and moved away from Justingrad, and with some rich arendator's children, got to study in Uman.

With this background, most who emigrated came to America and a few to South America. The few exceptions went to Uman, Odessa, and Kishinev. For the most part, those coming to America lacked money, skills, or friends. The beginning jobs were menial. Survival, of course, was the first necessity.

In America

Over the years, Joe Gillman and his wife, Etta, kept in touch with many of the immigrant family members. They kept in contact with someone in every segment of the family groups, which by 1960 involved more than 26 cities. By 1962 they determined to survey the B'nai Khaim, developing an inventory with pertinent data regarding the members themselves and their spouses and children. "Lieutenants" served as helpers. We developed a card catalog for every baby, including those newly born. At the time Joe and Etta began collecting data, the family numbered more than 350 (with children but not spouses). For statistical purposes, there were more than 250 family members 16 and over, and now including spouses.

The project included developing:
Questionnaires for distribution.
Information on immigrants regarding vital statistics on education and occupation.
Similar questions to American born and their spouses regarding degree of schooling, religions, education, occupation.

Adaptation to America, including:
Degree of adherence to tradition in rituals, etc. (Dietary laws, Sabbath).
Attitude toward intermarriage.
In adapting, forming new prejudices – attitudes toward the Negro for instance.
Cultural interests.
Sense of identity as Jews – attitude toward Israel, their Jewishness.
Participation in Jew community services.

Other comparisons

Education and Occupations of Immigrant B'nai Khaims

Those who achieved command of English had the best adjustments and determined the potential for economic achievement and identification with the new culture. The higher the age at arrival, the less possible became the formal education required for success. Only three B'nai Khaim immigrants who arrived above age eight achieved professions. [A317] Harry Dudwick at 8, [A026] John Robboy at 17, and [A457] Joe Gillman at 18.

263

Those who did not become professionals were involved mainly later in a small retail business, e.g., handicrafts, paper hanger, scrap iron, wholesalers, at first stalls and peddlers, but later stores and wholesalers. In America as in Russia, the B'nai Khaim members engaged mostly in trade and services. Women were primarily housewives, but many worked wholly or part-time to help in the factory (needle trades, stores, seamstresses). The earlier the age of arrival correlated with the more likely one got formal education and had the potential for achievement. Those under eight did exceptionally well.

Native-Born (including those who came before age 8) – Occupation and Education.

Males: Sixty-eight percent were college graduates and mostly in white-collar occupations and the professions (doctors, lawyers, dentists). Some were engineers or professors.
Among the native-born women, 35% went to college, and 94% graduated high school.
Religious Education:
Among the native-born, only half had received training (mostly for bar mitzvah). Sixty-four percent of the males attended a Jewish Sunday School or Jewish secular school.

Dietary Laws

The members trended away from observance of dietary laws and were influenced by the neighborhood in which they lived. Those living in mixed areas had a built-in aversion to eating pork – none ate bacon, shellfish, etc. The beard vanished as a symbol of piety.

Sabbath

Eighty-six percent of married males work on Sabbath. Fifty percent of B'nai Khaim women and 80% of native-born cook on Saturday. Many continue to light candles on Sabbath eve.

Synagogue membership

A surprisingly large population of women of native-born regularly attended synagogue. What stood out was the shift away from Orthodoxy to Conservative to Reform to no affiliation. Among native-born: 1/29 belonged to an orthodox congregation, 8 Conservative, 8 Reform, 12 none.

The native-born had the most holidays. The B'nai Khaim observed High Holidays, but only 35/211 observed the other major holidays. Passover was the most celebrated as it was joyful. The seder was popular; about a quarter celebrated with just a family dinner.

Intermarriage
There was a 10% intermarriage rate for 2nd generation B'nai Khaim

Jewish Identity

Eighty-five percent of B'nai Khaim retained an affinity for Israel. "Because I am a Jew – it's my country. But America is my country. The B'nai Khaim are not yet ready to give up their identity. Eating or not fasting is one thing, but giving up Jewish identity means giving up the security of belonging."

#59 KNYAZHE'S CONTRIBUTION TO AMERICA

The Jewish population of [C01] Knyazhe during my 17 years of childhood consisted of 164 Jews. During this same period, I recall but two who moved away and four who died, leaving a total of 158 Jews. Of this total, some 65 to 70 migrated to America, leaving 85 to 90 Jews, men, women, and children.

The life these people endured was not to be envied. They lived under most primitive conditions: poor housing, poor hygiene, most restrictive economic resources, tyrannical government, and hostile neighbors. Yet, they rose way above their neighbors in all phases of life.

This small group of Jews ran a municipal government with a mayor and scribe of its own. It maintained a synagogue and spiritual leader, a butcher to supply them with kosher meats, a school, and rebbe for their children and, of course, a public bathhouse. It was also this same small group of Jews who provided the much more prosperous peasantry with a carpenter, blacksmith, furriers, seamstress, grocers, and other merchants and even winnowers of grain and a miller to crack the millet seeds for kasha.

The same small, but energetic group also managed to contribute some 65 to 70 of its members to America as part of the significant Jewish immigration at the turn of the century. Contrary to the pleas of Emma Lazarus,[98] it was not the weak or the lame who were dispatched. The weak, the old, and the indolent remained at home. It was the young, the vigorous, the restless, the ambitious, the freedom-seeking young men and women who left in search of opportunities.

I arrived in the States in 1910 as one of these immigrants. The most striking thing then was the scarcity of older people. Few men over 40 years of age were seen. All were young. We lived life with intensity, mediated through the enzymatic action of the vigor, imagination, and the aspirations of youth. The pure American air expanded the new immigrants' lungs. It invigorated his muscles and reactivated his brain. It aroused his ambition and widened his horizon.

The Cleveland Jewish district then extended from East 22nd Street to East 65th Street in the East and from Woodland to Cedar Avenue on the north. It was one giant beehive of activity with Woodland Avenue carrying the lifeblood to all nooks and crannies of the vibrating organism.

Here there was love, play, and work. There was music, hope, and aspiration. Here industry and commerce flourished. Shops, factories, and banks were built. Unions formed, strikes fought, and synagogues, temples, movies, and theaters erected. Halls, all kinds of them, dance halls, concert halls, lecture halls, and schools, public and private, were opened. The youth were reading, talking, and debating Zionism, Socialism, Communism, Anarchism, philosophy, and literature. All these were discussed, debated, digested, and assimilated at school, at parties, at home, or at picnics in Gordon or Garfield Parks. It was this atmosphere that chemists, engineers, lawyers, and judges grew up. Here is where and how the new citizen shaped and re-shaped, molded, and adjusted to the environmental stresses of "The New American."

---

[98] American author of poetry, prose, and translations, as well as an activist for Jewish causes. Lines from her sonnet "The New Colossus" (Give me your tired, your poor, your huddled masses yearning to breathe free ...) appears inscribed on a bronze plaque installed in 1903 on the pedestal of the Statue of Liberty.

#60 THE NEW LIFE IN AMERICA

July 1, 1927, was my first day facing the working world. I was utterly unprepared. I had no guidance and was penniless.

In those days, our fathers were merely poor tailors, barbers, or peddlers, and, as is well known, poverty and stupidity go hand in hand.

I did have a vision. I came home with the idea that Warner Road in Garfield Heights would be an ideal place for my office. For two weeks, I searched for a spot on Warner Road and then gave up the pursuit in disappointment.

I needed a license, an office, and furniture as well as an automobile. [A011] Mother was dying; [A011] Father's earnings were meager. [A023] Tobie and [A024] Joe were exhausted. Within a few weeks, I found myself in debt and burdened with a home and its responsibilities. Adding to this was the famous crash, which soon overtook us all. No wonder it took me ten years to get to my feet.

By the spring of 1936, I was free of all debts and encumbrances. Now, I was ready to start again. I moved into a more respectable office and was prepared for the next venture. [A023] Sister Tobie, my friend [A814] Izzy Cantor, and [A654a] Viva Gressel (who never even knew me) sensed the spirit of the moment and collaborated independently in a conspiracy against me. [A674a] Miriam Shapiro ([A654a] Viva's sister) and Miriam's husband, [A674] Uriah, joined them. Even [A675] Dotty ([A674a] Miriam's daughter) fell in step and proclaimed her consent to my marrying her Aunt [A026a] Sarah.

Things went at a rapid pace. It was a question of striking the iron while it was hot, and so were the telephone wires reaching [A686] Ezra Shapiro (Uriah's brother) and [A686a] Sylvia Shapiro on their vacation in Canada. No wonder [A677] Yonny (Miriam's son) was puzzled and insisted on knowing what was to happen on August the first. Even the Veterans Administration scrapped all red tape and handed me my bonus check of $250 within minutes, while [A665.1a] Father Shapiro hurried to tie the knot the very next day. This was a simple, unceremonious one, but as you know, it held well since.

[A026a] Sarah made our home comfortable. My practice improved. The in-laws were kind, loving, and helpful. Sarah proved herself productive. [A027] Myrna arrived unhesitatingly, while [A031] Stanley managed to pull his first surprise (for we were suspecting twin girls) and he has surprised us ever since.[99] These were years of great satisfaction, both personally and professionally. I do not claim distinction in medicine, profundity of thought, or high scholarship. My very simplicity and softness of character filled me best for general practice. Practice in my earlier days was much more challenging and less remunerative than at present. However, though we were helpless and restricted in our armamentarium, a practice carried kindness, sympathy,

---

[99] Stanley was adventuresome throughout his life, which not infrequently left [A026a] Sarah anxious. But when she received a letter from him during his travels or his weekly telephone calls from wherever he might be, she knew he was at the moment, neither 10,000 feet about the earth nor 10,000 feet below. In a letter dated in 1973 to a Maine cousin, John hoped/prophesized that at sometime long in the future, Stanley would become the family's historian.

warmth, respect, and intimacy, which sustained me highly. The loss of the latter is what people bemoan with the disappearance of the general practitioner, but what is gone will never return.

As far as I am concerned, I have given more succor and comfort in my own crude way to thousands of men, women, and children in their struggle for existence than many a high towered professor. I had the strength of character to withstand all difficulties, privations, and all temptations and remained true, not just to the ethical traditions of the profession, but to that of my fellow man. I felt that I successfully preserved my integrity and am, therefore, at peace with myself.

Now I can count my blessings. [A027] Myrna and her husband, [A027a] Herbert Groger, brought us three splendid grandchildren, [A028] Laurel, [A029] Richard, and [A030] Debra. [A031] Stanley and his wife, [A031a] Anita Wyzanski, likewise gave us two beautiful grandchildren [A032] Elizabeth and [A033] Caroline. All of them are still very young. Hopefully, each one will provide us with much joy in future years.

[A026a] Sarah is, of course, the ONE who made all this possible.

#61 [A034] MORDECHAI AND SARAH SPECTOR ROBBOY
By [A050] Stephanie Judith Yellen-Mednick

[A034a] Sarah Spector, [A034] Mordechai Robboy's wife, was petite but mighty. She was a great cook, loving and caring, especially to the family. After marrying her, Mordechai moved to her home town of [C43] Zashkov, where he became the community's Cantor and, besides, ran a small chicken farm.

The Spector family had nine children. In later years, Sarah often spoke to her grandchildren about her extended family, her cooking, and how they did so much together. One discussion piece was how each of the various cooks might make the same dish but slightly differently. The family members were also most opinionated, but close.

Fig. 61-1: [A047] Sylvia Robboy

Mordechai and Sarah had seven children: [A035] Nathan (1897) [A047] Sylvia (1900), [A057] Morton (1901), [A059] George (1907), [A064] Rose (1909), [A071] Dorothy (1911), and [A075] Eddie (1914).

Fig. 61-2 [A034] Mordechai Robboy clan in Russia: ?1918
Top: Mother [A034a] Sarah Spector Robboy, [A047] Sylvia, Father [A034] Mordechai Robboy, and [A057] Morton;
Bottom: [A064] Rose, [A071] Dorothy, [A059] George.

Fig. 61-3: [A034] Mordechai Robboy clan in Russia: c1919. Picture are deceiving, for Eddie, the youngest, holds the photograph shown as 61-2 (cropped and not seen).
Top: [A047] Sylvia, [A064] Rose, [A071] Dorothy , [A059] George
Bottom: [A034a] Sarah, [A075] Eddie, [A057] Morton.

Girls of that era generally never received any formal education. Yet Mordechai felt differently, believing and taking it upon himself that every girl should know how to read and write. He ensured that happened. And he so taught Sylvia to read and write, as he did with the other sisters, [A064] Rose and [A071] Dorothy. Sarah, too, could write, but whether she knew it before marriage, or learned it from Mordechai or at some later time is uncertain. But it is her writing which is the only Yiddish handwritten script the Editor of these letters has found.

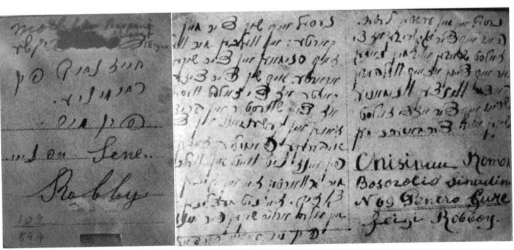

Fig. 61-4 Letters, likely postcards, [A034a] Sarah Spector wrote in Yiddish script.

269

Both Mordechai and Sarah were family-oriented, but then again, many in their village of [C43] Zashkov felt similarly. Indeed, many relatives lived there, and they were family. Whenever there was a wedding or significant event, the relatives in the various communities would all come together to celebrate. It was a warm and close community with family. Mordechai traveled frequently to the neighboring towns selling eggs, and also visiting with relatives.

Mordechai was thought of as loving and hands-on. He was open and conversed with all. He never paid attention to class systems. He freely spoke with the street sweeper as to another learned man.

And then tragedy came. Circa 1919, after World War I had ended, the pogroms had devolved into the Russian Civil War with the Bolshevik revolutionaries. Because Mordechai was both the Cantor and scholar, he was one of the first people purposely attacked when the revolutionaries entered. They beat him over the head with a bat. The midwife was called and asked to care for him. She immediately sent Sylvia and Dorothy to the nearby swamp to obtain leeches, the standard practice at that time, which "relieved" the pressure on the head. Mordechai died three days later.

Brother [A035] Nate, who was a great horseman, had also been sought by the Bolsheviks. Cousin [A026] John Robboy, who was already in America, had made it possible for him to leave and travel to America by providing the needed monies.

Sarah understood the immediate danger for the entire family and began making plans to leave. John, once again, helped provide the funds needed to escape. The family traveled in a wagon, usually at night and undercover, so to avoid exposure. To the extent possible, the older children walked while the younger children hid under the hay in the wagon. There was little food on the trip. During part of the journey, they stowed away on a cattle car.

Sarah gave whatever she could obtain to the children. In many ways, people thought that Sylvia's small frame was linked to malnutrition, mostly as Sylvia's children born later in the United States were so much taller. Sarah's family had to travel over 300 miles to reach Cherbourg, a port city on the French Atlantic coast. Sylvia had been age 14 when the journey commenced, but 16 years old by the time she and the family boarded the ship to America. They remembered nothing of the route taken, but it was clear that the path was well-trodden and known to many, much like the underground railroad slaves in the United States took to freedom. Sylvia was very much impressed by the people they met during their travels and commented that so many of them were helpful. Yet, it was also apparent that many did not wish to become too involved. In part, the background of World War I flavored many persons' behavior. Many people were uncertain of how to act. Were they dealing with friend or foe? They just wished to avoid calamity. Sarah was never too specific but did remark about how the family celebrated the holidays during the journey, at least to the extent possible. It was minimalist. They celebrated wherever and however they could. They did not and could not always keep the Sabbath. Often they were unable even to keep the holidays.

The oceanic crossing was particularly rough. Many passengers were sick throughout the journey. The healthy mothers communally cared for all the children and all of the other sick passengers. The ship offered little room and privacy. They traveled in steerage, and nothing more than "curtains" separated the small amount of space each family had from the other families in the hold.

[A035] Nathan made arrangements with people in New York to meet the family once they cleared immigration in 1921 at Ellis Island. He provided the tickets that brought the family by train to Cleveland.

Fig. 61-5: Ellis Island immigrant registration for Sylvia Robboy Isbitz.

Cleveland meant freedom and love once again. Family with many cousins from both the Spector and Robboy sides were present and loving. The family flourished.

Fig. 61-6: [A034] Mordechai Robboy's children) at Mort's wedding 1948
L-R: [A035] Nate, [A059] George, [A047] Sylvia, [A075] Edward, [A075a] Sylvia, [A064] Rose and [A057] Mort.

Fig. 61-7: [A034] Mordechai Robboy's Cleveland descendants) in 1948.
L-R: [A059] George with [A060] Rhoda, [A075] Eddy, [A035] Nathan (NM) and Rhea with [A036] Mitch and [A042] Stan, [A064] Rose and Dave Rein with [A094] Susan and [A065] Bill, [A057a] Helen and [A057] Mort with [A058] Mel, [A018a] Rose and [A018] Nate with [A020] Marcia and [A019] Nancy.

Fig. 61-8: [A034] Extended Robboy clan at Mort's wedding 1948
L-R Top: [A059] George, [A013] Bernie, [A059a] Mary, [A013a] Rosalie, [A026a] Sarah, [A026] John, [A057a] Helen, [A057] Mort, [A075] Edward, [A075a] Sylvia, [A035a] Rhea, [A064a] David Rein, [A035] Nathan, [A064] Rose
Middle: [A031] Stanley J, [A027] Myrna (upper), [A056] Betty Isbitz (lower), [A063] Merle, [A058] Melvin, UKN, [A047] Sylvia Isbitz
Front: [A042] Stanley G, [A036] Mitchell, [A065] Bill Rein

One cousin with whom Sylvia, Sarah's daughter, was particularly close was [A026] John Robboy. Curiously, Sylvia disliked the cold, even though the area in Ukraine from where she came was frequently cold and with snow. Sylvia wished warmth.

Because of this desire and after some four years of living in Cleveland, Sylvia, together with her cousin Lillian, from the Spector side of the family, left for Los Angeles, where Sylvia promptly found work as a seamstress. Friends arranged for her to meet [A047a] Joe Isbitz, a meeting that took place on a streetcar. They dated for a short while and married. Her mother, Sarah, came from Cleveland for the wedding.

Fig. 61-9: Isbitz family C1850 [A048] Marilyn,[A047a] Joe and [A047] Sylvia, [A056] Betty, [A055] Sarah-Fay, [A053] Rosalie.

Sylvia and Joe lived initially in Boyle Heights, where [A053] Rosalie was born (1930). The family then moved to San Pedro, where [A055] Sarah-Fay and [A056] Betty were born. Joe was a tailor, and more specifically, had become a tailor to the admiral and the higher-ranking clientele working at the Navy Yard in San Pedro. Marilyn began school at the Cabrillo Avenue Elementary School.

#62 [A079] MENDEL ROBBOY AND PHILADELPHIA
By [A090] Howard Robboy

[A079] Mendel and [A079a] Anna Desatnick Robboy and their three children, [A080] Phyllis, [A083] Sidney, and [A088] Benjamin (ages 10-12) settled in Philadelphia in 1923, a city where Anna's sisters and brothers already lived and where others were to come. They had come from Knyazhe during the time of the pogroms. They settled in the Port Richmond area, which was a predominantly Polish Catholic neighborhood.

By way of background, the families, Kranzel and Desatnick, also heralded from the nearby Ukrainian shtetls, [C43] Zashkov, [C31] Stavishtsh and [C35] Tsybuliv. The former was where Mendel's brother, [A034] Mordechai Robboy, and his wife, [A034a] Sarah Faiga lived. [A026] John Robboy, the son of Mendel's other brother, [A011] Shmuel, in 1908, also lived with Mordechai and Sarah while attending school there.

Other cousins, from John Robboy's Kaprove side, also died in the 1919 pogroms in these villages.

Another cousin from Knyazhe, [A350] Froim Dudnik married Sarah Dayan, from Zashkov, and in 1922, after Sarah's death during a childbirth, his three children emigrated to Palestine, followed later by Froim. Their nephew [A829] Moshe Dayan was the chief of staff of the Israel Defense Forces (1953–58) during the 1956 Suez Crisis and Defense Minister during the Six-Day War in 1967.

[C31] Stavishtsh was where Cousin Rabbi [A515] Avrom Kaprov, another cousin on John's mother's side, was sent to work. [C35] Tsybuliv, located about 4 miles to the southeast of Knyazhe, was the home of some Desatnick relatives.

Mendel and his family were fortunate for just one year after they arrived in Philadelphia, immigration would have proved problematic, if not impossible. The United States passed a new law:

> The **Immigration Act of 1924**, or **Johnson-Reed Act**, including the **Asian Exclusion Act** and **National Origins Act** was a United States federal law that prevented immigration from Asia, set quotas on the number of immigrants from the Eastern Hemisphere, and provided funding and an enforcement mechanism to carry out the longstanding ban on other immigrants.

> The 1924 act supplanted earlier acts to effectively ban all immigration from <u>Asia</u> and set a total immigration quota of 165,000 for countries outside the Western Hemisphere, an 80% reduction from the pre-World War I average. Quotas for specific countries were based on 2% of the U.S. population from that country as recorded in 1890. As a result, populations poorly represented in 1890 were prevented from immigrating in proportionate numbers—mainly affecting Italians, Eastern European Jews, Greeks, Poles, and other Slavs. According to the U.S. Department of State Office of the Historian, the purpose of the act was "to preserve the ideal of U.S. homogeneity." Congressional opposition was minimal.

> (Source: Wikipedia).

Shortly after coming to Philadelphia, the family moved to Cleveland. Mendel attempted to make a living picking trash and to sell whatever he could, but this was insufficient, and so the family returned to Philadelphia. Mendel took a job at the Budd Company, which made railroad cars. Unfortunately, he hurt his back and had to quit.

Mendel and Anna went into the produce business in Port Richmond. After saving enough to rent a store, they then took in produce (e.g., fresh fruits and veggies and salads) and not just groceries (all of the other foods commonly purchased, such as milk and eggs.) The store sold no meats. On Fridays, fish were available.

In actuality, the store was their home. The store on the main floor was a converted living room. A small kitchen was behind. Seventeen steps led to the second floor, where there were three bedrooms. The basement, which had an exceedingly shallow ceiling and a dirt floor, was primarily used for storage. The cat controlled the mice, and the dog, the potential burglars.

The work was grueling. The store opened at 8 a.m. and closed at 9 p.m. Vacations were virtually nonexistent. Mendel and Irma closed the store one day a year and used that to go to the beach.

Antisemitism was rife in this region. Gangs of Italians, Germans, Irish, and Polish adolescences attacked each other and Jews. Each nationality had its own turf. The Jews had none. Ben used to tell stories of these gangs waiting outside of the library on Ann Street for him and said he could expect to get beaten when leaving the library. There was also a railroad bridge on Richmond street that served as a barrier. Any Jew who dared go under the bridge was subject to beatings. It was not surprising that Ben told his children that if someone is not Jewish, they are antisemitic.

In addition to antisemitism, during the depression era, the Mafia would call upon the small business owners demanding protection money. The business done in Mendel's store was so negligible that they never bothered.

Mendel and his son, [A088] Ben, and [A083] Sidney would then huckster the food. They would rent a horse for a dollar a day and, on Friday, go into the neighborhoods peddling the goods. Many times, Mendel spoke of a horse he rented that would kick him. Mendel also spoke of carrying 100-pound bags of coal up to the third-floor of peoples' homes. Later, as the business grew, the store always sold fish on Fridays. Mendel and Ben would take the Number 15 trolley home from the wharf and then carry the fish and produce three blocks west to the store.

[A080] Phyllis, their daughter and oldest, had a heart of gold, but she was troubled and erratic, though due mainly to having had to witness her father put up against a wall to be shot by the firing squad (described in Chapter #36). Phyllis was shy and concerned. She trained as a nurse, most likely as a licensed practical nurse (LPN), and did private duty nursing. Much of the time, she also helped her parents in the store.

Phyllis married late. [A080a] Perry Gomel, her husband, was a good man and worked as a union glazier. He had from a former marriage two teenage children, Bobby and Francis. Perry had won custody of the two children, but as was not uncommon in those days, the judge ordered that the two children live and be raised in an orphanage, allowing Perry to see them only on weekends. Perry, in addition to his work as a glazier, had a motorcycle cart and went around selling water at ballgames and playgrounds. [A090] Howard Robboy, [A088] Ben's son, remembers well the enjoyable rides on the scooter.

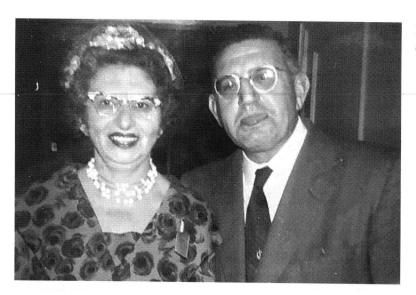

Fig. 62-1: [A080] Phyllis and Perry Gomel.

DO NOT DETACH THIS SHEET FROM DUE BOOK

DESIGNATION OF BENEFICIARY

The undersigned hereby designates as his beneficiary

Phyllis Gomel, Name — Wife, Relationship (if any)

1427 Keyser St, Address — Phila, City — Pa., State

Signature of Member Perry Gomel

Date 7/26, 1966 Signed Wm C Melnick, Fin. Sec.

CHANGE OF BENEFICIARY

The undersigned hereby changes his beneficiary

from ....

to .... Relationship (if any)

Address — City — State

Signature of Member ....

Date ...., 19..... Witness .... Fin. Sec.

OFFICIAL MEMBERSHIP BOOK

BROTHERHOOD OF PAINTERS, DECORATORS & PAPERHANGERS OF AMERICA

Social Security No. 150 [redacted] — Receipts For Dues Assessments — Card No. 125429

From Perry Gomel

Initiated in L. U. 55N No. of Atlantic City, City — N.J., State

Date of Initiation 1937

Date of Birth 10/15/06 — Age at Initiation 30

Initiation Fee (Amount actually paid) 5.00

President Wm C Melnick

Local Union No. 252 of Phila - Pa, City — State

Members must designate the name of beneficiary or change of beneficiary on blank provided on preceding page which must be signed also by the Financial Secretary.

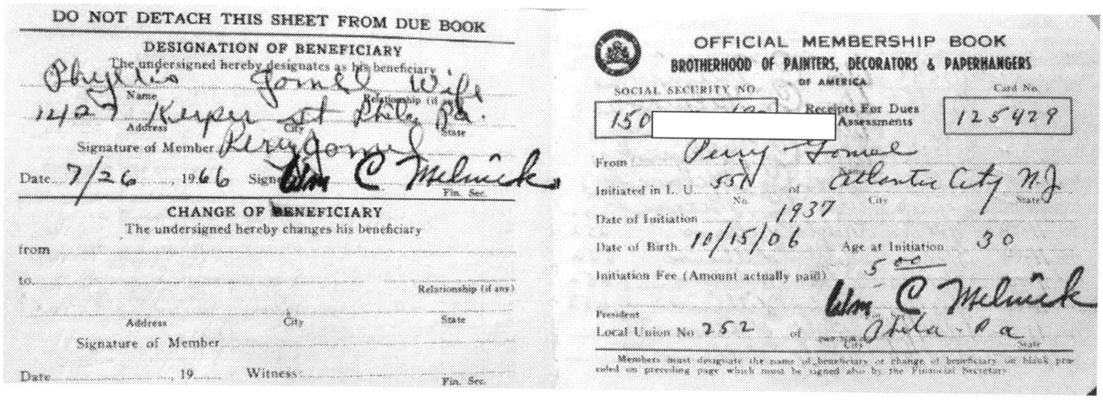

Fig. 62-2: Savings bank book.

[A081] Francis, Perry's daughter, married David Levy, a judge. They later divorced. Their two children were John and Ricard Levy. [A082] Robert Gomel, Perry's son, also had two children.

[A083] Sidney worked in the grocery store with his parents after he left school in the eighth grade. Among his duties on Fridays at 5 a.m. was to buy fish at the City Market for his parents to then resell in their store. In 1948, having completed his army tour of duty, he went into the auction business, along with other members of the Desatnick family. Sid later bought a used truck, a Dodge, from Frank Kranzel and then became an auctioneer at farmers markets in the Philadelphia metropolitan area. He auctioned and pitched hardware and seasonal merchandise and did quite well for someone in that business. His success in part was that he was smooth, articulate, and could convince people to buy items that they might not normally purchase. Sometime in the mid-1950s, he sold the truck and opened up a hardware store in the Pennsauken Merchandise Mart in New Jersey, just across the river from Philadelphia.

Fig 62-3: [A083] Sidney Robboy in the US Army, 1944.

Fig 62-4: July 4th, 1946 parade in Philadelphia, Feltonville section, Robboys, and Kranzel relatives. L-R Rear: Isador, Samuel, and Elka Kranzel; Front: Frances Kranzel, [A083] Sidney Robboy, [A084] Gita Robboy, Fannie Kranzel, and unknown.

Sid married [A083a] Eva Desatnick, a first cousin, who was a schoolteacher in Philadelphia in the Solis Cohen school. Eva's job teaching provided their principal income. But life is not always straightforward.

Earlier, Sid was dating Frannie Kramer, a first cousin on the Desatnick side. Fannie's mother, Nima Tessie Kramer, was [A079a] Anna's sister. Nima had a grocery store about six blocks away, with parakeets that were always chirping away. Sidney, at one time, took a trip to Cleveland. Eva, who also was Anna's niece on the Desatnick side and Fannie's sister, wished to go along. By the time they returned from the trip, Sid and Eva were dating, and shortly after that, married at Niagara Falls.

Sidney and Eva had two children [A084] Gita and [A087] Bruce. The latter was a compulsive gambler. After winning $10,000 one evening playing blackjack, the next evenings left him with cleaned out credit cards. He died later in an auto accident, leaving a wife, [A087a] Leslie, who was a schoolteacher, but no children.

[A088] Benjamin, the youngest brother, met his wife to be, [A088a] Irma, in 1935 when he was age 19. Irma had been orphaned early. Her mother died when she was age 11, and her father was in a sanatorium with tuberculosis. Her family was so poor they often could not afford toilet paper. As it happened, Mendel and Anna's gross grocery store carried fruits that came wrapped in blue paper, which proved a satisfactory substitute for toilet paper. That was certainly an upgrade from having to use old newspapers. And Irma loved coming to the grocery store. Irma went to a dance where she was to meet Lew Kranzel, but he never showed up. Ben did come, and soon they were married.

Ben began Drexel University at night and, in 1937, obtained a certificate in mechanical engineering. Problematically, he could not get a job in mechanical engineering due to both antisemitism within the field and that the country was not yet entirely out of the depression. He became an apprentice machinist at 37.5 cents an hour at a link belt company in Philadelphia. His job enabled Ben and Irma to marry on Memorial Day, in 1937. Thus, a day's employment was not lost. Their honeymoon consisted of one night spent in a Center City hotel. The job kept Ben out of the military during World War II since it was critical to the war effort. In 1944, Ben came to realize he needed to leave the machine shop and get into the front office of an engineering firm, for otherwise, he would always remain a machinist.

In 1954, Ben quit his job, bought a Ford truck with money he inherited from an aunt who just died, and also entered the auction business. He would commonly go to the Center City, where there were wholesalers and buy remainders essentially. What he purchased was still largely principally war surplus. The concept of discount stores had just begun; the fad would only come later, at which time Ben's type of auction business would ultimately disappear. Many of the items sold, negotiated, auctioned, such as a hammer, would sell for a dollar, which was the average price paid for any item. He did, though, sell all sorts of tools. Some slightly larger items were electric toasters and fans. More expensive items were electric drills, toolboxes, or fishing gear, but the price for any item never exceeded $100. In other words, it was a hardware store on wheels. Some of the items sold were seasonal, grass seed. Ben's motto, with tongue-in-cheek, was, "if it doesn't grow, I'll take it back."

Most of the selling was confined to four nights of the week. During the day, he would shop for new merchandise. His two favorite places to sell were at the Cow town in South Jersey, where there was a western rodeo. Also, he liked to sell at the farmers market.

By 1959, business being so poor, Ben quit the auctioneering business and returned to engineering.

Ben and [A088a] Irma had two children. [A089] Stanton taught for 36 years, principally business subjects such as retail selling.

[A090] Howard, the younger son by five years, attained a Ph.D. in Sociology and taught for 40 years, 34 years at the College of New Jersey, where he headed the Sociology Department for eight years. Howard became renowned for writing the definitive studies on the food, the po'boy,[100] and later became instrumental when volunteering in the Philadelphia History Museum. One of his family's most treasured possessions, a menorah, was among the first items they purchased when coming to Philadelphia. The menorah was passed on and later became Howard's. One branch was bent. Howard mused, "That's what happens in real life. Things get bent." The story of the menorah appears in Chapter #76.

---

[100] The po'boy, a traditional sandwich from Louisiana, invariably consists of meat, usually in the form of roast beef or fried seafood. The latter may be shrimp, crawfish, crab, fish, or oysters. The specialty is served on New Orleans French bread, which has a crispy crust and fluffy center.

Mendel and Anna's family, like most families, developed likes and dislikes over the years, favorites, and persons ignored. This family was no different. [A083a] Eva, Sidney's wife, was the most strong willed of the entire family, indeed, the matriarch. It was said, no tears were shed at the funeral. Eva did not like Perry. As one example of her taste for the entire family, she and Sid in the 1950s took a cruise through South America, which at that time was quite an expedition. Upon returning, they brought lovely presents for nearly all. Francis and Robert, though, received only a menu from the ship. In the earlier years, when most of the family were working in the grocery store or had begun working in the auction business, most believed Eva would help raise all the children, communally. But that was not to be. Instead, Mendel and Anna's home remained the focal point, and that is where Howard came to know Phyllis's children, Francis and Robert, well.

Mendel and Anna were Orthodox and prayed in the neighborhood Orthodox shul. Ben and Irma, whose home was kosher, were conservative Jews but remained observant.

Fig 62-5: [A079] Anna Robboy lighting Shabbat candles.

Mendel died in 1953 at age 90. Phyllis left, and Anna ran the grocery for another eight years. It was also thought that Francis, Phyllis's daughter, might move to be with Eva and Sidney, who by then had a large home in New Jersey. But this too was not to be. Eva wouldn't permit it. Ben and Irma's house was too small, so Francis ended up living with her mother, Phyllis.

#63 [A298] YOSSEL (JOSEPH) DUDNIK – WHERE TO LIVE, USA OR RUSSIA?
By [A302] Trudy Borenstein-Sugiura

[A298] Yossel (Joseph) Dudnik, the second of [A293] Aaron and Tzipora Dudnik's nine children and their oldest son, came to the US in 1909, when he was age 23. Five years later, in 1914, he and Minnie Bellis married. Their first daughter, [A299] Beatrice, was born two years later, in 1916, in Cleveland. World War I was about to commence. As the war was ending, Yossel found living in the United States was difficult, at which point the family returned to [C06] Bershad, the Ukrainian village from where Yossel was born. But life was not so easy in Russia. This time was the period of Russia's great Civil War, discussed elsewhere as the time of the pogroms, the ending of the czarist regimes, the advent of the White Russians, and finally, the Bolsheviks (Red Russians) heading the State. Irene, the second oldest child, was born in Russia during this mayhem (Mar 25,1920). In returning, they anticipated the Bolsheviks would no longer attack Jews and would have become far more hospitable and entrepreneurial. Unhappy with the new Russian regime, the family returned to Cleveland, where [A307] Selma, the third daughter, was eventually born some years later.

Fig. 63-1: Dudniks c1918
Top: Ukn, Ukn, Ukn, [A294] Gita;
Middle: [A298a] Minnie, [A317] Harry, Ukn, Ukn, [A298] Joe Dudnik and [A299] Bea on lap; Front: [A026] John Robboy, Ukn.

Joseph was not a particularly good businessman. He was an intellectual and dreamer. He always had ideas for business. For example, he devised how to create shoes from cardboard, but forgot to assess what would happen when it rained. Family lore told that when coming to the United States to the port of Galveston, another passenger with whom he had become friends asked him to start a clothing shop in Texas. Would Joseph join as a partner? Joseph turned him down because he felt it was important he go to Cleveland to join his family. Of course, the man's last name was either Neiman or Marcus, presumably of what would later become Neiman Marcus. In actuality, Neiman Marcus had begun three years earlier. Herbert Marcus, Sr., a former buyer for another Dallas' department store, had already left to begin a new business with his sister and her husband, A.L. Neiman.

During the Depression years, the family moved to the Sunrise Farm, a collective or co-operative located in central Michigan that the chewing gum Wrigley family from Chicago established. They helped support, constructively, families willing to start a new form of living. Joe loved the experience. The children lived, played, and were schooled in the children's area. Some youngsters loved that. Many of the older children did not. Being a commune, [A299] Beatrice found herself assigned to share a room with a man. Refusing, she left the commune altogether and moved in with her uncle [A317] Harry Dudwick and aunt [A317a] Ida. Others liked the concept, for, overall, the broader community consisted of Jewish intellectuals who enjoyed each other. Many notables came through, including artists, actors, teachers, some of whom taught violin. Ultimately, the collective failed as the participants were not used to either the physical labor or the nature of farming life. Some felt the commune fell apart because the women were arguing in the kitchen, which probably was not true. More likely, factions built among the Jewish families made co-existence problematic.

Fig. 63-2 [A299] Beatrice Dudnik and friend at the Sunrise Farm, the Agricultural Commune.

As the cooperative's experience was later described:[101]

---

[101] Sutton, Robert P. (2004). "Sunrise". *Communal Utopias and the American Experience: Secular Communities, 1824–2000*. Greenwood Publishing Group. pp. 122–127. ISBN 978-0-275-97553-1

[The members had] no farm experience and did not realize what they were getting themselves into. Others were "negligent in taking care of tools and machines, negligent in performing their assigned duties, negligent in preparation of food." Sunrise became too isolated and "lost all interest in what was going on in the world outside." The residents had naively accepted the unrealistically attractive picture painted for them in Cohen s promotional literature. "They were carried away by the beautiful vision of the promised land and listened only to the words that pleased them." "The reality, when it turned out to be nothing like the dream, irritated them to such an extent that they wished to kill the thing that had disappointed their expectations." Ultimately, they lost confidence in utopian communal life. Sunrise had been conceived, as had the other Great Depression utopias, in a desperate effort to provide a haven from the unemployment and insecurity of economic bad times. But when the depression receded the reason for Sunrise's existence, like the rationale for the other cooperatives, seemed irrelevant. Most people began to realize that they could once again find economic opportunity and the good life in mainstream America.

Despite the commune's dissolution, Joseph remained idealistic, read widely, and had socialist tendencies. At one point he translated Sigmund Freud's works into Yiddish. Books found in Joseph's library at the time of his death are shown below. As a sign of the time, the cost was five cents.

Fig. 63-3: Books in Joseph's library. The latter was a Russian Children's book translated into English that [A306] Susan brought back from a trip to The Soviet Union.

Many immigrants who came to the United States during that period were flush with ideas for businesses. Most failed, were impractical or never begun. But some form of employment was necessary.

Joseph did eventually open a spice store that was located at the Reading Terminal Market in Philadelphia. He was handy, and by himself built all the shelving shown in the picture. He sold the company sometime in the 1960s, although often returned there. The store remained active until sometime in the early 2000s.

Fig. 63-4 Left: [A298] Joseph Dudnik in his Reading Terminal Market, the shelving of which he built himself. Right: [A298a] Minnie, Joseph's wife, standing by the spices sold in the store.

After returning to Philadelphia, Joseph and Minnie began a luncheonette located on North Broad Street in Philadelphia. The family all lived in the floor above the store.

[A298a] Minnie is remembered as the woman always boiling chicken for the family. One story remembered was her having retained her thick Russian accent. One cousin loved to ask her, "Grandmom, What's a wrench?" And she would answer, "A wrench is a place where cowboys raise kettle."

Parents always look out for their children. Not uncommonly, mothers mostly served as matchmakers. In 1945, the family had an extra room that could be let. The parents conspired with and offered [A299a] Max Borenstein, who had been injured in Berlin at the end of the war and whose parents were friends, that he could occupy the room. Max's mother and new stepfather told him there was no more room in their house, so he must find somewhere else to recuperate. Max soon married Beatrice. Not long after, Beatrice's sister, [A305] Irene, married Max's brother, [A305a] Julius Borenstein. And so, it was that two sisters married two brothers.

Fig. 63-5 [A299] Beatrice (left), [A305] Irene (middle) and [A307s] Selma Dudnik (right).

Fig. 63-6: [A298a] Minnie and [A298] Joseph Dudnik, 1958.

Shortly before World War II began and before Beatrice and Max married, Max joined the US Army and was sent to Iceland, where he was responsible for helping set up the Armed Forces Postal Service for its anticipated theater of operations in Europe. He remained there for 4.5 years when he became wounded, but not by the war. He had jumped off an army truck and smashed his knee. Having a love for math, Max later worked for the IRS in its fraud division. He was thorough and the person whom no one would wish to come up against.

One of [A302] Trudy Borenstein's likes (Beatrice and Max's daughter) was to draw portraits of her father using easily obtained products, such as supermarket circulars. Max found it impossible to discard anything, even a piece of paper. They thus became scratchpads, but unusual scratchpads at that, for many were extensively marked with mathematical symbols. One portrait of him used these materials. Trudy became an artist and goldsmith.

Fig. 63-7: Portraits of [A299a] Max Borenstein with his markings on his used scratchpads by [A302] Trudy Borenstein-Sugiura), Left: "Champs" 2016 (Max had been the Pennsylvania State Table Tennis Champion); Right: "For a Limited Time" 2017

Max later worked for the Internal Revenue Service (IRS). When at a family picnic with other Dudniks, someone contacted the IRS suggesting the IRS investigate Max as being a potential communist. Such happenings occurred during the McCarthy period. Such a possible association could be made as various members of the extended mishpocha had such leftist leaning. [A305] Irene Borenstein's daughter, [A306] Susan, indeed worked in the sugarcane fields in Cuba in the 1960s.

Joseph and Minnie's middle daughter, [A305] Irene, became an architect. She later developed difficulties when working with her hands, learning she had Dupuytren's contractures. This condition forced her to undergo several corrective operations.

#64 [A317] HERSHEL DUDNIK, THE INTERPRETER
by [A319] Nora Dudwick

[A317] Hershel Dudnik, later Harry Dudwick, was the eighth of the nine children born to [A292] Rivka Kaprove and [A292a] Noah Dudnik.

Harry's birthdate is officially August 25, 1904, which would have made him 19 when his sojourn from Russia began in 1923. In actuality, Harry may have been older. His mother, [A293a] Cipa, best transliterated as Tsipora, was friends with the local commissar, who helped change Harry's date of birth on his documents so he would be allowed to emigrate and avoid the Red Army draft.

Another critical decision Cipa faced was who would come. The father, [A293] Aaron, had died long ago. Two sisters, [A313] Olga and [A314] Dora, were married, had families, and chose not to leave. Thus, the four that finally left together were Cipa and the three youngest children, [A316] Dina, Harry, and [A320] Kenia (Kay).

Fig. 64-1: [A293] 1923 Passport photos of Cipa Dudnik and her daughters coming to America. The travel documents for son [A317] Harry are in next chapter.
Left: Dudniks [A293] Cipa, [A316] Dina, and [A320] Kay. Cipa, who could not write Ukrainian, initially signed her photo with three Xs, then crossed them out and wrote the names of the three in Yiddish.
Right: [A320] Kay and [A293] Cipa Dudnik.

The passports to leave Russia were issued in Kiev on August 8, 1923. The papers for the voyage from England to the US were obtained on August 26, 1923. The papers needed for the border crossing came on August 29, 1923. The family obtained visas in the Riga Latvian American Consulate on September 19, 1923 (after a three-day stay) to first travel to England, which (arriving on October 2, 1923). From there, they were to continue on the White Star Line[102] to the

---

[102] The White Star Line, a name used by the Oceanic Steam Navigation Company, was a prominent British shipping company that provided passenger and cargo services between the British Empire and the United States. The White Star branded itself for steady and comfortable passages and not for speed, unlike other shipping companies. It treated both the upper-class travelers and immigrants well. The company merged during the Great Depression with its chief rival, Cunard Line, and since now part of the Carnival Corporation.

United States. The person listed on the application to serve as their reference was Cipa's son, [A298] Joseph, who lived at 2240 E 97th St. in Cleveland. The travel documents are covered more fully in Chapter #65.

After arriving in England, Dina was refused entry due to tuberculosis. She was forced to return to Russia, where she died soon after. Harry remained in England for two years. During this period, Cipe broke her leg and was housed in the home of a local English family, who were exceedingly kind to her. Years later, Harry and his wife, Ida, when the family lived in Reading (1950-54), had a very happy reunion with this couple. The shipping company put the family in barracks and paid all the costs. Harry remembered this time as a lovely period of their life. He volunteered in a local garage, where he learned the rudiments of fixing cars and was popular among local English girls. A postcard Tsipora and Harry sent from Southampton, England to Joseph and Minnie in the US, dated October 19, 1924, confirmed the stay.

Harry and the family arranged to come to the United States before the Immigration Law of 1924 went into effect. Still, the documents also allowed for a later entry, which did occur. It seems the group may have split up with the women coming to Cleveland earlier and Harry later. They lived initially with [A298] Joseph Dudnik, a son and sibling. Acculturation in the new country was both fruitful and fraught with difficulties.

Harry soon met Ida Gross in an acting club at the local settlement house. She had been born on February 18, 1909, in Farrell, PA, a small community outside of Sharon, PA. Her parents were Hungarian Jews. Her father had various jobs, including running a shop and peddling goods in the south. He was known as impractical but most kind. Ida's mother died when she was a teenager.

Harry and Ida married on March 18, 1933, in Cleveland. Sometime between then and when their first daughter, [A318] Nancy, was born, Harry changed the family's last name from Dudnik to Dudwick to be more American. He worried about his and Ida's new child suffering prejudice attached to a "foreign" last name. Given that there is a Hill of Dudwick in Scotland, the name change was not an unreasonable choice at the time.

Harry, like most of the youths arriving in the United States, needed to survive and was forced into relatively unskilled jobs, such as clerking in a shoe store. His first real break into the professional ranks came due to his fluency in Russian. The new Russian government hired Harry as an interpreter. The new Bolshevik government had sued the US for the return of Russian gold bullion deposited in US banks. The US argued that asset seizure compensated for the Bolsheviks refusal to honor debts accrued by the tsarist government, which had borrowed money to fund its participation in World War I. With the case being heard in the US federal courts in New York, NY, Harry found it impossible to attend night school and still have time to study and work full time as an interpreter. He had to choose one or the other. It seems Harry may never have completed his studies for even a bachelor's degree, despite that he could read incredibly well and translate one language into another with such ease, proficiency, and elegance. Harry had become the polyglot reader and superb technical translator. He translated from Russian, but also Ukrainian and Bulgarian, and of course, knew Yiddish and some German.

This first job as an interpreter then led Harry to his first serious job. He was asked to work for the Russian trade mission, which was later to become the Russian Embassy. This position carried serious responsibilities. He would meet dignitaries and many well-known personalities when they arrived at the airport and attended to them during their entire stay in the United States. His family recounts his many encounters with famous opera singers, politicians, and the like. Harry's new role required him to attend many of the associated cultural events. An unusual responsibility was to maintain the organization's wine cellar. Harry didn't drink much, which possibly explains the assignment. He loved the job.

Harry soon obtained, like other new immigrants, his US citizenship. After the US recognized the Soviet Union and the first Soviet embassy was established, Harry and other employees who were US citizens were let go.

Soon after, Harry began working for the US State Department. The family used to joke that Harry was the first person who had gone directly from serving in a Russian spy agency to go directly to the US government spy agency. This group, in 1942, would become the Office of Strategic Services (OSS), the US's wartime intelligence agency, and predecessor to today's Central Intelligence Agency (CIA).

Harry's position in the State Department as an interpreter meant he moved frequently. The family was first in Portland, OR, and then in Los Angeles, where [A319] Nora, their second, was born. And soon they were back in Washington D.C. In 1950, they left for Reading, England, near the BBC listening station in Caversham Park. Harry monitored the Soviet broadcasts as part of the US-UK coordinated efforts to contain communism.

Fig. 64-2: [A317] Harry Dudwick and Mother [A293] Tsipora Dudnik.

Harry and the family returned to the US in 1954, but then encountered dangerous difficulties due to Sen. Joseph McCarthy and the fear that Harry might be a Soviet collaborator. From the late 1940s through the next decade, McCarthy accused many citizens of subversion without any regard for evidence. This period became known as the "Second Red Scare." Many of the accused, the alleged communists, were blacklisted and lost their jobs, even though, in reality, they never belonged to the Communist Party. Of course, many of the books and pamphlets that Harry kept in his library were turn-of-the-century anarchist pamphlets. But never was there any indication that Harry, himself, was a communist.

Harry was known to lean left. Many visitors to his home had foreign-sounding names and, importantly, for his neighbors, foreign accents, including his relatives. And so Harry was questioned quite regularly. About six months later, likely due in part to the tremendous pressure placed upon him, Harry suffered a massive heart attack. He, fortunately, negotiated a medical retirement in 1957. This compromise removed him from both government service and the attendant pressures. This change freed Harry to work as a freelance translator. He lived for another 20 years only to die of lung cancer. Harry had stopped smoking at the time of the heart attack, but, nonetheless, the timing was too late. The damage had been done. Harry died in 1976 at age 72.

[A317a] Ida, Harry's wife, never obtained a college degree. She attended high school in Cleveland Heights. She loved to write and desired to become a journalist, but her parents switched her into business high school before completing high school at one of Cleveland's best public high schools. Initially, in defiance of her parents, she attempted to begin work as a journalist on the night shift, but her parents forbid it. Coming from a low-income family and being in the middle of nine children, she was forced to work in stores that, unfortunately, would not lead to a substantial career. Good jobs at that time were scarce and exceedingly scarce for Jews. Once she and Harry married, it became a hardship to take a job as they moved so often. After Harry became a freelance translator, Ida became Harry's full-time transcriber and editor.

Harry and Ida had two daughters, [A318] Nancy and [A319] Nora. The parents wished to give Nora the middle name of her grandmother, but for Nora to be "Nora Tzipora" had an ill ring.

Nora, when growing up and then as a student, traveled to Russia several times. In the early 1980s, she established contact with a remaining cousin, most likely one of [A315] Aaron's grandchildren. While a graduate student in anthropology, she hoped to do her fieldwork in Moscow. Already in Armenia in 1987, she spent the first couple of months trying to work with the bureaucracy to secure permission to return to Moscow. Then the political world exploded.

Armenia and Azerbaijan were at odds. The area, now part of the Soviet Union, consisted of two neighboring republics located between the Black Sea and the Caspian Sea. The contested area was east of Armenia in the Republic of Azerbaijan. The Nagorno-Karabakh conflict, as it became known, was territorial and ethnic. Nagorno-Karabakh (Armenians refer to the territory as Artsakh), and the seven districts now occupied and claimed by Artsakh are still internationally considered part of Azerbaijan. Sometimes the circumstances of life dictate strange twists. The concept of Nora's dissertation changed. It suddenly became a study on Armenian nationalism and the recreation of the nation.

Harry had eight brothers and sisters.

[A294] Gitie Dudnik, the oldest, born in 1883, married Eli Dudnik, who likely was not a relative, at least not a close one. They had one son, [A295] Abraham, who became one of the most well-known trial lawyers in Cleveland. [A031] Stanley Robboy, the editor of this compendium, remembers having returned from medical school when the newspapers began calling our home on June 3, 1962. Abe had died in an airplane crash. Astonishingly, Abe, himself, called several hours later. He had been refused permission to board, despite having a purchased ticket. One hundred six Atlanta cultural leaders, together with the Symphony Orchestra players, had been given the plane as a charter. When Abe died the next year, the flags in Cleveland flew at half-mast. One family story was that Abe and Harry loved to go off and tell off-color jokes.

Fig. 64-3: [A294] Gitel Dudnik and grandson [A296] Bobby C1848.
Fig. 64-4: [A295] Abe Dudnik with Aunt [A298a] Minnie Dudnik.
Fig. 64-5: [A295] Abe and Rose, [A296] Robert and [A297] Joan Dudnik.

[A309] Pearl and her husband, Louis Guralnick, had no children but were remembered as always being most generous. They always left $20 gifts to at least Nora on Valentine's Day and so many other special occasions.

[A320] Kenia or "Kay," the youngest, was the beauty of the family. Her elegance enamored all. She modeled for the various local department stores and later designed clothing lines. One son, [A321] Sidney became the Dean and professor at the Illinois Institute of Technology.

Fig. 64-6: Kay's hat line.

[A320] Kenia or "Kay," the youngest, was the beauty of the family. She modeled for Wanamaker's, a local department store in Philadelphia. She married Philip Guralnick, who operated a dental practice from their house. One son, [A321] Sidney, became an engineering professor at the Illinois Institute of Technology. He was the dean for five years, provost for seven, and helped in many other roles.

#65 PASSPORT DE RIGEURS IN THE 1920s
By [A558] Gene Katzman

Editor's note: The physical aspect of traveling during the 2020s is less than appealing to most people. Obtaining documents needed for travel, such as passports and visas are relatively straightforward and, in no small extent, can be done by the Internet. Traveling one century before was a different experience. This chapter describes the documents [A317] Harry Dudnik, later Dudwick, needed for him and similar documents for his mother and two sisters to leave Ukraine and emigrate to the United States.

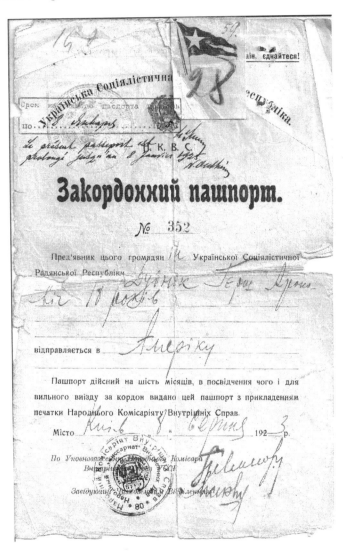

Ukraine and Russia had two different passports. One allowed internal travel within the country for identification purposes. The second was for external trips of which this is an example. Most Russian documents at the time, for travel, were in native Russian and French, reflecting the relations and aspirations of the Russian nobility. This document is also in Ukrainian; some are also in Latvian.

This passport, Number 352, is from the Ukrainian Soviet Socialist Republic. The large lettering says external passport (i.e., an exit visa.)

The attached red flag with a white star indicates the person with this passport will be leaving Russia on a White Star Steamship.

The red circular stamp near the top is in Ukrainian; the rectangular stamp is in Russian. The handwriting just beneath it in French states the passport expired on January 8, 1925.

Fig. 65-1 Passport, top sheet.

The writing beneath number 352 is in Ukrainian. It reads the owner of this document is a Ukrainian citizen. The name says Dudnik Gersh Aaronovitch (typical Russian patronymic), 18 years old, and going in the direction of America.

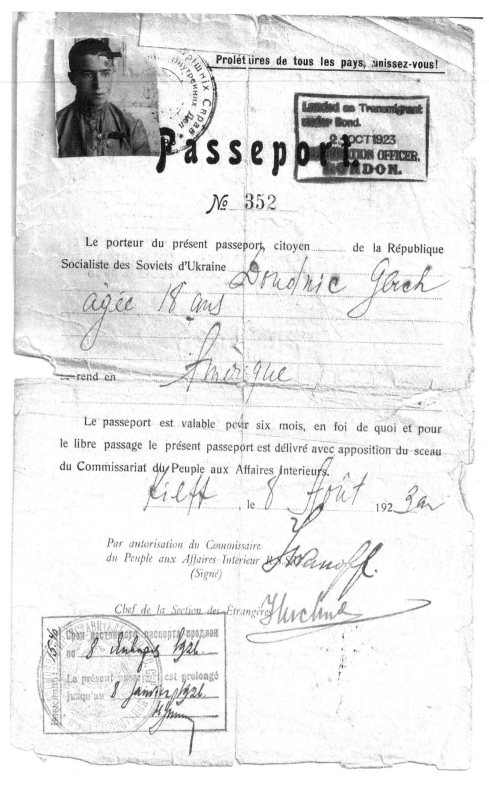

Fig. 65-2 Passport, 2nd half.

The passport's second half repeats the information given above. The document, from the Bureau, Commissariat of the People of Internal Affairs, states the passport expired in six months. Dated at the bottom: Kiev, 8 August, 1923.

The top rectangular stamp indicates the holder entered London, England, on Oct 2, 1923.

Two stamps at the bottom. Both are rectangular, and the Ukrainian and French give the expiration date of Jan 8, 1926.

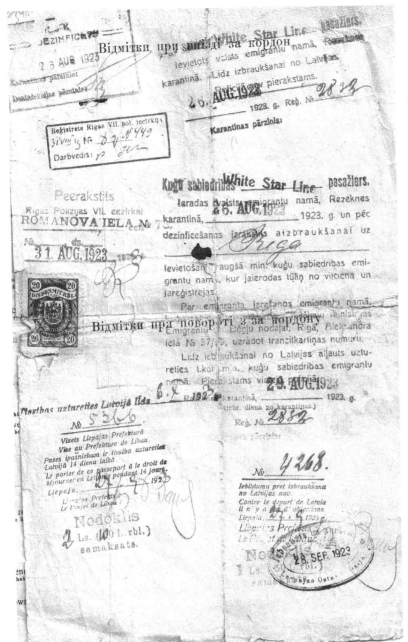

Fig. 65-3: Exit visa

Harry Dudnik, Exit visa to leave the border.

Title: "Right to leave border."
Upper right (in Latvian): Visas to leave Latvia (Riga), stamped 26 Aug 1923.

Upper left (in Latvian, dated 26 Aug 1923): The bearer entered Latvia and may purchase currency. Just beneath (dated 31 VIII, N449).

Middle Right: Star Passenger No. 26 Aug 1923, city Riga.

Middle Left, Above red revenue stamp: Riga police, Aug 31, 1923, signed (Official) Iela Romanova No 75?

Bottom left: Oct 6, 1923, in Latvian and French, Must leave the country in 14 days, going from Port of Liepaja (Libau) (on Baltic Sea), about 100 miles south, dated Sept 27, 1923. Cost 2 Ls (100 L rubles).

Bottom right, in Latvian and French: "Must leave the country within 14 days from Port of Liepaja (Libau)," about 100 mi south, Sep 28, 1923.

293

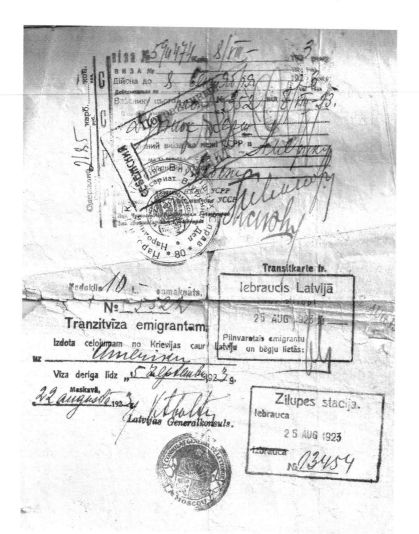

Fig. 65-4: Border stamp

Harry Dudnik, Border stamp, pg-2.

Upper half: Paid 2185 Rubles.
Ukrainian CCPP translates to USSR in Ukrainian. Visa No. 594474, Expires Aug 8, 1923. Corresponds to Passport 352.
The lower part of the block repeats in Russian. Circular stamp at the bottom: In Russia from Moscow.

Lower left: Latvian transit for emigrants (not to stay) dated Aug 22, 1923, expiring Sept 5, 1923. Going to America. Issued at Latvian Embassy in Moscow.

Right: Two Transit stamps. Enters Latvia on Aug 25, 1923; 2nd gives stamp number.

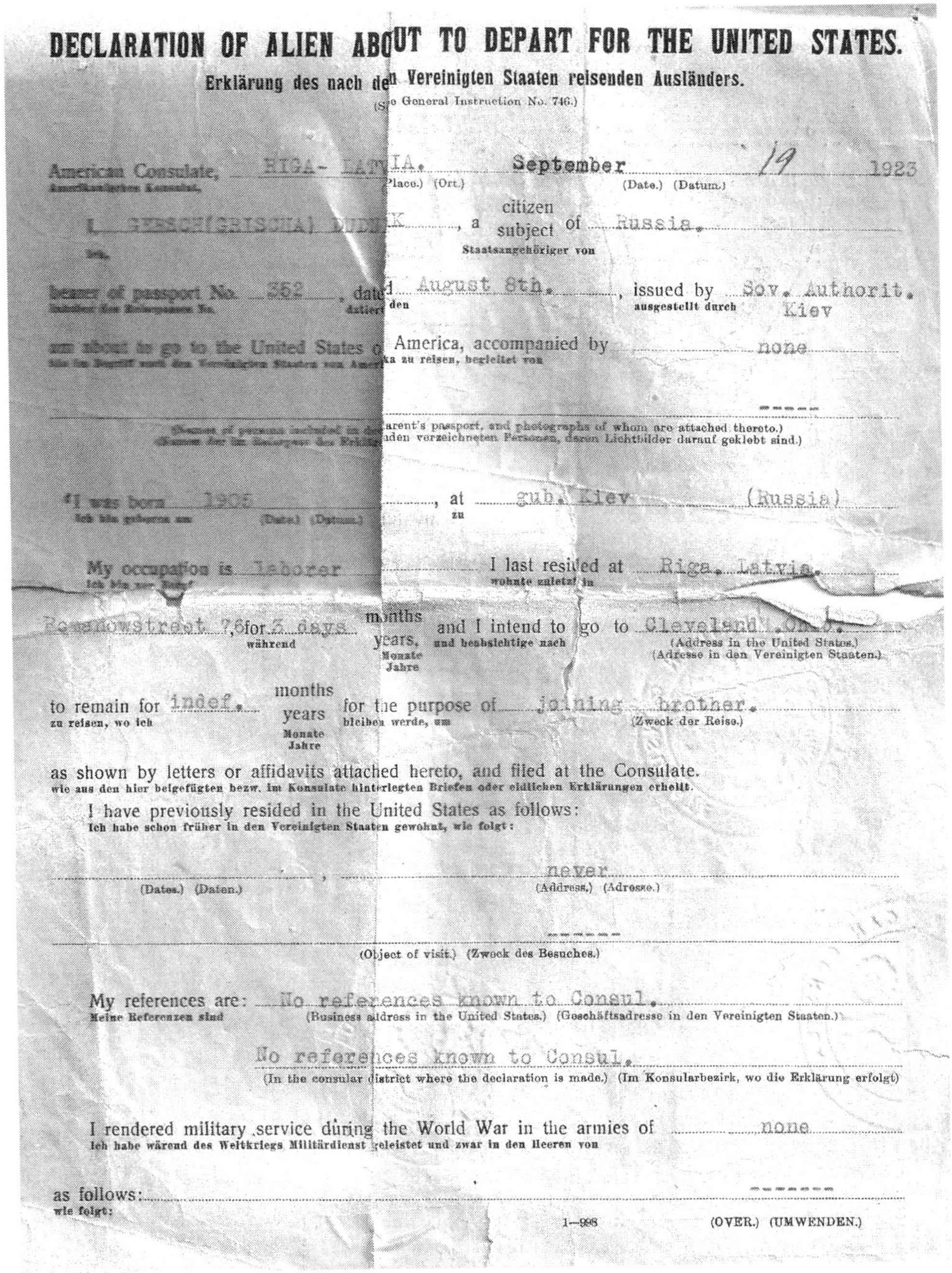

DECLARATION OF ALIEN ABOUT TO DEPART FOR THE UNITED STATES.

Erklärung des nach den Vereinigten Staaten reisenden Ausländers.

(See General Instruction No. 746.)

American Consulate, RIGA - LATVIA. September 19 1923
Amerikanisches Konsulat, (Place.) (Ort.) (Date.) (Datum.)

I, L. GERSCH (GRISCHA) LUDNIK, a citizen subject of Russia.
Ich, Staatsangehöriger von

bearer of passport No. 352, dated August 8th, issued by Sov. Authorit.
Inhaber des Reisepasses No. datiert den ausgestellt durch Kiev

am about to go to the United States of America, accompanied by none
bin im Begriff nach den Vereinigten Staaten von Amerika zu reisen, begleitet von

(Names of persons included in declarant's passport, and photographs of whom are attached thereto.)
(Namen der im Reisepass des Erklärenden verzeichneten Personen, deren Lichtbilder darauf geklebt sind.)

I was born 1906, at gub. Kiev (Russia)
Ich bin geboren am (Date.) (Datum.) zu

My occupation is laborer I last resided at Riga, Latvia.
Ich bin nun Beruf wohnte zuletzt in

Rosenowstreet 76 for 2 days months years, and I intend to go to Cleveland, Ohio.
während Monate Jahre und beabsichtige nach (Address in the United States.)
(Adresse in den Vereinigten Staaten.)

to remain for indef. months years for the purpose of joining brother.
zu reisen, wo ich Monate Jahre bleiben werde, um (Zweck der Reise.)

as shown by letters or affidavits attached hereto, and filed at the Consulate.
wie aus den hier beigefügten bezw. im Konsulate hinterlegten Briefen oder eidlichen Erklärungen erhellt.

I have previously resided in the United States as follows:
Ich habe schon früher in den Vereinigten Staaten gewohnt, wie folgt:

never

(Dates.) (Daten.) (Address.) (Adresse.)

(Object of visit.) (Zweck des Besuches.)

My references are: No references known to Consul.
Meine Referenzen sind (Business address in the United States.) (Geschäftsadresse in den Vereinigten Staaten.)

No references known to Consul.

(In the consular district where the declaration is made.) (Im Konsularbezirk, wo die Erklärung erfolgt.)

I rendered military service during the World War in the armies of none
Ich habe wärend des Weltkriegs Militärdienst geleistet und zwar in den Heeren von

as follows: 1—998 (OVER.) (UMWENDEN.)
wie folgt:

Fig. 65-5a: Declaration to leave. Passed through Latvia on Sept 19, 1923.

Sponsored by brother Joseph in Cleveland.

Transit stamp for America via England, issued Sept 19, 1923, good for 1 year.

295

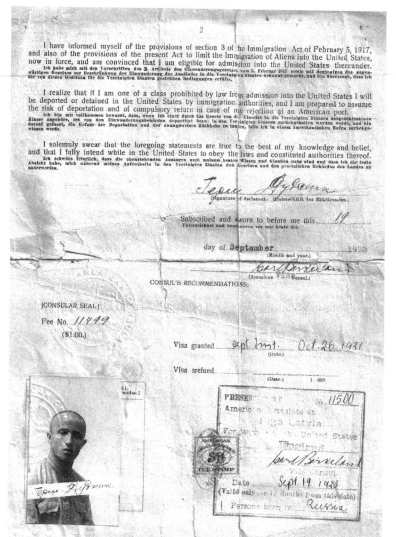

I have informed myself of the provisions of section 3 of the Immigration Act of February 5, 1917, and also of the provisions of the present Act to limit the Immigration of Aliens into the United States, now in force, and am convinced that I am eligible for admission into the United States thereunder.

Ich habe mich mit den Vorschriften des 3. Artikels des Einwanderungsgesetzes vom 5. Februar 1917 sowie mit denjenigen des gegenwärtigen Gesetzes zur Beschränkung der Einwanderung der Ausländer in die Vereinigten Staaten bekannt gemacht, und bin überzeugt, dass ich die von diesen Gesetzen für die Vereinigten Staaten gestellten Bedingungen erfülle.

I realize that if I am one of a class prohibited by law from admission into the United States I will be deported or detained in the United States by immigration authorities, and I am prepared to assume the risk of deportation and of compulsory return in case of my rejection at an American port.

Ich bin mir vollkommen bewusst, dass, wenn ich einer durch das Gesetz von der Einreise in die Vereinigten Staaten ausgeschlossenen Klasse angehöre, ich von den Einwanderungsbehörden deportiert bezw. in den Vereinigten Staaten zurückgehalten werden werde, und bin darauf gefasst, die Gefahr der Deportation und der zwangsweisen Rückkehr zu laufen, falls ich in einem amerikanischen Hafen zurückgewiesen werde.

I solemnly swear that the foregoing statements are true to the best of my knowledge and belief, and that I fully intend while in the United States to obey the laws and constituted authorities thereof.

Ich schwöre feierlich, dass die obenstehenden Aussagen nach meinem besten Wissen und Glauben wahr sind und dass ich die feste Absicht habe, mich während meines Aufenthalts in den Vereinigten Staaten den Gesetzen und den gesetzlichen Behörden des Landes zu unterwerfen.

(Signature of declarant.) *(Unterschrift des Erklärenden.)*

Subscribed and sworn to before me this 19
Unterzeichnet und beschworen vor mir heute den

day of **September** 1928
(Month and year.)

(American Vice Consul.)

CONSUL'S RECOMMENDATIONS:

[CONSULAR SEAL.]

Fee No. *11499*

($1.00.)

Visa granted ...... Oct. 26 1931
(Date.)

Visa refused ......
(Date.)

Date **Sept. 19 1928**

#66 [A374] JOSEPH GALLER
([A379] Lucy Coleman recounts)

[A368] Israel Galak, from [C02] Justingrad married and moved to [C36] Uman, one of the larger Jewish cities in Ukraine, Russia, to live with [A368a] Rivka Surak.

Fig. 66-1: [A368a] Rifke (Surak) Galak who died in Uman, wife of Israel (from Yustingrad).Fig. 66-2: Galak (Galler) Family in Uman, [A397] Sarah in braids, [A371] Pearl, [A385] Morris who stands tall, [A372] Ruchel, and [A381] Yochanon.

The family was orthodox Jewish, i.e., Chassidim. [A368] Israel spent most of his time in the synagogue. [A368a] Rifke ran a tea house, which meant, early every morning, their children went from house to house with hot tea. When their customers and friends awoke, a glass of hot tea would be awaiting them. The three daughters, [A371] Pearl, [A372] Ruchel, and [A397] Sarah, became excellent seamstresses and sewed largely in the homes of the wealthy.

Fig. 66-3: [A374] Joseph Galler (from Uman) on arrival to USA, 1913.

Fig. 66-4: Galak (Galler) family, 1927, [A374a] Rose, [A374] Joseph / Yossel (adults) and children (left to right) [A375] William, [A377] Jeanette, and [A379] Lucy.

[A374] Joseph, the fifth of the family's eight children, attended cheder until he reached bar mitzvah age. Soon after that, he left for America using the money his uncle Velvel had given him. He first went to Hamburg, having swum across a river and taking a train for the rest of the journey. From Hamburg, he sailed to Argentina to "see the world." His older brothers, [A369] David and [A370] Sam, were already in Chicago. Joseph met relatives on his mother's side in Buenos Aries, where he was given work by running errands. Lucy's sister, [A377] Jenny, noted that in Buenos Aires, it was the uncle who wished not to care for Joseph, and so Joseph went to the [A831] Baron de Hirsch[103] colonies to learn agriculture. Hirsch established these colonies to absorb Jewish refugees from Europe and Russia and provide them a sustainable living and productive employment. The pogroms had forced many destitute Jews to flee abroad.

In a short while, he got enough money and sailed to America in 1914 and once there, to Chicago, where he changed the last name to Galler, just as had his older brothers, David and Sam. Joseph ironed shirts in a sweatshop for a period until brother Sam took him into his business, and he became a peddler.

One evening, Joseph attended a "greenhorn dance" where he met [A374a] Eva (later known as Rose) Friedman. Before long, in 1917, they married.

Rose had immigrated some years before with her parents and five or six siblings. The father was a cabinet maker and so had a fair trade. Rose was born in a shtetl. Like so many, her family was poor and had primitive housing with a dirt floor. Water, which was Rose's task to obtain, came from a creek down a nearby hill. Their home was in the province of Grodno, near Lithuania, which was then part of Russia. Like most Jewish girls raised in a shtetl, Rose lacked any formal schooling. She spoke only Yiddish at the time she married.

[A375] William was their first child. [A379] Lucille, the third child, was born a decade later in a French Hospital in Chicago. The nurses gave her a French name, but her parents, after that, named her Tzvia, a Hebrew name after her mother's grandfather. From then on, she was Lucille or Lucy.

Brother [A375] William (Bill) and Lucy were outside one snowy cold winter day. [A377] Jenny, the second child, who was born five years after Bill, was indoors with a contagious disease, probably the German measles. Bill built an igloo, into which they crawled, and it was warm! Jenny watched from the window. Bill always had a dog, typically some stray he had befriended. His dogs were always named Rover. In the winter, Bill harnessed the dog to the sled, putting Lucy on the sled, and both would mush off, she was falling into the snow within minutes! Bill once built a boat in the basement of the Keeler Avenue home. He and his friends took it out, which was no small feat, and launched it in the park lake nearby. It promptly sank. After that, he became intensely interested in chemistry and built a laboratory in the basement. Every weekend, for years, the stink that arose drove everyone from the house, and sometimes out of the yard. So

---

[103] [A831] Moritz (Zvi) von Hirsch, known also as Maurice de Hirsch (1831-1896), was a German Jewish philanthropist who established charitable foundations that promoted Jewish education and improved the lives of oppressed European Jewry. His greatest charitable enterprise was to support the Jews persecuted in Russia by offering them a way to become established and productive once moved. He funded and established emigrations and colonization schemes affording the persecuted Jews opportunities to develop in agricultural colonies located in Argentina, Canada, Palestine, and the US. The Woodbine Colony in southern New Jersey was the model in the US. It failed in the 1940s as the settlers lacked needed farming experience and the distance to viable markets.

knowledgeable did he become that while a student at Marshall High School, he served as the chemistry teacher's assistant. His proficiencies exempted him from many chemistry classes at the University of Illinois. Instead, he assisted his professors.

[A377] Jenny, the middle child, was active early on, especially with roller skates. Later she loved to bike and swim. In her teens, Jenny joined Habonim,[104] which became the all-important aspect of her life. Many of the boys and girls she met during those years remained close friends forever. After entering the University of Illinois, Herman Finkel, also a Chicagoan and member of Habonim, romanced her, and at age 19, they married. After a few years, they made their home in Israel.

Fig. 66-5: [A375] Bill and [A377] Jenny Galler.

Fig. 66-6: [A379] Lucy Galler Coleman.

Before Lucy began school, Bill and Jenny had already taught her to count, read, and write the alphabet..

On the very first day of school, she and her mother arrived late, by which time the kindergarten class was already overfilled. Hence, she began the first grade. It, too, was crowded. Lucy and several other children were seated on little chairs in the aisle

The rest of the children had fixed seats with desks. Because Lucy knew already how to write her name and all the other letters, she quickly earned a seat at the front and her own desk! Her teacher, Miss Pine, had a wig and always wore a yellow brocade dress with a high crochet collar. After a short time, Lucy was permitted to walk to school alone. After several years, she entered the accelerated program. Two classes of fourth-grade students finished three full years in only two and a half years.

Lucy and her siblings had always thought that since their father attained citizenship, Rose was also included. But it was not so. The laws changed just before Joseph got his citizenship. Registration of aliens began sometime in the '30s, and thus Rose was included. Lucy helped her with her civic lessons, but despite the lack of formal training, Rose was clever, good at calculations, and able to read a bit in English. But studying who the presidents were and the rest of US history was both problematic and uninteresting for her. The requirements for citizenship seemed more stringent then than they do now. Rose lived in a sheltered, narrow environment.

---

[104] Habonim Dror ("the builders of freedom") evolved in 1982 from two Jewish Labour Zionist youth movements that merged, Habonim, founded in 1929 in England and Dror, founded in 1915 Poland.

The neighbors were all Jewish and naturally spoke primarily in Yiddish. Even the Negro salesman in the dairy store, which sold milk and milk products, spoke Yiddish fluently to all the women customers. For Rose, her home and her children were her entire life. She often baked "babkes,"[105] a type of raised coffee cake with cinnamon and sugar.

When in high school, Lucy also joined Habonim, a Labor Zionist youth group, and traveled throughout the city for meetings. It was through this group, and also through the family, she became aware of current events. Uncle [A370] Sam received an urgent message from two German young men to save them from Nazi Germany. This event occurred in the early thirties. They had picked his name from a telephone book. He helped them, and they came to the United States. One remained in Chicago and worked for Sam. The other went to medical school, becoming a doctor later practicing in Israel. During World War II, the Chicago papers carried the terrible headlines about the siege of the Warsaw Ghetto and its downfall. It dominated the news for nearly a week. During those years, it was impossible to walk the neighborhood streets when President Roosevelt gave a speech and not hear it on all the neighbors' radios, especially in summer, when the windows were open. Pearl Harbor Day was as memorable as it was horrific. Like so many other Americans that Sunday afternoon, Joseph and Lucy were leaving the movies when the news flashed worldwide.

Joseph had three brothers and three sisters living in Chicago. Their father, [A368] Israel Galak, came to Chicago after the first World War. He had 17 grandchildren and over 35 great-grandchildren. He became immersed in his synagogue's activities. He had a long white beard and wore the familiar Chasiddik costume and spoke only in Yiddish. Being only one of the many children, Lucy and her grandfather never got to know each other well.

Lucy remembers several run-ins she had with her father, like those many other children experienced with their parents. Once, while young and after playing with the neighborhood children, she became excited and called her father a "bastard." Of course, he was surprised. Rather than getting angry, he took her aside and asked, "Do you know what you said and what it means?" Of course, the answer was "no." Then he told her precisely what the word meant. Lucy never used that word again. She also remembers pleasant times spending many an evening in the winter playing checkers or five hundred rummy with her family. Summers meant drives to Michigan and time spent in South Haven or Union Pier, by the beach. Stopovers in Gary, IN, meant banana ice cream.

But unhappy times also happened. In the summer of 1943, after returning from summer camp Tel Chai in Michigan, she learned her parents' marriage had dissolved. Without warning, Lucy was told to decide with whom she wished to live with- Jenny and Herman or Bill and Beady. In short order, Lucy was off to be with her sister Jenny in upstate New York to begin a new chapter in her life.

---

[105] Babka, a sweet braided cake of Ashkenazi Jewish origin, prepared with a yeast-leavened dough, rolled out and covered with chocolate, cinnamon, cheese and fruits, and then rolled up and braided and finally baked.

#67 [A013] BERNIE ROBBOY, AN AMERICAN CHILDHOOD

Editor's note: This chapter is based on an interview Bernie's son, [A014] David Gerson Robboy, conducted during July 2006, and is supplemented by notes from another son, [A016] Ronald Robboy.

[A013] Bernard Robboy, the only child of [A012] Khaim (Hymie) and Rebecca (née Meshenstein) Robboy, was born on August 29, 1919, in Cleveland's Mt. Sinai Hospital. Like Hymie, Rebecca had immigrated from the Ukraine but was from Bratslav (pronounced Breslov),[106] a larger town 40 miles slightly southwest from Hymie's native [C01] Knyazhe. The new family lived at 3269 E. 116th Street, off Kinsman Road, in the Mt. Pleasant section of Cleveland's east side.

Fig. 67-1: [A013] Bernie Robboy, Left, as the sailor man 1923, age 4; Right, with his goat. Age 7.

Hymie had been working for a manufacturer of men's clothing, H. Black Company, but when Bernie was four, in late 1923, Hymie developed allergies to the dust materials and had to give

---

[106] Bratslav (also called Breslov) was also the birthplace of the one of the most famous and enigmatic of Hasidic masters, Nahman of Bratslav (1772–1810), revered not only by his pious followers but by literary scholars as well for his extraordinary mystical tales. Nahman, as it happened, died in [C36] Uman, a larger city that was even closer to Knyazhe than was Bratslav. Uman was also home to numerous relatives of the Voskoboiniks and Kaproves, that is, to Hymie's mother's family, and Hymie himself had been sent to a yeshivah in Uman in his youth. Uman has furthermore been, ever since Nahman's death, the destination of legions of Breslov Hasidim making a Rosh Hashanah pilgrimage to their rebbe's tomb. Though Hymie was not Hasidic, he would inevitably have been aware of the Breslov cult when he was there in Uman—with thousands converging on the city every year—and one wonders if he found a note of irony in his having moved half way around the world only to then marry a woman from Bratslav.

that up. So, the parents purchased a small business near what was known as the Central district, an area adjacent to downtown Cleveland. It was a small neighborhood candy store located at 7706 Kinsman Road (at E. 77th St.). The building was not unlike a tenement; the family lived on the second floor. After several years, they moved into private quarters in a duplex around the corner at 3027 77th Street.

The store proved a tough way to make a living, but the parents eked a living and slowly improved upon the business. Initially selling only candy, they enlarged it to sell other products, including smoked meats and a few foods, though it never became a full-service grocery store. Bernie worked in the store as a youth. Among other things, he made take-out sandwiches for customers. It never made much money, and financially, it was always touch-and-go. The Depression, which began in 1929, made life exceedingly difficult, yet the store continued to provide a living, however meager.

The neighborhood at first was predominantly a lower working-class white community where there were many industrial endeavors. Slowly, it became more mixed and then mostly Black. Due to the local poverty, made all the worse by the failing national economy, crime became rampant.

Bernie remembers that his Aunt Clara, his mother's older sister, did not like where the family lived. She considered the neighborhood too dangerous. Her solution was to have Bernie come live for a time with her family in Cleveland Heights, which Bernie considered "one of the fancy suburbs." Clara had two sons, Albert and Sanford. The younger of the two, Sanford, was close to Bernie in age. Clara's husband, Ben Stein, also an immigrant, was poorly educated but well-off financially. He was a so-called "jobber," which was to say a wholesaler. He operated the Buckeye Pants Company. "Actually, just pants," Bernie remembered it in 2006. "No suits, just pants." It was modest in size, but prosperous. He had only one salesman, "who would go on the road to all the small towns in Ohio." When Bernie stayed with them, Aunt Clara became upset when he would return home from playing baseball, which he loved to do, with his clothing dirty, especially his socks. How could one not become dirty playing ball on a sandlot, especially after sliding into a base? Bernie soon left and was "glad to get out of there."

Ever since the 1910s, Hymie's parents and his other siblings, [A017] Nessie, [A023] Tobie, [A024] Joe, and [A026] John, all lived together in a primarily Jewish neighborhood off E. 105th Street in Cleveland. By the 1920s, though, John went off to medical school, and Joe and Tobie appear to have each frequently moved about, trying out life in California or New York, but then returning to the parents' home as a kind of base.

Hymie's business survived the Depression but never thrived. The work was demanding, with the store remaining open from 7 a.m. until 11 p.m. Hymie worked the hours continuously. Mother helped, but with her illnesses and caring for young Bernie, she spent much less time there. Only on the holidays of Rosh Hashanah, Yom Kippur, and Passover did the store close, but then not for the full day. It just closed early.

Unlike his siblings, who lived with their parents, Hymie and his family had set up their own household some distance away, so they had relatively less to do with his parents and other siblings. [A011] Grandpa Schmiel remained Orthodox. The family did get together on Jewish holidays, but Bernie remembers Schmiel conducting the services almost entirely in Hebrew, which bored him. Bernie also remembers the paucity of substantive discussions they had as a group. After grandfather Schmiel died, the family, in general, became wholly secular, not even having a joint seder at Pesach. Schmiel lived for several years after grandmother [A011] Malka died.

Bernie went to school near his home, and as the area changed, so did the school. During the years of elementary school, the region was mostly white. By junior high, though, he was in a "tough school," as he later recalled, that was predominantly Black. Rawlings Junior High School (7520 Rawlings Ave., Cleveland) had six educational tracks, determined by ability. Section 1 consisted of higher-qualifying students. Section 6 had the lowest achievers and was almost entirely Black.

In 1933, while in junior high school, Bernie volunteered to work on the school newspaper. Vividly recalling after more than seventy years, the faculty advisor told him she was recruiting students for the paper's staff. She hoped he would join "because they expected more from the Jewish pupils," as he recalled her saying. But Jews were a distinct minority there. There were a total of four, counting Bernie, all in Section 1. After a short while, the paper folded.

By 1934, the high school Bernie was to enter had become almost entirely Black. As such, it was underfunded compared to schools in whiter and more affluent neighborhoods. Academics were weak, and Bernie would have been one of the few white students to attend there at that time. (They "could be counted on one hand," as he remembered in his late-life interview.) He would allude over the years to how he was a target for bullying and worse. By stealth, he transferred to another high school in an entirely different neighborhood consisting of, as he called it, a "more cosmopolitan population." To do so and improperly, he gave a relative's address as his legal residence and was thus admitted to the school. To attend, though, was not easy, for Bernie had to take three streetcars each way to go between home and the school. John Adams High School (East 116th Street and Corlett Avenue) was touted throughout Cleveland for its academic programs. Many of its graduates later became notable achievers.[107] Bernie remembers the school's orchestra being of such quality that it performed in New York City. He graduated from the school in 1937.

Bernie began college at Adelbert College, the undergraduate school of Western Reserve University. After two years, he entered its podiatry school, which then was the Ohio College of Chiropody (now Kent State University College of Podiatric Medicine). He graduated in 1942.

Hymie's wife died in 1945 after a lingering struggle with lupus. Soon after, he was hospitalized with asthma. In later years Bernie told how he visited his mother every day in the hospital for many months until her death. Not long after, cousin [A496] Minnie Trachtman invited Bernie to a dance held at Cleveland College, a school for adult learners established jointly by Western Reserve University and Case School of Applied Science.[108] There Bernie met his future wife, [A013a] Rosalie Smotkin, a student at Western Reserve. Rosalie's parents, Bessie and Morris

---

[107] See https://en.wikipedia.org/wiki/John_Adams_High_School_(Ohio)

[108] This was soon before the latter was renamed Case Institute of Technology, and more than twenty years before the two merged to become Case Western Reserve.

Smotkin, had moved to Cleveland several years earlier after their son, Alex, accepted a job working at the Cleveland research facility of the National Advisory Committee for Aeronautics, the forerunner of today's NASA. Rosalie had remained in school in her native Des Moines, Iowa. But wanting to join her family, she moved to Cleveland and enrolled at Western Reserve, from which she had graduated by the time Bernie married her in 1946.

After graduating from podiatry school in 1942, Bernie began practicing in space rented from a dentist, Lee Leslie. The area was physically changing from a mostly white to a considerably poorer, black population, which was not conducive to a podiatry practice. Also, it was difficult to procure sufficient supplies at that time, so his practice was not good. On top of all that, there had been the long decline of his mother and then Hymie's hospitalization. Since his practice was going nowhere, Bernie chose to neglect it and, instead, man the store in which his father had invested more than twenty years. In the end, though, that made no sense, either. Hymie couldn't maintain the store by himself, and Bernie vacillated between it and his practice. Hymie decided to sell the store and retire, and he came to live with Bernie and Rosalie, whose first child, [A014] David, was born in the 77th Street home. They decided to move from the neighborhood, which had become much too dangerous. They feared venturing out at night due to the excessive crime. It was about this time that Bernie also decided to leave the business location where he was, for the area and the practice had not picked up sufficiently. He decided to switch fields. He closed the practice, sold the equipment, and became a representative for a pharmaceutical company.

The Smotkin parents lived nearby. The building in which they resided was sold, and the new owner wished to occupy the space himself. As housing was exceedingly difficult to find during the immediate post-World War II period, the Smotkins moved in with Bernie, Rosalie, and Hymie. They were now in a single house, not a duplex, meaning they were a bit crowded. Furthermore, Alex, who was still single, joined them also. Unfortunately, Alex was difficult, and harmony was not strong in the household.

Eventually, the entire group moved to E. 153rd Street, into a duplex, with Bernie and family living in the downstairs half and the Smotkins residing upstairs. [A016] Ron was born in the new home. But as the living did not feel ideal for Hymie, he decided instead to leave for California to live with his sister, Tobie, in Santa Monica. In turn, Tobie turned out to be a difficult person with whom to live, and after a while, Hymie left to live and work on a chicken ranch in Fontana, east of Los Angeles near San Bernardino. (One day just weeks before turning eighty, Bernie spontaneously recalled the name of the chicken farmer. It was Shater.)[109] As Ron remembers being told years before, Hymie's asthma was exacerbated on the farm, and that was why he left it after a short while. He returned to Cleveland and lived in East Cleveland.

---

[109] Jewish chicken farmers were a distinct phenomenon well into the post-World War II years. Though certainly to be found elsewhere in the country, they were especially prevalent in southern New Jersey—where the Baron de Hirsch had in 1891 established an agricultural school for Eastern European Jewish immigrants—and California, where, besides the many in the ideally suited valleys surrounding Los Angeles, such as where Hymie worked, there was a close-knit community of mutually supportive Jewish chicken farmers around Petaluma, north of San Francisco. Many, especially those settling in the Petaluma colony, had been blackballed from other work because they had been communists or other leftists, and they sought the relative autonomy and anonymity as farmers. See Kenneth L. Kann, *Comrades and Chicken Ranchers: The Story of a California Jewish Community* (Ithaca, N.Y.: Cornell University Press, 1993).

After four or five years, Bernie and Rosalie decided they must move, for it was exceedingly difficult to live with the Smotkins. The mother was overly domineering. And so Bernie and Rosalie chose to move to California, where Bernie found a job with another pharmaceutical company. [A016] Bill was born in California. Bernie's later move to San Diego was entirely accidental. One child had asthma, which led to Bernie and Rosalie deciding to move away from the foothills, where they had been living, and find a place in Santa Monica, by the ocean, where the air was relatively pollen-free. But Bernie's boss at the pharmaceutical company thought if he was to relocate, he could be much more useful in San Diego, where eventually the family moved.

Fig. 67-2:

Standing L-R: Robboys. [A012] Hymie, [A026] John, [A023] Tobie, [A024b] Bessie and [A024] Joe Robboy;

Kneeling [A015] Ron and [A014] David Robboy (Hymie's grandchildren). 1957, Los Angeles CA.

Fig. 67-3: Robboys and Smotkins (in-law family): Back L-R: Evie Smotkin, [A013a] Rosalie Robboy, [A026] John Robboy, [A013] Bernie Robboy, Morris and Bessie Smotkin, [A012] Hymie Robboy; Front: [A015] Ron Robboy and [A014] David holding [A016] Bill. Hymie is the father of Bernie, who is the children's father. Bernie's wife is [A013a] Rosalie (nee Smotkin), daughter of Bessie and Morris. Evie married Rosalie's brother, Alex, (absent from photo). 1957, Los Angeles, CA.

Somewhat earlier, two of Hymie's siblings also had moved to California (and a third, Nessie, had died relatively young). Joe, after a short-lived marriage in Buffalo, had returned to Cleveland, where he worked as a paperhanger. There, he met [A024b] Bessie Kimmelman, and the two married. He retired from the work of paperhanging, and they moved to Los Angeles, where he then worked for the paperhangers' union.

Joe and Bessie settled in Boyle Heights, an ethnically diverse district near Los Angeles city center. It was home to many Japanese families and institutions (despite the forcible relocation of most during the war), along with similar numbers of Mexicans, as well as working-class Eastern European Jews, for whom Boyle Heights had been a central hub. Joe and Bessie had already owned their house there for several years when, in 1954, Bernie joined them for some weeks before his wife and children arrived from Cleveland. In 1962, Bessie fell and died from a traumatic hematoma to the skull. Joe was devastated. He began neglecting himself and his house. Bernie moved him to an apartment in an upscale neighborhood off Wilshire Boulevard. Being closer, Bernie could better care for his uncle. But Joe remained despondent. Besides profoundly missing his wife, the old radical was utterly out of his element in the new neighborhood. He died shortly after that in 1964.

Fig. 67-4: Joe and Bessie's home at 119 N. Mathews Street as it appears today in the Boyle Heights district in Los Angeles.

Tobie was the veritable Gypsy, moving several times among New York, Los Angeles, and Cleveland. In New York, she had a terrific job as a dressmaker for a leading fashion shop. Everyone was impressed with her eye.

She often walked by a fashionable dressmaker's store, saw a dress in the window display that intrigued her, and returned to her house where she sketched it out and then made it. After moving to Los Angeles, Tobie worked for a time in Hollywood, where, according to cousin [A048] Marilyn Yellin, she was a designer and draper for MGM costume designer Adrian Greenberg ("Gowns by Adrian"). Marilyn's mother, [A047] Sylvia Isbitz, had moved to Boyle Heights even before Joe did, and, though after marrying and moving to the more distant San Pedro, she remained in close contact with Tobie for many years.

After a series of apartments in Hollywood and closer to downtown Los Angeles, Tobie moved to one in Santa Monica and then bought a house there, into which Hymie moved with her. Tobie was chronically unhappy, and she and Hymie never got along. As an example, Hymie wanted to buy the house from her, but she refused and then sold it to somebody else. And that was how they parted.

Few of our melamdim (plural of melamed) were scholars. Most were poor, sick men who turned to teaching because they were unfit in the competitive world even of their time. The most crucial requirement then was discipline, but most failed even in the latter. The few more scholarly ones succeeded in teaching us the Bible, reading and writing.

During the year 1906-07, four of us were fortunate to have [A401] Liova Dolgonos, our cousin, as our teacher. Liova was a bookkeeper but had a knack for teaching. During that year, we covered the Pentateuch, the Prophets, and Kings. We learned some Hebrew and Russian history, Hebrew and Russian composition, and grammar as well as arithmetic.

My first teachers in Cleveland were [A809] Esther Swick (Morris), [A728a] Rebecca Ragoff, [A457] Joseph M. Gillman, [A755] Haide, and [A756] Henrietta Peiser. In his enthusiasm as to how the school should be taught, Joe made me use Webster's Intercollegiate Dictionary. As a result, I was always forced to look up a dozen or more words to clarify the first one. I still appreciate the laborious job.

[A756] Henrietta was a high school teacher. She was the only one who guided me to a goal and finally entered me into the sophomore class of Old Central High School, where [A740] Ruetnik was principal and [A741] Bathrien his assistant. Old-timers probably remember our teachers there: [A748] Mrs. Hanna, [A747] Mrs. Fliedner, [A743] Mr. Bissel, [A759] Mr. Winkler and [A752] Mr. Lewis, [A754] Mr. Marple, [A751] Mr. Chas Hozan, [A746] Mr. Cook, [A745] Miss Brown and [A742] Miss Avery, [A758] Miss Roberts, [A753] Miss Malorie, [A744] Miss Brio and [A757] Mr. Petersilge. They were a group of wonderful men and women truly dedicated to the profession. As human beings, some of them succumbed to the prevalent prejudices, while a few had the genuine spark that distinguished them among teachers. [A751] Mr. Hozan belonged to the latter. His course in ancient history surpassed that given in college.

[A757] Mr. Petersilge was another one of this type. Keeping a class in algebra spellbound for one and a half hours on a hot summer day was certainly an art and he was master in that. Yet a third one in this class was [A745] Miss Brown, who replaced [A742] Miss Avery for six weeks. She presented the characters in "The House of Seven Gables" vividly and in animated form. I am still sorry that she left us so soon.

[A748] Miss Hanna was an aged, fatigued woman whose method of teaching probably dated back to her graduation day. Her room was on the fourth floor. I had to run from [A743] Mr. Bissel's room in the basement to the fourth floor to reach her room. Hence I always arrived after the bell rang. Assuming that I was playing somewhere, she always called on me as soon as I entered her room. Though breathless, my recitation was perfect since I worked hard to translate my Latin into meaningful English. I knew the Latin very well and felt confident of myself. Imagine, therefore, the shock when Miss Hanna failed me in the exam covering the first six weeks of work. When I protested, she showed me the exam paper where I left two questions completely unanswered. I was stunned. There was no explanation possible except possibly as a result of excitement. All I could do was to ask for on the spot immediate examination. I must have been very earnest and impressive to have her accept such a suggestion. My recitation was excellent, and my standing thus fully restored.

The above experience made me reevaluate my methods of study. I put in too much time in preparing my homework. I felt there must be some better way. I had two classmates, [A762] Serina Friedman and [A763] Regina Dorid, whose translation of the Latin was too good, too smooth. I suspected that it was not their own. Both girls were very friendly and willing to help but refused to divulge the source that helped them. I decided to read the story of Caesar in English and at least have some understanding of what the story was about. I entered the bookstore of Burrows, asking for Caesar in English. "O, you want a Pony?" said the salesman. "No," said I, "not a pony." A pony to me was still a horse. Just fifty cents and I went home with the story of Caesar in my hand. Within 20 minutes, my lesson was done. What a relief! I saved some three hours of hard work. The next morning my recitation was delivered carefully and purposely and still in broken English so as not to give myself away to Miss Hanna. However, when I convinced myself that my sudden polished English was accepted unquestioned, I became as bold as the rest of the students. Of course, I never knew the Latin as well as before, but I did save time, and my grades did not suffer.

I was fond of [A747] Miss Fliedner. She was a kind, good woman and able teacher, but how she let me pass Ivanhoe is beyond me. I had absolutely no concept of knight or tournament, understood absolutely nothing, and was irretrievably lost in the book.

[A743] Mr. Bissel lacked fineness and fanfare but worked hard to teach us something and was highly disappointed to find the majority of his students not knowing the meaning of a sentence or a subject and frequently turned to me for the definition. [A754] Mr. Marple was an eccentric. His physics course suffered much because of his eccentricities. All of us were much too young to appreciate [A746] Mr. Cook's exposition of the New England town hall meeting. Nevertheless, some imprint was left on our minds.

[A759] Mr. Winkler talked quietly and very monotonously. Since I left school early and had no chance to communicate with the schoolmates, I was forced to leave whatever I did not understand undone and thus flunked algebra. To my surprise, I was reassigned to his class to which I objected, stating that Winkler was a poor teacher. [A741] Mr. Bathnien, who was very friendly to me, could not accept such audacity. The fact that I was seven years older than the average high school student mattered nothing to his erudite mind. At any rate, I won my point and was transferred to the class of [A750] Mr. Hitchcock. I did excellently in the class but lost the friendship of Mr. Bathnien.

[A758] Miss Roberts was an attractive woman and a fine teacher but was consumed by hatred. Her antisemitism was veiled by spewing venom at the foreigner. This was her daily ritual in a class where over 50% of the students were either Jewish immigrants or children of immigrants. At the end of the first six weeks, she flunked me in the exam of Hamlet. Several days later, she was so overwhelmed by my excellent English and expression of thought in the reexamination that not only did she read my paper to the class, but also gave me five points above the regulation for originality. Nevertheless, she gave me a final grade of 75 in the course.

Central High School was integrated. There were few Negroes present then. Hence there was no Negro problem. Antisemitism, if present, was clandestine. Only one teacher, [A758] Miss Roberts, was tainted, but she was careful and only attacked foreigners. In general, the teachers were dedicated and superior to those I met later in college and graduate schools.

At Adelbert School, in contrast, the teaching was poor, and the teachers were neither impressive nor inspiring. I remember most for their mediocrity, some for their meanness or stupidity, and but a very few for their finer qualities.

Dr. [A702] (Pinkey) Schmidt was an autocrat and severe disciplinarian. His door would close at the first ring of the bell. No one could then enter until the end of the hour. One of the students was thrown out of the class because he came dressed in a sweater coat. Dr. Schmidt considered a sweater coat as an ungentlemanly dress.

My experience with him was good. He treated me gently and passed me in history without having taken the final exam given on May 25, 1917, the day I left for the Army camp, although he offered me a special exam before then.

Students dreaded physics and [A703] Dr. Mountcastle, but for me, physics was one of the prescribed courses. I did quite well yet managed to carry away two unpleasant experiences.

[A764] Joe Rossen, my partner, and I were engaged in the experiment on "torsion." Joe carried a copy of the experiment, successfully well done by some other student of previous years in his bosom pocket, and managed to copy the figures from that copy rather than the ones we obtained. I used my own with a resulting poor grade because of a high percent of error. Apparently, the lab instructor punished me for honesty.

The final examination consisted of four problems. When subtracting two from five, I marked down a remainder of five. The answer to that problem was, therefore, wrong and 25% was taken off. The result was that I did not pass physics. When I asked [A703] Dr. Mountcastle whether he felt that I really didn't know the most elementary math, he answered, "You are going into medicine. You give your patient the wrong injection, and you kill him." However, he was willing to pass me provided I remain at Adelbert for the fourth year. Naturally, it was better to do that than to repeat physics with him and I acquiesced.

It was not until years later that I learned the reasoning power of this man's mind. Students drafted for Army service during World War I were granted one-half year's credit by the school towards graduation. This naturally appeared on record and followed the student wherever he went. From my experiences later, I became suspicious whether or not this credit seemed to some teachers at least like the "Mark of Cain" whom they were to watch carefully as the "incomplete." [A457] Dr. Joseph M. Gillman, who was then teaching economics at Pittsburgh University as well as other schools, agreed that my suspicion was entirely correct. At some later time, however, he denied having agreed with me.

Fortunately, teachers are but human and differ in ability, characters like the rest of us. There was [A704] Dean Lectner whom many students did not love much, and yet I succeeded to establish excellent rapport with him. On our first meeting during the interview for admission to Adelbert, he examined my record and found that [A758] Miss Roberts, my teacher at Central High School, had given me a 75 in English. Reserve required an average grade of 82 and no less than 80 in each course. He turned to me and said: "I won't give you any exam in English. You'll do well with us," and I never disappointed him. Though I did best in languages and social sciences, I felt the need of English and physical sciences and took as many as possible of both.

Upon returning from service, I had another interview with [A704] Dean Lectner, who wanted my impressions and observation of my army days. I told him that I found the boys from the south and small communities illiterate, but clean, while the boys from the north were filthy and diseased. I thought that he was quite impressed. We then proceeded in outlining my program, and I asked for the course, "The English Novel," which fascinated me. Because of particular difficulties in programming, he could not fit the novel course in at the time but promised to let me take the course sometime before I left Adelbert. To my surprise, he remembered and kept his promise. Unfortunately, I was greatly disappointed. I thought that [A705] Dr. Emerson could do a great deal better. But if Dr. Emerson failed me here, he made up in the course on daily theme writing. It was a challenging and time-consuming course. Finding topics was a job in itself, and then to condense the subject to 200 words was even more challenging. The Tuesday morning conferences with him were highly enjoyable, although his criticism of the sources of my information and correction of slang expressions, which I was unable to discern, led to continuous debate. Despite all that, I received an "A" for the course and always felt thankful for his great help.

Another fine teacher and person was [A706] Dr. Gruenes, an organic chemistry teacher. During the very last few days of the year, I, unfortunately, undertook to boil sulfuric acid outside the hood. When Dr. Gruenes saw the dense, acrid smoke, he came running and jumped at me furiously, ready to devour me. He spouted sarcastic questions at me. I knew I was guilty, yet I threw similarly loud and sarcastic answers at him. The students, attracted by our shouting, surrounded the two of us just when I made the brilliant remark, "and furthermore, I don't know a damn about your course." No sooner was this uttered than I realized that I might be thrown out of school. Dr. Gruenes was stunned. He turned to the students, and fortunately as if organized, they all supported me. To my surprise, not only did he give me a good grade, but we remained friends as well.

Another fine man and a good teacher was [A707] Dr. Gaelke, professor of sociology. I have never read so much as I did for that course. The weekly conferences were enjoyable and rendered thus by his personality.

#70 WESTERN RESERVE MEDICAL SCHOOL

The BA degree at Adelbert College opened the door of Western Reserve University medical school for me. The school was quite familiar to me as I worked there for about six and a half years. This included the times when I attended Central High School and Adelbert College. I have described above my first experiences working at the Medical School for [A691] Dr. George Neil Stewart, the Director of Experimental Medicine, and of [A692] Dr. David Marine, his associate. I worked for them starting at the lowest echelon and gradually rose to a respectable position and was known to all as Dr. Stewart's boy. After three years of working full time, I entered high school and continued as a part-time worker for another three and a half years when I entered Adelbert College. In the fall of 1921, I returned to the same place, this time as a medical student. This audacity of mine, as I discovered later, must be ascribed to my naivete, for I was completely unaware of the dangers facing me.

The medical school consisted of a massive three-story stone building on the corner East 9th and St. Clair flanked by two smaller brick buildings housing on the Physiology Department and the Experimental Medical Department on the east side of the court. The main building was constructed in the form of a hollow shell. On each side of the entrance were steps leading to two massive platforms running along the east, west, and south walls punctuated by doors leading to the numerous offices, classrooms, and laboratories. On the southwest corner of the first floor was also a deep amphitheater for class meetings.

The lecture is not a new invention. It was utilized as a medium of teaching since time immemorial. Moses used it to instruct the Israelites. Jesus and Paul were impressive lecturers. Our prophets Isaiah and Jeremiah were effective lecturers, just like the itinerant preachers of modern times.

The schools of my own days embraced this method of teaching more because of convenience and economy by means of which they were able to reach masses of students, but apparently never worried about the ability of the lecturer to perform. When students failed to listen to these men, the schools made attendance mandatory. During my days in school, the lecture was, and probably still is, the universal plague, torturing the students since most lectures are boring, poorly presented, and waste the best hours of the student's day. In twelve years at college and medical school, the entire staff, the chief of the department down to the lowest intern, lectured, feeding us mostly improperly mixed, poorly seasoned foods. The exceptions were few.

Even during my practice days, the guest lecturer was rarely well organized or inspiring. The man is usually certain of his erudition, hence in no need of proper construction or planning and delivery of his talk. He considers himself above all criticism.

The February issue of the *Family Physician*, page 196, carries an item titled "Medical student concentration during lectures," the study of which hopefully will induce the lecturer to improve his technique. All I can say is that it is about time. The medical student finds himself suddenly thrown into a vast and deep ocean full of various sizes and shapes of structures microscopical and microchemical, highly complex both in structure and activities. The student is asked to learn all of them in the minutest detail. With the help of an excellent guide, he gradually finds his way to carry on by supplemented reading of the textbook two to three or more times until he attains a mental picture of the structure. Nowadays, visual aids may help to speed the process and alleviate his pain. Those of us who remember the time when the chief was endowed with absolute power, as well as cruelty and meanness, wish heartily for improvement, not only in the teaching, but also in the selection of students and abolition of restrictions.

Here is the introductory statement made by [A693] Dr. Frederick Clayton Waite, Professor of Microscopic Anatomy. Precisely at 8 a.m. on October 1, 1921, Dr. Waite came running down the steps. As he reached the amphitheater floor, he made a swift turnabout and without greeting us or introducing himself, began with the wise dictum of a great educator: "I have never had any trouble with anyone except with those boys who read from the back." What effect this introductory statement made on others I don't know. Most students were five to seven years younger than me and were gentile. Thus, this was not directed to them anyhow, but every word remained indelibly imprinted upon my mind, together with even his nasal tone.

Consumed by hatred and endowed with power most probably through influence, Freddie Waite revealed himself as the crudest, meanest, most sadistic and jealous watchdog. He was feared and hated by all. Like a trained dog, he never tired. He always searched for blemishes, and when one was uncovered, he would hound the student till the end.

Soon after [A760] Mr. McDonald and I refused to join the ROTC, Dr. Waite felt he had uncovered two communists to be eliminated. From then on, every drawing of mine carried an unsatisfactory mark.

To his credit Dr. Waite was a good teacher and his course was splendidly organized. What I never understood was why he and all teachers of this course in the various schools expected us to be artists in drawing. He was known to have devised his own I.Q. tests to help him determine the awareness or thinking power and observations of his students. His favorite tests were to have the student identify the man on the picture hanging on the wall next to his seat or he would ask the student for the number of steps from the first to third floors. He really had a great time.

My schoolmate, [A761] Mr. Krenicky, who worked part-time in Dr. Waite's office and with whom I walked home daily, told me that the talk in the office about Jews was abominable, but would not elaborate much about what exactly was said. He urged me to change drawings with him, for he was certain that my drawing then would be satisfactory. I refused, fearing discovery, and then Dr. Waite would have the chance to charge me with cheating.

Then after my first 6 weeks in school and just 2 days after I received a grade of 88 in his course of histology and being only one of five students who passed the exam in Embryology, I was summoned to his office where I was subjected to the following third degree: I had no idea that for the Jewish student he had a favorite set of questions.

Q. John, is your father educated?
A. He had a Jewish education.

Q. Is your mother educated?
A. She had a Jewish education.

Q. Do you have any doctors in your family?
A. "No." (This was wrong. Two cousins Brodskys practiced medicine before Waite was born.)

Waite – "Then how do you expect to become a doctor? I want you to go into dentistry."

When I protested showing how well I did in my recent exams, he answered: "I don't doubt your industry, but you'll never make it in medicine. I won't pass you unless you go into dentistry."

Me: "I'll wait and see how I'll do in June."

Waite: "You must make up your mind right now."

Me: "I will wait till June."

Waite: "In that case, I will never pass you."

Two or three days later, after the final exam, I ran into the building, hoping to get some information when I met [A694] Dr. Todd, Professor of Anatomy. Without stopping to talk to me, he said: "John, I had nothing to do with it." That, of course, was enough said.

Dr. Waite remembered his promise and gave me an "X" in histology. The others passed me, and the school magnanimously granted me the privilege to repeat the freshman year.

Next, I saw [A695] Dr. Hitchcock, the registrar. He remembered me and talked to me in a very kind and fatherly way. He felt returning would be a great risk as there was no assurance for any better results. He was quite convincing to me. Though crushed, I was not lost and decided to look around further.

During my first year at the medical school, I also had a number of other teachers who were unsavory. [A696] Dr. Bradley Patten, a famous embryologist who later wrote the definitive textbooks on the embryology of the chick and pig, was Dr. Waite's associate. Whether he was naturally so or merely imbibed all the unsavory qualities from those that the chief suffered, Dr. Patten proved that he hated the student with a venom equal to that of his chief. During the second semester, Dr. Patten ran a course in biochemistry. We learned how to use the delicate and intricate scales to weigh out infinitesimal amounts of chemicals. These drugs were used in prepared solutions in Kjeldahl glasses that had to be used under a hood. Since there were but four to five glasses, the students had to queue up. One of the fraternity boys allowed his friend to get into line ahead of him. Soon the boys made a game of this and broke into line just ahead of me. Dr. Patten stood in the middle of the room, observing this. I asked him to stop the game, but he answered, "I have nothing to with this." The game was now sanctioned. The boys continued. I naturally got behind and had to make up my work in the late afternoon. The technician did not like to work overtime, and I was reported as falling behind. I was then declared incompetent and unable to get along with my fellow men.

[A694] Dr. Todd and [A697] Dr. Ingersol headed the Department of Gross Anatomy. There were also several student assistants whom the students feared lest instead of helping they would spy on our competence. The dissections were done with the help of a most detailed dissection book. The students were greatly confused but did the best under the circumstances. [A698] Dr. Headly, another teacher, would usually appear in the late afternoon but never said anything. He appeared like he either was drunk or drugged and grunted as he ran through the lab.

Dr. Todd spoke to us always after lunch. His speech and diction were beautiful. I remember the talk on the development of the leg. It was the best after-dinner speech for ladies I could ever imagine.

We met Dr. Ingersol during the final exam. The students waited in line the whole morning and came in twos to face the ordeal. Dr. Ingersol was sitting at the side of the body in which the lower abdomen was open, and the open urinary bladder was visible. The question was, "What is it?" Regardless of what was the answer, he repeated the question in various forms for the next 15 minutes. What he wanted was never learned. Next, we met with Dr. Todd, who presented part of an organ, sometimes turned upside down. He tried to see how we would come out of the dilemma.

#71 THE UNIVERSITY OF WEST VIRGINIA MORGANTOWN MEDICAL SCHOOL

After my experience at the medical school at Western Reserve University, I went to the University of West Virginia at Morgantown to take a summer course in histology. I went there hoping for a solution to my problem.

At Morgantown, I met a man whom I took for the Dean. I sat facing him. He put his hand on my knee and slowly managed to climb up until he felt my phallus. Apparently, my reaction was strongly adverse, for he instantly removed his hand and sent me to the cashier's office to pay for the course ($30 or $40) and matriculate $25. That done, I went to the class where I met several boys and a red-headed Pittsburgh girl who suffered from hay fever. All were viewing slides and drawing what was on the slides. The girl told me that the teacher left for three weeks of vacation, and all one has to do is to study the slides. After lunch, I met with the Dean once more. He, too, told me that the teacher would be away for three weeks. He also told me that he couldn't assure me of admission to the school for the coming year. I thought fast now, and to my answer, he said that my money would be returned only in the first 24 hours. I rushed to the office, got my money, and returned home.

Immediately I began writing to the various medical schools. Western Reserve could not be mentioned for now such a student was absolutely blacklisted. Every school asked for a record of the college work, a photograph, and a personal interview. Buffalo Medical School even asked for $10 with the application blank. Michigan, to my surprise, admitted me readily, probably because of my BA degree.

#72 THE UNIVERSITY OF MICHIGAN MEDICAL SCHOOL

The medical department in 1922 was leaderless and in the process of finding a chief. There were at least 28 teachers whom I remember, but clearly, there were many more, and every one of them lectured. The physical diagnosis course was the only one that brought us to the ward. Unfortunately, it was in the hands of the lowest echelon. Since the University of Michigan served as the center for the state, most patients were chronic and stayed there for weeks. They were repeatedly questioned and examined by different groups of students so that they learned to give us a complete history and even helped along in the physical by pointing out where and what to look for in the chest, abdomen or other areas.

Most of the teachers were good and devoted and tried to give us what they could. Apparently, because of the lack of leadership, the subject of tuberculosis was entirely neglected. The rumor among the students was that the whole class goes to Mt. Clemens, where we study tuberculosis at the VA Hospital, but this never took place. Thus, we left school with hardly a lecture on this very vital disease.

Most teachers tried their best to transmit what they could to us. Among them, the prominent ones were [A738] Neubrugh for his philosophical thought-provoking differential diagnoses, [A739] Thomas Weller's analytical discussions of his cases (later won the Nobel Prize), and [A737] Dean Cabot's direct way of presentation and treatment of his cases. Dean Cabot was a staunch conservative, but a just man. By logic and good horse sense, he rose to greater qualities than his colleagues.

It was Cabot who came to the help of our Jamaican Negro who made two trips at great expense to New York for interviews and examinations for an internship but failed to get the appointment. Dr. Cabot thought this outrageous. He called the hospital and succeeded in placing the man. It was Cabot who came to the rescue of one of our junior students enabling him to finish his studies. And it was Dr. Cabot who came to the rescue of one other man, [A776] Dr. M.A. Fine.

Though I made no honors, I did quite well, and I am sure that I was in the upper ten or at least 20% of the class. This average or even better I kept up through my internship and all through my 46.5 years of private practice. I made hundreds or possibly even thousands of good friends among my colleagues and patients who trusted, honored, and loved me throughout my years of practice and even in my retirement.

As late as July 1973, criteria for the selection of students to the medical school was still a serious issue, as the article in the Journal of the American Physician by [A709] Dr. Philip B. Price shows. Dr. Price, who was the Dean Emeritus of the University of Utah Medical School, stated that several comprehensive studies showed that a "safe" physician should have 87 desirable traits and be free from 26 undesirable characteristics. He also said that 35 of these traits exist in a recognizable form in high school students. Therefore, he advises that students should be selected from this group. However, he failed to list these traits.

#73 THE INTERN

Not all men are destined to play a significant role in the great eventful things in life. My internship belongs to the category of simplicity, but it enriched my life just the same.

[A765] Sister Ray was about 50 years old. She had been in the nunnery at St. Vincent's Hospital, Toledo, Ohio, for many years, where she served God and humanity. She fulfilled her duties well but did not allow her austere life to eradicate her innate sense of humor. This humor added flavor to her otherwise rigorous life. It enabled her to see the comedy, even in tragedy. Yet this did not alleviate her aloneness, and she apparently sought someone to share her feelings with her.

For some reason, Sister Ray found what she sought in me. We became good friends so that she would show me whatever bizarre or interesting event occurred in the hospital.

Once, she called asking me to come up. Her voice, though hilarious, betrayed a sense of urgency so that I answered her call promptly. What I beheld on entering the room almost shocked me. It looked as if a murder and violent struggle of the victim had taken place. Sister Ray, however, readily destroyed my conclusion. She assured me that there was no murder, only a phlebotomy performed by a [A766] Dr. Shapiro.

I knew of this man though I never met him. He was a graduate of Western Reserve University and an admirer of a young lady who was destined to become my cousin at a later date. Surgery was his aspiration. Whether he ever reached his goal, I don't know because I left Toledo within a few months. It was of interest to know that nearly every appendectomy of his had some tragic consequence. That is why Sister Ray showed me his handiwork. Both of us felt that he should have been eligible for the Nobel Prize.

The fool enters where the wise fears to tread. But young men have no doubt. If they escape tragedy, it is but accidental.

The Medical School at the University of Michigan awards the diploma, but the State grants the license to practice medicine upon satisfactory completion of one year's internship. While this law aims to protect the public against inadequately trained physicians, it gives the hospital dictatorial powers over the intern.

In my days, there were many more interns than available internships. The hospital, therefore, took full advantage to exploit the young men who were at their mercy. Thus: 1) one had to present an official record of his grades at school; 2) a picture had to be submitted with the application; 3) an interview was required; 4) some hospitals required competitive exams, and finally, 5) infraction of these rules could lead to severe consequences, including termination of the internship and then no possibility of external practice.

Though aware of all this, I ventured into no man's land as narrated below. During my late teens, while working for [A692] Dr. David Marine in the Department of Experimental Medicine at Reserve, I acquired considerable experience in administering ether and chloroform anesthesia to animals.

[A715] Dr. Phil Katz, a recent graduate of Michigan and a friend of mine, was aware of my qualifications and induced me to administer anesthesia in a home delivery. Thus, late one summer evening, the two of us arrived at the home of the patient. We found the husband resting outside the house. The wife was found in a small windowless room, which, if I remember correctly, had no light available at all. The patient was in active labor. Dr. Katz found the presentation was a breech and the cervix dilated. Water was heated in a large basin, and I anesthetized the patient. The extraction of the baby was prompt and successfully accomplished with the help of a strong push from the mother. No episiotomy or repair was necessary. The uterus was firm, and there was no bleeding. We felt jubilantly ran to congratulate the father. The latter, however, apparently felt entirely unconcerned and was not to be found. Most probably, he went to drown his sorrows.

I never inquired whether Dr. Katz collected for his services, but he did pay me $5 on the spot. I returned to the hospital, and only after I relaxed did it dawn on me the risk I had taken.

The emergency room at the hospital had evolved gradually from a first aid station to a very vital organ of public service. At any active center, the problems vary tremendously and are of great educational value for the inexperienced young physician. I remember vividly the Detroit grandmother who brought her beautiful little granddaughter to the Emergency Room of St. Vincents Hospital. The girl had been treated to a memorable automobile ride to Toledo to honor her recovery from measles but electrocuted herself by some electrical gadget as she played with her cousin. While in the bathroom, she had inserted her finger into the electric socket. All of us doctors, nurses, and orderlies were standing impotently, unable to help and crying with that wretched grandmother. All through that day, when anyone attempted to describe that distraught, painful grandmother, we burst into laughing and crying, not at her, but at our own impotence. I see her now, and if I were not ashamed, I would burst out crying even now.

Four accident cases came into the emergency room at one time. When I first looked at the patient assigned to me, no face was visible. On closer inspection, however, I realized that the scalp was split at the vertex of the skull. It was turned inside out and pulled down, covering the face. The whole area appeared clean. In my excitement, I forgot all surgical principles and quickly replaced the scalp to its proper location and sutured the wound. The patient was otherwise in good condition. My task was accomplished, and the patient was admitted to the house for further observation. The criticism from the elders came later, but fortunately, my results were beyond criticism. I am sure no well-trained or tried surgeon could ever get away with as great a result as mine.

A young woman met with an accident and was brought into the emergency room, where she asked for her own doctor. I knew the man. He was a young, neatly dressed, bold, livewire type. He held an excellent job with a company in Toledo and, judging by his dress and carriage, was quite successful in practice. I watched him examine the young lady. He seemed not only thorough but also extremely gentle and solicitation of her well-being. Had this ended at this point I would have always respected him, but just as I left him, he ran over to me, calling the patient a bitch. To me, he remained the ugliest creature and a disgrace to his profession.

The important surgeons at St. Vincent's: 1) [A767] Fred Douglass; 2) [A768] Dr. George – last name escapes me; 3) [A769] Dr. Cunningham; 4) [A770] Dr. Crinion; 5) [A771] Dr. R. L.

Bidwell; and 6) his brother. By general consent, Dr. George, though less dramatic than Dr. Douglass, was considered the better of the two. He was careful in his diagnosis. His patients were usually sick because of real pathology, and his postoperative care was excellent. We ascribed this to his proper technique and gentle handling of the tissues.

Late one summer a young doctor, the son of a wealthy Toledo furniture dealer, brought a patient into the hospital whom he had examined at a drug store and suspected of having a perforated gastric ulcer. After examining the patient with me, this young doctor asked me to report the vital signs and differential count to him every hour at the hotel where he took a room for the night. I did as he requested. By 2:00 a.m. or 3:00 a.m., he decided that it was time to explore the patient and summoned [A768] Dr. George. Because the patient was a wealthy man's son, he was always attended to by the rich man's doctor. The young physician, therefore, felt obliged to wake the doctor from his sleep and request him to come down to the hospital.

When I came up to the second floor, I found some nurses, sisters, and interns excitedly awaiting the arrival of the great personage. As a stranger in town, I couldn't quite understand it. I thought possibly [A281] Nicholas II was resurrected and was coming to St. Vincent's. Finally, the great man did arrive. He was too great to greet or talk to anyone, but he did speak to the young physician and Dr. George. The patient was explored, and a pinpoint perforation was found and repaired. The patient made an uneventful recovery and was discharged in due time only to return some several weeks later with a diagnosis of pelvic abscess. Again Dr. George operated on him. After he had closed the wound, he took off his glove, shook hands with the young physician saying "my hat off to you."

Another case in which Dr. George was involved was that of a young nurse labeled as a case of appendicitis but was treated for acute bilateral salpingitis. Nurses and sisters knew that appendicitis required immediate surgery, but this girl was running a high fever, yet was treated medically. Some of them understood the problem well, but those of us directly involved had to protect the girl against the vitriolic moral censure of the nuns, the gossip of the nurses and other personnel as well as against the known scandal monger physician, who never failed to be where he was unwanted.

The treatment in those days lasted six weeks, after which surgery followed. Those were long and tedious weeks. Finally, the day of judgment arrived. This was a day to remember. All eyes and ears were directed to the one operating room. Even the scandalmonger managed to show his face there. Dr. George now had the opportunity to play his part and managed his part so skillfully that no one realized when or what he removed or what he did with the specimens removed. The wind now dispersed, the nurse made an excellent recovery, and nothing more was heard about this.

[A767] Dr. Fred Douglass was the most honored, most popular, busiest, and most successful surgeon in the city. His daily operative schedule was fantastic, operating on 10 to 14 patients a day. His intern never came to lunch on time. Because of this, there was a constant feud with the sister of the Intern dining room who would refuse to feed the late comers. Dr. Douglass was clean and swift at his work and well organized. He removed the gallbladder in six steps. His patients had easy recoveries. All of us admired him and his technique. It was only after I came into practice and saw other work that I realized why Dr. Douglass did so well. Every year Dr. Douglass would pick one intern and place him in some different part of the city. Out of gratitude, this young man felt obliged to refer his surgery to Dr. Douglass. The latter's policy was never to question the former's diagnosis. As a result, he removed more appendices and gall bladders than the combined surgical staff. Moreover, most of the patients were young, healthy, and without any pathology. The surgery, therefore, was clean, smooth, and quick while the recovery rate was very high.

Once a niece of Dr. Douglass' came in with a diagnosis of acute appendicitis. The intern, [A776] Dr. M.A. Fine, made a diagnosis of early pregnancy and marked that boldly on the chart. As usual, Dr. Douglass never looked at the intern's diagnosis. This time, he blushed plenty. Fortunately, the patient did not lose the baby. Douglass was very critical for not having been informed, but Fine told him, "It was all there for you to see."

Hospitals are nests of dirty politics and serious jealousies. [A769] Dr. Cunningham and [A770] Dr. Crinion were the lesser known surgeons and fair ones for the time. For some reason, Cunningham enjoyed more favoritism from the hospital. Dr. Crinion, who endowed one of the surgical rooms, felt deserving the greater consideration. If Dr. Cunningham occupied Dr. Crinion's room and thus interfered with his schedule, Dr. Crinion's protest was loud enough to reach the Pope in Rome. The Bidwell brothers were not very popular. [A771] R.L. Bidwell was considered the better surgeon of the two. In fairness, I must say his diagnostic acumen was good and technique fair, but I felt that his postoperative care could be improved. Naively I asked permission to follow Dr. George's method. The poor man jumped as if stung by a bee. I never realized how seriously I injured his pride.

R.L. Bidwell's brother was a stocky but handsome man, always well dressed and gay. He traveled a great deal and spoke much and loudly. He was therefore referred to as "Wind." Over time, his practice and skill dwindled. I am certain he was gravely aware of it. I remember he brought in a young lady, apparently a patient he had operated on many years earlier. Every nurse, intern, and sister knew that the poor woman was dying from postoperative obstruction. Revision of the operation was indicated, but Dr. Bidwell remained steadfast to the end, probably fearing exposure.

The best display of politics mixed with a bit of antisemitic flavor was displayed in the medical department. [A772] Dr. Levison and [A773] Dr. Saltzman were two outstanding keen and progressive Jewish internists. [A774] Dr. Waggoner was a homeopathic physician and chief of staff. The animosity between MDs and homeopathic physicians was still very much alive. Dr. Levison somehow managed to keep the peace, but not Saltzman. Waggoner not only succeeded in throwing the latter off the staff but curbed his privileges even further.

The intern was always eager to accompany Dr. Saltzman on his rounds at 8 a.m. for Dr. Saltzman liked to teach as he walked from patient to patient. Dr. Waggoner, therefore, insisted that the intern spend that particular hour in the lab. This was strictly enforced so that actually the intern was the innocent victim.

The attitude to and the treatment of the medical student now, as compared with that accorded to us and particularly to the Jewish student, is so vastly different that the new graduate will never understand the scarring their colleagues sustained during the years of study.

In Russia, Jews were simply excluded from the higher schools. Because of this exclusion policy, there developed the "extern," i.e., one who studied under a private tutor and then applied for an entrance exam. I knew several such students. One, [A261] Mr. Krasnyansky, a teacher of mine in [C43] Zashkov for several months, a handsome, angelic, and brilliant man was examined so many times that he finally gave up the struggle. Most of these externs finally landed in Austria or Germany, where they finished their studies.

The medical school in the United States, until recently, secretly practiced exclusion. The Jews, of course, knew this. Non-Jews did not care to know it. I remember when Harvard admitted its policy of exclusion. Many Jewish students, like myself, somehow managed to break the barrier with but a small loss of time. In the first two months of school, the great educator, [A693] Dr. Frederick Waite, promised me a failure. In very frank words, he alleged that since my parents were not educated, I couldn't possibly become a physician. Other students experienced greater losses and more serious scars, while some gave up the fight altogether.

Dr. [A776] M.A. Fine, co-intern of mine at St. Vincent's in Toledo, was an excellent intern. All liked him, and he was well recognized for his good qualities. The two of us, as the only Jews, grew close and very friendly. Despite this friendship, he nursed one secret all through the year. Finally, in desperation and looking for advice, he divulged it to me.

In addition to the policy of restriction, all our medical schools at that time engaged in what I consider now to be morally criminal acts, that is, swindling the young students. All enrolled many more students than they were able to accommodate during the junior or senior years. Western Reserve University, for instance, admitted 54 men to its freshman class. Four of these were Jews. Every fourth year one Negro was admitted. By the end of the sophomore year, 24 men were forced to fall out because the school only had room for 30 men. Anything at all was sufficient to get rid of the student. The Jewish student was the first one in line. That is how Dr. Fine was eliminated from the University of Maryland in Baltimore in his sophomore year. Also, such a student carried the mark of Cain on his forehead so that no other school would admit him unless the student was able by cheating or lying. Some tried to hide the mark on his forehead.

The choice left for Fine was to enter a class "C" school in, I believe, Philadelphia or Boston, which then granted him his M.D. in 1926. By some miracle, St. Vincent's Hospital gave him an internship. The AMA strictly forbid this. Now at the very end, the State of Ohio would not recognize his M.D. and wouldn't allow him to take the state board exam of Ohio. This was the secret Fine revealed to me in June 1927. I felt but two men could possibly help. Both [A767] Drs. Douglass and [A775] Stone were quite fond of Fine. He followed my advice. The two men were shocked by this discovery. Dr. Douglass lost no time and immediately dispatched Dr. Stone to talk to [A737] Hugh Cobot of the University of Michigan. The latter, whom I knew and respected, was a very conservative, but just and upright man. He recognized the injustice done to Fine, but being bound by law and regulations, he could only admit Fine to the junior year. Fine thus lost two years but did get his M.D. I saw him some ten years later in Baltimore. Like myself, he was married. His office was poor and unattractive, but like me, he was happy. I have never heard or seen him since.

#74 AN AMERICAN JEW BORN TO
IMMIGRANT PARENTS FROM CZARIST RUSSIA

Excerpted from "On Being a Jew and a Boston Braves Fan: Alone and Afraid in a World I Never Made" From Moral Outrage in Education (2004) by [A584] David Purpel. Reprinted with permission of Nancy Kaprov Gore and Peter Lang Inc., International Academic Publishers.

Editor's note 1: We all intuitively understand we carry a familial history going back more than hundreds of years but understand little of why we think and act as we do. David addresses the culture our parents have given to us, and what their parents have given to them. This incisive essay goes to the heart of why we are who we are and understanding more of why we are. Note 2: We have all heard of unexpected encounters. A more memorable one for me was to learn at my childhood shul, Park Synagogue, Cleveland Heights, OH, about a woman of foreign birth who spoke virtually no English came on a Saturday morning for services. Living the concept about welcoming the stranger, congregants conscientiously went and chatted with her. One invited her to her home for lunch. The stranger froze when entering the house. She pulled from her wallet a picture – the exact picture on the piano. The two were relatives. That is how I felt when I received a letter in the late 1980s that read, "We are a brother and sister in search of our family." We spoke almost immediately, and within minutes, I had them placed on the family tree. From having no relatives, they suddenly had more than a thousand. Little did we suspect that the brother and I lived only a block apart in Cambridge for some time.

Much of my family's story is achingly and painfully familiar, part of the narrative of Jewish experience that allows one to use the words routine and tragic in the same sentence. Both my parents were born in the same shtetl in what is now Ukraine, just south of Kiev, and each of them witnessed the murder of a parent by bandits in the chaos and tumult of the Russian civil war. Both fled in terror and made their individual ways as teenagers across Europe by the grace of luck, grit, bribes, some kind people, a network of Jewish agencies, and God knows what else. They eventually arrived in Boston in the early twenties, got married and settled down to a life of poverty, struggle, fear, and grief.

Their life spans coincided with World War I, the Bolshevik revolution, the Red scare, the Depression, the rise of Fascism, the New Deal, World War II, the Holocaust, the Atomic age, the Cold War, McCarthyism, the establishment of the state of Israel, the Korean War, the Civil Rights Movement, the war in Vietnam, the Watergate scandals, and the assassinations of Archduke Ferdinand, Leon Trotsky, Mohandas Gandhi, John Kennedy, Martin Luther King, and Robert Kennedy.

Politically, they were basically radicals but their commitment to socialism was always delimited by their fear of Stalin and the traditions of virulent Russian antisemitism. They adored FDR but were tempted to vote for Norman Thomas as they strongly supported the labor movement. They also thought that a role of government was to protect us from big business. They almost always voted and followed political campaigns with great interest and acumen.

They had read Gogol and Tolstoy in Russian, Sholom Aleichem and the brothers Singer in Yiddish, and Dorothy Parker and Philip Roth in English. They had seen Menashe Skulnik, Maurice Schwartz, and Molly Picon on the stage, in the movies and on television and heard them on the radio, likewise Mary Martin, Helen Hayes, and Paul Newman. They loved Sid Caesar's comic genius, were scornful of Milton Berle's vulgarity, and were much more devoted to Playhouse 90 than to any sitcom. They never went to a proper school.

They did this in between the frustrating and backbreaking tasks of running a small grocery store, beset with a shrinking clientele and ferocious competition from "the chain stores" and the overwhelming chores that come with parental responsibilities. They had five children (one of whom died from a ruptured appendix at the age of two) each one of whom provided them with opportunities for pride, aggravation, hopes, and disappointments. They had their share of existential crises, marital disputes, major illnesses, and probably less than their share of joys, triumphs, and celebrations.

They were indeed complicated folks, often loving and generous, sometimes mean-spirited and spiteful; always worried and fearful; usually secretive and guarded; capable of genuine gaiety and laughter, and yet ultimately presenting a morose image of themselves as victims, surviving with poignant dignity but struggling to control their demons of terror, fear, and despair. They were very intelligent, even wise; well read; politically sophisticated; sort of open-minded but also wary and skeptical of change. Their attitudes toward their Jewish and American identities were complicated, full of fierce loyalties but laced with ambivalence, ambiguity, and paradox.

They certainly wanted their children to be Jewish, but their modes of acculturation were irregular and unfocused. For one thing, and probably for reasons much more psychological than ideological, they purposefully decided not to live in a Jewish neighborhood, which gave us all the opportunity to interact with a predominantly Irish Catholic, working-class community, one which at best aspired to and occasionally reached attitudes of strained toleration toward "kikes." My parents put heavy stress on Yiddishkeit, were only mildly observant although strict on some issues (no mixing of dairy with meat, no pork or shrimp, no school on the Holidays, at least most of the time). Although they were both quite knowledgeable about religious practices and traditions they expressed a skeptical if not cynical attitude towards religious institutions. They were apprehensive, suspicious, and patronizing of goyim and contemptuous of assimilating and socially ambitious Jews, whom they called "all-rightniks." They taught us to read Yiddish authors but not the Torah; they discussed/argued political and social but not theological issues with us; and they insisted that we remember and revere our heritage as Jews, even as they disavowed the Jewish God.

I went to Hebrew school four days a week (after public school and on Sundays) and became a bar mitzvah. That was the only formal Jewish education I ever had, and although I learned to read and write Hebrew, it was a very threadbare education at best. And yet I have become convinced that with all the mixed signals and missed opportunities, and all the other craziness in my home, my parents provided me with some critically important and energizing notions that have helped to shape my worldview, one that clearly has a strong Jewish flavor.

In retrospect these Jewish influences that came from my childhood seem to have influenced my professional work more than they did my personal life, (But that's another story.) In some ways my professional foci (citizenship education, critical thinking, clinical supervision, critical pedagogy, moral education), even as they shifted, all seemed to have common resonance with some of the more visible Jewish values. However, this did not become clear to me till I came to write *The Moral and Spiritual Crisis in Education*, the work that best represents my professional concerns and value commitments.

I have to confess that I often felt inspired while I was actually writing this book. By that I emphatically do not mean that the book was ghostwritten by some divine author but rather that I sensed that I had entered a different kind of space, a mysterious space made special and exciting because it seemed to be sacred, I do not believe that I would have been open to this experience had I not just read Abraham Joshua Heschel's monumental and truly inspired work The Prophets. When I read it I was afraid I would hyperventilate, so powerful, so profound, and so compelling was it to me. I knew that the paradigm of prophetic thought focusing on a God of history, justice, and mercy who strives in covenant with humanity to create a loving and just community that Heschel so eloquently and passionately describes was and is the one for me. What was so extraordinary was the way Heschel's book was simultaneously familiar and new to me. The substantive elements were all new to me, in truth, up to that point I had zero idea of the significance of the Prophets—who they were, what they did and said, and what they represented. And yet the essential message seemed to be in harmony with my intuitive sense of what constitutes the ultimate meaning and purpose of life. What was annoying to me was that it had taken me so long to find this paradigm. What was mysterious to me was how I had somehow come to resonate with this basic language in spite of my unfamiliarity with the particular literature.

What was also inspirational was that I was struggling with something far more important and worthwhile than my usual limitations and constraints, nothing less than the opportunity to write within that sacred paradigm. How successful or unsuccessful I was in this responsibility is not totally clear to me but one thing did become apparent to me. I had discovered that an essential part of the moral and spiritual grounding of my work had always been there. The exciting thing was that this came to me in such a mysterious way, and the embarrassing thing was that I didn't really know very much about this grounding.

This account only partially explains why the book that eventually emerged, while certainly stressing the centrality of the prophetic tradition, does not speak directly to the Jewish sensibility that permeates it. It took me a long time to fully recognize, as some of my colleagues told me early on, that I had written a Jewish book without saying so. It took me much less time to recognize that if I indeed had written within Jewish traditions, I had done so as an amateur. Hence my agenda became clear. I needed to know a lot more about this grounding, and so I have read and continue to do a lot of reading and studying of traditional Jewish sources. I am finding it to be both exciting and frustrating, both accessible and opaque, simultaneously compelling and remote. I also realized that I needed to be a lot more explicit about my Jewish orientation and have made some tentative and modest steps in that direction in my writing and teaching.

I have taken the time to write about my parents and my personal background partly to highlight the difficulty of factoring out the Jewish dimension of my life from the myriad of other influences and factors, be they psychological, historical, sociological, or characterological in nature. It is easy enough to say that my parents were Jewish, that I grew up in a Jewish home, and that I consider myself to be a Jew. After that it's very hard. Not only is it excruciatingly difficult to explain what I have said about my Jewish background and identity but it is also exceedingly difficult to sort out and explain the enormously complicated dynamics of the matrix of personal, cultural, circumstantial, contingent, and societal events that shape my consciousness. Indeed, it is this complexity that makes this writing assignment so challenging, so difficult, and so risky. Furthermore, when it came time for me to begin to work on the assignment, I realized that my customary professional discourse and writing style were not going to be of much help and more likely would be counterproductive in addressing the questions of the integration of my personal and professional lives.

The task would seem to require serious self-interrogation, a process that I have so far assiduously and successfully neglected and avoided. Indeed, I have been so successful that I've had to think hard about a different approach that would at least enable me to make a good faith effort at writing this essay. This led me to understand that even though until fairly recently I had largely avoided careful, systematic self-examination of my Jewish identity, my Jewish consciousness has surely not evolved randomly, nor is it disconnected from my persona nor from my work. Rather, it is expressed in my attitudes, behaviors, and sensibilities and is lodged in the crowded, messy, and unswept compartments of my inferiority.

In order to bring some order to this clutter, I decided to rely on, of all things (you should excuse the expression) my intuition. My intuition told me that I would have to dig deep to find some gems, but that these gems are stored in places that are dear and accessible to me. These places turn out to be the vast treasure of Jewish stories of all varieties, be they legends, tales, jokes, anecdotes, allegories, or midrashim. More particularly, the richest source of self-insight would be those stories that I especially love to read, hear, and tell over and over again. My intuition-driven reasoning is that I can learn a lot from those specific stories precisely because I continue to tell them. Their very persistence in my nervous system indicates that they resonate with my innermost sense of meaning. Therefore, I would like simply to tell a few of these stories and then reflect on their meaning and significance for me.

In some ways the questions and quandaries concerning these connections are similar and parallel to the ones regarding my Jewish identity. Did I choose to be a Braves fan any more or less than I chose to be Jewish? Why is my loyalty to the Braves and Jews independent of anything Jews or Braves believe, do, or say? If the recruiter for the Red Sox Knothole Gang had been at the park a day earlier, would I have become a Red Sox fan? Was my initial bonding to the Braves a matter of obsession? A genuine symbiosis? An instance of self-indulgent pride and chauvinism? Or was it an example of true and profound commitment? Am I Jewish only because of the happenstance of birth, and do I have any more capacity to renounce my Jewish identity than I did to reject my Braves fandom? Did I continue to support the Braves because they were, presumably like my perception of Jews, oppressed, despised, and pitiful? Or was it vice versa? Did I resent the Red Sox because they were a metaphor for the smug, entrenched, and powerful goyim? Perhaps my two major identities were related by dint of their affording me the opportunity to have a unique identity in my neighborhood and/or to be oppositional; perhaps they both represented my status as marginal and minority; perhaps they reflected a concern for justice and mercy for the oppressed, or perhaps they both allowed me to wallow in martyrdom and victimization.

Epilogue
As I expected, the process of writing this paper has clarified some issues, confused others, and raised brand-new ones for me. Perhaps the issues all come under the heading of the problematics of choice. I did not choose to be a Jew, I do not believe that I can choose not to be a Jew. I am

absolutely clear that among other important things, I am a Jew, and I have no problems with any of this. As the adage says, one does not choose to be born or to die, or as George Santayana said, "No one speaks language, everyone speaks a particular language." Or, as the saying goes, everybody has to come from somewhere. Frankly, I don't know if it would be better if I could have chosen or what I would have chosen if I could, but in any case the issue is moot to me.

Of course, I have much more choice about how I express and manifest my Jewish identity, and the fact that I have such a lot of choice stems in large part from the happenstance of my living in twentieth- century America. As I navigate between the freedom and autonomy that comes with the territory of the Enlightenment American style and the commitments that come with the territory of Jewish traditions, I struggle with several questions. Is it OK for me to pick and choose the Jewish traditions that are appealing to me and resonant with my work? (I sort of think it is but I need some help with this.) Is it all right to see Jewish sources as, to use Roger Simon's term, fertile grazing areas for finding support for my ideas? Should I define myself as a Jew living in exile or as an American "who happens to be Jewish"? Should I become more attached to a particular Jewish tradition and work to deduce its relevance to American education? Is my work as an educator about encouraging goyim to be more Jewish or better informed on Jewish thought, or both, or neither? Perhaps I should accept and even embrace a life of multiple and shifting professional identities, moving from one paradigm and context to another. As a matter of fact, can I just give up fussing over these issues and forget all about this identity thing?

The most complicated question for me personally, however, has to do with my realization that, as with my connection to the Boston Braves, my deepest and strongest ties are at base irrational. In a very real sense, these bonds have absolutely nothing to do with the content of Jewish history, nor its religious teachings, nor its literature, as much as I love and treasure them, I came to treasure them because I am Jewish; I did not become Jewish because I treasured them. I know this kind of visceral bonding resonates with the consciousness of the physicist's mother, but there it is and I remain very, very puzzled by it all. As far as my work is concerned, would it have had a similar orientation if I were born an Episcopalian? Or if I were a fourth-generation Jew? Or if I were an Israeli? I'm not even sure I need to know.

I end with even more questions than I had when I began, which reminds me of a story.

Two people, one a Jew, the other not, are having a long and heated conversation. One of them, in a moment of frustration, asks, "Why is it that every time I ask a Jew a question, they always answer with another question?" The Jew replies, "So what's wrong with asking questions?"

#75 HOW ONE DEFINES ONESELF
By [A402] Dave Douglas to [A457] Joe Gillman circa 1962

Editor's note: This letter tackles the question so many of us are asked so often.

Having been a citizen of four countries during my lifetime (Russia, Romania, Canada, and America), and if asked to which I belong, my answer is simple and definite:
I AM AN AMERICAN!

If asked, do I consider myself an Atheist, Agnostic, Protestant, Catholic, Unitarian, or Jew, my answer remains definite and straightforward:
I AM A JEW.

I find my American citizenship does not interfere nor conflict with my Jewishness, nor do these two definitions conflict in any shape or form. We enjoy a separation of State and Church as a matter of national policy and Law. I chose to become an American citizen because I embraced the principles of this national idealism.

It is not meaningful to try and sever or fragment these two, i.e., my Americanism and my Jewishness, because they are separate entities:

I am an American,
I am a Builder,
I am a Jew,
I am a Realtor,

I have included two other definitions and placed all four definitions in alphabetical order, to bring into sharp focus the fact that none of these compete with each other and all define me correctly. Specifically, I have included two facets of my commercial activity – builder and realtor – you might ask: Are you a Realtor-Builder or a Builder-Realtor? Are you more of a builder than a realtor, or visa versa? Is that a logical question, no? And although most people will answer this question without thinking, one way or another – the truth, in fact, is they would be wrong – because when I build, I am a builder, and when I sell real estate, I am a realtor. I can be on a construction job in the morning when I am 100% builder, and later I may be offering a property for sale, and I am then 100% a realtor.

I am an American and I am a Jew; I am an American Jew; I am an American of Jewish extraction; I am an American who was formerly a Canadian; I am an American who had been born in Russia. All these are accurate descriptions, and none of these definitions compete, conflict, or contradict each other.

THAT'S A LONG ANSWER TO A SHORT AND SEEMINGLY INNOCENT QUESTION.
I am, however, a rabid individualist and refuse to be classified by any other standards than those I believe in, and those I have set for myself.

#76 ROBBOY FAMILY MENORAH c1820
Gifted to Philadelphia History Museum

Editor's note: Cousin [A090] Howard Robboy gifted this menorah in 2012 to the Philadelphia History Museum at the Atwater Kent (Photograph by Sara Hawken); The collection is now at Drexel University. The story comes from the Encyclopedia of Greater Philadelphia (https://philadelphiaencyclopedia.org/archive/artifact-menorah/). Leslie Peck, who earned a master's degree in history at Rutgers University-Camden, wrote the text. Reprinted with permission of Mid-Atlantic Regional Center for the Humanities, Department of History, Rutgers, The State University of New Jersey, Camden, NJ.

Fig 76-1 Menorah with the word "Zion" on the star at the top

Menorahs have a very ancient connection with Judaism. The instructions for making them appeared in the first five books of the Hebrew Bible, known as the Torah – the foundational text of Judaism. According to the book of Exodus (or Shemot), craftsmen were to construct them with "three branches from one side of the lampstand and three branches from the other side" (Exodus 37:18). Since ancient times, this classic shape and design have been a recognizable symbol of Judaism.

The menorah at the top of this page came from M. Wolozin Inc. of New York, a Judaica store that operated on Eldridge Street on the lower East Side of Manhattan. Its silver-plated branches appear to have wax stains from the dripping of candles. Rather than three branches on each side, as the Torah instructs, this menorah has four. The center is topped with a Magen David (Star of David), and it is inscribed in Hebrew with the word "Zion." If we look closely at this menorah from the collection of the Philadelphia History Museum, what does it suggest about how it might have been used? Would it have been owned by someone very wealthy or someone of more modest means?

This kind of menorah, different from the traditional Jewish menorah, is called a Hanukiah or Hanukkah Menorah. The eight branches hold the candles lit for the eight nights of Hanukkah, while the center holds the shamash, or helper candle, which lights the others. Hanukkah begins with the lighting of the shamash and one candle, and each evening a new candle is added until the final night when the Hanukiah is fully lit. Hanukkah menorahs are made in a wide range of styles from simple yet elegant designs (like the one shown here) to very intricate and elaborate. Modern Hanukkah menorahs range from the traditional to the abstract. The classic shape and design of this Hanukiah, however, is one that even the earliest Jewish residents of the Philadelphia area would have recognized.

The first Jewish inhabitants of Philadelphia were a small group of Sephardic and German Jews who lived in the city in the 1730s. Among them were families that became prominent in local Philadelphia history, such as the Gratz family, for whom Gratz College was named. In 1782 this group dedicated the city's first synagogue (Congregation Mikveh Israel) on Cherry Street, and Benjamin Franklin (1706-90) was among the donors to its building fund.

For almost a century the Jewish community in the United States was predominantly German or Western European. But as the pogroms and persecutions increased in Eastern Europe in the 1880s, Jews from Poland, Russia, and other eastern European countries flooded into the major cities of the United States in a wave of immigration that lasted from 1880 to 1924. Philadelphia was no exception, and the established German/Jewish community in the city was inundated with refugees who were foreign to them in almost every way. They dressed differently, they worshiped differently, and they even spoke a different language – Yiddish. The large numbers of Jewish immigrants forever changed Jewish life in Philadelphia and the nation.

Among those many millions seeking to escape the poverty and persecution in Eastern Europe were the owners of this menorah. In 1923 [A079] Mendel Robboy (c. 1884-1953), a native of Kiev, his wife, [A079a] Anna (c. 1884-?), and their three children intended to travel on board the *Constantinople* from Constanta, Romania, to New York. Passenger lists indicate they never made it on board, and they instead traveled on the SS *Canada* destined for Providence, Rhode Island. They were one family among thousands who left their homeland in search of economic opportunity and religious freedom in the United States. They became part of that tremendous wave of immigration that forever changed American Jewry. Settling in Philadelphia, their American story began in Port Richmond, where the Robboys lived and operated a small grocery store. Port Richmond had a large Jewish population at that time, enough to support two synagogues at Tulip and Auburn Streets in the heart of an area that became known as "New Jerusalem."

One of the many Jewish holidays the Robboy family would have celebrated was Hanukkah, with this Hanukiah. The holiday was not prescribed in Jewish scripture like Passover and Yom Kippur, but it became a celebration of Jewish resilience in the face of persecution. Rabbi Joseph Telushkin, in his book *Jewish Literacy* (1991), commented that it is indeed "one of the happiest Jewish holidays." It recalls the oppression of the Jews by the Seleucid ruler Antiochus IV Epiphanes (215 B.C.E.-164 B.C.E.), who sought to outlaw Judaism and put idols in the Jewish temple in Jerusalem. In 166 B.C.E. the Jews, led by the Maccabees, rebelled and purified the Temple by destroying the idols. When they sought to light the menorah, they had only one container of oil—enough for one day. According to the story, that one flask lasted for eight days, and the Hanukkah Menorah has eight candles to commemorate that miracle.

Hanukkah was not a major holiday on the Jewish calendar until the twentieth century. However, Hanukkah played an important role for new Jewish immigrants to the United States, who associated Christmas with a potential for violence, such as the attacks on Jewish businesses that occurred at Christmastime during the Warsaw pogrom of 1881. In the new world, "Hanukkah served as a counter-balance to this fear of Christmas in Jewish communities," wrote Emma Green in her article "Hanukkah Why?" in the December 2015 issue of *The Atlantic.* In Philadelphia, the Jewish community was free to worship without fear. If we try, we can imagine Mendel Robboy, his wife, Anna, and their children, gathered around this Hanukiah, celebrating the miracle of oil and celebrating their new lives, their faith, and their new freedom in America.

Stories of Practice

#77 YOUNG DOCTOR

The bachelor, if at all promising, may become part of the hunting game. Many mothers, sisters, and friends of unmarried girls, as well as some spinsters, may join the game, a game which is apt to provide the hunted one rich and unique experiences. There came in many a call for my services, which really were intended for the introduction. Occasionally these were discernible, and I felt like the doctor in the picture examining the flask of urine while the mother and daughter questioned him.

Customs are outgrowths of time and necessity. Bundling was resorted to during colonial days because of distances and difficulties in transportation. In our day, the matchmaker, though still holding sway among the well-to-do, had lost his reputation among the immigrant boys and girls. Coupling was a strange phenomenon to them. The young met in lecture and dance halls, at picnics or home parties. I participated in many of these and frequently had my full share of the fun.

Mrs. K., a proprietress of a hardware store on East 105th Street, managed to seat herself next to Mother in the synagogue on Saturday mornings. This allowed her to inquire about Mother's children, particularly the doctor. Her central theme was that one need not carry the entire burden of tuition and suggested to Mother to have me meet her beautiful and accomplished daughter. Mother was not averse to the idea and begged me to do so as a special favor to her. This I did and reported to Mother that the girl was much too young and not particularly attractive. The lady was greatly offended and accused Mother of "wiping the floor with her daughter." The young lady did manage to find a medical student whom she married. She was jubilant. I saw her frequently.

The spinster, the widow, and the divorcee may provide the bachelor a glimpse into the life of a group of women whom the Russians labeled as sufferers. These women may be of various walks of life and levels of culture and intelligence but yet have failed somewhere in their social adjustment. They are laughed at, spoken of with derision and often ostracized by society. Each one, therefore, must shift for herself and devises her own solution for her problems.

Edith was a petite, dark, and timid young woman. She was intelligent but not very attractive. She was always overlooked in the dance hall, although she smiled and tried hard to be noticed. Her visits to me as a patient were not frequent, and her complaints were always vague. It was evident what she lacked, and I was ministering more as a psychiatrist than a physician. Once she had an exciting date for the weekend in Akron, Ohio, and as it frequently happened, she came down with a severe upper respiratory infection just a day or two before the expected date. The poor girl was frantic. I felt the opportunity must not be wasted, and so I did all possible and insisted that she keep the date. She returned euphoric and most appreciative of me. Some years later, she married a widower and was happy for a few years until he died.

A young woman off East 105th Street took sick, and I made a house call. I found her on a cot in the dining room. She did not appear ill nor were her complaints serious. Her history also was vague. Her problem was not too difficult to discern as I began to question her about her social life. Finally, as most doctors do, I started advising, telling her to make friends, go out to movies, concerts, etc. She listened and let me go on for a while and then said: "Can't you?" I could advise her no further.

[A778] Mildred tried a different approach altogether. Mildred was an attractive young divorcee in the neighborhood. One morning as I turned the car onto Hough Avenue on my way to downtown, I saw Mildred waiting for the streetcar. Out of courtesy, I invited her to come along. She welcomed the opportunity and lost no time in introducing the subject. On opening the door, she remarked, "Do you have enough space for my Torah?" Without waiting for a response, she continued quoting her mother – "not to give it to the worms." Soon she changed the subject reaching down to her navel. She wanted me to see it. Possibly I could help her since the navel is part of my business. I offered to do what I always do. That same afternoon I found Mildred all dolled up in the waiting room ready for me. Since patients there were a rarity, Mildred was certainly of no interference. Thus the examination was begun. Really, I was far from prudish and what she presented was not unattractive either. But stupidly, I was always afraid of the gold digger, scandal, and infection.

Finally, I managed to get rid of her, only to find that my services impressed her so much that the next day she called by phone: "This is Mildred. When should I come?" "Which Mildred?" I asked. After identification, I told her my office was open till 4 p.m. and that she may come anytime. Within minutes Mildred appeared, and I must confess she did deserve earnest consideration. Instead, I managed to get rid of her with dispatch. This time, Mildred must have sensed my attitude and never returned since.

[A779] Mrs. S.F., whose sister and brother-in-law were close friends of mine, had left her husband in California and came to Cleveland. When I found her in the waiting room, she did appear sick, and I took her into the consultation room at once. She spoke openly and bluntly, "Men can get relief anytime, but women can't. I can't pick men from off the street. You need not fear me. All I need is relief, and you can give it to me." These were the days before the pill, but she was fully equipped with the paraphernalia to prevent pregnancy. Frankly, she was quite an attractive, petite brunette, but my better judgment kept me from becoming involved.

Five days later, her sister and brother-in-law invited me to go with them to Mentor Beach (Medina, Ohio), where I found this poor woman frantic and claiming not to be relieved by the sedative I had prescribed. She almost raped me, but I managed to withstand her temptation and promised to find someone who would help her. I contacted [A815] Mr. Armstrong, a tall, very handsome, energetic, young teacher at the Workmen's Circle School. I promised him a great weekend. Upon returning, I found him a wreck and ready to murder me. He was utterly exhausted and never could satisfy her.

The practice of obstetrics was much more straightforward in our earlier days than at present. Prenatal care was unknown. Delivery was done at home where the natural process of birth was practiced, often without even the whiff of ether to alleviate the pain. It was late one evening when the call came. [A780] Mrs. S., a para IV or V on Greenview and Linn Drive, was in active labor, and her [A716] Dr. Perskey was unavailable. Upon arriving, I found the patient standing at the bedside. The baby's head was already delivered, and the body of the child, including the afterbirth, readily followed. The patient then returned to bed, relieved as if after a good bowel movement. All were happy as befits such an occasion, and I went home.

Returning three days later, the sister of the patient wanted to know what the patient might eat. Since she was quite well, I felt no restriction necessary and began to enumerate what she may have, including eggs. "Well," the sister interrupted, "everything yes, but no eggs!" This absolution and the characteristic motioning with the index finger from right to left is the custom of our people. To argue was superfluous.

It was a beautiful summer Saturday afternoon, and not a patient was in sight when the telephone rang. "I have a patient who is at full term, and I must leave town. All is normal. Would you be interested in handling the case now? If yes, the patient will call you soon." Who could refuse such an opportunity? Fifteen minutes later, a woman called, "Come to see us. If we like you, fine. If not, we will pay you for the visit."

After, office hours I drove up to the patient's home on East Boulevard near Buckeye, a charming neighborhood where the patient's mother met me. The mother was loquacious and talked incessantly until I said I want to see the patient, whose abdomen was twice her size. Innocently, I said: "What a beautiful twin." This remark, I found out later, convinced both ladies of my high competence and ability as an obstetrician, and they used my services in the future. We agreed upon the sum of $75. This was a good fee at the time.

It was not a typical case for, in addition to having multiple pregnancies, she was toxemic. She had a generalized pruritus and a markedly elevated blood pressure. Despite these things, I decided to take the case because should any difficulties arise, I would not be at fault, and the other physician would be charged with neglect. Exactly 24 hours later, just as I was to leave for some important celebration, the call came in that the patient was in labor. I ran over there just in time to deliver two beautiful little girls. All three were well. All of us were happy. Early the next morning, one of the babies developed acute respiratory difficulties. I contacted [A718] Dr. Dembo, and the baby was admitted to St. Lukes, where she was treated with x-rays for enlargement of the thymus and recovered within a few days. Unfortunately, this same child died in Toledo from whooping cough.

This ended the story of a very normal pregnancy. I can't recall who the doctor was, nor his reason for abandoning her at that late hour. I can only come to one conclusion. No competent or responsible man would ever handle such a case the way this man did, and all involved, including myself, were merely fortunate.

A frantic couple came for help. [A781] Mrs. B. was in the second month of gestation, and they hoped that I would abort the girl. I knew the girl and her parents well. I was, therefore, anxious to guide them properly. Fortunately, I found them receptive to reason. My advice, therefore, was to elope, then have me take care of the pregnancy. Upon the birth of the child, I would declare it premature and thus heal all wounds. My advice was well taken. Monday of the next week, they returned home married. To their surprise, the couple was well received, and everybody was happy. Even the natural force cooperated with us. B.'s labor started with profuse hemorrhage due to placenta previa or rather, a low implantation of the placenta. She was rushed to the hospital, where she was delivered vaginally with both patient and infant in good condition. Needless to say, during this great storm, all questions or doubts were forgotten. Although I have not seen these people since that time, I know that three more children joined the family. By this time, some have graduated from professional schools and are responsible citizens themselves. The entire family is happy. I feel compensated by their happiness.

[A782] Miss Cook was late in the first trimester of pregnancy. She wanted me to take care of her and under the following stipulation: 1) I and no one else was to be her obstetrician; 2) I must not take her to St. Ann's Hospital or allow anyone to force her to go there; and 3) she would be called "Mrs." during the hospital stay. I promised to do as she wished and carry her through, provided she would have her teeth put into decent shape. She was otherwise well. A reservation for delivery was then made at Glenville Hospital, and [A719] Dr. M. Gray filled her with a complete set of teeth. For the next three months, everything was well until she came in great excitement, telling me the nurse insists she go to St. Ann's. I quieted her down, assuring her of my promise. Everything went well. She had a fine husky boy, and all carefully observed the guaranteed title of "Mrs."

Three days following the delivery, a Czechoslovakian immigrant appeared at the hospital claiming paternity of this young son. No one could dispute his claim. Upon recovery, there was a furnished apartment prepared for the couple on Euclid Avenue. All bills were paid, including dental, medical, and hospital services, and there was cheer everywhere. Her employer, who was suspected, was, to my mind, a man of honor and decency. I haven't seen any of them again, but I must say he certainly was an upright man to stand by her and see that she was fully cared for. Not only did he provide for all necessities, but he also managed to provide a husband for her as well as a father for the son. This was a man with a soul.

Lander Rd., 35 years ago, was in no man's land, and $5 was a good sum of money. I was relatively young yet and very appreciative of even a night call. My response to the late call was understandable. I found a [A783] young lady quite excited and complaining of abdominal pain. From the history and examination, it was evident that the pains were due to congestion consequent to sporting with her lover. The young lady, ignorant of the actual meaning of "sexual relations," imagined herself pregnant. Naturally, she was assured of this impossibility, for not only was there no penetration, but there also wasn't even any actual contact. Both were relieved, and the pain subsided.

The young man was now very grateful and asked for the bill that, of course, was $5. To this came a very definite and uncompromising answer: "Me pay $3. When I call, you must come." This impression is familiar to many people. They feel that the doctor must respond at all times or circumstances and must submit to the whims of the citizens. Naturally, I felt $3 better than nothing. It also taught me that [A787] Rabbi Akiba was not the only one privileged to transmit the entire Torah within a minute's time.

The lady came in quite disturbed. One of her legs grew heavier than the other, and indeed it was somewhat swollen. It was, therefore, only natural for me to examine the other leg since bilateral swelling is due to conditions entirely different from unilateral swelling. The lady, however, refused to let me see the other leg. I explained the necessity, but she refused to let me have a peek at her other leg. Now I became quite curious and insisted upon seeing her leg as I felt that she was concealing something. Hard-pressed, the lady said, "But doctor, I only washed the one leg."

[A431a] David Perlman was the ex-husband of my cousin [A431] Alta and was now married to Sadie. Both considered themselves close relatives of mine. One summer night, Sadie called, insisting that I must come. David was very sick. She lived six miles away off Kinsman Rd, but I responded, thinking that he must be terribly ill. On opening the door, Sadie met me with these words: "John, I want you to tell me did he give it to me or I give it to him?" My response must have shown well upon my face. I said, "good night," leaving the question unanswered.

Natural instincts are difficult to suppress. A mother brought her pregnant 15-year-old daughter in to see me. The mother was frantic and expected me to abort the young girl. After a lengthy talk, I convinced the mother that she would do best to change neighborhoods after the baby came and raise it as her own. Both mother and daughter saw the wisdom and left my office with this plan in mind. Thus, they planned and arranged for everything. When the child arrived, the young girl suddenly matured and loudly announced that the child was hers and that she wanted to be called "Mother." This young mother was smarter than all of us. She was to face the world and her problems squarely.

Arranged from Above, tragedy and comedy travel together as if in partnership, albeit on opposite sides of the coin. Without this partnership, the life of the medical practitioner, involved as he is in continuously fighting the tragic effects of disease, would be devastating were it not for his ability to adapt the philosophical attitude to help mitigate his frustration. Even in his later years, sudden flashbacks of his long-forgotten experience act as antidotes enabling him to laugh again.

#78 MEDICAL PRACTICE IN THE EARLY 1900s

Most physicians in the earlier part of the present century were in general practice. A very few endowed developed greater knowledge or skills than their colleagues and proclaimed themselves as specialists.

The hospitals were small, poor, and ill-equipped, and patients entered only in extreme conditions. Anesthesia was ether or chloroform, and nitrous oxide anesthesia was just being introduced. Hospitalization insurance was unknown. Mortality, despite good basic nursing, was high and added to the fear of patients entering the hospital.

Surgeons and practitioners alike performed many minor operations at home, with success varying under the circumstances. Since I had some practical experience in administering anesthesia (for more than six years, I anesthetized dogs, cats, guinea pigs, and other animals in the experimental medical lab at Western Reserve), several physicians called on me for help.

The tonsil at that time was believed the culprit causing rheumatic fever, arthritis, and other diseases. Since every adult and child possess at least two tonsils and they are not too difficult to get at, most felt it was their duty to remove them not only when diseased but even prophylactically. Dilatation and curettage is another condition frequently tackled at home.

No doubt, many men had or developed some skills, while others lacked the ability and learned not to indulge. Yet some refused to learn. One, Dr. G., an egotistic man not realizing his inabilities, never learned even to grasp the tonsil properly and seldom recovered a whole tonsil, only bits of it. Somehow, he managed to get them without killing the child. Never have I seen such clumsiness and complete ineptitude. I helped him on a few and was delighted when he stopped calling me. Whether he had any complications afterward, he never told me.

The irony is amusing. For my daughter, [A027] Myrna, I had a well-trained ENT man, my friend [A723] Dr. Samuel Lemel, take out her tonsils. He did a beautiful and clean job, yet three or four hours later, he was forced to leave an office full of patients and run to Mt. Sinai to control her hemorrhage. All I can say is, "the dummy gets the prize."

Dr. V., a frustrated surgeon, engaged me to help him. This man was more able but very negligent and unhygienic. He was poorly equipped. Twice he called me, and each time behaved the same way. After the child was anesthetized and just after he started to work, he would leave the table and run to speak to the parents about his great deed, leaving the child with a mouth full of blood and gurgling. He repeated this two or three times. These are great moments for enjoyment for the anesthetist. Finally, with the operation over, I was thinking about how to avoid his calling me again. When he asked how much my services cost, I asked for $25, hoping this would be so high that he'll never call me again. He paid me $10, and it worked.

Dr. R., whose reputation was unsavory, asked for my services for a D&C. That was the only one I performed as I did not care to be involved in possible abortions. Again, I made my price high. He never called after that.

Substituting for other doctors is not an easy matter. One must be careful not to displease the patients for fear of ruining his practice. At the same time, one must not go overboard so as not to entice them to come to you, thus stealing his patients, a complaint frequently charged against some colleagues. The most difficult thing is to carry on in the treatments as outlined by the doctor you displace.

Dr. [A724] Peggy E., who practiced in northeast Cleveland in an industrial area with a high Slavish population and knew that I was eager to move my office, invited me to spend a Wednesday afternoon in her office. The intention was to sell her lucrative practice to me. Frankly, I found it extremely profitable. I have never seen such a flow of patients from all parts of the city though she was in no way the known physician in town. Whether she had an x-ray machine or an electrocardiograph was not clear. At any rate, it did not require much intelligence to find the secrets. Practically every patient came for a "shot" of vitamins or had some similar type of case. No history or examination was required, and I took in over $70 in cash that afternoon. What Peggy netted for using the diathermy and quartz lamps, and the amount collected or charged was not known. Needless to say, I felt the office was not for me as I could not handle such an affair.

In early childhood [A011] Mother used to tell us stories about ghosts, even though she, herself, never believed in them. Later I read about ghosts in Shakespeare dramas. Still, I never saw them until one afternoon about 1940 when on entering my office, I found some eight or 10 patients whose extreme pallor and depressed appearance made me make such a diagnosis.

My diagnosis was soon verified. As I called them in, each one turned out to be an addict. The same druggist whom I never knew referred all of them to me. I resolved quickly that I couldn't heal them and referred them all to the Metropolitan Hospital, then known as the City Hospital for care. One of these patients came in with her husband. For some reason, I thought I could conceivably help her. I began to treat her, hoping to get the husband's cooperation. I wrote to the narcotic division asking for guidance. Within two weeks came a large amount of literature from the Chicago office telling me all the rules and left the rest for my discretion. In the meantime, I found the husband's cooperation lacking. After that, I discontinued handling her. Thus, my venture into rehabilitation ended as abruptly as it began.

I learned later that Dr. B., who had treated these addicts, left the state precipitously, probably to escape prosecution. The druggist then referred them to me.

#79 A DAY IN MY MEDICAL PRACTICE

Responding to an early morning call, I found the patient, [A785] Mrs. D. Williams, drunk, lying on the floor and unable to get up because of an injury to her leg. The foot was turned back almost perpendicularly to the leg. Without much ado, I seized the foot and replaced it to its proper position. An x-ray verified this. Ignorance is bliss!

A traveler passing through Cleveland was seized with diarrhea, and I had him admitted to Mt. Sinai Hospital, which was then still relatively small. By error, the patient received a stiff dose of a drug with a name similar to but rather than Trop (camphor-paregoric), the intended drug. The error was discovered immediately after the drug was administered. The patient was watched carefully through the night by the nurse, who felt guilty. Nothing unusual happened, but the patient was incredibly pleased with the exceptional attention given. I am certain he is probably still praising the hospital, nurses, and me for the care given to him in Cleveland.

The evening was pleasant, it being summer, and my date, [A817] Grace White, came along for the call at 36th and Payne. It was then still a respectable neighborhood, and there was as yet no fear of attack by hoodlums.

On entering the home, I found the lady of the house and the boarder playing cards. Both were drunk and motioned, indicating to me where the patient was. Upon entering the bedroom, I found the patient dead drunk and unable to sit or lie quietly. He just kept rolling. The stench was terrific, and I became nauseated. Since this was in the pre-hospitalization insurance era, there were plenty of beds available, and all hospitals granted us privileges. Hence, I sent the man to Charity Hospital and managed to leave the house without vomiting, but I felt filthy and rushed to the nearest gas station to wash. All evening long, I continued to wash myself every time I passed a gas station, though Grace assured me that I was pristine clean.

#80 [A720] DR. SANFORD ROSEN'S CASE

When covering the practice of Dr. Sanford Rosen, I was summoned one morning to deliver one of his patients at home on the West Side of the city of Cleveland.

Arriving, I found a young Italian woman in active labor. Her young husband and parents were also there. The last three seemed even more nervous than the patient, mainly because they knew me not and could not trust me.

The patient was laboring well with intense pain, yet accomplished little, possibly also because of her apprehension. The parents and husband reacted almost violently to her every scream. They paced the floor, wrung their hands, and prayed. They also chattered in Italian, which I could not understand.

By afternoon the patient looked tired and was not progressing. It looked like she would need special help, and I suggested hospitalization. My suggestion was not accepted. Instead, the husband began calling doctors who seemed Italian to him, asking them for help. What he told them I don't know, but no one volunteered. I presumed he said to them that I was in the home, and they naturally refused to come. I was frightened to stay there any longer yet could not leave the patient unattended. Again, I asked for permission to hospitalize the patient. Finally, at about 4 or 5 p.m., the husband consented. The patient was now transported to City Hospital, where she normally delivered by the next morning. Then I had my first good laugh. I never even asked for any remuneration for my services. Even now, as I write this probably 40 or more years later, I still laugh.

#81 [A722] DR. FOXY, THE ABORTIONIST

Bound by the Hippocratic Oath, the physician must never enter into deals shady in character or into collusions with men of criminal intent. Nevertheless, the doctor, hard-pressed by the frantic, illegitimately pregnant patient, frequently feels compelled to yield to her pleas and refers her to the abortionist even at the risk of being accused of being an accomplice. Though the physician holds the abortionist in contempt and shuns him as an associate or colleague, he usually knows little of these men's characters or their activities. He is, therefore, utterly ignorant of the dangers to which he exposes his patient.

Typifying the abortionist, Dr. Foxy, so-named because of his crafty behavior and sharp, piercing eyes, was my neighbor, and for years we were on friendly terms. He always deplored the fact that doctors refused to recognize him as a physician and envied me because I was able to do as I pleased and sleep nights quite peacefully. He tried to induce me to join his activities, assuring me with complete safety. The room would be dark. A mask could cover my face, and the patient was fully anesthetized. I wouldn't even have to utter a word. Just come in, perform a dilatation and curettage (D&C) and leave.

The lure of gold always serves as a snare of entanglement from which there is no escape. Once entangled, one is forced into deeds never earlier conceived. Before long, one finds himself in a ring and the underworld. Having no recourse to the hospital nor training or facilities to meet complications, the abortionist must abandon his victim and leave her to fate. Many of them die or are disposed of in various ways, including the methods employed by Dr. Harvey Lautringer, as the New York Times of May 21, 1964, reported.

The baby black market constitutes a lucrative by-product of the abortionist's business. Thus, a young woman had already sold one infant and was now pregnant with a second. She was under the auspices of the ring, fully cared for during the entire period of gestation, and was to be transported to California for delivery and disposition of the newborn child. The baby market may even afford the abortionist the appearance of a benefactor. The victim needs only to pay the immediate expenses involved. The abortionist provides room and board, nursing care, delivery, and disposition of the newborn, as the following case history illustrates.

Twenty-four hours following an anonymous call to ascertain whether I do home births, Mrs. Foxy called on Jul 20, 1935, saying that Dr. Foxy had a 23-year-old illegitimately pregnant girl who was at term and whom he was unable to deliver because of illness. Furthermore, the poor woman had only $40. I was still young and idealistic and it was natural to volunteer. Mrs. Foxy was happy and sent the patient to my office that same afternoon. Carrying all her belongings in a suitcase, the patient appeared at 2:00 p.m. She told me that she lived with people on the West Side of the city and that afterward, a nurse would take care of her. I found her in good physical condition and at term. She left with instructions to notify me when labor set in. On July 25th, I visited her at home and found everything well.

At 8 a.m. on August 2, I was notified that the patient had been in labor since 4 a.m. I saw her within the hour. She was in active labor and seemed to progress well. However, by noon when she slowed up, all progress had stopped, and she was growing weak. I felt that help was indicated, but she objected to any advice without consulting Dr. Foxy or the nurse. I thought it too risky to waste time. Hence, I called on my colleague, a young obstetrician. The latter responded readily. The patient was anesthetized, and a healthy baby girl was delivered. The mother was also in good condition, but the obstetrician, finding the uterus not well contracted, sent me to a somewhat distant supply house for pituitrin. At the same time, he remained at the scene to massage the uterus.

While we were busy delivering the patient, a young woman appeared dressed in white like a nurse. We were too occupied to bother with her, but when I returned from the drug house, she was no longer there. The pituitrin was now administered, and the obstetrician left with my promise that I would pay him as soon as I received my money. Next, I instilled silver nitrate into the baby's eyes. The patient now seemed well. I left orders for the care of both patients with the landlady and left for the office. However, upon my return late that evening, I found none of the orders had been carried out. I was quite upset, but the landlady promised better care later. The next morning, I still found both patients uncleaned since the delivery. This time, I spoke in no uncertain terms, and my orders were respected from then on. On August 5, 1935, I made out the birth certificate and mailed it to the Bureau of Vital Statistics. A day or two later, I was paid the $40 with the assurance that no more had been given to Dr. Foxy. Of my sum, I gave the obstetrician $15 for his services, to which he gracefully consented.

Since the delivery of the baby, an abrupt change took place in the atmosphere about me. I wasn't quite aware of what was going on, but statements were made, and puzzling questions were thrown at me. Finally, Dr. Foxy wanted to know why I reported the birth and asked me to leave the case. Now, of course, I realized that I had foiled his business and promised to quit as soon as I could arrange for both patients' proper disposition. The mother now promised to leave for home on August 10. That morning, however, she broke down and told me the following story.

She was referred to Dr. Foxy by one of my colleagues during her sixth month of pregnancy. No abortion was now possible. She paid $200 to Dr. Foxy for the room, board, and nursing care. The nurse was to "do away with the baby." What that meant, she did not know. When the nurse saw the obstetrician watching the patient, she thought he was guarding her against the nurse. She was thus much frightened and did not carry out her mission. The next day she was still willing to do so provided the mother came along. Since I had been given fictitious names, it was thought that the mother would never be traced. The mother, however, was reluctant to yield, and the plan collapsed.

A new birth certificate was now made out and mailed to the authorities. All concerned were now warned against any foul play. I attempted to have Dr. Foxy return the $200, but the mother and her brother were so afraid of exposure that this demand was dropped. Mother and baby were later admitted to the retreat of the Jewish Social Service on August 16.

Ten years later, I had the occasion to see the mother. She appeared gay, well-groomed, and wearing a fur coat. Both of us pretended not to know each other.

#82 THE STUPID PRIEST

The priest, as the spiritual leader, and the physician as the healer often fail in their efforts since higher training and education do not replace common sense. The case of [A784] Mrs. Frau Pudlimer illustrates this most vividly. Mrs. Pudlimer, an asthmatic for years, was a simple, kind, and humble woman and would have been happy with life if not for the numerous hysterical symptoms that plagued her. The Pudlimers lived next to my office. They were pleased with each other and quite compatible. Her Catholicism presumably had no difficulties with his Protestantism. The husband was always sympathetic and gentle with her.

In the summer of 1934, she began to have attacks of pain that were diagnosed as gallstones proven by x-ray. I advised operation and referred her to [A717] Dr. Gibson, a general surgeon at Lakeside Hospital. As customary, I was notified of her admission, but shortly afterward, I learned that because she had become highly frantic and had undue anxiety, she was discharged from the hospital just some 10 minutes after admission. This procedure repeated itself three to four times though she experienced most agonizing pain. Psychiatric care was not within her reach. Besides, psychiatry was not yet in vogue or as popular as it is today. Finally, after suffering a full weekend of agonizing pain without any relief, she submitted to surgery and returned home well.

The recovery apparently had a significant effect on her psyche, and she made the following confession to me. As a Catholic and married to a Protestant without the benefit of the church, she appealed to the priest for dispensation for her sin before submitting to surgery. The latter, however, not only refused her request but actually demanded that she leave her husband and threatened her with death. In desperation, she countered: "You are not a father. No father would make one leave the man she loves." She was convinced that she would not recover without his blessing. No wonder she was so frantic.

Mrs. Pudlimer died about two years later during one of her asthmatic attacks. I am not prepared to say how much the priest contributed to her agonies and death. Still, I do say that any of the above professionals devoid of kindness, sympathy, or plain horse sense would be of greater credit when out of the profession.

#83 HYPOGLYCEMIA

Recently, [A711] Dr. Saul Genuth, an internist at Mt. Sinai Hospital, in discerning a case of hypoglycemia, reminded me of a situation I observed and helped to treat when I was about ten years old and living in Knyazhe.

Fasting on Yom Kippur day was obligatory. Even the Epicurus (a philosophy taught to attain the happy, tranquil life, with peace and freedom from fear together with the absence of pain, achieved by living a self-sufficient life surrounded by friends) still respectful of His all-discerning eye above, and followed the dictum of the day. Fainting, due to the prolonged fasting, was, therefore, a frequent experience during that day. But fainting on Simchat Torah was unheard of and was therefore of grave significance.

Simchat Torah was a holiday unique in its importance and its form of celebration. While solemnity and prayer celebrated most holidays, unusual pageantry, hilarity, and gaiety marked this one. All but the incapacitated Jews in town participated. All of us gathered in the Bet Hamidrash[110] for the occasion. We had but one synagogue in the town, which served not only as the house of prayer but also as the community house for all purposes.

All men and women, including infants and children, gathered in the one large room that constituted our sanctuary. People were standing on tables, benches, and even on windowsills. But a narrow circular path was left about the periphery for the procession.

[A202] Yankel Weinstein, the Shamash,[111] took his position at the ark and with a sharp, strong-carrying voice, began to summon the various congregants to honor the Torah:

Rise Reb Chaim B'reb Noah to honor the Torah!

Rise Reb Shmuel B'reb Ben Zion to honor the Torah!

Rise Reb Yakov B'reb Shuel to honor the Torah!

As a democratic society, every male, regardless of age, was given the equal right and privilege to march. Since we had but three scrolls in our possession, the procession led by [A197] Rabbi Yankel, or better known as Yankel, the shochet, was carried on until late at night.

As the procession passed, everyone, even every child, knew exactly what to say and what to wish to each marcher. These kids knew who was rich and who was poor, who was well and who was ill, whose daughter was over age, and whose wife was barren. Thus, the procession progressed marked with great hilarity and enthusiasm, though without a morsel of food or a drop to drink until late at night when they left for home only to return the next morning for a repeat performance, which lasted until about 2 p.m.

As one can discern, the Reformation had not yet reached our Knyazhe. Our adult males were still orthodox in their beliefs. As they always abstained from consuming any food before the morning

---

[110] A school where Jews, especially in eastern Europe, study the Bible, the Talmud, and later Hebrew literature.

[111] A person who assists in the running of a synagogue or its religious services, especially the reading of the Torah.

hakafot (walking or dancing around a specific object, generally in a religious setting) were over, the adults had fasted for 16-18 hours. They were now ready to partake in the grand march marked by singing, dancing, and the gaiety that had been anticipated all through the year.

The walk went on from home to home where all were fed prakes (stuffed cabbage)[112], taiglach (triangular dough baked in honey), gefilte fish, honey cake, strudel, jelly wine, vodka, and other goodies. Just how much one consumed of either drinks or the food was a matter of one's tolerance and capacity, but until this time, never had anyone been stricken ill. Then [A326] Chaim Dudnik was discovered perched against a wagon in front of [A005] Sarah Faiga Kalman's house, oblivious to the entire world.

It was soon evident that this was not drunkenness but a deep coma. Chaim was then carried home and put to bed with all the marchers following. There was neither a doctor nor a feldsher available in our town. Every Jew, as is well known, knows something about medicine. Those who gathered suggested various remedies, and some of them actually were put to use. Thus, his ears were pulled, and his nose pinched. He was pierced with needles and pulled by the tongue, but there was no response.

Now came my turn. Someone suggested horse dung. As an active participant in all events and activities in town, I was promptly dispatched to fetch some fresh horse manure, an easy task. Knyazhe lacked many things, but horse dung was available everywhere and aplenty. Within minutes I returned with an abundant supply of the new panacea. This was now squeezed, and the juice poured into the victim's mouth. We never really learned just how Chaim liked it. Suffice to say that it proved as disappointing as all previous measures. Father, recalling that Chaim had suffered a similar episode once before, now persuaded all to leave while he remained at the victim's bedside nursing him through the night. By morning he regained consciousness and soon returned to his duties as businessman and manager of the Graf's estate.

Vicissitudes in life separated us until the Russian Revolution, and the pogroms that followed forced Chaim and his family to emigrate to the United States.

We know that prolonged starvation will produce hypoglycemia (low blood sugar) with resulting unconsciousness. We also know that alcohol may intensify the hypoglycemia and thus lead to deep coma. Both criteria were present in this case. Chaim had fasted for at least 16 hours, then consumed some wine and possibly vodka along with some food.

The discussion of hypoglycemia by Dr. Genuth brought this entire picture to my mind.

---

[112] In Europe, it's commonly stuffed with ground beef, pork (for non-Jews) or lamb, grains like rice or barley, and seasoned with onions, garlic, paprika and cumin. The cabbage rolls aren't just about the filling; the tomato sauce is equally as important. With the addition of pickled vegetables and some sugar, the sauce can be sweet-and-sour, or with more tomatoes and herbs the sauce can be savory. The origins can be traced across Europe, Russia, the Balkans, and as far east as Iran and Northern China. https://www.myjewishlearning.com/the-nosher/8-comforting-stuffed-cabbage-recipes-for-sukkot/

#84 [A818] MRS. HALPERIN AND THE ITINERANT CANTOR

To err is human. That is correct. But that God is just and perfect is questionable. Eve was the first to defy God's injustice. She ate the apple, thereby breaking His monopolistic power. She paid heavily for her action, but thankfully, her knowledge became available to all humanity.

God Himself admitted his mistake when he acknowledged that man whom He created was wicked and sought to destroy him.

Abraham, the great advocate, argued against God's injustice. Though he lost his case, Abraham succeeded in rescuing Lot and his family before Sodom and Gomorrah were destroyed.

Other men also found fault with God's rule. In our day, [A226] Rebbe Lech from [C07] Berdichev had his annual arguments with God.

One of the great injustices committed was His granting a few selfish people most of the wealth of the world and leaving little to the vast mass of people who must live in poverty and degradation. Even the Jews, whom He chose as His favorite, He repeatedly surrendered them into the hands of others to be tortured and murdered.

Even in the endowments of personal characteristics, He is unjust. Only a few people are endowed with the greatest gifts of scholarship, beauty, grace, and skills. The rest are left ugly and unattractive.

I recall, for instance, that [A250] Zeidel Rovner, the famous Russian cantor, was to conduct services on a specific weekend at the "Hacker Shul" in the city of [C14] Kishinev in 1909. I was then a young boy and apprenticed to a [A246] Mr. Shankman, a mechanic, on a salary of 5 rubles for the year without room or board. In my hometown, there was no cantor, just a plain "bal-tfile," a (lay) prayer leader. My curiosity and desire were, therefore, fired immediately. The price of admission was no problem. The height of the fence, on the other hand, was of much concern. With a friend's help, I scaled the fence and ripped the seat of my pants. I did hear Mr. Rovner and his choir sing.

Years later, I had the occasion to meet a New York itinerant cantor to whom my friend, Mrs. Halperin, introduced me. For two months, this cantor has been traveling through the province from New York to Cleveland, stopping at the various Jewish communities where he displayed his talents. He finally landed in Cleveland. Nowhere was anyone particularly interested in him or his abilities. No one paid any attention to him nor offered him as much as a decent bed or meal. There was no special committee waiting for him either. Only Mrs. Halperin, the messenger of goodwill, was there to extend her services to this beloved guest. Mrs. Halperin was the familiar Jewish mother, now extinct, of our former generation. She was a woman rich not in dollars but spirit. Her home and children were her empire. She was happy and content and yearned to share her happiness with those less fortunate than herself, of whom there was quite an abundance in our Jewish neighborhoods. She was the Peoples Relief, an unorganized organization to collect whatever pennies were available for the Jewish victims of the pogroms that followed the Revolution in Russia. She was the Bikur Cholim, a group that provided actual help as well as visiting the sick and helped arrange dowries for poor orphaned Jewish maidens. And of course, she was the Welcome the Stranger, a precious Jewish tradition.

That the cantor should find his way to Mrs. Halperin was, therefore, not accidental. Her doors were wide open, especially for a cleric, such a respected guest. All comforts she could provide were offered to him, yet he seemed uncomfortable and indisposed. This made her think of me, her doctor and friend, and neighbor on North Blvd. She knew me for years during my school days and had the utmost faith in me as a friend and doctor. She knew that I would restore her guest to full strength readily and efficiently.

My response was prompt, as was expected. The cantor indeed appeared somewhat ill and indisposed yet insisted on being left alone and was in no need of medical care. Gradually his opposition was overcome so that I could take his temperature, pulse, respiration, and blood pressure. But when it came to the heart, he just wouldn't let me open his shirt, assuring me that he was quite well. The doctor gets accustomed to this type of character and, in time, becomes bold, more or less forcing his way. On opening the shirt, there was such an unusually significant overabundance of lice that further search was unnecessary. The diagnosis now was evident, and so was the treatment. I told Mrs. Halperin to merely dunk the cantor in a tub of hot water and cook him together with all his clothes and lice. But for Mrs. Halperin to perform the act was more than formidable. She pondered her problem all through the night, and early next morning began her campaign of collection. Within a few hours, she had enough money collected to dispatch the poor cantor to his family in time for the Sabbath.

"You sure were funny, both [A721] Dr. Howard Gans and you." This was [A657a] Hanna Gressel talking to me just days or possibly weeks after [A658] Carmi, her son, had made a good recovery from his recent operation and returned home in excellent condition.

These records were of interest to me. It just so happened that I considered my bit of service excellent, and I was to commend myself for the accomplishment when Hanna delivered her thanks. It was in response to this that I did preserve a partial record of Carmi's case.

Carmi was a month premature at birth, which is usually of no consequence, but he was not too well in early childhood. He suffered frequent upper respiratory infections with fever, nasal congestion, and swollen glands. At two years of age, nasal polyps were removed due to nosebleeds. At three years of age, he had a tonsillectomy. He also had ear infections recurrently, which presented in addition to chickenpox, measles, and mumps.

Beginning on May 11, 1938, Carmi developed episodes of abdominal pain with tenderness over McBurney's point[113] but had no history of vomiting, nausea, nor abdominal rigidity. The urine was normal. It was still the era before antibiotics. The diagnosis of chronic appendicitis was still acceptable and entertained here to some extent, but not entirely. In February and May 1940, he had the same complaints with some findings and slight fever. In April 1941, he again presented with the same findings, but to a much greater degree. This time, it was accompanied by a high fever (102.6°), which lasted for several days. He also developed diarrhea. This time sulfa was prescribed, and mesenteric adenitis, i.e., glandular fever, was entertained. [A721] Dr. Howard Gans was consulted and advised hospitalization and observation to rule out appendicitis. The condition did not improve. Dr. Gans then explained to the mother that he must explore the son immediately to avoid the 1% of cases that rupture, making the operation too risky to do. The operation, performed on April 30, 1941, showed the appendix to be normal. Carmi returned to his room and, within a few days, was discharged, recovered, and in good condition.

This story has an addendum.[114] Years later, when cousin [A672] Donald Shapiro visited Carmi in Israel, the two had a great time. Carmi convinced Donald that he wasn't even sick at the time. He only pretended and was able to put it over on the doctor.

Donald, in turn, was also convinced that his troubles in 1946 were psychosomatic and not due to blood disease. My records, however, were incontestable. I am, however, pleased that the

---

[113] The name given to the point over the right side of the abdomen located one-third of the distance from the anterior superior iliac spine to the umbilicus (navel). This point roughly corresponds to the most common location of the base of the appendix where it attaches to the cecum.

[114] Editor's note: Many stories have an aftermath. Carmi's malingering according to him was induced by a borderline psychotic grade schoolteacher who had falsely accused him of laughing out loud to something that [A672] Don Shapiro had said. Carmi said that [A721] Dr Gans who had recently immigrated to the USA was chosen to perform the surgery as his fees were less costly than the more established surgeons. When Dr. Gans visited Israel in 1968, he told Mom and Dad that Carmi's operation gave him the academic acceptance in the USA due to Carmi's malformed appendix.

treatment Donald received was excellent so that no competent hematologist can find any trace of his troubles.

That is a feather in my cap.

Follow-up 1: Cousin [A660] Macky Gressel (now Mike) wrote that his brother [A658] Carmi passed away just as the coronavirus pandemic swept across the world in the spring of 2020. Although Carmi, his two brothers [A659] Jonathan and [A660] Macky, and sister [A661] Beth were all born in the US, they and their parents, [A657] Louis and Chanah Gressel, made aliyah about 1950, shortly after Israel's founding. Carmi left first with several Brudno cousins. The remaining family followed several months later. At Carmi's eulogy, Macky related that when Carmi was but five or six years old, he declared: "I want to be a farmer in Palestine." That was before World War II had ended and the world learned of the Holocaust tragedy. That also predates John's story about Carmi by about five years.

Some 45 years later, when Lou and Chana died, a newspaper clipping dated September 14, 1945, from The Cleveland Jewish Center Bulletin was found in their belongings. Its title was "A Youth's Reaction,", and penned in Carmi's unique style, was believed to be his.

> Dear Ma and Dad:
>
> Today we received news of the end of the war. Somehow, I couldn't make myself rise to the occasion and rejoice. Nothing seemed real, for I didn't feel that my war was over. Instead I felt that a [missing words] which advanced me many years, and I was forced to make up my mind as to the course my life would take. I was thinking that the right to rejoice belongs only to the parents whose sons were not killed. I fear that the war of pounding the sword to the plowshare is greater and longer, but will never reach such a decisive victory. It will put more innocent people in misery. This has been a war against my own people to whom I shall give the better portion of my life. I hope that my feelings are not forced ones which I might say in a serious moment. These are my honest thoughts.
>
> Your loving son

Macky also remembers that Carmi was most creative and recently finally solved a fundamental problem that had long stumped the greatest mathematicians and engineers in the world of electronic cryptography: how to generate perfect random numbers. Perfect random numbers are the basis for all of today's modern cryptography systems. For 30 years, Carmi labored on the problem until he solved it, also implementing a system based upon this generator. His meticulous software architecture planning and creative design minimized to a small volume a hardware system that encrypts huge messages and deciphers them reliably as well as virtually error-free. Indeed, messages once encoded cannot be hacked by current computation systems nor by those in the foreseeable future.

Just one year before his death (2019), Carmi presented the system at an International Electronic Cryptography conference at the Technion in Haifa. Three weeks before his death at age 89, Carmi was granted his latest patent.

Follow-up 2: Macky also relates that Carmi contracted scarlet fever in 1946. [A026] Dr John nailed the pink quarantine sign on our front door. Antibiotics at that time were scarce and reserved for the armed services. Lou, however, was able to secure the medicine Carmi needed.

Some fours later, Dr. John diagnosed sister Beth as suffering from a ruptured appendix, which was operated on and treated successfully.

In April 1994, [A660] Mackie suffered horrible abdominal pains while at work. The company physician had him hospitalized immediately. An appendectomy was performed, which took 20 minutes longer because the inflamed appendix was on the backside of the intestine. The two surgeons who did the operations wrote academic papers on the case.

If genetic predisposition has anything to do with appendectomies, then one might muse that indeed Carmi was sick. Carmi had a very high pain threshold. That and his self-medication tendencies coupled with anti-narcissism in which good health took second place to work was the root of many problems that afflicted him throughout his life.

Philosophies and Medicine

#86 PROFESSOR [A708] CORLTON JAERSON

Professor Corlton Jaerson, Western Kentucky University, Bowling Green, KY 42101

Dear Professor Jaerson:

My flu experience is limited to my observation in the army. Inducted on May 25, 1917, I was given the basic infantry training and shifted to the base hospital at Camp Gordon, GA, where I served as orderly until February 1918, when I was discharged, enabling me to enter the sophomore class of college.

On entering the ward early Monday morning, I beheld a scene the kind of which I never saw again, although I practiced as a general practitioner in Cleveland for 45 years. I was there on the staff of a large hospital and had visited others as well.

There was one other orderly and two nurses with me. I don't recall if there were any others nor if any instructions were given. The ward held three rows of beds, 12 in each row, two rows inside, and one on the porch.

Upon entering the ward, one's attention was immediately drawn to about half a dozen beds on the far left-hand side. They had sideboards roped across to prevent the patients, who were raving mad in delirium, from getting out of bed. Further, the patients had their arms tied and held by sheets to the bed. Their teeth were as black as charcoal.

Instinctively I knew what to do. Apparently, this was genetically transferred to me. My [A010] grandmother, illiterate and unschooled, practiced midwifery gratis for many years in her town in Russia. Her daughter-in-law, my [A011] mother, though extremely busy running a home with five children, a sewing establishment as well as a small dry goods business which she transported to the bazaar in town as well as to the neighboring town, served as the general practitioner, also gratis. She never refused help to anyone in need. She somehow did learn to read but was otherwise unschooled.

These few delirious soldiers received my utmost attention. There were no effective drugs then, and intravenous fluids were unknown. The army, however, did supply water and plenty of linens. Sponges and linens were frequently changed and with gratifying results.

I do not know what the mortality rate in the camp was. It must have been great as we soon became accustomed to the clatter caused by the wheeling of corpses along the boardwalk to the morgue. But our boys here did quite well. One New York boy was smart enough to volunteer for kitchen duty so as to stay with us until he regained his strength. I am still sorry that I failed to communicate with him.

One other soldier was a southern boy whose mother was stricken by flu on her way to camp and died en route. The youngster cried, calling her continually. He suffered from marked diarrhea, was weak, and moaned all the time. We, therefore, named him Sadie. I doubt whether any patient in the world ever received better nursing care or a more frequent change of linens. We were happy with his recovery and very proud of our accomplishments.

From what I learned on returning home in February 1918 was that mortality was incredibly high in the city. All, including the doctors, were in a panic. The medical armamentarium was still weak. The hospitals were quickly filled. The number overwhelmed the doctors. All that the doctor could advise was isolation, which the people took for abandonment. [A023] Tobie, my sister, failed to heed this advice and nursed mother who recovered and lived for many years with us. I am certain other mothers survived under similar circumstances.

At present, our armamentarium is greatly enlarged. We have various intravenous fluids as well as numerous potent drugs, but we are creating physicians' assistants instead of physicians, and the art of nursing has been allowed to deteriorate. Just how we'll handle another pandemic flu remains to be seen.

#87 [A820] PARACELSUS (PHILIPPUS AUREOLUS THEOPHRASTUS BOMBASTUS VON HOHENHEIM)

He called himself Paracelsus in contempt of Celsus and other authors dead for thousands of years and whose medical texts were still in use in the 1500s.

He was born in Zurich in 1493 and died in Salzburg at age 42 in 1541. He challenged all academics and fought the oldest traditions in medicine. He had many theories, some contradictory, most outrageous. He was Rabelaisian, picturesque, cold, drank with students, ran after women, and traveled much. He was considered a quack in science but was not. He was a profound genius. He was a practical man. He was a superb diagnostician. He preached diagnosis, felt that the doctor must give the direct application of self. "He broke with the tradition by which the physician was a learned academic who read out of an old book, and the patient was in the hands of the assistant who carried out orders."

"There can be no surgeon who is not also a physician." "Where the physician is not also a surgeon, he is an idol that is nothing but a painted monkey."

For his ideas, he encountered many enemies. He was brought to Basel in 1527, where he cured the infected leg of the printer Johann Frobenius, which other doctors had wanted to amputate. His procedure was a great triumph. Iconoclastic ideas in medicine came cheek by jowl during the Reformation in 1517. The University of Basel had a democratic tradition. Paracelsus, therefore, was allowed to teach the Frobenius printed book by Erasmus and other liberals.

In 1543, three books appeared which changed Europe: 1) *The Anatomical Drawings of Andreas Vesalius*; 2) *Translation of Greek Mathematics and Physics of Archimedes*; 3) *On the Revolutions of the Heavenly Spheres* by Nicolaus Copernicus.

#88 THE INSURANCE MONSTER

Letter in response to the article in The Cleveland Physician by Dr. Wm. E. Forsythe, Academy of Medicine, Cleveland, OH.

Dear Dr. Forsythe:

I read your letter and brochure attentively, and I am giving you my comments, although you asked for none. I hope you'll take the time to decipher my handwriting and that many of our members will also send you their comments.

The utilization and tissue committees must not be placed in the same category. The Tissue Committee deals with specific items, is limited in scope, and affects but a small group of men, the surgeons, within the hospitals only. The Utilization Committee, on the other hand, is of much greater scope. It includes every physician in the hospital and is transmitting information to clerks within and outside the hospital, all of whom may wield tremendous power over every physician in the hospital. It is more of a spying agency sponsored by outside forces that have the audacity to persuade the doctor to do the dirty work for them. It is remarkable how we physicians are trapped and talk the way those outside forces wish us to.

Insurance is sold as protection when needed, but with the hope that it will never be used. The number of hospital beds is kept to a minimum for fear that the greater use of the beds will break the insurance companies. Attempts are now made to curtail further the use of the beds by instituting measures fit for the police station. Even now, a battery of officials and clerks rule us. One cannot admit a patient unless the admitting clerk or resident approves the diagnosis. Not very long ago, I was forced to recite by phone to the superintendent the complete differential diagnosis before he graciously consented to give me a bed. Then to ascertain the emergency, he checked the same with the resident on service.

Do we need additional supervision to tell us what tests to use and how long to keep patients in the hospital?

Are all obstetrical cases able to leave within five days? Suppose one is hysterical or just dainty or is blessed with two or three little ones and no mother or nurse at home and needs an extra 2-3 days for recuperation?

What about the aged or debilitated patient who cannot be subjected to assembly line handling or the single man or woman who has no home to go to and must remain for an extra two days until strength is regained so that they can navigate on their own?

Hospitals differ in equipment and cannot work the patient up as readily as the better-equipped hospitals. Doctors also differ in acumen. Not all are [A832] Paul Dudley Whites.[115]

What will the academy do to protect us against this monster? Hire more advocates? Of what use are our highly trained men if they are to be left to the mercy of insurance companies, their clerks

---

[115] White (1886-1973) was an American physician, who was one of the leading cardiologists of his day. He was a prominent advocate of preventive medicine.

who follow elaborate charts, and who never deal or come in contact with human ailments or emotion?

With the deepest respect, I am

John Robboy, MD

#89 PREJUDICE IN MEDICINE

The student of medicine before, during, and since my days had to face not only language and financial difficulties but also great hatred and prejudices. The latter, in particular, was directed at the Jew.

Most physicians of my day were either immigrants or sons of immigrants whose fathers had just risen from the peddler stage. These men could ill afford elaborate well-equipped offices with nurses and receptionists. Some did not even consider the white coat of any importance, and most of them, including myself, engaged in general practice. However, it was less financially remunerative than the other specialties of which surgery was the most glamorous as it is to date. General practice, however, offered its own forms of satisfaction due to its unusual variety, challenges, and experiences that soften or sweeten the many frequently unpleasant tasks. It is the most trying discipline on the doctor's energy and time. Unless one loves children and is tolerant of people in general, the aged in particular, he should avoid this discipline. It is not for the dowdy who is afraid of the cockroach or of soiling his finger on the dirty diaper.

During my early days, people generally were less affluent than nowadays, and very few had ready conveyances to carry them to the doctor's office or hospital. Hospitalization insurance was yet unknown. Hospitalization was limited to the very sick. X-rays and laboratory procedures were still extremely limited. Home visits were most common. The practice was, therefore, challenging, but not inferior and sometimes even superior to that of the present day. The doctor simply resorted to greater observation and evaluation of the signs and symptoms encountered. This favored warmth, respect, and intimacy that were mutually sustaining. It is this warmth, kindness, sympathy, and intimacy that people long for today.

As far as I was concerned, it was the strength of will and perseverance that helped me to overcome all obstacles and prejudices to reach the goal. I have not attained any particular distinction, but I can say happily that I kept abreast of my colleagues all through my years. I have given more succor and comfort to many thousands of men, women, and children than has many a high-powered man, while at the same time, I did not compromise myself in any way. I lived up to the ethical standards of the profession and held membership in national and local organizations, including the Cleveland Medical Library. I was on the staff of the pediatric department at Mt. Sinai and served as a clinician all through my practice. (Many years later, cousin [A690] Sidney Wolpaw became the CEO, which also was during the 1965-1966 time when [A031] Stanley interned there.) As a result, I am now at peace with myself.

Medical practice is as old as is humanity. Eve was born with the aid of anesthesia and surgery. Even the engineer or sociologist made use of it in forming her into a beautiful and attractive mate and companion. Yet no significant progress followed for over the many thousands of years since.

Both the doctor as well as his medicine and practice are the by-products of man, time, and circumstances. The doctor is only the mirror of the society that raises and nourishes him. The criticism leveled at the doctor for his wrong behavior is, therefore but a reflection upon the teachings and philosophies of the responsible society.

During 50 years as a general practitioner, I mingled with colleagues of all specialties in the hospital, clinics, or homes and am unable to agree with the numerous severe criticism and charges leveled at them and especially at the general practitioner. The general practitioner lost ground because of his own myopia in failing to keep up with the requirements of time and his professional competence, not because of dishonesty. The general practitioner, as I know him, served his patient well and gave of himself freely in time and effort. Few of these practitioners could afford to roam over Europe or other places for sightseeing, nor could they afford the price of postgraduate studies. I did not know of any that accumulated fortunes.

The affluence of society during the past four to five decades brought the downfall of the practitioner who is so much missed and highly praised now. It was this wealth that gave rise to the expansion of our hospitals and schools. With it also came the rise in medical, scientific skills, which young men of affluent parents were now enabled to achieve in years of postgraduate training. The general practitioner welcomed these men. We recognized them for their superior standing and introduced them gleefully to our patients. Unfortunately, the patients embraced the latter and quietly left their friends and counselors behind. Gradually the general practitioner disappeared but was not replaced. The specialist now is forced to do the general practice, which he considers below his dignity and poorly remunerative. The results were changes in practice with a serious impact on health care. The changes were most pronounced in the aged. A clamor for aid has resulted in Medicare and Medicaid. At the moment, these measures are already of great help. No doubt, time will bring about the needed improvement to make it a universal helpful system for all.

#90 CHANGES IN THE MEDICAL PROFESSION

Our world is in flux. As part of this world, we change with it, and so do all our activities. The changes in medical practice have been so fundamentally great that it's nearly impossible for the older practitioner or the patient to grasp what it truly entails.

The general practitioner was the backbone of medical practice. Now he has become a rarity. Specialization during the last 40 to 50 years substantially fragmented the medical practice. The patient now is bewildered, not knowing where to turn when sickness strikes. Is he to see the nose man for his cold or the ear man or possibly the chest man because he also coughs? Furthermore, he better not get sick at night, at the weekend, or for God's sake on Wednesday (the, commonly, the general practitioner's day off). At night he still has some chances for the emergency room is still open, and an ambulance is available at $35 per trip.

The patient looks at the internist as his family physician, but the latter is not what he once was. He is now a specialist. He doesn't care to treat simple ailments. It is way below his dignity to waste his time on cold or coughs or even aches and pains. Give him leukemia or porphyrias or other exotic ailments, and he'll brighten up. He will ship you right off to the hospital for the resident to write up your case, order x-rays, and other laboratory procedures so that when he arrives the next morning, the diagnosis is presented to him. Meanwhile, Medicare, Medicaid, and private hospital insurance pay for all his troubles. Am I giving a particularly dismal picture of medical practice? Possibly yes, but that is how it appears to many.

I was in general practice for over 46 years. I don't recall any time when the practitioner was in such low esteem as he is now. Why?

The specialist came into being during these past 30 to 40 years. We, general practitioners, recognized them as better trained, as men with four to five years of postgraduate training. We, therefore, welcomed them into our midst. We introduced them to our patients and praised them highly. As a result, they captured the leadership ready, usurped all the beds in the hospital, but were utterly disinterested in what happened to the great mass of practitioners, although I must admit in their great compassion, they did apportion 5% of the beds for us. Fortunately, penicillin came at that moment to our rescue. Penicillin made us independent of the hospital. We were now able to treat our patients at home and in the office.

The specialist continued to grow. The people fell for his pedigrees while the practitioner continued to lose ground. To counteract this movement, the profession responded by creating the generalists or primary physician who will be a man with a better training level, not limited to one field. How the people will react to him or how he will adjust to his practice is too early to tell, for, at this same time, the PA (physician's assistant) came into being. This is a one-quarter baked man who will work under the supervision of his chief, who, in time, may have a half dozen PA's carrying out his orders without him ever seeing the patient.

I am not a disgruntled practitioner. I had a decent practice of my own and was happy with it. I did well and had many patients, both white and black, who loved and respected me. It was only because of the infirmities of age that I felt it was time to retire.

357

#91 GENERAL PRACTITIONER AS VICTIM

The proverb, "the patient died of improvement" may be now extended to the practice of medicine, which is also "dying from improvement." This will continue until the profession wises up and institutes measures to improve the practice. Formerly specialists grew up slowly from the ranks by continuous effort and development of their knowledge and skills. During the past 25 years, opportunities to develop a specialty increased so that the specialists multiplied in number. The general practitioner recognized the superior qualities of the specialist and welcomed him and spread his name to the public. In due time the specialists usurped the crucial posts in the hospital and not only degraded the practitioner in the eyes of the public but eliminated him from the prestigious hospitals in the city.

Formerly, the specialist accepted the patient when recommended by his doctor. Now he accepts him directly and independently. Under these conditions, he does not feel obligated to send any reports to the doctor, or he sends them late and in an abbreviated form. The result is that neither the patient nor the referral has any benefit. Referrals for consultation are considered transfers and treated as such. Many a patient returns. The practice of the referral is thus shrinking while that of the specialists grows.

The newest development is that of the full-line man, a person until now found only in the university hospital.

Having topped the biblical age by ten, it is commonly considered now time to make room for others. Ordinarily, I would agree with this principle. However, with the presumed shortage of physicians and remaining energy, this could be postponed for a few years were the changes in practice and attitudes of the public more conducive.

Practice in earlier days was much less financially remunerative and more complicated than presently, but it was a great deal more pleasant and exciting than now. The public had a friendly, positive attitude toward the physician. He was loved and respected. There was a halo about him exuding love and affection that the present-day doctor will never know despite his greater knowledge and skill.

There was an enviable intimacy and trust. The practice was full of great variety, challenge, and romance. All this is now gone. The doctor now is looked upon as a robber and a cheat. Time destroyed the intimacy. People now are greatly scattered, and it is not feasible to make calls. This inner city is so fearfully dangerous that one couldn't do so even under police protection. The doctor works under surveillance not only in the hospital but in his office as well. The peer review committee is always behind his back. Medicare watches him, and the lawyers lie in wait to pounce upon him. The doctor is afraid of performing any incision or giving an injection because of possible lawsuits. The surgeon is particularly scrutinized and charged with malpractice. His insurance cost is prohibitive, and courts and jurors treat him with hostility. Much of this, I must confess, emanates from the greed of the doctor himself. Medicare is probably the greatest blessing bestowed upon the people. It was meant to help the elderly and not to enrich the doctor. Medicare and other insurance safeguard his fee, an assurance he never had before. Unfortunately, because of greed, he is killing the goose that laid the golden egg. This applies also to the hospital emergency room. Instead of emergency room care, the emergency room became an expansive and expensive diagnostic department. No wonder many refuse to pay these bills. The milking is everywhere, but even the supply of milk is also exhaustible.

Medical knowledge and skill continue to increase rapidly, forcing greater specialization. Many men limit themselves to individual diseases. While this gives the doctor a chance to grow more prominent in the specialty, the patient is not profiting from it at all unless there will be one man to gather all the accumulated facts and apply them to the case on hand. This must be either the general man or the internist. It also means that the various specialists will have to learn to cooperate so as to enable the one to coordinate all the findings and act accordingly.

Instead of being thrown out of the institution, the general man must be given access and possibilities created for him to perfect himself. Some specialists already treat the internist as the former general practitioner. This view will entail mini-residences for these men for a month or two in the various departments. Such additional training will keep the men abreast of newer developments. The present postgraduate courses fall short of these accomplishments.

#92 REFLECTIONS ON PRACTICE

Regrettably, one fails to keep a diary of events in his daily practice, particularly during the earlier years. The experiences of my first 20-25 years in practice were incredibly rich in episodes and memories that now are impossible to recapture.

Practice then was much less sophisticated than it is at present. The physician claimed no superiority over the laity. He visited their home, occasionally even partook of a cup of coffee, and took part in their grief and calamities as well as their joy and celebration.

Most people lived in compact areas. The homes were simple. Most physicians were general practitioners whose offices were in the neighborhood. There were few specialists.

The general practitioner was well trained for his time. His office was simple but adequate, and he served the people with all the means at hand. The doctor was a friend and advisor. It was pleasant to walk down the street. There was respect and kind greeting from all passersby while the little one whispered, "There goes my doctor."

The doctor knew his patient firsthand. A glance at his home was revealing and of greater importance than the elaborate report of the caseworker or the questionnaire of his administrative assistant. There were great intimacy and confidence, which is now missing.

All of the above vanished during the past 20-25 years as a result of social, economic, and scientific changes. What is of interest is that all these changes worked out contrary to logical expectations.

The cities have grown tremendously due to the great migration of the people to the suburbs as a result of the great prosperity of the land and explosive scientific advancement in all fields as well as in medical knowledge and its skills.

The success enabled the new medical graduate to perfect himself in some chosen specialty before venturing into practice. The same wealth filled all the beds in the hospitals. Instead of advertising for people to spend their vacations in the hospital, they are now refused beds, often when in dire need.

The specialized physician now became the dominant character of the hospital while the public became enamored by the halo surrounding him. The latter had no difficulty in eliminating the general practitioner. The method was usually subtle. He was just denied beds or was assigned but a 5% maximum of all available beds. In the case of strong objections, the old bugaboo of "fee-splitting" was resorted to. Thus, our best and finest hospitals succeeded in becoming "Judenrein" (Jew-free). The old general practitioner, rather than being improved, was excluded.

In olden days, the old practitioner and specialist had no difficulty in finding juniors to answer their emergency or house calls. Now that also changed. The young specialist is of a new breed. Few ever knew poverty or privation. He was well supported all through school and properly equipped with excellent office, secretary, and all necessary paraphernalia. He does not need the old man's calls. Home calls and night calls soon became a national problem. Patients turned to the emergency room as their solution.

#93 ABORTION

Editor's note: The subject of abortion remains one of today's most controversial societal issues. The practice of terminating a pregnancy is well known since ancient times. The Catholic Church forbids abortion, whereas, from a Jewish perspective, abortion is treated more from a social than a theological perspective, with how the mother's life is affected taking priority. Since the 1920s, the US abortion laws have progressively liberalized, with the right to have abortion becoming legal. Within a year after New York State legalized abortion, the maternal-mortality rate plummeted there by 45%, proclaiming it a public-health triumph. Today, the issue remains palpable, as evidenced by the numerous articles seen almost continuously in newspapers and the antagonistic fights of the pro-life and pro-choice court and congressional battles. John's views are an honest perspective of his beliefs and experiences in the daily practice of caring for patients and the issues forever confronting them.

The physician's creed is to preserve life and alleviate pain. By and large, most physicians live these principles. Only the exceptional dissents.

Abortion, to the practitioner, always presented a knotty problem. The religious man had no difficulties. To him, the fetus is divine and not to be interfered with. All other mortals, however, must contend with the other obligations associated with the social, economic, and health problems. Those who are law-abiding felt dutifully obligated to help the victim somehow extricate herself from the mire into which she had fallen. The transgressor, married or unmarried, is in greatest need.

The committee of wisemen, when making the decision to deprive the unfortunate transgressor of her baby, are usually satisfied, not realizing they may have created a victim who will be tormented throughout the rest of her life.

One such woman was my patient during my senior year at the University of Michigan. For years, she had been searching for the lost child whom she imagined was now being tortured by her captivators. I encountered several such patients during my years in practice. All were victimized by men whose honestly and purpose were beyond question.

These victims always came to mind when the question of abortion came up, and I always felt there was a need for a better solution to this problem.

Most of these girls were frantic. They could not face the world and suddenly came to realize the complications and difficulties they were about to meet.

I found that many such situations could be handled by simple methods, thus avoiding the later tragedies.

Wherever possible, I tried, after calming these people, to persuade them to bring their parents with them to discuss the situation. With the parents present, solutions were usually near. For the religious Jewish boys and girls, I had some success in convincing them that even the critics of the Jewish religion recognized the fetus as having represented the consummation of a marriage.[116] To prevent gossip and shame, a weekend elopement and procurement of a marriage certificate by a justice of the peace was sufficient.

Today, this advice sounds ancient. The question of abortion now engulfs the land. Abortion has become a national disease, nay an epidemic the "enlightened" fan. It is a widespread calamity of drugs, promiscuity, and disease and presents on a scale never seen before in any civilization. The longer-term effects have yet to be evaluated. In years, the enlightened will have perished and thus escape the knowledge of what they had accomplished.

---

[116] Editor's note: During my childhood years, Father's answer to my question how long it takes for a child to be born was always puzzling. The firstborn child could come even after only a day of marriage, whereas each succeeding one nine months. How mysterious.

#94 AUSCULTATORY ACUMEN

Editor's note: Father, in his later years, was critical of the medical and education systems present in the USA and wished better. His displeasure appeared nationally in his Letter to the Editor published in the *Journal of the American Medical Association* (JAMA) in 1961 in Vol 175, #5, pg 415.

To the Editor: The article "Auscultatory Acumen in the General Medical Population," in THE JOURNAL, Sept. 3, page 32, is entirely unrevealing. During the past 30 years, I have had the opportunity to observe and to comment frequently on the fact that at rounds, when they were still held at the bedside, doctors differ considerably in localizing and recognizing heart sounds and murmurs. It is, therefore, evident that most of us would profit by extra training.

The better showing by present-day senior students and diplomates is, of course, expected. There certainly must have been some progress in teaching at our medical schools during these past 30 years. It would be tragic, indeed, if the diplomate with 5 years of postgraduate work were unable to localize a murmur correctly.

The teaching in my days, and I speak from my own experience only, was abominable. It was through our own efforts and perseverance that our training was enhanced. Those with superior intellect, ability, and industry naturally reached a higher level than the colleague not so blessed.

Unfortunately, the average physician could seldom afford the price of a worthwhile postgraduate course. Possibly, in time, our large hospitals will recognize it as a duty to open their doors, enabling a physician to spend at least 1 or 2 months in general medicine on the same basis as an intern or resident. Such an event would be a boon to the profession as well as to society.

In rubbing shoulders with specialists and diplomates since 1926, I find them very well trained and possessing superior knowledge, but they are not supermen. The old-timer need not feel any more inferior than the infantryman in comparison with his more specialized colleague. Each one performs his job well.

JOHN ROBBOY, M.D.
412 Commonwealth Bldg.
Cleveland 6. Ohio

Philosophies and Religious Commentaries

#95 A CHAPTER OF THE BIBLE

The imperfections of man are the result of God's inexperience. The creation of man was His very first mistake. It is man who kept Him provided with crime and other trouble since the day of creation.

The second mistake was in creating Eve.

God made man – Adam on Friday – and rested on the next day, which we later hallowed as the Sabbath. It was during this day of relaxation when He realized that Adam would be doomed to loneliness unless a female companion is provided for him. Eve thus was but an afterthought. God now brushed up on anesthesia, surgery, and sculpture. Instead of making a rough-shod figure of clay, He removed one of the ribs of Adam surgically under anesthesia, shaped a beautifully attractive and graceful form, and blew the spirit of life into it, creating Eve.

The result was love at first sight. The two cleaved to each other and became one flesh.

The two were very happy in their garden. It was but natural for the young bride to be attracted by the aroma of the fruits and flowers and as she was promenading through the garden, how could she withstand the alluring red-cheeked apples on the tree of knowledge, though admittedly, they were on the proscribed list of forbidden fruit?

To Eve this seemed but a minor transgression. God, however, considered this a serious offense. The release of knowledge would now threaten His power and rule. Adam and Eve were banished from the garden at once. Adam was sentenced to a life of labor, and Eve was punished with the pangs of labor.

Their sons became the first victims of this knowledge. It led to jealousy and strife, which culminated in the murder of Abel by his brother Cain.

The third mistake came next.

Jealousy, strife, and all types of wickedness and crime quickly spread through the young world, and God decided to wipe humanity off the earth. He enlisted Noah, a great mechanic and shipbuilder, to help him in this task. Instead of the original decision, Noah was to construct an ark into which he was to gather his wife, his sons and their wives, pairs of clean animals, and two pairs of all unclean animals, male and female of each species. When all was done, God caused a great flood on the earth. It continued for 40 days, during which all life on land perished except that in Noah's ark. Soon the waters receded, and Noah landed his ark on Mt. Ararat, where it remains to this day.

Life on earth was soon replenished, and the ancient civilization with all its characteristics returned. God found it challenging to cope with all the problems Himself and sought out Abraham to help Him.

Abraham was a man of stature, a great anti-pagan iconoclast. He was a radical, and not too welcome in his native city, Ur, in Chaldea.[117] Like the radicals of our own time, he sought refuge in other lands. Before leaving his city, Abraham made a pact with his Almighty, who blessed him and promised him and his followers the land of Canaan. Fortified with this pledge, he now gathered his family, herds, as well as his nephew, Lot, and his herds. Together, they started the journey. Abraham thus became the "Wandering Jew," and his followers the "Chosen People."

Abraham wasn't only a scholar. He was a fine and upright man as well. Wherever he went, he managed to gain respect and proper treatment for himself and his wife, Sarah. He also remained a splendid uncle. When his herdsmen fought with those of Lot, he managed to arrive at a fair settlement and peaceful separation of the two camps. That is when Lot settled in Sodom.[118] Uncle's vigilance, however, never ceased. When the neighboring kings carried Lot, his men, and herds away, Abraham came to help. He pursued these robbers, rescuing Lot and all. Years later, when the people of Sodom and Gomorrah became so incredibly wicked and sinful that God decided to wipe them off the earth, Abraham displayed his great powers of advocacy. His impassioned plea for justice continues to be admired to this very day in its clearness and eloquence, even though he lost his case. However, he did rescue Lot and his family. Whether Lot, the drunk, deserved all that effort is another question.

Rich as the life of Sarah and Abraham was in experiences, it yet remained incomplete, for they had no children. Abraham did have a son, Ishmael, by his wife's maid, Hagar, but Sarah had no children of her own and was unhappy. By now, she was even too old to expect any. Old Abe, however, refused to give up. Again and again, he pleaded until the Lord yielded and granted them a son. Sarah was about 90 years old, and Abraham was around 100 years of age.

The arrival of Isaac brought new problems. Sarah was worried lest Ishmael would want to claim his legacy from the father. Abraham bowed to her pleas and banished Hagar together with his son Ishmael into the wilderness.

Isaac grew up to be a good, healthy, lovable and obedient, though apparently not too bright a son. Had it not been for the superior intellect of his father, Isaac would have been sacrificed on the altar.

When Isaac reached mid-adolescence, his protective father imported his niece as the wife for his beloved son. The young couple was quite happy with each other and, in due time, were enriched with twin boys, Esau, the older, and Jacob, the younger. Following their natural inclinations, Esau became a hunter and Jacob, a herdsman.

---

[117] Ur Kaśdim, commonly translated as Ur of the Chaldeans, is the city mentioned in the Hebrew Bible as the birthplace of the Israelite and Ismaelite patriarch Abraham. It is located on the Euphrates River, near where it joins the Tigris River, in the area of Sumer in the southern Ancient Mesopotamia.

[118] One of the five biblical cities, also known as the "cities of the plain" (from Genesis), now synonymous with impenitent sin. Sodom was located on the Jordan River in the southern region of Canaan. While the region was compared to the garden of Eden as being well-watered and green, suitable for grazing livestock, after divine judgment was passed, both Sodom and Gomorrah were consumed by fire and brimstone.

Jacob failed to inherit the beautiful upright characteristics of his illustrious grandfather, Abraham. Instead, he inherited the qualities of his scheming mother, Rebecca, and those of his uncle, Laban, the cheat. Jacob's life, rich in experiences, was marred by jealousy, strife, murder, and other crime.

Anxious to protect her favored son, Rebecca involved Jacob in the swindle of his blind father, Isaac, in which he obtained the legacy due Esau. Soon after this, he managed to have Esau himself surrender the legacy to him by a similar unsavory method, an act that caused strife between the brothers for many years.

When Jacob reached early adolescence, Rebecca dispatched him to her brother, Laban, in Haran[119] to find a wife among her own people. There Jacob fell deeply in love with his charming cousin, Rachel, Laban's younger daughter. After serving Laban seven years, he discovered ugly Leah substituted for Rachel. Seven more years of service did in no way deter Jacob's love for Rachel. She deserved it and more. In fact, he continued serving Laban for six more years and would have continued longer had not his cousins found him plundering their father's herds.

Jacob, by now, was a wealthy man possessing many herds as well as four wives, eleven sons, and one daughter, and he fled, fearing their anger. Laban pursued, caught up with Jacob, and even searched him, for Jacob even robbed him of his goods. Laban failed to find them because Rachel had them hidden in the saddle she was sitting upon, and the father dared not disturb his daughter, who was pregnant at the time.

No sooner had Laban left, when Jacob was notified that Esau, with 400 of his men, were on their way to meet him. Jacob was now severely shaken and prayed for help. That night he dreamed of a struggle with a man of God, and not only was he victorious, but he was given an additional name, Israel, as a portent of victory. Thus fortified, Jacob now presented Esau a substantial gift, and the two departed in amity and peace.

Continuing his journey, Jacob reached the city of Shechem (first capital in the Kingdom of Israel and today, the present-day Nablus). Here the young prince Shechem violated Jacob's daughter, Dinah. Jacob and his sons were distraught. Young Shechem offered to marry her, but Jacob refused the offer unless all the males of the city submitted to circumcision. To this, the people acquiesced. But on the third day following the circumcision, the brothers fell upon the city, killed all the inhabitants, plundered all they could, and left.

Continuing his journey further, Rachel went into labor, delivered her second son, Benjamin, and died. She was buried in Bethlehem, and the family continued the journey to Hebron, where Isaac was dying. Esau now joined Jacob, and the two buried their father. Jacob then remained permanently in Hebron.

The brilliance of Joseph and his appearance, added to the favoritism shown to him by the father, generated a severe animosity for him from his brothers, who actually plotted his murder. Because Reuben and Judah objected to murder, the brothers yielded and sold Joseph to the Ishmaelites. The latter brought him to Egypt, where he was sold to Potiphar, a high officer of Pharaoh. Joseph

---

[119] Now universally identified with Harran, a city whose ruins lie within present-day, most southern border of Turkey, just north of the present-day Syrian border.

was made overseer of Potiphar's household. His attractive appearance aroused Lady Potiphar. She made advances toward him, which he refused. Offended by being spurned, she accused him of attempted rape and had him imprisoned. Here among the prisoners, he gained a reputation as a great interpreter of dreams. This reputation soon reached the ears of Pharaoh, who, displeased with his astrologers, summoned Joseph to his court to have Joseph's interpretation of his most recent dreams. Joseph felt the dreams meant seven years of plentiful crops for Egypt, which would be followed by seven years of drought. He, therefore, advised and even outlined the plans to prevent such calamity. Joseph's interpretation seemed most logical, and Pharaoh appointed Joseph to the post as Viceroy enabling him to carry out his plans. Time proved Joseph correct. Egypt, therefore, emerged as the only country free from starvation in the vast region around.

Starvation elsewhere forced Jacob to send his sons to Egypt to buy grain. Joseph recognized his brothers and identifying himself to them. They celebrated the reunion. He then supplied them with the desired food and asked them to bring the rest of the family to Egypt. Jacob was very skeptical of the entire story and plan but spurred on by the hunger, he yielded. He gathered the whole Israelite clan, 70 strong, and journeyed to Egypt. There, they settled in the province of Goshen (located in the eastern delta of the Nile River), a province that modern research shows the Hyksos, a Semitic tribe, had invaded much earlier.

About one and a half centuries later, the Egyptians reconquered the area and enslaved both the Hyksos and Israelites.

That a people who grew in number and prosperity over several centuries would refuse to bow to enslavement and obliteration never dawned upon the Egyptians. Russia is learning that now.

A great, well organized, and coordinated popular underground movement developed. Even the midwives cooperated by refusing to kill the newly born males. The foundling Moses may have been an act of sabotage by court personnel.

The leadership of Moses was open and audacious, one of strength. He had at least ten confrontations with the powers that be, asking for emancipation and freedom, and finally took the most dramatic and successful step, a step that remains unmatched in the history of the world.

It took 40 years of wandering in the wilderness during which domestic rebellion was suppressed, wars with the various tribes fought, and starvation overcome. A constitution was proclaimed, and courts of law and order established.

Moses was not destined to bring his people into the Promised Land, but he left his people in good hands. His labor was not lost. This is the story of the Passover that all of us Jews, regardless of where we live, our color or belief, observe and cherish.

#96 EMANCIPATION

Tonight, Jews everywhere gather to commemorate and to celebrate the exodus of the Israelites, our ancestors, from the land of their enslavement.

About 400 years earlier, Jacob and his family, the Israelite, some 70 strong, driven by hunger, immigrated to the land of Egypt, where Joseph, son of Jacob, was a leading government official. Because of Joseph, the immigrants were well received. They were allowed to settle in the city of Goshen, in the fertile northeastern part of the Nile Delta. Here the immigrants multiplied and prospered for some time, but, with the rise of new dynasties, the attitude towards these immigrants changed, which finally led to their enslavement.

No clear explanation for this phenomenon has ever been advanced. Egypt's powers and influence in the political field had been waning. Egypt was harassed and frequently invaded by its neighbors. The Israelites constituted a small minority group with a culture and religious belief vastly different from that of the Egyptians. They were looked upon with suspicion, and this led to the mistreatment by the Egyptians. The Israelites, in turn, grew restless and rebellious. The Egyptians now had reason to consider them disloyal. Gradually, the Israelites were disenfranchised and finally enslaved, a condition prevalent and practiced widely throughout the world at that time.

The fear generated by this small minority, now reaching about 500,000 men, must have been unusually great. Enslavement alone was apparently not sufficient to contain this insurgent group. More extreme measures were needed. The manual tasks were now increased, and the supervision was made harsher. Finally, actual extermination was decided upon. Pharaoh ordered the slaughter of all newborn Israelite males.

To the student of psychology, these measures are of great interest, for they indicate the human intellect had not changed much in these 3,000 years. During World War II, the Nazis mobilized a most scientific machine whose sole purpose was to devise all possible forms of torture in their effort to exterminate the Jews, their imaginary enemy. During the post-war period, the sophisticated and presumably more enlightened Soviet Union, in its desire to be supreme in scientific endeavor, undertook to improve upon the crude method of the Nazis by instituting a more refined way to exterminate.

Just when the Jews will overcome this Russian enemy is difficult to predict. Still, I venture to say that their emancipation will arrive and will be another victory added to those in Jewish history.

"Why is this night different from all other nights?" is the question asked by the child, and the father answers, "We were slaves in Egypt."

Thus begins the dramatic story depicting the self-liberation of the Jews from 400 years of enslavement in Egypt. This great event takes us back over 1,400 years before the birth of Christ at a time when the Jews staged a spectacle unique in significance and character ever since. Though history records other similar heroic events in later centuries during times of endangerment, none equals in character that of the Jews.

The sound of liberty and freedom was reverberating through the atmosphere everywhere, for the entire world was one great camp of slavery with but a very few number possessing all the rights and wealth. Many a heroic figure using his own genius would gather an army among the unfortunate and rise against the oppressors. Still, regardless of strength, all eventually were overcome by the powers that be and massacred or re-enslaved.

Of more ancient times, the Bible records the revolt and exodus of the Jews from Egypt. The rebellion differed both in the form of bloodshed and consequences from all before and after its occurrence. The exodus was an uprising led through years of negotiation during which a leadership and plans developed. The persuasiveness of Moses, like that of Mr. Henry Kissinger, the U.S. Secretary of State of today, was significant enough to obtain permission for the Jews to leave. Possibly, Moses' difficulty in speech was responsible for this method, but it worked, and 600,000 Jews succeeded in throwing the yoke of slavery from off their shoulders and walk out from Egypt.

Pharaoh's error in changing his mind and pursuing the Jews led to his own demise and the great success of the Jewish feat. The pharaoh's vast army of well-equipped men and modern chariots was swallowed by the waters of the Red Sea, then giving the Jews the chance to rest and consolidate their ranks.

Soon after the walkout, Pharaoh realizing his weak-mindedness, went in pursuit of the Jews, which resulted in his vast army of horses and chariots being swallowed in the Red Sea. This crushing defeat added even greater significance to the feat shown by the slaves and must have sent dangerous shockwaves and fears throughout the world of that day. But Moses now was in no hurry. Now he had the chance to rest, consolidate, and coordinate his powers and plan ahead. He formed a government with a constitution and laws.

He took 40 years to accomplish what he started. During these years, he struggled with restlessness in the ranks, suppressed the revolt of Korah,[120] polished the Jews, formed a national government with a constitution, an army, laws and judges, and before he departed, even appointed his successor who was to lead the Jews into Canaan.

---

[120] Numbers 16:1–40 indicates that Korah rebelled against Moses along with 249 co-conspirators and were punished for their rebellion when God sent fire from heaven to consume all 250 of them. ... God then smote 14,700 men with plague, as punishment for objecting to Korah's destruction (Numbers 16:41ff.)

Foremost were the problems of water, shelter, and food. Also, he had to repair the wounds and take care of the hazards of the environment. Here the experience of his wandering days through the wilderness was of great help to Moses. He knew the terrain well and knew how or where to find water and food. He then established a civil patrol to guard against the hostile elements in the environment. Now that he had taken care of these problems, Moses began his primary task, to polish, educate and shape this degraded people into a nation worthy of the name. It was here where the "Fireside chats"[121] began. He spoke to his people from up the mountain. They listened and learned. Here he gave them a written constitution of a series of fundamental laws that serve as the model for all democratic governments to this day. He also formed district courts and appointed judges to administer the laws of justice and equality to all.

Moses was now 120 years old, tired, and unable to do anymore. He, therefore, entrusted the leadership to his Joshua,[122] his general, and off he went up the mountain never to return.

Thus ends the unique story of the Exodus, which was unique in several ways. 1) It was a first revolt in the history of Jews for freedom. 2) It was also the first revolt in history against bondage. 3) It was a bloodless revolt accomplished by negotiations and persuasion. And 4) it was the first democratic government based on law and order, justice, and equality.

As children of our ancient ancestors, we agree with their philosophies of law and order, justice, and equality and are happy to celebrate Passover as if we are ourselves members of the first exodus.

---

[121] A series of evening radio addresses U.S. President Franklin D. Roosevelt gave between 1933 and 1944.

[122] For whom [A026] John Robboy, the author of these reminiscences, named his son, [A031] Stanley Joshua Robboy.

#98 CHAD GADYA

The Aramaic version of Chad Gadya made its first appearance in Europe in 1590 in the Prague Haggadah. Since then, it had been incorporated in all haggadahs. It is still being sung by the Jewish children everywhere during the siddurim.

To the Jew, the allegorical significance of the song was obviously evident: Father meant God; the kid, Israel; and the two coins, the two tablets of the covenant.[123] The song also depicts the principle of Jewish morality that there is no sin without punishment.

Within time the phrase "Chad Gadya" itself became part of the Yiddish language and curiously assumed the slang meaning of "prison." The Polish Jews used the latter connotation to confuse the censor who was utterly ignorant of the term.

It is only in the past few years that the philosophy and the profound meaning of the song came to be realized. The author, whose identity was lost in antiquity, endowed with the vision of the genius, understood the laws of nature and the interrelationships of all life in their respective environments. He foresaw what man is capable of doing to himself and others. His warning remained unheeded for all these centuries. It is only in our most recent past few years that Rachel

---

[123] The Passover Haggadah ends with the fun but peculiar song, Chad Gadya – An Only Kid, in which the repetition in each stanza underscores the ebb and flow of Jewish history – sometimes we're down, but then we rise up. While most of the song looks backwards, it ends with an optimistic view toward the future, a fitting conclusion to the Seder. The Vilna Gaon explained the song symbolic meaning of this sequence with each verse alluding to one person or event in Jewish history with Angel of Death being ultimately vanquished at the conclusion of the song by the Holy One, Blessed be He.

The kid is the birthright mentioned in Genesis 25. This is the right to take the baton that had been passed from Abraham to Isaac, to continue Abraham's mission to build a world full of loving kindness and monotheism and devoid of idolatry, child sacrifice and other evils.

My father is Jacob who bought the birthright from his twin brother Esau, who had been born first and thus had the natural right to the birthright.

The two zuzim are the bread and stew Jacob paid Esau for the birthright.

The cat represents the envy of Jacobs's sons toward their brother Joseph's, leading them to sell him into slavery in Egypt.

The dog is Egypt, where Joseph landed, and where eventually the entire clan of Jacob and the subsequent Israelite nation lived, were enslaved, and were redeemed.

The stick is the famous staff of Moses, used to call forth various plagues and part the waters of the Sea for the Israelites to cross.

The fire represents the thirst for idolatry among Israelites that proved to be a persistent bane for over 800 years, from the year they left Egypt until the destruction of the First Temple in the Fifth Century BCE.

The water represents the Fourth Century BCE sages who eradicated idolatry.

The ox is Rome (Esau's descendent) who destroyed the 2nd Temple in 70 CE.

The butcher is the "Messiah Son of Joseph" (Mashiach Ben-Yoseph) who will restore full Jewish sovereignty in the Land of Israel.

The Angel of Death needs no introduction; in this song he represents the death of Messiah Ben-Yoseph

The Holy One of course also needs no introduction; here He arrives with Messiah Ben-David.

Carson[124] and other ecologists and scientists brought the question of pollution to the fore. Will man have the courage and intelligence to prevent his own destruction?

---

[124] American marine biologist, author, and conservationist whose book Silent Spring and other writings are credited with advancing the global environmental movement.

#99 [A024] JOE ROBBOY AND COMMUNISM
[A014] David Gerson Robboy relates

Editor's note: Having experienced early lives of oppression and pogroms, several family members, after coming to the United States, politically leaned heavily to the left. Some wished for, and indeed a few openly advocated on behalf of their fellow workers for a life where their children should never experience the difficulties they endured early on. [A024] Joe Robboy was probably the most activist member of the family. Several of us who knew him in his later life remember him as kind and loving.

[A024] Joseph Robboy, the fourth of [A011] Shmiel (Samuel) and Malka (Mollie) Robboy's five children, was born on November 4, 1890. He was the first of their children to emigrate to the United States (1907 or 1908). He settled in Cleveland, Ohio. Other siblings and parents came shortly after that. Joe married his first cousin, once removed, [A428] Gertrude Gelman. The marriage was short-lived. They had one child.

Joe worked as a paperhanger in Cleveland, where he met his second wife, [A024b] Bessie Kimmelman. The 1930 Census places them in East Los Angeles, living next door to Joe's first cousin, [A047] Sylvia (Robboy) Isbitz and her husband, [A047a] Joe Isbitz. But as the following news clippings indicate, Joe was in Los Angeles at least as early as 1928. Subsequent public documents show that Joe and Bessie were to move back and forth between Los Angeles and Cleveland, though it is unknown how many times. The 1940 Census, for example, places them back in Cleveland. But by 1948, voter registration records show he and Bessie had settled in the Boyle Heights neighborhood of Los Angeles in the duplex where they were to remain in retirement to their last years.

On July 23, 1928, the Los Angeles Times headlined the article:

ACCUSED REDS ARRESTED
Launching of Communist Drive Here Leads to Raids; Suspected Books Found in Possession

Eight persons described as Reds, one of them a woman, were arrested yesterday by Detective Lieutenant Hynes and the police red detail when it became known that the Communist party had launched a secret membership campaign in Los Angeles.

Each of the suspects, when searched, was found to be in possession of several books of so-called solidarity certificates to be sold ostensibly for the relief of striking coal miners and their families. The prices stamped on the certificates ranged from 10 cents to $10.

In reality, he said, the money collected is to be used to foster and encourage the breaking of laws of the United States and for the spreading of Communistic propaganda.

"There is no doubt," Hynes said, "that this 'drive' is similar to that conducted by the Anti-Imperialistic League, which we already have shown has been engaged in collecting funds for Sandino, to be used in killing United States Marines in Nicaragua. In fact, on the reverse side of the certificates it states: 'This solidarity certificate has helped to win the miners' strike, save the miners'*union, encourage mass picketing and fight the injunctions.' "

The slips also urge the purchaser to "agitate for organizing the unorganized, for one national agreement and a national miners' strike."

Other pamphlets found in the possession of the prisoners set out that the Communists "do not restrict ourselves to our expression of solidarity and comradely spirit to the American working class." It urges "a flight [sic] for a militant union, mass picketing and mass violation of injunctions against the workers and the union." In conclusion, it advocates the erection of a Communist society in the United States.

Those arrested were booked on charges of violating Sections 2 and 3 of City Ordinance No. 34983. which prohibits the soliciting of money for charitable purposes. They gave the following names: Aaron Grossburg, 34 years of age. 229 West Second street: Mrs. Mary Ostrow. 50, of 722 Mt. Washington Drive: Ben Farber, 43, of 3367Ramona Boulevard: Joseph Robboy, 37, of 3625½ Brooklyn avenue: Edward Tampfer. 45. of 824 West Tenth street; Aaron Feinberg, 41, of 529 North Cumming street; Mike Schenvoneck, 33. of 339 Rush avenue. San Gabriel; Dave Fradkin. alias Stein, 810 Forest avenue.

10 months later, on May 28, 1929, the trial was held, after which the Los Angeles Times headlined the article:

FOUR BOAST COMMUNIST AFFILIATION
Handbill Passers Admit Red Sympathy in Court; Judge Reserves Decision

Four self-asserted Communists yesterday went on trial before Municipal Judge Northrup on charges of violating the handbill ordinance by passing out asserted Red propaganda. The four, Joseph Robboy, 3625½ Brooklyn Avenue: George Kiosz, 1302 West Pico Boulevard: Vartin Galalin, 1023 Wall street, and George A. Abajian, 342 East Fourth street, were arrested by Detectives Pfeiffer and Hays of the police Red squad last April.

Robboy and Kiosz were accused by Deputy City Prosecutor Weller of passing out "May Day" handbills put out by the Communist party urging a demonstration "for the defense of the 'soviet' union." The other two were arrested after invading laundries and passing out handbills asking employees to strike.

Frank Walden, called as a witness for the defense by Attorney Leo Gallagher, identified himself as a member of the Communist party and an organizer for the Trade Union Unity League, which, he said, had no direct connection with the Communist party.[125]

"We are now attempting to organize the laundry workers so they may strike for higher wages," he declared on the stand when questioned by Judge Northrup as to his activities. Gallagher's defense was that the Communist party is a charitable organization and as such does not come under the ordinance.

After hearing the testimony, the court took the case under advisement until June 7, next.

On June 24, 1929, the Los Angeles Times reported:

COURT FINDS COMMUNIST PAIR GUILTY
Robboy and Kiosz Fined for Handbill Distributing and Give Notice of Appeal

---

[125]The then-new Trade Union Unity League was in fact an industrial union umbrella organization created that year by the American Communist Party (CPUSA). It was abandoned in 1935, when the Party pivoted to its Popular Front strategy.

After having the case under advisement for several weeks, Municipal Judge Northrup has handed down a decision finding Joseph Robboy, 3625 ½ Brooklyn avenue, and Georg Kiosz, 1302 West Pico Boulevard, both self-asserted Communists, guilty of violating the city handbill ordinance by passing out radical literature. He fined them $15 each.

At the same time he found Vartin Galalin, 1023 Wall street, and George A. Abajian, 342 East Fourth street, not guilty of the same offense. In this case, Judge Northrup held, Galalin and Abajian were distributing handbills tending to be of an educational nature.

The dodgers passed out by Robboy and Kiosz advertised a "May day" Communist picnic and urged a demonstration "for the defense of the soviet union," evidence produced at the trial showed. The two men gave oral notice of appeal from the court's decision, Judge Northrup setting their appeal bond at $25 each, which was furnished.

In 2019, Joe's great-nephew [A014] David Gerson Robboy established "The Joe and Bessie Robboy Memorial Annual Scholarship" at Portland Community College, in Oregon. He attached the following text to the scholarship:

Joe Robboy, born in 1890 to a Yiddish-speaking family in Knyazha Krynytsya, Ukraine, emigrated to the United States, where he became a labor activist. On July 22, 1928, he was arrested by the Los Angeles Police red detail. According to the *L. A. Times*, "Each of the suspects, when searched, was found to be in possession of so-called solidarity certificates to be sold ostensibly for the relief of striking coal miners...." In 1929 he was arrested and convicted "on charges of violating the handbill ordinance by passing out asserted Red propaganda" (*L. A. Times*, Jun 24, 1929). In 1930, a Congressional committee to investigate Communist activities heard testimony that named Joseph Robboy among a list of immigrant radicals (almost all Jewish), arguing for greater limits on immigration. By the 1950's, Joe and his wife, Bessie (Kimmelman) Robboy, lived in the Boyle Heights section of Los Angeles, where Bessie was known as one of the most active anarchists. It was a mixed marriage: he a communist and she an anarchist.[126] Bessie died in 1962 and Joe in 1964. This scholarship is dedicated to the memory of two trouble-makers for social justice, and the recipient is encouraged to follow in their footsteps.

---

[126] As British anarchist Fermin Rocker described it, "In Los Angeles one of the most active anarchists (of a very active group) was Bessie Kimmelman. They all used to congregate at her place. Hers was another case of a devout anarchist married happily to a devout Communist." Interviewed in New York City, 1972, for Paul Avrich, *Anarchist Voices: An Oral History of Anarchism in America* (Edinburgh, Scotland, and Oakland, Calif.: AK Press, 2005), 40. The AK Press edition is a paperback re-issue of the original edition by Princeton University Press, 1995 (not to be confused with an abridged Princeton edition of 1996). Fermin Rocker was the son of the eminent anarchist Rudolf Rocker, who, though a German and not a Jew, wrote extensively in Yiddish.

#100 [A665] COUSIN DR. ELI GRAD AND THE HEBREW COLLEGE IN BOSTON

The following article appeared in the Israeli paper "Al Hamishmar" on February 10, 1977. Additional material appeared in the same paper on Feb 17, 1977.

The Hebrew College in Boston

Abraham Yas'ur

When I read in the catalog of the Hebrew College about the attitude of the College's fifth President (1970-1986), cousin Dr. [A665] Eli Grad,[127] the member of the Board, and the students of the College to the central issues of our time, I decided to check the institution with my own eyes.

I was not disappointed. This is the institution of my choice due to its being the intellectual and cultural center of Boston's Jewish community. The institution was established in 1921 as the Beit Midrash Le'Morim, the Hebrew Teachers College. The language of instruction in the College and the Prozdor (high school division established shortly after that) was and continues to be Hebrew. In 1927 the State of Massachusetts empowered this institution to grant bachelors, masters, and doctoral degrees and certificates. The first bachelor's degree was granted in 1930.

Among the better-known early teachers of the institution, I will only mention Dr. [A789] Nisson Touroff[128] and Dr. [A790] Samuel I. Perlman,[129] blessed be their memories. Today, Torah is spread to 200 college students by an outstanding faculty, which includes Professors [A791] Mordechai Wilensky, [A792] Aaron Weider, [A793] Sol Schimmel, and [A794] Dov Eron of Tel Aviv University, among others. Other visiting Israeli scholars have spent their sabbaticals there. Recent visiting scholars include [A795] Reuven Kritz, [A796] Moshe Bar Asher, [A797] Yochanan Silman, and others.

The leadership of the College invites outstanding personalities to visit and meet with students and faculty. [A802] Shaul Tchernichovsky[130] was an early visitor. [A827] David Ben Gurion met with students and faculty on two occasions. Recent guests included Professor [A798] A. B. Yehoshua and Professor [A799] Abraham Kaplan.

Many of the graduates are involved in Jewish education in the United States. Quite a few have achieved significant leadership roles in American Jewish education. Many live and work in Israel.

---

[127] Dr. Eli Grad, wrote The Brudno Family: A family tree and biographical sketches, 1984 (self-published)

[128] Nissan Touroff (1877–1953), born in Nesvizh near Minsk, was a founder of the School in 1921 and its first dean.

[129] Samuel Perlman, second dean (1926-1932).

[130] Shaul Gutmanovich Tchernichovsky (1875 –1943) was Russian-born and considered one of the great Hebrew poets. The ancient Greece culture greatly influenced his works about nature.

The student must complete 104 academic credits at Hebrew College to qualify for a certificate. Earning a degree requires sixty additional credits in the humanities, which can be taken at one of the several educational institutions in the area with which Hebrew College maintains consortium relationships. This cooperation with other area colleges is an excellent achievement for Hebrew College.

I came here to hear the "Ani Maamin" ("I believe") of Professor Eli Grad, who has now headed College for ten years. His ardent devotion to the texts and comprehensive sources of the Jewish heritage as indispensable to the creative survival of the American Jewish community is exemplary.

First, as an advocate of the Jewish people, he is superb. He knows our people. He knows our roots, and he knows our culture.

Second, he insists that the bonds which unite all Jews are much more significant to Jewish survival than the differences which separate us. He insists that Hebrew is the language of our Jewish heritage and our national renaissance in Israel, that it is indispensable to the fullest achievement of Jewish consciousness and to that kinship of soul and spirit without which worldwide Jewish unity is in jeopardy.

At Hebrew College, Dr. Grad inherited a noble tradition of commitment to our Hebrew heritage from a line of distinguished Hebrew scholars, which included Professor [A800] Isaac Zilberschlag,[131] and Professor [A801] Jacques Mikliszanski, among others.

Reflecting on the realities of Jewish life in America, Dr. Grad points out that for the young American Jew, group memory no longer has any of the taint of immigrant squalor, and little of the trauma of six million deaths without reason. It appears that the young American Jew has not really come to grips with the meaning of the peoplehood of Israel in his life. To be sure, Grad says, the pain of his brethren hurts him, and he responds wholeheartedly to their cries for help, but that sense of kinship does not extend to fellow Jews who are not in trouble. The young American Jew shares the suffering of his fellow Jews. He does not share their identity. His observations do not lead Grad to pessimism. He believes in the possibilities of Jewish life in America.

Referring to the rapid growth of Judaic studies at many American universities, Dr. Grad sees in this phenomenon expression of a need for Jewish learning. Turning the conversation back to the rationale and raison d'etre of Hebrew College, Dr. Grad emphasizes that above all else, the Jewish heritage represents teaching, the communication from one who possessed vitally significant Jewish knowledge to one who lacks that knowledge.

Central to Grad's concerns and plans is his vision of the College's special obligation to make available to ever-widening circles the very best in learning and Jewish cultural opportunities. In short, he strives to develop in Boston a learning community that will give purpose and substance to Jewish life.

---

[131] Member of "Ivriya Society" post World War I, whose mission it was to revive Hebrew as a spoken language.

#101 HASIDUT AND JEWISH HISTORY

Two opposing principles were struggling between themselves in historical Judaism: the individual vs. the collective or national. The origin of belief is, as it is known, buried in the depth of the human mind. We desire to determine where it comes from and where it is going. It desires to reach the essence of life to unite divinity in thought and emotion. From this psychic spring also comes the Jewish belief. However, as soon the Jewish people in their monotheistic world outlook became a separate, unique unit in the pagan world, its leaders, to prevent the loss of the Jews while mixing in strange surroundings, made use of the power of their religion. That is how the two principles have intervened so that now it is quite difficult to determine what is needed to support the nation or vice versa so that Judaism, with its world outlook, may serve the world as the "light for the Nation."

Already in ancient times, the "God Nation," i.e., a nation unusual in its relation to God, surrounded itself by a wall of "Torch of Priests." The latter developed in parallel with the "Torah of the Prophets" as a religion of law and moral religion. At the same time, both Torahs reflected the needs of the mass rather than the individual.

In the Judaism of the Bible, the principle of the public rather than private supervision dominates. The Creator watches all his creatures: nations, generations, or leaders of nations or generations, but the individual does not find himself, so to say, under supervision. The real rationale of the Torah recognizes not the remains of the individual's body, for after all, "it is but dust and returns to dust," but only the notion that the spirit and body are forever part of the chain of generations. We understand that all children should follow in the right path. The Torah also decreed reward/punishment on earth as the natural result of the human deed.

Objections to the collective appear in the songs of Psalms and the Book of Job. The individual is dissatisfied with his national religion because it makes him, but a means to the collective. He wants to unite his soul with his Creator and pour out his heart for his own sake. He wants to believe that each individual is to be awarded for his particular deeds and that each individual soul has its own limitless existence.

These were the arguments of the original Hasidim if the conception of Hasidut[132] is to be defined in the sense of striving to a direct relationship between man and God. The Essenes represent this type of Hasidut. The Essenes blossomed during the reign of the Greek/Roman power, at the time when the national existence was in peril, and the Pharisees tried to strengthen Judaism as they understood it "Fence to Fence." The religious laws as tools for protecting the nation forced the Hasidim to move away from the community and to separate themselves into the wilderness to pray in solitude in small groups (God seekers). They were seeking moral perfection.

Later an open rebellion broke out against the nationalism and religion of ancient Christianity, which is, by nature, a particular religion. Since that time, religion is turning more nationalistic, and its many laws limited. The Torah becomes a Talmud, a science of lawmakers and learned jurists. To observe the 630 commandments and their history became a goal of its own

---

[132] Popular mystical mass movement in Judaism influenced by the Kabbalah ideas. Hasidut stresses the innate ability of every individual to achieve closeness to God through intense prayer and other ritual activities.

importance. It is all accomplished as a national discipline to fortify oneself with psychological power.

When the Talmud during the scholars (Geonim)[133] became a second Torah, the Karaim[134] formed a protesting group. Their protest, however, is in the name of pure belief, but only because of their fanatical attitude to the first Torah, which they interpreted in their own way, as a frozen law, without adjusting to exigencies of time and needs of the nation. Because of this, they left the Jews.

Examples of the struggle between the two principles of religion, the individual and national, are found in a later period. The orthodox Rabbis, with the religious philosophy, fought with the Mystical Cabala. However, this debate remained within the circles of the learned and writers and did not hurt the masses. Only when the practical Cabala joined the messianism of Sabbatai Zevi,[135] which aroused the world, did the masses become aware of the double-sidedness of Judaism. Individual repentance became a means with which to help in the redemption of the Jew and the nation. The preparation of each soul became a preparation for the messianic period. The fierce desperation that followed the fall of the messianic movement brought cleavage psychology and strengthened the masses in striving for religious perfection of the individual within the national limits. This striving called forth the revival of the new Hasidut.

This religious movement spread among the Polish Jews of the 18th century and, within a short time, reached a height never seen in Jewish history. During the first few decades, this movement became referred to as a sect. However, this faction quickly broke through its limits so that in many places in Poland and Russia, its numbers exceeded the opposition. The split between the Hasidim and their opponents (Misnagdim)[136] had already reached its end when the 19th century began. The Misnagdim remained loyal to the Rabbinical line.

---

[133] Geonim were the presidents of the two great Babylonian Talmudic Academies during the Abbasid Caliphate, and were the generally accepted spiritual leaders of the Jewish community worldwide in the early medieval era. Geonim, the plural of Gaon, means "pride" or "splendor" in Biblical Hebrew, and "genius" today. As a title of a Babylonian times, it was akin to "your Excellency". The Geonim played a prominent and decisive role in the transmission and teaching of Torah and Jewish law. They taught Talmud and decided on issues on which no ruling had been rendered during the period of the Talmud. The Geonim were also the spiritual leaders of the Jewish community in their time.

[134] Karaite Judaism or Karaism is a Jewish religious movement where the written Torah alone is recognized as the supreme authority in halakha and theology.

[135] Sabbatai Zevi was a Sephardic ordained rabbi, though of Romaniote origin and a kabbalist, who was active throughout the Ottoman Empire and claimed to be the long-awaited Jewish Messiah. He founded the Sabbatean movement, and subsequently the Dönmeh crypto-Jews.

[136] Misnagdim, meaning "Opponents"; were Eastern Europe Jews who resisted the rise of Hasidism in the 18th and 19th centuries. Most lived in Lithuania, where Vilnius served as the bastion of the movement, but anti-Hasidic activity occurred in many locales. The most severe clashes between the factions took place in the latter third of the 18th century; the failure to contain Hasidism led the *Misngadim* to develop distinct religious philosophies and communal institutions, which were often innovative and not merely a perpetuation of the old status quo. The most notable results of these efforts, pioneered by Chaim of Volozhin and continued by his disciples, were the modern,

The Jewish communities at the time were divided. In the northern regions of Eastern Europe (Latvia and Russia) the Misnagdim were in the majority. In the southern regions, Ukraine and East Galicia, central Poland, Romania and Hungary, the Hasidut was the majority. Thus, one may conclude that in the 19th century, most East European Jews were Hasidim, i.e., the sect was greater than the orthodox opposition.

The Hasidic Movement, therefore, caused the greatest split in Judaism. However, it was an inner split, one in belief but not in the religious community.

Hasidim was the exact opposite of the Karaim of 1,000 years earlier. The latter strove to change the content of the practical religion in opposition to the Rabbinate, which formed the practical theology according to their ideas and public understanding. They thus caused an outer split that excluded them from the national total, a split impossible to unite.

The creators of Hasidim never interfered in the religious traditions and manner except to make minor changes in the order of prayer and some customs. It is, therefore, self-evident that they never even thought to deny the principles of Judaism. They had a positive approach. They emphasized the individual inner belief of the religion that was entirely within the national outer faith. They added meaning to each religious step, to return evolutionism to the fossilized prayers that lost their meanings and which touch the very roots and branches of religion. The movement desires to reform not the belief but the psychic of the believer, to strengthen his feelings over reason, the union with God, the understanding of God, the Torah of the heart above the Torah from the book. True Hasidism taught various fantasies and mysticisms, stories and incredible miracles, the Tzadikism,[137] miracle makers who intervene between God and man in that way brought strange and unknown elements into pure Judaism. Because of this, Hasidot brought Judaism out of the abstract world down into the nether world, adjusting it to the reach or goals of ordinary human beings. In this way, it succeeded in attracting the great mass, to arouse a deep change of soul, and to plant new life in psychic and new hopes.

The effects of Hasidim are great and important, particularly in its rise and development in the eyes of our ancestors and those of the generations that are yet in us. It lies amid our history and forms an entire mystic cult with a chain of wonder stories whose heroes are the creations of Hasidot. They are our relatives, ancestors, and inheritors.

---

independent *yeshiva*. Since the late 19th century, tensions with the Hasidim largely subsided, and the heirs of *Misnagdim* adopted the epithet "Litvaks".

[137] Tzadik is a title in Judaism given to people considered righteous, such as Biblical figures and later spiritual masters. The root of the word ṣadiq, is ṣ-d-q, which means "justice" or "righteousness". When applied to a righteous woman, the term is inflected as tzadeikes/tzaddeket.

"Recent" Events

#102 MODERN VIEW OF AMERICA (1965)
Letter from Harry Robin to Joe Gillman, 1965

Editor's note: Cousin Joe Gillman's B'nai Khaim in America (1969, Dorrance & Company, Philadelphia) documents the adaptations that nearly 100 immigrant Jews, all stemming from a common ancestor, and their American-born offspring made all coming to America and being the first generation born in the United States. Nearly all of the immigration occurred in the years 1903-1914 and 1921-1925. The book chronicles the religious and cultural values the immigrants brought from their native Ukraine (Pale of Settlement) and the changes the economic, sociological, and cultural experience they and their American offspring experienced here during the ensuring 60 years affected their lives.

The years following World War II (1945 through the 60s) brought unbelievable prosperity, opportunity, and freedom to the children unknown to the parents. Religious persecution was unknown to the newer generation.

The letter below describes one family member's extraordinary optimism typical of the new generation. It also expresses the dismay felt when the United States became entangled and entered into the Vietnam War, which was both costly in life.

Gillman was well known for his several academic economic treatises (*Prosperity in Crisis*, 1965, Marzani & Munsell Publishers; and *The Falling Rate of Profit*, 1957, D. Dobson London, Publisher)

Dearest Joe and Etta,

Your book arrived several weeks ago, and your card from the USSR.

We received both with delight, and it's good to know that you're home now and back at work.

"Prosperity in Crisis" should be made into a feature film, for distribution throughout the WESTERN ALLIES, the NATO Countries and the countries of the OAS, SEACO, etc. It would be an excellent thing for the numb-minded American public to be so neatly reminded of a few facts and ideas. I am especially delighted with your occasional references to the younger American economists, and how their situations (at universities, corporations, and banks, etc.) help to delude them even about economic theory. It's the first time I've read a book on economics which is everywhere lucid. You write like a wizard, and I've been learning things about my own writing from you, indirectly of course, but quite significantly.

Life here moves; the children are beautiful, bright, developing into independent and intelligent personalities. All are very musical: Raissa at the piano, Gregor on the trumpet, and little Alexandra at anything that makes tones. Erica is now with us, turning 17 in Aug. She's just graduated from high school (at the end of her junior year) and accepted by the University of Wisconsin, where she may major in psychology. Mary and I think her extraordinarily musical and are trying to urge her to keep at it. She plays the piano and the guitar exquisitely, sings like an angel, has perfect pitch, and all the attributes of a fine musician. She must somehow keep at it, along with a more "earnest" profession.

Mary's been teaching more and more, as the children get more house-broken. She's still marvelous, perhaps more so.

My job gets more and more fascinating and responsible. I am now preparing a script, which I shall direct, for a film sponsored by the National Science Foundation. I intend it to explain to parents of HS chemistry students why the Chemistry curriculum and general teaching methods need changing to become more experimental when compared to previous memorization and didactic approaches. A good deal of the work is to be done in San Francisco, at the University of California (Berkeley), so that you will infer – correctly – that life is quite pleasant for me.

Love to you all. Keep writing! Let us know about B'nai Khaim, et al.

HARRY ROBIN, 1358 N. SPAULDING AVE, HOLLYWOOD 46, CALIFORNIA

July 24, 1965

#103 THE FBI AND ME: A TEACHER'S STORY
By [A498a] Ken Goodman
Reprinted with permission of [A498] Yetta Goodman

Editor's note: Ken Goodman, married for 62 years to cousin [A498] Yetta Goodman, died in early 2020. The story that follows was told during the memorial service held on December 22, 2020. It relates all too well the fears of Jews and their history with pogroms, dangers, and destruction that follow poorly controlled political assassination. Fortunately, Ken and Yetta were young enough to regroup after the decade-long hiatus in their lives, later to become pioneers in the field of literacy education. Both were to become distinguished professors and world-famous for their research on how people learn to read.

The Federal Bureau of Investigation (FBI) with the State of California's collusion took ten years of my professional career from me. From when I was 15 years old in 1943, until 1964, the FBI had me under surveillance. They invaded my privacy and used deceit to obtain information about where I lived, where I worked, and with whom I met. Ultimately the FBI had me fired and black-listed from teaching during the McCarthy era.

The FBI, the Justice Department's investigative arm, has at times gone beyond investigating to use the information it gathers to intervene in the lives of American citizens. In the 1950s, Senator Joseph McCarthy caused many prominent people to lose their jobs. That story is well known. Less known is that the FBI's director, J Edgar Hoover, used his agents to supply most of the information McCarthy used. Few know but many suspect that thousands of teachers, civil servants, social workers, doctors, professors, and others also lost their professions and livelihoods through the FBI's illegalities. I was one of their victims. To accomplish the FBI's goal required individual state and school district administrators to participate actively. In my case, the State of California's Department of Education used the FBI's information to have my school district Superintendent fire me.

After finally gaining access to my 500-page FBI file only recently through the Freedom of Information Act, I understood the FBI had deprived me of my Constitutional right to assemble with other citizens of like belief peaceably. Colluding with the US Attorney General, they determined that certain political parties and groups shouldn't have the right to "peaceably assemble." Without warrants, they surveilled American citizens who were not engaged in any illegal activities and then used that information to intervene in those citizens' lives and livelihoods. They used deceit and illicit means to monitor individuals and groups. And they both forced and paid citizens to provide information about their friends and colleagues.

Shortly after graduating from high school in 1943 at age 15, I visited my grandparents, whose apartment was located where Wayne State University's athletic facilities now stand. It was a strange time. The newspaper headlines proclaimed race rioting had occurred the night before on the nearby Belle Isle.

Adolescence, a time of self-discovery, is a difficult age. Some kids experiment with drugs or liquor while some join gangs. I joined the Communist Party and the Young Communist League. In 1943, to me, at age 15, it was a logical thing to do. I never publicly admitted this before, for doing so would have subjected me to all manner of injury. In the context of the McCarthy era, it would have required me to betray others.

Jewish immigrants to the United States were refugees from violent antisemitism and were often participants/victims in the political upheavals of the social revolutions in Eastern Europe. My father came to the United States as a child in late 1905. My aunt had been active in the 1905 failed uprising against the Czar. His family was conflicted between religious tradition and political activism. My father spent his life rejecting both and yet tried to make a place for himself with only three years of formal education. My mother was born in South Bend to immigrants who had only recently come from Poland. My mother's father owned the "Jew" store in Lasalle, IL, where he raised nine children. She left school before 9th grade.

I was born in Chicago in 1927 as the 3rd and youngest child. I started school during the depth of the depression with an impoverished family. We moved frequently, and hence, I was always the new kid -- the outsider. We rarely lived in Jewish communities, which meant I experienced incidental antisemitism. Occasionally, acts were overt when classmates or neighbor kids learned I was Jewish. My second grade teacher called me a dirty little Jew and told me to return to Russia, where I belonged.

I also realized early that life is short, and time lost can never be reclaimed. That means doing something about solving the problems of human society. At some point in my youth, I realized that progress does not come without conflict. Revolution is necessary to overcome the forces in society that produce inequality, injustice, and use the institutions of democracy to control and maintain their privilege. But revolution is not a matter of replacing one power group with another. The true revolution has to change the conditions that prevent progress toward social and economic justice. Hence, I chose to define myself as a teacher, researcher, and scholar. I needed to produce knowledge and use it and my voice to make my life of value. My revolution was the change I could bring through education.

Growing up Political

My sister, who was nine years my elder, became a student at the University of Illinois. She began my political education during her visits home,. She talked about how working people were badly treated. She spoke about how something called "capitalism" caused the Great Depression and how she and her new friends would change things. I listened as my father, who was forever starting failing businesses, defended the system, dismissing her enthusiasm with, "You can't change human nature." My sister brought us more than political insight into my life. She introduced me to essential books, an appreciation of art and classical music, and a desire for more learning.

Her ideas impressed my brother and me. By age 16, he was deeply engrossed in politics. In 1938, when my mother and I followed my father to Los Angeles for yet another start-over, having failed in Chicago, New York, New Jersey, and Detroit, my brother remained in Detroit to complete high school. He stayed with my newly married and newly graduated sister and brother in law who struggled with low paying jobs. He immersed himself in political activities during the weekends.

On December 7, 1941, the Japanese attacked Pearl Harbor. My brother and brother-in-law joined the navy. My sister became a teacher, and my mother got a job in a defense factory. As a high school graduate, I worked in a factory and sold pins for Russian War Relief (They were an ally then).

Soon I entered Wayne State University, where I found people with my interests and values. We formed a chapter of American Youth for Democracy. My new, stimulating, and diverse friends shared my concerns and growing political awareness. I knew I wished to help to change the world. We would fight Fascism and bring about a better world when the war ended. I wrote for the Daily Collegian (later The South End), the Wayne State newspaper, and became a leader. I attended political rallies. I joined picket lines at Briggs Stadium, protesting the absence of non-white players. We picketed the Dutch Consulate over their treatment of Indonesia. Detroit was indeed segregated at that time.

In 1946 I moved to the University of Michigan, where I lived in a coop house. By age 18, I was a board member of the coop house association. I learned to cook meals for 30.

With the undergraduates and grad students I met, we discussed Marxism, race discrimination, current political issues, and antisemitism. We joined other groups helping to integrate barbershops. We were only now learning the extent of the Holocaust. Some of our incoming mates were returning vets. A few had seen the concentration camps.

I need to differentiate the radical left of the forties from the New Left of the '60s. We were the children of the Great Depression. Our need to make a living took priority over politics. We engaged in no violence and broke no laws. The revolution we believed would come would be achieved through unions and legal means. After all, many of Roosevelt's ideas and those of the New Deal came from Marxism. In the concepts of Marxism, I understood institutions and the need for social solutions to the profit motivations of capitalism. My friends also had high personal commitments to opposing the injustices of the system. Nothing we ever did was improper, nor was I asked to do anything illegal. We committed to no violence. No organization I belonged to was ever illegal, including the Communist Party.

My record

In reading my file, my first discovery was that the FBI observed and spied on my friends and me from our first meetings. That is no exaggeration. The FBI files showed that some friends were not my friends. A bowling partner had recorded my average was 88. The G-men must have had a good laugh over that information. Someone at a party of maybe a dozen people at my home filed a report on all the other guests too. Despite reporting on every meeting I attended, every petition I signed or circulated, nothing I was alleged to have done was illegal. No record suggested I committed any crime or criminal act. As early as 1947, the agent in charge requested the FBI cease keeping an active file on me.

A notation in my file dated March 1947 read:

> "It is noted that since the date referenced in the report only two sources of information have been furnished relative to subject's communist activities by confidential informants and that it is believed that the subject according to information furnished by informants

would not be deemed dangerous to the internal security of this Country. It is recommended therefore that subject's name be removed from the security index files and this office is so advised."

By 1948, the Detroit agents lost interest in me. But in 1950, I committed the apparently subversive act. I became a teacher.

In 1946, at age 19, I married a "red diaper" baby. Her family moved to Russia, where her father helped start an auto industry in Gorky. Soon she and her mother returned to Detroit, after which my parents ceased providing me with any support, even though I was now attending the University of Michigan. In 1948 I left school to work for the election of Henry Wallace on the Progressive Party ticket. I also worked that year in the Packard auto factory in Detroit. I attended the Young Progressives convention in Philadelphia as a delegate from my United Auto Workers local. By the year-end, we moved to Los Angeles, and I enrolled at UCLA and finished my bachelor's degree in labor economics. I then took courses at the new Los Angeles State University to qualify for elementary and secondary teaching certificates, continuing my political interests as time permitted. My first marriage ended during this period.

In 1950 the complete history of my 1943-47 activities with pictures and artifacts appeared in a new file the Los Angeles FBI Office kept. Conspicuously missing was the statement I was deemed not to be a risk to the Country's security and that my Detroit file had been closed.

The McCarthy Years late 1940's through the 1950s

In the spring of 1950, I completed California's requirements for both Elementary and Secondary Teaching certificates by student teaching in 7th grade in Torrance Elementary School in the Torrance Unified School District. During that summer, I worked at the Eastside Jewish Community Center's Day camp, and there met [A849] Yetta Trachtman, my wife-to-be.

I began teaching the 8th grade in September 1950. By the year-end, I was asked to renew my contract for the following year.

I worked again at the same day camp during the summer of 1951. Yetta and I began dating and married in June 1952. My second year of teaching eighth-grade students was highly successful. I learned to treat 12 and 13 year-olds like adults, even though expecting them to act like children. I participated in school committees and attended the California Teachers Association in San Francisco as a delegate from my local Teachers Association. I finished a Master's Degree in education. Yetta began teaching in Redondo Beach in a new middle school, also in the eighth grade. She was successful from the start.

Now some background to the McCarthy period and the hunt for Communists:

J. Edgar Hoover, the FBI director, designed the US loyalty-security program, and the FBI agents carried out all background investigations. Between 1946 and 1952, the number of agents assigned doubled from 3,559 to 7,029. The standards of evidence they applied resulted in thousands of government workers losing their jobs. The informers' identities remained secret. The people reviewed were never permitted to cross-examine those who accused them, let alone usually to know who they were. Often, those accused never knew of what they were charged.

From 1951 to 1955, the secret "Responsibilities Program" the FBI operated distributed anonymous documents with evidence the FBI collected about teachers', lawyers', and others' Communist affiliations. Those accused in these "blind memoranda" were often summarily fired without any further process, certainly not "due" process. The FBI engaged in many illegal practices, including burglaries, opening mail, and illicit wiretaps in pursuing to collect information on suspected Communists.

The reason I had a new file established about me in the Los Angeles FBI office was unrelated to any new activities. It was due only to me becoming a school teacher. The Detroit FBI misinformed the LA FBI why I had moved. They said I moved in 1950 to become a teacher in Torrance, California. Actually, I was in California since 1948, having completed my BA and earning my teaching certification.

The FBI was neither subtle nor careful about its data gathering. The school clerk asked me, "Is some bill collector trying to get information about you?" Neither were they subtle about parking an unmarked car with two men in suits inside the wrong way in front of our house. On occasion, they confused Yetta, my second wife, with my first.

The earliest report was from 1950; a policeman had stopped me from circulating a peace petition in a Los Angeles park. A redacted report dated 1952 included names of several other teachers under surveillance. By January 1953, the FBI decided to go beyond investigating teachers. The Responsibilities Program" zeroed in on me. Several liberal governors worried they might be attacked as soft on Communists, so they asked the FBI for state employees' information. Under the Responsibilities Program, the governors routinely received reports orally or on paper lacking a letterhead.

My file made clear the sequence of events that led to my firing. Dated January 9, 1953, a letter in my LA FBI file directs the San Francisco FBI office to inform then-Governor Earl Warren that I was a teacher and lists in detail information gathered from 1943 through 1947. The last paragraph of the letter was most telling:

> "None of the information may be attributed to the FBI…The information is furnished in the strictest confidence, and…no reference can be made to the FBI in any manner with any action taken based on the information furnished."

The San Francisco FBI did so, forwarding the information to a special agent in the State Department of Education, who then contacted the Torrance Superintendent and School Board. The FBI wanted me fired, but would not take responsibility for doing so. This fact was no small thing, for had I known this, events might have gone differently. The school might have fired me without any indication of why. But there would have been a complication. In May 1953, the school board had awarded me permanent tenure.

Some two weeks later, my principal came to my room in mid-morning and told me to go directly to the Superintendent's office. Upon entering, I was surprised to see a dozen men. One I recognized as an advisor to the National Education Association and its California affiliate.

Supt. Hull got right to the point. The only person he introduced was Special Agent Dresser, whom I assumed, erroneously, was FBI. I only learned later from my file was he was from the

California Department of Education. The delineation of my "subversive" activities read by SA Dresser at my firing was identical to what the FBI provided to Governor Warren in its letter. The events all occurred when I was age 15 to 19. Since I assumed he was an FBI agent, it never occurred to me to challenge the source.

When he finished, Supt Hull asked for my response. I replied, had I known the nature of the meeting, I would have come with a lawyer. He said that this was not a legal hearing. The board had already revoked my tenure and voted to end my employment at the school year's ending. They would permit me to finish the year provided I took no public action to protest or fight my dismissal.

When I pointed out my good recommendations over the years, he said, "This is not about your teaching. It is about your subversive activities."

What could I say or do? Do I challenge the truth of the alleged activities? Do I point out that nothing in the list was illegal? Do I threaten to sue the district? The hysteria of the time meant none of these were possible choices.

Both the ACLU and the left Civil Rights Congress offered me sympathy, but they were overwhelmed with cases like mine and were losing all of them in court. I was surprised to read in my file that an attorney had called the Superintendent on my behalf.

So I finished the school year saying nothing to my colleagues or students about why I was not returning. The following summer, I learned no district to which I applied would hire me. Within a few weeks, many other of my teacher friends were similarly dismissed. It became evident that the FBI had moved beyond investigation to actively using selected information from informants to intervene in the employment and lives of teachers, government employees, social workers, lawyers, doctors, and university professors.

Yetta's Superintendent called her after my friend informed him I was fired. Her Superintendent told her he wasn't renewing her contract but would give her a recommendation. She was, in fact, able to find a job in another district. We may never know what pressure he may or may not have resisted.

In my case, as I began to apply for jobs, it became obvious something had been inserted in my placement file, which was an absolute requirement that all requests for information would clearly state why I was fired.

SA Dresser reported to the FBI that based on its information, I had been fired. The file also depicted the hysteria of the times. It also showed how citizens willingly used the information to their advantage. My file notes that Supt. Hull inquired about two other teachers, both Jewish. One, who taught with me, was the president of the local Teachers Association. The other, whom I hardly knew, resigned after I was fired. Supt. Hull thought that was suspicious.

Governor Warren asked the State Attorney General to interview me. He replied I had already been fired. My file shows that Dresser called me in to tell me he was recommending revoking my teaching certificates (that never actually happened). Dresser asked me to respond to "certain information in our possession." He allowed me to "clarify my position" regarding the allegations. He asked if I was willing to answer questions concerning my "affiliations, associations and activities." I replied that I could not answer those kinds of questions. I told him I was standing on my constitutional right under the 5th amendment and that I would be betraying my profession if I answered. He asked me if I knew the National Educational Association (NEA) was advising teachers to answer questions. I said shame on them for doing that. I asked him to understand my belief that I should be judged based on my classroom record and my ideas and methods. Nothing else should matter.

As the interview ended, he offered me the stool-pigeon alternative. Cooperation would help my situation. I impolitely declined.

I have been unable to obtain my records from the California Department of Education. Only after reading my FBI files was it apparent the FBI information was the foundation of my firing. But the FBI explicitly forbid the information to be attributed to it. Was this the policy of the California government or the act of an overzealous individual? It was certainly not the proudest moment in Earl Warren's political life.

Purgatory, 1953-1962

The FBI was not satisfied just to get me removed from my teaching job, even though they were aware I was a highly regarded teacher. It used every means to keep track of me subsequently. 'Pretense' is their favorite phrase for deceit. Someone used trickery to learn I was not teaching, and someone pretending to be a colleague got my wife to reveal I was working for my father. Someone reported on a meeting held at our home to raise funds for other fired teachers fighting their dismissal. Did someone take the bait Special Agent Dresser offered? In November 1953, responding to a LA FBI office request, someone, presumably from the Detroit FBI, prepared a detailed list of all meetings I was reported to have attended and sent it to the LA Office suggesting they maintain a security card on me.

Concluding this file was old, Special Agent John J De Bello recommended my file be closed:

> "As all outstanding in re rep have been covered, with the submission of amended administrative passages to the Bureau, this case is closed administratively."

Yet, in January 1955, the FBI found I was now an assembly-line worker for Chrysler in Southgate, Ca, a "key facility" the army and navy so designated. My job was to hang doors on cars. So my file was re-opened. Perhaps, not coincidently, some unknown person, who testified at the House of Unamerican Activities Committee, said I was active in the Communist Party in 1945-46 (at age 17).

They used deceit to get information from Yetta and the plant security to confirm I was working there. My file was re-opened since the company did business with the armed forces. Later, in 1955, my file was once again closed. It appears that someone believed I was involved in underground activities, but there was no evidence I was or even knew about such an underground.

Now for the third time, my file was closed. Note Hoover personally signed the report (see JEH initials next to "director".

STANDARD FORM NO. 64

Office Memorandum • UNITED STATES GOVERNMENT

TO : SAC, Los Angeles (100-32880) DATE: May 27, 1955

FROM : Director, FBI (100-344117)

SUBJECT: KENNETH SAWYER GOODMAN
SECURITY MATTER - C

Reurlet dated April 29, 1955.

A review of referenced Los Angeles letter by the Bureau shows that the only basis for the continued retention of the subject in the Security Index is information reflecting that as of August 8, 1954, the subject was being considered for possible assignment in the Los Angeles County Communist Party underground apparatus. A review of your letter and Bureau files fails to show that the subject did participate in the Los Angeles County Communist Party underground activities or that there is evidence that the subject had knowledge of his possible consideration for an underground assignment. In view of the above, the subject does not meet the standards set forth in SAC Letter 55-30 and his Security Index card is being cancelled by the Bureau. Your office is instructed to take similar action and cancel the Security Index card maintained for the subject.

If, in the future, your office develops any information showing the subject's actual participation in Communist Party underground activities or develops other information justifying his retention in the Security Index, you should resubmit your request in accordance with instructions in SAC Letter 55-30.

SI Cancelled

1 sent to Detroit by Fd 128a 11/5/64 slp

100-32880-70
SEARCHED ... INDEXED ...
SERIALIZED ... FILED ...
MAY 31 1955
FBI-LOS ANGELES

51376 DocId:32684492 Page 223

Fig. 103-1 FBI memo signed by J Edgar Hoover

What follows in my file was a series of semi-annual notations updating where I worked and lived.

In 1960 the LA FBI interviewed me, hoping I might be cooperative. Their terse report states:

> KENNETH SAWYER GOODMAN was interviewed on January 13, 1960, at 11006 Arbuckle Avenue, Pacoima, California. The jurisdiction of the FBI in the internal security field was explained to GOODMAN, and he stated he had nothing to discuss with Agents of the FBI. The interviewing Agents attempted to explain to GOODMAN the nature of the Communist Party and its international association with the Communist Party, Soviet Union, at which time he interrupted the Agents to state that the Agents were wasting their time and his and that he had nothing to say to Agents of the FBI. At this point GOODMAN was asked what his attitude would be and where his allegiance would lie in the event of hostilities between the United States and Russia. GOODMAN stated, "I would be right here telling you that I had nothing to discuss with the FBI."

Fig. 103-2

From 1953 through 1963, I was unable to teach in any public school. Although I had a variety of part-time and full-time jobs, I was also unemployed and unemployable at times. Several other fired teachers worked at the same auto plant in Southgate, Ca, as I. Later, I worked nights at another auto plant in Van Nuys, taught Jewish Sunday school, and directed day camps for the Los Angeles Jewish Centers Association.

Eventually, I found full-time employment as a social group worker for the Valley Cities Jewish Community Center in Van Nuys Ca. To progress in that position, I needed to complete a two-year program leading to a Master's degree in Social Work. Instead, I decided to risk pursuing a doctoral program in education at UCLA. Tuition there was nominal at the time. I had some support with teaching and research assistantships and taught for a year at a startup private secondary school in Beverly Hills staffed entirely with black-listed teachers.

My file shows that the FBI renewed its surveillance about me every six months lasting into the 1960s.

<u>Informants</u>

Though redacted, my file listed names I knew. It wasn't hard to determine who were some of the informants. I have asked what caused people to become informants? Did the FBI hire young people to penetrate our groups? Did they pressure members using inducements and threats? Were they members who became disillusioned or angry at others and volunteered to be informants? Some of these informants probably are victims themselves, trapped into giving names.

In the 1960s, each annual report contained a statement from informants who seemed to know me stating that: 1) I am no longer in the party and 2) probably not even sympathetic. In November 1964, when the LA FBI discovered I was now an assistant professor at Wayne State University, they asked the Detroit FBI for verification, once more redundantly sending my 1943-47 record back to them.

My file ends at that time.

Life after survieilance:

After 20 years of surveillance, the FBI lost interest in me, and just as my career in education was resuming. Reflecting back, the reason may have been that the new left was emerging, and that group was far more contentious. Campuses were exploding. Or perhaps, the many informants in the old-left got out of hand and were now informing on each other.

I graduated with a Doctor of Education Degree in 1963 from UCLA. To my surprise, I had three job offers. The most attractive came from Wayne State University.

I didn't know until I arrived that Fall that my contract ran for three years. The baby boom was exploding, and so was teacher education. Wayne State had been part of the Detroit public schools until World War II when it became a State University. The new Dean had recently moved from NYU and brought several prominent progressive educators.

Assuming that I would be at risk and vulnerable unless I established myself as a researcher and scholar, I immediately launched literacy research. Detroit was an ideal laboratory for me. The graduate students were teachers in the schools who welcomed me in their classrooms. I avoided the middle-class suburbs. Instead, I chose to study why black and Appalachian white kids were less successful in school. I learned much about urban dialects.

I presented at conferences, wrote articles, and began a book with my new colleagues. After publishing, I provided copies of my work to crucial scholars. Soon graduate students wished to work with me.

Only when I achieved tenure and promotion did I again begin to feel secure in my profession. At that time, my Dean, in his monthly newsletter, quoted Oliver Wendell Holmes on academic freedom. A short time later, I learned the faculty knew of my history but took a chance to hire me.

Yetta completed her doctorate at Wayne State.

We later spent a semester at the London Institute of Education. One evening, after a stimulating seminar, we dined at an Italian restaurant with other faculty and students. As the seminar discussion veered to Marxist views of language, Yetta and I found ourselves instinctively looking over our shoulders for the FBI.

No one truly knows how many other victims the Hoover/McCarthy systematic interventions caused. Many teachers I knew were personally involved. They were dedicated teachers who mostly never returned to teaching. When I decided to pursue the doctorate at UCLA, many friends advised me I wasted my time. Another friend who ran a liquor store was particularly bitter. Of greater significance, the NEA and AFT, the official organizations representing teachers, proved complicit in getting teachers fired. At its convention, the NEA voted teachers should cooperate with the authorities. School authorities such as the California Department of Education were active in getting teachers fired, knowing the FBI would not permit itself or its informants to be involved in any court actions. Even more tragic was the long-lasting effect the fears put into us stifled our teaching and curriculum by limiting productive controversy and innovative teaching methods.

The history recorded here shows what can happen when the government in a democratic society abuses power and uses agencies to squash what they perceive as anti-democratic agendas. Could the FBI again become the tool of limiting the rights of citizens to assemble peaceably? Who doubts that it could?

#104 RESCUE OF THE DANISH JEWS
Letter from [A334a] Charlotte Milstein to [A457] Joe Gillman on Mar 2, 1964

<u>Editor's note:</u> Many of our family members died during World War II when the Germans invaded Russia. [A334a] Charlotte Milstein's uncle and aunt, [A835] Aage and Greta Bertelsen, were principal organizers in multiple somewhat coordinated events that saved more than 7,000 Danish Jews.

Their letters highlight the distinction in word usage of "evacuation" and "rescue" when applied to historical events. "Rescue" implies action and bravery to the rescuer and a somewhat helpless victim to the rescued. The Danes, who helped the Jews escape to Sweden as shown by these letters, confirmed the Danish Jews' and their friends' conduct during the time; they displayed courageous decisions and active participation made under exceedingly difficult circumstances.

<u>From [A334a] Charlotte Milstein</u>

It may interest your readers to know that the Lyngby Resistance Group performed the successful evacuation of Denmark's Jews in October 1943. My uncle, [A835] Aage Bertelsen, was one of the principal organizers. It was he, who with six others, spirited almost 6,000 people across the narrow channel between Denmark and Sweden's town of Malmo. This episode is one of the few bright spots in an otherwise black period of history.

My uncle, Aage Bertelsen, tells of this in his book "October 1943," which is one of the first English-language works about the Danish Jews' flight (published in 1954). It is a firsthand account telling of his experiences to help Jews escape to Sweden. In a tribute to him, [A821] Albert Einstein met with him in New York in 1953. He was much honored by many organizations and lectured across the country during that year. He spent an evening at our home in Los Angeles with the [A385] Galler's and my husband's parents. He now teaches at Aarhus University near the small native town of Silkeborg, Denmark. The book, which is poorly translated and hurriedly written, presents the facts without embroidery.

<u>Events as summarized by the editor:</u>

Within a few weeks in October 1943, the Danes moved about 95% of the country's Jewish population, over 7,000 people, to safety in neutral Sweden. Even as vessels were carrying the fugitive Danish Jews across the Øresund strait to Sweden, the news had already reached England and the USA, where expatriate Danes sought some encouraging news useful to alter Denmark's dubious reputation as "Hitler's pantry." With Denmark's rapid capitulation once the Nazi's occupied it in 1940, and their extensive cooperation with German forces after that had marked the Danes as "opportunist cowards." By the war's end 1945, however, the Danes had maneuvered themselves to the winning side and achieved de facto status as part of the allied war effort. But another 20 years had to pass for the world to become fully aware of the remarkable events in that fateful month of October 1943.

The Danes knew that Jews had to pay for their illegal crossings to safety. It was never a secret. A 1945 cartoon in the satirical magazine, *Svikmøllen*, tells not only of how widely known were the payments and payment demands, but how much people commonly discussed them at the time.

A gentleman stands at the ticket counter for the Copenhagen boat to Malmö and asks,
"How much is a ticket to Sweden?"
"Five kroner and 60 øre."
"That's cheap! The last time I paid 3,000 kroner!"

Some families paid up to 50,000 kroner for the crossing, even though the price to buy an actual fishing boat was 15,000 to 30,000 Danish kroner in 1943. Fortunately, the passage for many was 1,000 kroner and some less. At that time, a fully trained worker's monthly salary was 414 kroner.

On August 28, at the German plenipotentiary in Denmark, Dr. Werner Best, the chief executive officer of the occupying German power, presented the Danish government with an ultimatum that would abrogate fundamental Danish civil rights. The Danish government rejected the ultimatum, after which the following morning, the German army imposed a state of emergency. Martial law then went into effect. No longer did the Danes, including its Jews, have the protection of its elected government. On September 8, Best sent a telegram to Berlin recommending "that measures should now be taken toward a solution of the problem of the Jews." The night of October 1 was set for implementation.

Best had ensured that Danish Jews would receive advance warning of the Aktion planned for the 1st. In reality, he also had become a "big softy." Though antisemitic, he felt that a hunt for Jews did not serve the Nazi regime's strategic interests. The aim was to make Denmark "judenrein" (cleansed of Jews) while avoiding widespread unrest amongst the wider population. Whether this happened via deportation to German prison camps or via illegal flights to Sweden was irrelevant to him.

On September 28, German shipping attaché Georg Duckwitz informed several Danish Social Democratic Party leaders of the pending action against the Danish Jews. These political leaders quickly set about using their large labor union and other contacts to warn as many Jews as possible of the coming action scheduled two nights hence.

September 29, 1943, was the first night of Rosh Hashanah. While much of the population was yet unaware of the forthcoming "Aktion," the warnings spread as a wildfire might spread across the country. Knocks came to neighbors' doors. Contemporary diaries and memoirs tell of many spontaneous offers of assistance from extended family networks, friends, acquaintances, and even total strangers.

Sea crossings to neutral Sweden were quickly organized. But terrible dilemmas arose for families with young children. There were terrifying rumors about children being strangled or smothered or even thrown overboard to keep them quiet during the illegal crossing. Some routes had doctors present who could anesthetize the children during the crossing. Full anesthesia was risky and occasionally had a perverse effect. A crying child could expose and endanger everybody, whether fugitives/refugees or fishermen. Also, the October weather could be harsh – wet, windy, and cold. Crossings through choppy waters in pitch darkness were precarious at best. And even if successful, what were the Jewish families to do once arriving in Sweden? At least 150 children (about a tenth of all Jewish children) remained instead hidden in Denmark when their parents fled. Amazingly, no Dane betrayed even one single child to the German police authorities.

Also, to the Danes' credit, the Danish state mechanism enacted measures right in the middle of the Nazi occupation to ensure the absent Jews' possessions and their property remained safeguarded.

[A835] Aage Bertelsen, then a teacher at the Leader Lyngby School in Copenhagen, was a key member organizing the transfer of Jews. His house served as the center of rescue activities. Several hundred Danish Jews passed through it. Pasteur Krohn, Vicar of Lyngby and others, helped him and his wife, Greta, is this endeavor. After the Germans discovered his role, he fled to Sweden, where he became the headmaster of the Danish school for the years 1944-45. The two Bertelsens remained apart for ten months later, and the whole family reunited only 20 months later at the liberation in May 1945.

Bertelsen recalled later: "It was our wish that it should become universally known that there was a travel agency open any time and to anybody who felt impelled to go on a vacation to Sweden. We were well aware of the risk, but we hoped that by the time the Germans got on our heels and closed down the shop, we should have finished a useful piece of work."

Greta, his wife, was arrested in November 1943. The German, during the interrogation, asked why did she help Jews: "We know you have participated in helping Jews to Sweden, isn't that true?" "Of course it is, all decent people did." "And why did you help the Jews? Was it to make money?" "Because of sympathy with poor, persecuted people, who came to us confidentially placing their lives and fates in our hands…." The two Bertelsens discussed earlier how the rescue work made them feel. "It's as if we never realized before what it means to live."

Jan Oberg and Johan Galtung, in their work, describe Berkelsen as "a tall man and a great man, a visionary, pacifist, civil resister, educator, and philosopher. He took life more seriously than most, and he could be playful and fun like a child. His life's guiding principle was "Engage in your time!" and while he wrote and talked a lot, he also did it. His weapon was non-violence – both in life and politics.

Later in his life, Bertelsen said he had known many Jews but few Arabs or Palestinians. He hoped that with the birth of Israel, future pogroms might be averted. He reports that [A822] Chaim Weizmann, Israel's first President, whom he had met, believed antisemitism, in the best of cases, could be reduced, but likely not totally. Weizmann believed antisemitism was rooted in the very existence of the Jew.

Bertelson saw antisemitism as a complex construct. It incorporated culture (values, norms and ethics), politics, psychology (xenophobia), and law (minority status). The psychology of hatred against a group, he said, can be as strong as instincts. When questioned whether he has felt such an instinctual, unconscious reaction, his response was "Yes…We are all to some extent prone to react negatively to what is foreign, to the stranger, to those who are fundamentally different in some aspects from ourselves."

References:

Bertelsen, Aage, October 1943, (tr. By Milly Lindholm). London: Museum Press, 1955).
https://archive.org/stream/october43aageber001971mbp/october43aageber001971mbp_djvu.txt

Humanity in Action in 2013 in Civil Society and the Holocaust: International Perspectives on Resistance and Rescue.

Oberg J and Galtung J: Danish Citizens who Saved Jews in Denmark, https://www.holocaustrescue.org/danish-citizens

Aage Bertelsen (1901 – 1980) – Danish educator for peace. http://blog.transnational.org/2014/07/aage-bertelsen-1901-1980-danish-educator-for-peace/

#105 A DANISH HERO
Letter from [A335] Norman Milstein to [A031] Stanley Robboy, Feb 14, 2020)

I have some information that will be of interest related to [A835] Aage Bertelsen. Beside me is the signed copy of Bertelsen's book that he inscribed to Aunt Serena and Cousin Myrtle, my Great Grandmother and Grandmother on my mother Charlotte's side of the family. Bertelsen's book, by the way, in translation, is freely available on the web.

The Lyngby Group was central in rescuing Jews, but *they were not the only rescuers. That should not be forgotten. M*y mother, in her letter, may have implied that they were acting alone.

"Even after the Lyngby Group had started its route, we continued our connections with other organizations, most frequently by taking over some of their passengers, or vice versa." -- p. 131, October '43

Secondly, an essential and unusual ethical matter took place relevant to present history, which dealt with Bertelsen's interactions with the Hollywood people who desired to make a movie based on his book. I verified these memories from long ago with my brother [A336] David Milstein.

Bertelsen, a man of high integrity, humility, and honesty, had been asked to release his story for the making of a Hollywood movie. Bertelsen refused because they wanted to alter a fundamental truth of his story significantly. They wanted to make a Hollywood romance between an unmarried duo smuggling Jews, NOT a story about a married couple heroically working closely together to foil the Nazis. I suppose that seemed too pedestrian and commercially untenable to the big shots of Hollywood.

We are in a troubling era of "fake news" reminiscent of the so-called "news" generated by totalitarian regimes. Both Hollywood, with its habits of manipulating the truth in the interest of profit, and our politicians and media, all share serious blame for these problems. Foreign powers with their own agendas are also involved. Bertelsen reminds us that in the battle between big money and integrity, the latter integrity should be victorious.

According to my parents, Bertelsen's response to Hollywood was, "You insulted my wife." Therefore, the movie was never made. He simply returned to Denmark.

Bertelsen's courageous humanitarian interventions to save many lives remain a great inspiration!

[A335] Norman Milstein also provided a letter reprinted from a book that a member of the Danish resistance wrote before the Nazis executed him. This letter communicates the profound, humane values that motivated so many Danes during those terrible times. It is a testament to the courage, kindness, and heroic sacrifices that many people made.[138]

---

[138] VESTRE PRISON, German Section Cell 411, 4 April 1945

Dearest Mother

Today, I went before the military tribunal together with Joergen, Niels and Ludwig. We were condemned to die. I know that you are strong and that you will be able to take this. But listen to me, Mother. It isn't enough that you are able to take it. You must also understand it. I'm not of importance and will soon be forgotten, but the ideas, the life, the inspiration which filled me will live on.

You will find them everywhere-in the new green of spring, in people you will meet on your way, in a loving smile. Perhaps you will also find what was of value to me, you will love it and you won't forget me. I would have liked to grow and mature, but I will still live in your hearts and you will live on because you know that I am in front of you on the road and not behind, as you had perhaps thought at first. You know what has always been my greatest wish and what I thought I would become. Mother dear, come with me on my journey. Don't stop at the last stage of my life, but instead stop at some of the preceding ones you may find something which will be of value to the girl I love and to you, Mother.

I have followed a certain path and I don't regret it. I've never betrayed what is in my heart, and now I seem to see the unbroken line which has run through my life. I'm not old, I ought not to die, and still, it seems so simple and natural to me. It's only the brutal way which at first terrifies us. I have so little time left; I don't quite know how to explain it, but my mind is completely at peace. I have always wanted to be like Socrates, but although I have no one to talk to as he had, I feel the same tranquility of spirit and very much want you, Hannie, and Nitte to understand this....

How strange it seems to be writing this testament! Each word will stand; it can never be amended, never revoked, never changed. I'm thinking of so many things. Joergen is sitting here in front of me writing a letter to his daughter for her confirmation-a document for life. We have lived together as friends and now were going to die together.

Finally there are the children who have recently come to mean so much to me. I had so been looking forward to seeing them and being with them again. Just to think of them makes me happy and I hope they will grow up to be men will be able to get more out of life than what lies on the surface. I hope that their character will develop freely and never be subjected to prejudice.

Give them my love, my godson and his brother

NOTE: Kim Malthe-Bruun, born in Denmark in 1923, was 16 when the German Army invaded Denmark. He quickly joined the resistance. He served as a sailor when the Gestapo arrested him in December, 1944 while transporting weapons from Sweden to Denmark. After being tortured, he was executed on April 6, 1945. After the war, his mother, Vibeke Malthe-Bruun, arranged for the publication of his letters (1949). The book included sections of his diary and a collection of his letters to his mother, aunt and his girlfriend, Hanne. The book, titled _Kim_, became a bestseller in Denmark and made Kim revered as a national hero. An English version appeared in 1955 with the title _Heroic Heart: the Diary and Letters of Kim Malthe-Bruun_.

#106 [A556] ANNA MICHALOVNA KAPROVE, AFTER THE NAZIS
by [A558] Gene Katzman

[A556] Anna Gilman (nee Kaprav), in the early summer of 1941, began medical school at the Moscow Medical University. Her beloved grandfather, Leib Greenberg, had just passed away in the shtetl of Pliskov in Podolia (central Ukraine). The entire family, including mother [A451.4a] Leah Kaprov Grinberg, plus her aunts and uncles and many cousins living in Moscow, came to pay last respect and take care of their Grandmother, Surrah Chaya Greenberg, planning for her to return with them to Moscow. Anna had exams and was unable to go. Unfortunately, two weeks later, the Nazis invaded the western frontiers of the Soviet Union, where Pliskov happened to be (150 kilometers from the Soviet/Romanian border). The family, trapped in Ukraine, spent their last days in the [C38] Vinnitsa Ghetto. They all perished in a fire the Nazis began and kept sustained by local sympathizers of Hitler's ideas. Thus, Anna lost her entire family in a single moment. She had already lost her father, [A555] Michal Kaprov, in one of the many pogroms when she was less than a year old. Now, not yet quite 21, she was utterly alone in a horrible war-stricken world.

By the summer's end, she was drafted to the medical train division as a war nurse. She spent the next four years (1941-45) on a medical train traveling to the front line to pick up the wounded from the places of battle to then transporting them to the rear where it was safer. The picture dated late fall 1943 shows Anna on the lower row, to the extreme right. [A828a] Yelena Bonner,[139] who later married physicist [A828] Andrei Zakharov,[140] is in the center next to Anna. Yelena became a famous human rights advocate, and her later husband became known as the "Father of the Russian hydrogen bomb." He later became a prominent dissident.

For her work, Anna received the medal, "For the victory over Germany in the Great Patriotic War of 1941-1945."

Kaprav Anna Mikhailovna
Award presentation
Rank: ml. lieutenant
Location: VSP 122
Record number: 1536453285

---

[139] Yelena Georgievna Bonner (1923 – 2011), wife of physicist Andrei Zakharov, was a Russian human rights activist. During her lifetime as a dissident, she was known for her great courage and characteristic blunt honesty.

[140] Andrei Zakharov was the father of the Soviet hydrogen bomb, but later opposed the Russian's abuse of power. In 1975, he was awarded the Peace Prize for his work for human rights. Furiously, the Soviet leadership refused him permission to travel to Oslo. Instead, Yelena Bonner received it on his behalf. Subsequently, Zakharov lost all his Soviet honorary titles, and for several years the couple remained under strict surveillance at their home in Gorki. In 1985, Gorbachev, now in power, permitted them to return to Moscow.

Fig. 106-1: Anna's (Lower right, front row) medical team. Center, front row, Yelena Bonner, future wife of Andrew Sakharov, father of Russian hydrogen bomb and later dissident fighting for human rights; Right: Medal "For the victory over Germany in the Great Patriotic War of 1941-1945." English:

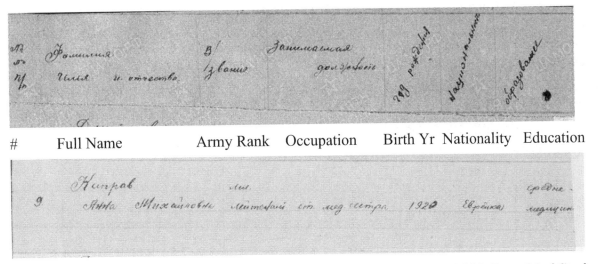

#	Full Name	Army Rank	Occupation	Birth Yr	Nationality	Education
9	Kaprav Anna Mikhalovna	Jr Lieutenant	Registered Nurse	1920	Jew	Med Student

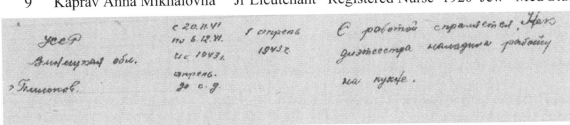

Place birth	Yrs in Red Army & current place	Characteristics

401

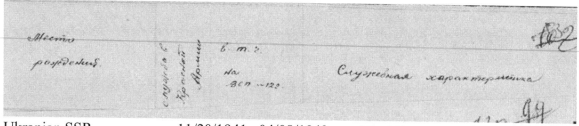

| Ukranian SSR Vinnitsa District Pliskov | 11/20/1941 | 04/08/1943 | Meet the expectations, performs dual duties as a nurse and supervises kitchen. |

Fig. 106-2 Documentation associated with the medal.

Fig 106-3 [A556] Anna Michakovna Kaprove and [A556a] Yosef Salomonovich Gilman 1951.

#107 GLASNOST AND COMING TO AMERICA
by [A558] Gene Katzman

[A558] Gene (Gennady – birth name) Katzman was born in 1971 in Moscow. His parents, [A557] Elena and [A557a] Konstantin Aron Katzman, were two years apart in age (father born 1948, mother born 1950), and both had met when they were college students. In the USSR, each major city had a single University and multiple institutes organized by specialty, such as printing, engineering, law, medicine, etc. Both parents were at the Moscow Polygraphic Institute, which focused on large-scale printing. Konstantin's training dealt more with the engineering associated with big operational, highly complex printing systems. Elena trained in accounting and economics. Their schooling programs were five years long, and their degrees would be equivalent to a master's degree that one might receive today.

Gene was about five years old when he first learned about antisemitism.

He lived near his grandparents, at Sokolniki, a neighborhood on the northeast side of Moscow. Their home was in an apartment complex where the typical buildings were uniform and five-six stories high. Children from all areas would play together. There were no computers back in the 1970s with which to play. Kids then would all hang out together for the day. Homework from school would be completed, allowing the children to resume play in the common area.

Their neighborhood was largely made up of children of Russian background. His playmate, who was also about the same age, would call out "Yid, Yid" to describe another child who might look slightly different. Gene then did the same when he came home. Gene's father asked him if he knew what "Yid" meant, to which he had to say he did not. His father then told him that the word meant Jewish and that he, Gene, was Jewish, his father was Jewish, his mother was Jewish, his grandparents were Jewish, and so were all his uncles, aunts, and grandparents. They were all Jewish. Gene was surprised. The next question that came out of his mouth was, "So Aunt Sopha (Sophia Davidovich, cousin of Konstantin Katzman) is a Jew?" The answer was affirmative. Gene had another question ready. Was her husband, Uncle Gene (Davidovich), a Jew too? The rest looked like a ping pong match. Gene was shouting the names of the relatives and friends of the family and was getting the defiant "Yes" back. It probably would last forever, until Gene asked the last question. "So Aunt Olga's (Olga Sorokin – Elena Katzman sister) dog "Boruch" is Jewish?" Konstantin smiled and answered, "Do you think someone would name a dog like this if it wasn't Jewish."

Gene came to understand that calling someone a "Yid" was done purposefully in a most derogatory manner. It was meant to be hurtful. It was meant to mean that you were different than all others.

In school, Gene also learned that many of the facts about your life were not anonymous. The teachers knew much more about you than you might have believed. The classroom list of students included not just your name, but your religion or ethnicity and where you lived. Nothing was hidden. Even if the student or the parents did not wish for the teacher to know, all knew that the teacher did know.

Another story from Gene's childhood describes the child's reaction to the Anti-Jewish and Anti-Israeli atmosphere dominant in Moscow during the early to mid-1980s. Gene attended the elementary school in the Southern Yuzhnoe Izmailovo neighborhood on the East side of Moscow. He was in third grade. In his class was another Jewish child whom Gene befriended, Valery Yazmir (now living in Petach Tikva, Israel), who has remained a good friend. These two Jewish kids in a class of gentiles started to fill their real identity, and their sense of Jewish belonging grew exponentially. Both learned the Hebrew alphabet through an old textbook found in Val's grandfather's library. An after-school activity was to beautify the school building and surrounding territory. They were given a job to paint a playground located in the school vicinity. The paint was blue. After the job was completed, and some paint was still available, the two wondered how they might utilize it as intended. Gene suggested,

"See the Boiler Room Hut, just north of the school?"
"Yes," replied Val.
"What if we paint ISRAEL in big Hebrew letters on a wall of the Hut?"
"Yes. It is a good idea. Let's write it in Hebrew so no one will know what it is and will not bother to clean it up."

The two eagerly start painting the letters, filling a true sense of their Jewish pride. Val then suggested a second idea,

"Let's paint an Israeli Flag and wave it on my balcony."
"But you live on the 14th floor. Who would see it? I live on the 4th, and it easily could be seen from the street, offered Gene."
"Good idea," Val agreed.

The moment they came to Gene's apartment, they found pillowcases in a linen closet. With scissors, they cut a big white rectangle from it. Then using a deep blue paint, they painted the flag of Israel as best they could. They found a hair dryer in a bathroom by which to dry the painted flag. Several hours later, they raised the flag of the Jewish State from their 4th-floor balcony so it would wave over Moscow, the Soviet capital. Soon after that, Gene's father, Konstantin, came home from work and noticed immediately the Jewish star and stripes waving on his balcony. Konstantin came up with a wise decision. Let's lower the flag from the balcony and express our Jewish pride inside the Jewish apartment. All three of them, with dignity and pride, went to the balcony and had a lowering of the flag ceremony. Gene and Val blew Hatikva through their lips. Val was given the honor to hold the flag in his room.

Gene's mother-in-law (Ina Feldstein (Starik)) told a story when the entire family was traveling to the Caucusus (Georgia) on vacation. A young college student on the train asked her where she was from since she looked more Georgian or Armenian than Russian. The person was surprised when she said Jewish. He asked why was she being so harsh on herself. "I just wanted to know what is your ethnic background, and here you are, shouting you are Jewish."

[A567] Yacov lived in Kiev, where antisemitism was far more pronounced than in Moscow or elsewhere in many other regions of Russia. Just the surname name could make it easy to suspect a Jewish heritage. Berdichevsky sounded Jewish; without question, Katzman signified Jewish. Yacov was one of the first family members who determined to emigrate and was speaking about it with Gene's parents early in the 1970s when he decided to leave. By 1973, Gene's parents had already decided they, too, would emigrate.

Throughout Gene's teenage years, people did not hide their feelings towards Jews. If you felt Jewish and not particularly Russian, then you were asked when you were going home (meaning to Israel). Even though one's parents, grandparents, and earlier ancestors had already lived in Russia for over 200 years.

To emigrate was not easy. One needed an invitation, which generally meant from a relative in Israel. Having a sponsor was mandatory.

Yacov, by 1973, had already collected all of the papers about the family history that would be needed for the authorities. The organization to which one applied in Moscow was named OVIR (Office of Visas and Registrations). In 1978, Gene's parents decided definitely to emigrate and turned in their documents to try to obtain exit papers. It was not until over a year later that the Russian officials announced that they had reviewed the documents and that the family definitely could not leave the country.

And that is when the real difficulties began. The Russian officials would ask, "How could you want to go? Because if you're a real Russian, no Russian would want to leave." But if you did wish to leave, then you were a traitor, because only traitors would leave. [A557a] Gene's father at that time held a relatively senior engineering position in the printing shop of the Moscow Academy of Science. Still, since he intended to leave, it was felt there would be no reason that he should be allowed to continue in the printing Institute, and so was fired. [A557] Elena, too, was deemed unworthy to hold her job, as she too had become a traitor, and she was let go. To complicate this period, grandmother [A556] Anna had developed cancer.

For the next year, life was most difficult as both parents could only find the most menial jobs. Eventually, Elena got her old job back, but not for Konstantin. Only after several years did he find a new more substantial position, but with a different company.

Some of their relatives were also refuseniks.[141] Gene Davidovich had had a Ph.D. in mathematics but was unable to find a job. His wife (Sophia Davidovich), one of the first persons in the Soviet Union to specialize in information technology (IT), lost her position and, for the next decade, could only find a job as a mail carrier.

By the time Gene's parents left in 1989, he was coming of age and finally beginning to understand what antisemitism was, and all that was happening. Friends got depressed when trying to leave. Starvation was to be avoided, a difficulty without reasonable jobs. And the employers could be harsh and would give any excuse conceivable except the real reason why good jobs and promotions were so scarce. Being Jewish was an economic curse.

By the mid-1980s, many families had been refused permission to emigrate, and their lives became exceedingly difficult subsequently. Gene's family just accepted that going would be

---

[141] An unofficial term for individuals, who typically were, but not always Soviet Jews, whom the Soviet officials refused permission to emigrate, primarily to Israel.

difficult, but didn't raise a fuss. And that helped some; life was not as bad as it might have become.

In April 1987, their relatives, the Davidovich family, announced they were leaving. Their son, Alex, was three months older than Gene.

By 1987 perestroika had begun.[142] At that time, it was being said that only 6,000 people desired to leave, and since they were all so vocal and making such trouble, it was thought, or so it was said, it was just more straightforward to get rid of these dissenters and have quiet again. Of course, the number that left during the coming years was about 2 million.

One piece of fortunate luck that helped Gene and his parents was the visas they had procured earlier did not have an expiration time limit. Thus, they were still active. During this period, acquaintances were no longer friendly, but at least not overly hostile as before. The exit visas came through. Gene's family had choices. They had family in Israel, and the Davidoviches, who were now already living in Chicago, were willing to act as sponsors.

Of course, nothing was simple, especially in comparison to today. The exit visa was for Israel. It could not be for the United States. But at that time, the Soviets and Israel had no formal relations, which meant there were no direct flights between the two countries. Everything had to be conducted through third parties. And the moment Gene and his family left Russia, their citizenships were declared null and void.

Using [A567] Yakov Berdichevsky's name and address in Israel for exit visa purposes, on April 6, 1989, the family flew to Vienna, Austria. As with other families leaving Moscow and coming to Vienna, few had their own family there. What had begun with just an occasional family departure now was numbering at least 100 a day.

---

[142] Soviet Pres. Mikhail Gorbachev, in 1990-1991 was the person single most important in allowing Russian Jews to emigrate. Leonid Brezhnev, his predecessor (General Secretary, Soviet Union Communist Party, 1964-1982), began the practice of reforming the Russian economic and political system in 1979. The changes truly came into full force when Soviet President Mikhail Gorbachev promoted what was called "perestroika," the policy permitting greater awareness of economic markets, as well as ending central planning. Perestroika lasted from 1985 until 1991. Its goal was to make socialism work more efficiently. It was not to end the command economy. Gorbachev also popularized "glasnost," which meant "openness and transparency."

On December 5, 1965, a Glasnost rally took place in Moscow, which was the key event leading to the emerging Soviet civil rights movement. Specifically, early on, it allowed the public, independent observers, and foreign journalists to attend trials in person. Trials until then were closed to the public. As Chapter #105 relates. Andrei Sakharov did not travel to Oslo to receive his Nobel Peace Prize as he was publicly protesting about another political trial that was then occurring. Gorbachev's new policy or transparency now allowed the Soviet citizens to discuss their system's problems and potential solutions publicly. Glasnost allowed greater contact between the Soviets and Westerners and loosened restrictions on travel. Ultimately, this led to the policy permitting Jews to emigrate to Israel and elsewhere. Reference https://en.wikipedia.org/wiki/History_of_the_Jews_in_Russia and https://www.foreignaffairs.com/articles/russia-fsu/1991-03-01/glasnost-perestroika-and-antisemitism. For additional material about later emigration, see https://en.wikipedia.org/wiki/1990s_post-Soviet_aliyah

Fig. 107-1: Exit visa from Russia and Entrance Visas to Austria for [A558] Gene, [A557a] Konstatin and [A560] Sarah Katzman.

The arriving passengers quickly met inspectors where officials from Israel were also present (Austria had diplomatic relations with Israel). Unlike today's airports where ramps led directly from the plane to the terminal, the passengers had to walk down the stairways and across the tarmac to the building where the Viennese officials met them. The Israeli immigration officials, who were there also, quickly determined whether the passengers were coming to Israel or did they wish to go to the United States or elsewhere. If to the United States, the family was shunted to yet a different line and taken to meet with officials from the "Joint" (Distribution). This meant meeting with officials from HIAS (Hebrew Immigrant Aid Society), a Jewish-American nonprofit organization operating since 1881 to provide humanitarian aid and assistance to refugees, especially Jewish refugees. To this new family, it felt like they were on a conveyor belt, but an exemplary conveyor belt at that.

Gene's family stayed in Vienna for ten days and worked with the US Embassy to claim refugee status. The Austrians were clear that they did not want Russian Jews in the country, and so the stay was restricted to 10 days and not more. Other non-Jewish groups, it seemed, were treated differently and more generously.

From Vienna, the family left by train for a transit camp in Ladispoli, a seaside village about 10 miles east of Rome.[143] The family was given a small cottage, a monthly allowance, and a Russian-Italian Dictionary. Heads of the families were told to start looking for a place to stay elsewhere. The time given was a week due to the growing wave of Russian Jewish emigration. The cottage needed to be readied for another group of Jewish immigrates who left USSR the week later. Konstantin Katzman and Peter Sorokin (husbands of Elena and Olga) were given a difficult task. Without knowing the language, culture, and the topography of Italy, limited money (Italian liras) and a small pocket-size Russian-Italian Dictionary, find a place to live for their families during what proved to be a three-month stay in Italy. On the last day of their stay at the camp, the men found the place at Nettuno (Italian seashore countryside 45 miles south of Rome), which precluded them from becoming the "Italian Homeless."

All monies given for a monthly allowance suddenly had to be used for monthly rent. The deposit to the landlord meant there was virtually nothing left for day-to-day survival, food, etc. It was tough. The food stock gathered as an emergency supply back in Moscow (instant soup cubes, canned meats, and fish) was depleting rapidly. Families wanted to hide their survival needs, but it was impossible to do so now. The local neighbors, who were simple Italian farmers, helped to determine the needs of the new people in their village. They did not ask if they needed help. Just one day, baskets of fruits and vegetables, as well as freshly baked home bread, appeared on the footsteps of their front door. They wanted to help but also wished not to harm their feelings. They preferred their help to remain incognito. The family received nominal monies, but as it was insufficient to live, the men who *could* work found illegal, relatively menial positions. The family had come in April 1989 and left on July 13, 1989.

The children enjoyed the experience and the new location. They liked living in a seaside village, and as it was summer, the beach was an attraction. It was different for the parents. Not only did they need jobs to support their family, but they also had to prepare for interviews and obtain the necessary papers for immigration to the United States.

Then came the interview at the US Embassy (Via Veneto, Rome). Sophia Davidovich (cousin of Konstantin Katzman) provided a letter of sponsorship to the HIAS Italian office. HIAS purchased the family's airplane tickets to Chicago. The Katzmans and Sorokins soon came to America on a TWA Rome–New York–Chicago flight. At 9:10 p.m., the TWA plane landed in O'Hare.

Once there, Gene's father got a job as a technician in a printing shop, and by August 1989, Gene's mother began work as an accountant. After another four months (March 1990), Elena secured a new job involved with payroll accounting. She later became a COBOL developer and stayed in that line of work for another 15-20 years until she retired. Gene's father had difficulty moving from his role as a technician to finding a job as an engineer. Also, the entire printing

---

[143] For Gene and his family, this was heaven. But it was not always so for the Italians. Compromises had to be made by all. See https://www.jta.org/2005/09/26/archive/first-person-a-camp-for-soviet-jewish-refugees-lives-on-but-only-in-peoples-memories, https://www.jta.org/1989/04/11/archive/ladispoli-bulging-at-the-seams-as-soviet-jews-cram-seaside-town, https://www.latimes.com/archives/la-xpm-1989-02-19-mn-420-story.html, and https://www.timesofisrael.com/why-189000-soviet-jews-fled-to-italy-rather-than-the-promised-land/.

industry was changing tremendously due to automation. Gene's father continued working for the rest of his career as a high-level technician.

In March 1991, Gene entered the University of Illinois at Chicago and four years later graduated with Bachelor in Statistics Degree. But his career in actuarial science did not happen to be. Gene found a job as a computer programmer, later becoming a database system analyst. He now is a Database Architect at the Wintrust Bank. In 2002, Gene received a master's degree in computer science at Keller Graduate School of Business. On June 1, 2001, Gene married Stella Leyzerova, also a Russian Jewish émigré who came to Salt Lake City, Utah, in 1995 from Donetsk, Ukraine. Aaron Katzman was born in 2008 in Park Ridge, Illinois, 19 years after the Katzman family left the Soviet Union.

[A560] Sarah Katzman, [A557a] Konstantin and [A557] Elena Katzman's daughter, came to the USA at age 14 years. She started in 9th grade at Ida Crown Jewish Academy, and after the family moved to the suburbs, she continued at the Main East High School in Des Plaines. The school is famous for its students, Hollywood actor Harrison Ford and First Lady Hilary Clinton. Sarah then went to the University of Illinois in Chicago and graduated from its Information System program. Since 1997, she has worked as a computer system analyst and developer.

Fig. 107-2: [A558a] Stella Katzman, [A563] Anna Sorokin, [A562] Jane Sorokin, [A557] Elena Katzman, [A560] Sarah Katzman, [A564] Lisa Sorokin, and [A561] Olga Sorokin (an aunt). 2011.

Fig. 107-3 [A558] Gene Katzman family. [A558a] Stella, [A558] Gene, [A559] Aaron.

The [A561] Olga Sorokin (nee Gilman) family, [A557] Elena Katzman's younger sister, came to the US in 1989 together with the group. Olga's husband, [A561a] Peter Sorokin, was a medical doctor back in Moscow, and taking series of medical exams and completing the residency, he continued his medical career as a physician in one of the Chicago hospitals. Olga went into public health by obtaining a research position in the College of Nursing at the University of Illinois at Chicago. She worked there until retiring. Their daughters, [A562] Eugenia ("Jane"), [A563] Anna (named in honor of her grandmother), and [A564] Elizaveta (Lisa), attended the Solomon Schechter Day Jewish Schools and Stevenson high school at Buffalo Grove. After graduating from high school, Jane and Anna got their medical degrees at the University of Michigan at Ann Arbor and the University of Wisconsin at Madison, respectively. Jane practices obstetrics, and Anna, neurology. Lisa obtained her degree in art and then worked in one of the art museums in Minneapolis, MN. All three have families.

#108 OUR ARGENTINIAN FAMILY

by [A537] Valeria Sabrina Ideses)

Editor's note 1: Throughout this book, we mention relatives or villagers who visited or emigrated to Argentina. Residents from Kynazhe include [A205] Aaron Weinstein and [A195] Lemel Shudler (the blacksmiths), Brothers [A196] Hershel and [A195] Lemel Shudler, children of [A207] Laizer and [A208] Yossel, or members of the family, including [A325] Charni-Gitel, children of [A606] Avrom Kaprove, [A374] Joseph Galak (later Galler). In particular, [A531] Gedalia Kaprow's grandson, [A532] Gedalia Kaprow, established a large family there with many descendants. We recently reunited with the family. The up-to-date family tree now appears in Appendix B3 and supplemental stories will appear in the future as available on our Dropbox account. The present information is sketchy.

Editor's note 2: Days before this book went to print, Mr. Rolando Gail, Secretary of the Buenos Aires Genealogical Society and a relation by marriage, contacted us inquiring about a potential new branch of our Argentinian family. The key ancestor was [A605] Israel Kaprov, the son of [A578] Simkha Kaprov, who was a brother of [A290] Khaim Kaprov, from whom the name "B'nai Khaim" originates. Three forms of evidence link the association: 1) DNA genetic matches between members of this new cluster and other known members of the family tree; 2) the exceedingly close match in names of three children, explained by the Americanized names in Joseph Gillman's files made in the 1960s, and the Argentinian form of the word ([A606] Avrom → Abraham, [A608] Simkha → Simon, and [A609] Yoel → Julio); 3) the near-identical name for Israel's wife, [A605a] Chiah Dvorah in Joe Gillman's records → Chaia Dvorah in Argentina. Some of the family subsequently moved to Israel. By 1980, this new branch consisted of more than 40 members, all listed in Appendix 3. Additional information as learned will be available in the Dropbox file.

[A532] Gedalia (Gregorio) Kaprow, born 1884, came to Argentina about 1910, saved money, and several years later, circa 1913, helped his wife, [A532a] Sara Futeransky, immigrate with the children [A546.1] Motel (Mateo), [A542] Elisa, [A543] Hersh and [A547] Ana. They settled in the La Plata region, the capital of the province, which is just south of Buenos Aires. Three of the children, [A548] Isaac, [A550] Saul, and [A551] Maria, were born later in Argentina. In total, they had seven children. It is unclear whether Mateo ever attended high school, but he was entrepreneurial, having had a bakery, bazaar, and a toy store. He was remembered as having a "strong personality."

One of Mateo's brothers wished to play the violin and become a musician, but Gregorio [A532] was unhappy about this and refused permission. It seems the son left home and was not heard from again.

One of Mateo's granddaughters, [A537] Sabrina, remembers that her non-Kaprov grandfather also emigrated from Russia and was immediately settled in a Jewish agricultural commune that Baron Maurice de Hirsch funded. As the earlier communes in Mauricio and Moïseville had been filled, Mateo, as the newcomer, went to the one newly opened in the province of Entre Rios (the colony Clara).[144]

Relatives introduced Sabrina's mother, [A534] Dora Ana Caprav, when age 21, to her future husband, [A534a] Isaac Ideses. He had completed high school in Buenos Aires and then served in the Army, where he was good with machines. After that, he became a mechanic at Aerolíneas Argentinas, formally Aerolíneas Argentinas S.A., Argentina's largest airline and the country's flag carrier. Dora lived in La Plata, where she had a Jewish upbringing. She had wished to make aliyah but never had the option.

Dora's three children, [A535] Javier Horacio Ideses, [A536] Ariel Esteban Ideses, and [A537] Valeria Sabrina Ideses all grew up in a Jewish culture. Indeed, during their childhood, the only realistic opportunity for an education was one that was Jewish and in a Jewish school. Ariel, the middle child, later moved to Israel. Sabrina also moved to Israel, made aliyah, but eventually returned to Argentina before emigrating to the United States.

Another of Gregorio's sons, [A543] Hersh, as a young adult, owned a bar and was the bartender. Before retiring, he served as a governmental security guard at the seaport. His son [A544] Adalberto, who became religious and became a shochet (butcher licensed by rabbinic authority), married Sophia Freue, who was of Sephardic origin. Their oldest son, [A545] Alejandro, when a teenager, went to a Chabad summer camp in Argentina, and within a month, was frum (highly observant) and became a rabbi practicing in Argentina. Tragically, at age 31, he died in an accident.

Adalberto also interested his brother, [A546] Eliahu Kaprov, in the rabbinate. In 1991, Eliahu went to Brooklyn, NY, to study with Menachem Mendel Schneerson,[145] who many knew as the Lubavitcher Rebbe, or just as the "Rebbe." In Brooklyn, Eliahu met his wife to be, Batia Levi, and after completing his studies, returned with her to her home town of Rio de Janeiro where Eliahu is now a Chabad Rabbi.

Virtually nothing is known about Gregorio's other children or their descendants. [A548] Isaac was said to have had an argument with his father and never seen again.

Eliahu relates that some years ago, a woman from Spain called confusing his father [A544] Adalberto with [A548] Isaac's son, [A549] Alberto, claiming to be his cousin.

We have much to learn about our Argentinian family.

One of [A546.1] Motle's grandchildren, [A537] Sabrina Ideses, now lives in the United States and supplied the family picture. Her daughter [A538] Gal, currently attends college in Florida.

---

[144] http://www.jewish-tours.com.ar/news/news0386)

[145] Menachem Mendel Schneerson was Russian born, and led the Lubavitcher Hasidic dynasty. As an American Orthodox Lubavitcher rabbi, many considered to be one of the single most influential Jewish thinker of the last century.

Fig. 108-1 Capravs in Buenos Aires at beach ~1965. [A533] Mateo and Maria Caprav with children [A539] Oscar (Queque) and [A534] Dora (now Ideses).

Fig. 108-2 [A546] Adrian Gustavo ("Eliahu") Kaprov, a Chabad rabbi in Rio de Janeiro, and his wife [A546a] Batia.

#109 [A026] FATHER'S GOODBYE NOTE

Editor's note: John wrote this letter when at Mt Sinai Hospital, where he was undergoing lung surgery from what was thought to be cancer, but proved to be a massive bronchial infection. He died, actually, eight years later on July 3, 1980, at age 87.

Monday, 31 January 1972

To all my dear and near ones,

Crises mark the life of man. During my 78.5 years of life, I experienced my share of situations, all of which resolved successfully.

Somehow, I feel this is not my last one. I feel confident I will yet enjoy you for a few years more. I just don't feel ready to leave this earth, mean as it may be.

Mine has been a rich life. Though unwanted and born in poverty, I enjoyed the great love, warmth, and affection from all. I never experienced riches, wealth, or luxury, yet I had all the necessities of life.

My people gave me all they could, by endowing me with a strong constitution and ambition. Because of this, my accomplishments were not of the greatest but did enable me a life of expression, which others, under better circumstances, failed to obtain.

I enjoyed my life's work, though I felt I should have known and done more. Even so, I feel great satisfaction in having served all equally and without any prejudice, rich and poor, black or white, and particularly that I managed never to compromise my integrity, though in great stress at times.

None of you cry, should I leave you. Not only did I love you all, but also I genuinely felt as part of you.

Sarah, you now have two daughters and two sons and five wonderful grandchildren. Cultivate their love and affection. Your life will be greatly enhanced thereby.

Love to all,

John

Dr. John Robboy

Dr. John Robboy, 87, died Wednesday at Mount Sinai Hospital, where he was a staff member for more than 50 years. He had been ill for six weeks and had a history of heart disease.

Dr. Robboy retired from the hospital's pediatrics staff in 1973 at 80.

He was born in Knuaja Krenitza in the Ukraine and came here in 1910. He worked with animals in the laboratories at Western Reserve University School of Medicine.

University doctors helped him learn English and with his classes at school. He also obtained U.S. citizenship during those early years here.

He lived in University Heights. He was graduated from Central High School and Western Reserve University. In 1926 he completed studies toward a degree in medicine at the University of Michigan.

Dr. Robboy's college studies were interrupted by World War I when he went in the Army and served as a hospital orderly.

He was a scholar of Judaism, studied the Bible and took part in many activities of the Jewish Community Center in Cleveland Heights.

In addition, he wrote memoirs telling of his early life in the Ukraine and of his experiences here.

He was a member of the American Medical Association and Phi Lamda Kappa, a medical fraternity.

He is survived by a daughter, Myrna Groger of University Heights; son, Dr. Stanley Robboy, associate professor of pathology at Harvard Medical School, and five grandchildren. His wife of 43 years, Sarah S., died last year.

Services were private.

Fig. 109-1: Newspaper obituary for [A026] John Robboy.

APPENDICES

APPENDIX A: CHRONOLOGY OF JOHN ROBBOY'S LIFE

1893-06-01	Born, Shares home (bathhouse) with [A202] Yankel Weinstein
1893+	Family moved into home of [A228a] Urpina, widow of Uchrem Skrivenuk
1897	Begins school with [A251] Katzap
1899	Taught by [A252] Rebbe Moshe
1901	Lives in Sokolivka with [A431] Alta Gilman; Taught by [A257] Israel Kiegele
1902	Sokolivka, living with [A237] Virins
1903	[A221] Avrom Aaron leave town; parents obtain the home from the [A160] Graf
1903-4	Taught by [A258] Rebbe Laib in Knyazhe
1905	Taught by [A259] Rebbe Avraham in Knyazhe
1906	Taught by cousin [A401] Liova Douglas (Dolgonos)
1907	Lives in Sazhkov with [A034] Mordechai and Sarah Faiga Robboy and 7 children
1909	Monasterishte with [A263] Mr. Schlemensohn, a grain dealer, and schooling with son [A264] Aaron
1909-09	Lives with Aunt [A502] Leah and Uncle Itz in Kishinev and worked for [A246] Mr. Shankman, a mechanic
1909	Fire destroys home in Knyazhe; John returns home, and temporarily lives with Yudel (the pharmacist) and Frima
1910	John temporarily lives in the home of Lefko and then emigrates
1910-11-07	John and brother Hymie arrive in Quebec
1910-11-10	Enters United States and travels to Cleveland, coming to the home of [A806] Dora Roodman on Scovill and E. 30th Street.
1910-12-01	Work for Dr. George Stewart, at Western Reserve University Medical School
1913	Begins Central High School, Cleveland
?	Family purchases home on E 39th St near St Clair Avenue.
1915	Becomes an American citizen, and officially becomes John
1916	Graduates high school
1917	Begins Adelbert College of Western Reserve University (Premed), Cleveland
1917-05-25	Drafted in WW1, a conscientious objector, reports to Camp Gordon, GA
1918-02	Discharged from Army and begins sophomore class at Adelbert College of Western Reserve University, Cleveland
1921-10-01	Begins medical school, Western Reserve University, Cleveland
1926	Graduates medical school, University of Michigan, Ann Arbor
1926-07	Intern, St Vincent Hospital, Toledo, OH
1927-07-01	Enters private practice
1928	Joins staff, Mt Sinai Hospital, Cleveland (remains until death)
1936-04	Becomes free of all debts
1936-07	Moves office to 681 E 105 St by St Clair Ave, Cleveland
1936-08-01	Marries [A026a] Sarah Shapiro
1938	[A027] Myrna born
1941	[A031] Stanley born
1950?	Moves office to 10616 Euclid Ave, Cleveland
1965?	Moves office to 102nd and Euclid Ave, Cleveland
1975?	Moves office to about 12400 Cedar Ave, Cleveland Heights, OH
1980-07-03	Death

APPENDIX B1: VOSKOBOINIK ROBBOY GERSON & KNYAZHE FAMILIES

	Family member	**Spouse**
[A001]	Laizer Eli Voskoboinik	Paya
[A002]	- Yakov Hersh Voskoboinik	Aidi
[A003]	- Haskel Voskoboinik	Faiga
[A004]	- - Donia Voskoboinik	
[A005]	- Sarah Faiga Voskoboinik	Kalman
[A005b]		Boruch (h2 Sarah)
[A006]	- - Moshe Voskoboinik	
[A007]	- - Yossel Voskoboinik	
[A008]	- - Baila Voskoboinik	

BEN-ZION ROBBOY FAMILY

[A010]	Leah Voskoboinik	Ben Zion Robboy
[A011]	- Shmiel Robboy	Malka Kaprov
[A012]	- - Khaim|Hyman Robboy	Rebecca Meshenstein
[A013]	- - - Bernard Robboy	Rosalie Smotkin
[A014]	- - - - David Gerson Robboy	Deborah Herzberg
[A015]	- - - - Ronald Robboy	Susan Severtson
[A016]	- - - - William|Bill Robboy	
[A017]	- - Nessie Gerson Robboy	
[A018]	- - - Nathan Gerson →Robboy	Rose Nedelman
[A019]	- - - - Nancy Robboy	Mark W Cooper
[A020]	- - - - Marcia Robboy	Jonathan Ames
[A021]	- - - Pauline Robboy	Milton Siegel
[A022]	- - - - Donald Robert Siegel	Roselle|Rosie Schwartz
[A023]	- - Tobie Robboy	
[A024]	- - Joseph|Yossel Robboy	Gertrude Gelman A2B2C2D1
[A024b]	- -	Bessie Kimmelman
[A026]	- - John Robboy	Sarah Shapiro
[A027]	- - - Myrna Robboy	Herbert Groger
[A028]	- - - - Laurel Groger	Alijandro Espinosa
[A029]	- - - - Richard Groger	Kaili Fan
[A030]	- - - - Debra Groger	Mark Robinson
[A031]	- - - Stanley J Robboy	Anita Wyzanski
[A032]	- - - - Elizabeth Alice Robboy	Orde Kittrie
[A033]	- - - - Caroline Sarah Robboy	Pete Gearhart
[A031b]	- -	Marion Meyer (Loeb) (w2 Stanley)
[A034]	- Mordechai Robboy	Sarah Spector
[A035]	- - Nathan Robboy	Rhea Heiser
[A036]	- - - Mitchell Robboy	Leslie Ann Shnaeder
[A037]	- - - - Robin Robboy	
[A038]	- - - - Jeffrey David Robboy	Marlene Luz Perez
[A039]	- -	
[A040]	- - - - Deborah Robboy	Joel Doliner
[A041]	- - - - Brian Douglas Robboy	
[A042]	- - - Stanley Gail Robboy	Marion Lee Malkin
[A043]	- - - - Rebeca Malkin Robboy	Lawrence Saul Busansky
[A044]	- - - - Rachel Beth Robboy	Jeremie Orin Waterman
[A045]	- - - - Sara Gail Robboy	___ Munday
[A046]	- - - - Michael Robboy	

[A047]	- - Sylvia Robboy	Joe Isbitz
[A048]	- - - Marilyn Isbitz	Stanley Yellin
[A049]	- - - - Rhea Eve Yellin	Albert Turek
[A050]	- - - - Stephanie Judith Yellin	Kenneth Mednick
[A051]	- - - - Beverly Elizabeth Yellin	
[A052]	- - - - Joseph David Yellin	
[A053]	- - - Rosalie Isbitz	Robert Eggleston
[A054]	- - - - Maurice Eggleston → Waterman	Shelly Gould
[A055]	- - - Sarah-Fay Isbitz	Ira Manson
[A055.1]	- - - - Karen Michelle Manson	
[A055.2]	- - - - Jeffery Michael Manson	
[A056]	- - - Betty Isbitz	Robert Koondel
[A056.1]	- - - - Jennifer Arin Koondel	
[A057]	- - Morton Robboy	Ira Manson
[A058]	- - - Melvin Lee Robboy	
[A059]	- - George Robboy	Mary Frankel
[A060]	- - - Rhoda Deloras Robboy	Richard Stamm
[A061]	- - - - Blake William Stamm	Lisa Wilson #1
[A062]	- - - - Michael Stamm	Patricia Eberbardt
[A063]	- - - Merle Robboy	Linda Robinson
[A064]	- - Rose Robboy	David Rein
[A065]	- - - William Rein	Joan Kest
[A066]	- - - - David|Sonny Rein	Kathlene Springer
[A067]	- - - - Marcie Rein	Scott Pate
[A068]	- - - Susanne F Rein	Richard|Dick S Bailys
[A069]	- - - - David Bailys	Gayle Cohen
[A070]	- - - - Frederick Bailys	Allison Levy
[A071]	- - Dorothy Robboy	Nathan Strauss
[A072]	- - - Martin Strauss	Harlene Gaylord
[A073]	- - - - Steve Strauss	Allyson Kay
[A074]	- - - - Dan Strauss	Leslie Gerhardt
[A075]	- - Eddie Robboy	Sylvia Davis
[A076]	- - - Marc Robboy	Marilyn Meyers
[A077]	- - - Howard Paul Robboy	Susan Kurzrock
[A078]	- Sosi Robboy	
[A079]	- Mendel Robboy	Anna Desatnick Aunt)
[A080]	- - Phyllis Robboy (Freida)	Perry Gomel
[A081]	- - - Francis Gomel	David Levy
[A082]	- - - Robert T Gomel+	Randi Singer
[A082.2]	- - - Jessica L Gomel	Steven Veksland
[A083]	- - Sidney Robboy	Eva Desatnick
[A084]	- - - Gita Robboy	David M Levin
[A087]	- - - Bruce S Robboy	Leslie Eileen Goldstein
[A088]	- - Benjamin Robboy	Irma Levin Lee
[A089]	- - - Stanton L. Robboy	
[A090]	- - - Howard Alan Robboy	Candace Clark
[A091]	Itzhak Voskoboinik	
[A092]	- Shava	
[A093]	Dinah Voskoboinik	

GERSON FAMILY

[A094]	Hanna Voskoboinik	Levi Gerson
[A095]	- Avrom Shmiel (Samuel)	[A017]Nessie Robboy

	- - (Adopted as Robboy)	
[A098]	- Paya	
[A099]	- Fullie	married uncle
[A100]	- Ruchel	
[A101]	- Nathan	Anna Sobel
[A102]	- - Irvin Kaffen	Marg Grossman
[A103]	- - - Ronald Kaffen	Sharon Lowery
[A104]	- - - Neal E Kaffen	Romayne Tussey

MORE VOSKOBOINIK FAMILY

[A105]	Golda Voskoboinik	#1 Annulled
[A105b]		Meir Groysman (h2 Golda)
[A107]	- Jennie | Shaindel Voskoboinik	Harry Pritzker
[A108]	- - Rose	
[A109]	- - - Marvin Pritzker	Rose Kanovsky
[A110]	- - - - Helene Pritzker	Murray Berkowitz
[A111]	- - - - Alan Gedalia Pritzker	Brenda Silverman
[A112]	- - - - Nachman Nathan J Pritzker	Henny Bressler
[A113]	- Rayah	
[A114]	- - Golda	Irv Schulman
[A115]	- - - Roger C. Schulman	
[A116]	- - - Randi	__ Starling
[A117]	- - Naome	Julian Newman
[A118]	- - - Rayah	Bruce Heins
[A119]	- - - Karen	Arthur Adler
[A120]	- Pauline	Julius Friedman
[A121]	- - Marvin Friedman	Susan Benjamin
[A122]	- - - Melanie H. Friedman	Scott Weltman
[A123]	- - - Robert Gary Friedman	
[A124]	- - Herschel Harry Wolf Friedman	Rochelle (Shelly) Skolnik
[A125]	- - - Stephanie Friedman	__ Schneider
[A126]	- - - Robin Friedman	__ Galkin
[A127]	- - - Ken M Friedman	
[A128]	Haskel Voskoboinikà Weiss	Reva Leah
[A129]	- Phillip Weiss	Elsie Schmuckler
[A130]	- - Harry Weiss	
[A131]	- - - Joy Weiss	
[A132]	- - - Larry Weiss	
[A133]	- - Herman Weiss	Jeannie
[A134]	- - - Ronnie Weiss	-
[A135]	- - Daniel Weiss	Jeannie
[A136]	- - - Dale Weiss	Karen Kilroy
[A137]	- - - Roberta Weiss	
[A138]	- - - Charles Weiss	
[A139]	- Dave	Mollie Broth
[A140]	- Bessie (Betty Babe)	Jack Mesnick
[A141]	- - Rosalind Lee Mesnick	Jack A Sharwell
[A142]	- - - Dana Sharwell	
[A143]	- - - David Hal Sharwell	
[A144]	- - - Jack J Sharwell	Jenna Thompsen
[A145]	- - Allen F Mesnick	Francine _____
[A146]	- - - Faith Pamela Mesnick	Chris Lilley
[A147]	- - - Scott Howard Mesnick	

[A148]	- Hyman (Hy) Weiss	Sally Saltzberg
[A149]	- - Ronald Weiss	Doris Cohen
[A150]	- - - Hope Weiss	
[A151]	- - - Paul Weiss	
[A152]	- - - - David Kravitz	
[A153]	- - - - Daniel Kravitz	
[A154]	- - Judy Weiss	Harvey Nudelman
[A155]	- - - Scott Nudelman	
[A156]	- - - Lee Nudelman	
[A157]	- - David S. Weiss	Eta S. Berner
[A158]	- - - Daniel Weiss	
[A159]	- - - Jacob Weiss	

APPENDIX B2: KNYAZHE FAMILIES AND OTHERS

Town's people

[A160]	Graf Krasitzki, wife Justina	
[A161]	Pan Pavlovsky, manager	
[A162]	Mechanic	
[A163]	Water carrier	
[A164]	Anton	Farmer guarding Graf's cow pastures

Korsunski family

[A165]	Korsunski, Hershel & Rivka	
[A166]	- Faivel	
[A167]	- David	
[A168]	Korsunski, David Dudy	Obese, Rich-
[A168a]	Korsunski, Tzirl (f)	Mean, buried alive by peasants during pogrom
[A170]	- Ben & Wife,	Cousin [A241a] Boruch Mordechai)
[A171]	- Brocha - sister	
[A172]	Korsunski, Mendel & Zipa -	Cantonist
[A173]	- Shimon & wife	(moved away)
[A174]	Korsunski , Aaron (Gonta) & Wife	
[A175]	- Chaia	Cretin
[A176]	- Esther	
[A177]	Korsunski, Shaia	
[A178]	- Ruchel	m Meir Deutch [A214]
[A179]	- Rachmiel (m)	
[A180]	Korsunsky, Moshe	Moshe Bear, stepbrother [A252] Shaia Korsunsky
[A181]	- 2 children	
[A182]	Diuba & Boruch Mordechai	Korsunski Cousin; Blackmailed [A263] Bennie

Ber Laib family

[A183]	Hersh, Avrom	Russi Gerson, ? wife or separate person, grain dealer
[A184]	- Frima Gerson	Yudel, Feldsher fm [C28] Ochhmativ
[A185]	Hersh, Beryl	
[A186]	Hersh, Samuel Udi	

Kapalushnik family

[A187]	GedaliaEsther Kapalushnik	Stepbrother [A252] Shaia Korsunski
[A187.5]	- 3 sons, 7 daughters	
[A188]	- Moshe	
[A189]	Chaichic __,	Esther Kapalushnik's [A189a] sister in Zashkov
[A190]	Shuke Kapalushnik -	Owned oak ruler

Shudler family

[A191]	Isaac & Esther Shudler	Grain dealer & winnowers
[A192]	- SamuelMinnie	Grain dealer & winnowers
[A193]	- Yakov| Yankel	Grain dealer & winnowers
[A194]	- Chaia	m Meir __, a Butcher
[A195]	Lemel Shudler	Blacksmith
[A196]	Hershal Shudler, ? Chaim	Blacksmith

Yankel, Shochet's Family

[A197]	Rabbi YankelBrucha	Shochet, not Yankel Weinstein
[A198]	- Tevice	Son, became cantor
[A199]	- Ruchel	
[A200]	- Young boy	John's schoolmates

[A201]	- Young boy	John's schoolmates

Weinstein family

Moved Winnipeg

[A202]	Weinstein Yankel Faiga -	Kept Bathhouse, Shares house John's birth, deacon
[A203]	- Shlomo	Furrier, m girl from Terlitza
[A204]	- Chaim Hersh	Furrier, m [A216] Rivka Deutch
[A205]	- Aaron Weinstein	Blacksmith
[A206]	- Bessie	m __ Keinman, fm Yedenitz
[A207]	- Laizer	Furrier
[A208]	- Yossel	Furrier
[A209]	- Dvosia	Dwarf
[A210]	- Nechoma	
[A211]	- Ishika	
[A212]	Weinstein, Sara -	Yankel's sister

Deutch family

[A213]	Aaron Deutch,	Furrier
[A214]	- Mayer Meir	m [A255] Ruchel Korsunski]
[A215]	- David	
[A216]	- Rivka	m [A204] Yakov Hersh Weinstein

Radlideciatnik family

[A217]	Radlideciatnik Beryl & Sossie (Sonia)	Cattle dealer; Sossie disabled
[A218]	- Shmiel	Lame left arm
[A219]	- Yohel	Shoe repairman
[A220]	- Tema Teura	Congenital neck injury

Other Knyazhe residents

[A221]	Avrom Aaron	Owned 12 duplex w [A326] Chaim Dudnik
[A222]	- Pupa	[A011] Shmiel's girlfriend (first love), in Zashkov
[A223]	Yudel Dectar	Childhood friend [A026] John
[A224]	Shuke Gedaliah	
[A225]	Yankel Isaac	Flown
[A226]	Rebbe Lech	From Berdichev
[A227]	Shimon Pessis	
[A228]	Urchem Urpina Skriveniuk	Grandfather's landlady - latter
[A229]	Rachel Tzipes	Father escorted privy
[A230]	Lefko	Landlord after [A252] Shaia Korsunski moved home
[A231]	Musii	Bone setter
[A232]	Tarhatutu	1906, Student with John in Kiegele's class
[A233]	Urpina	Peasant girl,[A263] Bennie Korsunski impregnated
[A234]	Yudel's mother	Exposed herself father
[A235]	- Yudel Frima	Pharmacist

Residents of [C02] Justingrad

[A237]	Yankel Sarah Virin	Cousin & steamship travel agent; father lived there 1 yr
[A238]	Itzi	[A237] Yankel's brother, grain dealer
[A239]	- Abraham	Grandson, medical student
[A240]	- Nyashke	Grandson, gymnast
[A241]	- Yossel|Joe	Grandson, blind right eye
[A242]	Pinchas Chochazoh	Sokolievker Rabbi
[A243]	Karolnick family	
[A244]	- Duddey Dubovis	Red officer, hated Jews

Residents of [C09] Christinovka

[A245]	Zanvel	Commissioner, grain dealer

[A003a]	Faiga	m [A003] Haskel Voskoboinik

Residents of [C14] Kishinev

[A246]	Mr. Shankman	Father apprenticed to, in 1909 in Kishinev
[A247]	Yankel	Chief mechanic for Shankman
[A248]	Haskel	Worked at anvil for Shankman
[A249]	Yankel	Another apprentice for Shankman
[A250]	Zeidel Rovner	Cantor from Kishinev

Teachers (Rebbes)

[A251]	Katzap	1897 Knyazhe
[A252]	MosheMonicha	1898-01 Knyazhe, superb teacher
[A253]	- Feivel (m)	
[A254]	- Tzalik (m)	
[A255]	- Rissel (f)	
[A256]	- Sister (f)	
[A257]	Israel Kiegele,	1901-02 Justingrad
[A258]	Rebbe Laib,	1903-04 Knyazhe, from [C03] Arotof
[A259]	Rebbe Avraham,	1905-06, Knyazhe
[A401]	Dolgonos, Liova,	1906-07, Knyazhe, Odessa bookkeeper (Cousin)
[A261]	Mr. Krasnyansky	1908, from [C43] Zashkov
[A262]	Aaron Sohlemonsohn,	1908, gymnast [C24] Monasteristshe

People from Elsewhere

[A263]	Mr. Schlemensohn	Grain dealer, [C24] Monasteristshe
[A264]	- Aaron (duplicate)	Gymnast; help school John
[A265]	- Misha	Medical student
[A266]	Rabbi Rohbonchvamatz	Malka's rabbi from Monasteristshe
[A267]	- Hoshuah	
[A268]	Mr. Ochanowich	Owned private bank in Rezina
[A269]	Shalom	tax collector fm [C22] Lukashivka
[A270]	- Daughter	Lived in John's home

Health Care persons, elsewhere

[A271]	Dr. Kuzminsky	
[A272]	Dr. Braverman	[C43] Zashkov
[A273]	Tzentlor	Ophthalmologist, [C36] Uman
[A274]	Faiga	Feldsher from [C22] Lukashivka

RUSSIAN CZARS Rulers

[A275]	Ivan the Terrible (1547-75)	
[A276]	Catherine the Great (1762 – 96)	
[A277]	Alexander I (1801-25)	
[A278]	Nicholas I (1825-55)	
[A279]	Alexander II (1855-81)	Reformist
[A280]	Alexander III (1881-94)	
[A281]	Nicholas II (1894-1917)	
[A282]	Leon Trotsky	Communist theorist

Antisemites, pogroms

[A283]	Krushevan	
[A284]	Terpylo Danylo Ilkovych, aka Ataman Zeleny	
[A285]	General Denikin	
[A286]	Semyon Petliura	

APPENDIX B3: B'NAI KHAIM FAMILIES, PART 1
DESCENDANTS [A290] KHAIM KAPROV'S SON, [A291] YOSSEL

ID	Family member (Born < 1980) Generation 1-9 (#8 & 9 mostly omitted)	Partner
[A290]	Khaim Kaprov	Osna (w1 [A290] Khaim)
[A291]	- Yossel Kaprov	Perl
[A292]	- - Rivka Kaprov	Noah Dudnik
[A293]	- - - Aaron Dudnick	Cipa | Zipora Weinberg
[A294]	- - - - Gitie| Githa Dudnik	Eli Dudnik
[A295]	- - - - - Abraham H Dudnik	Rose Cohn
[A296]	- - - - - - Robert M Dudnik	Lynda| Lynn Cohen
[A297]	- - - - - - Joan Dudnik	
[A298]	- - - - - Yossel| Joseph Dudnik	Minnie J Bellis
[A299]	- - - - - - Beatrice| Breine Dudnik	Max Borenstein
[A300]	- - - - - - - Richard Douglas Borenstein	Virginia Hampton
	- - - - - - - - Douglas Richard Borenstein	
	- - - - - - - - Jeffery David Borenstein	Susan Hayes
[A301]	- - - - - - - Paul Elliott Borenstein	Jane Shanoskie
[A302]	- - - - - - - Gertrude| Trudy Borenstein	Yasuo Sugiura
[A303]	- - - - - - - - Maximillian S Sugiura	Carmella S Re
[A304]	- - - - - - - - Alex Jiro Sugiura	
[A305]	- - - - - - Irene Dudnik	Julius Borenstein
[A306]	- - - - - - - Susan Borenstein	
	- - - - - - - Bonnie Tina Borenstein	
	- - - - - - Michael Borenstein	___ Kalinowski
	- - - - - - - Benjamin Eli Borenstein	
[A307]	- - - - - - Selma Dudnik	Oscar S Bortner
	- - - - - - - Amy Bortner	?John Gialuco
	- - - - - - - Heidi G. Bortner	
[A308]	- - - - - - Jody M Bortner	John Everett Strawn
	- - - - - - - Adopt	
[A309]	- - - - Pearl Dudnik	Louis Guralnick
[A310]	- - - - Sarah Dudnik	Fyodor| Fred Dan Danilyuk → Dan
[A311]	- - - - - Aaron Dan	Miriam Levine
[A312]	- - - - - - Max Fred Dan	
[A313]	- - - - Olga | Golda| Golda Dudnik	Isaiah Maidansky
[A314]	- - - - Dora Dudnik	Meyer Goldenberg
[A315]	- - - - - Aaron Goldenberg	
	- - - - - - Kira Goldenberg	
	- - - - - - - Vava Goldenberg (m)	
[A316]	- - - - Dina Dudnik	
[A317]	- - - - Herschel| Harry A. Dudwick	Ida Gross
[A318]	- - - - - Nancy L Dudwick	
[A319]	- - - - - Nora Dudwick	___ Gallagherduff
		Igor Ashot Barsegian (h2 Nora)
[A320]	- - - - Kenia| Kay Dudnik	Philip Guralnick
[A321]	- - - - - Sidney Aaron Guralnick	Eleanor Albane
	- - - - - - Sara Diane ?Dion Guralnick	___Dubin
	- - - - - - Jeremy Guralnick	
[A322]	- - - - - Paul Boris Guralnick	Shirley Grossman
	- - - - - - Gail Guralnick	Criston Sloan
	- - - - - - - Child	
	- - - - - - Robert Penn Guralnick	Leanne _____
[A323]	- - - Isrul| Israel Dudnik	Chana
[A324]	- - - - Khaim Dudnik	
[A325]	- - - - Charni-Gitel Dudnik	??

[A326]	- - - Chaim| Khaim Dudnik	Brucha| Bertha [A413] Dolgonos
[A327]	- - - - Fania| Fanny Simone Dudnik	YevaLiova| Leon Moravsky →Morrison
[A328]	- - - - - Donald Dov Morrison	Shirley Lillian Mizes
[A329]	- - - - - - Leonette Sheryn Morrison	Michael Doran
		Clifford Irwin Gould (h2 Leonette)
	- - - - - - Leon Sandor Morrison	Pamela Caldwell
[A330]	- - - - - - Elliot Howard Morrison	Susan Milstein
	- - - - - - - Douglas Ezra Morrison	
[A331]	- - - - - - Barbara Joy Morrison	Scott Bresler
[A332]	- - - - Polia| Polya| Pearl Gittel Dudnik	Morris Galler [A385]
[A333]	- - - - Sarah: Surka Dvossi Dudnik	Aron Milstein
[A334]	- - - - - Alex Milstein	Charlotte A Clark
	- - - - - - Steven Howard Milstein	Alexis Scott
	- - - - - - - Heather Milstein	Jan Richmond
	- - - - - - - Charlotte Milstein	Kalene _____
[A335]	- - - - - - Norman Scott Milstein	
[A336]	- - - - - - David Reid Milstein	Betsy Blechman
[A337]	- - - - - David| Duzz Nathan Milstein	Barbara Wells
[A338]	- - - - - Cynthia| Cindy Bernice Milstein	Ian Grimmer
	- - - - - Judith Anne Milstein	
	- - - - - Karen Elizabeth Milstein	
	- - - - - Martha Rachel Milstein	Willis Scott
		Niuck Donder (h2 Martha)
	- - - - Ruchl Dudnik	
[A339]	- - - - Yosel| Joseph Noyach Dudnik	Dvora Korsonsky
	- - - - - Bina Dudnik	Arie Kaplan
	- - - - - - Dvorah| Debbie Kaplan	Ahron Ghivan
	- - - - - - Noga:?Nola Kaplan	Joseph Zvi
	- - - - - - Boaz Kaplan	Lin Gerenrot
	- - - - - Ofra: Diron Dudnik	
		Hedvig Mandl (w2 Yosell)
	- - - - Isrul Dudnik	
[A340]	- - - - ItzchakIsaac Dudnik	Sabina Frank
[A341]	- - - - Zahava Dudnik	Ronald Blum (h1 Zahava)
[A342]	- - - - - Elana Bracha Blum-Doering	Roy Howard Lubit
		Jon Christopher Geissmann (h2 Elana)
[A343]	- - - - - - Tamara Lea Doering	Michael Richard Brent
[A344]	- - - - - - Don Shimon Blum-Doering	Miryam Frieder
		John P Doering (h2 Zahava)
	- - - - - - Laurence J. Doering	
	- - - - - - Karl Peter Doering	Paula Carrington
	- - - - - - Andrea Elaine Doering	
	- - - - - - Stefanie Allison Doering	J Dirk Schwenk
[A345]	- - - - - Eliasaf Elliott Dudnik	Laura Mall
	- - - - - - Nina Simone Dudnik	Peter Killian
	- - - - - - Sara Arona Dudnik	Dave __
[A346]	- - - - Lillian| Lisa| Liza Dudnik	Edw| Julius Schwartz
[A347]	- - - - - Robert Norman Schwartz	Carole Celia Lesses
	- - - - - Stephen Michael Schwartz	Kristy Cook
	- - - - - Barbara Ruth Schwartz	Louis Nuchereno
	- - - - - Edward Allen Schwartz	Sharon Fine
		Sharon Fine (w2 Edward)
	- - - - - - Lewis Lesses Schwartz	Patricia Pierson
		Jean Suto (w2 Robt)
[A348]	- - - - Betty Dudnik	Leon Hayman (seeA1B3C2?)
[A348.2]	- - - - Miriam| Mimi Hayman	Allen Brown
	- - - - - Toby Sharon Brown	William White
	- - - - - - Robert Howard Brown	Arlynne Debra Pack

424

[A348.8]	- - - - - David Arthur Hayman	Barbara Amram
	- - - - - - Mark Steven Hayman	
[A349]	- - - - Vera Dudnik	
	- - - - Pinchas Dudnik	
	- - - - Raya Dudnik	
[A350]	- - - Froim| Efraim Dudnik	Sarah Dayan
[A351]	- - - Noach Dayan Dudnik	
[A352]	- - - - Tzipora Dudnik	Mordechai Kreisman
	- - - - - Noach Krouzman	Yoheved (Yovi) Horesh
	- - - - - - Roni Krouzman	Shirley
	- - - - - - Donna Krouzman	Barak Laks
	- - - - - Abraham Kroizman	Paula (Pnina) ___
	- - - - - - Ami Kroizman	
	- - - - - - Moran Kroizman	Toni Ben Gal
[A352.5]	- - - - - Chaya Kroizman	Israel Greenberg
	- - - - - - Efraim (Effi) Greenberg	Shiri Kozokaro
	- - - - - - Sharon Greenberg	
	- - - - - - David (Dudi) Greenberg	
[A353]	- - - - Miriam Dudnik	Samuel Gilai (Wesolowski)
	- - - - Ruth Sarah Gilai	Amos Mar-Haim
[A354]	- - - - - Gai Mar-Chaim	Vered Hagit Hoch
	- - - - - Tal Mar-Haim	Benjamin Yekutiel
	- - - - - Shachar Mar-Haim	Ram Gerson
	- - - - - Michal Mar-Haim	Liron Liptz
	- - - - - Sharon Mar-Haim	Ethan Mantzuri
	- - - - - Shay Gilai	Ruth Gelmond
	- - - - - Dana Gilai	Alon Frank
	- - - - - Adi Gilai	Shachar Familia
	- - - - - - Yael Familia	
	- - - - - - Daniella Familia	
	- - - - - - Yoav Gilai	Evelina
[A355]	- - - Leib Dudnik	Tsiril Tichman
		Sima Seinberg Yaffe (w2 Efraim)
[A356]	- - - - Reva Dudnik	
[A357]	- - - - Polya Dudnik	
[A358]	- - - - Chaya| Kaika Dudnik	
[A359]	- - - Yankel Dudnik	Leah _____
[A360]	- - - Olga Dudnik → Morrison (adopted)	Sam Perman
[A361]	- - - Nathan Dudnik	Reva Arnold
	- - - - Jacqueline Dudnik	Marshall Schaffner
	- - - - - Claudia Schaffner	___ Crawford
	- - - - Allen Dudnik	
	- - - - - Nancy Sharon Schaffner	
	- - - - Natalie Dudnik	
	- - - - Alice Dudnik	
[A362]	- - - - Betya| Betty Dudnik	Usher Lupetsky
	- - - - - Son	
[A362.1]	- - - - - Yasha| Yankel Lupetsky	
[A362.4]	- - - - - Fiti| Feivel Lupetsky (m)	
	- - - - - - Laura?	
	- - - - - - boy	
[A363]	- - - Pearl| Mimi Dudnik	Asher Gudisblatt
	- - - Rivka| Rebecca Gudisblatt	Marvin Kaplan
	- - - - Bruce Kaplan	?, marry 1963
	- - - - Andrew Kaplan	
[A364]	- - - Sarah| Sirka| Surcah Dudnik	Zeina| Zoma| Zuma Sol Morrison
[A360]	- - - - Olga Morrison Dudnik A1B1C6D1 adopt	Sam Perman
	- - - - - Gerald Perman	Judith Barkey

ID	Name	Spouse / Notes
[A366]	- - - - - Leonard Perman	Linda Koenigsberg, w1 Leonard
[A366b]		Eva Isabel Wallace à Kosberg, w2 Leonard
	- - - - - - Lori Ruth Perman	
	- - - - - - Stacy Ann Perman	
	- - - - - - Stephanie Morrison Perman	Sean Sosa
[A367]	- - Genendy Kaprov	Shmuel Galak
[A368]	- - - Israel Galak	Rifke Shurak| Surak
[A369]	- - - - David Galler	Zelda Shapiro
	- - - - - Charles Galler	Florence Lucas
	- - - - - - Dolores Galler	Morris Lachman
	- - - - - - - Sheri Lee Lachman	____ Malkin (h1)
		____ Jelinek (h2 Sheri)
	- - - - - - - Donna Lee Lachman	Rick Tuttle
	- - - - - - - David Lachman	
	- - - - - - Edwin J Galler	Lillian| Leah Davidson
	- - - - - - Julius Galler	Sherri _____
	- - - - - - David Galler	Donna _____
	- - - - - Gerald Galler	Susan Verb
	- - - - - - Stephen Franklin Galler	Becky _____
	- - - - - - Leslie Galler	Adam Sharrin
	- - - - Berl Galler	
	- - - - Samuel Galler	Bernice Mar Goldstein
	- - - - - Roberta Rosilyn Galler	
	- - - - - Ronald Galler	Ilene Roberta Bernstein
	- - - - - - Bruce Marc Galler	Nancy Anne Weissman
	- - - - - - Audrey Lynn Galler	Michael Shawn Lopez
	- - - - - - Scott Lawrence Galler	Holly Van Winkle
[A370]	- - - - Shmuel| Samuel Galler	Rose Wolfberg
	- - - - - Frances Leah (Twin) Galler	Arthur Spitz
		Charles Block (h2 Frances)
	- - - - - - Darcy Alison Spitz	____ Yucikas
	- - - - - Jean Genendy(Twin) Galler	Harold Phillip Robbin
	- - - - - - Shaun Elyse Robbin	Stuart Fishman
	- - - - - Robert Galler	Charlotte Schwartz
	- - - - - - Mark Scott Galler	
	- - - - - - - Juliana Galler	
	- - - - - - Reid Galler	
	- - - - - - Elizabeth Galler	
	- - - - - - Natalie Galler	
	- - - - - Lance Galler	
		Geraldine ____ (w2 Robert)
	- - - - - William Galler	Etta Joan Buzo
	- - - - - Susanne Evita Galler	Michael Caplan
	- - - - - Richard Jesse Galler	Valerie Ann Lichter
[A371]	- - - - Pearl Galler ?Galak	Meyer Sabath
	- - - - Aron| Harry Sabath	
	- - - - Velvel| William Sabath	Lois ____, ?Charlotte
	- - - - - Barbara Sabath	____ Merkin
	- - - - - - Barry Allen Sabath	
		Gladys Friedman
		Lois _____
[A372]	- - - - Ruchel:Rose Galler	Nathan Chasman
[A373]	- - - - Hyman E. Chasman à Chase	Elaine Brown
	- - - - - Leslie Sylvia Chase	Jeffrey Spirito
	- - - - - - Lance Jeffrey Spirito	
	- - - - - Ronald David Chase	Terry Goldstein
[A374]	- - - - Yossel| Joseph Galler	Eva | Rose Friedman

[A375]	- - - - - William Galler	Beatrice Pirchesky
	- - - - - - Marc Galler	
[A376]	- - - - - - Lynne Galler	Hezzy Dattner
[A377]	- - - - - Jeanette Galler	Haim Jacob| Herman Finkel
	- - - - - - Moshe| Moses| Mosey Finkel	Deganit Carmeli
	- - - - - - Uri Finkel	Michal Wetstein
	- - - - - - Michael Finkel	Never married
	- - - - - - Ofer Joseph Finkel	
[A378]	- - - - - Aliza Rachel Finkel	Richard Sanders
[A379]	- - - - - Lucille| Lucy Galler	Richard Coleman
[A380]	- - - - - - Renee Louise Coleman	Dan Ritzo
	- - - - - Anita Elaine Coleman	Carlos Portello
	- - - - - Daniel Alan Coleman	
	- - - - - Sharon| Sherry Debra Coleman	Barry ___
[A381]	- - - - Yochanon| Yefim Galler (Galak)	Adele Gaysina
[A382]	- - - - - Lazar Galak	Hana| Anna Perel
	- - - - - - Michael Galak	Raisa Polevoy
	- - - - - - Julius Galak	
	- - - - - Ilya Galak	Tatyana Kosobruhova
		Galina ____ (w2 Ilya)
[A383]	- - - - - Rifke| Raya Galak	Aron| Alex Zaika
[A384]	- - - - - - Grigory| Garik| Gary Zaika	Olga Karabash
	- - - - - - Semion Zaika	Leah Groysman
[A385]	- - - - Motel| Morris Galler	Pearl| Polia Dudnik [A332] A1B1C3D2
[A386]	- - - - - Rifka| Vivian Galler	Irving Korn
[A387]	- - - - - - Stephen (Shmuel) Alan Korn	Andrea:Andee Buckspan
[A388]	- - - - - - - Jeffrey Robert Korn } tw	
	- - - - - - - Richard| Rick Leslie Korn } tw	
	- - - - - - - Brian Scott Korn	
[A389]	- - - - - - Victoria Alisa Korn	Andres Lerner
[A390]	- - - - - - Howard (Khaim) Norris Korn	Susan Grossblatt
	- - - - - - - Carolyn:Carrie Ayn Korn	Alex Greenshield
	- - - - - - Laurence| Lazar| Larry Duane Korn	Carolyn Devol
[A391]	- - - - - - - Lia Korn	
[A392]	- - - - - Bernard| Buzz Aaron Galler	Enid Louise Harris
[A393]	- - - - - - Bruce Irving Galler	Grace Whang
[A394]	- - - - - - Elaine Beth Galler	Jim Levine
[A395]	- - - - - - Glenn Norman Galler	Carol Deutsch
[A396]	- - - - - Marilyn Ann Galler	Alan M Koschik
[A397]	- - - - Sarah Dolores Galler ?Galak	Isadore Nemiroff
	- - - - - Abraham Nemiroff	
	- - - - - Rifke| Vivian Nemiroff	
	- - - - - Jean Genendy Beverly Nemiroff	Lawrence Salkind
	- - - - - - Alan Reid Salkind	Kathy ____
		Carol _____
	- - - - - - Randy Scott Salkind	
	- - - - - - Sue Renee Salkind	Stuart Scott Feldman
	- - - - Milton William Nemiroff	Rhoda Veiner
	- - - - - - Lori Ann Nemiroff	David Worley
	- - - - - - Robert Steven Nemiroff	Nancy _____
[A398]	- - - Khaim Galak	Golda
	- - - Perl Galak	Moishe Ingber
	- - - - Genny| Golda| Jane	Salem Joubran
	- - - - - Vic Joubran	
	- - - - - John Joubran	
	- - - - - E2-4	
	- - - - - E5-6	
	- - - Yocheved Galak	Abraham Skolnik

	- - - - Bube Skolnik	
	- - - - Dvossie Skolnik	
	- - - - Gennie Skolnik	
	- - - - - Son	
	- - - - - - Karl	
	- - - - - - girl	
	- - - Perl Galak	Iskike
	- - - - Lisa	
	- - - - Pessie	PR Sukhoe
	- - - Baruch Galak	Yudis
	- - - - Large family Dx	
[A399]	- - Leah Kaprov	Dov| Beryl Dolgonos
[A400]	- - - Israel Dolgonos->Douglas	Tuba| Toby Mazur
[A401]	- - - - Liova| Louis Douglas	Golda| Olga Mauldaur
[A402]	- - - - - Dov| Dave Douglas	Rose Starkman
[A403]	- - - - - - Myrna Douglas	Morley Koffman
	- - - - - - - Lori Gail Koffman	Ken Ziebelman
	- - - - - - - Theodore Ian Koffman	Debby Lerner
	- - - - - - - Robert David Koffman	Tara Jacobowitz
	- - - - - - Lorne Douglas (m)	Carol Sherman
	- - - - - - Elyse Douglas (f)	
	- - - - - - Leslie Joy Douglas (f)	Nicolas Pruett
	- - - - - ?? Douglas	
	- - - - - Max Douglas	
[A404]	- - - - - Tzvi| Harry Douglas	Libby Grant (?Rodney)
	- - - - - - Lionel Douglas	
	- - - - - - Max Douglas	
	- - - - - - Laurel Douglas	David Shugarnan
	- - - - - - Sarah Shugarnman	
		A Frenchman (h2 Laurel)
	- - - - - Douglas	
[A405]	- - - - Polia Douglas	Moshe| Morris Fuks| Fouks
[A406]	- - - - Jacob| Jack Fouks	Jennie Shector
	- - - - - Toby Michelle Fouks (f)	Yoginder Nathan Sadana
	- - - - - - Steven Twist, b. Jefferey Sadana	Ayako Koike
		Kenneth Cunnington (h2 Toby)
[A407]	- - - - - Leslie Fouks (m)	Faith Sperling
	- - - - - - Carey Paul Fouks	Not married
	- - - - - - Jodie Michelle Fouks	Not married
[A408]	- - - - - David Fouks	Ruth Pearl Zimmerman
[A409]	- - - - - Wendy Ann Fouks	John Anthony
	- - - - - Terry Joan Fouks (f)	
	- - - - - Marsha Jane Fouks	Ralph Edwards
[A410]	- - - - - Gertrude Fouks	Sidney Zack
	- - - - - - Rosalind Meryl Zack	Howard Mark Karby
	- - - - - - Michelle Karby	Daniel Kotlowitz
	- - - - - - Debra Karby	Adam Rootman
	- - - - - - Sara Karby	Shaughan Halls
	- - - - - - Richard| Rafi Allan Zack	Michal Baruch
	- - - - - - Sharon Zack	Oren Moran → Zack
	- - - - - - Maya Zack	
	- - - - - Joanne Louise Zack	Allan Pakes
[A411]	- - - - - Arthur Fouks	Ancie Koshovoy
	- - - - - Sondra Fouks	Robert Ritter
	- - - - - - Paul Ritter	
	- - - - - - Romy Ritter	
		Bruce Green (h2 Sondra)

	- - - - - - Janice Fouks
[A412]	- - - Mischa| Moshe Douglas
	- - - - 5 other children died young
[A413]	- - - Bracha| Bertha Douglas
[A414]	- - - Itzhok Dolgonos - → Douglas
[A415]	- - - - Lisa Douglas
	- - - - - Son
[A416]	- - - - Sonia Douglas
	- - - - - Lucia Arnopolski
[A417]	- - - - Abram Dolgonos
[A418]	- - - - Josip Dolgonos

- - Beila\| Berta Kaprov
- - Sarah Kaprov
- - Rokhel Kaprov

Butch Blum
Paula ___

Chaim Dudnik [A510] A1B1C3
Esther _____
Sonal ?

__ Arnopolski
__ Rosen

APPENDIX B3: B'NAI KHAIM FAMILIES, PART 2
DESCENDANTS [A290] KHAIM KAPROV'S SON, [A419] BERYL

ID	Family member (Born < 1980) Generation 1-9 (#8 & 9 mostly omitted)	Partner
[A419]	- Beryl Dov Kaprove	Dvossie Brodsky
[A420]	- - **Khaye Golda Kaprove**	Velvel Gilman
[A421]	- - - Khana Esther Gilman	Isruel Tepilsky
	- - - - Rose Teplitzky	Jacob Feldman
	- - - - - Sylvia Feldman	Frank Schwartz
	- - - - - - Ellen Schwartz	___ C. Azorin
	- - - - - - Victor Stephen Schwartz	Gail Diane ____
	- - - - - - - Male Schwartz	
	- - - - - - - Female Schwartz	___ Pawlak
	- - - - - - - Male Schwartz	
	- - - - - Alvin Feldman	Joan Gotleib
	- - - - - - Kenneth Paul Feldman	
	- - - - - Bernice Feldman	Martin Landau
	- - - - - - Madeline Landau	
	- - - - - - Claudia Landau	
	- - - - Sarah Teplitzky	Jacob Rosen
	- - - - - Sidney Rosen	Elaine Stein
	- - - - - Ronald Rosen	Phyllis J Ditkoff
	- - - - - Dennis Rosen	
	- - - - - Edwin Rosen	Rosalyn Brody
	- - - - - - Michelle Rosen	
	- - - - Mary Teplitzky	Harry Friedman
	- - - - - Ina Friedman	Benjamin Lieberman
	- - - - - - Michael Lieberman	
	- - - - - - Daniel Lieberman	
	- - - - - - Chester Lieberman	
	- - - - Rudolf Taplitz	Frieda Candler
	- - - - - William Chester Taplitz	
	- - - - - Richard Taplitz	Phyllis Lerner
	- - - - - - Sheri Taplitz	
	- - - - - - Daniel Taplitz	
	- - - - - - Susan Taplitz	
	- - - - - - Randy Taplitz	
	- - - Morris Teplitzky	Ruth Berman
	- - - - Judith Teplitzky	Donald Davidovit
	- - - - - Michael Davidovit	
	- - - - Henry Teplitzky	
	- - - Benjamin Teplitzky --> Taplitz	Miriam Schachter
	- - - - Joel Harris Taplitz	Judith ___
	- - - - - Keith Teplitzky	
	- - - - - Julie Anne Teplitzky	
	- - - - Mitchell Taplitz	___ Robson
		Unknown Khaya's H2
[A422]	- - **Pessie Kaprov**	Moshe Shestunov- → Gillman
[A423]	- - - Chaye| Haya Sarah Gillman	Eliezer Pribludny
[A424]	- - - - Rachel| Rose Strayer Pribludny	Morris Green
	- - - - - Pauline Green	Harold P Gannis
	- - - - - - Terry Lee Gannis	
	- - - - - - Darian Gaye Gannis	
	- - - - - - Lynette Joy Gannis	
	- - - - - - Marla Denise Gannis	

	- - - - - Aaron Green	
	- - - - - Allan Green	
	- - - - Avraham Pribludny	
[A425]	- - - - Bayla Liba Pribludny	
[A426]	- - - - Khaim| Hyman Strayer Pribludny	Masha Portnick
	- - - - Leonard Biederman Pribludny	Phyllis Siegel
	- - - - - Jay Bradley Pribludny	
	- - - - - Ira Walter Pribludny	
		Sadie Strayer Berman (w2 Hyman)
	- - - - - Martin Strayer	
	- - - - - Leah Strayer	
[A427]	- - - Daniel Gelman	Sarah| Sheva Kaprow
[A428]	- - - - Gertrude| Gisi Gelman Twin-1	Joe Robboy A2B7C4 [A024]
		Sam Mittleman (h2 Gertrude)
[A429]	- - - - - Gordon Mittleman	Ferne Elaine Phillips
	- - - - - - Daniel David Mittleman	Eva Darga
	- - - - - - David	
	- - - - - - Alexandra	
	- - - - - - Jacob	
	- - - - - - Michael Mittleman	
	- - - - - Susan Shelley Mittleman	Robert Zent
	- - - - - Jeri Judith Mittleman	
	- - - - Khaim Gelman Twin-2	
	- - - - Pessie Gelman	
[A430]	- - - - Dvossi| Dorothy Gelman	Benjamin Kareff
	- - - - - Natalie Kareff	Jerome Miller
	- - - - - Cheryl Lynn Miller	Richard I Leff
	- - - - - Debra Gaye Miller	Ronald Fink
	- - - - - - Eric Benjamin Fink	
	- - - - - - Andrew Lawrence Fink	
	- - - - - Eileen Kareff	Morton Haber
	- - - - - - Jill Lorry Haber	Jeffrery Kramer
	- - - - - - Jody Lynn Haber	Mathew Hale
	- - - - - - Joy Denise Haber	Norman Dunstan
		Michael Enck (h2 Joy)
[A431]	- - - Alta| Anna (orig Baila Liba) Gelman	David Hirsh Pearlman (h2 Alta)
[A432]	- - - - Abe Pearlman	Freda| Frieda ___
[A433]	- - - - - Annette Pearlman	Howard Stanley Lynn
	- - - - - - Ronald Lynn	
[A434]	- - - - - Shirley Pearlman	Joseph Amato, Jr
[A435]	- - - - - - Cheryl Lynn Amato	___ Ladawer
	- - - - - - Kenneth Michael Amato	
[A436]	- - - - - Emanuel: Sonny Pearlman	Simone Dechelle Wllingford
[A437]	- - - - - - Vicky Pearlman	___ Kuczynski
[A438]		Alva Baily (w2 Abe)
[A439]	- - - - - Rita Sue | Susie Pearlman	James Albin Bogart
[A440]	- - - - - - Lesa K Bogart	Louis G Woyton
[A440b]		Gregg Edward Jusko (h2 Lesa)
	- - - - - - Robert Allan Bogart	
		Donald Mahle (h2 Rita Sue)
[A441]	- - - - - - Barbara Mahle	Michael Marzec
[A442]	- - - - - Joyce Pearlman	Michael Segulin
[A443]	- - - - Beryl| Ben Perlman	Sylvia Plumka
[A444]	- - - - - Arleen B. Perlman	Allen W Rossen
[A445]	- - - - - - Ellen Marcia Rossen	David Maman
[A446]	- - - - - - Sandra Rossen	Avner Lahrey
[A447]	- - - - - - - Moriah Lahrey (f)	
[A448]	- - - - Pessie| Pauline Pearlman	Julius | Jack Fox

[A449]	- - - - - Robert Fox	Martha Kerner
[A450]	- - - - - Denise Fox	——
[A451]	- - - - - Michelle Fox	Rick Moss
[A452]	- - - - - Julius| Jay Fox	
	- - - - - Lisa Fox	
[A453]	- - - - - Diane Fox	Irving Chaitoff
[A454]	- - - - - - David Kaye Chaitoff	
	- - - - - - Ronald Chaitoff	
	- - - - - - Joy H Chaitoff	
[A455]	- - - - - Marlene Beverly Fox	Richard Rock div
	- - - - - Mitzi Robin Rock	Craig Donoff
	- - - - - - Chase B Donoff	
		Herbert F. Zweig (h2 Marlene)
[A456]		Motel Gelman (h2 [A620] Alta Perlman)
[A457]	- - - Yossel| Joseph Gillman	Etta Judith Cohen
[A458]	- - - - Leonard Gillman	Reba Parks Marcus
	- - - - - Jonathan Webb Gillman	Elizabeth Lewis
	- - - - - - Mark Gillman	Erin Boggs
	- - - - - - Philip Daniel Gillman	Heidi Curtiss
		Pamela Nomura (w2 Jonathan)
	- - - - - Michal| Miki Judith Gillman	Walter Read
	- - - - - - Aletha Read	
		Larry Batchelder (h2 Michal)
[A459]	- - - - Robert David Gillman	Katherine Backus
[A460]	- - - - - Daniel Webb Gillman	Emily White
		Julie A. Black (w2 Daniel)
	- - - - - Matthew William Gillman	Clair Moritz
		Eileen Costello (w2 Matthew)
	- - - - - Jane Elizabeth Gillman	Raymond McMackin
	- - - - - David Wallace Gillman	
[A461]	- - **Daniel (Rabbi) Kaprov**	Khaya
	- - - Ettie Rachel Kaprov	
	- - - Khaim Kaprov	
	- - - Tobie Kaprov	
	- - - Gershon Kaprov	
[A462]	- - **Yenta Kaprov**	Yankel| Jacob Trachtman
[A463]	- - - Motye| ?Mordecai| Max Trachtman	Khana| Hannah| Anna Charnopolsky
[A464]	- - - - Rochel| Ruth Trachtman	Alex Teplitsky
[A465]	- - - - - Marilyn Teplitzky	Leonard I Weinstock
	- - - - - - Jill Alison Weinstock	Robin Klombers
	- - - - - - Sharon Leslie Weinstock	Jacques Steinberg
	- - - - - - Mark Jason Weinstock	Robin Klombers)
	- - - - - Son Teplitsky	
	- - - - Yakov| Jack Trachtman	Rose Kosutsky
[A466]	- - - - Moishe| Morris Trachtman	Leke| Lilly Chertow
	- - - - - Muriel Trachtman	Howard F Hirt
	- - - - - - Victoria Jane Hirt	
	- - - - - Paula Trachtman	Peter L Rothholz
	- - - - - - Amy Elizabeth Rothholz	
		Edward Butscher (h2 Paula)
	- - - - Louis Trachtman	Lena Krasson
	- - - - - Evelyn Trachtman	Murray Abrams
	- - - - - - Alan Bruce Abrams	
	- - - - - - Pamela Abrams	Marvin Reinglass
	- - - - - - Lawrence Paul Abrams	Elanit Radmi
	- - - - Carl| Colman Trachtman	Anita Klass ?Glass

- - - - - - Stacey| Sarah Trachtman		Nancy Pollack
- - - - - - Leslie| Lazar Trachtman		Cherie E. Pell
- - - - - Albert Trachtman		Jim Chavis
- - - - - Joy Victoria Trachtman		Dinnis Post
- - - - - - Liane Mara Chavis		Vincent Isaac (h2 Liane)
		Kathleen Marie Freis
- - - - - - Aaron Louis Chavis		Raymond Tordini (h2 Joy Victoria)
		Rachel Munoz
- - - - - Lyle Howard Trachtman		Adele Foigelman A2B4C3D5E1
- - - - - Jack Trachtman		Lynn Black
- - - - - Lawrence Howard Trachtma		Karon S McCoy (w2 Jack)
		Alyssa Graber
- - - - - Louis Joseph Trachtman		Melissa Lynn Heller
- - - - - Lee William Trachtman		Frank Kanefsky
[A467] - - - Dora Trachtman		Sarah Blyn Linder
[A468] - - - Samuel Trachtman		Sam Wald
- - - - Shirley Trachtman		Howard Polman
- - - - - Barbara Ann Wald		David Wegin (h2 Barbara Anne)
- - - - - Michael Wald		
- - - - - Jeffery Wald		
[A469] - - - - Marcia Trachtman		Jeffrey Scheer
- - - - - Jennifer Scheer		Ali Hammud
- - - - - David Scheer		
[A470] - - - ZalmanShlomo Trachtman		? w1
		Bracha Zatkoritsky- (w2 Zalman)
[A471] - - - Yacov| Jacob Trachtman		Ahuva Colodny
[A472] - - - Svi Trachtman		Bracha Jaloshitsky
[A473] - - - - Eyal Trachtman		Janice Sussman
- - - - - Noah Trachtman		Orin Katz
- - - - - Sharon Trachtman		
- - - - Ofra Trachtman		Chaim Tsfati
- - - - - Timna Tsfati		Ishar Neumann
- - - - - Ohad Tsfati (m)		
- - - - - Naoma Tsfati		
- - - Nehama | Sonya Trachtman		Israel Sinkofsky
- - - - Pinchas Sinkofsky		
- - - - Tseila Sinkofsky		
- - - - Shlomo Sinkofsky		
- - - - Itzak Trachtman		Nehana| Yona Tankus ?Tanhus
- - - - Shlomit Trachtman		Gad Enoch
- - - - - Yohin Trachtman (m)		Tal Gotlieb
- - - - - Irit Trachtman (f)		Amnon Litvak
- - - - - Micahel Trachtman		
- - - - - Yehuda Trachtman		Lea Toronchk
- - - - - Adi Trachtman		
- - - Rivka Trachtman		Itzhak Lubitz
- - - - Elana Lubitz Amir		Itshaki Amir ?
- - - - Nina Itshaki (f)		
- - - - Merev Itshaki (f)		
- - - - Nava Lubitz (f)		Arey Eshad
- - - - Hannah Lubitz		Yuval Eker (see Janette Rosenbaum)
- - - - - Efrot Eker		
- - - - - Yael Eker		
- - - Beryl| Dov Trachtman		Judith ? Tehudit Kessler
- - - - Itzhak Trachtman		Ziva Jacobi
- - - - - Erez Trachtman		Smadar Rubenstein
- - - - - Tomar Trachtman		

	- - - - - - Oren Trachtman	
	- - - - - - Shlomo Trachtman	
		Shoshanna Baratz (w2 Dov)
	- - - - - Arieh| Arye Trachtman	Achsa Cohen
	- - - - - Esther Trachtman	Yoni| Jonathan Gershstein
	- - - - - - Mala Gershstein (f)	
	- - - - - - Dafna Gershstein (f)	
	- - - - - - Shlomit Trachtman (f)	Ghomein| Rane'm Yaacobi
[A474]	- - - Hyman Trachtman	Edassy| Hadassah Kaprov (A7B4)
[A475]	- - - - Haika| Ida| Chicki Trachtman	Samuel Kaprove- →Kaplan
[A476]	- - - - - Edith Kaprove	David Newler
	- - - - - - Ilene Ann Newler	Dennis Herman
[A477]	- - - - - Jeannette Kaprove	Robert Rosenbaum
	- - - - - - Lenore Ann Rosenbaum	Richard Rossi
	- - - - - - Diane Ruth Rosenbaum	Victor Reinhold
	- - - - - Shirley Kaprove	Jules Tintinfass
[A478]	- - - - Golda Trachtman	Harry Berman (also Yusti)
	- - - - - Edith Berman	Bernard Kurtz
	- - - - - - Barry Kurtz	Beverly Hammer
	- - - - - - - Brandon Scott Kurtz	
	- - - - - - Debbi Kurtz	Joe Weidinger
	- - - - - Marilyn Berman	Gerald Silverman
	- - - - - - Richard Silverman	
	- - - - - - Mark Scott Silverman	
	- - - - - - Lori Silverman	Richard Fuzl
[A479]	- - - - Yankel| Jacob Trachtman	Eva Rudin
	- - - - - Eugene Trachtman	Esther Schwartz
[A480]	- - - - - Howard Daniel Trachtman	
[A481]	- - - - - Louis Trachtman	Elizabeth| Betty Breland
	- - - - - - William Clay Trachtman	
[A482]	- - - - Itzik| Isadore| Isaac Trachtman	Rose Epstein
	- - - - - Elaine Phyllis Trachtman	Henry W Pieta
		Bernard Shrybman (h2 Elaine)
	- - - - - - Debra Sue Shrybman	Alan Mills
	- - - - - - Cindi Shrybman	William Lasher Crowley
		Henry Peita (h2 Elaine Phyliis)
	- - - - - David Lawrence Trachtman	Linda Margot Braithwaite
	- - - - - James Benjamin Trachtman	Karen Lee Lane
	- - - - - Jennifer Beth Trachtman	Peter Earle Rooks
[A483]	- - - - Bluma| Bella Trachtman	Marvin Foigelman
	- - - - - Adele Foigelman	Jack Trachtman
		Harry Gan (h2 Adele)
	- - - - - - Children: See Father	
[A484]	- - - - Bracha| Bertha Trachtman	Isadore| Dan Levitsky
	- - - - - Sheldon Levitsky	Ellen Lidman
	- - - - - - Steven Levitsky	
	- - - - - - David Levitsky	
	- - - - - Eileen Levitsky	Robert Fine
	- - - - - - Lisa Fine	
	- - - - - - Julie Fine	
		Mariam Kaprov (b Yachnis) (w2 Hyman?)
[A485]	- - - Yossel| Yosef Trachtman	Haika| Chaia Taratuta (fm Kanala)
[A486]	- - - - Tova Trachtman	Moshe Ariely I
	- - - - - Shlomo Ariely	Nahima Osherov
	- - - - - - Yuvall Ariely	Smadar ____
	- - - - - - Hadass Ariely	Moshe Papo
	- - - - - - Daphna Ariely	Amnon Shalmon)
	- - - - - - Gal Ariely (m)	

	- - - - - - NIr (m) Arielli	Dvora Girshtain (w2 Shlomo)
	- - - - - Benjamin Ariely	
	- - - - - Assaf Ariely (m)	Ayala Shtamler
	- - - - - Efrat Ariely (f)	
[A487]	- - - - Leah Trachtman	Michel Bogomilny- → Palchan
	- - - - - Moshe| Ernst Palchan	Imna Hodes
	- - - - - Geula Palchan	
	- - - - - Yehuda Palchan	
		Liana Bekkerman (w2 Moshe)
	- - - - - Yael Lisa Palchan (f)	
	- - - - - Itzak- Israel Palchan	Mila Bogdanov
	- - - - - Liza Palchan	
	- - - - - Tali Palchan	
[A488]	- - - - Miriam Trachtman	Israel Wilnai
	- - - - - Amos Wilnai	Ruth Arieli
	- - - - - Sigal Wilnai (f)	
	- - - - - Yael Wilnai (f)	
	- - - - - Nitzan Wilnai (m)	
	- - - - - Dan Wilnai	Sarah Weingarten
	- - - - - Guy Wilnai	
	- - - - - Iris Wilnai	
	- - - - Rivka Pria Wilnai	Sergio Hart
[A489]	- - - Sarah Batya Trachtman	Nahemia Gesserl
	- - - - Hannah Gesser	Peretz Viletsky
	- - - - - Mihal Viletsky	
[A490]	- - - Bat-Ami Trachtman	Israel Rapoport
	- - - - Ehud| Udi Rapoport (m)	Gilat| Gili Noiman
	- - - - - Efrat Rapoport (f)	
	- - - - - Noa Rapoport (f)	
[A491]	- - - - Amnon Rapoport (m)	Inka Klinn
	- - - - - Matan Rapoport (m	Tal Briskin
	- - - Yacov| Jacob Trachtman	Tzilla Furman
	- - - - Gil Trachtman	Ora Hurwitz
	- - - - - Nir Trachtman (m)	
	- - - - - Rotam Trachtman (m)	
	- - - - - Tal Trachtman (f)	
	- - - - Irit Trachtman	Moti Kafry
	- - - - - Anat Kafry (f)	
	- - - - - Ifat Kafry (f)	
[A492]	- - - Shneur| Schnayer Trachtman	Batya| Bessie Gelman
[A493]	- - - - Grisha| Hershel Trachtman	Sima Sima Zebiskay
	- - - - - Shaika Trachtman	
	- - - - - Enna Trachtman	
	- - - - - Anna Trachtman	Chaim Bellman
	- - - - Boris| Beryl Trachtman	Eda Kapin
	- - - - - Rivka Trachtman	Bori Averbach
	- - - - - Ula Trachtman	Alal Oserbys
	- - - - - Velvel Trachtman	Marina ___
	- - - - Sona Trachtman	Tova Feedler
	- - - - - Alexander Trachtman	Larisa ____
	- - - Ben-zion Trachtman	Lena Sweedel
	- - - - Alex| Schnayer Trachtman	Vera ____
	- - - - - Natalie Trachtman	____
		____ (h2 Natalie)
	- - - - - - Child	
	- - - - Moshe Trachtman	Galina ____
	- - - - - Svetlena Trachtman	Leonet _____

435

	- - - - - Olga Trachtman	Galina (Ben-Zion)
[A494]	- - - Velvel| William| Feigel Trachtman	Alexander ____
[A495]	- - - - Yankel| Jacob Trachtman	Dvora| Dora Shapiro
[A496]	- - - - Minnie Trachtman	
	- - - - - Dorey Janice Brandt	Erwin Brandt
[A497]	- - - - - - Arieh Chaim Finell	David Finell
	- - - - - - Etan Reuven Finell	
	- - - - - Judith Ellen Brandt	
[A498]	- - - - Yetta Mollie Trachtman	Alex Giloff
[A499]	- - - - - Debra Lynn Goodman	Kenneth Sawyer Goodman
	- - - - - Karen Jean Goodman	David Goodman
	- - - - - Wendy Jo Goodman	Rodolfo Ilizal Castro
	- - - - - - Julia Goodman	Robert Hood
[A500]	- - - Ephraim| Frank| Froika Trachtman	Fannie Pratter
[A501]	- - - Girl Trachtman	
[A502]	- - **Leah Kaprove**	Itzhak Gelman (m Kishinev)
[A503]	- - - Moishe Gelman	Freda Grabois
	- - - - Hona| Ana Gelman	Mordecai| Markus Feldman
	- - - - Polia Gelman	Moritz Leibovitch
	- - - - - Edji Leibovitch	Lenny Lezko
	- - - - - - Tatiana Lezko	Andrei Botea
	- - - - - Suzanne Leibovitch	
[A504]	- - - - Boris Gilman	Slava Bronea Beilus
	- - - - - Michael Gilman	Mariola Blech
	- - - - - - Alexandra Gilman	
	- - - - - - Adrian Gilman	
		Pearl Seeger (w2 Boris)
	- - - - Froika| Froim Gelman	Hava Bershasky
	- - - - Moishe| Michael Gelman	Galina Liphetz
	- - - - - Alexander Gelman	
	- - - - - Sophie Gelman	Mark Vaisman
	- - - - - - Boris Vaisman	
	- - - - Yossel| Joseph Gelman	Olga Lowe
	- - - - Raia| Ruchel Gelman	Alexander Barandvsky
	- - - - - Tanya Barandvsky	Moris Lyublinsky
	- - - - - - Michael Lyublinsky	
	- - - - - - Rimma Lyublinsky	
[A505]	- - - Rivka Gelman	Yossef Galperin
	- - - - Faiga Galperin	Zisa Kramer
	- - - - - Lily Kramer	Aviv Con
	- - - - - - Joesph	____
	- - - - - Miron Kramer	Margarita ____
	- - - - - - Anatoli Kramer	
[A506]	- - - Motel| Mark Gelman (h2 Alta)	Alta Perlman
[A507]	- - - Genendal| Gwendel Gelman	Shloma ____
[A508]	- - - Yankel| Jacob Gelman	Frima| Sarah Rabinowitz
[A509]	- - - - Leah Gelman	
[A510]	- - **Itzik Gelman ?Rabbi**	Khana Sarah
	- - - Velvel Gelman	
[A511]	- - - Tobie Gelman	____ shohet ?
	- - - Daniel Gelman	
	- - - Hillel Gelman	

ID	Name		Spouse/Related
[A011]	- - **Malka Kaprov**		Shmiel Robboy
[A012]	- - - Khaim| Hyman Robboy		Rebecca Meshenstein
[A013]	- - - - Bernard Robboy		Rosalie Smotkin
[A014]	- - - - - David Gerson Robboy		Deborah Marion Herzberg
			Elizabeth Booher (w2 David)
[A015]	- - - - - - Ronald Robboy		Susan Severtson
	- - - - - - - Julian Hintz+		
	- - - - - - - Joseph Hintz+		
[A016]	- - - - - William| Bill Robboy		Christopher (Chris) Hurley
			Pearl Roth Gabaeff (w2 Bernard)
[A017]	- - - Anna Nessie Gerson Robboy		Avrom Shmiel Gerson
[A018]	- - - - Nathan Gerson->Robboy		Rose Nedelman
[A019]	- - - - - Nancy Ann Robboy		Mark W Cooper
	- - - - - - Deborah Ann Cooper		Leon Jay Adato, Jr
	- - - - - - - Kaleb Raphael Adato		
	- - - - - - David Joel Cooper		Pamela Crisel
	- - - - - - Eric Juan Cooper (Adopted)		Elizabeth (Bessie) Eaton
			Cassie Letourneau, (w2 Eric)
	- - - - - - Andrew (--> Monica) Cooper		
[A020]	- - - - - Marcia Lee Robboy		Johnathan Ames
	- - - - - - Jason Lawrence Ames		Kathleen E. Parente
			Madelin Mendez (w2 Jason)
[A021]	- - - - Pauline Gerson Robboy		Milton Siegel
[A022]	- - - - - Donald Robert Siegel		Rosetta| Rosie Schwartz
	- - - - - - Terry Lynn Siegel		Robert Alan Harvey
	- - - - - - Karen Ellen Siegel		Brandon Fielder
[A023]	- - - Tobie Robboy		
[A024]	- - - Joseph| Yossel Robboy		Gertrude Gelman A2B2C2D1
	- - - - Zachary Robboy		
[A024b]			Bessie Kimmelman (w2 Joseph)
[A026]	- - - John| Yankel Robboy		Sarah Shapiro
[A027]	- - - - Myrna Loise Robboy		Herbert Groger
[A028]	- - - - - Laurel Groger		Alijandro Espinosa
[A031]	- - - - Stanley J Robboy		Anita Wyzanski
[A032]	- - - - - Elizabeth Robboy		Orde Kittrie
[A033]	- - - - - Caroline Robboy		Peter Gearhart
			Marion Loeb Meyer (w2 Stanley)
[A515]	- - **Avrom : Abraham Ershel Rabbi Kaprow**		Sima Schwartz
	- - - Died 1 in infancy		
	- - - Died 2 in infancy		
	- - - Died 3 in infancy		
[A516]	- - - Fishel| Edward Philip Kaprov		Malka| Mollie Molly Reich
[A517]	- - - - Irene Gertrude Kaprov		James Shiro
	- - - - - Sandra Toby Shiro		Robert S. Lipman
	- - - - - - Meredith Lipman		Jonathan B. Ladov
	- - - - - - Kathryn Lipman		Kenneth Hausman
			Arie Kanofsky (h2 Kathryn)
	- - - - - - Allyson Lipman Jaffe		Andrew N. Jaffe
	- - - - - - Andrew Benjamin Lipman		Andrew Rubin
	- - - - - Alan Bruce Shiro		
[A518]	- - - - Gerald Louis Kaprow		Roslyn Cohen
[A519]	- - - - Gail Lee Kaprow		Robert Allen Ginsberg
[A520]	- - - - - Marcia Rachel Ginsberg		Scott Alibertl
	- - - - - - Lauren Michele Ginsberg		Jeffery Halperin
	- - - - - - Amy Beth Ginsbergc		Joseph SantaLucia
	- - - - - Michael Bruce Kaprow		Carol Ann Malcolm
	- - - - - - Tammy		Michael Moore

	- - - - - - Amey Malloy	
	- - - - - - Robert J Rosewall	Heather Rosewall
[A521]	- - - - Rhoda Kaprow	William Matson
	- - - - - Kevin Jon Matson	Pamela Marcil
	- - - - - Child 2	
[A522]	- - - Dvossi| Dorothy Kaprov	Yankel| Jake| Jacob Zitaner
[A523]	- - - Shirley Zitaner	Stanley Charm
	- - - - Anne Sima Charm	Andrew Abel
[A524]	- - - - Susan Charm	Kurt Schwartz
[A525]	- - - - Elizabeth Martha Charm	Richard Jerome Long
[A526]	- - - Moishe Kaprov	
[A527]	- - - Pessie| Pauline G Kaprov	Frank S Lerman
	- - - - Herschel Marvin Lerman	Gail Neiman
	- - - - Sally Beth Lerman	David Weiss
	- - - - Sima Joy Lerman	Leonard Naymark
	- - - - Sharon Ilana Naymark	Marc Daniel Rose
[A528]	- - - Gedaliah| Gordon,Rabbi Kaprow	Gittel| Geraldine Shapiro
[A529]	- - - - Rab Sholom Moishe Kaprow	Sheila Bernstein Weinstein
	- - - - Marc G. Kaprow	Ivy Dawn Schillinger
	- - - - Philip Scott Kaprow	Marissa Mencherd
	- - - - -	Sara Nemis (2)
	- - - - Simi Joyce Kaprov	Leonard Lerman
		___ Velley (Simi h2)
		? Name, w2 [A600] Beryl
		? Name, w3 [A600] Beryl

APPENDIX B3: B'NAI KHAIM FAMILIES, PART 3
DESCENDANTS [A290] KHAIM KAPROV'S CHILDREN,
[A530] SHMUEL, [A531] GEDALIA, [A573] KHAYA,
[A574] ITZIK-YOEL & [A577] ISROEL DOVID

ID	Family member (Born < 1980) Generation 1-9 (#8 & 9 mostly omitted)	Partner
[A530]	- **Shmuel Abba Kaprov**	
	- - Children	
[A531]	- **Gedaliah Kaprov**	Nessie __
	- - Abroham| Abraham Kaprow	
[A532]	- - - Gedalia | Gregorio Kaprow	Sara Futeransky
[A533]	- - - - Motle | Mateo Caprav	Maria Monastersky
	- - - - - Carlos Charles Caprav	Katy
	- - - - - - Rosana Claudia Caprav	Marcelo ___
[A534]	- - - - - Dora Ana Caprav	Isaac Ideses
[A535]	- - - - - - Javier Horacio Ideses	
[A536]	- - - - - - Ariel Esteban Ideses	
[A537]	- - - - - - Valeria Sabrina Ideses	Javier Malik
[A538]	- - - - - - - Gal K Malik	
[A539]	- - - - - Oscar | Quique Caprav	Ana ___
[A540]	- - - - - Gerardo Andres Caprav	
[A542]	- - - - Elisa Caprav	Mauricio Mijalovich
	- - - - - Maximo Mijalovich	
	- - - - - Maria Daniela Mijalovich	
	- - - - - __ Mjalovich	__ Farace
	- - - - - Roberto Mjalovich	
	- - - - - - Marcelo Mijalovich	
	- - - - - - Claudia Mijalovich	
	- - - - - Teresa Mjalovich	?? __ Profeta
	- - - - - - Chil 1	
	- - - - - - Child 2	
[A543]	- - - - Hersh Kaprow	Maria Lenbersky
[A544]	- - - - - Adalberto Carlos Kaprow	Sophia Mirta Freue
[A545]	- - - - - - Alejandro Cezar Kaprow	
[A546]	- - - - - - Adrian Eliahu Kaprow	Batia Levi
	- - - - - - Marcelo Daniel Kaprow	
	- - - - - Mabel Kaprow	___ Lanconi
[A547]	- - - - Ana Caprav	Luis Einhorn
	- - - - - Marta Einhorn	
	- - - - - Eugenia GracielaEinhorn	
[A548]	- - - - Isaac Caprav	Rosa ____
[A549]	- - - - Alberto Caprav	
	- - - - - Emiliano Caprav	
	- - - - - Gabriela Caprav	
	- - - - - Luciano Caprav	
[A550]	- - - - Saul Caprav	
[A551]	- - - - Maria | Mary Caprav	Mauricio Fuks
	- - - - - Silvia Fuks	
	- - - - - - Luciano Caprav	
	- - - - - Alejandra Minervini	
	- - - - - Patricia Fuks	
[A552]	- **Shemariah Kaprov**	Perl
	- - Naftali Kaprov	
	- - Yankel Kaprov	

[A553]	- - Yakov Kaprov	Hanna Litvak
[A554]	- - - Samuel Kaprov --> Kaplan	Miriam Geisingsky
	- - - - Edward Kaplan (Kaprov)	
[A555]	- - - Michael Kaprov	Leah Grinberg
[A556]	- - - - Anna Michalovna Kaprove	Yosef Salomonovich Gilman
[A557]	- - - - - Elena Gilman	Konstantin Aron Katzman
[A558]	- - - - - - Gene Joseph Katzman	Stella Yurievna Leryzerova
[A559]	- - - - - - - Aaron Max Katzman	
[A560]	- - - - - - Sarah Maria Katzman	
[A561]	- - - - - Olga Gilman	Peter Sorokin
[A562]	- - - - - - Evgeniya "Jane" Sorokin	Gabriel Sean Schaab
[A563]	- - - - - - Anna Sorokin	
[A564]	- - - - - - Elezaveta "Liza" Sorokin	
[A565]	- - - Velvel Kaprov	
[A566]	- - - Ratsa Kaprov	Samuel Berdichevsky
[A567]	- - - - Yakov ?Velvel Berdichevsky	
[A568]	- - - - Anna Berdichevsky	Boris Tokar
[A569]	- - - - - Aleksandra Tokar	Ukn
	- - - - - Arthur Tokar (adopted)	
[A570]	- - - - Leonid Tokar	Marina Pritssker
[A571]	- - - Belchik Kaprov	Chaya ___
[A572]	- - - - Yakov Kaprov	
[A573]	- **Khaya Kaprov**	
[A574]	- **Itzik-Yoel Kaprov**	Osna Kaprov
	- - Noah Dovid| Daniel Kaprov	
	- - Yankov Moishe Kaprov	
	- - Nehhama| Nachomi Kaprov	Yossel Puchatilofsky
	- - - Osna Puchatilofsky	
	- - - Gedalia Puchatilofsky	
	- - - Ethel Puchatilofsky	Louis Dratch
	- - - - Joseph B Dratch	Estelle Goodman
	- - - - - Michael William Dratch	
	- - - - - Edward Gary Dratch	
[A575]	- - - - - Eliot Mark Dratch	Gail Ann Thal
	- - - - Leah Dratch	Arthur Shifren
	- - - - - Alan Shifren	Lois Kamison
	- - - - - - Lisa Shifren	
	- - - - - - Jaimie Shifren	
	- - - - - Arlene Shifren	Arnie Rubin *
	-	Gary Charlestein ? Kernosh (h2 Arlene)
	- - - - Nathan M Dratch	Joan Lipshutz
	- - - - - Frances Dratch	___ Bornstein
	- - - - - Edward Dratch	
	- - - - - Anne Dratch	Robert Berman
	- - - - Sylvia Dratch	Robert Scheinoff
	- - - - - Ellen Scheinoff	Steven Wolf
	- - - - - -	
	- - - - - Richard Scheinoff	Holly Abrams
	- - - Nathan Puchatilofsky→Grossman	Esther Kaplan
	- - - Gloria Grossman	Harold Bernhard
	- - - - Robin Joy Bernhard	David Kurss
	- - - - Lisa Gail Bernhard	
	- - - Joseph Grossman	Dolores Isenberg
	- - - - Barbara Ellen Grossman	Sheldon Macks
	- - - - - Rachel Macks	
	- - - - - Lori Nan	Randy Benderson

- - - - - - Evan Benderson
- - - - - - Sarah Benderson
- - - Pinnie| Pinchos Puchatilovsky
- - - Leible Puchatilofsky
-   Khaye (w2 Itzik-yoel)
- - Hadassah| Edassy Kaprow   Hyman Trachtman-A2B4C3
- - KhaimHyman Kaprove   Mariam Yachnis (w2 Hyman)
- - - Leah Kaprove   Louis| Pinye Brodsky
- - - Julius Brodsky   Marlene Lieberman
- - - - Linda Beth Brodsky   Div
- - - - - Danielle
- - - - Marc Brodsky   Marina ?
- - - - Susan Brodsky
- - - Female, die   Cecelia Friedland
- - Yitzchak| Isadore Kaprove   Judith Panar
- - - Robert Kaprove   ___ Penn
- - - - Sara Ilene Kaprove
- - - - Alison Kaprove   ___ Smith
- - - - Matthew Simon Kaprove
- - - - - Son
- - - - - Dau
- - Menucha Kaprov
- - Itzak Kaprove   Leah
- - Velvel Kaprov
- - - ??
- - - ?
- - - ?
[A290b]   Edassey Edossy (w2 [A290] Khaim)
[A577]   - **Isroel| Yisrael Dovid Kraprov**

                                                 Khaya (w2 [A690] Itzhak)

441

APPENDIX B3: B'NAI KHAIM FAMILIES, PART 4
DESCENDANTS [A578] SIMCHA & [A620] YOEL ELI KAPROV

ID	Family member (Born < 1980) Generation 1-9 (#8 & 9 mostly omitted)	Partner
[A578]	**Simkha Kaprove**	Fayge| Fegah
[A579]	- Shlomi Kaprov	Bassie| Buni
	- - Yoel Kaprove	Dvorah Kaprov
	- - - Samuel Kaprove	Ida Trachtman
	- - - Rose Kaprove	
[A580]	- - David Kaprove| Caprov	Ethel| Ette| Ete Rabinowitz
[A581]	- - - Velvel Kaprov (Israel Perepelitsky->Purpel	Soybel Bergelson
[A582]	- - - - Nathan Purpel	Jacqueline Dinerstein
	- - - - - Amy Purpel	
[A583]	- - - - - Michael Purpel	
[A584]	- - - - David Edward Purpel	Elaine Annette Ladd
	- - - - - Mark Purpel	Rachael ___
[A584.2]	- - - - - Rachel Ann Purpel	Frederick Robert Bryant
	- - - - - - Susan Louise Bryant	
	- - - - - - Sara Elizabeth Bryant	
[A585]	- - - - - Nancy Purpel	Luis Eduardo Gonzales
		Michael John Gore (h2 Nancy)
	- - - - Ethel D Purpel	
[A586]	- - - - Marilyn (Molly) Purpel Marcus	Paul Marcus
	- - - - - Gary Marcus	
	- - - - Esther Rachel Purpel	Theodore G. Scott
	- - - - - Benjamin Scott	
[A584b]		Bayla Fleishman Waxman (w2 David)
[A588]	- - - Khaim| Charles Caproff	Pearl Shapiro
[A589]	- - - - Marion Caproff	Ronald Jack Kashin
	- - - - - Brian Kashin	Alison Davis
	- - - - - Debra Gail Kashin	Robert William Schacter
	- - - - - Robert Steven Kashin	
	- - - - - Aaron Elliot Kashin	
	- - - - - Albert Kashin	
[A590]	- - - - David Caproff	Tracy Knouse
	- - - - - Charly Ariel Caproff	
	- - - - Joan Caproff	Merle Andrews
	- - - - - Josh Andrews	
	- - - - - Justin Andrews	
[A591]	- - Chavah Dvorah Kaprove	Motel
[A592]	- Moshe Kaprove	Golda Rachel Schulnik
[A593]	- - Shalom Kaprove	Fageh Haverback
	- - - Rifki| Rose Ann Kaprove	
	- - - Yoel| Louis Kaprove	
	- - - Esther Kaprove	
	- - - SimchaSamuel J Kaprove	
	- - - Sarah| Sally Kaprove	Theodore Zisserson
	- - - - Howard Zisserson	Arlene Decof
	- - - - Bonnie Zisserson	Paul Hildred
	- - - - - ?Matthew Hildred	
	- - - - - Male 2 Hildred	
	- - - - - Male 3 Hildred	
	- - - - - Male 4 Hildred	
	- - - - Kenneth Zisserson	Elizabeth Very
	- - - - - Male 1 Zisserman	
	- - - - - Male 2 Zisserman	

	- - - - Ann Zisserson	Richard Hochman
	- - - - - Debbie Hochman	Louis Sanchez
	- - - - - - Sarah Sanchez	
	- - - - - - Rachel Sanchez	
	- - - - - - Male Sanchez	
	- - - - - Derek Hochman	
	- - - Abraham| Abie Kaprove (Downs)	
	- - - Lillian Kaprove	Ari Newman
	- - - Mariam Kaprove	Paul Shulman
	- - - - Donna Shulman	Barry Hartstone
	- - - - - Alan Hartstone	Allison Bertuch
	- - - - - Eric Hartstone	
	- - - - Carl Shulman (sing)	
[A594]	- - Schmuel| Samuel Kaprove à Cooper	Sara Lasensky
	- - - Frimi| Florence Cooper	Harry Ari Fishman
	- - - - Ruth Fishman	Joseph Gritz
	- - - - - Neal Martin Gritz	Marci Passmore
[A595]	- - - - - Larry Richard Gritz	Tracy Lynne Marquardt
	- - - - - Shelly Joy Gritz	Lewis Scharfberg
	- - - Simcha| Sidney Cooper	Sadie Edna Ross
[A596]	- - - - Gary Russell Cooper	Bonnie Linda Suskauer
	- - - - - Stephanie Michelle Cooper	___ Scherr
	- - - - - David Ari Cooper	Tricia Lee Ann English
[A597]	- - - - Marc Bruce Cooper	Roslyn Susan Rice W1
	- - - - - Allison Hillary Cooper	Michae Lee Folmsbee
		Bruce Dyke ?Dyche (h2 Allison)
		Wendy Dormont (w2 Mark Cooper)
		Donna Hasse (w3 Mark Cooper)
	- - - Yoel| Joseph Robert Cooper	Rita Dolores Aaron
	- - - - Erica Dawn Cooper	Arthur Jay Friedman
	- - - - - Monica Ilene Friedman	
	- - - - - Stacy Elise Friedman	
[A598]	- - - - - Brad Aaron Friedman	
	- - - - Stephanie Barbara Cooper	Wm Fredrick Scherr
	- - - - Betsy Debra Cooper	Steven Spector
[A599]	- - SimchaSamuel Kaprove	Sophie Fialky
	- - - Fred Kaprove	Mae Karp
	- - - - Beth Kaprove	Charles Ratner
	- - - - Michael Steven Kaprove	Debbi Adler
	- - - Ruth Kaprove	Harold Alpert
	- - - - Susan Alpert	Charles Comey
	- - - - Hollis Alpert	Steve Gomberg
	- - - - Brian Alpert	Robbin Breslow
	- - - - Shelley Alpert	Alan Sherman
[A600]	- - ChikiChava Kaprove	Yisrael Weinekov
	- - - Simon Weinekov	
	- - - Ruth Weinekov	
[A601]	- - Esther Malka Kaprove	Berel| Ben Varinsky
	- - - Betty Varinsky	Irving Shuman
	- - - - Marilyn Shuman	Joseph A Smith
	- - - - - Ira Smith	Donna Mondro
	- - - - - Michelle Smith	Bruce Gitt
	- - - - Janet Faye "Didi" Shuman	Steve Katz
	- - - - - Tamar Katz	___ Holloman
	- - - - - - __ Holloman	
	- - - - - Joshua Katz	
	- - - Philip Varinsky (d)	Dorothy Gomer
	- - - - Howard Varinsky	Leslie Gould

- - - - - Dana Varinsky		
- - - - - - 2nd		
- - - - Michel Varinsky	Tina Dolin	
- - - - - Abbie Varinsky		
[A602] - - FegehFeika Kaprove	Hershel Wolozin	
[A603] - - Eva| Chavah (Cooper) Kaprove	Dave Herman	
- - - Frederick R Herman	Ilene __	
	Ruth Jean Spoont (w2 Fred)	
- - - - Lee Herman	Patricia Foster Yusem	
- - - - Susane Carol Herman	Ray Cohen Williams	
- - - Ruth Herman	Morris Lift	
- - - - Carl Eric Lift	Lisa Michelle Aycock	
- - - - - male		
- - - - - fem		
- - - - - fem		
	Varsha Suhukla (w2 Carl)	
- - - - Alan Lift	Brenda Toscani	
- - - - Marc Lift		
[A604] - - - Rabbi Shimon Herman	Charlotte Mae Golub	
- - - - N'tina Malka Herman	Yehoshua Dov Ber Kamensky	
- - - - Yehuda Zev Herman	Stephan Glick	
- - - - Moshe Dov Herman	Andrea Ruth Becker	
- - - - Shmuel Arvah Herman	Gilit Devorah Rieser	
- - - - Reuven Shalo Herman	Ariela Miriam Wiener	
[A605] Israel Kaprove	Chiah |Chaia Dvorah	
[A606] - Avrom	Abraham Kaprove → Caprov	Sirke	Sara Sirota	
- - Bertha Caprov		
- - Elisa Caprov	Samuel Gendelman	
- - - Oscar Alberto Gendelman		
- - - Roberto Daniel Gendelman		
- - Piñe Caprov		
- - Peisse Caprov		
- - - Mario Caprov		
- - Simón Caprov		
[A607] - Gitel Kaprove (?no such person)	Zelik	
[A608] - Simcha	Simon Kaprove → Caprow	Adela Grobocopatel	
- - Clara Caprow	Luis Melamed	
- - - César Melamed		
- - - Saúl Melamed		
- - Pedro Caprow	Celia Kessler	
- - Adolfo Caprow		
- - - Marta Susana Caprow		
- - - Marcos Caprow	Elida Esther Montes	
- - - Leticia Gladys Caprow		
- - Carlos Caprow		
[A609] - Yoel : Julio Kaprove → Caproff	Maria Gelman	
- - Clara Caproff	Marco ___	
- - - Liliana ___		
- - Sara Caproff	Abraham Nudel	
- - - Ruty Nudel		
- - - Gady Nudel		
- - - David Nudel		
- - Fanny Caproff	Yaakov Skiva	
- - - Eldad Skiva		
- - - Huzy Skiva		
- - - Orna Skiva		
- - - Nava Skiva		
- - Israel Caproff	Betty ___	

	- - - Hudy Caproff	
	- - - Moran Caproff	
	- - - Abigail Caproff	
	- - Dorit Caproff	
	- - Salomon Caproff	Clarie __
	- - - Mahain Caproff	
	- - - Tal Caproff	
	- - - Gal Caproff	
[A610]	- Reichel| Ruchel Kaprove	Pessie (Peyack) Sklar
[A611]	- - Ezra Sklar	?
	- - - Michel Sklar	
	- - - Mendel Sklar	
[A612]	- - Chaim Sklar	**Perel Kaprov (see *3A5B5)**
	- - - Chiki Sklar	
	- - - Pini Sklar	
	- - - Nachomi Sklar	
	- - - Shayah Sklar	
	- - - - ??	
	- - - - ??	
	- - - - ??	
	- - - - ??	
	- - - Simcha Sklar	
	- - - - ??	
	- - - - ??	
	- - - ??	
[A613]	- - Baruch Sklar	
	- - - ??	
	- - - ??	
	- - - ??	
	- - - ??	
[A614]	- - Hershel Sklar	
	- - - David Shapiro	
	- - - Ann Shapiro	
	- - - Bessie Shapiro	
	- - - Jeanette Shapiro	
	- - - ??	
	- - - ??	
[A615]	- - Shayndel Sklar	
	- - - ??	
	- - - ??	
[A616]	- - Fayge Sklar	
[A617]	- - Chaya Sklar	Schmiel ___
	- - - Simon _____	
	- - - Shandel _____	
	- - - Ann _____	
[A618]	- Yonkel David Kaprove	
	- - Motel Kaprove	
	- - Pini Kaprove	
	- - Pesse Kaprove	
[A619]	- Chanah Dvorah Kaprove	
[A620]	Yoel Eli Kaprove	
[A621]	- Simchi Kaprove	Fegah
[A622]	- Leib Kaprove	
[A623]	- Chiki (Chayka?) Kaprove	
[A624]	- Raisel Kaprove	
[A625]	- Pinchas| Pini Kaprove	Bat Shavah| Sheva
[A626]	- - Laiki Kaprove	Mechel Shuman
	- - - Pini Shuman	

	- - - ? Son Shuman	
[A627]	- - - Bar Sheva Kaprov	
[A628]	- - Nachomi Kaprove	
[A629]	- - Chanah| Ania Kaprove	Married
[A630]	- - Chrisi Kaprove	
[A631]	- - Perel Kaprove (Follow under Sklar)	Chaim Sklar (*2A4B2)
	- - Tubi Kaprove	Pini| Pinchas Tishler
	- - - Nusel| Nathan Tishler	Fayge
[A632]	- - - - Chanah Tishler	Sam Beckerman
[A633]	- - - - Sasha Tishler (3 children)	Pessia
[A637]	- - DvorahDobi Kaprove	Yoel Kaprove (*2A1B1)
	- - - Bessie| Buni Kaprove	Moshe| Morris Cooper
	- - - - Louis Cooper	Sylvia Toplin
	- - - - - Alan J Cooper	Karen Altman
	- - - - - - Jennifer Cooper	
	- - - - - - Jeffery Cooper	
	- - - - - - Jeremy Cooper	
	- - - - - Sanford Cooper	
	- - - - Rose Cooper	Lester Popiel
	- - - - - Michele Popiel	
	- - - - - Phyllis Popiel	Richard Dickinson
	- - - - - - Ryan Dickinson	
	- - - - Harriet Popiel	Howard Powers
[A638]	- - - Simcha| Samuel Kaprove	Ida Trachtman *1A2B4C3D1 Follow Ida
		Dora Sholitzky
[A639]	- - - Reiche| Rose Kaprove	Benny Sadkin
[A640]	- - - - Leonard Sadkin	Judith Lippman
	- - - - Howard Sadkin	Sue Clement
	- - - - Lawrence Sadkin	
	- - - - Martin Sadkin	
	- - - Esther Sadkin	Stuart Kaufman
	- - - - John Kaufman	
	- - - - Barbara Kaufman	
	- - - Donald Sadkin	Barbara Lippes
	- - - - Jennifer Sadkin	Mark Lofman
	- - - - - Noah Lofman	
	- - - - - Zachary Lofman	
	- - - - Jonathan Sadkin	Wendy Swadron
	- - - - Rachel Sadkin	

APPENDIX B4 Cleveland Families and Others

BrudnoShapiro Clan

[A650] Rabbi Menashe (ben Porat) ben Joseph (1767-1831)
[A651] Hannah bat Menashe

Ezra Selig Brudo

Partial listing Brudno descenants

[A652] Batya bat Ezra Selig Brudno
[A653] Balebrine Rolnick (sister [A652] Batya
          And [A652a] Wolf's 2nd wife)

Wolf Rogovin --> Brudno

Children of Leah Brudno

[A654] Albert Sam Gressel
[A655] Sarah Gressel
[A656] Miriam Gressel
[A657] Louis Gressel
[A658]   Carmi Gressel
[A659]   Jonathan Gressel
[A660]   Malcolm (Macky) Dean Gressel
[A661]   Beth Gressel
[A662] Esther Gressel

Yael Ber Gresssel
Viva Lewin
Leon Shapiro [A669]
Uriah Shapiro [A674]
Chanah Kaplan
Shlomit Levin
Miriam Safer
Tamar Kishony
Eitan Israeli
Jack Fallenberg

Children of Rachel Brudno

[A663] Viva Lewin
[A664] Mania Lewin
[A665]   Eli Grad

Mendl Lewin
Sam Gressel

Geraldine Pescov

[A665.1] Children of Esther-Rochel Brudno

[A666] Jake Shapiro
[A667] Chyeneh Shapiro: d Russia
[A668] Chaim Shapiro: d Russia
[A669] Leon Shapiro
[A670]   Divi Shapiro
[A671]   Yola Shapiro
[A672]   Don Efraim Shapiro
[A673] Joseph Shapiro: d Russia
[A674] Uriah Shapiro
[A675]   Dorothy (Dotty) Shapiro
[A675b]
[A677]   Jack (Yonny) Shapiro
[A678] Rivka: d teenager in fire
[A026] Sarah Shapiro
[A027]   Myrna Robboy
[A031]   Stanley Robboy
[A031b]
[A682]   Manuel Shapiro
[A683]   Joel Shapiro
[A684]   Paul Shapiro
[A685]   Ellen Shapiro
[A686] Ezra Zelig Shapiro
[A687]   Rena Shapiro
[A687b]
[A687c]
[A688]   Daniel Shapiro

Rabbi Osias Shapiro
Fanny Bat Nathan

Sarah Gressel
David Lewin
Herb Lev
Zeva Rahel

Miriam Gressel
Jack Dannhauser
Sally Schenker (w2 Uriah)
Felicia

John Robboy
Herbert Groger
Anita Wyzanski
Marion Meyer (w2 Stanley)
Helen Suit
Sylvia Tigges
Susan Teichman
Forrest McDonald
Sylvia Lamport
Barry Newman
Michael Blumberg (h2 Rena)
Bernard Olshansky (h3 Rena)
Ellen Spingarn

Children of Isaac Brudno

[A689] Ethel Brudno

Hannah Modell
Jacob Wolpaw

Western-Reserve University

[A691]   Dr. George Neil Stewart
[A692]   Dr. David Marine
[A693]   Dr. Frederick Clayton Waite (Microscopic Anatomy)
[A694]   Dr. Todd (Anatomy)
[A695]   Dr. Hitchcock (Registrar)
[A696]   Dr. Bradley Patten (Embryologist)
[A697]   Dr. Ingersol (Anatomy)
[A698]   Dr. Headly
[A699]
[A700]   Charles Burn
[A701]   Max Charkin
[A702]   (Pinkey) Schmidt
[A703]   Dr. Mountcastle, physics
[A704]   Dean Lectner
[A705]   Dr. Emerson, English
[A706]   Dr. Gruenes (or Kuener), organic chem
[A707]   Dr. Gaelke, Sociology

Other Universities

[A708]   Corlton Jaerson
[A709]   Philip B Price, Dean Emeritus, U Utah Med School

Other Physicians, most from Cleveland

[A710]   Dr. Moses Garber
[A711]   Dr. Saul Genuth
[A712]   Dr. Sam Quitner
[A713]   Dr. Krepehl
[A714]   Dr. Skeel
[A715]   Dr. Phil Katz
[A716]   Dr. Perskey
[A717]   Dr. Gibson, genl surgeon, Lakeside Hosp
[A718]   Dr. Dembo
[A719]   Dr. M. Gray
[A720]   Dr. Sanford Rosen
[A721]   Dr. Howard Gans
[A722]   "Dr. Foxy"
[A723]   Dr. Samuel Lemel, ENT specialist
[A724]   Dr. Peggy E.
[A725]   Dr Salman
[A726]   Dr. Foda
[A727]   Dr. McLeod
[A728]   Dr. Julius Rogoff
[A729]   Zuker, chemist
[A730]   Dr. George Crile
[A731]   Dr. Stone
[A732]   Dr. Slom
[A733]   Dr. Mentin
[A734]   Dr Richard Dexter
[A735]   Dr Clyde Cummer
[A736]   Dr. Castile

University Michigan

[A737]   Dean Hugh Cabot

| [A738] | Dr. Neubrugh |
| [A739] | Dr. Thomas Weller |

School teachers

Old Central High School

[A740]	Ruetnik, principal
[A741]	Bathrien, his assistant
[A742]	Miss Avery, English
[A743]	Mr. Bissel
[A744]	Miss Brio
[A745]	Miss Brown, English
[A746]	Mr. Cook, Social studies
[A747]	Mrs. Fliedner, English
[A748]	Mrs. Hanna, Latin
[A749]	Henrietta, high school teacher.
[A750]	Mr. Hitchcock, Math
[A751]	Mr. Chas Hozan, teacher ancient history
[A752]	Lewis
[A753]	Miss Malorie
[A754]	Mr. Marple, Physics
[A755]	Haide Peiser
[A756]	Miss Henrietta Peiser
[A757]	Mr. Petersilge, algebra
[A758]	Miss Roberts, English
[A759]	Ms. Winkler, Math

School mates

[A760]	Mr. McDonnald
[A761]	Mr. Krenicky
[A762]	Serina Friedman
[A763]	Regina Dorid
[A764]	Joe Rossen, partner at WRU, undergrad, physics

Toledo hospitals

[A765]	Sister Ray, St. Vincent's Hospital
[A766]	Dr. Shapiro
[A767]	Dr. Fred Douglass, surgeon
[A768]	Dr. George last name, surgeon
[A769]	Dr. Cunningham, surgeon
[A770]	Dr. Crinion, surgeon
[A771]	Dr. R. L. Bidwell, surgeon
[A772]	Dr. Levison, progressive Jewish internists.
[A773]	Dr. Saltzman, progressive Jewish internists.
[A774]	Dr. Waggoner, homeopathic physician, chief staff
[A775]	Dr. Stone
[A776]	Dr. M.A. Fine, co-intern St Vincent's

Patients

[A777]	Edith
[A778]	Mildred
[A779]	Mrs. S.F.
[A780]	Mrs. S
[A781]	Mrs. B
[A782]	Miss Cook
[A783]	young lady from Lander Road
[A784]	Mrs. Frau Pudlimer
[A785]	Mrs. D. Williams

Rabbis

[A786]   Cantor Saul Meisel, Hazzen, Cleveland Heights, OH
[A787]   Rabbi Akiba

Hebrew Union College

[A655]   Eli Grad (President and Cousin)
[A789]   Nisson Touroff
[A790]   Samuel I. Perlman
[A791]   Mordecai Wilensky
[A792]   Aaron Weider
[A793]   Sol Schimmel
[A794]   Dov Eron
[A795]   Reuven Kritz
[A796]   Moshe Bar Asher
[A797]   Yochanan Silman
[A798]   A. B. Yehoshua
[A799]   Abraham Kaplan
[A800]   Isaac Zilberschlag
[A801]   Jacques Mikliszanski
[A802]   Shaul Techernichovsky

Merchants & Friends

[A803]   Zupnik, teller at Union Trust in Cleveland
[A804]   Mrs. Gabowitz, sweethart bank mng Cleve
[A805]   Mrs. Paley
[A806]   Dora Roodman
[A807]   Bessie Roodman
[A728a] Rebecca Rogoff, wife [A728] Julius Rogoff
[A809]   Esther Morris Zwick
[A810]   Mr. Sagolovitch, Singer Sewing Machine Agency
[A811]   Mr. Leventhal, Sunshine Broom Co
[A812]   Mr. Hirsch, tenant
[A813]   Young Ruskin
[A814]   Izzy Cantor
[A815]   Mr. Armstrong, teacher at Workmen's Circle School
[A816]   Anna Minaker
[A817]   Grace White
[A818]   Mrs. Halperin
[A819]   Ben Bernstein

Famous Personalities

[A820]   Paracelsus
[A821]   Albert Einstein
[A822]   Chaim Weizmann
[A823]   Vladimir (Zvi) Zhabotinsky, Zionist Activist
[A824]   Chaim Nachman Bialik, Poel Laureat Israel
[A825]   "Dr" David Rebelsky, Canadian Zionist (Poet Laureate Israel)
[A826]   Nahum Goldberg (Canadian Zionist)
[A827]   David Ben Gurion
[A828]   Andrei Sakharov, father Soviet hydrogen bomb, then dissident
[A829]   Moshe Dayan
[A830]   Sholem Aleichem (Solomon Naumovich Rabinovich)
[A831]   Baron Moritz (Zvi) von Hirsch
[A832]   Paul Dudley White
[A835]   Aage Bertelsen (Rescued Danish Jews)   Greta Bertelson

APPENDIX C: Gazetteer (Alphabetical)

	Russian town	Latitude, Long		Relations
		N	E	
	Principal towns			
[C01]	Knyazhe-Krinitsa	49 06	29 45	18.3 mi NW of Justingrad
				98.3 mi SSW of Kiev
				Zvenyhorods'kyi district, Cherkas'ka oblast
[C02a]	JustingradYustingrad	49 55	30 13	Same as Sokolivka
[C02b]	Sokolivka, Sokoliefke,			20 mi N of Uman
	Other towns			
[C03]	Arotof (Orativ)	49 12	29 32	
[C04]	Astakhan			On Volga River
[C05]	Bender	46 50	29 29	
[C06]	Bershad	48 21	29 32	40 mi SW of Uman
[C07]	Berdichev	49 54	28 34	
[C08]	Bucharest	44 25	26 06	
[C09]	Christinovka	48 50	29 58	
[C10]	Dunai			
[C11]	Gaisin	48 48	29 23	60 mi W of Uman
[C12]	KasiukaKashivka	51 10	23 21	
[C13]	Kiev	50 21	30 30	120 Mi N of Yustingrad
[C14]	Kishinev	47 01	28 50	146 mi from Yustingrad
				village in Podolia
[C15]	Knyazheki			
[C16]	Kodima (Kodyma)	48 06	29 07	
[C17]	Konela	49 04	30 06	3.8 mi N of Yustingrad
[C18]	Korsun	49 26	31 15	115 mi S of Kiev
[C19]	Kuritna (Korytne)	48 20	25 23	
[C20]	Libava (Libow, Lviv)	49 50	24 00	
[C21]	Lipovetz	49 11	29 01	"County" seat for Knyazhe
[C22]	Lukashivka	49 10	29 45	4 mi N of Knyazhe, Tax collector's home
[C23]	Lubovich			
[C24]	Monasteristshe	48 59	29 49	7 mi S of Knyazhe; Ben-Zion Robboy birth home
[C25]	Moscow	55 45	37 37	
[C26]	Nikolayev (Mykolaiv)	46 58	32 00	48 mi NE of Odessa
[C27]	Novosilka			3 miles west of Knyazhe
[C28]	Ochhmativ	49 10	30 21	20 mi NE or SW of Yustingrad
[C29]	Odessa	46 29	30 44	163 Mi N Yustingrad
[C30]	Szitomir (Zhytomyr)	50 15	28 40	
[C31]	Stavishtsh	49 23	30 11	24 mi N of Justingrad
[C32]	Tarashtscha	49 34	30 30	
[C33]	Terlitza (Terlytsia)	48 56	29 42	21 mi SW of Justingrad
[C34]	Tetiiv	49 33	29 41	18 mi NWW of Zashkov
[C35]	Tzibulev Tsybuliv	49 06	29 50	4 mi east of Knyashe, DesatnickKranzel home
[C36]	Uman	48 45	30 13	130 Mi S of Kiev; 21 mi S of Yustingrad
[C37]	Vilna	54 41	25 17	
[C38]	Vinnitza (Vinnytsia)	49 11	28 30	
[C40]	Volozhin	54 05	26 31	Near Vilna
[C41]	Voznesensk	47 34	31 18	
[C42]	Yedenitz (Edinet)	48 10	27 18	In Bessarabia (Moldova)
[C43]	Zashkov	49 15	30 05	

Location of towns, arranged from North South and from West East

	Town	N	E	<28E	28E	29E	30E	31E	>31E
[C25]	Moscow	55 45	37 37						37 37
[C37]	Vilna	54 41	25 17	25 17					
[C40]	Volozhin	54 05	26 31	26 31					
[C12]	KasiukaKashivka	51 10	23 21	23 21					
[C13]	Kiev	50 21	30 30				30 30		
[C30]	Szitomir (Zhytomyr)	50 15	28 40		28 40				
[C02a]	JustingradYustingrad	49 55	30 13				30 13		
[C07]	Berdichev	49 54	28 34		28 34				
[C20]	Libava (Libow, Lviv)	49 50	24 00	24 00					
[C32]	Tarashtscha	49 34	30 30				30 30		
[C34]	Tetiiv	49 33	29 41			29 41			
[C18]	Korsun	49 26	31 15					31 15	
[C31]	Stavishtsh	49 23	30 11				30 11		
[C43]	Zashkov	49 15	30 05				30 05		
[C03]	Arotof (Orativ)	49 12	29 32			29 32			
[C38]	Vinnitza (Vinnytsia)	49 11	28 30		28 30				
[C21]	Lipovetz	49 11	29 01			29 01			
[C22]	Lukashivka	49 10	29 45			29 45			
[C28]	OchrimovaOkhmatova	49 10	30 21				30 21		
[C01]	Knyazhe-Krinitsa	49 06	29 45			29 45			
[C35]	Tzibulev Tsybuliv	49 06	29 50			29 50			
[C17]	Konela	49 04	30 06				30 06		
[C24]	Monasteristshe	48 59	29 49			29 49			
[C33]	Terlitza (Terlytsia)	48 56	29 42			29 42			
[C09]	Christinovka	48 50	29 58			29 58			
[C11]	Gaisin	48 48	29 23			29 23			
[C36]	Uman	48 45	30 13				30 13		
[C06]	Bershad	48 21	29 32			29 32			
[C19]	Kuritna (Korytne)	48 20	25 23	25 23					
[C42]	Yedenitz (Edinet)	48 10	27 18	27 18					
[C16]	Kodima (Kodyma)	48 06	29 07			29 07			
[C41]	Voznesensk	47 34	31 18					31 18	
[C14]	Kishinev	47 01	28 50		28 50				
[C26]	Nikolayev (Mykolaiv)	46 58	32 00						32 00
[C05]	Bender	46 50	29 29			29 29			
[C29]	Odessa	46 29	30 44				30 44		
[C08]	Bucharest	44 25	26 06	26 06					

APPENDIX D: MAPS

Fig. Appendix D-1: The Pale of Jewish Settlement at the end of the 19th century. From commons.wikimedia.org. The boxed area is where Knyzhe and Sokolivka are located.

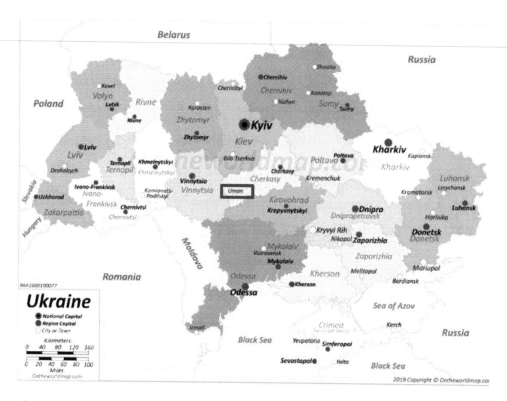

Fig. Appendix D-2: Map of Oblasts (provinces) of Ukraine. Uman is the major city located in the very Southwest of the Cherkasy Oblast. Knyazhe is located immediately northwest and Sokolivka, immediately North (neither appear in this map). Reprinted with permission of OnTheWorldMap.com.

Fig. Appendix D-3. Map of Ukraine. Reprinted with permission of MapOfEurope.com.
https://mapofeurope.com/wp-content/uploads/2013/06/ukraine.jpg?616c43

Fig. Appendix D-4: Ukraine w latitude and longitude markings. Circled area locates Knyazhe and Sokolivka, both in the catchment area of the Southern Bug River. Reprinted with permission from Britannica.com

Fig. Appendix D-5: Rivers of Ukraine. Circled area locates Knyazhe and Sokolivka, both in the catchment area of the Southern Bug River. Reprinted with permission from https://en.wikipedia.org/wiki/File:Map_of_Ukraine_political_enwiki.png

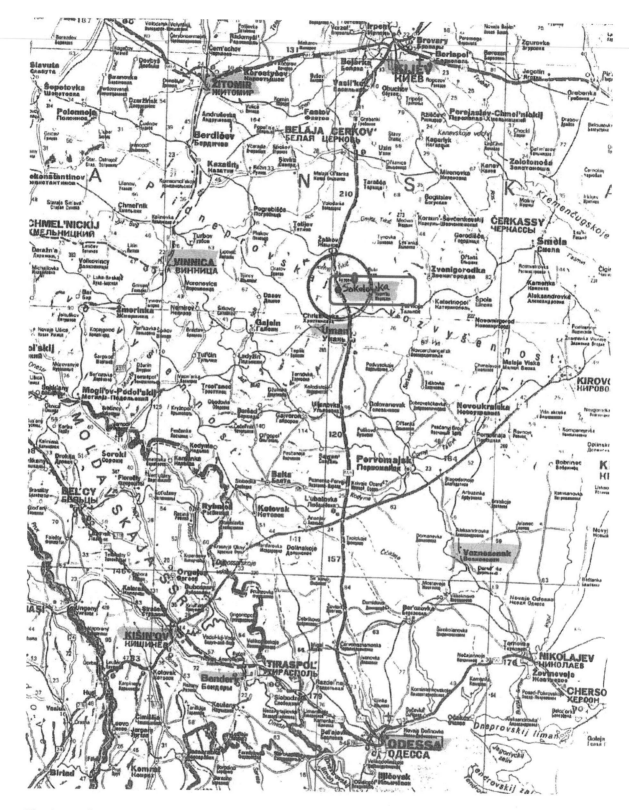

Fig. Appendix D-6 (Map Kiev to Odessa (Highlighting Sokolivka), in Memories of Sukoliefke/Ustingrad, B'nai Khaim reunion, Aug 17-18, 1991.

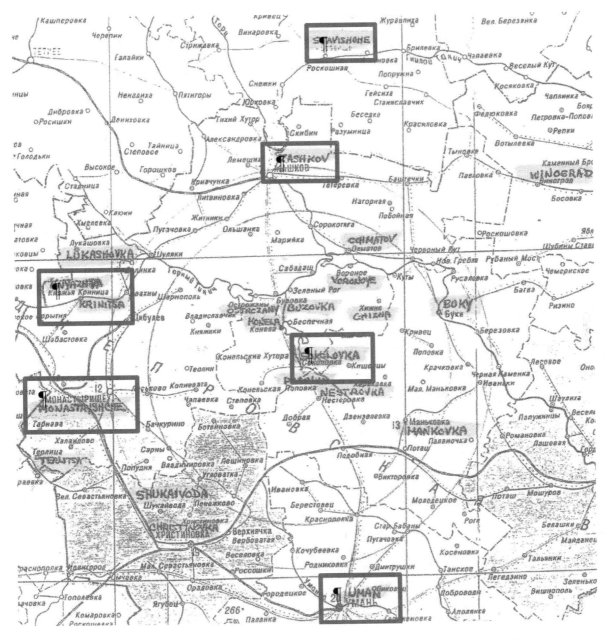

Fig. Appendix D-7: MAP Knyazhe-Krinitsa, Sokolivka-Justingrad, from Stavishne (North) to Uman (South) in Memories of Sukoliefke/Ustingrad, B'nai Khaim reunion, Aug 17-18, 1991.

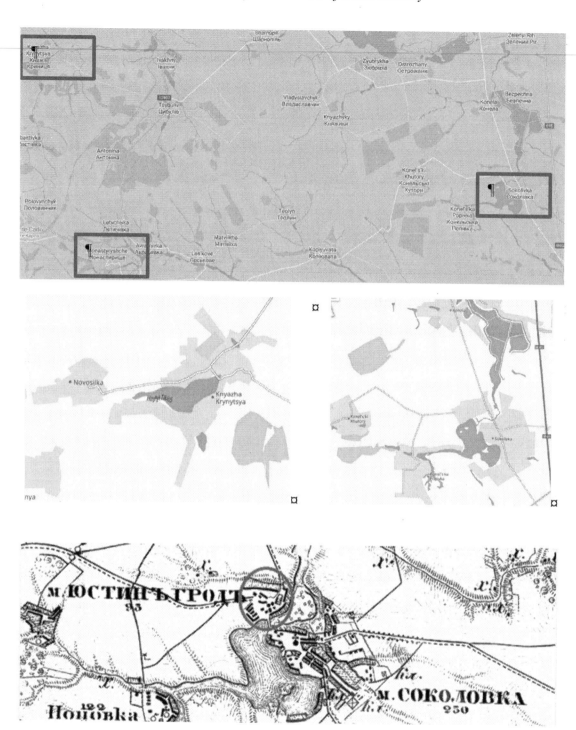

Fig. Appendix D-8: Map of Knyazhe (lower left) and Sokolivka / Justingrad (Upper right) and nearby major villages. From https://www.viamichelin.com/web/Maps/Map-Ukraine Reprinted with permission of Michelin North America; Detail of Justingrad / Sololivka 1846 http://jewua.org/justingrad/ Reprinted with permission.

Fig. Appendix D-9: Map Knyazhe (Knyazha-Kryntysya, aka Knyazhe) and Sokolivka Reprinted from
http://www.maplandia.com/ukraine/cerkaska/knyazhyky/. Map data @2020 Google Imagery @TerraMetrics

APPENDIX E: POGROM ANNIHILATING SOKOLIVKA (Aug 3-4, 1919)

Fig. App-E1: [A475a] Sam Kaprove (L) with a member of the Sokolivka Schule in Buffalo, admiring the plaque established to commemorate the pogrom victims of 1919 (Holy Order of the Living Cemetery, Cheektowaga, near Buffalo, New York, dedicated August 30, 1964). In addition, Sam also was instrumental in organizing the Sokolievker group in Philadelphia to contribute to the memorials at the Kibbutz Mash'bei Sadeh, which is located in the Negev desert just 8 miles north of Ben Gurion's home.

Age	Name	Relation
25	Alaitz, Baruch	Khaim-Moishe, blacksmith's son
17	Alaitz, Yidel	Khaim-Moishe, blacksmith's son
22	Albieter, David	Velvel, blacksmith's son
18	Alshansky, Avrora	Yisrael, Shochet's son
30	Arshadke, Khaye	Matel Shmoorak's daughter
25	Axelrod, Fishel	Kriensnepanner from Galicia
20	Beliovsky, Ezriel	From Kanala
32	Berestishevsky, Velve	From Knyashe
28	Berkovitch, Shraerel	Shimon, feldsher's (Nurse) son
32	Berlin, Herschel	Avrom Berlin's son
20	Bernstein, Yoshike	Hershel Israel Shmilek's son
26	Blank, Benny	Israel Litvak's son
24	Blecher, Yeshaye	From Antanavke
28	Bodurek, Zeidel	Usher Stelmach's SIL (wagon maker)
26	Bogoraolny	Rivke Liebe-Leah's SIL
23	Boord, Abraham	Pine Nesterivker's son

Age	Name	Relation
2	Boord, Abraham	Yidel Kripnick's (gritz maker) son
2	Boord, Chanah	Pine Nesterivker's son
25	Boorkat, Shamei	Blind Schlosser's (locksmith) brother
19	Boorshenka, Chaim	Ester-Chanah's son
28	Booshtein, Michael	Levi, Barber's son
20	Busier, Abraham	Kutzie, musician's SIL
58	Chernov, Menachem	egg dealer
30	Chernov, Moishe	Menachem, egg dealer's son
20	Cohen, Berel	From Zhashkow
19	Cooperman, Aaron	Eliezer Below's son
17	Dizak, Berel	Israel Dizak's son
24	Dizak, Boruch	Berke Brantzie's son
40	Dolgonos, Alec	Nachum Rachel's son
30	Doolman, Chaye	Moshe-Aaron Doolman's daughter
17	Doolman, Rafael	Moshe—Aaron Doolman's son

Age	Name	Description
25	Dozoretz, Chaim	Shmuel-Aba Stisie's son
28	Dozoretz, Mendel	Zelig Stisie's son
48	Dozoretz, Rachel	From Chizene
17	Dratch, Israel	Yechiel Dratch's son
21	Dratch, Mendel	Bennie Chayes son
19	Dratch, Motel	Shmuel Usher Chaye's son
29	Dratch, Yankel	Moshe—Lieb, butcher's son
21	Duchovne, Benny	Pine Abraham Kusie's son
21	Duchovne, Motel	Pine Abraham Kusie's son
16	Edelson, Chaim	From Bela Tzerkva
23	Eliatz, Itzchok	Chaim-Moshe, Blacksmith's son
20	Eliatz, Mayer	Chaim-Moshe, Blacksmith's son
19	Eliatz, Mendel	Yosel, Watercarrier's son
19	Eliatz, Yosel	Yosel, Watercarrier's grandson
26	Ezriels, Boruch	From Stavisht
23	Feldman, Velvel	Pinee Velvele's son
28	Fuhn, Herschel	Yitzchak Herschel-Menashe's son
18	Fuhn, Payse	Leib Hershel Menashe's son
18	Glantz, Ephraim	Pine, Gabbai's wife's son
28	Greenberg, Berel	Benny Chaye's son—in—law
36	Henzel, Benny	David Lazer's son
42	Kanevsky, Benny	Sony Valiaznick's son
24	Kaprow, Gedaliah	Yechiel, Hershel-Yosel's son
15	Kaprow, Hershel	Velvel, Yakov-Lieb's son
20	Kaprow, JocoCMoshe	Meir, Mason's son
18	Kaprow, Moshe	Abraham, Cantor's son
23	Kaprow, Velvel	Yankel, Israel—Aaron David's son
18	Kaprow, Yankel	Benny Mordchai Gedaliah's son
30	Karalick, Pesach-Lieb	Moshe Itzchok Nachman's son
16	Kazminsky, Alec	Shmuel, Shochet's son
20	Klatsman, Berel	Shimon, Blacksmith's son
22	Klatsman, Payse	Shimon, Blacksmith's son
17	Kulikov, Abraham	Shepsel, Baker's son
88	Kvasney, Shimon	Shimele, Barber
45	Kvasney, Sarah	"Shreierin" (yeller)
18	Kvasney, Shlomo	Shimele, Barber's son
35	Liametz, Esther	Yidel - Shlomo, Sexton's wife
25	Liametz, Yosel	Itzchok, water carrier's son
16	Lieps, Chaim	Efraim Abraham Motel's son
30	Lieps, Leeb	Efraim Abraham Motel's son
31	Linevitch, Yankel	Alter Avremele's son
35	Lisnavsky, Yosel	Baruch Grossman's SIL
17	Lovinsky, Simcha	Nachman Hirsh, Carpenter's son
20	Mandel, Abraham	From Stavisht
22	Mandel, Gedaliah	Rabbi's grandson
24	Manevitch, Chaim	Moshe Kalot's son
24	Manevitch, Motel	Menashe, Driver's son
32	Mayer	Shrouel Bershadsky's SIL
28	Metichin, Yankel	Efriam-Shimon, Baker
28	Miratshnick, Leeb	Moshe Kalat's SIL
28	Miratshnick, Shimon	From Zashkov
26	Mutshniek, Yankel	Lisi-Herer Teacher's son
16	Muzikant, Leb	Yankel Papush's brother
23	Nalubey, Motel	From Zashkov
28	Narachod, Simcha	David Moshe, Teacher's son
19	Nizkovolez, Shlomo	Yitzchok Wiener's son
24	Novominsky, Israel	From Baranatshev
17	Odesser, Moshe	Bennie Israel Chaim's son
27	Palianofsky, Shlomo	From Kislin
22	Palishtshak, Abraham- Lieb	Herschel, Harnesss-Maker's son
19	Palishtshak, Joseph	Herschel, Harnesss-Maker's son
16	Pekar, Abraham	Jacob Moshe-Hirsch's grandson
45	Poszarny, Abraham—Ber	Nachman-Abraharo-Ber's son
16	Poszarny, Berel	Mendel, Water-carrier's grandson
23	Poszarny, Michel	Levi, Shmuel-Lieb's son
17	Priblodny, Abraham	Eliezer, Black one's son
55	Priblodny, Lazer	Moshe, Beryl-Chaim's SIL
26	Pushkalinsky, Itzchok	Laske, Showmaker's son
19	Putchenick, Motel	David Hershel Bennie's son
85	Rabinowitz, Pinchas'l	Rabbi
26	Raskalenka, Reuven	Moshe Itzchok Nachman's SIL
18	Reck, Benny	Hoshike, Shoemaker's son
30	Reinadarsky, Itzchok	Chaim—Tandaitnick's son (ready made clothes)
23	Rekun, Benny	Alter Ruten's son
35	Rekun, Ephraim	Alter Ruten's son
22	Riabai, Fishel	From Zashkov
17	Rosenberg, Velvel	Hershel Deitch's son
20	Ruenberg, Payse	Levi, Red one's son
20	Shyman, Michel	Kaneler Grandmother's son
25	Shyman, Michel	Gedalia Peretz's son
20	Sirota, Liezer	Itzchok, Cap Maker's son
17	Sirota, Motel	Itzchok, Cap Maker's son
16	Sirota, Motel	Aba, Blacksmith's son
17	Sklar, Mendel	Ezra Payse, Glasier's son
23	Smikun, Chaim	Yakob—Moshe Tailor's son
60	Snitzer, Itzchok	deaf one
21	Spector, Abraham	Sholom, Rope twister's son
26	Spector, Lemel	Sholom, Rope twister's son
18	Spivak, Zeidel	Abraham Itzchok—Nachman's son
25	Suhenko, Ezekiel	Ezriel Esthel-Leah's grandson
17	Tarashtuk, Chaim	Levi, Musician's son
17	Tarashtuk, Sandor	Levi, Musician's son
23	Tarnofsky, Abraham	Hershel, Smiths's son
23	Telishevsky, Nani	Yosef Chaim, Teacher's son
24	Tishman, Yosel	Base, Storekeeper's SIL
55	Tsherbis, Leb	Nachum Tshebis's son
29	Umansky, Aaron	Shlomo, Sexton's SIL
20	Umansky, Mayer	From Uman
18	Valadarsky, Zeidel	From Stavishta
32	Vaskov, Moshe	David Lipenes' son
16	Vavnabai, Simcha	David, Groatman's son
17	Vinacour, Leb	Velvel, Teacher's son
18	Zabrinsky, Joseph	Berel, Hat Maker's son
28	Zadanofsky, Shlomo	Levi, Red One's SIL
32	Zaslavsky, Yankel	Chaim Zavel's son
18	Zubata, Herschel	Abraham, Hare-Lip's son
25	UNKNOWN, Moshe	Mordche, Chane-Rivka's grandson

SIL=SIL

APPENDIX F: HEADSTONES OF FAMILY MEMBERS

Gravestone markers the authors have are shown below.

Fig. App F-1: Headstones (From Left to Right):

[A012a] Rebecca Meshenstein Robboy
[A017]   Nessie Gerson Robboy
[A011] Malka (Mollie) Kaprov Robboy
[A034a] Sarah Spector Robboy

Fig. App F-2: Headstones (From Left to Right:
[A332] Polia Galler
[A333] Sarah D Milstein

Fig. App F-3: [A528] Tombstone Rabbi Gedaliah Kaprow

Fig. App F-4: [A528] Tombstones Dolgonos / Douglas Gedaliah Kaprow

[A400] DOUGLAS Israel, d 1943-01-16
[A400a] DOUGLAS Tohba, d 1938-02-21
[A405] FOUKS Paula, d 1964-03-06
[A405a] FOUKS Moses, d 1951-12-23

ACKNOWLEDGEMENTS

Many cousins generously offered their help in forms of commentary, reviewing the manuscripts, clearing up family relations, and procuring photographs. Many are named in John's writings. The listing below is complete, including those not named in the text, who have been given new code numbers, logically ordered by place in the family tree. Included are:

[A020] Marcia Robboy Ames
[A157a] Eta Berner
[A342] Elana Bracha Blum-Doering
[A344] Don Shimon Blum-Doering
[A440] Lesa K Bogart
[A300] Richard Douglas Borenstein
[A302] Gertrude| Trudy Borenstein
[A308] Jody M Bortner
[A043] Rebeca Malkin Robboy Busansky
[A539] Oscar Enrique Caprav
[A541] Gabriel Hernan Caprav
[A525] Elizabeth Martha Charm
[A373] Hyman Chase
[A380] Renee Louise Coleman
[A596] Gary Cooper
[A597] Marc Cooper
[A312] Max Fred Dan
[A343] Tamara Lea Doering
[A403] Myrna Douglas
[A575] Eliot Mark Dratch
[A299] Beatrice| Breine Dudnik
[A345] Eliasaf Elliott Dudnik
[A341] Zahava Dudnik
[A319] Nora Dudwick
[A028] Laurel Groger Espinosa
[A497] Arieh Finell
[A378] Aliza Finkel
[A409] Wendy Ann Fouks
[A407] Leslie Fouks
[A408] David Fouks
[A124] Harry Friedman
[A598] Brad Friedman
[A379] Lucy Galler
[A393] Bruce Irving Galler
[A396] Marilyn Ann Galler
[A376] Lynne Galler
[A395] Glenn Galler
[A460] Daniel Webb Gillman
[A520] Marcia Ginsberg
[A499] Debra Goodman
[A499.2] Karen Goodman
[A498] Yetta Mollie Trachtman Goodman
[A585] Nancy Kaprov Gore
[A082] Robert Gomel
[A082.2] Jessica L Gomel
[A595] Larry Gritz
[A027] Myrna Robboy Groger

[A029] Richard Groger
[A604] Shimon Herman
[A537] Valeria Sabrina Ideses
[A535] Javier Ideses
[A477] Jeannette Kaprove
[A546] Adrian Gustavo| Eliahu Kaprow
[A519] Gail Lee Kaprow
[A558] Gene Joseph Katzman
[A056] Betty Isbitz Koondel
[A387] Stephen Korn
[A588] Jeffrey Korn
[A390] Howard Korn
[A366b] Isabel Kosberg
[A084] Gita Robboy Levin
[A538] Gal K Malik
[A055] Sarah-Fay Isbitz Manson
[A354] Gai Mar-Chaim
[A586] Marilyn (Molly) Purpel Marcus
[A050] Stephanie Judith Yellin Mednick
[A338] Cindy Milstein
[A429a] Ferne Elaine Phillips Mittleman
[A329] Leonette Sheryn Morrison
[A330] Elliot Howard Morrison
[A331] Barbara Joy Morrison
[A111] Alan Gedalia Pritzker
[A584.2] Rachel Purpel
[A491] Amnon Rapoport
[A066] David|Sonny Rein
[A014] David Gerson Robboy
[A077] Howard Paul Robboy
[A090] Howard Alan Robboy
[A394] Elaine Galler Robboy
[A015] Ronald Robboy
[A016] William Robboy
[A036] Mitchell Robboy
[A445a] Ellen Marcia Rossen
[A347] Robert Schwartz
[A347.2] Stephen Michael Schwartz
[A074] Dan Strauss
[A072] Martin Strauss
[A073] Steve Strauss
[A480] Howard Trachtman
[A157] David S. Weiss
[A122] Melanie H. Friedman Weltman
[A384] Grigory| Garik| Gary Zaika
[A523] Shirley Zitaner
Rolando Gail

INDEX: ALPHABETICAL BY LAST NAME

The index's cornerstone is each person's code number, e.g., [A026] John Robboy, and his wife [A026a] Sarah Robboy. Second spouse have the code [A___b]. The index attempts to capture, insofar as is realistic, the multiple names any person may have. Women have a birth surname e.g., John Robboy's daughter was born [A027] Myrna Robboy, but became [A027] Myrna Groger after marriage. Second marriages have the suffix "b" and third marriages "c." Some members shortened (e.g., [A373] Chaseman → Chase) or changed ([A128] Haskel Voskoboinik → Weiss) their last name after coming to United States. Many, both female and males, also shortened or Anglicized their given name (e.e, A345] Eliasaf → Elliott). When a family member married, but the spouse's last name is unknown, the maiden surname is then the final surname.

The index in the electronic Kindle version lists each person's unique ID with all last names.

The print-on-demand (soft cover book) and PDF version lists a second index with the page numbers where each person's ID number is cited. The Kindle version omits this second indix as names can be electronically searched and the page number is a function of the viewing screen size.

[A019.1]]	**Adato**	Deborah Ann Cooper		[A305]	**Borenstein**	Irene Dudnik
[A119]	**Adler**	Karen Maness		[A299a]	**Borenstein**	Max
[A830]	**Aleichem**	Sholem		[A301]	**Borenstein**	Paul Elliott
[A563]	**Alenne**	Anna Sorokin		[A300]	**Borenstein**	Richard Douglas
[A520]	**Alibertl**	Marcia Rachel Ginsberg		[A306]	**Borenstein**	Susan
[A039]	**Alvarez**	Daphne Robboy		[A308]	**Bortner**	Jody M
[A435]	**Amato**	Cheryl Lynn		[A307]	**Bortner**	Selma Dudnik
[A434]	**Amato**	Shirley Pearlman		[A496]	**Brandt**	Minnie Trachtman
[A020]	**Ames**	Marcia Robboy		[A481a]	**Breland**	Elizabeth
[A348.8a]	**Amram**	Barbara		[A343]	**Brent**	Tamara Lea Doering
[A409]	**Anthony**	Wendy Ann Fouks		[A331]	**Bresler**	Barbara Joy Morrison
[A486]	**Ariely**	Tova Trachtman		[A419a]	**Brodsky**	Dvossie
[A416]	**Arnopolski**	Sonia Douglas		[A348.2a]	**Brown**	Allen
[A069]	**Bailys**	David		[A348.2]	**Brown**	Miriam Mimi Hayman
[A070]	**Bailys**	Frederick		[A652]	**Brudno**	Batya bat Ezra Selig
[A070.1]	**Bailys**	Gregory		[A665.1]	**Brudno**	Esther-Rochel
[A068]	**Bailys**	Susanne F Rein		[A689]	**Brudno**	Ethel
[A651]	**bat Menashe**	Hannah		[A580]	**Bryant**	David Edward Purpel
[A632]	**Beckerman**	Chanah Tishler		[A579a]	**Buni**	Bassie
[A298a]	**Bellis**	Minnie		[A043]	**Busansky**	Rebeca Malkin Robboy
[A827]	**Ben Gurion**	David		[A549]	**Caprav**	Alberto
[A650]	**ben Porat**	Menashe		[A539a]	**Caprav**	Ana
[A568]	**Berdichevsky**	Anna		[A547]	**Caprav**	Ana
[A566]	**Berdichevsky**	Ratsa Kaprov		[A534]	**Caprav**	Dora Ana
[A566a]	**Berdichevsky**	Samuel		[A542]	**Caprav**	Elisa
[A567]	**Berdichevsky**	Yakov		[A541]	**Caprav**	Gabriel Hernan
[A581a]	**Bergelson**	Soybel		[A540]	**Caprav**	Gerardo Andres
[A110]	**Berkowitz**	Helene Pritzker		[A548]	**Caprav**	Isaac
[A478]	**Berman**	Golda Trachtman		[A551]	**Caprav**	Maria
[A478a]	**Berman**	Harry		[A533a]	**Caprav**	Maria Monastersky
[A157a]	**Berner**	Eta		[A533]	**Caprav**	Motle
[A835]	**Bertelsen**	Aage		[A539]	**Caprav**	Oscar Quique
[A835a]	**Bertelsen**	Greta		[A550]	**Caprav**	Saul
[A824]	**Bialik**	Chaim Nachman		[A590]	**Caproff**	David
[A341]	**Blum**	Zahava Dudnik		[A589]	**Caproff**	Marion
[A344]	**Blum-Doering**	Don Shimon		[A588a]	**Caproff**	Pearl Shapiro
[A342]	**Blum-Doering**	Elana Bracha		[A580]	**Caprov**	David Kaprove
[A440]	**Bogart**	Lesa K		[A580a]	**Caprov**	Ethel Rabinowitz
[A439]	**Bogart**	Rita Sue Pearlman		[A454]	**Chaitoff**	David Kaye
[A487]	**Bogomilnya Palchan**	Leah Trachtman		[A453]	**Chaitoff**	Diane Fox
				[A453a]	**Chaitoff**	Irving
[A299]	**Borenstein**	Beatrice Breine Dudnik		[A525]	**Charm**	Elizabeth Martha
[A302]	**Borenstein**	Gertrude Trudy				

[A523]	**Charm**	Shirley Zitaner
[A524]	**Charm**	Susan
[A463a]	**Charnopolsky**	Hannah
[A373]	**Chase**	Hyman Chasman
[A372]	**Chasman**	Ruchel Galler
[A334a]	**Clark**	Charlotte
[A457a]	**Cohen**	Etta
[A379]	**Coleman**	Lucille Lucy Galler
[A380]	**Coleman**	Renee Louise
[A471a]	**Colodny**	Ahuva
[A019.1]	**Cooper**	Deborah Ann
[A596]	**Cooper**	Gary Russell
[A597]	**Cooper**	Marc Bruce
[A019]	**Cooper**	Nancy Robboy
[A594]	**Cooper**	Schmuel Kaprove
[A311]	**Dan**	Aaron
[A312]	**Dan**	Max Fred
[A310]	**Dan**	Sarah Dudnik
[A675a]	**Dannhauser**	Jack
[A376]	**Dattner**	Lynne Galler
[A056.4]	**Davidson**	Jennifer Arin Koondel
[A075a]	**Davis**	Sylvia Robboy
[A829]	**Dayan**	Moshe
[A350a]	**Dayan**	Sarah
[A079a]	**Desatnick**	Anna Robboy
[A083a]	**Desatnick**	Eva
[A582a]	**Dinerstein**	Jacqueline
[A343]	**Doering**	Tamara Lea
[A417]	**Dolgonos**	Abram
[A326a]	**Dolgonos**	Brucha
[A399a]	**Dolgonos**	Dov
[A418]	**Dolgonos**	Josip
[A399]	**Dolgonos**	Leah Kaprov
[A040]	**Doliner**	Deborah Robboy
[A329]	**Doran**	Leonette Sheryn Morrison
[A413]	**Douglas**	Bracha Bertha
[A402]	**Douglas**	Dov Dave
[A401a]	**Douglas**	Golda Mauldaur
[A400]	**Douglas**	Israel Dolgonos
[A414]	**Douglas**	Itzhok Dolgonos
[A401]	**Douglas**	Liova Louis
[A415]	**Douglas**	Lisa

[A412]	**Douglas**	Mischa Moshe
[A403]	**Douglas**	Myrna
[A405]	**Douglas**	Polia
[A402a]	**Douglas**	Rose Starkman
[A416]	**Douglas**	Sonia
[A400a]	**Douglas**	Tuba Mazur
[A404]	**Douglas**	Tzvi Harry
[A575]	**Dratch**	Eliot Mark
[A361.8]	**Dudnik**	Betty Lupetsky
[A360]	**Dudnik**	Nathan
[A293]	**Dudnik**	Aaron
[A295]	**Dudnik**	Abraham H
[A299]	**Dudnik**	Beatrice Breine
[A348]	**Dudnik**	Betty
[A413]	**Dudnik**	Bracha Bertha Douglas
[A326a]	**Dudnik**	Brucha Dolgonos
[A326]	**Dudnik**	Chaim Khaim
[A323a]	**Dudnik**	Chana
[A325]	**Dudnik**	Charmi-Gitel
[A358]	**Dudnik**	Chaya Kaika
[A413a]	**Dudnik**	Chaim
[A293a]	**Dudnik**	Cipa Weinberg
[A316]	**Dudnik**	Dina
[A314]	**Dudnik**	Dora
[A345]	**Dudnik**	Eliasaf Elliott
[A327]	**Dudnik**	Fania
[A350]	**Dudnik**	Froim Efraim
[A305]	**Dudnik**	Irene
[A323]	**Dudnik**	Isrul Israel
[A297]	**Dudnik**	Joan
[A298]	**Dudnik**	Joseph
[A320]	**Dudnik**	Kenia Kay
[A324]	**Dudnik**	Khaim
[A355]	**Dudnik**	Leib
[A346]	**Dudnik**	Lillian
[A298a]	**Dudnik**	Minnie Bellis
[A353]	**Dudnik**	Miriam
[A385]	**Dudnik**	Motel Morris Galler
[A351]	**Dudnik**	Noach Dayan
[A292a]	**Dudnik**	Noah
[A313]	**Dudnik**	Olga
[A365]	**Dudnik**	Olga Morrison

[A309]	**Dudnik**	Pearl		[A451]	**Fox**	Michelle
[A363]	**Dudnik**	Pearl Mimi		[A448]	**Fox**	Pessie Pauline Pearlman
[A332]	**Dudnik**	Polia Gittel		[A449]	**Fox**	Robert
[A357]	**Dudnik**	Polya		[A059a]	**Frankel**	Mary Robboy
[A356]	**Dudnik**	Reva		[A544]	**Freue**	Adalberto Carlos Kaprow
[A292]	**Dudnik**	Rivka Kaprov		[A432a]	**Frieda**	Freda
[A296]	**Dudnik**	Robert M		[A598]	**Friedman**	Brad Aaron
[A310]	**Dudnik**	Sarah		[A374a]	**Friedman**	Eva
[A364]	**Dudnik**	Sarah		[A124]	**Friedman**	Herschel Harry
[A350a]	**Dudnik**	Sarah Dayan		[A127]	**Friedman**	Ken M
[A333]	**Dudnik**	Sarah Dvossi		[A121]	**Friedman**	Marvin
[A307]	**Dudnik**	Selma		[A122]	**Friedman**	Melanie
[A352]	**Dudnik**	Tzipora		[A120]	**Friedman**	Pauline Voskoboinik
[A349]	**Dudnik**	Vera		[A120a]	**Friedman**	Pauline Voskoboinik
[A359]	**Dudnik**	Yankel		[A123]	**Friedman**	Robert Gary
[A339]	**Dudnik**	Yosel Joseph		[A126]	**Friedman**	Robin
[A341]	**Dudnik**	Zahava		[A125]	**Friedman**	Stephanie
[A317]	**Dudwick**	Harry A.		[A551]	**Fuks**	Maria Caprav
[A317a]	**Dudwick**	Ida Gross		[A532a]	**Futeransky**	Sara
[A318]	**Dudwick**	Nancy L		[A564]	**Gaibaldi**	Elezaveta "Liza" Sorokin
[A319]	**Dudwick**	Nora		[A367]	**Galak**	Genendy Kaprov
[A054]	**Eggleston**	Maurice Waterman		[A368]	**Galak**	Israel
[A053]	**Eggleston**	Rosalie Isbitz		[A398]	**Galak**	Khaim
[A547]	**Einhorn**	Ana Caprav		[A382]	**Galak**	Lazar
[A821]	**Einstein**	Albert		[A383]	**Galak**	Rifke Raya
[A028]	**Espinosa**	Laurel Groger		[A368a]	**Galak**	Rifke Surak
[A662]	**Fallenberg**	Esther Gressel		[A126]	**Galkin**	Robin Friedman
[A497]	**Finell**	Arieh Chaim		[A319]	**Gallagherduff**	Nora Dudwick
[A378]	**Finkel**	Aliza Rachel		[A392]	**Galler**	Bernard
[A377]	**Finkel**	Jeanette Galler		[A393]	**Galler**	Bruce Irving
[A483]	**Foigelman**	Bluma Bella Trachtman		[A369]	**Galler**	David
[A411]	**Fouks**	Arthur		[A394]	**Galler**	Elaine Beth
[A408]	**Fouks**	David		[A392a]	**Galler**	Enid Harris
[A410]	**Fouks**	Gertrude		[A374a]	**Galler**	Eva Friedman
[A406]	**Fouks**	Jacob Jack		[A395]	**Galler**	Glenn Norman
[A407]	**Fouks**	Leslie		[A377]	**Galler**	Jeanette
[A409]	**Fouks**	Wendy Ann		[A379]	**Galler**	Lucille Lucy
[A450]	**Fox**	Denise		[A376]	**Galler**	Lynne
[A453]	**Fox**	Diane		[A396]	**Galler**	Marilyn Ann
[A448a]	**Fox**	Jack		[A385]	**Galler**	Motel Morris
[A452]	**Fox**	Julius Jay		[A371]	**Galler**	Pearl
[A455]	**Fox**	Marlene Beverly		[A332]	**Galler**	Polia Gittel Dudnik

[A386]	**Galler**	Rifka Vivian
[A372]	**Galler**	Ruchel
[A397]	**Galler**	Sarah Dolores
[A370]	**Galler**	Shmuel Samuel
[A375]	**Galler**	William
[A381]	**Galler**	Yochanon Yefim
[A374]	**Galler**	Yossel Joseph
[A505]	**Galperin**	Rivka Gelman
[A033]	**Gearhart**	Caroline Robboy
[A554a]	**Geisingsky**	Miriam
[A431]	**Gelman**	Alta
[A427]	**Gelman**	Daniel
[A430]	**Gelman**	Dvossi Dorothy
[A503a]	**Gelman**	Freda Grabois
[A508a]	**Gelman**	Frima Rabinowitz
[A507]	**Gelman**	Genendal Gwendel
[A428]	**Gelman**	Gertrude Gisi
[A502a]	**Gelman**	Itzhak
[A510]	**Gelman**	Itzik
[A510a]	**Gelman**	Khana Sarah
[A509]	**Gelman**	Leah
[A502]	**Gelman**	Leah Kaprove
[A503]	**Gelman**	Moishe
[A506]	**Gelman**	Motel
[A505]	**Gelman**	Rivka
[A427a]	**Gelman**	Sarah Kaprow
[A511]	**Gelman**	Tobie
[A508]	**Gelman**	Yankel Jacob
[A017a]	**Gerson**	Avrom Samuel
[A095]	**Gerson**	Avrom Samuel [A017a]
[A099]	**Gerson**	Fullie
[A094]	**Gerson**	Hanna Voskoboinik
[A094a]	**Gerson**	Levi
[A101]	**Gerson**	Nathan
[A097]	**Gerson**	Nathan
[A095a]	**Gerson**	Nessie
[A017]	**Gerson**	Nessie Gerson Robboy
[A098]	**Gerson**	Paya
[A100]	**Gerson**	Ruchel
[A489]	**Gesser**	Sarah Batya Trachtman
[A423]	**Gillman**	Chaye Haya
[A460]	**Gillman**	Daniel Webb
[A457a]	**Gillman**	Etta Cohen
[A458]	**Gillman**	Leonard
[A422a]	**Gillman**	Moshe
[A422]	**Gillman**	Pessie Kaprov
[A459]	**Gillman**	Robert David
[A457]	**Gillman**	Yossel Joseph
[A556]	**Gilman**	Anna Michalovna Kaprove
[A504]	**Gilman**	Boris
[A557]	**Gilman**	Elena
[A421]	**Gilman**	Khana Esther
[A420]	**Gilman**	Khaye Golda Kaprove
[A561]	**Gilman**	Olga
[A519]	**Ginsberg**	Gail Lee Kaprow
[A520]	**Ginsberg**	Marcia Rachel
[A826]	**Goldberg**	Nahum
[A315]	**Goldenberg**	Aaron
[A314]	**Goldenberg**	Dora Dudnik
[A087a]	**Goldstein**	Leslie
[A081]	**Gomel**	Francis
[A082.2]	**Gomel**	Jessica
[A080a]	**Gomel**	Perry
[A080]	**Gomel**	Phyllis Robboy
[A082]	**Gomel**	Robert T
[A585]	**Gonzales**	Nancy Purpel
[A499]	**Goodman**	Debra Lynn
[A499.2]	**Goodman**	Karen Jean
[A498]	**Goodman**	Yetta Mollie Trachtman
[A503a]	**Grabois**	Freda
[A665]	**Grad**	Eli
[A424]	**Green**	Rachel Strayer Pribludny
[A352.5]	**Greenberg**	Chaya Kroizman
[A654]	**Gressel**	Albert Sam
[A661]	**Gressel**	Beth
[A658]	**Gressel**	Carmi
[A662]	**Gressel**	Esther
[A659]	**Gressel**	Jonathan
[A657]	**Gressel**	Louis
[A660]	**Gressel**	Macky Dean
[A674a]	**Gressel**	Miriam
[A663]	**Gressel**	Viva
[A338]	**Grimmer**	Cynthia Cindy Milstein
[A555a]	**Grinberg**	Leah

[A595]	**Gritz**	Larry Richard
[A030]	**Groger**	Debra
[A028]	**Groger**	Laurel
[A027]	**Groger**	Myrna Robboy
[A029]	**Groger**	Richard
[A317a]	**Gross**	Ida
[A105b]	**Groysman**	Golda Voskoboinik
[A105b]	**Groysman**	Meir
[A363]	**Gudisblatt**	Pearl Mimi Dudnik
[A320]	**Guralnick**	Kenia Kay Dudnik
[A322]	**Guralnick**	Paul Boris
[A321]	**Guralnick**	Sidney Aaron
[A309]	**Guralnik**	Pearl Dudnik
[A392a]	**Harris**	Enid
[A348.8a]	**Hayman**	Barbara Amram
[A348]	**Hayman**	Betty Dudnik
[A348.8]	**Hayman**	David Arthur
[A348.2]	**Hayman**	Miriam Mimi
[A118]	**Heins**	Rayah Maness
[A035a]	**Heiser**	Rhea
[A057a]	**Heller**	Helen Robboy
[A603]	**Herman**	Eva Chavah Kaprove
[A604]	**Herman**	Rabbi Shimon
[A014a]	**Herzberg**	Deborah Robboy
[A536]	**Ideses**	Ariel Esteban
[A534]	**Ideses**	Dora Ana Caprav
[A535]	**Ideses**	Javier Horacio
[A537]	**Ideses**	Valeria Sabrina
[A056]	**Isbitz**	Betty
[A047a]	**Isbitz**	Joe
[A048]	**Isbitz**	Marilyn
[A053]	**Isbitz**	Rosalie
[A055]	**Isbitz**	Sarah-Fay
[A047]	**Isbitz**	Sylvia Robboy
[A522]	**Jacob**	Dvossi Dorothy Kaprov
[A522a]	**Jacob**	Yankel
[A102]	**Kaffen**	Irvin
[A101]	**Kaffen**	Nathan Gerson
[A104]	**Kaffen**	Neal E
[A103]	**Kaffen**	Ronald
[A467]	**Kanefsky**	Dora Trachtman
[A554a]	**Kaplan**	Miriam Geisingsky

[A554]	**Kaplan**	Samuel Schmilik
[A627]	**Kaprov**	Bar Sheva
[A579a]	**Kaprov**	Bassie Buni
[A571]	**Kaprov**	Belchik
[A571a]	**Kaprov**	Chaya
[A461]	**Kaprov**	Daniel
[A522]	**Kaprov**	Dvossi Dorothy
[A474a]	**Kaprov**	Edassy
[A516]	**Kaprov**	Fishel
[A531]	**Kaprov**	Gedaliah
[A367]	**Kaprov**	Genendy
[A553a]	**Kaprov**	Hanna Litvak
[A517]	**Kaprov**	Irene Gertrude
[A574]	**Kaprov**	Itzik-Yoel
[A290]	**Kaprov**	Khaim
[A573]	**Kaprov**	Khaya
[A399]	**Kaprov**	Leah
[A555a]	**Kaprov**	Leah Grinberg
[A011a]	**Kaprov**	Malka Robboy
[A555]	**Kaprov**	Michael
[A290a]	**Kaprov**	Osna
[A422]	**Kaprov**	Pessie
[A527]	**Kaprov**	Pessie
[A566]	**Kaprov**	Ratsa
[A292]	**Kaprov**	Rivka
[A552]	**Kaprov**	Shemariah
[A530]	**Kaprov**	Shmuel Abba
[A565]	**Kaprov**	Velvel
[A553]	**Kaprov**	Yakov
[A572]	**Kaprov**	Yakov
[A462]	**Kaprov**	Yenta
[A291]	**Kaprov**	Yossel
A475]	**Kaprove Kaplan**	Haika Ida Trachtman
A475a]	**Kaprove Kaplan**	Samuel
[A556]	**Kaprove**	Anna Michalovna
[A606]	**Kaprove**	Avrom
[A419]	**Kaprove**	Beryl Dov
[A629]	**Kaprove**	Chanah Ania
[A619]	**Kaprove**	Chanah Dvorah
[A591]	**Kaprove**	Chavah Dvorah
[A623]	**Kaprove**	Chiki (Chayka?)

[A630]	**Kaprove**	Chrisi
[A419a]	**Kaprove**	Dvossie Brodsky
[A476]	**Kaprove**	Edith
[A601]	**Kaprove**	Esther Malka
[A603]	**Kaprove**	Eva Chavah
[A602]	**Kaprove**	FegehFeika
[A607]	**Kaprove**	Gitel
[A605]	**Kaprove**	Israel
[A477]	**Kaprove**	Jeannette
[A637]	**Kaprove**	Kaprove
[A420]	**Kaprove**	Khaye Golda
[A626]	**Kaprove**	Laiki
[A502]	**Kaprove**	Leah
[A622]	**Kaprove**	Leib
[A592]	**Kaprove**	Moshe
[A628]	**Kaprove**	Nachomi
[A631]	**Kaprove**	Perel
[A625]	**Kaprove**	Pinchas Pini
[A624]	**Kaprove**	Raisel
[A639]	**Kaprove**	Reiche Rose
[A610]	**Kaprove**	Reichel
[A593]	**Kaprove**	Shalom
[A608]	**Kaprove**	Simcha
[A638]	**Kaprove**	Simcha Samuel
[A621]	**Kaprove**	Simchi
[A578]	**Kaprove**	Simkha
[A609]	**Kaprove**	Yoel
[A620]	**Kaprove**	Yoel Eli
[A618]	**Kaprove**	Yonkel David
[A544]	**Kaprow**	Adalberto Carlos
[A546]	**Kaprow**	Adrian Gustavo
[A545]	**Kaprow**	Alejandro Cezar
[A515]	**Kaprow**	Avrom
[A519]	**Kaprow**	Gail Lee
[A532]	**Kaprow**	Gedalia
[A518]	**Kaprow**	Gerald Louis
[A528a]	**Kaprow**	Gittel Shapiro
[A543]	**Kaprow**	Hersh
[A521]	**Kaprow**	Rhoda
[A532a]	**Kaprow**	Sara Futeransky
[A427a]	**Kaprow**	Sarah
[A529]	**Kaprow**	Sholom Maurice

[A430a]	**Kareff**	Benjamin
[A430]	**Kareff**	Dvossi Dorothy Gelman
[A589]	**Kashin**	Marion Caproff
[A559]	**Katzman**	Aaron Max
[A557]	**Katzman**	Elena Gilman
[A558]	**Katzman**	Gene Joseph
[A557a]	**Katzman**	Konstantin
[A560]	**Katzman**	Sarah Maria
[A558a]	**Katzman**	Stella Leryzerova
[A024b]	**Kimmelman**	Bessie
[A032]	**Kittrie**	Elizabeth Robboy
[A403]	**Koffman**	Myrna Douglas
[A056]	**Koondel**	Betty Isbitz
[A056.4]	**Koondel**	Jennifer Arin
[A390]	**Korn**	Howard (Khaim)
[A388]	**Korn**	Jeffrey Robert
[A391]	**Korn**	Lia
[A386]	**Korn**	Rifka Vivian Galler
[A387]	**Korn**	Stephen (Shmuel)
[A389]	**Korn**	Victoria Alisa
[A396]	**Koschik**	Marilyn Ann Galler
[A577]	**Kraprov**	Isroel Yisrael
[A153]	**Kravitz**	Daniel
[A152]	**Kravitz**	David
[A352]	**Kreisman**	Tzipora Dudnik
[A352.5]	**Kroizman**	Chaya
[A437]	**Kuczynski**	Vicky Pearlman
[A435]	**Ladawer**	Cheryl Lynn Amato
[A447]	**Lahrey**	Moriah
[A446]	**Lahrey**	Sandra Rossen
[A527a]	**Lerman**	Frank
[A527]	**Lerman**	Pessie Kaprov
[A389a]	**Lerner**	Andres
[A389]	**Lerner**	Victoria Alisa Korn
[A558a]	**Leryzerova**	Stella
[A671]	**Lev**	Yola Shapiro
[A086]	**Levin**	Alan Michael
[A085]	**Levin**	Ellen Alisa
[A084]	**Levin**	Gita Robboy
[A088a]	**Levin**	Irma
[A394]	**Levine**	Elaine Beth Galler
[A484]	**Levitsky**	Bracha Bertha Trachtman

[A081]	**Levy**	Francis Gomel
[A670]	**Lewin**	Doris Divi Shapiro
[A663]	**Lewin**	Viva
[A146]	**Lilley**	Faith Pamela Mesnick
[A553a]	**Litvak**	Hanna
[A031b]	**Loeb**	Marion Meyer
[A525]	**Long**	Elizabeth Martha Charm
[A342]	**Lubit**	Elana Bracha Blum-Doering
[A362]	**Lupetsky**	Betya Betty Dudnik
[A362.4]	**Lupetsky**	Feivil
[A362.1]	**Lupetsky**	Yasha Yankel
[A433]	**Lynn**	Annette Pearlman
[A441]	**Mahle**	Barbara
[A313]	**Maidansky**	Olga Dudnik
[A538]	**Malik**	Gal K
[A537]	**Malik**	Valeria Sabrina Ideses
[A445a]	**Maman**	David
[A445]	**Maman**	Ellen Marcia Rossen
[A119]	**Maness**	Karen
[A118]	**Maness**	Rayah
[A055]	**Manson**	Sarah-Fay Isbitz
[A354]	**Mar-Chaim**	Gai
[A586]	**Marcus**	Marilyn Purpel
[A441]	**Marzec**	Barbara Mahle
[A521]	**Matson**	Rhoda Kaprow
[A401a]	**Mauldaur**	Golda
[A400a]	**Mazur**	Tuba
[A050]	**Mednick**	Stephanie Judith Yellin
[A012a]	**Meshenstein**	Rebecca Robboy
[A145]	**Mesnick**	Allen F
[A140]	**Mesnick**	Bessie Weiss
[A146]	**Mesnick**	Faith Pamela
[A141]	**Mesnick**	Rosalind Lee
[A147]	**Mesnick**	Scott Howard
[A031b]	**Meyer**	Marion Loeb
[A542]	**Mijalovich**	Elisa Caprav
[A334]	**Milstein**	Alex
[A333a]	**Milstein**	Aron
[A334a]	**Milstein**	Charlotte Clark
[A338]	**Milstein**	Cynthia Cindy
[A337]	**Milstein**	David Duzz
[A336]	**Milstein**	David Reid
[A335]	**Milstein**	Norman Scott
[A333]	**Milstein**	Sarah Dvossi Dudnik
[A429a]	**Mittleman**	Ferne Phillips
[A429]	**Mittleman**	Gordon
[A328a]	**Mizes**	Shirley
[A533a]	**Monastersky**	Maria
[A405a]	**Morris**	Moshe
[A405]	**Morris**	Polia Douglas
[A331]	**Morrison**	Barbara Joy
[A328]	**Morrison**	Donald Dov
[A330]	**Morrison**	Elliot Howard
[A327]	**Morrison**	Fania Dudnik
[A327a]	**Morrison**	Leon
[A329]	**Morrison**	Leonette Sheryn
[A360]	**Morrison**	Olga Dudnik
[A364]	**Morrison**	Sarah Dudnik
[A328a]	**Morrison**	Shirley Mizes
[A451]	**Moss**	Michelle Fox
[A451a]	**Moss**	Rick
[A045]	**Munday**	Sara Gail Robboy
[A397]	**Nemiroff**	Sarah Dolores Galler
[A476]	**Newler**	Edith Kaprove
[A117]	**Newman**	Naome Rubin
[A154]	**Nudelman**	Judy Weiss
[A156]	**Nudelman**	Lee
[A155]	**Nudelman**	Scott
[A687]	**Olshansky**	Rena Shapiro Blumber
[A820]	**Paracelsus**	
[A067]	**Pate**	Marcie Rein
[A432]	**Pearlman**	Abe
[A431]	**Pearlman**	Alta Gelman
[A433]	**Pearlman**	Annette
[A431a]	**Pearlman**	David
[A436]	**Pearlman**	Emanuel: Sonny
[A432a]	**Pearlman**	Freda Frieda
[A442]	**Pearlman**	Joyce
[A448]	**Pearlman**	Pessie Pauline
[A439]	**Pearlman**	Rita Sue
[A434]	**Pearlman**	Shirley
[A436a]	**Pearlman**	Simone Wllingfor
[A437]	**Pearlman**	Vicky
[A444]	**Perlman**	Arleen B.

[A443]	**Perlman**	Beryl Ben
[A443a]	**Perlman**	Sylvia Plumka
[A366]	**Perman**	Leonard
[A365]	**Perman**	Olga Morrison Dudnik
[A365a]	**Perman**	Sam
[A429a]	**Phillips**	Ferne
[A443a]	**Plumka**	Sylvia
[A500a]	**Pratter**	Fannie
[A425]	**Pribludny**	Bayla Liba
[A423]	**Pribludny**	Chaye Haya Gillman
[A426]	**Pribludny**	Khaim Strayer
[A424]	**Pribludny**	Rachel Strayer
[A570a]	**Pritssker**	Marina
[A111]	**Pritzker**	Alan Gedalia
[A110]	**Pritzker**	Helene
[A107]	**Pritzker**	Jennie Voskoboinik
[A109]	**Pritzker**	Marvin
[A112]	**Pritzker**	Nachman
[A108]	**Pritzker**	Rose
[A580]	**Purpel**	David Edward
[A582a]	**Purpel**	Jacqueline Dinerstein
[A583]	**Purpel**	Michael
[A585]	**Purpel**	Nancy
[A582]	**Purpel**	Nathan
[A584]	**Purpel**	Rachel Ann
[A581a]	**Purpel**	Soybel Bergelson
[A580a]	**Rabinowitz**	Ethel
[A508a]	**Rabinowitz**	Frima
[A491]	**Rapoport**	Amnon
[A490]	**Rapoport**	Bat-Ami Trachtman
[A825]	**Rebelsky**	David
[A066]	**Rein**	David
[A064a]	**Rein**	David
[A067]	**Rein**	Marcie
[A067.1]	**Rein**	Robert
[A064]	**Rein**	Rose Robboy
[A068]	**Rein**	Susanne F
[A065]	**Rein**	William
[A380]	**Ritzo**	Renee Louise Coleman
[A031a]	**Robboy**	Anita
[A079a]	**Robboy**	Anna
[A088]	**Robboy**	Benjamin

[A013]	**Robboy**	Bernard
[A024b]	**Robboy**	Bessie Kimmelman
[A041]	**Robboy**	Brian Douglas
[A087]	**Robboy**	Bruce
[A033]	**Robboy**	Caroline
[A039]	**Robboy**	Daphne
[A014]	**Robboy**	David Gerson
[A014a]	**Robboy**	Deborah
[A040]	**Robboy**	Deborah
[A071]	**Robboy**	Dorothy
[A075]	**Robboy**	Eddie
[A032]	**Robboy**	Elizabeth
[A083a]	**Robboy**	Eva Desatnick
[A059]	**Robboy**	George
[A428]	**Robboy**	Gertrude Gisi Gelman
[A084]	**Robboy**	Gita
[A057a]	**Robboy**	Helen
[A090]	**Robboy**	Howard Alan
[A077]	**Robboy**	Howard Paul
[A012]	**Robboy**	Hyman
[A088a]	**Robboy**	Irma Levin
[A038]	**Robboy**	Jeffrey David
[A026]	**Robboy**	John
[A024]	**Robboy**	Joseph
[A010]	**Robboy**	Leah Voskoboinik
[A087a]	**Robboy**	Leslie Goldstein
[A011a]	**Robboy**	Malka
[A076]	**Robboy**	Marc
[A020]	**Robboy**	Marcia
[A031b]	**Robboy**	Marion Meyer (Loeb)
[A059a]	**Robboy**	Mary
[A058]	**Robboy**	Melvin Lee
[A079]	**Robboy**	Mendel
[A063]	**Robboy**	Merle
[A046]	**Robboy**	Michael
[A036]	**Robboy**	Mitchell
[A034]	**Robboy**	Mordechai
[A057]	**Robboy**	Morton
[A027]	**Robboy**	Myrna
[A019]	**Robboy**	Nancy
[A035]	**Robboy**	Nathan
[A018]	**Robboy**	Nathan Gerson

[A095a]	**Robboy**	Nessie Gerson		[A378]	**Sanders**	Aliza Rachel Finkel
[A017]	**Robboy**	Nessie Gerson		[A510a]	**Sarah**	Khana
[A021]	**Robboy**	Pauline		[A562]	**Schaab**	Evgeniya "Jane" Sorokin
[A096]	**Robboy**	Pauline Gerson		[A469]	**Scheer**	Marcia Trachtman
[A080]	**Robboy**	Phyllis		[A125]	**Schneider**	Stephanie Friedman
[A044]	**Robboy**	Rachel Beth		[A114]	**Schulman**	Golda Rubin
[A043]	**Robboy**	Rebeca Malkin		[A116]	**Schulman**	Randi
[A012a]	**Robboy**	Rebecca		[A115]	**Schulman**	Roger C.
[A035a]	**Robboy**	Rhea Heiser		[A515]	**Schwartz**	Avrom Kaprow
[A060]	**Robboy**	Rhoda Deloras		[A346]	**Schwartz**	Lillian Dudnik
[A037]	**Robboy**	Robin		[A347]	**Schwartz**	Robert Norman
[A015]	**Robboy**	Ronald		[A515a]	**Schwartz**	Sima
[A013a]	**Robboy**	Rosalie		[A524]	**Schwartz**	Susan Charm
[A064]	**Robboy**	Rose		[A442]	**Segulin**	Joyce Pearlman
[A045]	**Robboy**	Sara Gail		[A688]	**Shapiro**	Daniel
[A026a]	**Robboy**	Sarah		[A672]	**Shapiro**	Don
[A034a]	**Robboy**	Sarah Spector		[A670]	**Shapiro**	Doris Divi
[A011]	**Robboy**	Shmiel		[A675]	**Shapiro**	Dorothy
[A083]	**Robboy**	Sidney		[A494a]	**Shapiro**	Dvora
[A078]	**Robboy**	Sosi		[A685]	**Shapiro**	Ellen
[A042]	**Robboy**	Stanley G		[A665.1]	**Shapiro**	Esther-Roche
[A031]	**Robboy**	Stanley J		[A686]	**Shapiro**	Ezra Zelig
[A089]	**Robboy**	Stanton L.		[A528a]	**Shapiro**	Gittel
[A075a]	**Robboy**	Sylvia		[A677]	**Shapiro**	Jack Yonny
[A047]	**Robboy**	Sylvia		[A666]	**Shapiro**	Jake
[A023]	**Robboy**	Tobie		[A683]	**Shapiro**	Joel
[A016]	**Robboy**	William Bill		[A669]	**Shapiro**	Leon
[A030]	**Robinson**	Debra Groger		[A682]	**Shapiro**	Manuel
[A455]	**Rock**	Marlene Beverly Fox		[A674a]	**Shapiro**	Miriam Gressel
[A455a]	**Rock**	Richard		[A684]	**Shapiro**	Paul
[A477]	**Rosenbaum**	Jeannette Kaprove		[A588a]	**Shapiro**	Pearl
[A444a]	**Rossen**	Allen		[A687]	**Shapiro**	Rena
[A444]	**Rossen**	Arleen B. Perlman		[A026a]	**Shapiro**	Sarah
[A445]	**Rossen**	Ellen Marcia		[A669a]	**Shapiro**	Sarah Gressel
[A446]	**Rossen**	Sandra		[A674]	**Shapiro**	Uriah
[A114]	**Rubin**	Golda		[A671]	**Shapiro**	Yola
[A117]	**Rubin**	Naome		[A142]	**Sharwell**	Dana
[A113]	**Rubin**	Rayah Voskoboinik		[A143]	**Sharwell**	David Hal
[A371]	**Sabath**	Pearl Galler		[A144]	**Sharwell**	Jack J
[A640]	**Sadkin**	Leonard		[A141]	**Sharwell**	Rosalind Lee Mesnick
[A639]	**Sadkin**	Reiche Rose Kaprove		[A517]	**Shiro**	Irene Gertrude Kaprov
[A828]	**Sakharov**	Andrei		[A511]	**shohet**	Tobie Gelman

[A626]	**Shuman**	Laiki Kaprove
[A022]	**Siegel**	Donald Robert
[A096]	**Siegel**	Pauline Gerson Robboy
[A021]	**Siegel**	Pauline Robboy
[A613]	**Sklar**	Baruch
[A612]	**Sklar**	Chaim
[A617]	**Sklar**	Chaya
[A611]	**Sklar**	Ezra
[A616]	**Sklar**	Fayge
[A614]	**Sklar**	Hershel
[A631]	**Sklar**	Perel Kaprove
[A615]	**Sklar**	Shayndel
[A013a]	**Smotkin**	Rosalie Robboy
[A563]	**Sorokin**	Anna
[A564]	**Sorokin**	Elezaveta "Liza"
[A562]	**Sorokin**	Evgeniya "Jane"
[A561]	**Sorokin**	Olga Gilman
[A561a]	**Sorokin**	Peter
[A034a]	**Spector**	Sarah
[A061]	**Stamm**	Blake William
[A062]	**Stamm**	Michael
[A060]	**Stamm**	Rhoda Deloras Robboy
[A402a]	**Starkman**	Rose
[A116]	**Starling**	Randi Schulman
[A074]	**Strauss**	Dan
[A071]	**Strauss**	Dorothy Robboy
[A072]	**Strauss**	Martin
[A073]	**Strauss**	Steve
[A308]	**Strawn**	Jody M Bortner
[A304]	**Sugiura**	Alex Jiro
[A302]	**Sugiura**	Gertrude Trudy Borenstein
[A303]	**Sugiura**	Maximillian S
[A368a]	**Surak**	Rifke
[A473a]	**Sussman**	Janice
[A485a]	**Taratuta**	Haika
[A421]	**Tepilsky**	Khana Esther Gilman
[A464]	**Teplitsky**	Rochel Ruth Trachtman
[A465]	**Teplitzky**	Marilyn
[A632]	**Tishler**	Chanah
[A633]	**Tishler**	Sasha
[A569]	**Tokar**	Aleksandra
[A568]	**Tokar**	Anna Berdichevsky

[A568a]	**Tokar**	Boris
[A570]	**Tokar**	Leonid
[A570a]	**Tokar**	Marina Pritssker
[A471a]	**Trachtman**	Ahuva Colodny
[A490]	**Trachtman**	Bat-Ami
[A483]	**Trachtman**	Bluma Bella
[A484]	**Trachtman**	Bracha Bertha
[A467]	**Trachtman**	Dora
[A494a]	**Trachtman**	Dvora Shapiro
[A474a]	**Trachtman**	Edassy Kaprov
[A481a]	**Trachtman**	Elizabeth Breland
[A500]	**Trachtman**	Ephraim Frank
[A473]	**Trachtman**	Eyal
[A500a]	**Trachtman**	Fannie Pratter
[A501]	**Trachtman**	Girl
[A478]	**Trachtman**	Golda
[A493]	**Trachtman**	Grisha Hershel
[A475]	**Trachtman**	Haika Ida
[A485a]	**Trachtman**	Haika Taratuta
[A463a]	**Trachtman**	Hannah Charnopolsky
[A480]	**Trachtman**	Howard Daniel
[A474]	**Trachtman**	Hyman
[A482]	**Trachtman**	Itzik Isadore
[A462a]	**Trachtman**	Jacob
[A473a]	**Trachtman**	Janice Sussman
[A487]	**Trachtman**	Leah
[A481]	**Trachtman**	Louis
[A469]	**Trachtman**	Marcia
[A496]	**Trachtman**	Minnie
[A488]	**Trachtman**	Miriam
[A466]	**Trachtman**	Moishe Morris
[A463]	**Trachtman**	Motye ?Mordechai
[A464]	**Trachtman**	Rochel Ruth
[A468]	**Trachtman**	Samuel
[A489]	**Trachtman**	Sarah Batya
[A492]	**Trachtman**	Shneur Schnayer
[A472]	**Trachtman**	Svi
[A486]	**Trachtman**	Tova
[A494]	**Trachtman**	Velvel
[A471]	**Trachtman**	Yacov Jacob
[A495]	**Trachtman**	Yankel Jacob
[A479]	**Trachtman**	Yankel Jacob

[A462]	**Trachtman**	Yenta Kaprov
[A498]	**Trachtman**	Yetta Mollie
[A485]	**Trachtman**	Yossel Yosef
[A470]	**Trachtman**	Zalman
[A049]	**Turek**	Rhea Eve Yellin
[A601]	**Varinsky**	Esther Malka Kaprove
[A082.2]	**Veksland**	Jessica Gomel
[A831]	**von Hirsch**	Baron Moritz
[A002a]	**Voskoboinik**	Aidi
[A008]	**Voskoboinik**	Baila
[A093]	**Voskoboinik**	Dinah
[A004]	**Voskoboinik**	Donia
[A003a]	**Voskoboinik**	Faiga
[A105b]	**Voskoboinik**	Golda
[A094]	**Voskoboinik**	Hanna
[A003]	**Voskoboinik**	Haskel
[A091]	**Voskoboinik**	Itzhak
[A107]	**Voskoboinik**	Jennie
[A001]	**Voskoboinik**	Laizer Eli
[A010]	**Voskoboinik**	Leah
[A006]	**Voskoboinik**	Moshe
[A120]	**Voskoboinik**	Pauline
[A113]	**Voskoboinik**	Rayah
[A005]	**Voskoboinik**	Sarah Faiga
[A092]	**Voskoboinik**	Shava
[A002]	**Voskoboinik**	Yakov Hersh
[A007]	**Voskoboinik**	Yossel
[A054]	**Waterman**	Maurice
[A044]	**Waterman**	Rachel Beth Robboy
[A293a]	**Weinberg**	Cipa
[A600]	**Weinekov**	Chiki Kaprove
[A529]	**Weinstein**	Sholom Maurice Kaprow
[A465a]	**Weinstock**	Leonard
[A465]	**Weinstock**	Marilyn Teplitzky
[A140]	**Weiss**	Bessie
[A138]	**Weiss**	Charles
[A136]	**Weiss**	Dale
[A135]	**Weiss**	Daniel
[A158]	**Weiss**	Daniel
[A139]	**Weiss**	Dave
[A157]	**Weiss**	David S.
[A157a]	**Weiss**	Eta Berner

[A130]	**Weiss**	Harry
[A128]	**Weiss**	Haskel Voskoboinik
[A133]	**Weiss**	Herman
[A150]	**Weiss**	Hope
[A148]	**Weiss**	Hyman
[A159]	**Weiss**	Jacob
[A131]	**Weiss**	Joy
[A154]	**Weiss**	Judy
[A132]	**Weiss**	Larry
[A151]	**Weiss**	Paul
[A129]	**Weiss**	Phillip
[A137]	**Weiss**	Roberta
[A149]	**Weiss**	Ronald
[A134]	**Weiss**	Ronnie
[A822]	**Weizmann**	Chaim
[A122]	**Weltman**	Melanie Friedman
[A353]	**Wesolowski**	Miriam Dudnik
[A832]	**White**	Paul Dudley
[A488]	**Wilnai**	Miriam Trachtman
[A436a]	**Wllingfor**	Simone
[A602]	**Wolozin**	FegehFeika Kaprove
[A690]	**Wolpaw**	Sidney
[A440]	**Woyton**	Lesa K Bogart
[A440a]	**Woyton**	Louis
[A031a]	**Wyzanski**	Anita Robboy
[A051]	**Yellin**	Beverly Elizabeth
[A052]	**Yellin**	Joseph David
[A048]	**Yellin**	Marilyn Isbitz
[A049]	**Yellin**	Rhea Eve
[A050]	**Yellin**	Stephanie Judith
[A410]	**Zack**	Gertrude Fouks
[A384]	**Zaika**	Grigory Garik
[A383]	**Zaika**	Rifke Raya Galak
[A823]	**Zhabotinsky**	Vladimir
[A523]	**Zitaner**	Shirley

INDEX, CHAPTER NUMBER WHERE MEMBERS' ID NUMBERS APPEAR IN FOOTNOTES

INDEX: BY ID NUMBER

[A033]	44, 51, 267, 416, 437, 469, 473
[A034]	8, 9, 13, 39, 44, 51, 87, 88, 102, 118, 268, 269, 271, 272, 274, 415, 416, 473
[A034a]	87, 88, 118, 268, 269, 274, 462, 474, 475
[A035]	13, 35, 44, 45, 49, 51, 88, 118, 244, 268, 270, 271, 272, 416, 473
[A035a]	272, 470, 474
[A036]	51, 118, 272, 416, 464, 473
[A037]	51, 416, 474
[A038]	51, 416, 473
[A039]	51, 416, 466, 473
[A040]	416, 467, 473
[A041]	51, 416, 473
[A042]	51, 272, 416, 474
[A043]	51, 416, 464, 466, 474
[A044]	51, 416, 474, 476
[A045]	51, 416, 472, 474
[A046]	51, 416, 473
[A047]	13, 51, 118, 268, 269, 271, 272, 273, 306, 373, 417, 470, 474
[A047a]	273, 373, 470
[A048]	51, 118, 273, 306, 417, 470, 476
[A049]	51, 417, 476
[A050]	51, 268, 417, 464, 472, 476
[A051]	51, 417, 476
[A052]	51, 417, 476
[A053]	51, 273, 417, 468, 470
[A054]	51, 417, 468, 476
[A055.1]	417
[A055.2]	417
[A055]	51, 273, 417, 464, 470, 472
[A056.1]	51, 417
[A056.4]	467, 471
[A056]	51, 272, 273, 417, 464, 470, 471
[A057]	13, 51, 268, 269, 271, 272, 417, 473
[A057a]	272, 470, 473
[A058]	51, 272, 417, 473
[A059]	13, 51, 268, 269, 271, 272, 417, 473
[A059a]	272, 468, 473
[A060]	51, 272, 417, 474, 475
[A061]	51, 417, 475
[A062]	51, 417, 475
[A063]	51, 272, 417, 473
[A064]	13, 51, 268, 269, 271, 272, 417, 473, 474
[A064a]	272, 473
[A065]	51, 272, 417, 473
[A066]	51, 417, 464, 473
[A067.1]	51, 473
[A067]	51, 417, 472, 473
[A068]	51, 417, 466, 473
[A069]	51, 417, 466
[A070.1]	51, 466
[A070]	51, 417, 466
[A071]	13, 51, 268, 269, 417, 473, 475
[A072]	51, 417, 464, 475
[A073]	417, 464, 475
[A074]	417, 464, 475
[A075]	13, 51, 268, 269, 271, 272, 417, 473
[A075a]	271, 272, 467, 474
[A076]	51, 417, 473
[A077]	51, 417, 464, 473
[A078]	13, 39, 51, 79, 417, 474
[A079]	8, 9, 13, 39, 41, 51, 79, 87, 88, 200, 220, 274, 279, 329, 417, 473
[A079a]	87, 200, 274, 277, 329, 467, 473
[A080]	39, 51, 200, 274, 275, 276, 417, 469, 474
[A080a]	275, 469
[A081]	51, 276, 417, 469, 472
[A082.2]	417, 464, 469, 476
[A082]	51, 276, 417, 464, 469
[A083]	13, 51, 200, 274, 275, 276, 277, 417, 474
[A083a]	277, 279, 467, 473
[A084]	277, 417, 464, 471, 473
[A085]	471
[A086]	471
[A087]	277, 417, 473
[A087a]	277, 469, 473
[A088]	13, 51, 88, 200, 274, 275, 277, 417, 473
[A088a]	277, 278, 471, 473
[A089]	51, 278, 417, 474

[A090]	51, 200, 274, 275, 278, 328, 417, 464, 473
[A091]	13, 39, 88, 417, 476
[A092]	13, 39, 417, 476
[A093]	13, 39, 417, 476
[A094]	14, 46, 47, 48, 272, 417, 469, 476
[A094a]	47, 48, 63, 469
[A095]	14, 417, 469
[A095a]	469, 474
[A096]	474, 475
[A097]	469
[A098]	14, 46, 49, 418, 469
[A099]	14, 46, 49, 79, 418, 469
[A100]	14, 46, 418, 469
[A101]	14, 46, 49, 418, 469, 470
[A102]	14, 49, 50, 418, 470
[A103]	418, 470
[A104]	418, 470
[A105]	14, 46, 47, 204, 418
[A105b]	14, 204, 418, 470, 476
[A107]	14, 46, 49, 204, 418, 473, 476
[A108]	46, 205, 418, 473
[A109]	46, 205, 418, 473
[A110]	418, 466, 473
[A111]	418, 464, 473
[A112]	418, 473
[A113]	14, 46, 204, 206, 418, 474, 476
[A114]	418, 474
[A115]	418, 474
[A116]	418, 474, 475
[A117]	418, 472, 474
[A118]	418, 470, 472
[A119]	418, 466, 472
[A120]	8, 14, 46, 204, 205, 206, 418, 468, 476
[A120a]	206, 468
[A121]	46, 418, 468
[A122]	46, 418, 464, 468, 476
[A123]	46, 418, 468
[A124]	46, 204, 206, 418, 464, 468
[A125]	46, 418, 468, 474
[A126]	46, 418, 468
[A127]	46, 418, 468
[A128]	14, 46, 48, 49, 418, 465, 476
[A129]	14, 46, 418, 476

[A130]	46, 418, 476
[A131]	418, 476
[A132]	418, 476
[A133]	46, 418, 476
[A134]	418, 476
[A135]	46, 418, 476
[A136]	418, 476
[A137]	418, 476
[A138]	418, 476
[A139]	14, 46, 418, 476
[A140]	14, 46, 418, 472, 476
[A141]	46, 418, 472, 474
[A142]	418, 474
[A143]	418, 474
[A144]	418, 474
[A145]	46, 418, 472
[A146]	418, 472
[A147]	418, 472
[A148]	14, 46, 419, 476
[A149]	46, 419, 476
[A150]	419, 476
[A151]	419, 476
[A152]	419, 471
[A153]	419, 471
[A154]	46, 419, 472, 476
[A155]	419, 472
[A156]	419, 472
[A157]	46, 419, 464, 476
[A157a]	464, 466, 476
[A158]	419, 476
[A159]	419, 476
[A160]	52, 58, 167, 182, 202, 210, 218, 242, 415, 420
[A160a]	73, 182, 242
[A161]	53, 96, 220, 420
[A162]	420
[A163]	420
[A164]	60, 420
[A165]	63, 420
[A166]	63, 420
[A167]	64, 420
[A168]	59, 60, 62, 236, 420
[A168a]	62, 83, 216, 218, 219, 231, 420
[A170]	62, 219, 420
[A171]	63, 420
[A172]	63, 100, 229, 420

[A491]	435, 464, 473
[A492]	15, 121, 435, 475
[A493]	121, 435, 475
[A494]	8, 15, 35, 98, 121, 133, 134, 135, 136, 436, 475
[A494a]	8, 133, 135, 474, 475
[A495]	133, 135, 436, 475
[A496]	115, 116, 121, 133, 135, 303, 436, 466, 475
[A497]	436, 464, 468
[A498]	115, 121, 133, 383, 436, 464, 469, 476
[A498a]	383
[A499.2]	464, 469
[A499]	436, 464, 469
[A500]	15, 121, 129, 134, 436, 475
[A500a]	121, 473, 475
[A501]	15, 129, 436, 475
[A502]	15, 34, 104, 121, 122, 133, 142, 169, 415, 436, 469, 471
[A502a]	8, 88, 121, 126, 133, 167, 169, 170, 238, 469
[A503]	15, 72, 112, 122, 124, 170, 436, 469
[A503a]	122, 170, 469
[A504]	124, 436, 469
[A505]	15, 122, 123, 124, 169, 170, 436, 469
[A506]	15, 123, 147, 148, 158, 163, 167, 170, 436, 469
[A507]	15, 72, 122, 123, 124, 170, 436, 469
[A508]	15, 72, 98, 123, 124, 168, 169, 170, 436, 469
[A508a]	99, 123, 469, 473
[A509]	72, 123, 124, 436, 469
[A510]	14, 15, 34, 81, 101, 124, 429, 436, 469
[A510a]	124, 469, 474
[A511]	101, 124, 436, 469, 474
[A511a]	124
[A515]	9, 15, 34, 81, 97, 124, 132, 253, 254, 256, 274, 437, 471, 474
[A515a]	97, 253, 254, 255, 474
[A516]	15, 97, 253, 254, 255, 437, 470
[A516a]	254

[A517]	254, 437, 470, 474
[A518]	254, 437, 471
[A519]	437, 464, 469, 471
[A520]	437, 464, 466, 469
[A521]	254, 438, 471, 472
[A522]	15, 97, 253, 254, 255, 438, 470
[A522a]	254, 470
[A523]	253, 254, 255, 438, 464, 467, 476
[A524]	255, 438, 467, 474
[A525]	255, 438, 464, 466, 472
[A526]	15, 132, 253, 438
[A527]	15, 253, 254, 255, 256, 438, 470, 471
[A527a]	35, 254, 471
[A528]	15, 161, 162, 163, 253, 254, 255, 438, 463
[A528a]	162, 254, 471, 474
[A529]	161, 162, 438, 471, 476
[A530]	15, 33, 439, 470
[A531]	15, 33, 410, 439, 470
[A532]	15, 410, 439, 471
[A532a]	410, 468, 471
[A533]	412, 439, 466
[A533a]	466, 472
[A534]	411, 412, 439, 466, 470
[A534a]	411
[A535]	411, 439, 464, 470
[A536]	411, 439, 470
[A537]	410, 411, 439, 464, 470, 472
[A538]	411, 439, 464, 472
[A539]	412, 439, 464, 466
[A539a]	466
[A540]	439, 466
[A541]	464, 466
[A542]	410, 439, 466, 472
[A543]	410, 411, 439, 471
[A544]	411, 439, 468, 471
[A545]	411, 439, 471
[A546.1]	410, 411
[A546]	411, 412, 439, 464, 471
[A546a]	412
[A547]	410, 439, 466, 468
[A548]	410, 411, 439, 466
[A549]	411, 439, 466
[A550]	410, 439, 466

[A551]	410, 439, 466, 468
[A552]	15, 33, 221, 439, 470
[A553]	15, 221, 224, 440, 470
[A553a]	224, 470, 472
[A554]	15, 222, 224, 440, 470
[A554a]	224, 469, 470
[A555]	9, 15, 221, 222, 224, 400, 440, 470
[A555a]	222, 223, 224, 225, 469, 470
[A556]	10, 221, 222, 223, 224, 225, 400, 402, 405, 440, 469, 470
[A556a]	402
[A557]	403, 405, 409, 440, 469, 471
[A557a]	403, 405, 407, 409, 471
[A558]	221, 291, 400, 403, 407, 409, 440, 464, 471
[A558a]	409, 471
[A559]	409, 440, 471
[A560]	407, 409, 440, 471
[A561]	409, 440, 469, 475
[A561a]	409, 475
[A562]	409, 440, 474, 475
[A563]	409, 440, 466, 475
[A564]	409, 440, 468, 475
[A565]	15, 440, 470
[A566]	15, 223, 224, 225, 440, 466, 470
[A566a]	223, 224, 466
[A567]	221, 223, 224, 225, 404, 406, 440, 466
[A568]	10, 221, 223, 224, 225, 347, 440, 466, 475
[A568a]	224, 475
[A569]	224, 440, 475
[A570]	224, 440, 475
[A570a]	224, 473, 475
[A571]	15, 223, 224, 225, 440, 470
[A571a]	224, 470
[A572]	224, 440, 470
[A573]	15, 33, 223, 439, 440, 470
[A574]	15, 33, 439, 440, 470
[A575]	440, 464, 467
[A577]	16, 34, 142, 439, 441, 471
[A578]	16, 410, 442, 471
[A579]	16, 442
[A579a]	190, 466, 470
[A580]	16, 193, 198, 199, 442, 466, 473

[A580a]	190, 193, 466, 473
[A581]	8, 16, 190, 192, 198, 442
[A581a]	466, 473
[A582]	442, 473
[A582a]	467, 473
[A583]	442, 473
[A584.2]	192, 442, 464
[A584]	322, 442, 473
[A584b]	198, 199, 442
[A585]	190, 442, 464, 469, 473
[A586]	442, 464, 472
[A588]	16, 198, 199, 442, 464
[A588a]	466, 474
[A589]	442, 466, 471
[A590]	442, 466
[A591]	16, 442, 470
[A592]	16, 442, 471
[A593]	16, 442, 471
[A594]	16, 443, 467
[A595]	443, 464, 470
[A596]	443, 464, 467
[A597]	443, 464, 467
[A598]	443, 464, 468
[A599]	16, 443
[A600]	16, 438, 443, 476
[A601]	16, 443, 471, 476
[A602]	16, 444, 471, 476
[A603]	16, 444, 470, 471
[A604]	16, 444, 464, 470
[A605]	16, 410, 444, 471
[A605a]	410
[A606]	16, 410, 444, 470
[A607]	17, 444, 471
[A608]	17, 410, 444, 471
[A609]	17, 410, 444, 471
[A610]	17, 445, 471
[A611]	17, 445, 475
[A612]	17, 445, 475
[A613]	17, 445, 475
[A614]	17, 445, 475
[A615]	17, 445, 475
[A616]	17, 445, 475
[A617]	17, 445, 475
[A618]	17, 445, 471
[A619]	17, 445, 470
[A620]	17, 432, 442, 445, 471

[A621]	17, 445, 471
[A622]	17, 445, 471
[A623]	17, 445, 470
[A624]	17, 445, 471
[A625]	17, 445, 471
[A626]	18, 445, 471, 475
[A627]	18, 446, 470
[A628]	18, 446, 471
[A629]	18, 446, 470
[A630]	18, 446, 471
[A631]	18, 446, 471, 475
[A632]	446, 466, 475
[A633]	446, 475
[A637]	18, 446, 471
[A638]	18, 446, 471
[A639]	18, 446, 471, 474
[A640]	446, 474
[A650]	37, 447, 466
[A651]	37, 447, 466
[A651a]	37
[A652]	37, 447, 466
[A652a]	37, 447
[A653]	37, 447
[A654]	447, 469
[A654a]	266
[A655]	447, 450
[A656]	447
[A657]	348, 447, 469
[A657a]	347
[A658]	347, 348, 447, 469
[A659]	348, 447, 469
[A660]	348, 349, 447, 469
[A661]	348, 447, 469
[A662]	447, 468, 469
[A663]	447, 469, 472
[A664]	447
[A665.1]	37, 447, 466, 474
[A665.1a]	37, 266
[A665]	10, 376, 447, 469
[A666]	37, 447, 474
[A667]	38, 447
[A668]	38, 447
[A669]	37, 447, 474
[A669a]	474
[A670]	447, 472, 474
[A671]	447, 471, 474
[A672]	347, 447, 474
[A673]	38, 447
[A674]	37, 266, 447, 474
[A674a]	266, 469, 474
[A675]	266, 447, 474
[A675a]	467
[A675b]	447
[A677]	266, 447, 474
[A678]	38, 447
[A679]	36
[A682]	38, 447, 474
[A682a]	102
[A683]	447, 474
[A684]	447, 474
[A685]	447, 474
[A686]	38, 266, 447, 474
[A686a]	266
[A687]	447, 472, 474
[A687b]	447
[A687c]	447
[A688]	447, 474
[A689]	447, 466
[A690]	355, 441, 448, 476
[A691]	36, 43, 108, 111, 311, 448
[A692]	43, 109, 111, 311, 317, 448
[A693]	109, 312, 321, 448
[A694]	313, 448
[A695]	313, 448
[A696]	313, 448
[A697]	313, 448
[A698]	313, 448
[A699]	448
[A700]	109, 111, 448
[A701]	109, 448
[A702]	309, 448
[A703]	309, 448
[A704]	310, 448
[A705]	310, 448
[A706]	310, 448
[A707]	310, 448
[A708]	10, 350, 448
[A709]	316, 448
[A710]	32, 113, 114, 448
[A711]	343, 448
[A712]	56, 448
[A713]	113, 448

[A714]	113, 448
[A715]	318, 448
[A716]	111, 333, 448
[A717]	342, 448
[A718]	333, 448
[A719]	334, 448
[A720]	9, 339, 448
[A721]	347, 448
[A722]	9, 340, 448
[A723]	336, 448
[A724]	337, 448
[A725]	109, 448
[A726]	109, 448
[A727]	109, 448
[A728]	109, 448, 450
[A728a]	113, 307, 450
[A729]	109, 448
[A730]	109, 111, 243, 448
[A731]	109, 448
[A732]	109, 448
[A733]	109, 448
[A734]	109, 448
[A735]	109, 448
[A736]	110, 448
[A737]	316, 321, 448
[A738]	316, 449
[A739]	316, 449
[A740]	307, 449
[A741]	307, 308, 449
[A742]	307, 449
[A743]	307, 308, 449
[A744]	307, 449
[A745]	307, 449
[A746]	307, 308, 449
[A747]	307, 308, 449
[A748]	307, 449
[A749]	449
[A750]	308, 449
[A751]	307, 449
[A752]	307, 449
[A753]	307, 449
[A754]	307, 308, 449
[A755]	307, 449
[A756]	102, 307, 449
[A757]	307, 449
[A758]	307, 308, 309, 310, 449
[A759]	307, 308, 449
[A760]	312, 449
[A761]	312, 449
[A762]	308, 449
[A763]	308, 449
[A764]	309, 449
[A765]	317, 449
[A766]	317, 449
[A767]	318, 319, 321, 449
[A768]	318, 319, 449
[A769]	318, 320, 449
[A770]	318, 320, 449
[A771]	318, 320, 449
[A772]	320, 449
[A773]	320, 449
[A774]	320, 449
[A775]	321, 449
[A776]	316, 320, 321, 449
[A777]	449
[A778]	332, 449
[A779]	332, 449
[A780]	332, 449
[A781]	333, 449
[A782]	334, 449
[A783]	334, 449
[A784]	342, 449
[A785]	338, 449
[A786]	80, 450
[A787]	334, 450
[A789]	376, 450
[A790]	376, 450
[A791]	376, 450
[A792]	376, 450
[A793]	376, 450
[A794]	376, 450
[A795]	376, 450
[A796]	376, 450
[A797]	376, 450
[A798]	376, 450
[A799]	376, 450
[A800]	377, 450
[A801]	377, 450
[A802]	376, 450
[A803]	88, 126, 450
[A804]	119, 450
[A805]	90, 450

490

Made in the USA
Columbia, SC
26 October 2021